Complete Guide to

SIZE SPECIFICATION and TECHNICAL DESIGN

Third Edition

PAULA J. MYERS-McDEVITT

FAIRCHILD BOOKS
NEW YORK • LONDON • OXFORD • NEW DELHI • SYDNEY

FAIRCHILD BOOKS
Bloomsbury Publishing Inc
1385 Broadway, New York, NY 10018, USA
50 Bedford Square, London, WC1B 3DP, UK
29 Earlsfort Terrace, Dublin 2, Ireland

BLOOMSBURY, FAIRCHILD BOOKS and the Fairchild Books logo
are trademarks of Bloomsbury Publishing Plc

First published in the United States of America 2003
This edition published 2016
Reprinted 2021, 2022

Library of Congress Cataloging-in-Publication Data
Names: Myers-McDevitt, Paula J., author.
Title: Complete guide to size specification and technical design / Paula J. Myers-McDevitt.
Description: Third edition. | New York: Fairchild Books, 2016. |
Includes bibliographical references and index.
Identifiers: LCCN 2015051279 | ISBN 9781501312717 (paperback)
Subjects: LCSH: Clothing and dress measurements–Handbooks, manuals, etc. |
Tailoring–Pattern design–Handbooks, manuals, etc. |
BISAC: DESIGN / Fashion. | BUSINESS & ECONOMICS / Industries / Fashion & Textile Industry.
Classification: LCC TT520.M974 2016 | DDC 687/.044–dc23
LC record available at http://lccn.loc.gov/2015051279

ISBN: PB: 978-1-5013-1309-7
ePDF: 978-1-5013-1304-2
eBook: 978-1-5013-1755-2

Typeset by Lachina
Printed and bound in Great Britain

To find out more about our authors and books visit
www.fairchildbooks.com and sign up for our newsletter.

Contents

Preface vi

Using This Text vii
Acknowledgments viii

PART I—GETTING STARTED

Chapter 1: Introduction to Size Specification and Technical Design 3

Brand Merchandise versus Private Label 3
Size Specification and Technical Design 5
Becoming a Technical Designer 8

Chapter 2: Tools of the Trade 10

Before You Begin 10
Determining Basic Body Dimensions 10
Measuring a Model or Body Form 13
Using a Spec Sheet 15
Computers in Fashion 19

Chapter 3: Basic Measurement Points 22

Measurement Preparation 22
Basic Measurement Points 24

PART II—WORKING WITH KNITS

Knits in Review 63

Chapter 4: Knit Tops 65

Measuring Knit Tops 68

Chapter 5: Knit Skirts 80

Measuring Knit Skirts 81

Chapter 6: Knit Pants ... 87

Measuring Knit Pants 88

Chapter 7: Knit Dresses ... 96

Measuring Knit Dresses 99

Chapter 8: Knit Jumpsuits and One-Piece Garments ... 111

Measuring Knit Jumpsuits and One-Piece Garments 114

PART III—WORKING WITH WOVENS

Wovens in Review 125

Chapter 9: Woven Tops ... 127

Measuring Woven Tops 130

Chapter 10: Woven Skirts ... 142

Measuring Woven Skirts 143

Chapter 11: Woven Pants ... 151

Measuring Woven Pants 152

Chapter 12: Woven Dresses ... 161

Measuring Woven Dresses 164

Chapter 13: Woven Jumpsuits and One-Piece Garments ... 177

Measuring Woven Jumpsuits and One-Piece Garments 180

Chapter 14: Blazers and Unconstructed Jackets ... 195

Measuring Blazers and Unconstructed Jackets 198

Chapter 15: Outerwear/Coats ... 210

Measuring Outerwear/Coats 214

PART IV—CHILDREN'S WEAR AND MENSWEAR

Chapter 16: Children's Wear Garments ... 229

Measuring Children's Wear 230

Chapter 17: Menswear Garments 242
Measuring Menswear 242

PART V—FITTING AND GRADING

Chapter 18: Achieving the Perfect Fit 259
Fit Evaluation Sequencing and Procedures 259
Rules for a Good Fit 260
Generalized Garment Fitting Tips 264
Common Fit Problems and How to Correct Them 266
Conducting a Fit Session 298

Chapter 19: Grading 300
How to Grade a Spec Sheet 300
Grading Guidelines for Misses/Women's, Children's, and Menswear Sizes 302

APPENDIXES

Appendix A: Basic Garment Croquis 333
How to Use a Garment Croquis 333
Woven Tops 336
Knit Tops 340
Skirts 344
Pants 347
Dresses 351
One-Piece Outfits/Jumpsuits 358
Blazers and Unconstructed Jackets 361
Coats 364

Appendix B: Metric to Imperial Conversion 369
How to Convert 369

Glossary—Important Terms and Definitions 371
Index 380

Preface

Complete Guide to Size Specification and Technical Design, Third Edition, is an essential tool for fashion students and professionals who are exploring a segment of the industry once kept a secret from consumers—private labeling. In today's economy, offshore production is a necessity for many companies, large and small, retail, and manufacturing. This text offers a comprehensive look at the basic knowledge needed to work as an industry liaison in both segments of the industry, retail or manufacturing, between design/product development staffs and production teams.

This text is a blueprint of size specification (size measuring) and technical design (size analyzing) for the missy/misses/women's wear market. It has been laid out in a simple manner consistent with most industry spec manuals of its type. It includes an introduction to the industry, chapters on measuring (ordered for easy use), and instructions on creating specification sheets, fitting garments, and grading. Industry spec manuals are often as diverse in layout as garments are in design; therefore, this text is taken from easy to use excel files, as not all students or professionals have access to state of the art CAD programs. Appendixes and a glossary of terms and definitions (for important industry terminology) have been added for referencing.

This text is not intended as a product development, patternmaking, production, or quality assurance tool. It does not cover material, trim, or color specifications (generally produced in product development); costing, piece lists, cut order sheets, assembly diagrams, order of operation sheets, or labor division instructions (generally produced in patternmaking and production); or garment inspection procedures (generally carried out in quality assurance departments).

New to this Edition

New to this edition of *Complete Guide to Size Specification and Technical Design* is the coverage of computer-aided design (CAD) tools including a brief introduction to PLM/PDM software such as Gerber, Lectra, and Optitex in Chapter 2. A new Chapter 16 on children's wear covers garments from newborn through juniors' sizes. There is also expanded information on fitting and grading in Part IV to address these important topics in greater depth. Appendix A includes 38 new body figure croquis and Appendix B offers a metric conversion table for easy reference. An online STUDIO for students includes downloadable templates, blank spec sheets, basic garment and figure croquis, and sample technical packages, among other learning resources.

Using This Text

Companies vary in how they apprentice technical design, and schools differ in how they present new material; therefore, the information in this text may not be presented in an order that follows everyone's criteria. For example, some prefer to present measuring woven garments first because the fabric is easier to handle. The industry often presents knit garments first because there are generally fewer style features to confuse the novice. Simply go to the section that makes you more comfortable. If needed, skip between knits and wovens, presenting the less complex garments first, then move on to the more complex garments.

Developing a first size specification sheet also varies in the industry. Spec sheets generated for offshore production generally start with a company sample. Private label spec sheets may begin with an evaluation of a designer sample (for copying), a factory sample, a sketch, a photograph, or a combination thereof. With the exception of a sketch or photograph, which requires the technician to use her experience and expertise to develop measurements without a garment, both the designer garment and the factory sample are usually measured first, fit onto a model or form, and then evaluated. This text works on the premise that a garment has been provided. CAD programs make this process much quicker and easier. Some programs even offer avatars, virtual fit models, to reduce samples.

Part I: Getting Started

Chapter 1, Introduction to Size Specification and Technical Design—This chapter explores and offers the reader an overview of size specification and technical design as it relates to private label and offshore production. It also examines technical design skill requirements.

Chapter 2, Tools of the Trade—Chapter 2 offers the reader important information needed before beginning. It includes standardized body dimensions, shows the reader how to measure a live model/body form with a recording chart, plus how to read and use a generic spec sheet. ASTM body measuring points are new to Chapter 2.

Chapter 3, Basic Measurement Points—Instructions are given to prepare a workstation for measuring and how to measure using step-by-step illustrated instructions for each basic measurement point.

Part II and Part III: Working with Knits and Working with Wovens

Chapters 4 through 15—Each chapter looks at specific garment types and the measurement points needed for each one. These chapters show the reader how to measure specific garments, with applicable measurement points. Basic garment spec sheets have been added for practical application and sample spec sheets for referencing.

Part IV: Children's Wear and Menswear

Chapter 16, Children's Wear Garments—New to the edition, this chapter looks at basic children's wear garments, from newborn through juniors' sizes. It covers how to measure them, and how to use what you learned from misses/women's wear to know which measurement points are needed for each garment. Basic garment sheets have been included for practical application and sample spec sheets are included for referencing.

Chapter 17, Menswear Garments—This chapter looks at the basic menswear garments, how to measure them, and how to use what you learned from misses/women's wear to know which measurement points are needed for each garment. Basic garment sheets have been included for practical application and sample spec sheets are included for referencing.

Part V: Fitting and Grading

Chapter 18, Achieving the Perfect Fit—This chapter should be explored only after one is comfortable with measuring. It offers common fit rules, common fit problems, and suggested solutions for correction.

Chapter 19, Grading—This chapter explores the last step in the technical design process. It offers grading spec sheet instructions for production, misses/women's size, children's, and menswear grading guidelines, and tolerance allowances. Expanded grade rules are new to this chapter.

Appendices

Appendix A, Basic Garment Croquis—Appendix A includes a sampling of flat garment sketches used in technical design and directions for croquis use. A blank spec sheet is provided for the experienced user who wishes to design individual garment spec sheets using the croquis provided and the measurement point chapters. New croquis for each garment type have been added to this text.

Appendix B, Mathematical Conversion—This appendix is included as a reference for those who work with the metric system versus the imperial system. It includes a table for converting fractions to decimals.

Glossary—The glossary provides all the important vocabulary terms and definitions that fashion students and professionals need to master.

Using the Complete Guide to Size Specification and Technical Design

STUDIO™ *Complete Guide to Size Specification and Technical Design*, Third Edition, now includes an online STUDIO accessible via www.BloomsburyFashionCentral.com, which provides easy access to content previously provided on the CD-ROM, as well as new online study tools aligned with each chapter of the book. With this valuable resource, students may:

- **Study smarter** with self-quizzes featuring scored results and personalized study tips
- **Review concepts** with flashcards of essential vocabulary
- **Downloadable templates**, blank spec sheets, basic garment and figure croquis, and sample spec sheets
- **Access additional resources** like a Care Labeling Guide, Ordering a Dress Form Guide and a Buttonline Card

Students can gain access to the STUDIO resources by purchasing a new textbook with a bundled access code. Access is free with purchase of Book + Studio ISBN 9781501313097 or eBook + Studio ISBN 9781501313080. Students may also purchase a STUDIO Access Card ISBN 9781501313073 at their campus bookstore or purchase Studio Instant Access ISBN 9781501313066 directly through Bloomsbury Fashion Central. Redeeming the access card will give students full access to the content on the CD-ROM packaged with previous editions of this book, plus material new to this edition. We are also pleased to now offer eBook rental options for this book. Visit *www.BloomsburyFashionCentral.com* for more information.

Instructor's Resources

- Instructor's Guide and Test Bank include sample syllabi, suggested projects, test questions, and evaluation guides
- *Learning with STUDIO* Student Registration Guide (PDF) and First Day of Class PowerPoint presentation (PPT)

To gain access to instructor resources, go to www.BloomsburyFashionCentral.com and create an account or log in to your account. Then visit the book webpage and in the instructor's module on the right hand side of the page, select "Instructor Resources" and click request. Within 48 hours of requesting, instructors will receive a confirming e-mail and may access requested review/exam copies, instructor's resources, and STUDIO content via the "My Course Material" section once logged in to the platform.

If you have any difficulties accessing the site or downloading material, please contact Customer Service at *www.bloomsburyfashioncentral.com/contact-us* for assistance.

Acknowledgments

I would again like to thank the wonderful staff at Fairchild Books for their invaluable experience and endless support, including, but not limited to Priscilla McGeehon, publisher; Amanda Breccia, senior acquisitions editor; Kiley Kudrna, assistant editor; and Edie Weinberg, art development editor.

The artwork thank yous once again go to Matrix Art Services, a division of Matrix Publishing services, Clay Weldon of Clay Weldon Design, and Graphic World, Inc. for providing new illustrations for this edition. Photo credits and thank yous belong to *JoAnn McGirr Turk*, Turk Photography.

I would like to thank again those who reviewed the first proposal and manuscript, offering insight that continues to inform the third edition: Catherine Black, Florida State University; Elizabeth Bye, University of Minnesota; Mary Ann Ferro, Fashion Institute of Technology; Cynthia L. Istook, North Carolina State University; Jo Kallal, University of Delaware; Marycarol Miller, Parsons School of Design; Anita Racine, Cornell University; Susan Suarez, Fashion Careers of California; Su Hwang, Texas Tech University; Jane Mountney, Art Institute Online; Dyana Harrison, Clary Sage College; Janace Bubonia, Texas Christian University; and Sheryl Farnan, Metropolitan Community College.

Lastly a big THANK YOU goes to my family for their love and support throughout this project.

PART I

GETTING STARTED

This text is designed for students and professionals as a comprehensive tool for size specification and technical design relating to the segment of the fashion industry known as private label and global garment production. By providing the basic knowledge needed to measure a garment, create a spec sheet, fit a garment, and grade, I hope to help fashion industry aspirants and professionals reach their goals as technical designers in the exciting field of garment production.

Chapters 1 through 3 explore the industry: "tools of the trade" used by technical designers, basic specification sheets, tips needed before beginning, how to measure a fit-model/form, how to prepare a workstation for measuring (giving systematically illustrated instructions for each basic measurement point), and basic measurement points for all garment types. Popular computer-aided design PLM/PDM programs are discussed as well.

Let's get started.

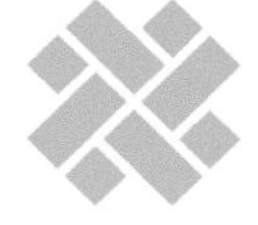

CHAPTER 1

Introduction to Size Specification and Technical Design

Brand Merchandise versus Private Label

National and designer brand merchandise is owned by manufacturing companies called wholesalers. The brands are produced in factories owned or contracted by the wholesaler, then purchased by various retail establishments. Brands are widely recognized by consumers, in part due to national advertising. *Free People*, *Stussy*, and *7 for All Mankind* are a few of the popular brands reported by blogger Olivia Newton of the hip British Youth market.[1]

"Private label" refers to merchandise that is manufactured by or for a retailer under a label owned by that retailer. Merchandise that carried retailers' names or any other names owned by them was once kept secret from the consumer. However, as the idea of private label or store-owned branding became popular and increasingly lucrative, the industry exploded. Anthropologie (by Urban Outfitters), Victoria's Secret, and Gap, including Old Navy and Banana Republic, are well-known private label retailers (see Figure 1.1). The retail store corporations own the labels. Corporate offices have designers or product development staffs that develop merchandise for their stores; this merchandise is produced at independent manufacturing factories or production plants. Manufacturers that produce their own lines have also been known to develop private brands for retailers. After production, the privately owned and labeled merchandise is shipped to distribution warehouses, and finally to their retail stores.

From the middle 1980s to the early 1990s, most fashion retail/buying offices started testing their own store labels. However, for retailers entering the manufacturing segment of the fashion industry, producing

Figure 1.1 Private label retailer.
(Bloomberg via Getty Images)

[1]*Which are the brands that Millennials love, hate or worse have no feeling towards?* Olivia Voxvurner. Report 2014, April 21, 2015, http://www.the-gma.com/brands-millennials-love-hate-worse-no-feeling-towards. Reprinted by The Global Marketing Alliance Accessed on June May 3, 2015.

clothing under private labels posed certain problems. As a variety of manufacturers produced garments under retail contracts, the retailers were finding inconsistencies in sizing and quality. Each sewing plant or factory was constructing garments with its own set of specifications. This resulted in specification buying and technical design, meaning merchandise was manufactured to the retail stores' standards, not the factories' standards. These private brand purchases allowed the stores to offer exclusive merchandise, giving them an edge over their competitors. It also offered the potential to increase profits, by providing a greater gross margin, through cutting out the middleman, and by enhancing the stores' image.

Today, private labels like Macy's *I.N.C.*, Bloomingdale's *Sutton Studio*, Saks Fifth Avenue's *Theory*, and Nordstrom's *BP* (*Brass Plum*) rival many of the designer labels (see Figure 1.2). In some cases, these retailers are spending money on in-house design staffs, store presentations, and national ad campaigns. The result is exclusive private brands that differentiate stores from one another.

Basically, a retail technical designer's job is to create and maintain size standards for this private brand merchandise. Have you ever noticed that you might be able to wear a pair of jeans in one size from one designer, but need a different size from another? The reason for this is that designers pride themselves on a unique fit, or brand standard, which represents the body image and profile of their customer, called their target market. Retailers have adopted this same philosophy for private labels. One retailer's brand may cater to a junior's market, so the cut of its clothing may reflect a younger, slimmer figure. Another retailer's brand may cater to an entirely different market, petites, for example. A petite figure less than five foot four inches in height is proportioned differently from a junior figure, perhaps of the same height, so the retailer must adopt size and quality brand standards that are unique to its customer. These are called retail standards. Once the retailer establishes its desired measurements, dress forms are custom made and models are hired so that garments can be checked against those standards.

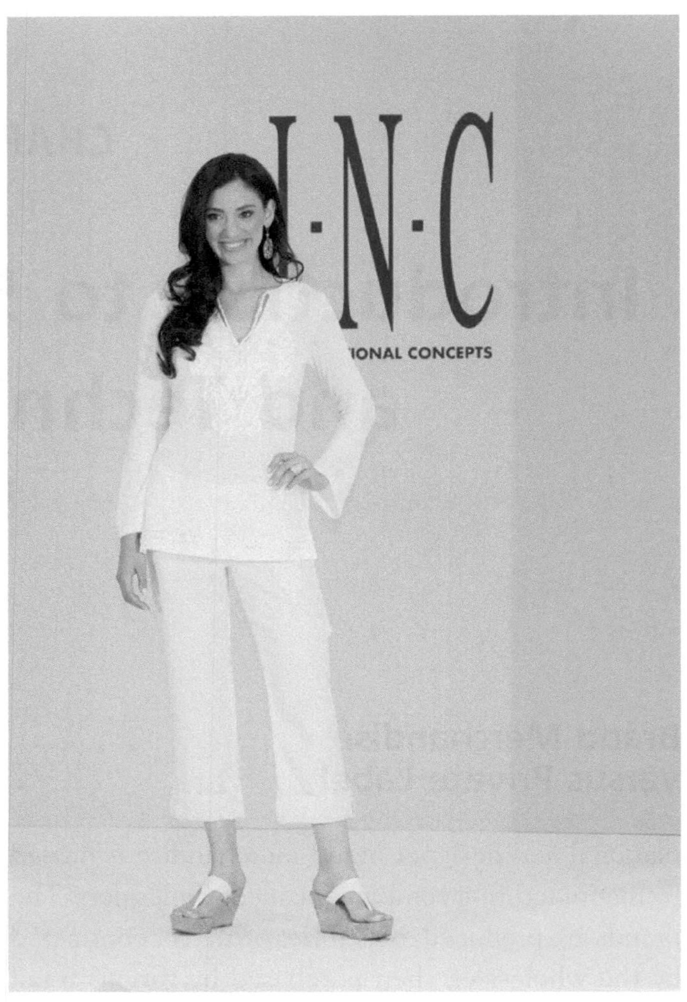

Figure 1.2 Private label brand.
(Getty Images for Macy's)

Retail standards are important because a retailer wants a customer to be loyal to its store. One of the best ways to ensure loyalty is to offer quality merchandise. Quality merchandise must of course look good, be priced right, hold up in laundering, be comfortable, and fit well. If the garment is not comfortable, chances are it does not fit properly. When a consumer is constantly pulling on the sleeve because the armhole is too small or tugging at the hem because a skirt rises, that customer will not be happy with her purchase and may not want to buy that store brand again. In private label, where the store's name is associated with the merchandise, a good standard fit is imperative.

Most branded merchandise and the majority of private label merchandise is produced overseas because costs are lower; therefore, profits are higher.

Retailers that produce private label merchandise have product development teams within their corporate offices that take care of production, while manufacturers have production managers to do the same. Unless factories are owned by retailers or manufacturers, both use people called sourcers who must locate the factories/plants. Some larger companies have staff that do nothing but locate and visit plants (manufacturing sources), looking for potential manufacturers of their merchandise. Other companies may give the job of locating these plants to the product development staff or they may hire independent sourcing companies. The independent sourcer often acts as a broker or liaison between the retailer, the manufacturer, and the production plant. Lai Apparel of New York is an example of a sourcing company that has had the prestigious TV retailer QVC as a client.

Once an agreement has been made between the retailer, the manufacturer, and the manufacturing plant, samples are produced. For private label companies, sample garments or prototypes can be created in several ways. The retailer might have staff designers create sketches of the desired garments, a product developer might find a great designer piece he or she would like to copy, or the factory might even offer design styles that it is currently producing. If samples are to be made from a sketch, specifications will be sent prior to the sample production. Sometimes samples are produced in advance of the retailer's finalized line in anticipation that they will be picked up (purchased under private label agreements), so style details may not be exact. Available buttons, zippers, fabrics, and trims that are close in style, type, and weight will be used for the first sample. However, sample styles that are copies or are accepted from a manufacture line for private label usually go through the process of being line approved; then specification sheets are written.

Branded manufacturers who source garments overseas also hire technical designers. The technical designers develop spec packages and follow through with production resources in other countries. They also develop production ready specifications, review prototypes or sales samples for construction and fit, and communicate with foreign agents, as well as work with the manufacturer's own merchandise and design teams.

Size Specification and Technical Design

Size specification is a term that has long been used in the fashion industry. It is simply a list of measurements for a particular size. Designers, patternmakers, and production personnel have all generated or used style sheets containing size specifications.

Designers use size specifications, also called specs, in several ways. One is to convey specific measurements to the draper or patternmaker. For example, if a designer wants the sweep of a specific garment to be 60 inches in circumference, she will note that on the spec sheet. A designer may also use a spec sheet if the garment is costing too much and costs need to be scaled back. The designer may look at the measurements and trim details and make appropriate style changes to save money.

A patternmaker uses a spec sheet differently. When he is making a first pattern from a sketch, he might estimate measurements, make the pattern, and then have a sample made from which a spec sheet is produced. On the other hand, a patternmaker may receive a set of specs that he must follow when drafting his first pattern.

Production personnel generally use specs for developing the cost of a garment; this is called costing.

Technical design is a relatively new industry term. As retailers entered the private label industry, they hired personnel to create size specification sheets, thus a title for this developing position was needed. Early on, some retailers like May Department Stores Co., Merchandising Services, used the title size specification analyst; Federated Department Stores and Macy's department stores used the title technical designer; Spiegel and J. C. Penney Company Inc. used the title quality assurance manager. Today, May, Federated, and Macy's have all merged to become Macy's Inc., and most companies use the term technical designer.

In retail, a technical designer is a person trained in design and patternmaking who can adjust garments to achieve a proper fit; compensate for variables such as movement, ease, and shrinkage; and act as a liaison between product development/design departments and manufacturers.

Some manufacturers hire technical designers to work with retailers to estimate cost sheets or to oversee offshore production of their lines. Specs are also used by garment manufacturers for estimating garment price quotes. Obtaining accurate garment measurements allows the manufacturer to better estimate marker yardage, which can help designers make important design and style decisions.

Once the line has been developed, the individual garments are sent to the size specification/technical design department for analysis. In larger retail companies, this department may be part of quality assurance or quality control. Occasionally, some companies will misuse titles for appearance or perceived prestige reasons, so let's look closely at the titles of these personnel.

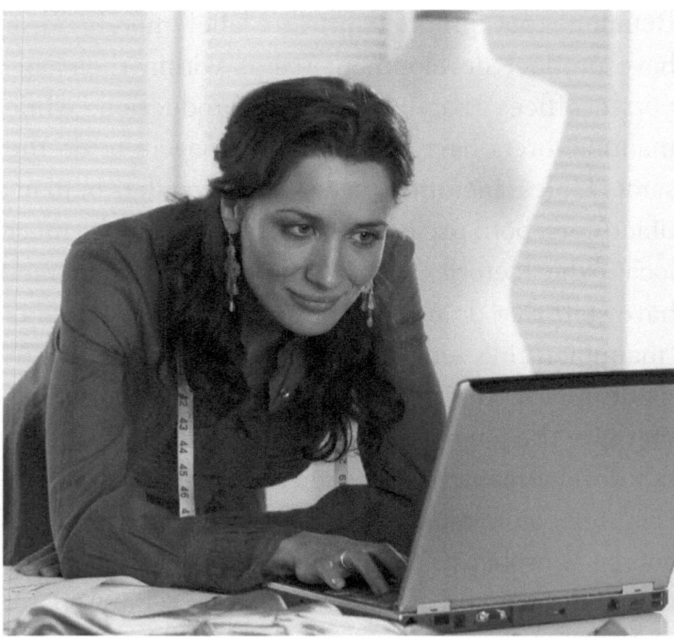

Figure 1.3 Technical designer working on computer.
(Tom Grill/The Image Bank/Getty Images)

- Style Clerk—A person working in a spec office who checks and records the style numbers of a garment for analysis. A secretary or assistant might also have this duty.
- Measurer—A person whose sole responsibility is to measure garments and record those measurements onto a spec sheet. This person reports to the technical designer. In many companies this position has been eliminated and the technical designer or assistant will measure the garments.
- Patternmaker—A person who can construct actual pattern pieces for a new style by adjusting a sloper (basic pattern) to meet the specifications required. The patternmaker who works in the specification/technical design/quality department often works with patternmakers at the manufacturing facilities. Many technical designers are also learning patternmaking, as some companies are eliminating patternmaking as well.
- Technical Designer—A person who analyzes garments, checking and adjusting fit as required and writing specification sheets (see Figure 1.3). This person also has a design background and can offer style changes as needed to solve production problems. Larger companies may have different levels of technical designers, e.g., junior technical designer and senior technical designer. The pay scale and levels of responsibility often dictate the title.
- Assistant Technical Designer—A person who performs clerical duties for the technical designer. This person knows how to measure and is apprenticing in fit analysis and design.
- Technical Design Manager/Senior Manager—A person who manages several technical designers, makes final fit decisions, writes specification sheets, and evaluates potential production risks. This person works closely with the general merchandise manager and/or a vice president/quality assurance-oriented partner, may offer style or design changes as needed for production, and sets the fit schedule.

Now let's look at the people who are responsible for creating the garments that are sent to the size specification analysts/technical designers for analysis. Not all companies have every position listed here. Depending on the size of the company and the nature of its business, some of the following positions will differ from company to company. Some positions can be combined; therefore, job responsibilities may overlap.

- Design Manager—A person who sets the brand or private label fashion direction, manages all aspects of design and development, and has final approval of materials, colors, patterns, and silhouettes for the season.
- Designer—A person engaged in creating new and original clothing or accessories by sketching and approving initial materials, colors, patterns, and silhouettes.
- Assistant Designer—A person who assists in interpreting the designer's creations. Depending on the company, this position may be more creative or more technical, based on whether the duties are more illustrative, designing or patternmaking, or sewing.
- Assistant Patternmaker—A person who works with the designer is an assistant to the designer and who can construct actual pattern pieces for a new style by adjusting a sloper (basic pattern) for sample making. This person may also apply draping methods to create a first design or sample.
- First Patternmaker/Patternmaker—A person who works with the designer or may be an assistant to the designer and who can construct actual pattern pieces for a new style by adjusting a sloper (basic pattern) for sample making. This person may also apply draping methods to create a first design or sample and then makes a final pattern for grading and production. Depending on the size of the company, patternmakers may have computer-generated systems to aid in the patternmaking. In smaller companies, the final patterns may be sent to an outside agency for grading and marker making.
- Illustrator/Sketcher—A person who illustrates/sketches for the designer, product development team, or technical team. Many illustrators/sketchers work freelance. In the past, illustrators were known for creating illustrations for ads, catalogs, or presentations, while sketchers did sketches for design, product development, and technical teams. The terms illustrator and sketcher have sometimes blurred in their definition, as some illustrators sketch and some sketchers illustrate.
- Assistant Product Developer/Manager—A person who helps develop and manage private label or brand merchandise within the sales and business plans.
- Product Development Manager—A person who oversees the development of private label or brand merchandise and monitors its production to ensure those garments meet the company's expectations.
- Product Manager—An executive who heads the product development team and is responsible for helping to plan, develop, and oversee the consistency of a style message for an exclusive product, product line, brand, or private label.
- Brand Manager—A person who is responsible for updating and maintaining brand identity, including private label, of a line and is responsible for planning, sales, and marketing of the brand.
- Merchandiser—A person who makes decisions concerning the direction of the company's line. The merchandiser studies market trends, conducts market research, works with the sales staff, and oversees product development, including private brands. This person is responsible for merchandise numbers in terms of the product and the stockkeeping units (SKUs).
- Fashion Director—A person who works closely with merchandisers, supplying important forecast information on color, trends, new fabrications, and market insights. The fashion director must stay at least one year ahead of the current industry trends. In some companies, the fashion director may have some of the same responsibilities as the merchandiser, without the numbers consideration.
- Sourcer/Sourcing Agent—A person who locates manufacturing facilities/factories to produce apparel merchandise. This responsibility may be part of the product development team's duties or can be contracted to an outside agency.
- Product Lifecycle Manager—A person who manages the Product Lifecycle Management System, a computer system that tracks the product development process from a garment's conception through design, manufacture, service, and disposal. A large company may have an entire Product Lifecycle Management (PLM) team.

- Stylist—A person who shops the market for style ideas that will fit the company's image. The stylist also translates those style ideas to fit the company's needs. A stylist often gives direction to the design department or product development staff and therefore must have a thorough knowledge of textiles and color.
- Assistant Merchandiser—A person who works for the merchandiser and is primarily responsible for clerical duties. This person is often an intermediary between the merchandiser and other company personnel.
- Department Merchandise Manager (DMM)—A person who manages a division or department of merchandise. This person manages several merchandisers and reports to a general merchandise manager.
- General Merchandise Manager (GMM)—A person who manages several divisions or departments of merchandise. This person reports to a vice president or a merchandise-oriented partner.
- Merchandise Product Director—A person who provides leadership to the divisional managers by driving and managing the core vendor business to deliver sales and margin results. Merchandise product directors provide strategic direction for private label and branded merchandise.

Whether you want to be a designer, buyer, merchandiser, patternmaker, or any number of other positions in the fashion business, chances are that you will encounter private label or offshore production in your career. Therefore, having knowledge of the workings of size specification/technical design can be useful in many ways. Here are a few examples.

Designers who work for manufacturers often work with buyers, where they design exclusive store merchandise. During a salesroom showing, a buyer might see a beautiful Indian lace dress at a vendor's house, but she doesn't like the style of the dress designed. She would like to have something made in that Indian lace, but it is exclusive to that vendor's house. The buyer has two options. Either have the lace copied at another fabric manufacturer or try to get an exclusively designed item by that vendor. If the vendor chooses to design and produce an exclusive item for the buyer, this merchandise will now compete with other merchandise that the buyer can get through private labeling. As a result, it is important for the designer and the vendor to know and understand the workings of private label in order to stay competitive.

Many of the industry's well-known retail stores, such as Gap, sell exclusive private branded merchandise. Even as a sales clerk, it is important to know your store's exclusive sizing, where the merchandise is manufactured, the quality of fabrics, care of fabrics, and so on. Consumers have become very savvy and expect a store's sales force to be knowledgeable.

As you can see, the industry is complex. The more you know, the more successful you will be. So let's take a look at what you need to know to become a technical designer.

Becoming a Technical Designer

Basic knowledge of garment construction and patternmaking is essential to becoming a technical designer, even though few are ever asked to sew a garment or make a pattern. However, technical designers constantly work with creative designers and patternmakers; therefore, they need to be informed in these situations. In addition, fitting apparel requires knowledge of quality garment construction, patternmaking, and an eye for detail. Having these skills is imperative when troubleshooting potential fit problems. Common fit problems and adjustments will be discussed in detail later in this text.

Basic, flat sketching skills are often required. This text offers basic style croquis (see Appendix A) to aid in drawing. Computer-generated sketches and digital photography are other tools used by technicians. Knowledge of computer photo and drawing programs (especially Illustrator, Corel, and Photoshop) is advised. Companies vary in their computer software, ranging anywhere from purchased specification packages (Karat Software), proprietary programs (Lectra and Gerber PDM) to spreadsheets (Excel) and databases (Access), so knowledge of those popular programs is advised as well. The majority of spec information is sent via email worldwide. Therefore, email communication skills are essential, including formatting and attachment capabilities.

Technical design requires an acute sense of detail. A person with an affinity for detail does well in this field. The pace is fast, and costly mistakes must be avoided. One incorrect or missed measurement can result in a neckline that doesn't fit or in a bulging hipline.

It takes time and practice to become a technical designer. At first, measuring is difficult because there are so many points of measurement. Individual companies will have different measurement points and different ways of measuring. It is easy to miss measurements and make mistakes. Companies also differ in the way they record measurements. Some are recorded flat or singular, while others are recorded in the circumference, or doubled. It is believed that wovens were originally recorded in circumference measurements because woven blouses were sold by chest measurements (32, 34, 36, etc.) rather than sized (6, 8, 10, 12 . . .). It is also believed that knits were originally recorded flat because most knitting machines, circular and flat, use singular measurements. Today, there is great debate among technicians/technical designers over the use of flat versus circumference. Some technicians prefer to record all measurements flat—knit or woven—feeling there is less room for human error when recording. Other technicians prefer to record their measurements in the circumference because those numbers better relate to fit adjustments or conversions from imperial to metric systems. Many of the large buying offices' technicians use both methods, recording knit garments via flat and woven garments via circumference methods. Since you will need to learn both, this text follows the knit-flat, woven-circumference methodology.

A mastery of fractional math is imperative. Although many companies use computers for grading, manual manipulation of numbers is necessary. For example, a technician might need to add ⅝ inch to a measurement of 12½ inches to achieve a desired fit. Don't let that scare you—in time, adding fractions will become as routine as simple addition. However, even imperial numbers with fractions may show up differently on various sheets; for example, 12.5 is the same as 12½.

Dedication is also an important attribute of technical designers. Depending on the size of the company, a single technician may evaluate several thousand garments a year. Market weeks, though not as popular in the industry as they once were, are still especially busy and meeting deadlines is imperative. The technician must be a company person, putting the needs of the company first. Hours can be long and grueling, but beyond self-satisfaction the rewards may be vast. Most technicians are well paid and may have comprehensive benefits packages, including healthcare and retirement plans, especially in larger companies. Some companies also offer bonuses, merchandise discounts, free or inexpensively priced samples, and dinner perks. There is often the opportunity for domestic and foreign travel. Technical designers are an integral part of the fashion business and are respected as such.

Any company that generates or utilizes specification sheets may hire a technical designer. The industry is widespread in the way it does business; manufacturers, consulting firms, sourcing offices, and warehouse quality control departments are just a few places where technical designers might work.

In the chapters that follow, you will learn how to measure models and body forms, measure garments, create spec sheets, fit garments for quality assurance, and grade sizes for production. It's a lot to learn. Patience and practice are essential to becoming a technical designer.

CHAPTER 1 TERMS

When working as a technical designer, you may come across the following terms. If you are unfamiliar with any of them, please look up the definitions in the glossary at the end of this text.

Brand/Branded merchandise
Private label merchandise
Retail standard
Size specification
Technical design
Technical designer

CHAPTER 2

Tools of the Trade

Before You Begin

Before any garment can be evaluated, a company sets up its technical design department. This involves getting body dimensions from the designer, patternmaker, or product development team and having dress forms custom made. Spec sheets are designed and measurement points are created. Then garments are measured, and fit sessions are conducted by evaluating garments using proper body ease, and approved sample specifications are graded into a full size range.

It is important to know that not only the layout of specification sheets (specs) vary within the industry but also the number of spec sheets that may be written per garment. Generally, there is a "first" or "working" spec sheet, a fully graded approval sheet, and as many in between as it takes to get the garment right. The method of developing a first size specification sheet also varies within the industry. Specs generated for offshore production generally start with a company sample. Private label specs may begin with an evaluation of a designer sample (for copying), a factory sample, a sketch, a photograph, or a combination thereof. With the exception of a sketch or photograph, requiring the technician to use her experience and expertise to develop measurements without a garment, both the designer garment and the factory sample are usually measured first, fit onto a model or form, and then evaluated. This text works on the premise that a garment has been provided.

In this chapter you will look at determining basic body dimensions, measuring a model or body form, and using a spec sheet.

Determining Basic Body Dimensions

Statistical tables compiled by the United States government have been adapted for most size categories used today in ready-to-wear apparel, whether designer, branded, or private label. Those tables reflect average of body measurements of large, random groups of people. ASTM (American Society for Testing and Materials) has done further analysis and compiled the statistical tables shown in Table 2.1 for adult female misses.

Neither ASTM nor the author proposes that these measurements are industry standards. They are simply an average of body measurements that may be used for individualized standardization. Furthermore, very few individuals have body measurements that exactly reflect the measurements given in Table 2.1. Any number of women who customarily wear a given size will have certain measurements that differ in relation to the table that follow. Posture and height are additional differential factors.

Table 2.1 STANDARD TABLE OF BODY MEASUREMENTS FOR ADULT FEMALE MISSES FIGURE TYPE, SIZES 2–20

Girth Measurements in inches.

Size	2	4	6	8	10	12	14	16	18	20
Bust	32	33	34	35	36	$37\frac{1}{2}$	39	$40\frac{1}{2}$	$42\frac{1}{2}$	$44\frac{1}{2}$
Waist	24	25	26	27	28	$29\frac{1}{2}$	31	$32\frac{1}{2}$	$34\frac{1}{2}$	$36\frac{1}{2}$
High hip	$31\frac{1}{2}$	$32\frac{1}{2}$	$33\frac{1}{2}$	$34\frac{1}{2}$	$35\frac{1}{2}$	37	$38\frac{1}{2}$	40	42	44
Hip	$34\frac{1}{2}$	$35\frac{1}{2}$	$36\frac{1}{2}$	$37\frac{1}{2}$	$38\frac{1}{2}$	40	$41\frac{1}{2}$	43	45	47
Mid-neck	13	$13\frac{1}{4}$	$13\frac{1}{2}$	$13\frac{3}{4}$	14	$14\frac{3}{8}$	$14\frac{3}{4}$	$15\frac{1}{8}$	$15\frac{5}{8}$	$16\frac{1}{8}$
Neck base	$13\frac{1}{2}$	$13\frac{3}{4}$	14	$14\frac{1}{4}$	$14\frac{1}{2}$	$14\frac{7}{8}$	$15\frac{1}{4}$	$15\frac{5}{8}$	$16\frac{1}{8}$	$16\frac{5}{8}$
Armseye	$14\frac{1}{4}$	$14\frac{5}{8}$	15	$15\frac{3}{8}$	$15\frac{3}{4}$	$16\frac{3}{8}$	17	$17\frac{5}{8}$	$18\frac{3}{8}$	$19\frac{1}{8}$
Upper arm	10	$10\frac{1}{4}$	$10\frac{1}{2}$	$10\frac{3}{4}$	11	$11\frac{3}{8}$	$11\frac{3}{4}$	$12\frac{1}{8}$	$12\frac{3}{4}$	$13\frac{3}{8}$
Elbow	$9\frac{3}{8}$	$9\frac{1}{2}$	$9\frac{5}{8}$	$9\frac{3}{4}$	$9\frac{7}{8}$	$10\frac{1}{8}$	$10\frac{3}{8}$	$10\frac{5}{8}$	11	$11\frac{3}{8}$
Wrist	$5\frac{5}{8}$	$5\frac{3}{4}$	$5\frac{7}{8}$	6	$6\frac{1}{8}$	$6\frac{1}{4}$	$6\frac{3}{8}$	$6\frac{1}{2}$	$6\frac{5}{8}$	$6\frac{3}{4}$
Thigh, max	$19\frac{1}{2}$	$20\frac{1}{4}$	21	$21\frac{3}{4}$	$22\frac{1}{2}$	$23\frac{1}{2}$	$24\frac{1}{2}$	$25\frac{1}{2}$	$26\frac{3}{4}$	28
Thigh, mid	$18\frac{1}{4}$	$18\frac{3}{4}$	$19\frac{1}{4}$	$19\frac{3}{4}$	20	21	$21\frac{3}{4}$	22	23	24
Knee	13	$13\frac{3}{8}$	$13\frac{3}{4}$	$14\frac{1}{8}$	$14\frac{1}{2}$	15	$15\frac{1}{2}$	16	$16\frac{1}{2}$	17
Calf	$12\frac{1}{2}$	$12\frac{7}{8}$	$13\frac{1}{4}$	$13\frac{5}{8}$	$14\frac{1}{8}$	$14\frac{1}{2}$	15	$15\frac{1}{2}$	16	$16\frac{1}{2}$
Ankle	$8\frac{3}{8}$	$8\frac{5}{8}$	$8\frac{7}{8}$	$9\frac{1}{8}$	$9\frac{3}{8}$	$9\frac{5}{8}$	$9\frac{7}{8}$	$10\frac{1}{8}$	$10\frac{3}{8}$	$10\frac{5}{8}$
Vertical trunk	56	$57\frac{1}{2}$	59	$60\frac{1}{2}$	62	$63\frac{1}{2}$	65	$66\frac{1}{2}$	68	$69\frac{1}{2}$
Total crotch	25	$25\frac{3}{4}$	$26\frac{1}{2}$	$27\frac{1}{4}$	28	$28\frac{3}{4}$	$29\frac{1}{2}$	$30\frac{1}{4}$	31	$31\frac{3}{4}$
Vertical Measurements in inches.										
Stature	$63\frac{1}{2}$	64	$64\frac{1}{2}$	65	$65\frac{1}{2}$	66	$66\frac{1}{2}$	67	$67\frac{1}{2}$	68
Cervical height	$54\frac{1}{2}$	55	$55\frac{1}{2}$	56	$56\frac{1}{2}$	57	$57\frac{1}{2}$	58	$58\frac{1}{2}$	59
Waist height	$39\frac{1}{4}$	$39\frac{1}{2}$	$39\frac{3}{4}$	40	$40\frac{1}{4}$	$40\frac{1}{2}$	$40\frac{3}{4}$	41	$41\frac{1}{4}$	$41\frac{1}{2}$
High hip height	$35\frac{1}{4}$	$35\frac{1}{2}$	$35\frac{3}{4}$	36	$36\frac{1}{4}$	$36\frac{1}{2}$	$36\frac{3}{4}$	37	$37\frac{1}{4}$	$37\frac{1}{2}$

(continued)

Table 2.1 STANDARD TABLE OF BODY MEASUREMENTS FOR ADULT FEMALE MISSES FIGURE TYPE, SIZES 2–20 *(continued)*

Girth Measurements in inches.

Size	2	4	6	8	10	12	14	16	18	20
Hip height	$31\frac{1}{4}$	$31\frac{1}{2}$	$31\frac{3}{4}$	32	$32\frac{1}{4}$	$32\frac{1}{2}$	$32\frac{3}{4}$	33	$33\frac{1}{4}$	$33\frac{1}{2}$
Crotch height	$29\frac{1}{2}$	$29\frac{1}{2}$	$29\frac{1}{2}$	$29\frac{1}{2}$	$29\frac{1}{2}$	$29\frac{1}{2}$	$29\frac{1}{2}$	$29\frac{1}{2}$	$29\frac{1}{2}$	$29\frac{1}{2}$
Knee height	$17\frac{5}{8}$	$17\frac{3}{4}$	$17\frac{7}{8}$	18	$18\frac{1}{8}$	$18\frac{1}{4}$	$18\frac{3}{8}$	$18\frac{1}{2}$	$18\frac{5}{8}$	$18\frac{3}{4}$
Ankle height	$2\frac{3}{4}$	$2\frac{3}{4}$	$2\frac{3}{4}$	$2\frac{3}{4}$	$2\frac{3}{4}$	$2\frac{3}{4}$	$2\frac{3}{4}$	$2\frac{3}{4}$	$2\frac{3}{4}$	$2\frac{3}{4}$
Waist length (front)	$13\frac{1}{2}$	$13\frac{3}{4}$	14	$14\frac{1}{4}$	$14\frac{1}{2}$	$14\frac{3}{4}$	15	$15\frac{1}{4}$	$15\frac{1}{2}$	$15\frac{3}{4}$
Waist length (back) (on Curve)	$15\frac{1}{2}$	$15\frac{3}{4}$	16	$16\frac{1}{4}$	$16\frac{1}{2}$	$16\frac{3}{4}$	17	$17\frac{1}{4}$	$17\frac{1}{2}$	$17\frac{3}{4}$
True rise	$9\frac{3}{4}$	10	$10\frac{1}{4}$	$10\frac{1}{2}$	$10\frac{3}{4}$	11	$11\frac{1}{4}$	$11\frac{1}{2}$	$11\frac{3}{4}$	12

Width and Length Measurements in inches.

Size	2	4	6	8	10	12	14	16	18	20
Across shoulder	$14\frac{3}{8}$	$14\frac{5}{8}$	$14\frac{7}{8}$	$15\frac{1}{8}$	$15\frac{3}{8}$	$15\frac{3}{4}$	$16\frac{1}{8}$	$16\frac{1}{2}$	17	$17\frac{1}{2}$
Cross-back width	$13\frac{7}{8}$	$14\frac{1}{8}$	$14\frac{3}{8}$	$14\frac{5}{8}$	$14\frac{7}{8}$	$15\frac{1}{4}$	$15\frac{5}{8}$	16	$16\frac{1}{2}$	17
Cross-chest width	$12\frac{7}{8}$	$13\frac{1}{8}$	$13\frac{3}{8}$	$13\frac{5}{8}$	$13\frac{7}{8}$	$14\frac{1}{4}$	$14\frac{5}{8}$	15	$15\frac{1}{2}$	16
Shoulder length	$4\frac{15}{16}$	5	$5\frac{1}{16}$	$5\frac{1}{8}$	$5\frac{3}{16}$	$5\frac{5}{16}$	$5\frac{7}{16}$	$5\frac{9}{16}$	$5\frac{3}{4}$	$5\frac{15}{16}$
Shoulder slope (degrees)	23	23	23	23	23	23	23	23	23	23
Arm length shoulder to wrist	$22\frac{15}{16}$	$23\frac{1}{8}$	$23\frac{5}{16}$	$23\frac{1}{2}$	$23\frac{11}{16}$	$23\frac{7}{8}$	$24\frac{1}{16}$	$24\frac{1}{4}$	$24\frac{7}{16}$	$24\frac{5}{8}$
Arm length shoulder to elbow	$13\frac{1}{4}$	$13\frac{3}{8}$	$13\frac{1}{2}$	$13\frac{5}{8}$	$13\frac{3}{4}$	$13\frac{7}{8}$	14	$14\frac{1}{8}$	$14\frac{1}{4}$	$14\frac{3}{8}$
Arm length center back neck to wrist	$30\frac{1}{8}$	$30\frac{7}{16}$	$30\frac{3}{4}$	$31\frac{1}{16}$	$31\frac{3}{8}$	$31\frac{3}{4}$	$32\frac{1}{8}$	$32\frac{1}{2}$	$32\frac{15}{16}$	$33\frac{3}{8}$
Bust point to bust point	7	$7\frac{1}{4}$	$7\frac{1}{2}$	$7\frac{3}{4}$	8	$8\frac{1}{4}$	$8\frac{1}{2}$	$8\frac{3}{4}$	9	$9\frac{1}{4}$
Neck to bust point	$9\frac{1}{4}$	$9\frac{1}{2}$	$9\frac{3}{4}$	10	$10\frac{1}{4}$	$10\frac{5}{8}$	11	$11\frac{3}{8}$	$11\frac{7}{8}$	$12\frac{3}{8}$
Scye depth	$7\frac{1}{8}$	$7\frac{1}{4}$	$7\frac{3}{8}$	$7\frac{1}{2}$	$7\frac{5}{8}$	$7\frac{3}{4}$	$7\frac{7}{8}$	8	$8\frac{1}{8}$	$8\frac{1}{4}$

Therefore, the body measurement points and dimensions listed in Table 2.1 have been added for your reference. Many companies have done private analysis or statistical gathering (possibly including this table) and have developed their own measurement tables. They use their own standards for sizing and an industry fit model that represents those standards. Nevertheless, the body dimensions shown here are good guidelines to use when analyzing size proportions. Classroom body forms are often donated by companies in the industry or are ordered according to individualized dress form company specifications. You may want to measure available forms against these measurements for size referencing.

Measuring a Model or Body Form

ASTM also proposes body-measuring points for a fit model. She should be measured thoroughly once a year and spot-checked monthly. It is important to use a fiberglass (plastic) measuring tape, as it will not stretch, and to have your model stand erect with a normal breathing pattern (see Figures 2.1, 2.2, and 2.3). A body form only needs to be measured once

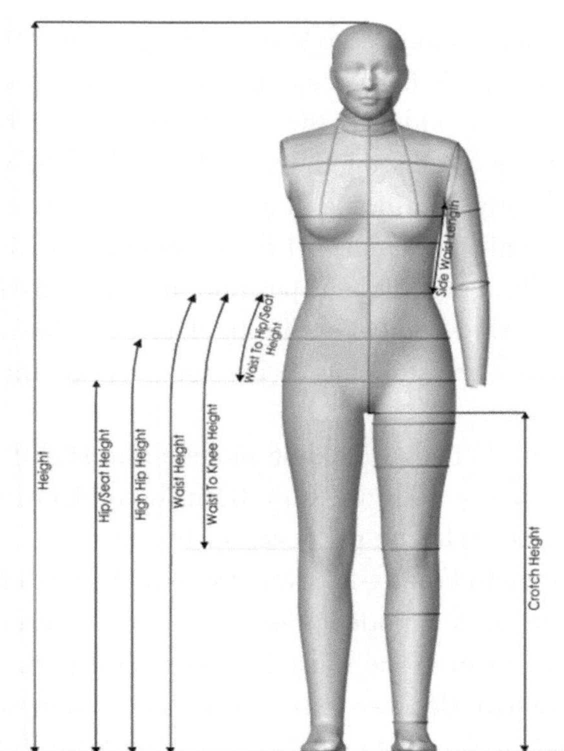

Figure 2.1 How to measure the body
(ASTM)

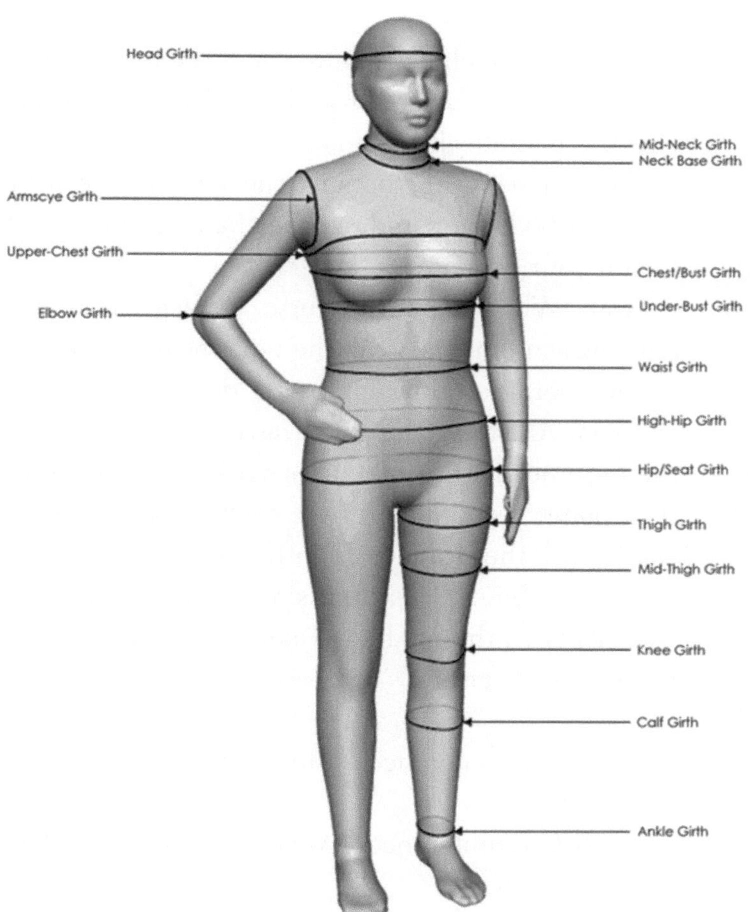

Figure 2.2 How to measure the body
(ASTM)

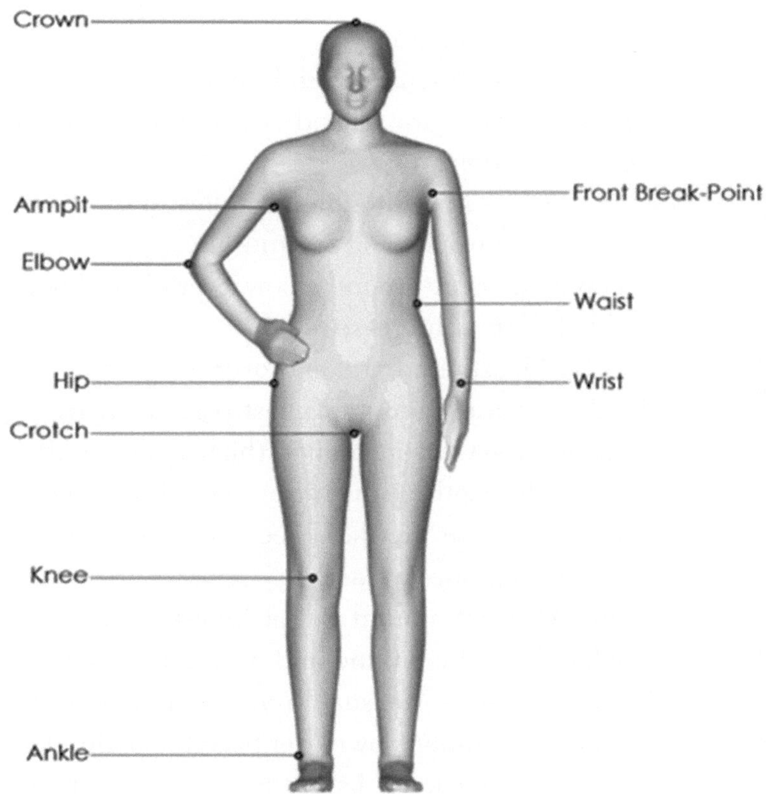

Figure 2.3 How to measure the body
(ASTM)

since it will not change. However, if the form is subject to severe wear or abuse, it is advisable to spot-check it periodically or replace it.

The following instructions can be used for a fit model or body form and may be changed or adapted to suit your needs.

Note: When measuring torso and leg circumference measurements, keep the tape measure parallel to the floor at all times; arms are down in a relaxed position. All stature/height measurements made on the form need a manufacturer mark on the stand to floor point. If you do not have such a mark, then be sure to ask the distance from the ankle to the floor (generally about 2¾"); then simply stop these measurements at the ankle and add the ankle to floor measurement given.

- Bust Circumference—Measure around fullest part of bust.
- Waist Circumference—Measure around smallest part of waist.
- High/Upper Hip Circumference—Measure around hip at a point 4" below waist.
- Low Hip Circumference—Measure around hip at a point 7" below waist.
- Mid Neck—Measure around middle of neck.
- Armseye—Measure around armseye at a natural relaxed position.
- Upper Arm—Measure around fullest part of upper arm without flexing the muscle.
- Elbow—Measure around elbow, over elbow bone, and between arm crease.
- Wrist—Measure around and over wrist bone.
- Thigh—Measure around fullest part of thigh.
- Mid Thigh—Measure around thigh at a point that is one-half length of thigh from crotch to knee.
- Knee—Measure around knee, over knee bone, and between knee crease.
- Calf—Measure around calf at fullest point.
- Ankle—Measure around and over ankle bone.
- Vertical Trunk—Measure from bottom of front neck at indentation down over front torso, through crotch, and back up back torso to top vertebra bone. [Note: Some companies prefer to take this measurement from right shoulder neck point, down over front torso, through crotch, and back up to starting point at right shoulder.]
- Cross-back Width—Measure at a point 4" down from back neck bone straight across back from armseye to armseye.
- Cross-chest Width—Measure at a point 4" down from shoulder at neck straight across chest from armseye to armseye.
- Bust Point to Bust Point—Measure from one bust point apex straight across to other bust point apex.
- Neck to Bust Point—Measure from neck at shoulder straight down to bust point apex.
- Armseye to Waist—Measure from the underarm, armseye, straight down the side of the body, to the smallest part of the waist.
- Waist to Hip—First mark the hip at a point 7" below the waist from the bottom of the waist at center front, then measure along the side of the body from the waist, at the smallest part, down to the hip at the point that intersects with the first point.
- Shoulder Length—Measure from the right shoulder to the left shoulder (feeling for shoulder bones) straight across the back.
- Arm Length, Shoulder to Wrist—Holding model's arm in a slightly bent position, measure from the top of the shoulder at the shoulder bone down the outer arm, crossing the top edge of the elbow bone slightly, continuing down to the wrist bone.
- Arm Length, Shoulder to Elbow—Holding model's arm in a slightly bent position, measure from the top of the shoulder at the shoulder bone down the outer arm, stopping at the top edge of the elbow bone.
- Underarm Length—Holding model's arm slightly away from the body, measure from the underarm straight down to the palm side of the wrist.
- Waist Length Front—Measure from the bottom of the front neck at indentation straight down over the front torso to the waist at the smallest part.
- Waist Length Back—Measure from the bottom of the back neck at the neck bone straight down the back to the waist at the smallest part.

- ❖ Stature—Measure from the top of the head straight down the back to the floor.
- ❖ Shoulder Height—Measure from the right shoulder bone straight down the front to the floor.
- ❖ Bust Height—Measure from the apex of the bust straight down to the floor.
- ❖ Waist Height—Measure from the center front waist straight down to the floor.
- ❖ High Hip Height—Measure from the high hip from a point 4" below the center front of the waist straight down to the floor.
- ❖ Low Hip Height—Measure from the low hip from a point 7" below the center front of the waist straight down to the floor.
- ❖ Crotch Height—Measure from the crotch from between the legs straight down to the floor.
- ❖ Knee Height—Measure from inside the leg, inseam, at the center of the knee straight down to the floor.
- ❖ Ankle Height—Measure from inside the leg, inseam, at the ankle bone straight down to the floor.

Using a Spec Sheet

A specification sheet, or spec sheet, is a technical rendering of a garment that identifies the points of measurement and size ranges. Every garment on the line requires a new set of specs because each garment is unique. All companies, large or small, now generate specs on a computer. The larger companies, as you learned earlier, use software packages, while small companies may simply draft specs using Word or Excel spreadsheets. Either way it is a good idea for technical designers to be able to develop specs by hand. For some companies, the trend to go global in order to keep up with competition has become so great that they have to outsource their specification services. Outsourcing to a consulting firm can offer companies instant access to qualified staff while they grow their own.

Developing a spec by hand or with the aid of a computer takes considerable training and experience. It is imperative that everyone in the production and manufacturing of clothing be able to read and use a spec sheet. Specs will vary in design throughout the industry. Let's look at the parts of a generic spec sheet (see Figure 2.4).

- ❖ Style—A numerical code or name is used to identify each style. Style numbers or garment names are often designated according to department, grouping, or style type.
- ❖ Season—Most retailers and wholesalers track styles by season. Even if silhouettes are repeated from season to season, a new style or color number/name is often assigned.
- ❖ Code—Codes are used for the method of measurement. There are more than 150 different codes used in the industry; only the most frequently used codes are printed on the spec sheets. Codes are important because they match the detailed measurement instructions found in the company's measurement manual. This text uses code numbers 1 to 155. Some spec manuals use three-digit codes or code numbers and letters. However designated, codes on the spec sheet in the code column will always match codes on the technical sketch.
- ❖ Point of Measure (Measurement Method)—A brief description of the method of measurement is listed beside the code. A single industry standard for measuring has not been set; therefore, it cannot be assumed that everyone using the spec sheet will measure the same way. The description is very important for this reason. It is also important if a common method needs to be changed to accommodate a particular style. The change is then noted next to the description. You'll learn more about that later.
- ❖ Tolerance—Sewing garments is not an exact science. Although every step is taken to ensure accuracy, no two garments will ever be exactly alike. Therefore, tolerance measurements are given to indicate how much of a measurement deviation, on the plus or minus, will be accepted. Tolerences are included on the misses, children's and menswear grade sheets for your reference (see Chapter 19).

GENERIC SPEC SHEET	STYLE
SEASON:	DESCRIPTION:
LABEL: (SIZE CATEGORY)	
DATE:	
TECHNICAL SKETCH	SKETCH/PHOTO

CODE	POINT OF MEASURE	TOL. +/–	4	S/6	8	M/10	12	L/14	16	XL/18

COMMENTS:

Figure 2.4 Generic spec sheet.

- Size Category—There are a number of different size categories, each carrying a size range. The children's wear category includes newborn 0 to 6 months, infant 6 to 24 months, toddler 2T to 4T, girls 4 to 6x, boys 4 to 7x, girls 7 to 16, and boys 8 to 20. Preteen sizes 8 to 14 are sometimes categorized with children's wear and other times are considered prejuniors. Juniors are generally a separate category with sizes ranging from 2 to 10 or 3 to 11. Women's wear is broken into misses/women's sizes, generally ranging from size 4 to 16, and large/plus sizes ranging from 18 to 30. The menswear category breaks down its sizes by style, for example, neck and sleeve length for shirts, waist for pants, and chest for suit jackets. Spec sheets will generally indicate the size category by department name, e.g., misses/women's wear.
- Size Range—Each size must be cut to its own measurements. The range of sizes (small, medium, large, extra large, for example) is listed across the top of the size columns. Generally, only the sizes that will actually be produced for that garment will be listed. A first or sample spec will only list the sample size measurements. Fully graded specs are developed after the sample has been approved for production. Chapter 19 covers grading instructions and includes grading charts for your reference.
- Sketch—A sketch or photo, often called a work sketch or work photo, is attached to the spec sheet. This gives everyone using the spec sheet a visual reference of the garment under production. It is important that exact style details are reflected on this sketch (the number of buttons, a pocket or a zipper, for example). Basic garment croquis can be found in Appendix A.
- Technical Sketch—The technical sketch is used as a key for visual code reference. The basic codes most frequently used are found on this sketch. If a style feature requires deviation from a basic or common code, then the new code must be added to the sketch for clarification. Details for clarification will be found in the Measurement Preparation section of this text found in chapter 3.

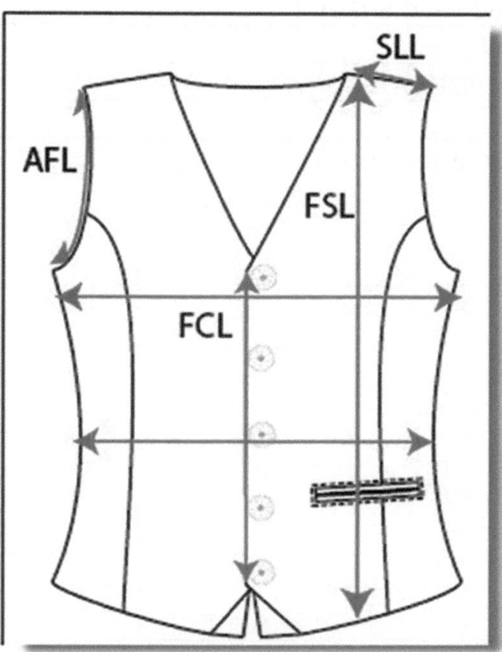

Figure 2.5 POM codes created in a Stylefile Program.
(Cathleen Fasanella)

Computer-generated sketches often allow the measuring details to be added right on the work sketch, eliminating the need for this sketch (see Figure 2.5).

A fit session worksheet (also known as a working specification/fit sheet), which we do not use in this text, is commonly used in the industry during the evaluation of production samples. Essentially, a fit session worksheet looks the same as a spec sheet with the exception of the measuring boxes. In place of the boxes for the size range and fully graded measurements, the fit session worksheet has the following (see Figure 2.6):

- Prototype—The prototype column is for the first measurements that were developed from a sketch or any garment under evaluation that is not from the contracted production plant.
- Revised Spec—The revised spec column is used after fitting a first garment. Changes or corrections are placed in this column. If first measurements are developed from a sketch, this column is not used.

GENERIC SPEC SHEET	STYLE
SEASON:	DESCRIPTION:
LABEL: (SIZE CATEGORY)	
DATE:	
TECHNICAL SKETCH	SKETCH/PHOTO

CODE	POINT OF MEASURE	TOL. +/–	PROTO-TYPE	REVISED SPEC	FIRST SAMPLE	FINAL SPEC	X	COMMENTS

COMMENTS:
NOTE: X INDICATES THE SAMPLE IS OUT OF TOLERANCE

(Tolerance 1/2-3/4 S, M, L, XL = 3/4" 4-18 = 1/2")

The measured garment spec sheets are for ***illustrative purposes only*** and should not be used as industry standards

Figure 2.6 Fit session worksheet.

- First Sample—The first sample column is used to list the measurements of the first sample as submitted by the contracted production plant. In some instances more than one sample will need to be submitted before production approval. If the garment is a second or third sample, the technician can simply make a note by changing this column or putting that designation in the comments column.
- Final Spec—The final spec column lists the approved specs decided upon after the sample evaluation. In most cases, these numbers reflect the revised spec or the sample spec measurements. However, there will be instances when new measurements are given. These changes should be noted in the comments column.
- X—This is the "out-of-tolerance" column. This column is used by the technician to let the contractor know that a measurement is not within allowed limits for sewing discrepancies. It is used to flag potential fit and construction problems.
- Comments—Any comments that need to be indicated to the production plant by the technician can go in this column.

In the chapters that follow, you will learn how to measure garments. These measurements are recorded onto the spec sheets. Later, when you are ready to evaluate garments for fit, those measurements will be analyzed one by one and changed or corrected as needed. But for now, it's time to get familiar with measuring. Read through and practice the measurement points in Chapter 3, then move on to the individual garment chapters for more measuring practice and spec sheet recording.

Computers in Fashion

PLM, PDM, CAD: What does it all mean and how is it affecting the industry? For some time, designers and technicians used simple programs like Microsoft Word and Excel. As they became more proficient they began to import Adobe Illustrator or Photoshop into their files. However, the industry has gone far beyond that technology, with the ability to import fabric samples into 3D images, and make virtual fittings on avatars. But before we look at the large companies that offer these services, let's look at the terminology they use.

- Product Lifecycle Management (PLM)—a system that tracks the product development process from a garment's conception through design, manufacture, service, and disposal.
- Product Data Management (PDM)—a system that tracks documents such as supplier sources and records, bill of materials, engineering tasks, and workflow.
- Computer-Aided Design (CAD)—a system used to design and develop products.

A few of the large companies offering technology solutions for fashion are Lectra, Gerber Technology, OptiTex, and Assyst Bullmer (see Figures 2.7, 2.8, and 2.9). They can offer services that range from image scanning, fabric design, pattern digitizing, and grading to virtual fitting. Technical designers work within these programs to record their specifications. It can take months to become proficient in these programs. Many large universities offer courses, but most beginning technicians apprentice on the job.

CHAPTER 2 TERMS

When working as a technical designer, you will come across the following terms. If you are unfamiliar with any of them, please look up the definitions in the glossary at the end of this text.

Body dimension
Computer-Aided Design (CAD)
Dress/body form
Product Data Management (PDM)
Product Lifecycle Management (PLM)
Prototype
Specification (spec) sheet

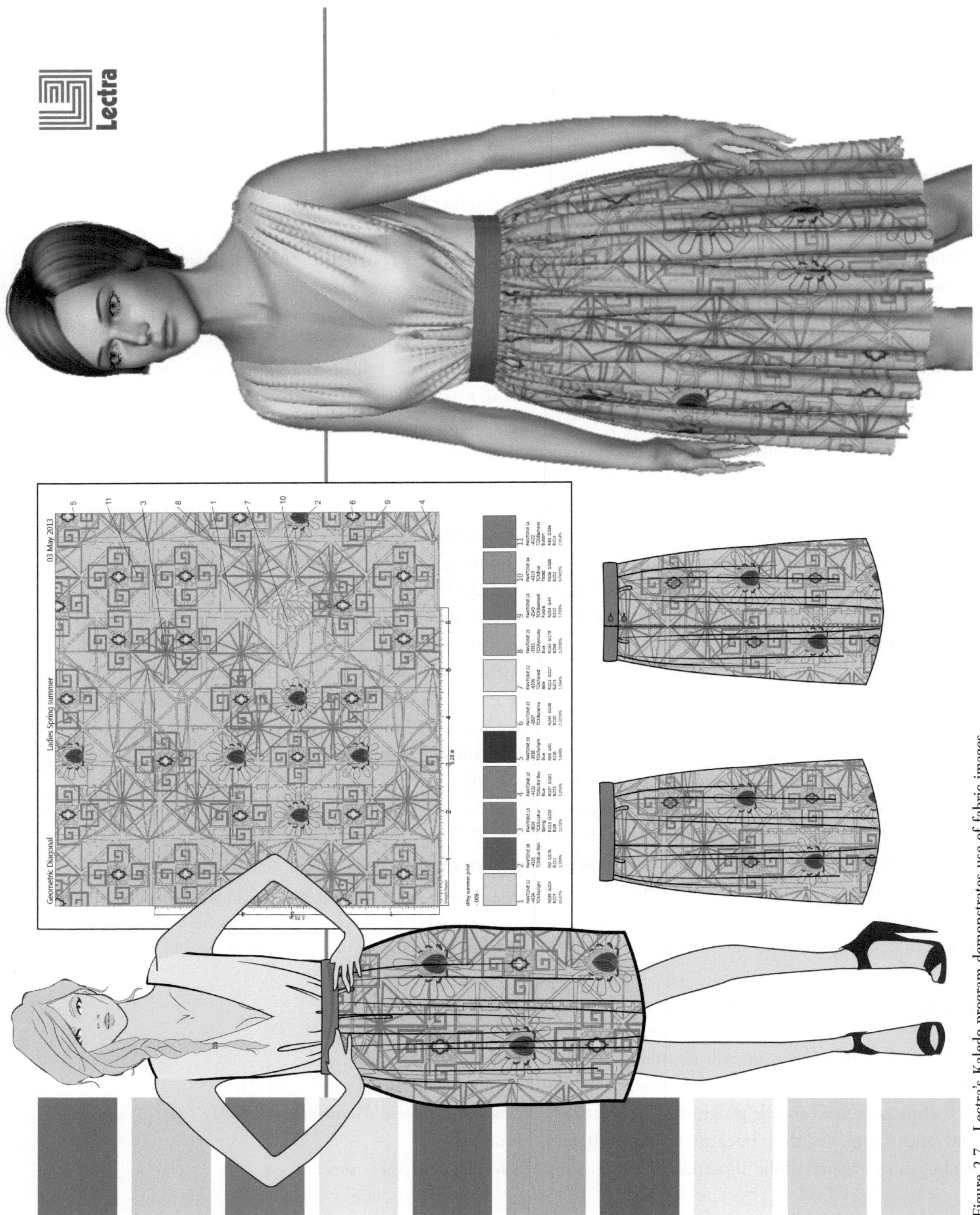

Figure 2.7 Lectra's Kaledo program demonstrates use of fabric images.
(LECTRA)

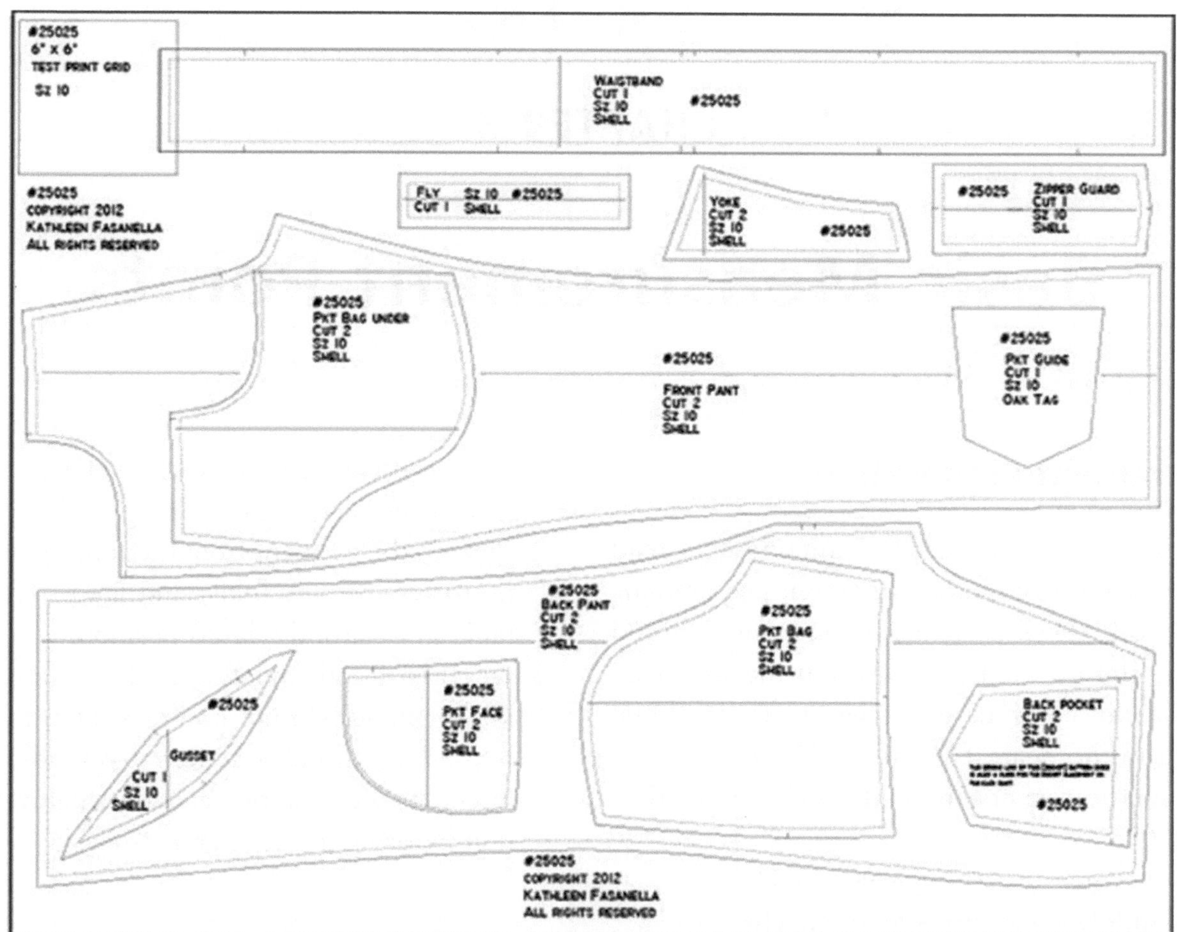

Figure 2.8 Creating pattern files in a Gerber Technologies Program.
(Cathleen Fasanella)

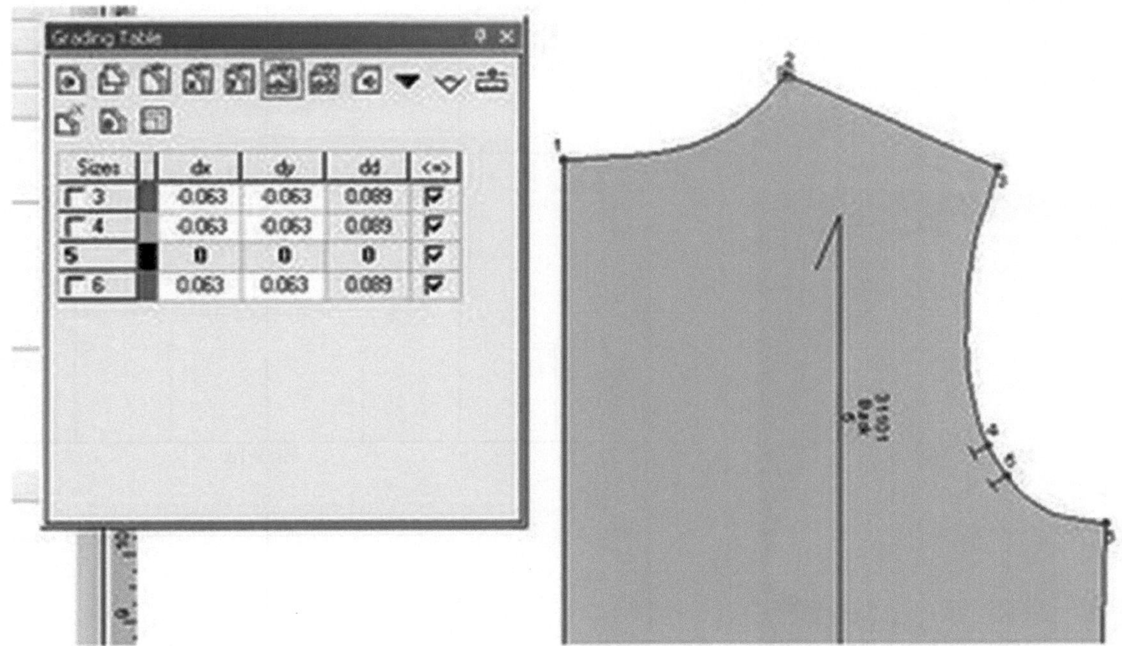

Figure 2.9 Optitex CAD program used to create pattern pieces.
(Cathleen Fasanella)

CHAPTER 3

Basic Measurement Points

Measurement Preparation

Before starting to measure, it is important to read and follow the list of ten measurement preparations that follow. If these preparations are not followed each time the garment is measured, the measurements may not be accurate. All garments should be measured to the nearest $\frac{1}{8}$" (see Table 3.1). For an imperial/metric conversion chart see Appendix B.

1. Always measure the garment lying flat, unless otherwise specified. The measuring surface must be clean and smooth without a rough texture or tabletop accoutrements. The area must be large enough to hold the entire garment lying flat without any folds or any part of the garment hanging over the edge of the table. A patternmaking table works well for measuring (see Figure 3.1).

Figure 3.1 Always make sure your garment is lying flat.

2. Pick up the garment from the top, shake it gently to remove any folds, and lay it flat on the table in a natural relaxed position.
3. Gently pat and smooth out all the fabric wrinkles by hand. Do not pull or stretch the fabric beyond its natural condition to remove wrinkles or compact the fabric beyond its natural condition by using inward hand strokes.

Table 3.1 FRACTIONS OF AN INCH

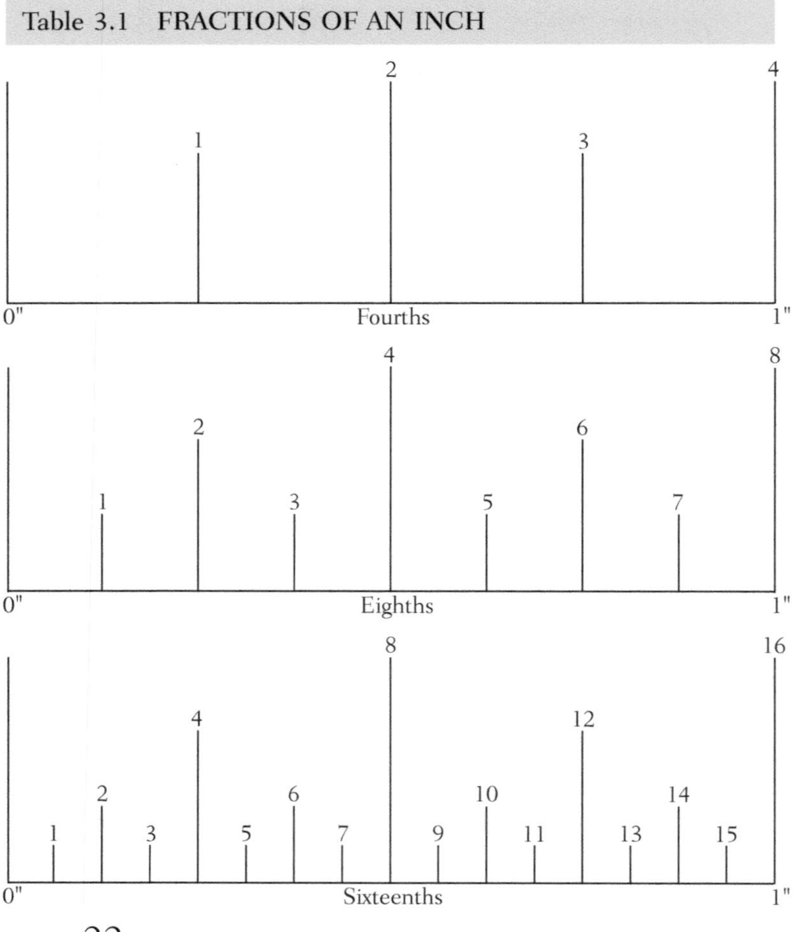

4. Take all the measurements with a plastic (fiberglass) tape measure. Do not use metal or fabric tape measures. Metal tape measures do not bend well when used on curves, while fabric tape measures can stretch with use and, therefore, both may result in inaccurate measurements. Periodically check your plastic (fiberglass) tape against a metal ruler to ensure its accuracy and replace it when the numbers become worn.
5. All measurements are taken with the tape measure lying flat against the garment, unless measuring a curved seam/contour. To get an accurate measurement on a curved seam/contour, stand the tape measure on its side edge and proceed with the measurement (see Figures 3.2a and b).
6. Take all the measurements with the buttons, snaps, zippers, hooks, ties, pleats, and vents fully closed and in a natural relaxed position. This is especially important for flared or pleated edges. They must lie with the pleats closed (pinned if needed) or with the gathers softly folding. Do not pull or stretch the garment, unless otherwise specified by the design (see Figure 3.3).
7. Extended measurements are taken on waist, leg, and cuff openings when elastic or drawstring draws areas or when a stretch fabric is used for contouring. Extended measurements are the only time a garment is to be stretched. Gently pull the garment to get a measurement of the fabric width before it's drawn by the elastic, drawstring, or contouring fabric, but do not stretch it beyond the natural relaxed position of the garment. Inert elastic should be measured with the garment extended until the fabric is smooth without breaking sewing stitches. Loosen the drawstrings and smooth out the gathers until the fabric is flat. Stretch materials are measured at a fully extended but not distorted position, without broken stitches.
8. For consistency, the front of the garment is always measured first, then the back. If the garment has a detachable item such as a collar or belt, it is measured last.
9. Always fold knitted garments for storage. Hanging knitted garments will cause them to stretch; therefore, measurements may not be accurate.
10. Before using a measurement method, be absolutely sure how that measurement is to be taken. Some garments may require a variation of that measurement due to highly detailed or unusual styling. Be sure to determine the measurement criteria and document any change on the specification sheet.

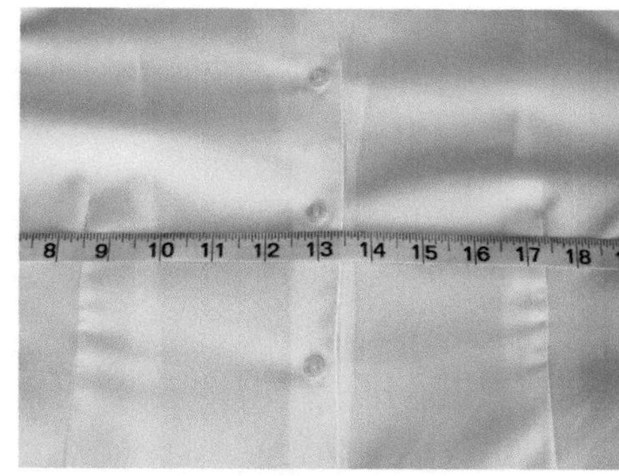

Figure 3.2a Your tape measure should lie flat against the garmet being measured.

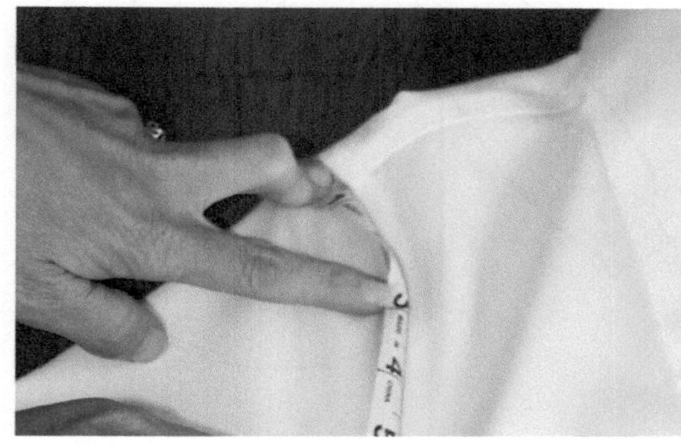

Figure 3.2b When measuring a curved seam, stand the tape measure on its side.

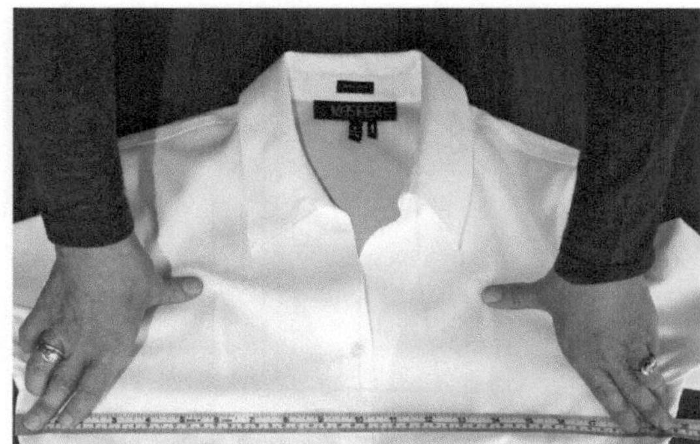

Figure 3.3 Make sure all buttons, snaps, zippers, etc. are closed when taking measurements.

A garment may contain a style or design feature that is not listed in the measurement terms and definitions section of this text. Those instances are very rare but are easily remedied by adding the required measurement point and a short description to your spec sheet.

Basic Measurement Points

1.

2.

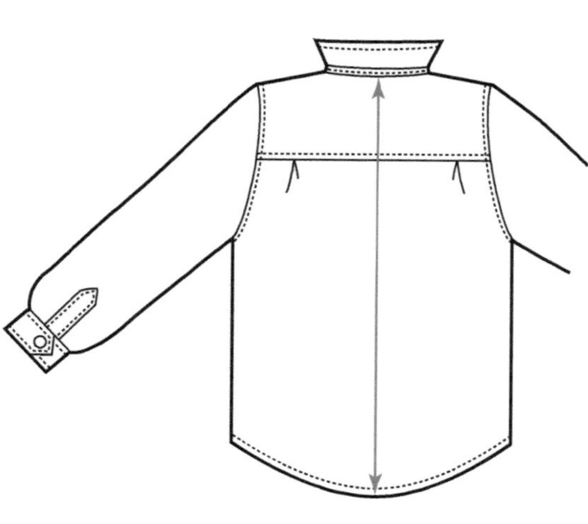

3.

Basic measurement points refer to the point of each measurement for a particular style/garment. A standard measuring method ensures that each person using the size specification, spec, will have the same understanding of the garment being created. This section consists of 155 basic measurement points. These points have been labeled, defined, and laid out in a manner that is consistent with top industry standards; however, this text does not propose to be a standard, but a reflection of other popular standards. These measurement points are offered in order of measurement, for example, length then width, rather then by garment style. Chapters 4 through 15 will regroup the basic body measurement points as required by a specific garment style.

It is an old industry practice for some measurement points to be taken flat, singular side to side, and some measurements to be taken in the circumference, also called total measurements. Circumference measurements are taken flat, then doubled. This may be confusing at first, but circumference measurements are clearly marked with doubling instructions. In many buying offices in larger industries, knits are generally measured singularly and wovens are doubled.

A few garment or partial garment illustrations have been chosen for each measurement point that follows, best representing that particular point of measure. However, a wide variety of garments are measured using these same measurement points. Again, this may be confusing at first, but further instructions for particular styles will be covered in Chapters 4 through 15.

Be sure you understand the ten measurement preparation instructions from the Measurement Preparation section at the beginning of this chapter before you begin to measure. At first, measuring may feel awkward. Practice each step until you feel comfortable with that measurement point, then move on to the next step. You will need to have several garments available for measuring practice. Use garments from your own closet, if you are a student, or ask to borrow garments from a design, technical, or quality assurance department if you work in the industry.

1. *Front Length (garments with a front opening)*—Measure from high point shoulder at neck straight down, parallel to center front, to bottom of garment at front. If garment has a collar, gently lift it away from shoulder-neck measuring point.

2. *Center Front Length (garments with a plain front; no front opening)*—Measure from center front neck joining seams straight down to bottom of garment at center front. [Note: A garment with a front opening may still require point of measure 1, Front Length, if neckline is unusual or is difficult to measure.]

3. *Center Back Length*—Measure from center back neck joining seams straight down to bottom of garment at center back. If needed, gently lift collar away from back neck to expose joining seam.

4. *Side Length*—Measure from bottom of armhole/side seam straight down to bottom of garment along side of garment. Do not follow natural curve of garment's side seam, unless otherwise indicated. If needed, gently lift sleeve away from armhole/side seam joining seam.

5. *Front Bodice Length (garments with a front opening)*—Measure from high point shoulder at neck straight down, parallel to center front, to top edge of waistband, joining seam, or rib. If garment has a collar, gently lift it away from shoulder-neck measuring point.

6. *Center Front Bodice Length (garments with a plain front; no front opening)*—Measure from center front neck joining seam straight down to top edge of waistband, joining seam, or rib. [Note: A garment with a center opening may still require point of measure 5, Front Bodice Length, if neckline is unusual or is difficult to measure.]

7. *Center Back Bodice Length*—Measure from center back neck joining seams straight down to top edge of waistband, joining seam, or rib. If needed, gently lift collar away from back neck to expose joining seam.

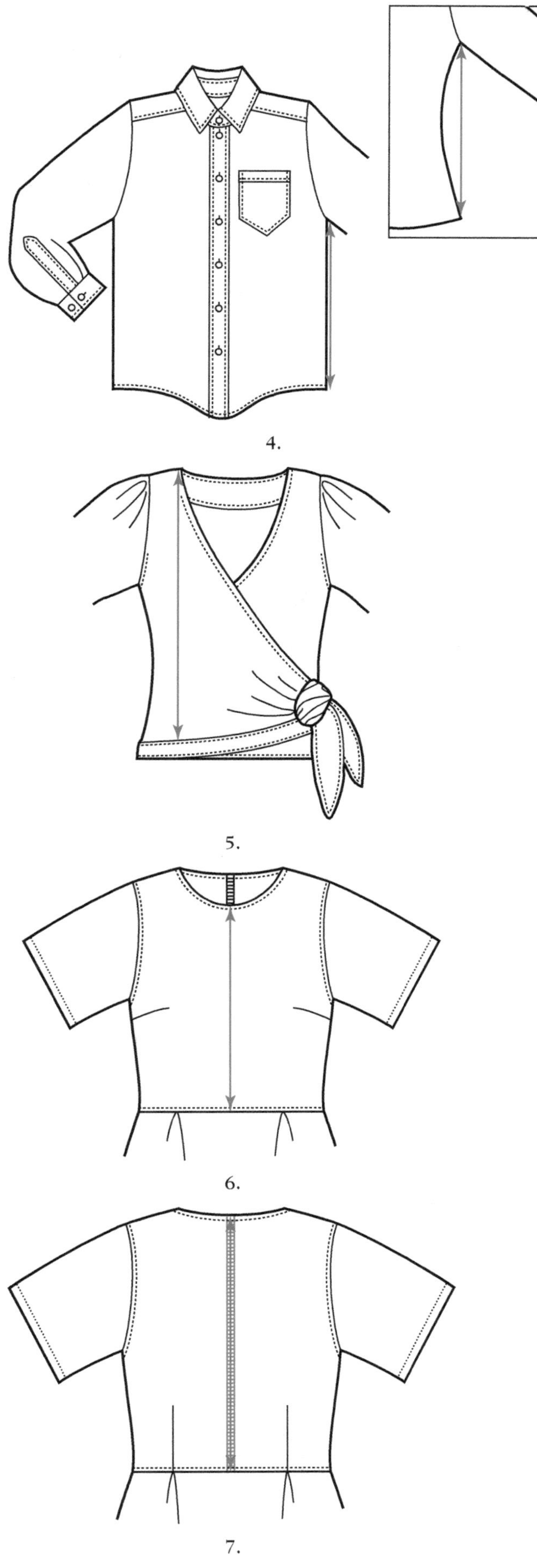

8. 9. 10. 11. 12. 13. 14. 15.

8. *Side Seam Bodice Length*—Measure from bottom of armhole/side seam straight down to top edge of waistband, joining seam, or rib, along side of garment, following natural curve of garment's side seam, unless otherwise indicated. If needed, gently lift sleeve away from armhole/side seam joining seam. [Note: You can take side seam bodice measurement straight rather than contoured if joining seam/rib can be extended, but indicate change on the spec sheet.]

9. *Chest Width (knit)*—Measure from edge of garment/side seam to edge of garment/side seam straight across garment at a point 1" below armhole.

10. *Chest Width Circumference (woven)*—Measure from edge of garment/side seam to edge of garment/side seam straight across garment at a point 1" below armhole. Double this measurement.

11. *Chest Width/Raglan Sleeve (knit)*—Measure from edge of garment/side seam to edge of garment/side seam straight across garment at a point _____" below high point shoulder. [Note: You will have to determine number of inches down from high point shoulder for each raglan sleeve style based on depth of sleeve. Then indicate this number on spec sheet.]

12. *Chest Width/Circumference Raglan Sleeve (woven)*—Measure from edge of garment/side seam to edge of garment/side seam straight across garment at a point _____" below high point shoulder. Double this measurement. [Note: You will have to determine number of inches down from high point shoulder for each raglan sleeve style based on depth of sleeve. Then indicate this number on spec sheet.]

13. *Across Shoulder*—Measure straight across front from armhole seam/edge to armhole seam/edge at shoulder seam or across natural shoulder fold line created if there is no seam.

14. *Shoulder Width*—Measure from neckband/collar/ribbing joining seam or neckline edge to top of armhole seam at shoulder, taken along shoulder seam or across natural shoulder fold line created if there is no seam.

15. *Across Chest*—Measure 2½" down from collar/rib joining seam at center front straight across front of garment from armhole seam/edge to armhole seam/edge. [Note: The 2½" measurement point is for misses/women's wear only and may need to be adjusted up or down ¼" to ½" accordingly for men's, children's, junior's, and large/plus sizes. Indicate any changes on spec sheet.]

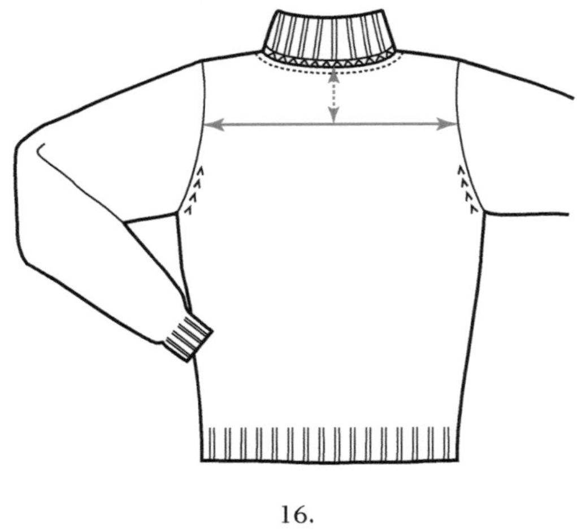

16.

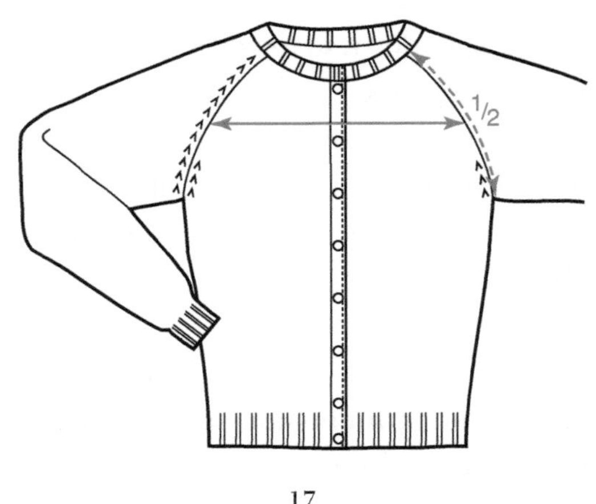

17.

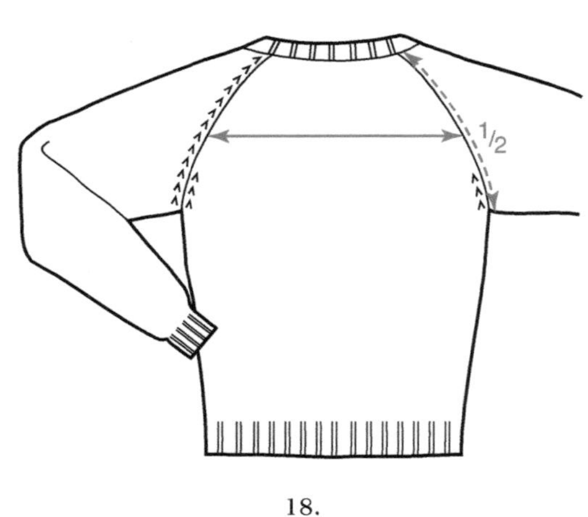

18.

19.

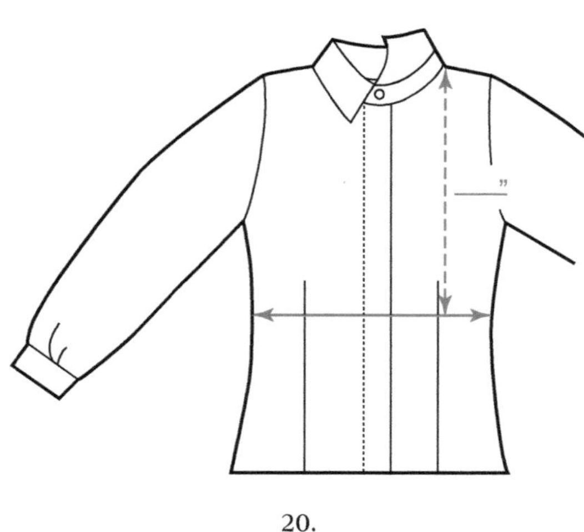

20.

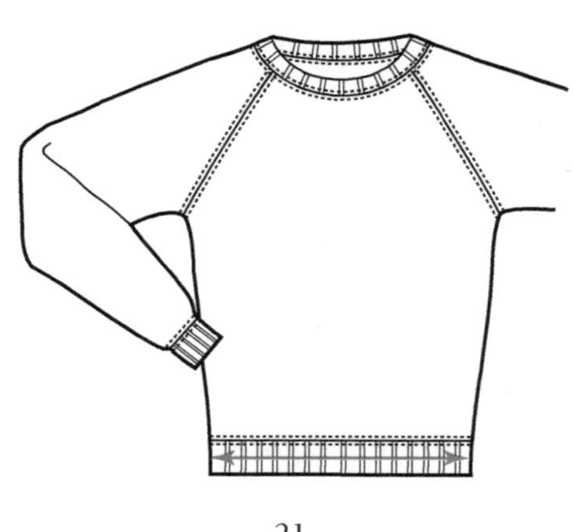

21.

16. *Across Back*—Measure 4" down from collar/rib joining seam at center back straight across back of garment from armhole seam/edge to armhole seam/edge. [Note: The 4" measurement point is for misses/women's wear only and may need to be adjusted up or down ¼" to ½" accordingly for men's, children's, junior's, and large/plus sizes. Indicate any changes on spec sheet.]

17. *Across Chest/Center Armhole*—Measure at one-half depth of armhole straight across front of garment from armhole seam/edge to armhole seam/edge.

18. *Across Back/Center Armhole*—Measure at one-half depth of armhole straight across back of garment from armhole seam/edge to armhole seam/edge.

19. *Waist Width (knit)*—Measure from edge of garment/side seam to edge of garment/side seam straight across garment on seam or at narrowest point of waist taper at a point _____" below high point shoulder. [Note: You will have to determine number of inches down from high point shoulder for each raglan sleeve style based on depth of sleeve. Then indicate this number on spec sheet.]

20. *Waist Width Circumference (woven)*—Measure from edge of garment/side seam to edge of garment/side seam straight across garment on seam or at narrowest point of waist taper at a point _____" below high point shoulder. Double this measurement. [Note: You will have to determine number of inches down from high point shoulder for each raglan sleeve style based on depth of sleeve. Then indicate this number on spec sheet.]

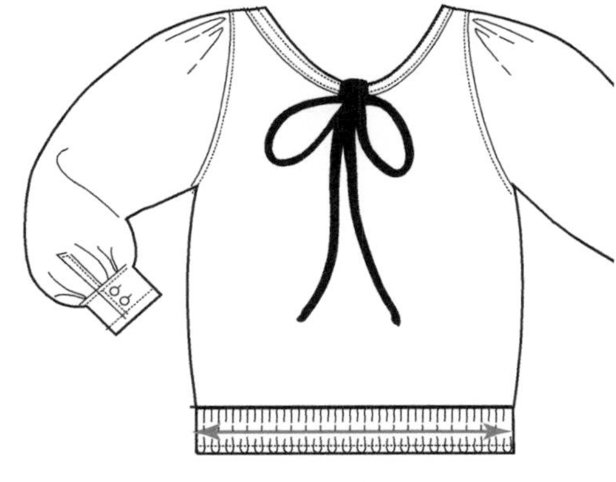

22.

21. *Bottom Band Width (knit top)*—Measure from side of bottom band to side of bottom band along center of band, following natural contour of waistband.

22. *Bottom Band Circumference (woven top)*—Measure from side of bottom band to side of bottom band along center of band, following natural contour of waistband. Double this measurement.

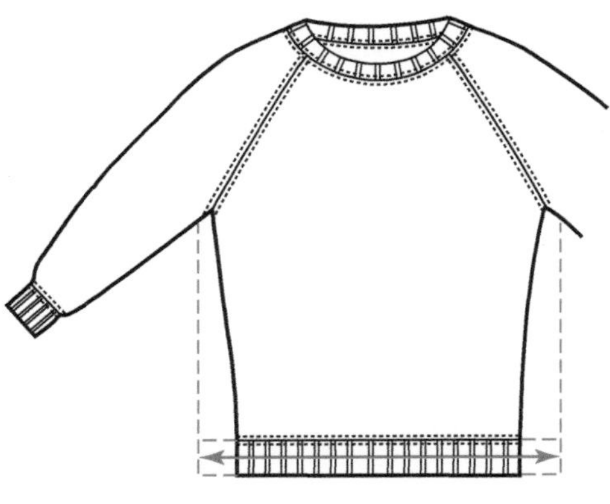

23.

23. *Bottom Band Width, Stretched (knit top)*—Measure from side of bottom band to side of bottom band straight across center of band in a fully extended position.

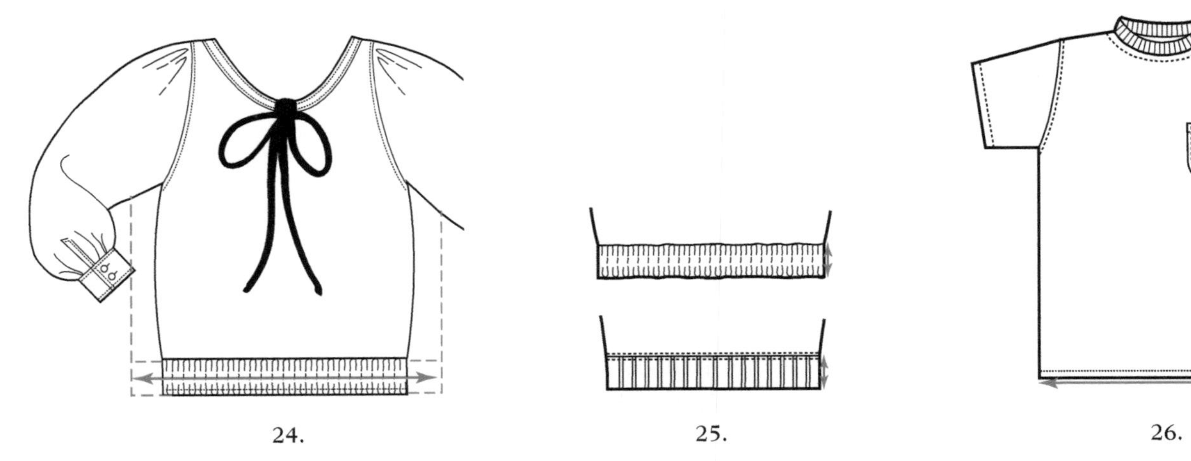

24.

25.

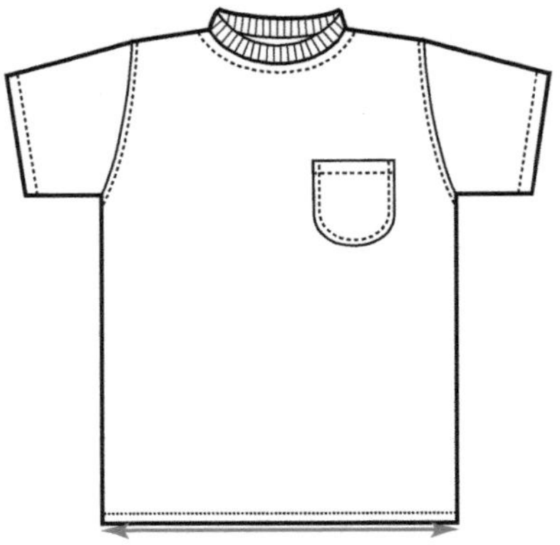

26.

27.

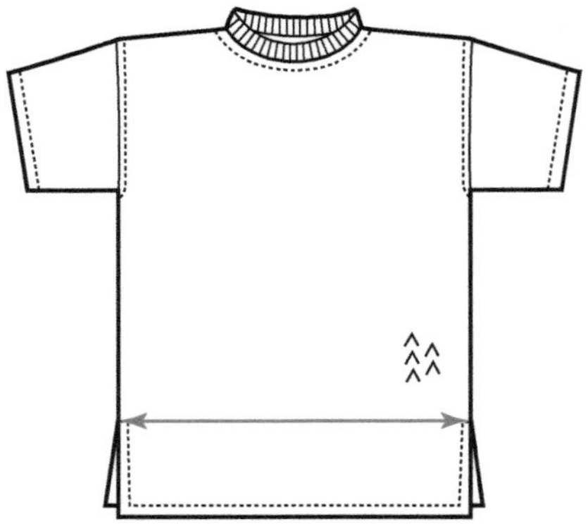

28.

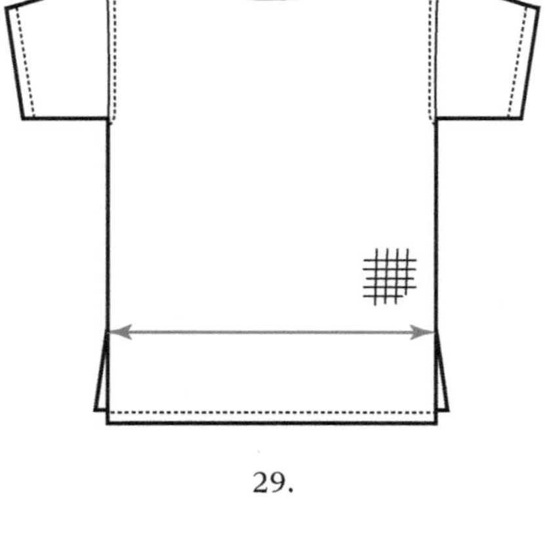

29.

30.

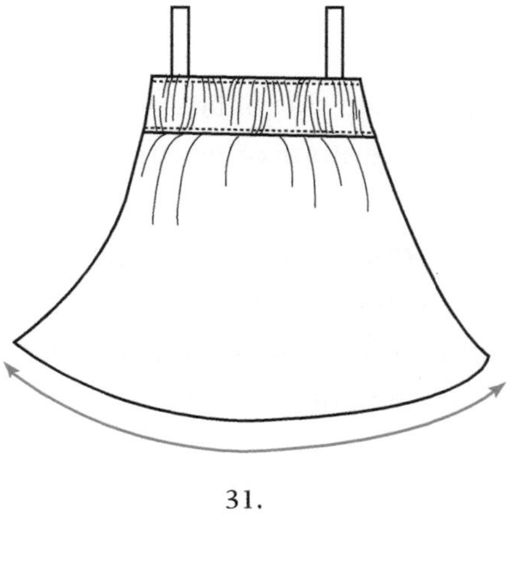

31.

24. *Bottom Band Width Circumference Stretched (woven top)*—Measure from side of bottom band to side of bottom band straight across center of band in a fully extended position. Double this measurement.

25. *Bottom Band/Ribbing Height (knit or woven top)*—Measure from band/ribbing joining seam straight down to bottom edge of band/rib opening. [Note: If band is shaped or contoured, indicate special measurement instructions on spec sheet.]

26. *Bottom Opening/Sweep (knit top)*—Measure from edge of garment/side seam to edge of garment/side seam straight across garment at bottom opening. [Note: If sweep has pleats, measure with pleats closed or relaxed.]

27. *Bottom Opening/Sweep Width Circumference (woven top)*—Measure from edge of garment/side seam to edge of garment/side seam straight across garment at bottom opening. Double this measurement. [Note: If sweep has pleats, measure with pleats closed or relaxed.]

28. *Vented Bottom Opening/Sweep Width (knit top)*—Measure from edge of garment/side seam to edge of garment/side seam straight across garment at top of side vents. Do not follow natural curve of garment. [Note: If vents are too high to measure sweep, indicate opening at appropriate position, e.g., midriff opening.]

29. *Vented Bottom Opening/Sweep Width Circumference (woven top)*—Measure from edge of garment/side seam to edge of garment/side seam straight across garment at top of side vents. Do not follow natural curve of garment. Double this measurement. [Note: If vents are too high to measure sweep, indicate opening at appropriate position, e.g., midriff opening.]

30. *Circular Bottom Opening/Sweep Width (knit top)*—Measure from edge of garment/side seam to edge of garment/side seam, following natural contour of garment at bottom opening.

31. *Circular Bottom Opening/Sweep Width Circumference (woven top)*—Measure from edge of garment/side seam to edge of garment/side seam, following natural contour of garment at bottom opening. Double this measurement.

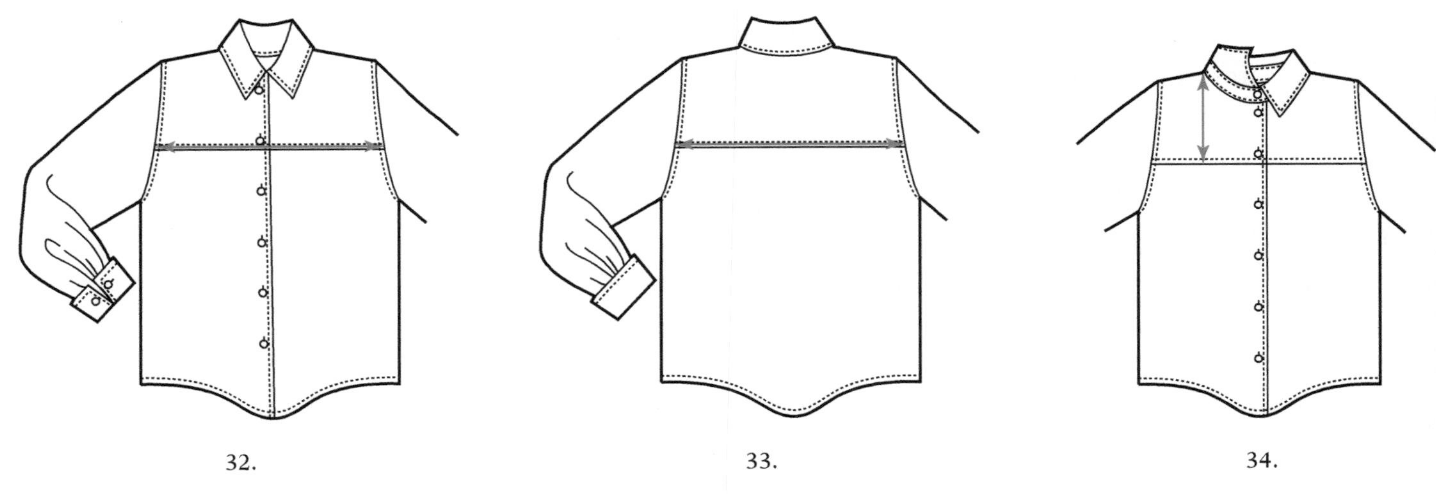

32. 33. 34.

35. 36.

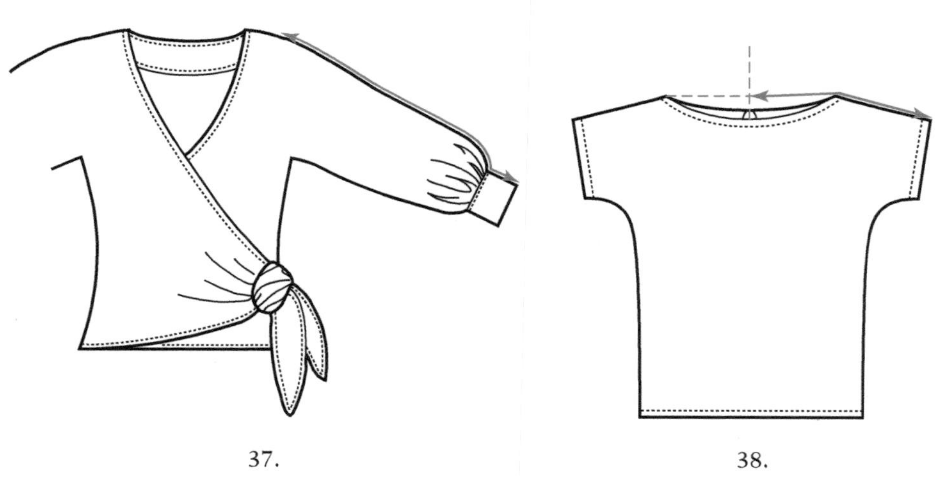

37. 38.

32. *Yoke Width Front*—Measure from armhole seam/edge to armhole seam/edge straight across front of garment, ignoring contours or points, at yoke-body joining seams. [Note: If yoke is asymmetrical, indicate changes in measuring as needed on spec sheet.]

33. *Yoke Width Back*—Measure from armhole seam/edge to armhole seam/edge straight across back of garment, ignoring contours or points, at yoke-body joining seams. [Note: If yoke is asymmetrical, indicate changes in measuring as needed on spec sheet.]

34. *Yoke Depth Front*—Measure from high point shoulder at neck straight down to bottom of front yoke-body joining seam. Gently lift collar away from shoulder-neck joining seam if needed.

35. *Yoke Back Depth*—Measure from center back neck joining seam straight down to bottom of back yoke-body joining seam. Gently lift collar away from back neck joining seam if needed.

36. *Sleeve Length Top Armhole*—Measure along top of sleeve/fold, following contour of sleeve from armhole seam at shoulder to bottom of sleeve opening, including cuff.

37. *Sleeve Length Top Neck*—Measure along top of sleeve/fold, following contour of sleeve from sleeve-neck joining seam/edge to edge of sleeve opening, including cuff. Gently lift collar at sleeve-neck joining seam if needed.

38. *Sleeve Length Center Back*—Measure from center back neck joining seam or from a point above neck at an imaginary line, that of a joining seam, along top of sleeve/fold, following contour of sleeve to edge of sleeve opening, including cuff.

39. *Sleeve Length Underarm*—Measure straight from bottom of armhole along sleeve seam to edge of sleeve opening, including cuff.

40. *Straight Armhole Width (knit)*—Measure from top of shoulder joining seam/edge straight down to bottom of armhole.

41. *Straight Armhole Width Circumference (woven)*—Measure from top of shoulder joining seam/edge straight down to bottom of armhole. Double this measurement.

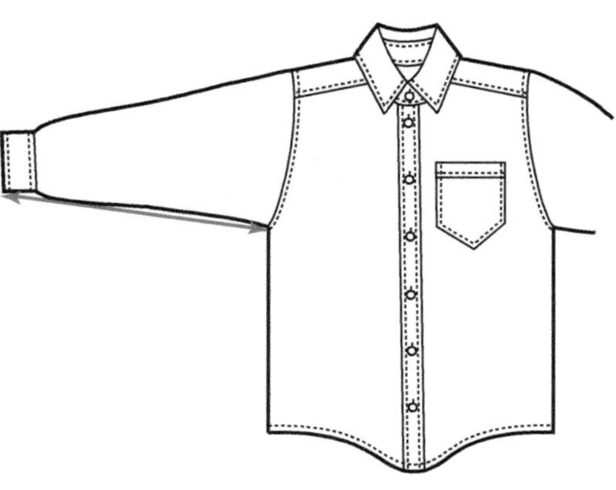

39.

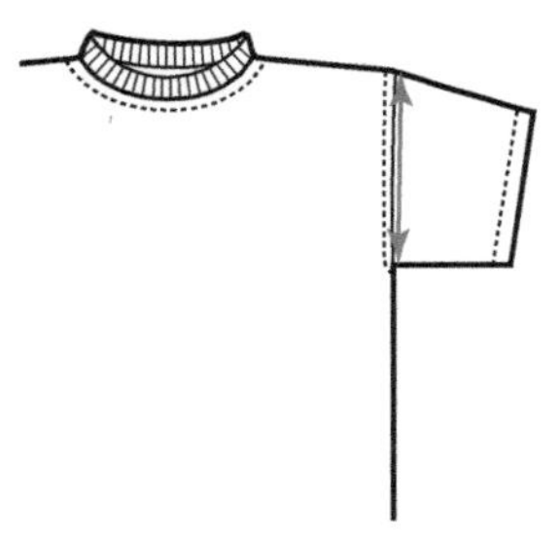

40.

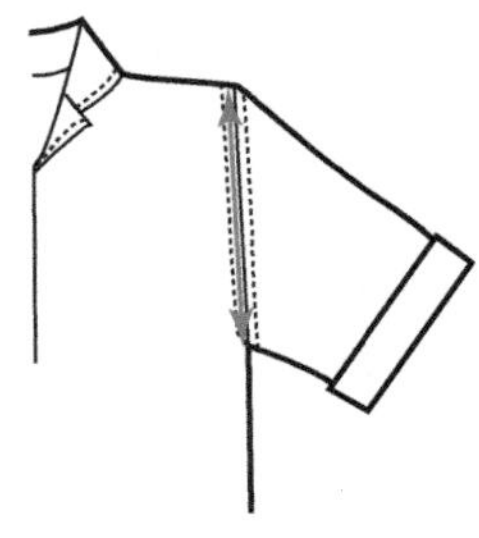

41.

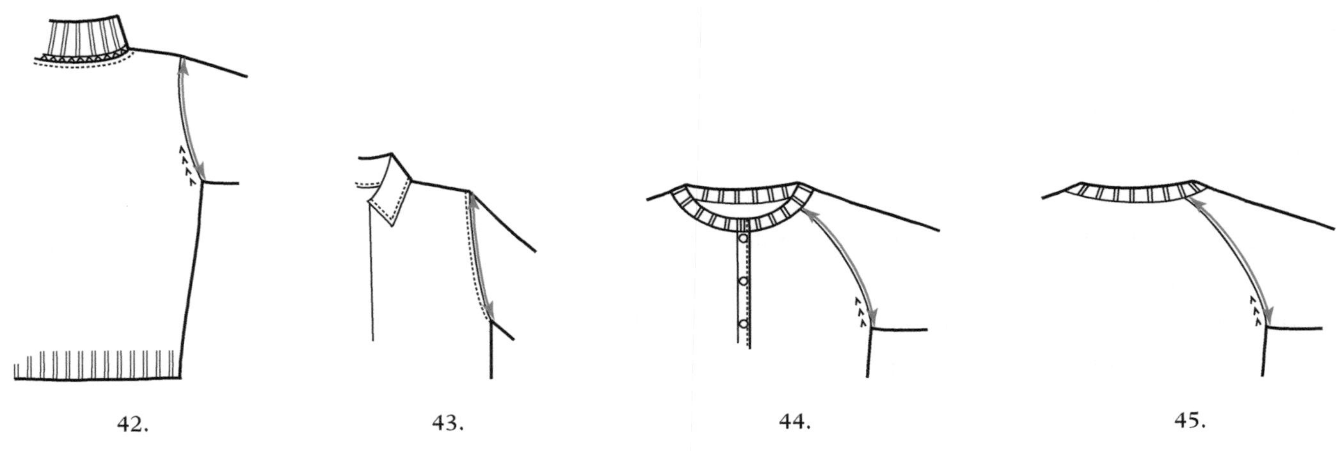
42. 43. 44. 45.

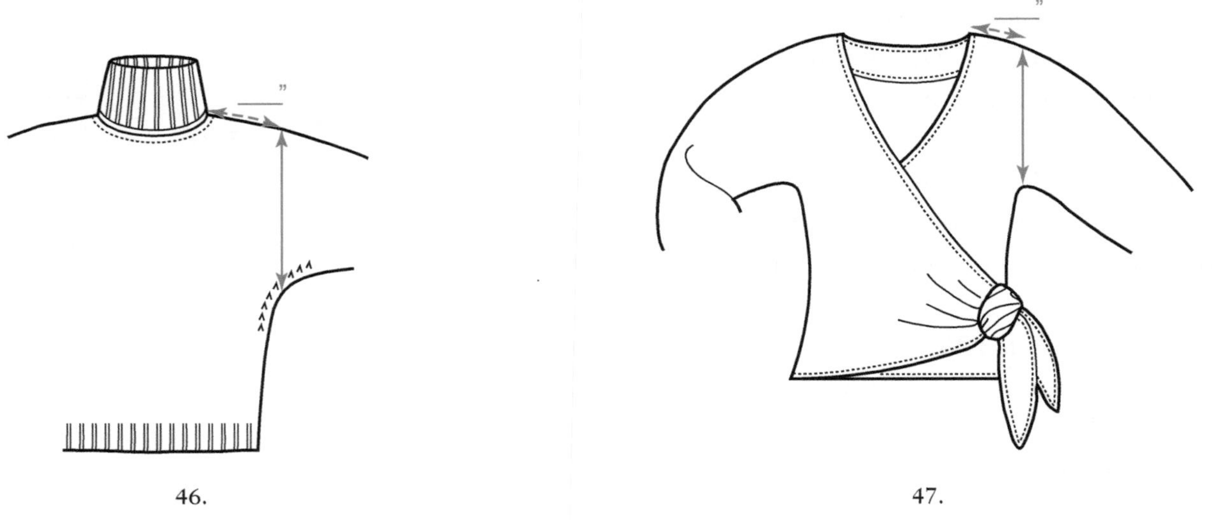

46. 47.

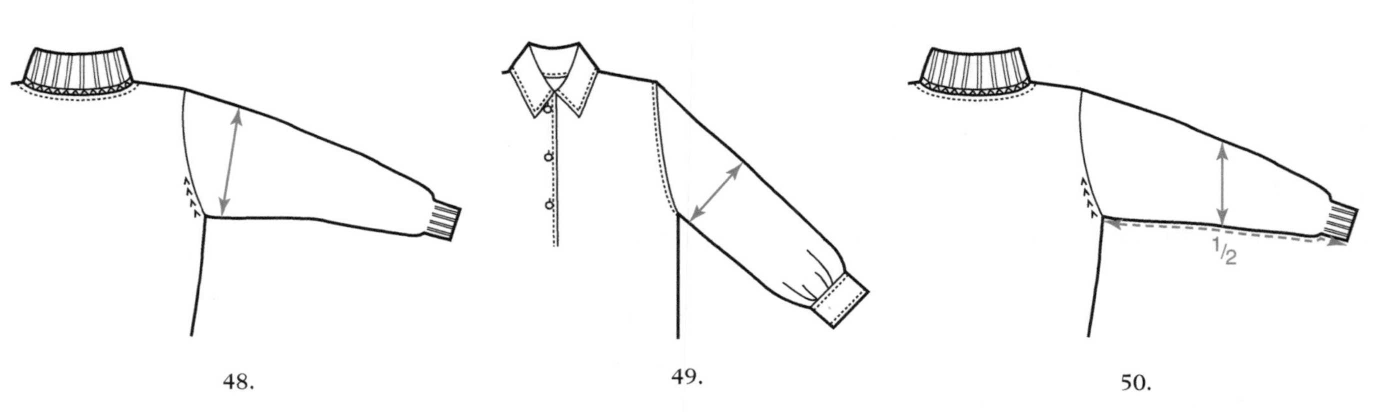

48. 49. 50.

42. *Curved Armhole Width (knit)*—Measure from top of shoulder joining seam/edge to bottom of armhole, following contour of armhole.

43. *Curved Armhole Width Circumference (woven)*—Measure from top of shoulder joining seam/edge to bottom of armhole, following contour of armhole. Double this measurement.

44. *Armhole Front*—Measure on front of garment from top of shoulder at neckline joining seam/edge to bottom of armhole, following contour of armhole. Gently lift collar away from neckline joining seam if needed.

45. *Armhole Back*—Measure on back of garment from top of shoulder at neck joining seam/edge to bottom of armhole, following contour of armhole. Gently lift collar away from neck joining seam if needed.

46. *Armhole Width Straight (knit)*—Measure from top of shoulder seam at a point _____" below neckline joining seam/edge straight down to bottom of armhole. [Note: Gently move collar away from neck joining seam if needed when measuring down _____" to armhole start point. Indicate number of inches measured down on spec sheet.]

47. *Armhole Width Circumference Straight (woven)*—Measure from top of shoulder seam at a point _____" below neckline joining seam/edge straight down to bottom of armhole. Double this measurement. [Note: Gently move collar away from neck joining seam if needed when measuring down _____" to armhole start point. Indicate number of inches measured down on spec sheet.]

48. *Muscle Width (knit)*—Measure from inner sleeve edge/seam to outer sleeve edge/fold at a point 1" below armhole and parallel to sleeve opening.

49. *Muscle Width Circumference (woven)*—Measure from inner sleeve edge/seam to outer sleeve edge/fold at a point 1" below armhole and parallel to sleeve opening. Double this measurement.

50. *Elbow Width (knit)*—Measure from inner sleeve edge/seam to outer sleeve edge/fold straight across sleeve at a point one-half of underarm sleeve length and parallel to sleeve opening at wrist or cuff. [Note: If sleeve is three-quarter length, indicate new point of measure on spec sheet.]

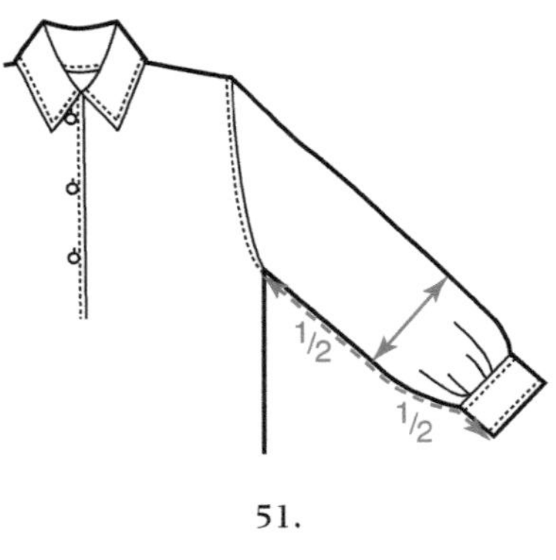

51.

51. *Elbow Width Circumference (woven)*—Measure from inner sleeve edge/seam to outer sleeve edge/fold straight across sleeve at a point one-half of the underarm sleeve length and parallel to sleeve opening at wrist or cuff. Double this measurement. [Note: If sleeve is three-quarter length, indicate new point of measure on spec sheet.]

52.

52. *Sleeve Opening Width (knit)*—Measure from inner sleeve edge/seam to outer sleeve edge/fold straight across bottom edge of sleeve opening.

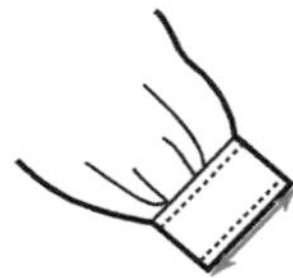

53.

53. *Sleeve Opening Width Circumference (woven)*—Measure from inner sleeve edge/seam to outer sleeve edge/fold straight across bottom edge of sleeve opening. Double this measurement.

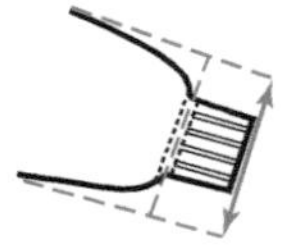

54.

54. *Sleeve Opening Width, Stretched (knit)*—Measure from inner sleeve edge/seam to outer sleeve edge/fold straight across bottom edge of sleeve opening in a fully extended position.

55.

55. *Sleeve Opening Width Circumference, Stretched (woven)*—Measure from inner sleeve edge/seam to outer sleeve edge/fold straight across bottom edge of sleeve opening in a fully extended position. Double this measurement.

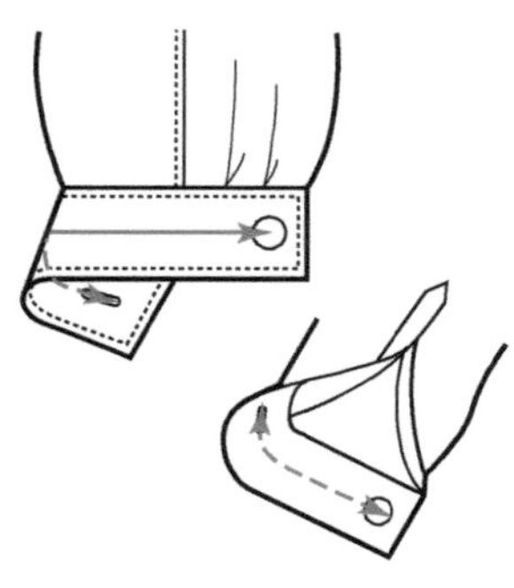

56.

56. *Cuff Length Sleeve*—Measure from outside end of buttonhole to center of button straight along center of cuff. Open cuff out as flat as possible when measuring. [Note: If cuff length is contoured, measure along center-most point.]

57. *Cuff/Ribbing Height Sleeve*—Measure from cuff joining seam or top of ribbing straight down to bottom edge of cuff or rib opening. [Note: If cuff is contoured, indicate changes made to measurement on spec sheet.]

58. *Neck Depth Front (garments with a plain front/asymmetrical front opening)*—Measure from center back neck joining seam/edge straight down to center front neck joining seam/edge.

59. *Neck Depth Center Front (garments with a center front opening)*—Measure from center back neck joining seam/edge straight down to center of first button at center front of garment.

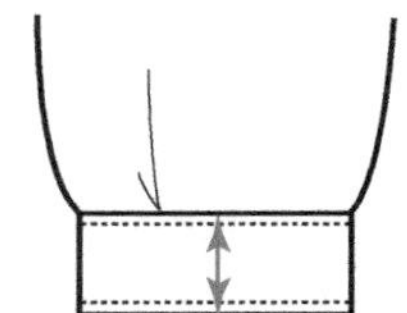

57.

60. *Neck Drop Front*—Measure from an imaginary line connecting neckline edges straight down to center front neck opening edge. Use a ruler if needed to connect top neckline edges.

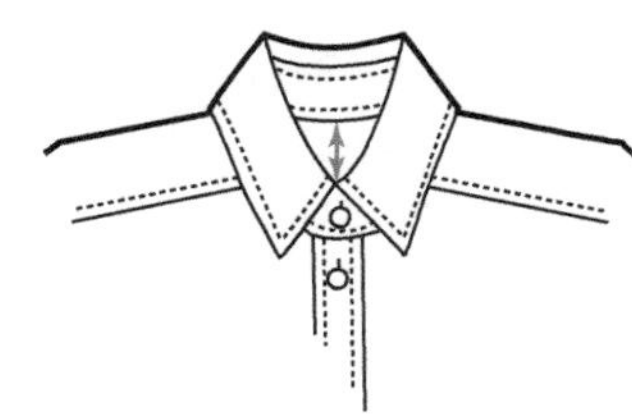

58.

61. *Neck Drop Back*—Measure from an imaginary line connecting neckline edges straight down to center back neck opening edge. This measurement is taken with front of garment faceup. Use a ruler to connect top neckline edges if needed.

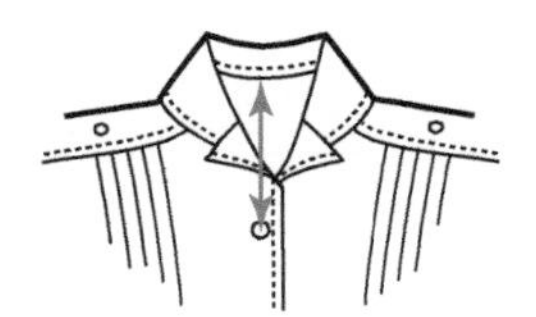

59.

62. *Neck Width, No Collar*—Measure from inside neck edge/seam to inside neck edge/seam straight across back neck at widest point. This measurement is taken with front of garment faceup.

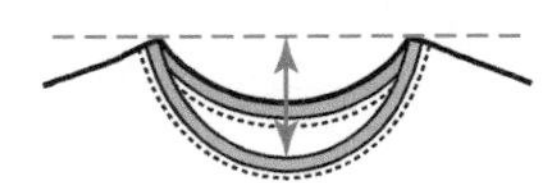

60.

63. *Neck Width, Collar*—Measure straight across back neck from neck-shoulder joining seam to neck-shoulder joining seam or natural shoulder line if no seam. This measurement is taken with back of garment faceup.

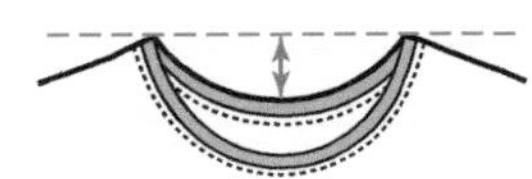

61.

64. *Neck Edge Width (knit)*—Measure from neck edge/seam/fold to neck edge/seam/fold along top opening edge, following natural contour of neck opening. Garment should be positioned with one shoulder on top of the other and with front and back neck edges meeting.

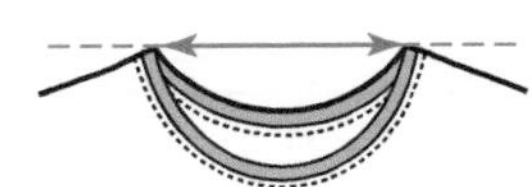

62.

65. *Neck Edge Width Circumference (woven)*—Measure from neck edge/seam/fold to neck edge/seam/fold along top opening edge, following natural contour of neck opening. Garment should be positioned with one shoulder on top of the other and with front and back neck edges meeting. Double this measurement.

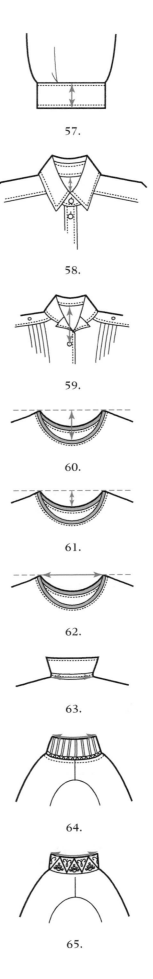

63.

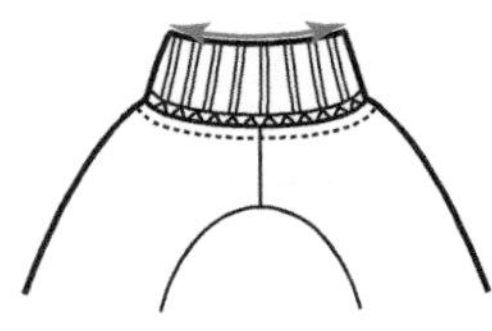

64.

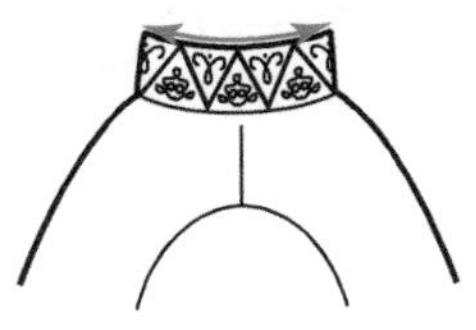

65.

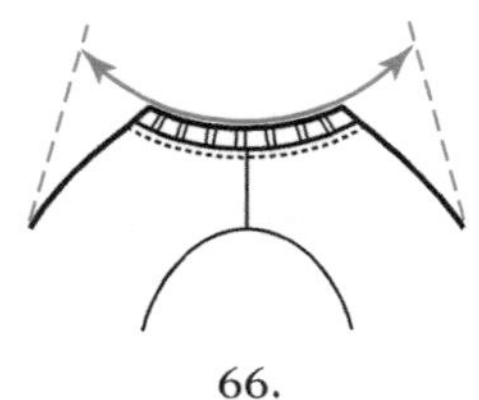
66.

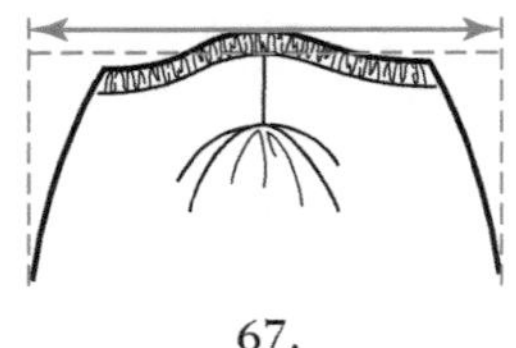
67.

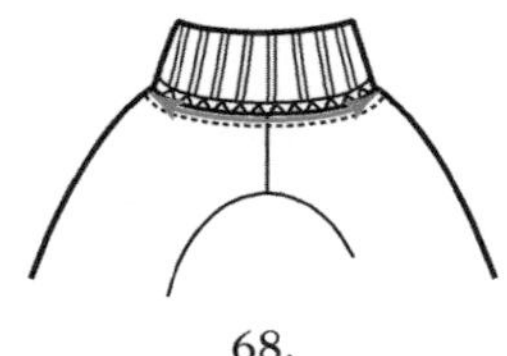
68.

69.

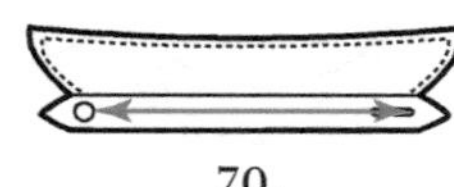
70.

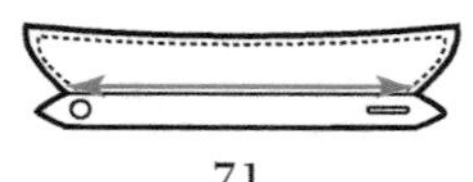
71.

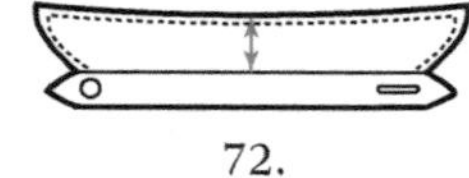
72.

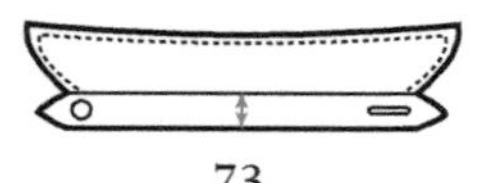
73.

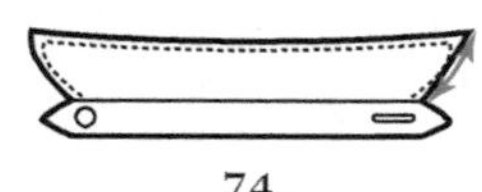
74.

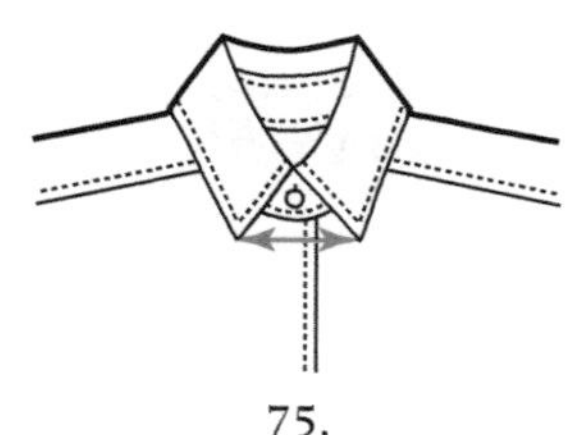
75.

66. *Neck Edge Width, Stretched (knit)*—Measure from neck edge/seam/fold to neck edge/seam/fold along top opening edge in a fully extended position. Garment should be positioned with one shoulder on top of the other and with front and back neck edges meeting.

67. *Neck Edge Width Circumference, Stretched (woven)*—Measure from neck edge/seam/fold to neck edge/seam/fold along top opening edge in a fully extended position. Garment should be positioned with one shoulder on top of the other and with front and back neck edges meeting. Double this measurement.

68. *Neck Base (knit)*—Measure from neck edge/seam to neck edge/seam along collar/rib joining seam or neckline edge, following natural contour of neck opening. Garment should be buttoned or zippered, if applicable, with one shoulder seam positioned on top of the other and with front and back neck edges meeting.

69. *Neck Base Circumference (woven)*—Measure from neck edge/seam to neck edge/seam along collar/rib joining seam or neckline edge, following natural contour of neck opening. Garment should be buttoned or zippered, if applicable, with one shoulder seam positioned on top of the other and with front and back neck edges meeting. Double this measurement.

70. *Neckband Length*—Measure from outside end of buttonhole to center of buttonhole across neckband, following contour of neckband.

71. *Collar Length*—Measure from one end of collar to other end of collar along neck joining seam.

72. *Collar Height*—Measure from collar/rib joining seam at center back neck straight up to outer edge of collar/rib.

73. *Collar Band Height*—Measure from collar joining seam at center back straight up to neckband joining seam at center back.

74. *Collar Point Length*—Measure from collar joining seam to outer edge of collar along collar point edge. [Note: If collar is rounded, measure at a point parallel to center back and indicate change on spec sheet.]

75. *Collar Point Spread (pointed collars only)*—Measure, with collar band buttoned and collar in place, from collar point straight across collar edge to collar point.

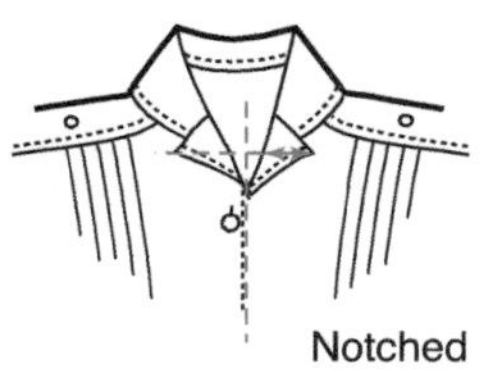

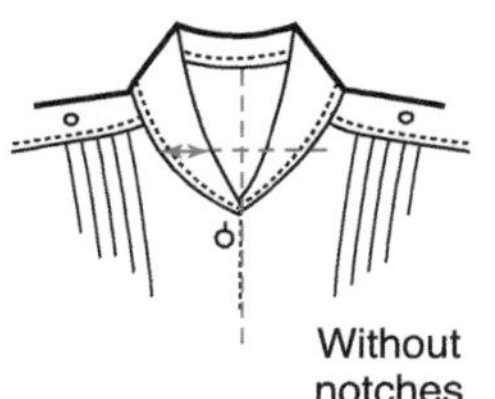

76.

76. *Lapel Width*

A. *Notched*—Measure from lower lapel notch straight across to lapel fold at a point perpendicular to garment center front.

B. *Without Notches*—Measure from lapel edge straight across widest point of lapel to lapel fold at a point _____" down from center back collar joining seam and perpendicular to front of garment.

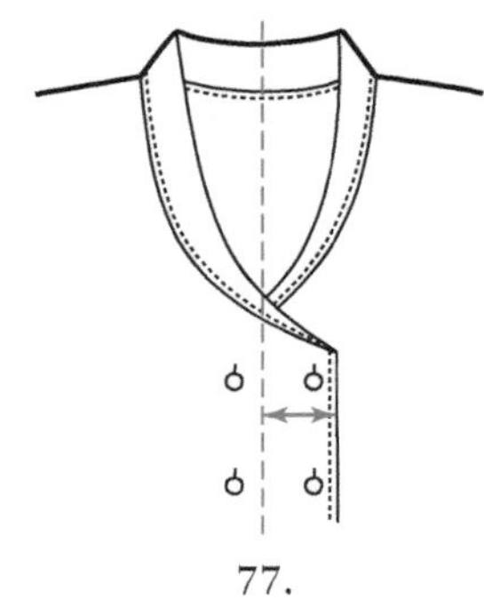

77.

77. *Center Front Extension*—Measure from an imaginary line at center front of garment horizontally to finished outer edge of front extended piece.

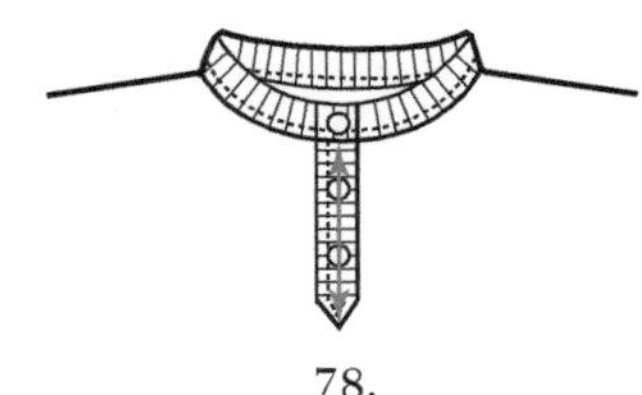

78.

78. *Placket Length*—Measure from top edge of placket straight down to bottom of placket opening along center of placket.

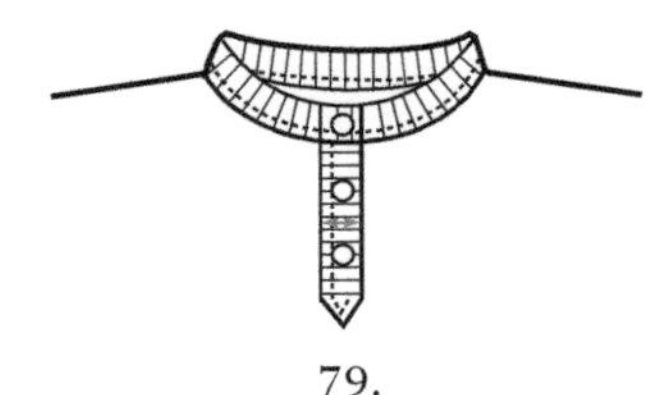

79.

79. *Placket Width*—Measure from placket joining seam straight across placket to placket edge at fold.

80. *Keyhole Length*—Measure from outer edge of neckline straight down to bottom of keyhole opening.

81. *Waistband Depth*—Measure from top of waistband edge straight down to bottom of waistband at waistband joining seam. [Note: If waistband is contoured, indicate measurement change on spec sheet.]

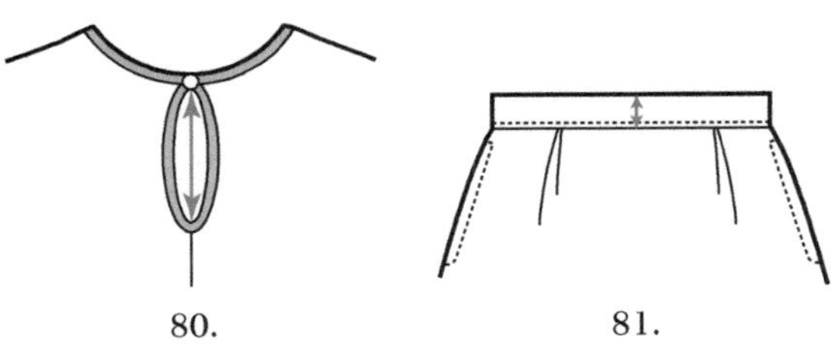

80. 81.

82. *Waistband Width (knit)*—Measure from side of bottom band to side of bottom band along center of band, following natural contour of waistband.

83. *Waistband Width Circumference (woven)*—Measure from side of bottom band to side of bottom band along center of band, following natural contour of waistband. Double this measurement.

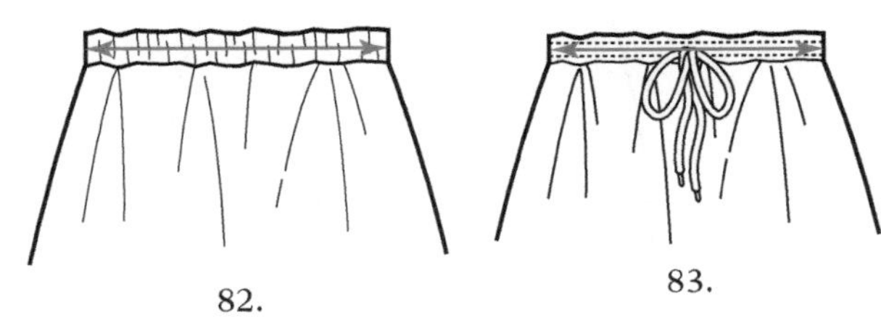

82. 83.

84. *Waistband Width, Stretched (knit)*—Measure from side of bottom band to side of bottom band straight across center of band in a fully extended position.

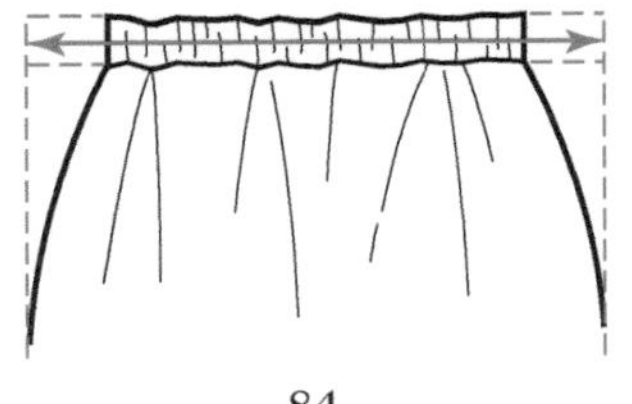

84.

85.

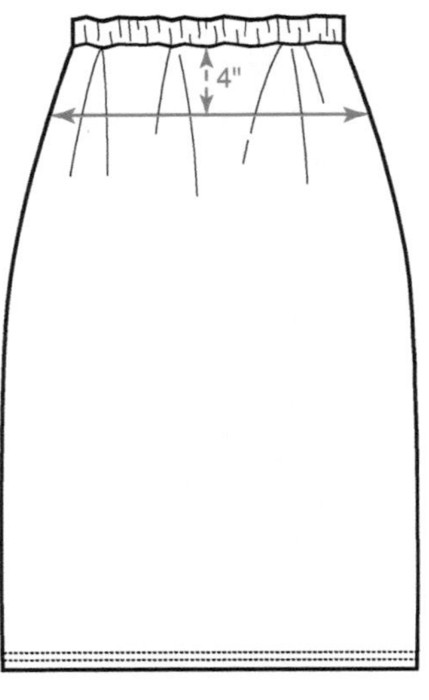

86.

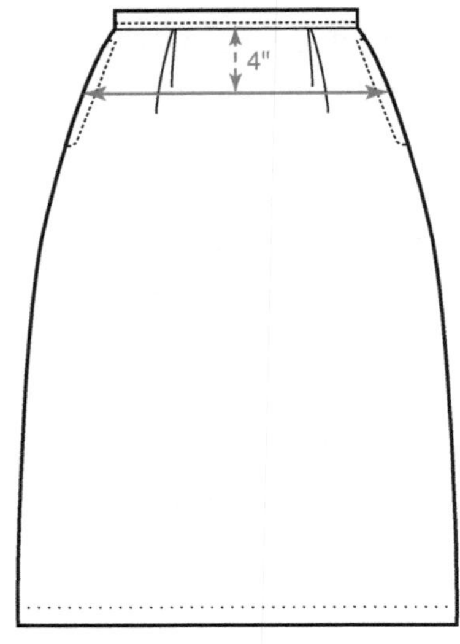

87.

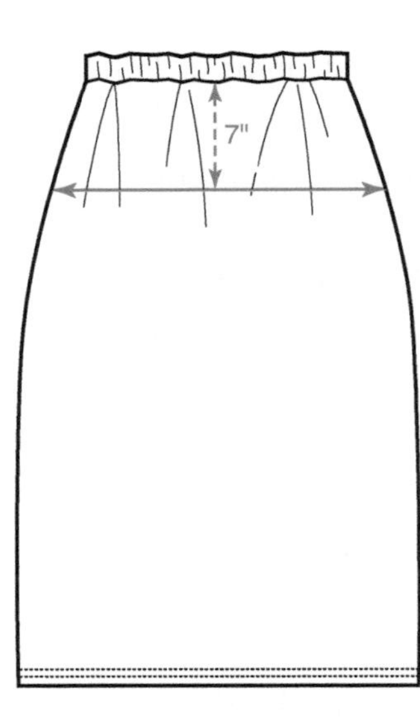

88.

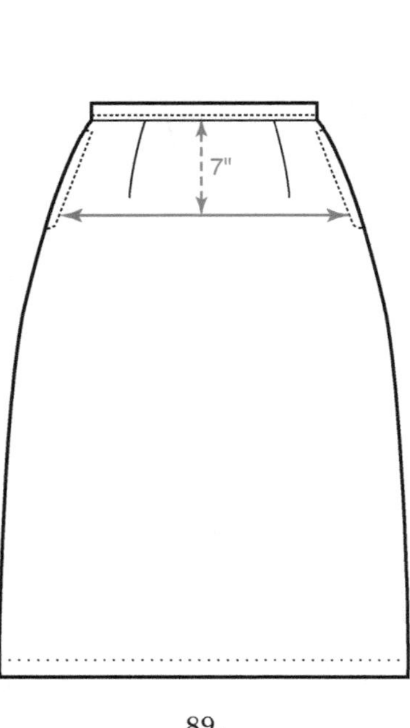

89.

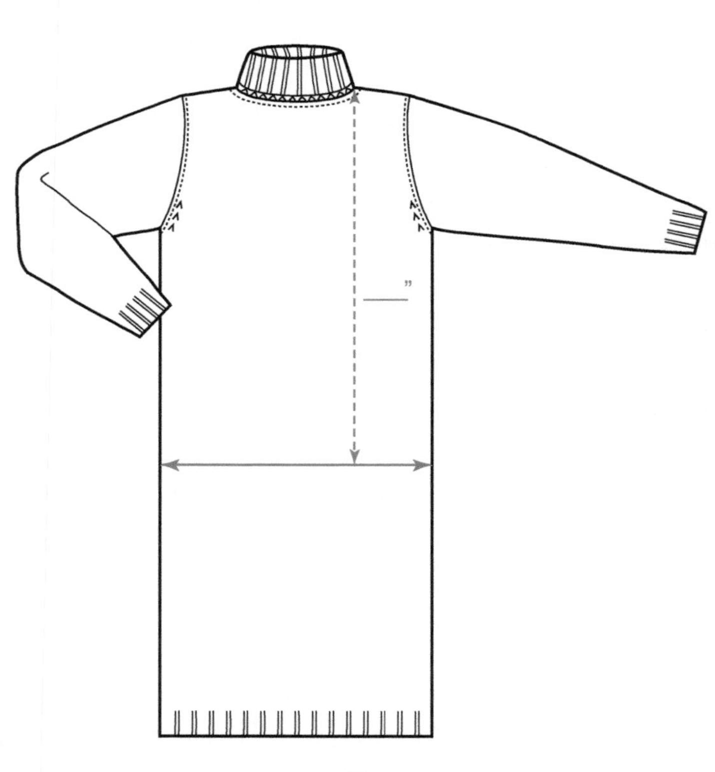

90.

85. *Waistband Width Circumference, Stretched (woven)*—Measure from side of bottom band to side of bottom band straight across center of band in a fully extended position. Double this measurement.

86. *High Hip Width (knit)*—Measure from edge of garment/side seam to edge of garment/side seam at a point 4" below bottom edge of waistband/seam, following contour of waist. [Note: The 4" point is for misses/women's wear only; adjust as needed ½" to 1" up or down for children's, petite's, junior's, or large/plus sizes. Indicate change on spec sheet.]

87. *High Hip Width Circumference (woven)*—Measure from edge of garment/side seam to edge of garment/side seam at a point 4" below bottom edge of waistband/seam, following contour of waist. Double this measurement. [Note: The 4" point is for misses/women's wear only; adjust as needed ½" to 1" up or down for children's, petite's, junior's, or large/plus sizes. Indicate change on spec sheet.]

88. *Low Hip Width from Waist (knit)*—Measure from edge of garment/side seam to edge of garment/side seam at a point 7" below bottom edge of waistband/seam, following contour of waist. [Note: The 7" point is for misses/women's wear only; adjust as needed ½" to 1" up or down for children's, petite's, junior's, or large/plus sizes. Indicate change on spec sheet.]

89. *Low Hip Width Circumference from Waist (woven)*—Measure from edge of garment/side seam to edge of garment/side seam at a point 7" below bottom edge of waistband/seam, following contour of waist. Double this measurement. [Note: The 7" point is for misses/women's wear only; adjust as needed ½" to 1" up or down for children's, petite's, junior's, or large/plus sizes. Indicate change on spec sheet.]

90. *Hip Width from High Point Shoulder (knit)*—Measure from edge of garment/side seam to edge of garment/side seam straight across at a point _____" below high point shoulder. [Note: You will have to estimate low hip point on garment if there is no waistband and fill in _____" from high point shoulder. This measurement will vary for children's, junior's, misses, and large/plus sizes.]

91. 92. 93.

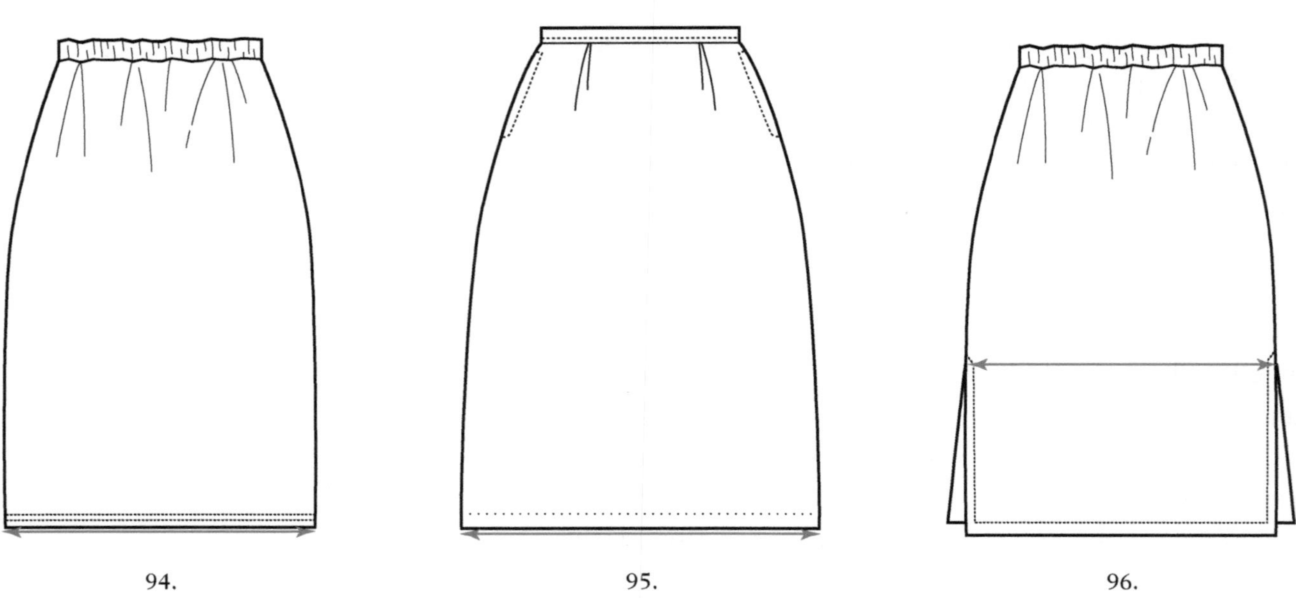

94. 95. 96.

91. *Hip Width from High Point Shoulder Circumference (woven)*—Measure from edge of garment/side seam to edge of garment/side seam straight across at a point _____" below high point shoulder. Double this measurement. [Note: You will have to estimate low hip point on garment if there is no waistband and fill in _____" from high point shoulder. This measurement will vary for children's, junior's, misses, and large/plus sizes.]

92. *Hip Seat Width (knit pant)*—Measure from edge of garment/side seam to edge of garment/side seam at a point _____" up from crotch seam, following contour of waist. [Note 1: This measurement is useful when waistband sits below natural waistline. Note 2: Adjust _____" up from crotch as needed for junior's and large/plus sizes. Note 3: A hip seat width of 2½" up for children's and 3" up for menswear can take place of low hip width.]

93. *Hip Seat Width Circumference (woven pant)*—Measure from edge of garment/side seam to edge of garment/side seam at a point _____" up from crotch seam, following contour of waist. Double this measurement. [Note 1: This measurement is useful when waistband sits below natural waistline. Note 2: Adjust _____" up from crotch as needed for junior's and large/plus sizes. Note 3: A hip seat width of 2½" up for children's and 3" up for menswear can take place of low hip width.]

94. *Bottom Opening/Sweep Width (knit skirt)*—Measure from edge of garment/side seam to edge of garment/side seam straight across garment at bottom opening. [Note: If sweep has pleats, measure with pleats closed or relaxed.]

95. *Bottom Opening/Sweep Width Circumference (woven skirt)*—Measure from edge of garment/side seam to edge of garment/side seam straight across garment at bottom opening. Double this measurement. [Note: If sweep has pleats, measure with pleats closed or relaxed.]

96. *Vented Bottom Opening/Sweep Width (knit skirt)*—Measure from edge of garment/side seam to edge of garment/side seam straight across garment at top of side vents. [Note: Indicate on spec sheet if there is only one vent or if vent hits at a point other than sweep, e.g., thigh opening.]

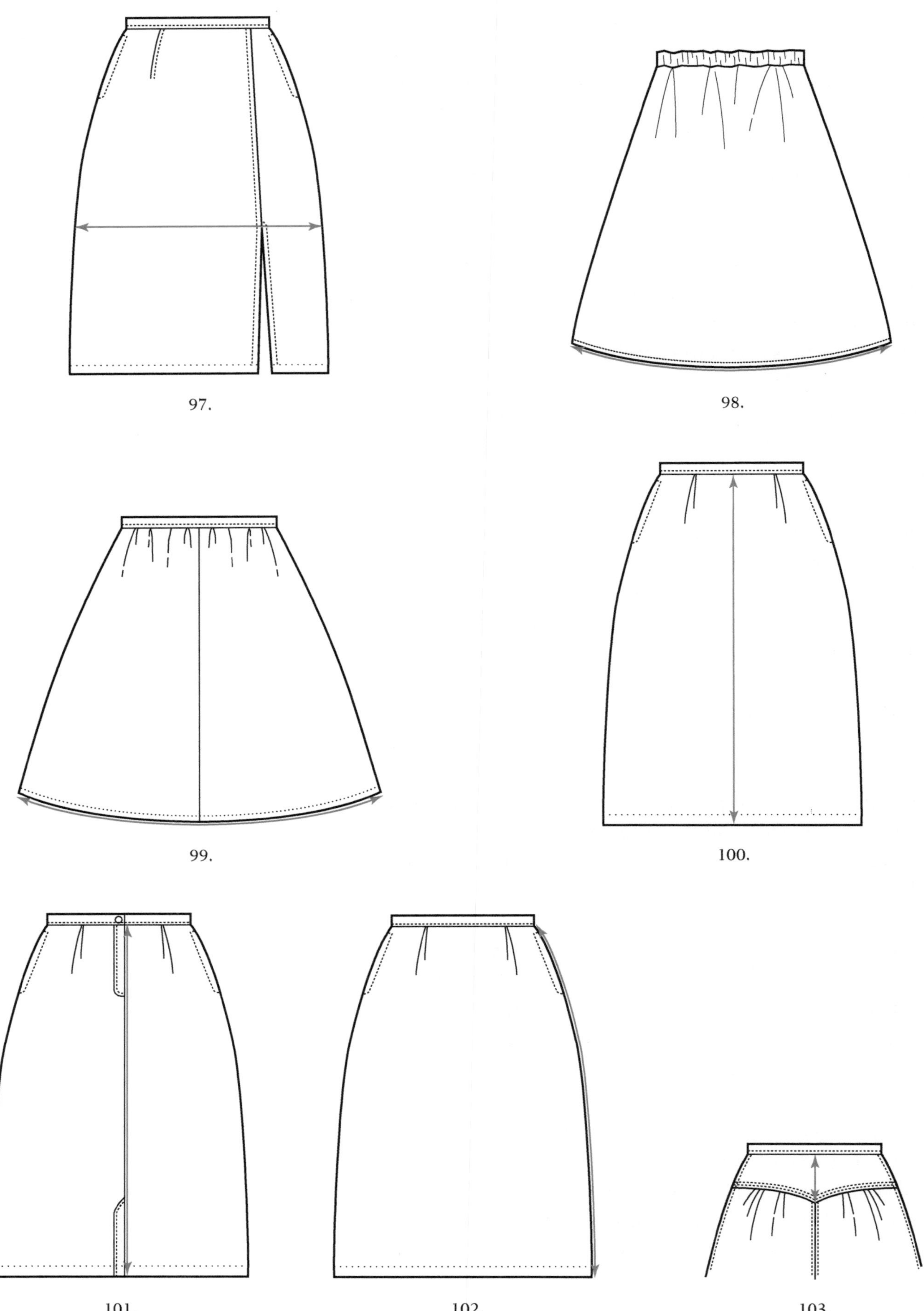

97.

98.

99.

100.

101.

102.

103.

97. *Vented Bottom Opening/Sweep Width Circumference (woven skirt)*—Measure from edge of garment/side seam to edge of garment/side seam straight across garment at top of side vents. Double this measurement. [Note: Indicate on spec sheet if there is only one vent or if vent hits at a point other than sweep, e.g., thigh opening.]

98. *Circular Bottom Opening/Sweep Width (knit skirt)*—Measure from edge of garment/side seam to edge of garment/side seam, following natural contour of garment at bottom opening.

99. *Circular Bottom Opening/Sweep Width Circumference (woven skirt)*—Measure from edge of garment/side seam to edge of garment/side seam, following natural contour of garment at bottom opening. Double this measurement.

100. *Center Front Skirt Length*—Measure from bottom of waistband/seam (top edge if not banded, or stitching if self-elastic/drawstring casing) straight down to bottom of garment at center front. [Note: A fashion-forward skirt may have an asymmetrical waist. Indicate top point of measure on spec sheet.]

101. *Center Back Skirt Length*—Measure from bottom of waistband/seam (top edge if not banded, or stitching if self-elastic/drawstring casing) straight down to bottom of garment at center front. [Note: A fashion-forward skirt may have an asymmetrical waist. Indicate top point of measure on spec sheet.]

102. *Side Skirt Length*—Measure from bottom edge of waistband/seam (top edge if not banded, or stitching if self-elastic/drawstring casing) to bottom of garment along side seam/fold of garment, following any contour.

103. *Skirt/Pant Yoke Depth Front*—Measure from bottom of waistband/seam (top edge if not banded, or stitching if self-elastic/drawstring casing) straight down to bottom of yoke joining seam at center front. [Note: If yoke is contoured, indicate point of measure on spec sheet.]

104. *Skirt/Pant Yoke Depth Back*—Measure from bottom of waistband/seam (top edge if not banded, or stitching if self-elastic/drawstring casing) straight down to bottom of yoke joining seam at center back. [Note: If yoke is contoured, indicate point of measure on spec sheet.]

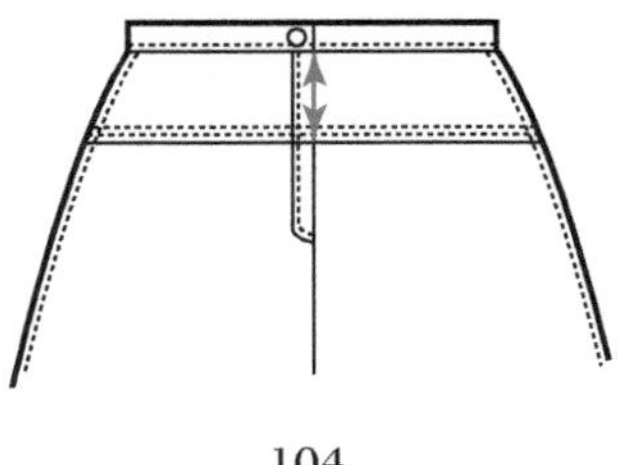

104.

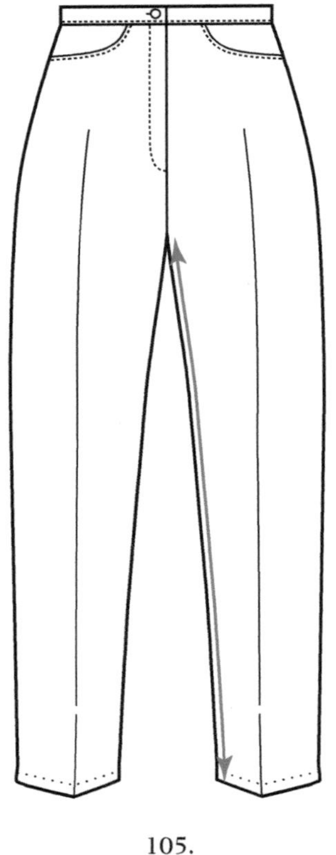
105.

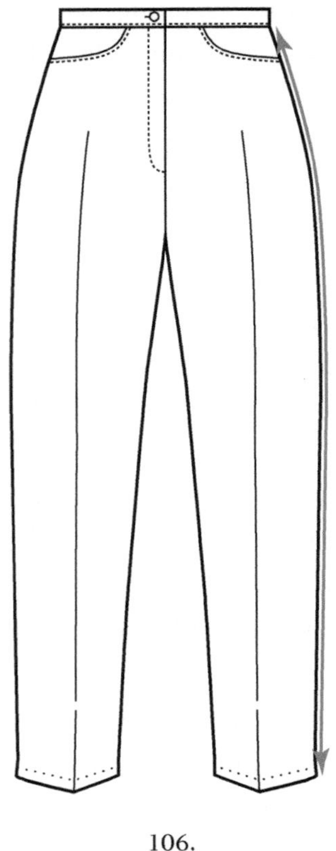
106.

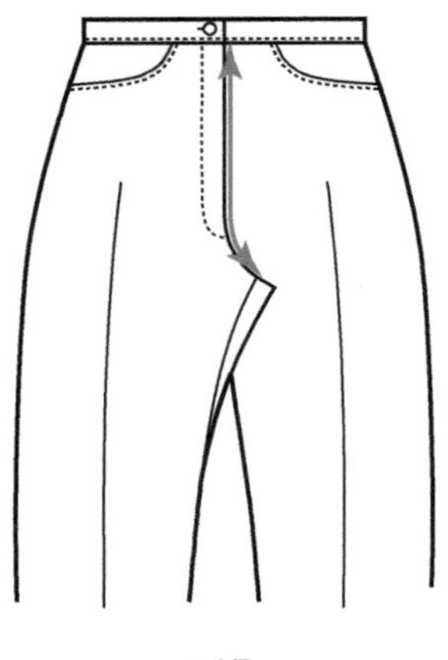
107.

108.

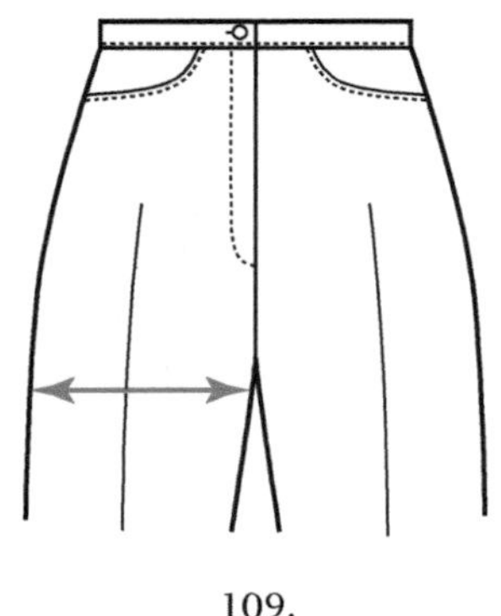
109.

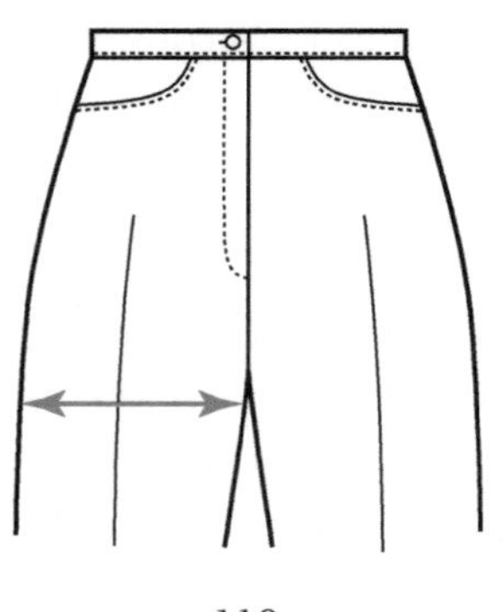
110.

105. *Inseam*—Measure from crotch joining seam to bottom of leg opening, following inseam/inner fold.

106. *Outseam*—Measure from bottom edge of waistband/seam (top edge if not banded, or stitching if self-elastic/drawstring casing) to bottom of garment along side seam/fold of garment.

107. *Front Rise*—Measure from bottom edge of waistband/seam (top edge if not banded, or stitching if self-elastic/drawstring casing) to crotch joining seam, following curve of front rise seam. [Note: Measure over zipper if in front rise seam.]

108. *Back Rise*—Measure from bottom edge of waistband/seam (top edge if not banded, or stitching if self-elastic/drawstring casing) to crotch joining seam, following curve of back rise seam. [Note: Measure over zipper if in front back seam.]

109. *Thigh Width (knit)*—Measure from pant leg edge/seam to pant leg edge/seam straight across pant leg at a point 1" below crotch and parallel to leg opening. [Note: If leg opening is asymmetrical, measure to a point that would be parallel to the leg opening.]

110. *Thigh Width Circumference (woven)*—Measure from pant leg edge/seam to pant leg edge/seam straight across pant leg at a point 1" below crotch and parallel to leg opening. Double this measurement. [Note: If leg opening is asymmetrical, measure to a point that would be parallel to the leg opening.]

111. *Knee Width (knit)*—Measure from pant leg edge/seam to pant leg edge/seam at a point one-half of the inseam and parallel to leg opening. [Note 1: If leg opening is asymmetrical, measure to a point that would be parallel to leg opening. Note 2: If pant leg is three-quarter length, indicate point of measure on spec sheet. Note 3: A general knee measurement from crotch seam of misses/women's 14", junior's 13", or large/plus women's size 15" can be used. Indicate change on spec sheet. Measure children's wear at one-half the inseam minus 1½", and for men's minus 2".]

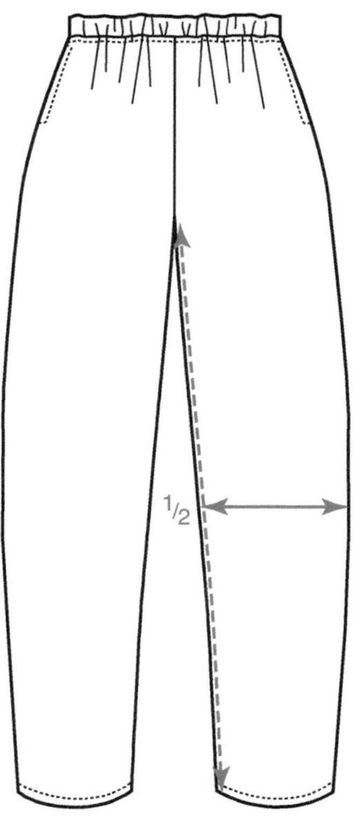

111.

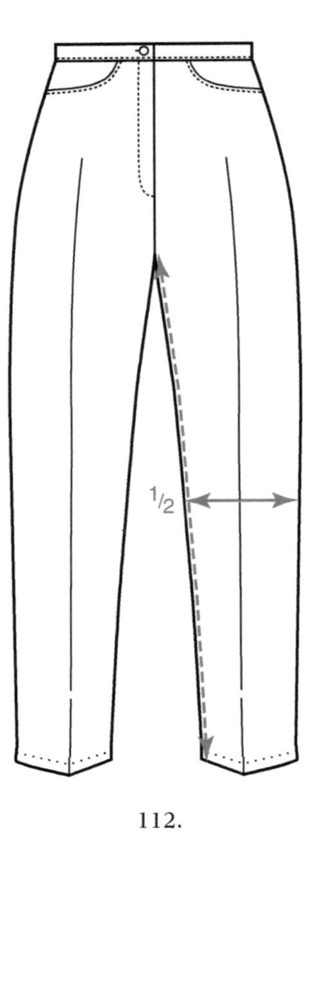

112.

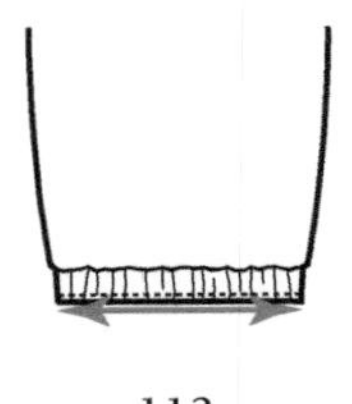

113.

114.

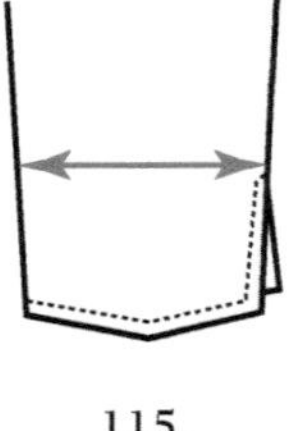

115.

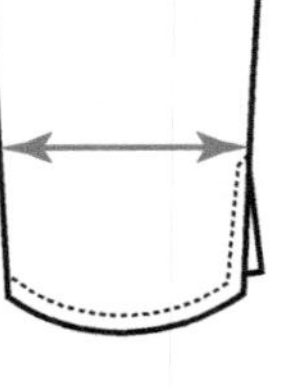

116.

117.

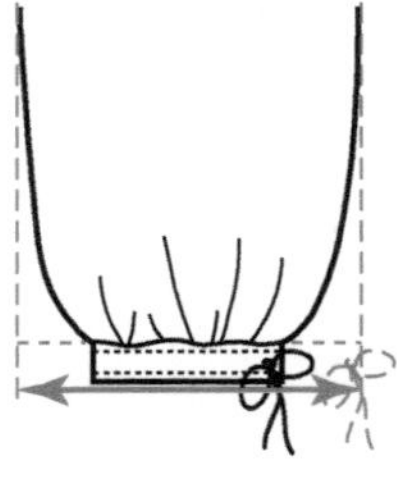

118.

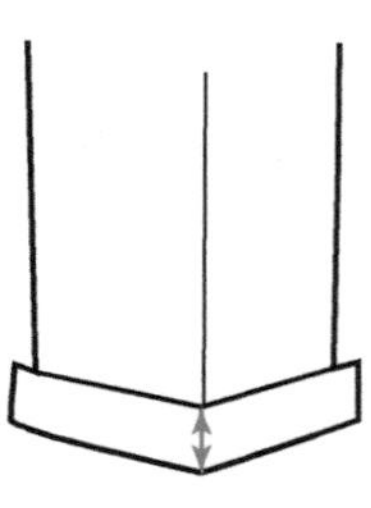

119.

112. *Knee Width Circumference (woven)*—Measure from pant leg edge/seam to pant leg edge/seam at a point one-half of inseam and parallel to leg opening. Double this measurement. [Note 1: If leg opening is asymmetrical, measure to a point that would be parallel to leg opening. Note 2: If pant leg is three-quarter length, indicate point of measure on spec sheet. Note 3: A general knee measurement from crotch seam of misses/women's 14", junior's 13", or large/plus women's size 15" can be used. Indicate change on spec sheet. Measure children's at one-half inseam minus 1½", and for men's minus 2".]

113. *Leg Opening Width (knit)*—Measure from pant leg edge/seam to pant leg edge/seam straight across bottom edge of leg opening. [Note: If leg opening is contoured, follow contour and indicate measurement change on spec sheet.]

114. *Leg Opening Width Circumference (woven)*—Measure from pant leg edge/seam to pant leg edge/seam straight across bottom edge of leg opening. Double this measurement. [Note: If leg opening is contoured, follow contour and indicate measurement change on spec sheet.]

115. *Vented Leg Opening Width (knit)*—Measure from pant leg edge/seam to pant leg edge/seam straight across pant leg at top of side vents.

116. *Vented Leg Opening Circumference (woven)*—Measure from pant leg edge/seam to pant leg edge/seam straight across pant leg at top of side vents. Double this measurement.

117. *Leg Opening Width, Stretched (knit)*—Measure from pant leg edge/seam to pant leg edge/seam straight across bottom edge of leg opening in a fully extended position.

118. *Leg Opening Width Circumference, Stretched (woven)*—Measure from pant leg edge/seam to pant leg edge/seam straight across bottom edge of leg opening in a fully extended position. Double this measurement.

119. *Cuff Height Pants*—Measure from top of cuff edge straight down to bottom of cuff fold and leg opening.

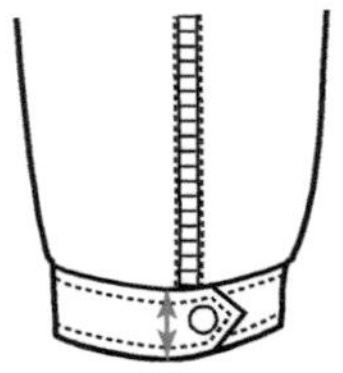

120.

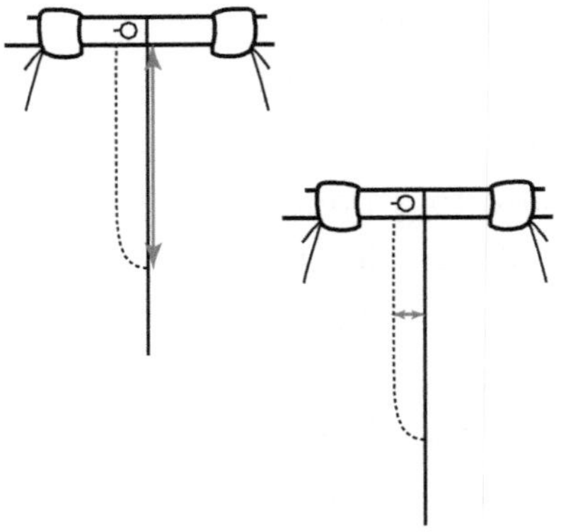

121.

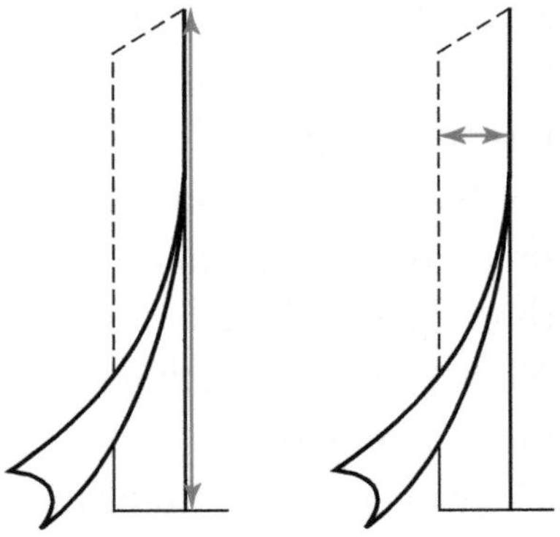

122.

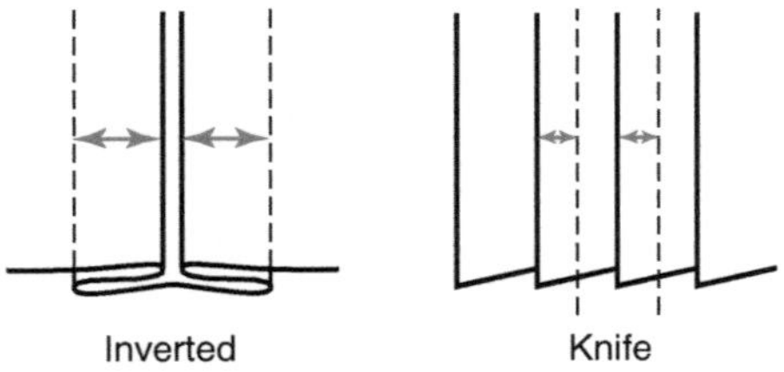

Inverted

Knife

123.

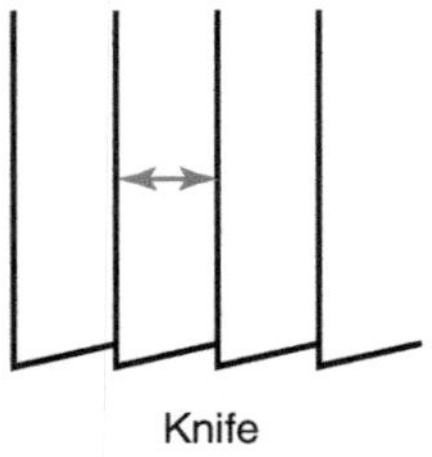

Knife

124.

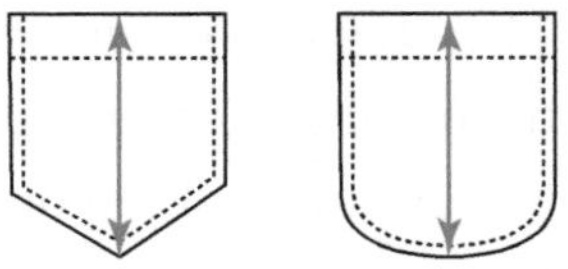

125.

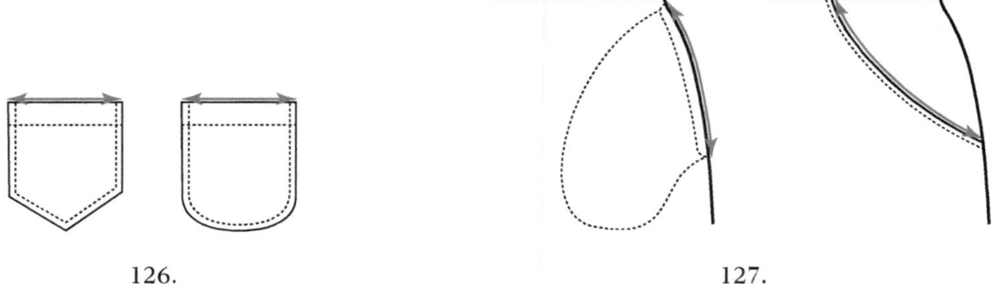

126.

127.

120. *Bottom Band/Ribbing Height Pants*—Measure from cuff joining seam or top of ribbing straight down to bottom edge of cuff or rib opening. [Note: For fashion-forward pants, you may want to include a cuff length. See point of measure 56, Cuff Length Sleeve, for measuring instructions and, if needed, indicate cuff length of pant on spec sheet.]

121. *Fly/Zipper*

A. *Length*—Measure from top of fly/zipper opening straight down to bottom of fly/zipper opening at zipper stop or bar tack.

B. *Fly/Zipper Width*—Measure top of fly/zipper at joining seam from edge/fold straight across to fly/zipper placket stitching.

122. *Vent/Slit*

A. *Height*—Measure from top of vent/slit straight down to bottom of vent/slit along edge of vent/slit.

B. *Width*—Measure top of vent/slit from edge/fold straight across to vent/slit placket stitching at a point parallel to garment hemline.

123. *Pleat Depth*—Measure from outer edge of pleat at fold/crease to inner fold of pleat. [Note 1: It is a good idea to indicate what type of pleat is being measured, e.g., box, inverted, knife, kick, kilt, or envelope. Note 2: If pleats are not parallel or symmetrical, indicate any special instructions on spec sheet.]

124. *Distance Between Pleats*—Measure from start of pleat to start of pleat, excluding pleat depth at a point directly below pleat joining seam. [Note: If pleats are not parallel or symmetrical, indicate any special instructions on spec sheet.]

125. *Applied Pocket Height*—Measure from top edge of pocket to bottom edge of pocket along center of pocket. [Note: For contoured or irregularly shaped pockets, take a second measurement and indicate point of measure on spec sheet.]

126. *Applied Pocket Width*—Measure from side of pocket to side of pocket along top edge of pocket. [Note: For contoured or irregularly shaped pockets, take a second measurement and indicate point of measure on spec sheet.]

127. *Pocket Opening Within a Seam*—Measure from top of pocket to bottom of pocket along edge of pocket opening.

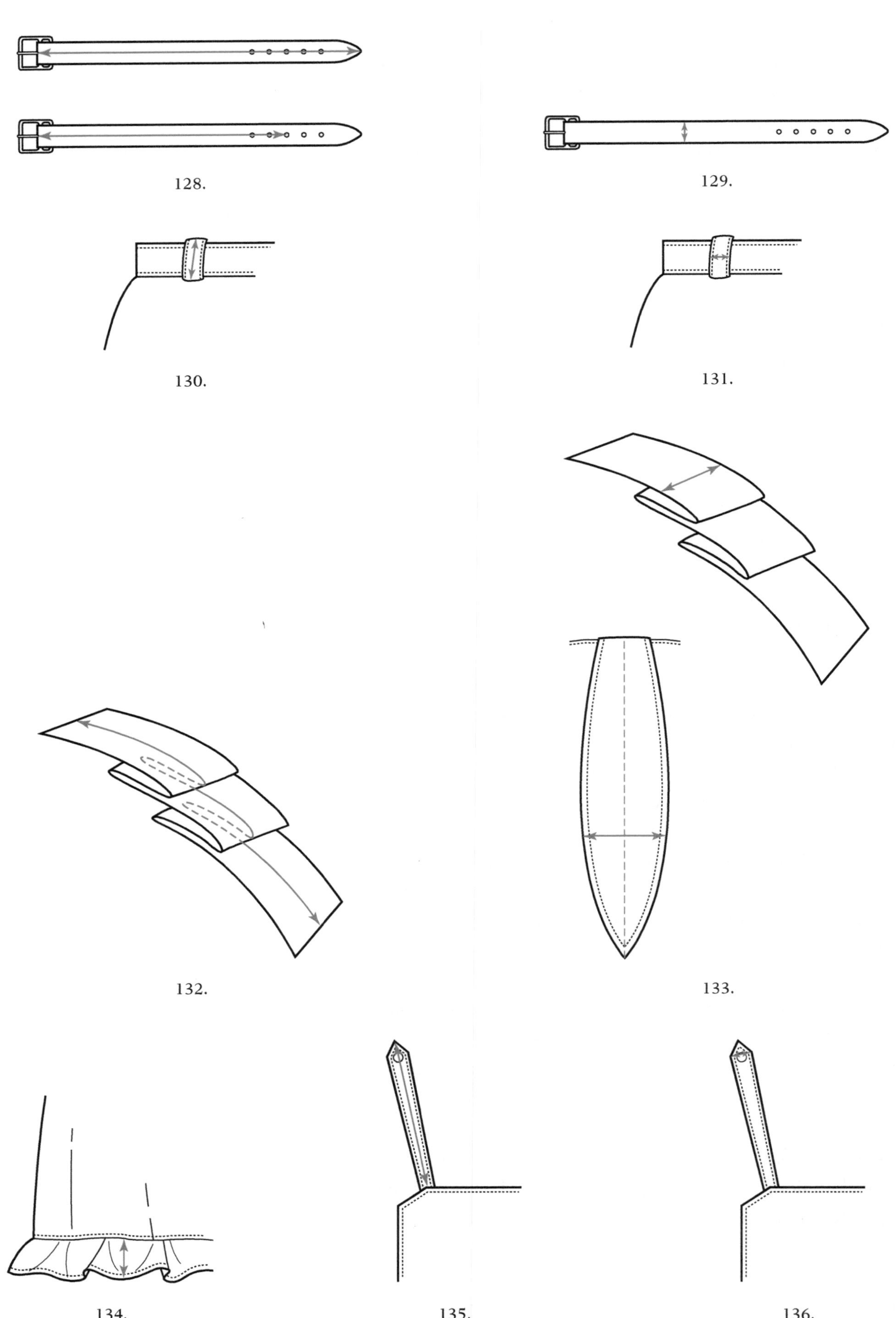

128.

129.

130.

131.

132.

133.

134.

135.

136.

128. *Belt Length*

A. *Total*—Measure from end of belt at buckle along center of belt to opposite end of belt, following contour.

B. *Circumference*—Measure from end of belt at buckle along center of belt to middle hole at opposite end.

129. *Belt Width (or Height)*—Measure from edge of belt straight across to edge of belt. [Note: If belt is contoured, indicate points of measure on spec sheet.]

130. *Belt Loop Length*—Measure from top of belt loop straight down/vertically to bottom of belt loop along center of belt loop. [Note: Fashion-forward or irregularly shaped belt loops may require further spec instructions. Indicate points of measure on spec sheet.]

131. *Belt Loop Width*—Measure belt loop from edge of belt loop straight across/horizontally to edge of belt loop. [Note: Fashion-forward or irregularly shaped belt loops may require further spec instructions. Indicate points of measure on spec sheet.]

132. *Tie Length*—Measure from end of tie/joining seam straight down to tie end along center of tie.

133. *Tie Width*

A. *Straight*—Measure from edge of tie straight across to edge of tie.

B. *Contoured*—Measure from edge of tie straight across to edge of tie at widest point of tie.

134. *Flounce/Ruffle Width*—Measure from flounce/ruffle joining seam straight across to outer edge of flounce/ruffle. [Note: If flounce/ruffle is contoured, measure along narrowest and widest points if possible and indicate changes on spec sheet.]

135. *Strap Length*—Measure from strap joining seam along center of strap to end of strap. [Note: If strap is contoured or has a contoured edge, measure along center, approximating center end point, or indicate instructions as needed on spec sheet.]

136. *Strap Width*—Measure from edge of strap straight across to edge of strap. [Note: If strap is contoured, measure along narrowest and widest points if possible and indicate changes on spec sheet.]

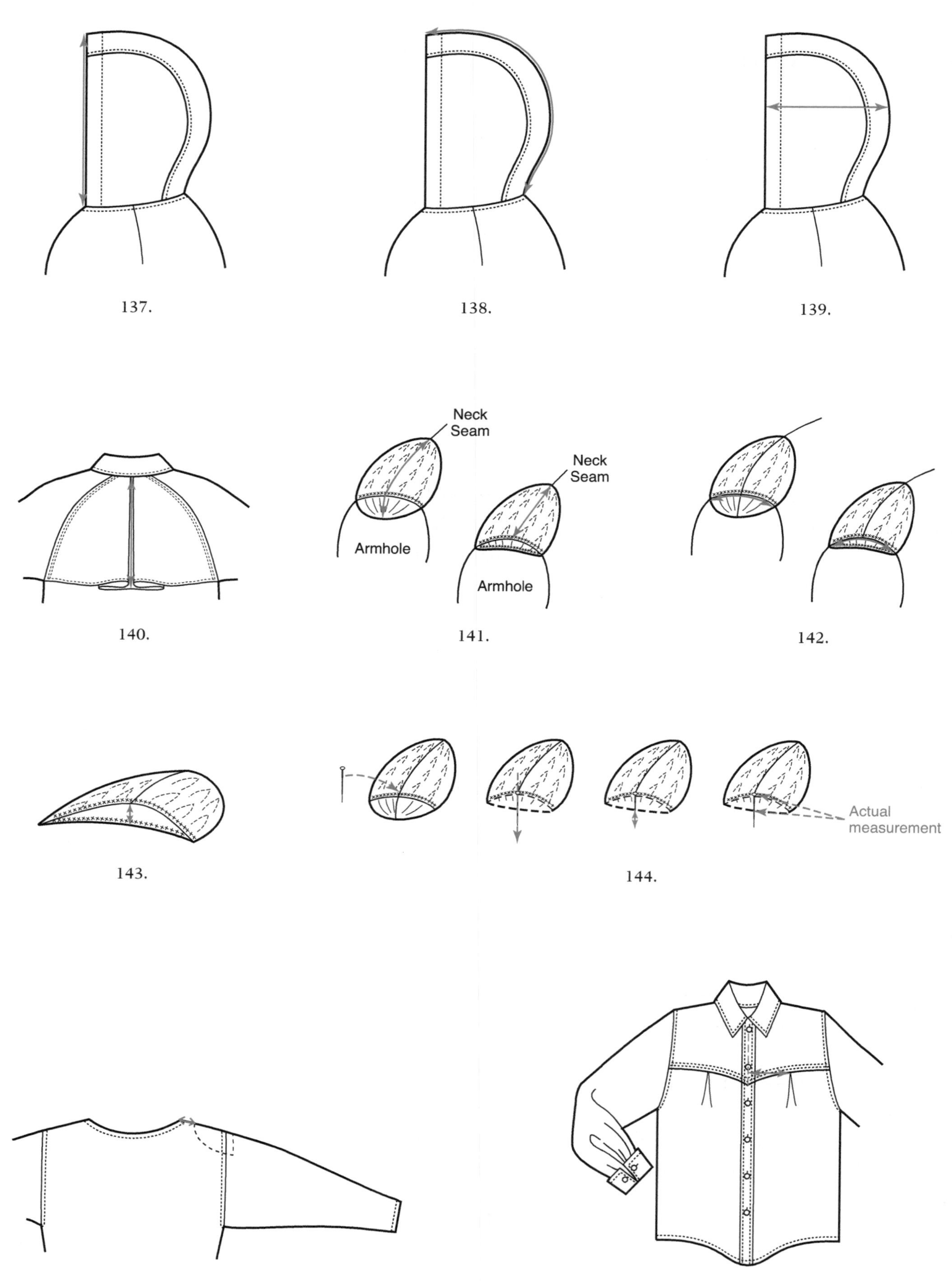

137.
138.
139.
140.
141.
142.
143.
144.
145.
146a.

137. *Front Hood Length*—Measure from top of hood to bottom of hood at center front joining seam along opening edge of hood.

138. *Back Hood Length*—Measure from top of hood at center front to bottom of hood at center back joining seam along outside curve of hood fold/seam.

139. *Hood Width*—Measure from front opening edge of hood straight across to back of hood at fold along widest point of hood.

140. *Flange Depth*—Measure from center back neck joining seam straight down to bottom of flange at center back. [Note: If flange is contoured or asymmetrical, indicate point of measure on spec sheet.]

141. *Shoulder Pad Length*—Measure from edge of pad straight across to edge of pad along center of pad or natural shoulder line of pad.

142. *Shoulder Pad Width*—Measure from side of pad straight across to side of pad along edge of pad if straight, or at widest point of pad if curved.

143. *Straight Edge Shoulder Pad Height*—Measure from top of pad straight down to bottom of pad along center of pad.

144. *Curved Edge Shoulder Pad Height*—Stick a 1" straight pin into thickest part of shoulder pad. Push pin all way through pad until head of pin rests on top of pad. Be sure not to crush pad. Measure portion of pin sticking out of pad. Subtract this figure from 1" (length of pin) to get shoulder pad height.

145. *Shoulder Pad Placement*—Measure from neck edge or joining seam straight across shoulder seam or natural shoulder line to start of shoulder pad.

146. *Pleats Placement*

A. *Front Pleat Top*—Measure distance from center front of garment straight across to start of first pleat at a point parallel to garment hem. [Note: You may need to use armhole or side seam as a starting point if there is no center front seam or placket.]

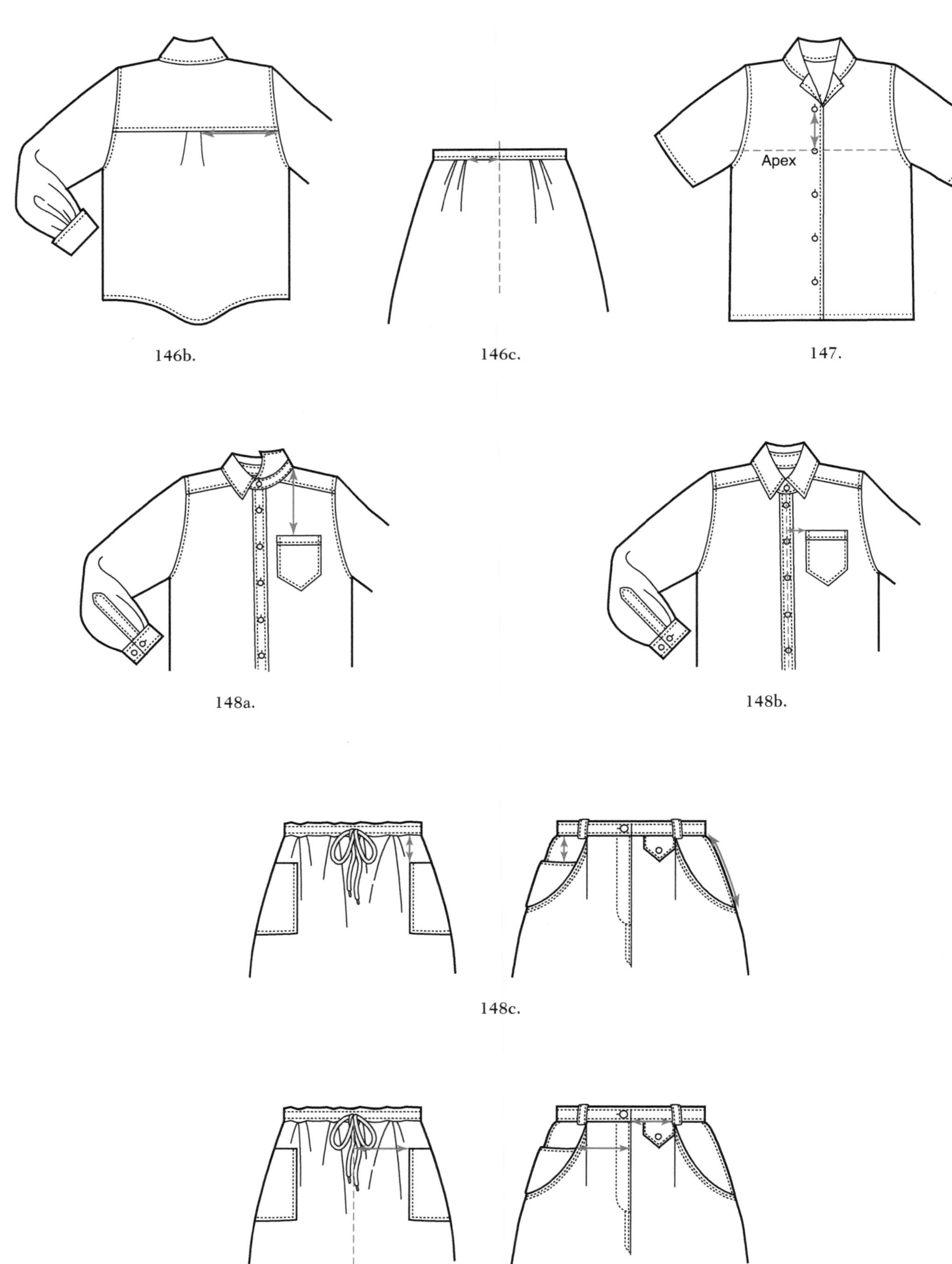

146b.

146c.

147.

148a.

148b.

148c.

148d.

B. *Back Pleat Top*—Measure distance from armhole seam/side seam (depending on pleat placement) to first pleat at a point parallel to garment hem.

C. *Front Pleat Skirt/Pant*—Measure distance from center front of garment waistband joining seam/edge straight across to start of first pleat.

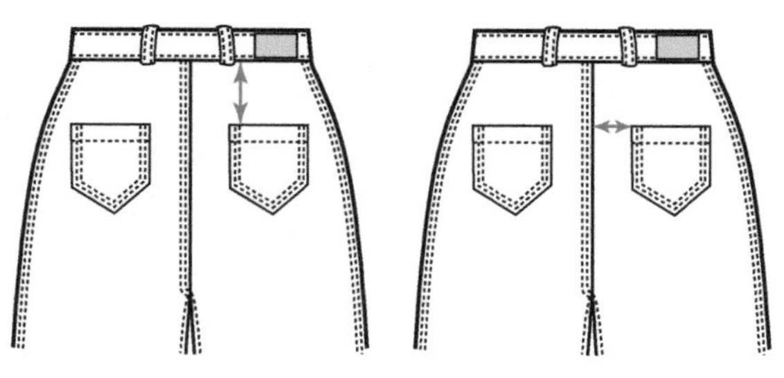

148e. 148f.

147. *Button Placement*—Refer to point of measure 59, Neck Depth Center Front, for placement of first button. Then measure distance of first button to second button. Be sure when measuring that button at bust point is lined up to apex of bust. Adjust all buttons accordingly and respace as needed.

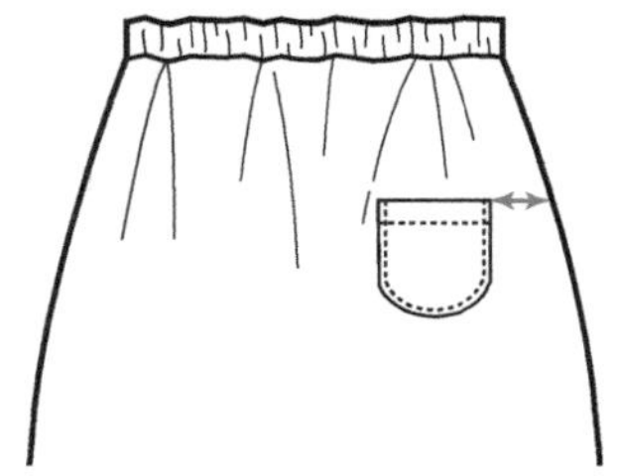

148g.

148. *Pocket Placement*

A. *Top Pocket Vertical*—Measure from shoulder-neck joining seam straight down to top edge of pocket.

B. *Top Pocket Horizontal*—Measure from center front straight across to side of pocket at top edge.

C. *Front Bottom Pocket Vertical*—Measure from waistband/joining seam/edge straight down to top edge of pocket.

D. *Front Bottom Pocket Horizontal*—Measure from center front straight across to side of pocket at top edge.

E. *Back Bottom Pocket Vertical*—Measure from waistband/joining seam/edge straight down to top edge of pocket.

F. *Back Bottom Pocket Horizontal*—Measure from center back straight across to side of pocket at top edge.

G. *Pocket from Side Seam*—Measure from side seam straight across to top of pocket. [Note: If pocket is contoured at sides, a top and bottom pocket size and placement must be measured and added to spec sheet.]

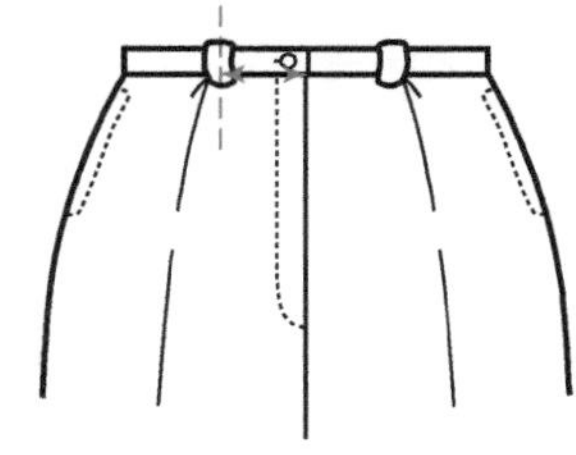

149a.

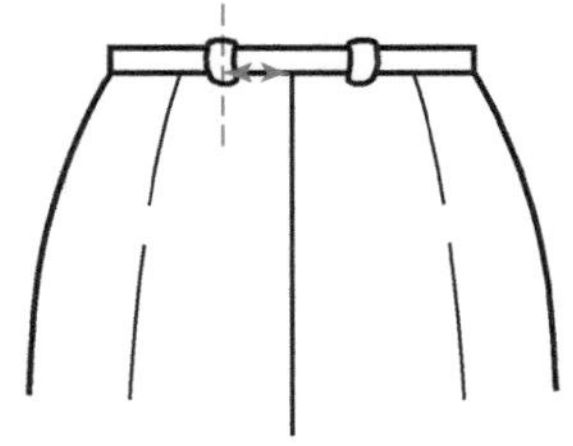

149b.

149. *Belt Loop Placement*

A. *Front*—Measure from center front of garment horizontally across to center of first front belt loop.

B. *Back*—Measure from center back of garment horizontally across to center of first back belt loop.

C. *Side Seam to Front*—Measure from center of side seam belt loop to center of front belt loop.

D. *Side Seam to Back*—Measure from center of side seam belt loop to center of back belt loop.

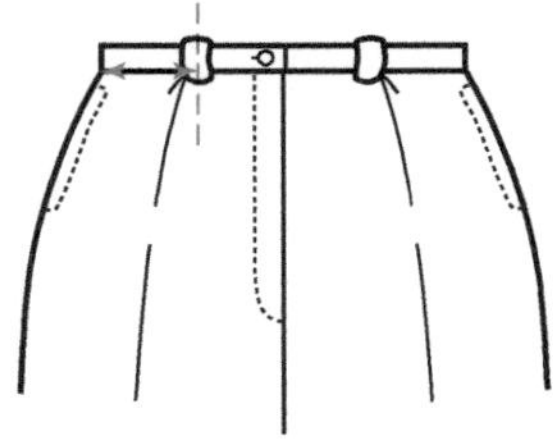

149c.

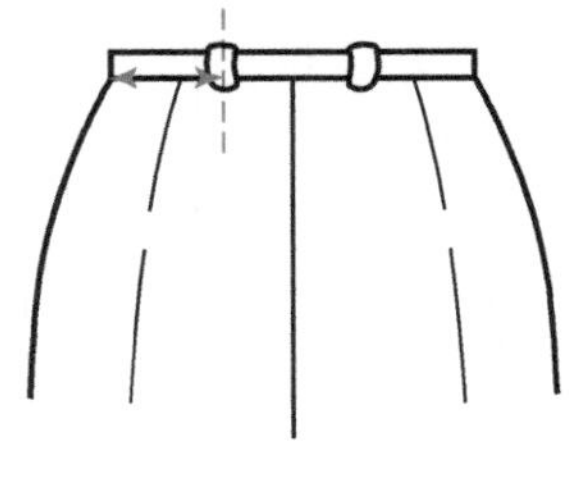

149d.

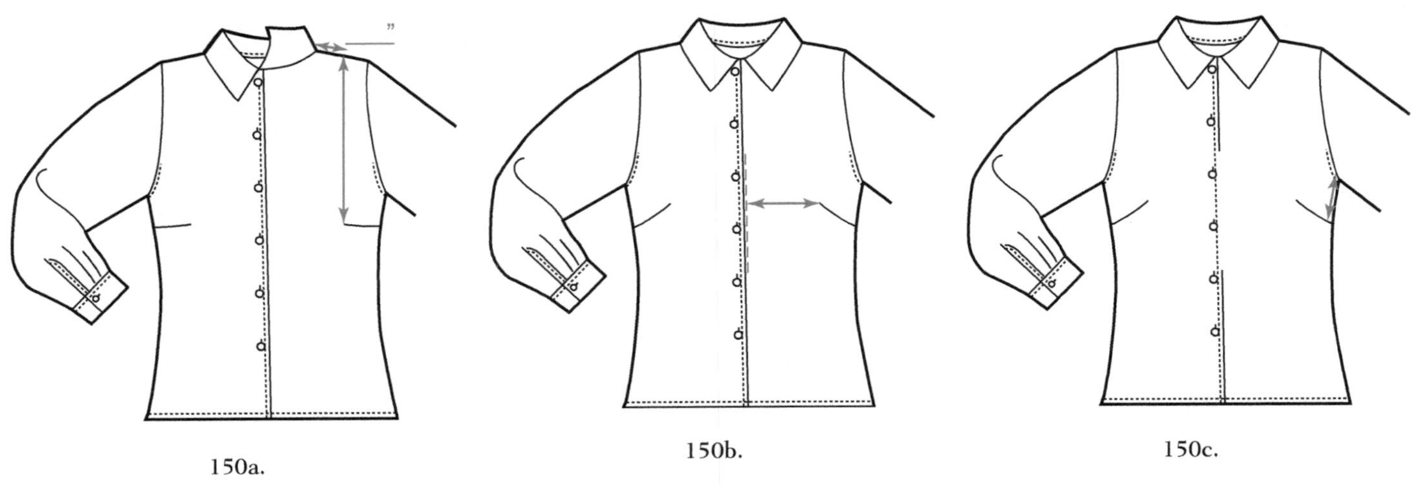

150a.

150b.

150c.

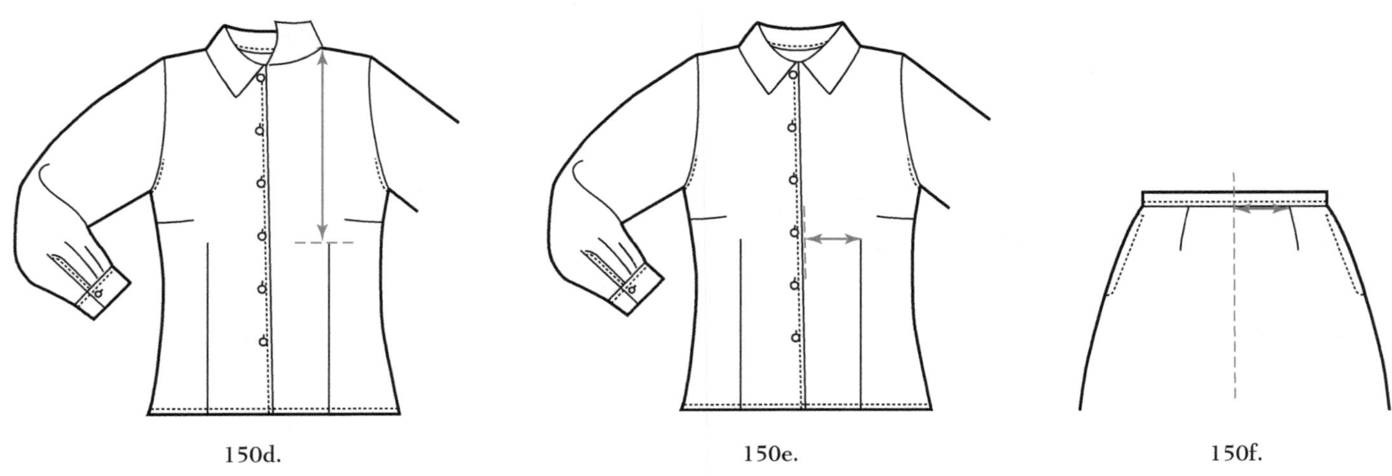

150d.

150e.

150f.

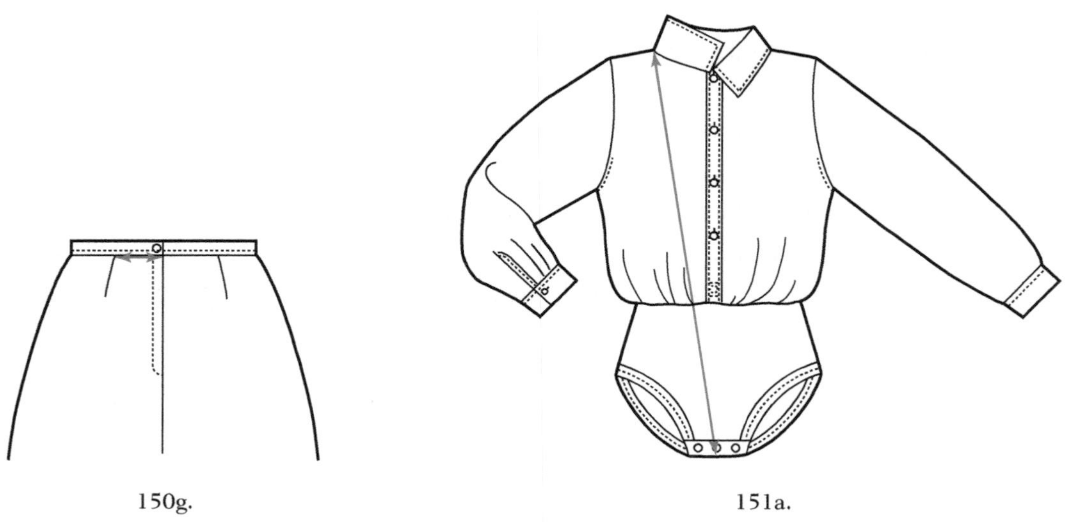

150g.

151a.

150. *Dart Placement*

A. *High Point Shoulder Bust Dart*—Measure from shoulder-neck joining seam or at a point _____" from shoulder-neck seam straight down, parallel to center front, to top of dart. [Note: The _____" from shoulder seam measurement is to be used for darts that are too short to be measured from high point shoulder. Be sure to indicate _____" measurement on spec sheet.]
B. *Center Front Bust Dart*—Measure from center front of garment straight across to top of dart.
C. *Side Seam Bust Dart*—Measure from underarm/side seam joining seam down along contour of side seam to bottom of dart.
D. *High Point Shoulder Princess Dart*—Measure from shoulder-neck joining seam straight down to top of dart.
E. *Center Front Princess Dart*—Measure from center front of garment straight across to top of dart.
F. *Center Front Skirt/Pant*—Measure from center front of garment at waistband joining seam/edge straight across to top of dart.
G. *Center Back Skirt/Pant*—Measure from center back of garment at waistband joining seam/edge straight across to top of dart.

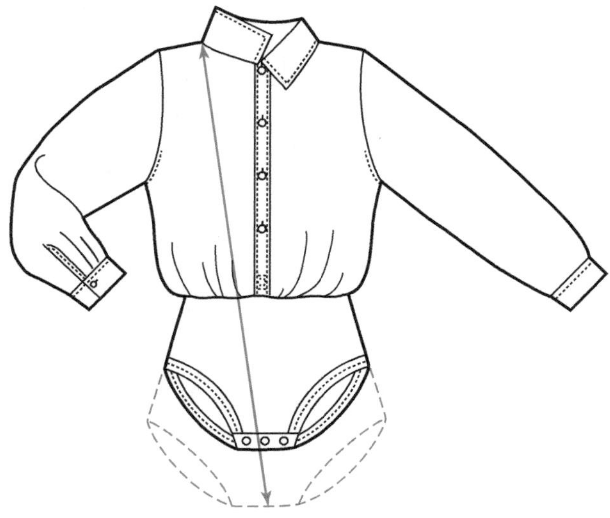

151b.

151. *Front Torso Length (jumpsuits and one-piece garments)*

A. *Garments with a Front Opening, Relaxed*—Measure from high point shoulder at neck straight down to crotch joining seam with garment in a relaxed position.
B. *Garments with a Front Opening, Extended*—Measure from high point shoulder at neck straight down to crotch joining seam with garment in a fully extended position.
C. *Garments with a Plain Front, No Front Opening, Relaxed*—Measure from center front neck joining seam straight down to crotch joining seam with garment in a relaxed position.
D. *Garments with a Plain Front, No Front Opening, Extended*—Measure from center front neck joining seam straight down to crotch joining seam with garment in a fully extended position.

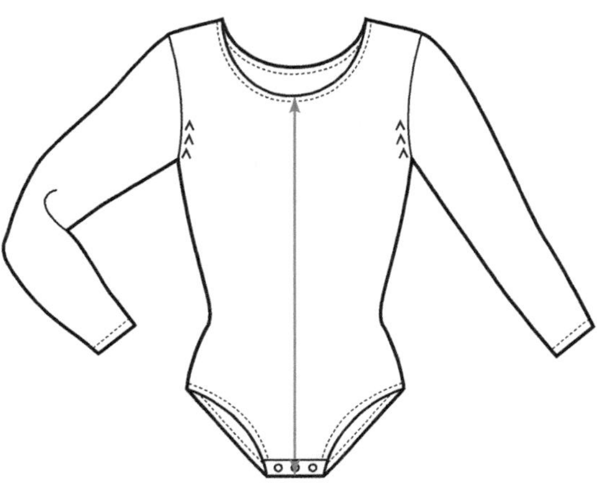

151c.

151d.

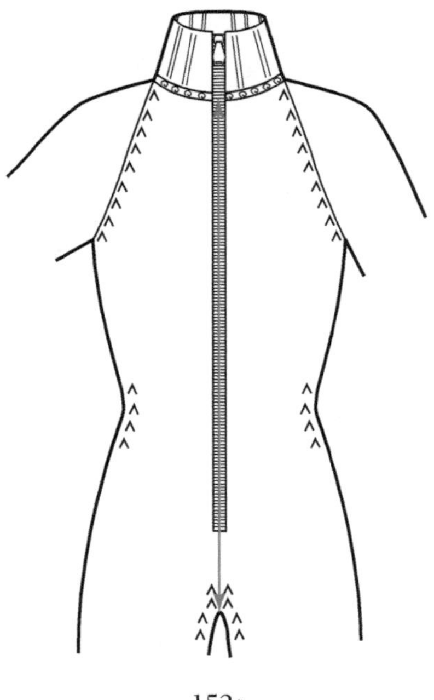

152a.

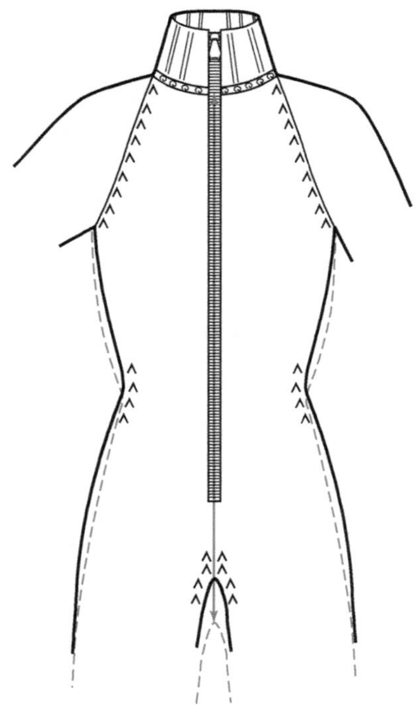

152b.

152. *Back Torso Length (jumpsuits and one-piece garments)*

A. *Relaxed*—Measure from center back neck joining seam straight down to crotch joining seam with garment in a relaxed position.

B. *Extended*—Measure from center back neck joining seam straight down to crotch joining seam with garment in a fully extended position.

153. *High Point Shoulder Length (jumpsuits and one-piece garments)*—Measure from high point shoulder straight down to bottom/hem of garment.

154. *Center Back Garment Length (jumpsuits and one-piece garments)*—Measure from center back neckline seam/edge straight down to bottom hem of garment. [Note: For pantsuits this point will intersect at an imaginary line formed by hemlines of pant legs and center of garment.]

155. *Crotch Width*—Measure straight across crotch from side to side along seam/bottom edge/fold.

CHAPTER 3 TERMS

As you become more familiar with the measurement points, you will come across the following terms. If you are unfamiliar with any of them, please look up the definitions in the glossary at the end of this text.

Center back (CB)
Center front (CF)
Circumference
Extended measurement
High point shoulder (HPS)
Measurement point (point of measure)
Natural relaxed position
Sweep
Total measurement

153.

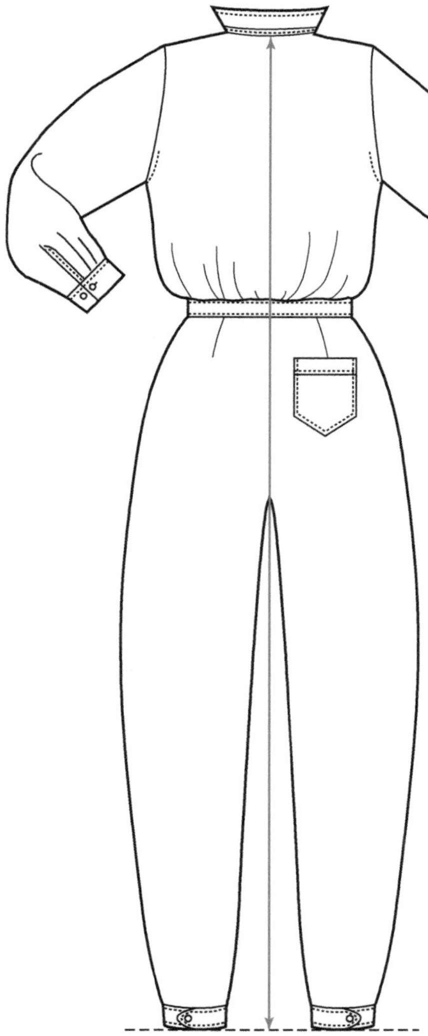

154.

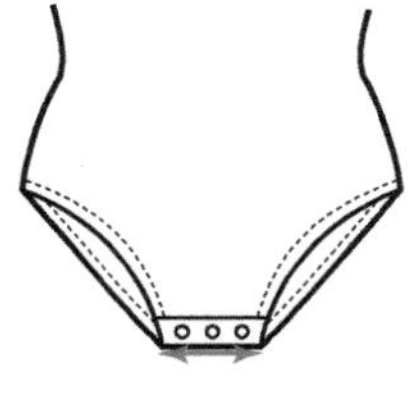

155.

PART II

WORKING WITH KNITS

- Before starting Chapters 4 through 8, be sure to read the Measurement Preparation instructions listed in Chapter 3.
- Only those measurement points that are used when measuring basic garments are included in the respective chapters. Not every measurement point listed will be used on every garment; however, every measurement point for that type of garment has been listed in each chapter.
- Ignore any skipped numbers.
- You may want to try several different points of measure at first to see which one may yield the most accurate measurement. It takes time choosing the best point of measure for your garment, but it is imperative that you consistently use the same method each time you measure that garment.
- Measuring knits will only include missy sketches.
- A generic missy spec sheet has been added to each chapter for your use. [Note: Although some in the retail industry call their missy departments contemporary, misses, or women's wear, the sizing is still considered missy; therefore, this terminology will be used on all spec sheets.]
- A completed example of a spec sheet has been added to each chapter for your reference.
- Basic garment illustrations and a blank spec sheet can be found in the croquis section of Appendix A, Basic Garment Croquis, at the back of this text. These can be used to create your own spec sheets.

Chapters 4 through 8 direct the user to measure knits flat or singular to be consistent with many technicians in the industry. For those in the industry or in the classroom who prefer to measure all garment circumferences, you may simply double these measurements and change your spec sheets accordingly.

Knits in Review

Knit fabric is constructed by interlooping and continuously forming a series of new loops consisting of one or more yarns. There are three classes of knit fabrics: circular knit, flat knit, and warp knit. This text does not entail fabric science, but several knit terms that may be helpful as you work through Chapters 4 through 8 are listed here.

Circular (tubular) knitting—the construction of a knitted fabric or garment on a knitting machine in a circular or tubular form.

Circular web—a fabric knitted in a tubular form, then cut and sewn to construct a garment.

Flat knit—the construction of a knitted fabric on a knitting machine in a flat form.

Full fashioned—a process of flat knitting in which the fabric is shaped by adding or reducing stitches.

Knitted courses (coarses)—rows of interlooping loops.

Knitting in the round—a term for circular or tubular knitting.

Selvage—the finished edge on a cloth that prevents raveling or fraying.

Warp knit—knit produced with yarns running lengthwise, as warp on beams are prepared with one or more yarns per needle.

Weft knitting—knit produced on both flat and circular knitting machines using one continuous thread (yarn) making all the loops of a course.

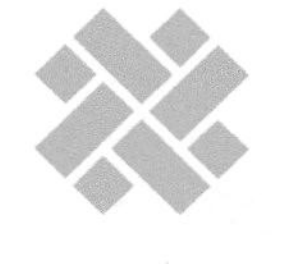

CHAPTER 4

Knit Tops

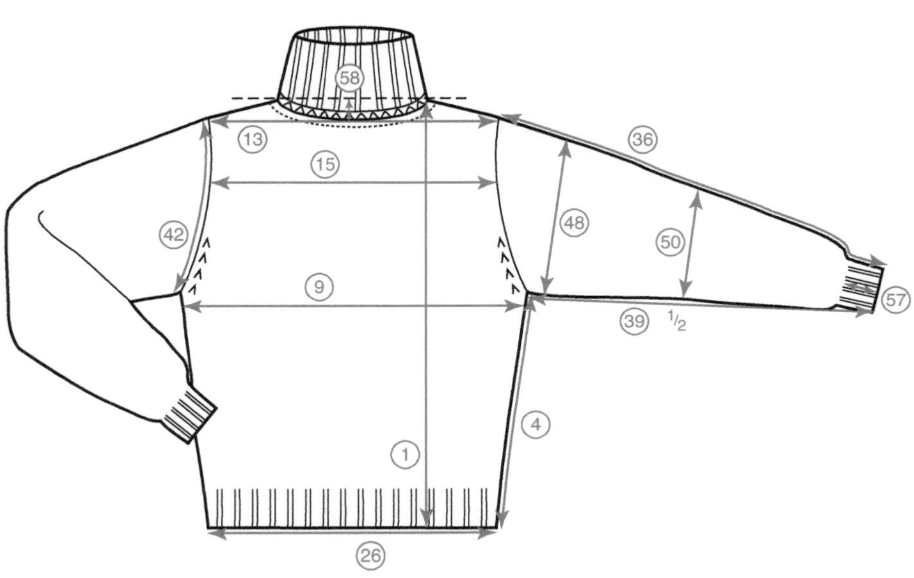

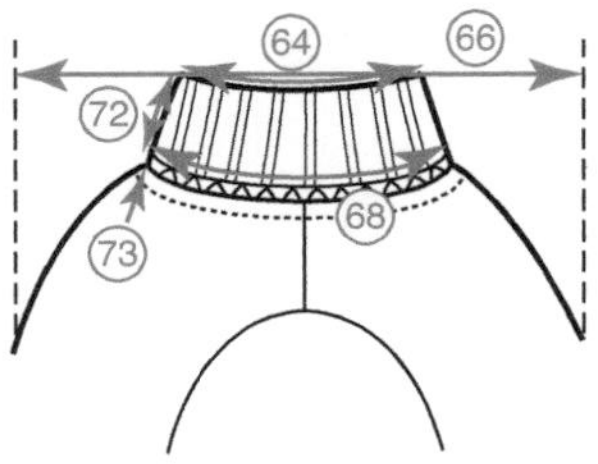

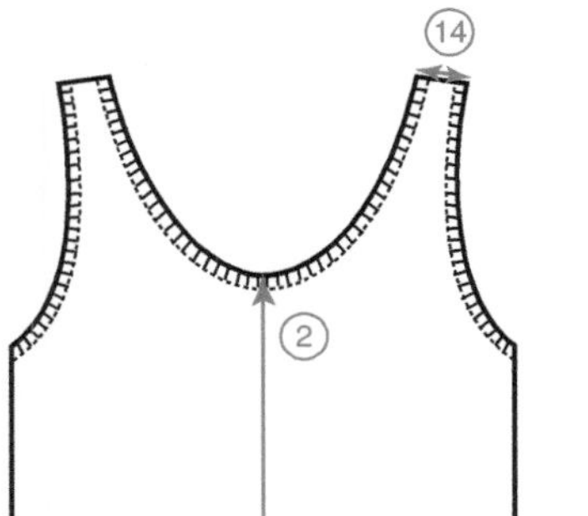

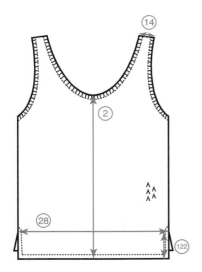

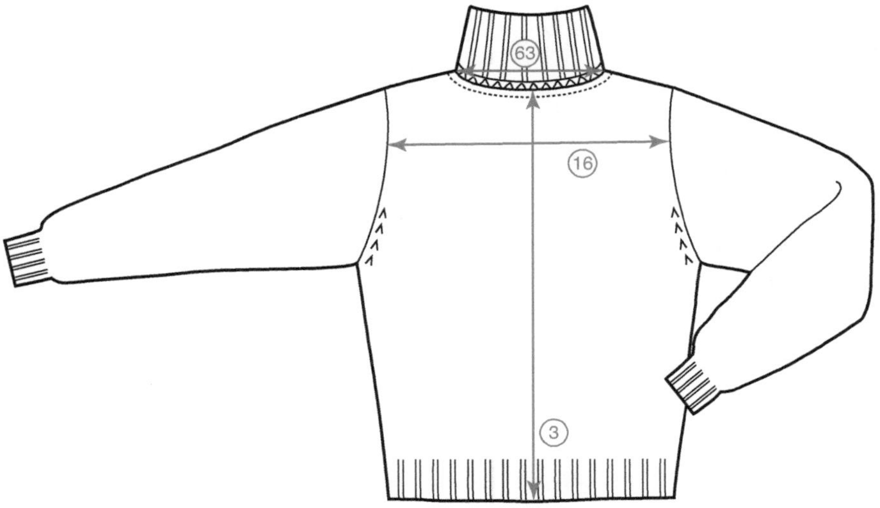

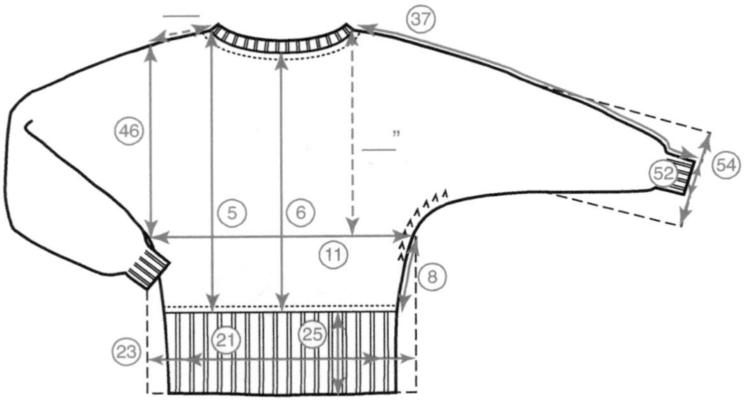

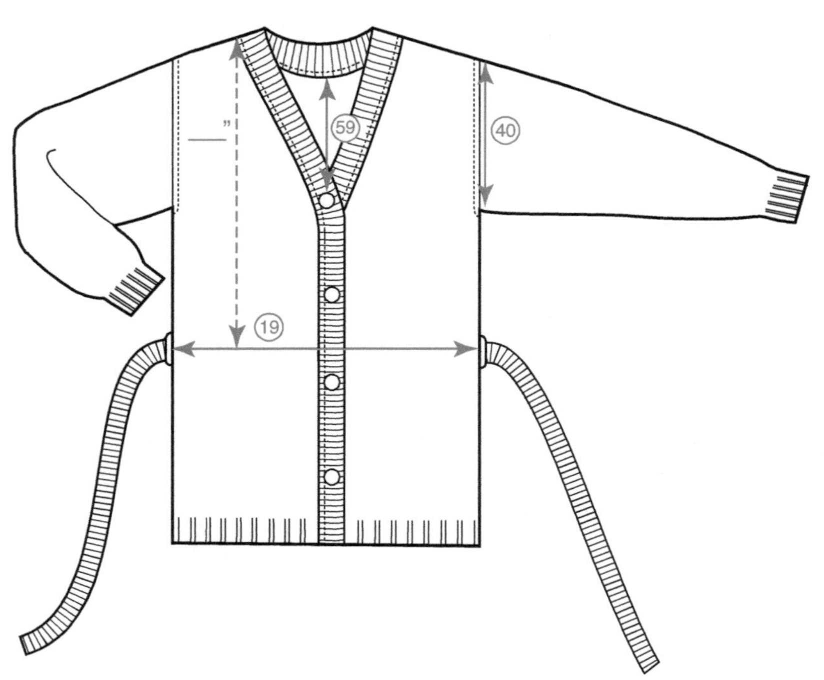
59
40
19

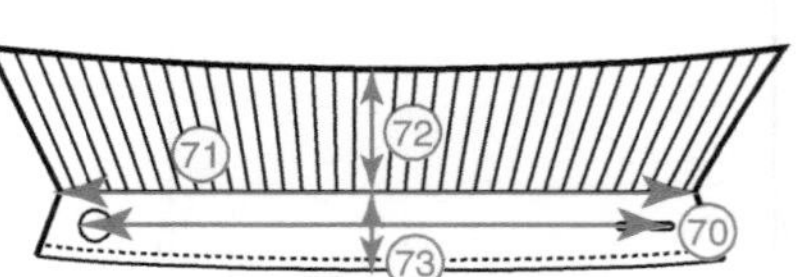
71
72
70
73

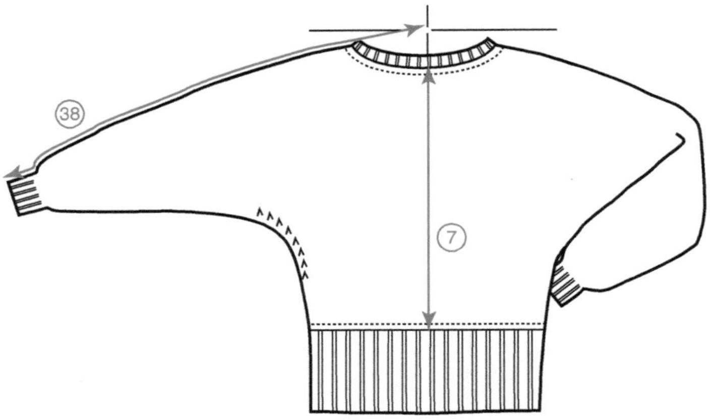

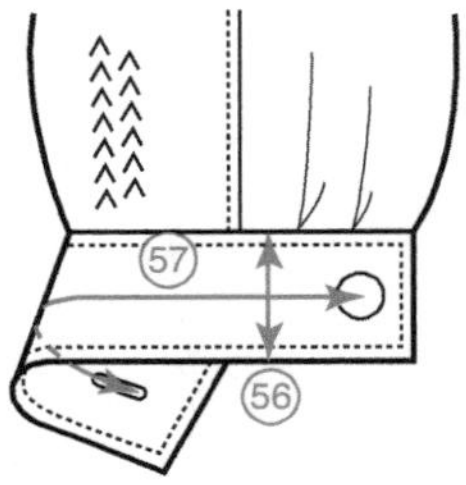

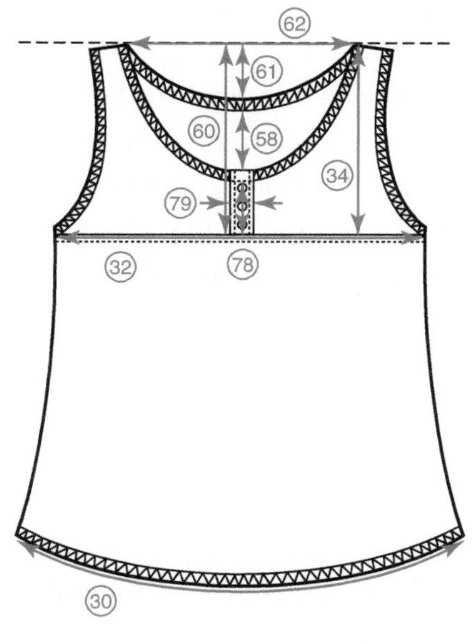
62
61
60
58
34
79
32
78
30

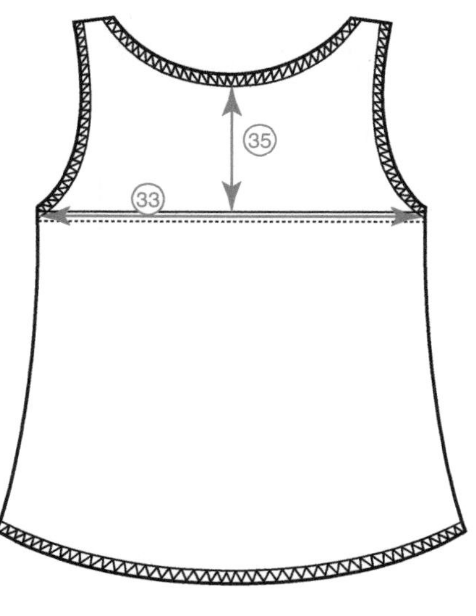
35
33

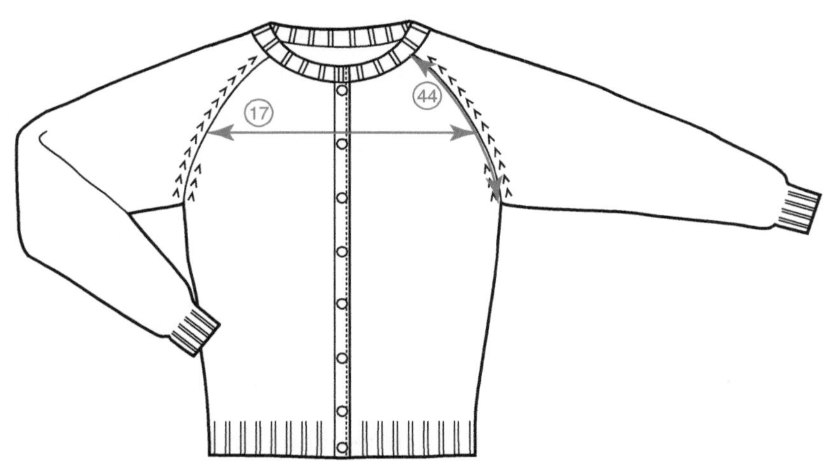
17
44

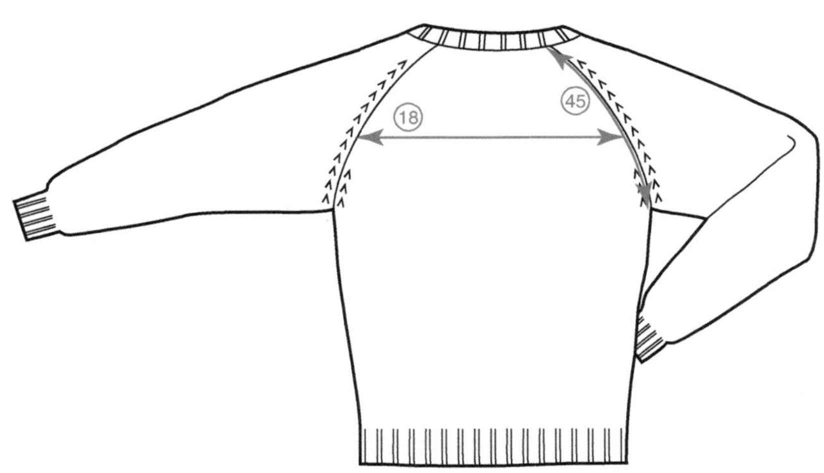
18
45

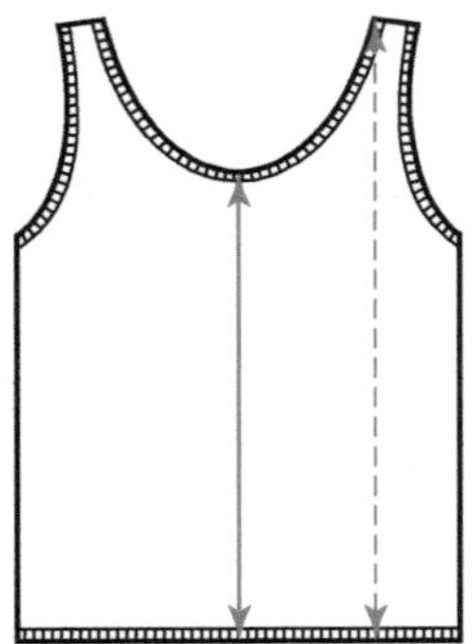

Figure 4.1 Choosing the best front length measurement point.

Measuring Knit Tops

Knit top spec sheets are used for knit garments, including shirts, sweaters, and vests. As you measure, you will find some instances when more than one method can be used for taking a measurement. For example, a knit top's front length can be measured from the high point shoulder or the center front. Most knit tops are measured from the high point shoulder even though they do not have a front opening. However, there are instances—for example, a tank top—when measuring from the center front is better than using the high point shoulder (see Figure 4.1). As the technician, you must decide which measurement method is best suited to your garment's style.

1. *Front Length (garments with a front opening)*—Measure from high point shoulder at neck straight down, parallel to center front, to bottom of garment at front. If garment has a collar, gently lift it away from shoulder-neck measuring point.

2. *Center Front Length (garments with a plain front; no front opening)*—Measure from center front neck joining seams straight down to bottom of garment at center front. [Note: A garment with a front opening may still require point of measure 1, Front Length, if neckline is unusual or is difficult to measure.]

3. *Center Back Length*—Measure from center back neck joining seams straight down to bottom of garment at center back. If needed, gently lift collar away from back neck to expose joining seam.

4. *Side Length*—Measure from bottom of armhole/side seam straight down to bottom of garment along side of garment. Do not follow natural curve of garment's side seam, unless otherwise indicated. If needed, gently lift sleeve away from armhole/side seam joining seam.

5. *Front Bodice Length (garments with a front opening)*—Measure from high point shoulder at neck

straight down, parallel to center front, to top edge of waistband, joining seam, or rib. If garment has a collar, gently lift it away from shoulder-neck measuring point.

6. *Center Front Bodice Length (garments with a plain front; no front opening)*—Measure from center front neck joining seam straight down to top edge of waistband, joining seam, or rib. [Note: A garment with a center opening may still require point of measure 5, Front Bodice Length, if neckline is unusual or is difficult to measure.]

7. *Center Back Bodice Length*—Measure from center back neck joining seams straight down to top edge of waistband, joining seam, or rib. If needed, gently lift collar away from back neck to expose joining seam.

8. *Side Seam Bodice Length*—Measure from bottom of armhole/side seam straight down to top edge of waistband, joining seam, or rib, along side of garment, following natural curve of garment's side seam, unless otherwise indicated. If needed, gently lift sleeve away from armhole/side seam joining seam. [Note: You can take side seam bodice measurement straight rather than contoured if joining seam/rib can be extended, but indicate change on spec sheet.]

9. *Chest Width (knit)*—Measure from edge of garment/side seam to edge of garment/side seam straight across garment at a point 1" below armhole.

11. *Chest Width/Raglan Sleeve (knit)*—Measure from edge of garment/side seam to edge of garment/side seam straight across garment at a point _____" below high point shoulder. [Note: You will have to determine number of inches down from high point shoulder for each raglan sleeve style based on depth of sleeve. Then indicate this number on spec sheet.]

13. *Across Shoulder*—Measure straight across front from armhole seam/edge to armhole seam/edge at shoulder seam or across natural shoulder fold line created if there is no seam.

14. *Shoulder Width*—Measure from neckband/ collar/ribbing joining seam or neckline edge to top of armhole seam at shoulder, taken along shoulder seam or across natural shoulder fold line created if there is no seam.

15. *Across Chest*—Measure 2½" down from collar/rib joining seam at center front straight across front of garment from armhole seam/edge to armhole seam/ edge. [Note: The 2½" measurement point is for misses/women's wear sizes only and may need to be adjusted up or down ¼" to ½" accordingly for men's, children's, junior's, and large/plus sizes. Indicate any changes on spec sheet.]

16. *Across Back*—Measure 4" down from collar/rib joining seam at center back straight across back of garment from armhole seam/edge to armhole seam/ edge. [Note: The 4" measurement point is for misses/ women's wear only and may need to be adjusted up or down ¼" to ½" accordingly for men's, children's, junior's, and large/plus sizes. Indicate any changes on spec sheet.]

17. *Across Chest/Center Armhole*—Measure at one-half depth of armhole straight across front of garment from armhole seam/edge to armhole seam/edge.

18. *Across Back/Center Armhole*—Measure at one-half depth of armhole straight across back of garment from armhole seam/edge to armhole seam/edge.

19. *Waist Width (knit)*—Measure from edge of garment/side seam to edge of garment/side seam straight across garment on seam or at narrowest point of waist taper at a point _____" below high point shoulder. [Note: You will have to determine number of inches down from high point shoulder for each raglan sleeve style based on depth of sleeve. Then indicate this number on spec sheet.]

21. *Bottom Band Width (knit top)*—Measure from side of bottom band to side of bottom band along center of band, following natural contour of waistband.

23. *Bottom Band Width, Stretched (knit top)*—Measure from side of bottom band to side of bottom band straight across center of band in a fully extended position.

25. *Bottom Band/Ribbing Height (knit or woven top)*—Measure from band/ribbing joining seam straight down to bottom edge of band/rib opening. [Note: If band is shaped or contoured, indicate special measurement instructions on spec sheet.]

26. *Bottom Opening/Sweep (knit top)*—Measure from edge of garment/side seam to edge of garment/side seam straight across garment at bottom opening. [Note: If sweep has pleats, measure with pleats closed or relaxed.]

28. *Vented Bottom Opening/Sweep Width (knit top)*—Measure from edge of garment/side seam to edge of garment/side seam straight across garment at top of side vents. Do not follow natural curve of garment. [Note: If vents are too high to measure sweep, indicate opening at appropriate position, e.g., midriff opening.]

30. *Circular Bottom Opening/Sweep Width (knit top)*—Measure from edge of garment/side seam to edge of garment/side seam, following natural contour of garment at bottom opening.

32. *Yoke Width Front*—Measure from armhole seam/edge to armhole seam/edge straight across front of garment, ignoring contours or points, at yoke-body joining seams. [Note: If yoke is asymmetrical, indicate changes in measuring as needed on spec sheet.]

33. *Yoke Width Back*—Measure from armhole seam/edge to armhole seam/edge straight across back of garment, ignoring contours or points, at yoke-body joining seams. [Note: If yoke is asymmetrical, indicate changes in measuring as needed on spec sheet.]

34. *Yoke Depth Front*—Measure from high point shoulder at neck straight down to bottom of front yoke-body joining seam. Be sure to gently lift collar away from shoulder-neck joining seam if needed.

35. *Yoke Back Depth*—Measure from center back neck joining seam straight down to bottom of back yoke-body joining seam. Gently lift collar away from back neck joining seam if needed.

36. *Sleeve Length Top Armhole*—Measure along top of sleeve/fold, following contour of sleeve from armhole seam at shoulder to bottom of sleeve opening, including cuff.

37. *Sleeve Length Top Neck*—Measure along top of sleeve/fold, following contour of sleeve from sleeve-neck joining seam/edge to edge of sleeve opening, including cuff. Gently lift collar at sleeve-neck joining seam if needed.

38. *Sleeve Length Center Back*—Measure from center back neck joining seam or from a point above neck at an imaginary line, that of a joining seam, along top of sleeve/fold, following contour of sleeve to edge of sleeve opening, including cuff.

39. *Sleeve Length Underarm*—Measure straight from bottom of armhole along sleeve seam to edge of sleeve opening, including cuff.

40. *Straight Armhole Width (knit)*—Measure from top of shoulder joining seam/edge straight down to bottom of armhole.

42. *Curved Armhole Width (knit)*—Measure from top of shoulder joining seam/edge to bottom of armhole, following contour of armhole.

44. *Armhole Front*—Measure on front of garment from top of shoulder at neckline joining seam/edge to bottom of armhole, following contour of armhole. Gently lift collar away from neckline joining seam if needed.

45. *Armhole Back*—Measure on back of garment from top of shoulder at neck joining seam/edge to bottom of armhole, following contour of armhole. Gently lift collar away from neck joining seam if needed.

46. *Armhole Width Straight (knit)*—Measure from top of shoulder seam at a point _____" below neckline joining seam/edge straight down to bottom of armhole. [Note: Gently move collar away from neck joining seam if needed when measuring down _____" to armhole start point. Indicate number of inches measured down on spec sheet.]

48. *Muscle Width (knit)*—Measure from inner sleeve edge/seam to outer sleeve edge/fold at a point 1" below armhole and parallel to sleeve opening.

50. *Elbow Width (knit)*—Measure from inner sleeve edge/seam to outer sleeve edge/fold straight across sleeve at a point one-half of underarm sleeve length and parallel to sleeve opening at wrist or cuff. [Note: If sleeve is three-quarter length, indicate new point of measure on spec sheet.]

52. *Sleeve Opening Width (knit)*—Measure from inner sleeve edge/seam to outer sleeve edge/fold straight across bottom edge of sleeve opening.

54. *Sleeve Opening Width, Stretched (knit)*—Measure from inner sleeve edge/seam to outer sleeve edge/fold straight across bottom edge of sleeve opening in a fully extended position.

56. *Cuff Length Sleeve*—Measure from outside end of buttonhole to center of button straight along center of cuff. Open cuff out as flat as possible when measuring. [Note: If cuff length is contoured, measure along center-most point.]

57. *Cuff/Ribbing Height Sleeve*—Measure from cuff joining seam or top of ribbing straight down to bottom edge of cuff or rib opening. [Note: If cuff is contoured, indicate changes made to measurement on spec sheet.]

58. *Neck Depth Front (garments with a plain front/asymmetrical front opening)*—Measure from center back neck joining seam/edge straight down to center front neck joining seam/edge.

59. *Neck Depth Center Front (garments with a center front opening)*—Measure from center back neck joining seam/edge straight down to center of first button at center front of garment.

60. *Neck Drop Front*—Measure from an imaginary line connecting neckline edges straight down to center front neck opening edge. Use a ruler if needed to connect top neckline edges.

61. *Neck Drop Back*—Measure from an imaginary line connecting neckline edges straight down to center back neck opening edge. This measurement is taken with front of garment faceup. Use a ruler to connect top neckline edges if needed.

62. *Neck Width, No Collar*—Measure from inside neck edge/seam to inside neck edge/seam straight across back neck at widest point. This measurement is taken with front of garment faceup.

63. *Neck Width, Collar*—Measure straight across back neck from neck-shoulder joining seam to neck-shoulder joining seam or natural shoulder line if no seam. This measurement is taken with back of garment faceup.

64. *Neck Edge Width (knit)*—Measure from neck edge/seam/fold to neck edge/seam/fold along top opening edge, following natural contour of neck opening. Garment should be positioned with one shoulder on top of the other and with front and back neck edges meeting.

66. *Neck Edge Width, Stretched (knit)*—Measure from neck edge/seam/fold to neck edge/seam/fold

along top opening edge in a fully extended position. Garment should be positioned with one shoulder on top of the other and with front and back neck edges meeting.

68. *Neck Base (knit)*—Measure from neck edge/seam to neck edge/seam along collar/rib joining seam or neckline edge, following natural contour of neck opening. Garment should be buttoned or zippered, if applicable, with one shoulder seam positioned on top of the other and with front and back neck edges meeting.

70. *Neckband Length*—Measure from outside end of buttonhole to center of buttonhole across neckband, following contour of neckband.

71. *Collar Length*—Measure from one end of collar to other end of collar along neck joining seam.

72. *Collar Height*—Measure from collar/rib joining seam at center back neck straight up to outer edge of collar/rib.

73. *Collar Band Height*—Measure from collar joining seam at center back straight up to neckband joining seam at center back.

74. *Collar Point Length*—Measure from collar joining seam to outer edge of collar along collar point edge. [Note: If collar is rounded, measure at a point parallel to center back and indicate change on spec sheet.]

75. *Collar Point Spread (pointed collars only)*—Measure, with collar band buttoned and collar in place, from collar point straight across collar edge to collar point.

76. *Lapel Width*

A. *Notched*—Measure from lower lapel notch straight across to lapel fold at a point perpendicular to garment center front.

B. *Without Notches*—Measure from lapel edge straight across widest point of lapel to lapel fold at a point _____" down from center back collar joining seam and perpendicular to front of garment.

77. *Center Front Extension*—Measure from an imaginary line at center front of garment horizontally to finished outer edge of front extended piece.

78. *Placket Length*—Measure from top edge of placket straight down to bottom of placket opening along center of placket.

79. *Placket Width*—Measure from placket joining seam straight across placket to placket edge at fold.

80. *Keyhole Length*—Measure from outer edge of neckline straight down to bottom of keyhole opening.

81. *Waistband Depth*—Measure from top of waistband edge straight down to bottom of waistband at waistband joining seam. [Note: If waistband is contoured, indicate measurement change on spec sheet.]

122. *Vent/Slit*

A. *Height*—Measure from top of vent/slit straight down to bottom of vent/slit along edge of vent/slit.

B. *Width*—Measure top of vent slit from edge/fold straight across to vent/slit placket stitching at a point parallel to garment hemline.

123. *Pleat Depth*—Measure from outer edge of pleat at fold/crease to inner fold of pleat. [Note 1: It is a good idea to indicate what type of pleat is being measured, e.g., box, inverted, knife, kick, kilt, or envelope. Note 2: If pleats are not parallel or symmetrical, indicate any special instructions on spec sheet.]

124. *Distance Between Pleats*—Measure from start of pleat to start of pleat, excluding pleat depth at a point directly below pleat joining seam. [Note: If

pleats are not parallel or symmetrical, indicate any special instructions on spec sheet.]

125. *Applied Pocket Height*—Measure from top edge of pocket to bottom edge of pocket along center of pocket. [Note: For contoured or irregularly shaped pockets, take a second measurement and indicate point of measure on spec sheet.]

126. *Applied Pocket Width*—Measure from side of pocket to side of pocket along top edge of pocket. [Note: For contoured or irregularly shaped pockets, take a second measurement and indicate point of measure on spec sheet.]

127. *Pocket Opening Within a Seam*—Measure from top of pocket to bottom of pocket along edge of pocket opening.

128. *Belt Length*

A. *Total*—Measure from end of belt at buckle along center of belt to opposite end of belt, following contour.
B. *Circumference*—Measure from end of belt at buckle along center of belt to middle hole at opposite end.

129. *Belt Width (or Height)*—Measure from edge of belt straight across to edge of belt. [Note: If belt is contoured, indicate points of measure on spec sheet.]

130. *Belt Loop Length*—Measure from top of belt loop straight down/vertically to bottom of belt loop along center of belt loop. [Note: Fashion-forward or irregularly shaped belt loops may require further spec instructions. Indicate points of measure on spec sheet.]

131. *Belt Loop Width*—Measure belt loop from edge of belt loop straight across/horizontally to edge of belt loop. [Note: Fashion-forward or irregularly shaped belt loops may require further spec instructions. Indicate points of measure on spec sheet.]

132. *Tie Length*—Measure from end of tie/joining seam straight down to tie end along center of tie.

133. *Tie Width*

A. *Straight*—Measure from edge of tie straight across to edge of tie.
B. *Contoured*—Measure from edge of tie straight across to edge of tie at widest point of tie.

134. *Flounce/Ruffle Width*—Measure from flounce/ruffle joining seam straight across to outer edge of flounce/ruffle. [Note: If flounce/ruffle is contoured, measure along narrowest and widest points if possible and indicate changes on spec sheet.]

135. *Strap Length*—Measure from strap joining seam along center of strap to end of strap. [Note: If strap is contoured or has a contoured edge, measure along center, approximating center end point, or indicate instructions as needed on spec sheet.]

136. *Strap Width*—Measure from edge of strap straight across to edge of strap. [Note: If strap is contoured, measure along narrowest and widest points if possible and indicate changes on spec sheet.]

137. *Front Hood Length*—Measure from top of hood to bottom of hood at center front joining seam along opening edge of hood.

138. *Back Hood Length*—Measure from top of hood at center front to bottom of hood at center back joining seam along outside curve of hood fold/seam.

139. *Hood Width*—Measure from front opening edge of hood straight across to back of hood at fold along widest point of hood.

140. *Flange Depth*—Measure from center back neck joining seam straight down to bottom of flange at center back. [Note: If flange is contoured or asymmetrical, indicate point of measure on spec sheet.]

141. *Shoulder Pad Length*—Measure from edge of pad straight across to edge of pad along center of pad or natural shoulder line of pad.

142. *Shoulder Pad Width*—Measure from side of pad straight across to side of pad along edge of pad if straight or at widest point of pad if curved.

143. *Straight Edge Shoulder Pad Height*—Measure from top of pad straight down to bottom of pad along center of pad.

144. *Curved Edge Shoulder Pad Height*—Stick a 1" straight pin into thickest part of shoulder pad. Push pin all way through pad until head of pin rests on top of pad. Be sure not to crush pad. Measure portion of pin sticking out of pad. Subtract this figure from 1" (length of pin) to get shoulder pad height.

145. *Shoulder Pad Placement*—Measure from neck edge or joining seam straight across shoulder seam or natural shoulder line to start of shoulder pad.

147. *Button Placement*—Refer to point of measure 59, Neck Depth Center Front, for placement of first button. Then measure distance of first button to second button. Be sure when measuring that button at bust point is lined up to apex of bust. Adjust all buttons accordingly and respace as needed.

148. *Pocket Placement*

A. *Top Pocket Vertical*—Measure from shoulder-neck joining seam straight down to top edge of pocket.
B. *Top Pocket Horizontal*—Measure from center front straight across to side of pocket at top edge.
C. *Front Bottom Pocket Vertical*—Measure from waistband/joining seam/edge straight down to top edge of pocket.
D. *Front Bottom Pocket Horizontal*—Measure from center front straight across to side of pocket at top edge.
E. *Back Bottom Pocket Vertical*—Measure from waistband/joining seam/edge straight down to top edge of pocket.
F. *Back Bottom Pocket Horizontal*—Measure from center back straight across to side of pocket at top edge.
G. *Pocket from Side Seam*—Measure from side seam straight across to top of pocket. [Note: If pocket is contoured at sides, a top and bottom pocket size and placement must be measured and added to spec sheet.]

149. *Belt Loop Placement*

A. *Front*—Measure from center front of garment horizontally across to center of first front belt loop.
B. *Back*—Measure from center back of garment horizontally across to center of first back belt loop.
C. *Side Seam to Front*—Measure from center of side seam belt loop to center of front belt loop.
D. *Side Seam to Back*—Measure from center of side seam belt loop to center of back belt loop.

150. *Dart Placement*

A. *High Point Shoulder Bust Dart*—Measure from shoulder-neck joining seam or at a point _____" from shoulder-neck seam straight down, parallel to center front, to top of dart. [Note: The _____" from shoulder seam measurement is to be used for darts that are too short to be measured from high point shoulder. Be sure to indicate _____" measurement on spec sheet.]
B. *Center Front Bust Dart*—Measure from center front of garment straight across to top of dart.
C. *Side Seam Bust Dart*—Measure from underarm/side seam joining seam down along contour of side seam to bottom of dart.
D. *High Point Shoulder Princess Dart*—Measure from shoulder-neck joining seam straight down to top of dart.

E. *Center Front Princess Dart*—Measure from center front of garment straight across to top of dart.

CHAPTER 4 TERMS

When working with knit tops, you may come across the garment terms listed here. If you are unfamiliar with any of them, please look up the definitions in the glossary at the end of this text.

Belted cardigan
Boat neck (bateau)
Classic cardigan
Cowl neck
Crew neck
Cropped top
Dolman sleeve
Flashdance
Mock turtleneck
Shrink
T-shirt (tee)
Tube top
V neck
V-neck cardigan
Vest

SPEC SHEET: Knit top | **STYLE**

SEASON:	DESCRIPTION:
LABEL: (SIZE CATEGORY)	
DATE:	
TECHNICAL SKETCH Turtleneck	SKETCH/PHOTO

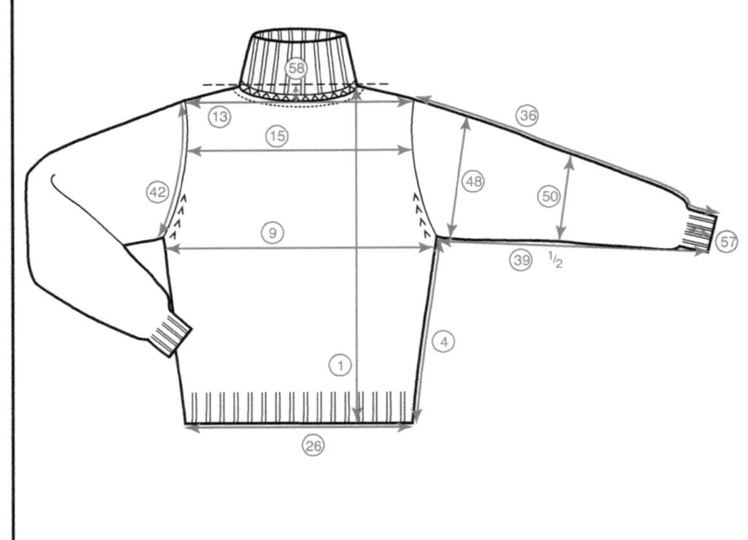

CODE	POINT OF MEASURE	TOL. +/–	4	S/6	8	M/10	12	L/14	16	XL/18
1.	Front length	1/2								
3.	Center back length	1/2								
4.	Side length	1/4								
9.	Chest width	1/4-3/8								
13.	Across shoulder	1/4								
15.	Across chest	1/4								
16.	Across back	1/4								
25.	Bottom band/ribbing height	1/8								
26.	Bottom opening/sweep	1/4-3/8								
36.	Sleeve length top armhole	3/8								
39.	Sleeve length underarm	3/8								
42.	Curved armhole width **(opening)**	1/4								
48.	Muscle width	1/8								
50.	Elbow width	1/8								
52.	Sleeve opening width	1/8								
54.	Sleeve opening width stretched	1/8								
57.	Cuff/ribbing height sleeve **(armhole)**	1/8								
58.	Neck depth front	1/8								

(Tolerance 1/4-3/8 S, M, L, XL = 3/8" 4-18 = 1/4")

The measured garment spec sheets are for ***illustrative purposes only*** and should not be used as industry standards

CODE	POINT OF MEASURE	TOL. +/–	4	S/6	8	M/10	12	L/14	16	XL/18
63.	Neck width collar	1/4								
64.	Neck edge width	1/4								
66.	Neck edge width stretched	1/4								
68.	Neck base	1/4								
72.	Collar height	1/8								
73.	Collar band height	1/8								

COMMENTS:

(Tolerance 1/4-3/8 S, M, L, XL = 3/8" 4-18 = 1/4")

The measured garment spec sheets are for ***illustrative purposes only*** and should not be used as industry standards

SPEC SHEET: Knit top

STYLE

SEASON: Early fall	DESCRIPTION: Sleeveless turtleneck
LABEL: (SIZE CATEGORY) Missy	
DATE:	
TECHNICAL SKETCH Turtleneck	SKETCH/PHOTO

CODE	POINT OF MEASURE	TOL. +/–	4	S/6	8	M/10	12	L/14	16	XL/18
1.	Front length	1/2				23				
3.	Center back length	1/2				21 1/2				
4.	Side length	1/4				14				
9.	Chest width	1/4-3/8				18 1/2				
13.	Across shoulder	1/4				14 3/4				
15.	Across chest	1/4				13 3/4				
16.	Across back	1/4				13 3/4				
25.	Bottom band/ribbing height	1/8				3/8				
26.	Bottom opening/sweep	1/4-3/8				18 1/2				
36.	Sleeve length top armhole	3/8								
39.	Sleeve length underarm	3/8								
42.	Curved armhole width **(opening)**	1/4				9				
48.	Muscle width	1/8								
50.	Elbow width	1/8								
52.	Sleeve opening width	1/8								
54.	Sleeve opening width stretched	1/8								
57.	Cuff/ribbing height sleeve **(armhole)**	1/8				3/8				
58.	Neck depth front	1/8				1				

(Tolerance 1/4-3/8 S, M, L, XL = 3/8" 4-18 = 1/4")

The measured garment spec sheets are for ***illustrative purposes only*** and should not be used as industry standards

CODE	POINT OF MEASURE	TOL. +/–	4	S/6	8	M/10	12	L/14	16	XL/18
63.	Neck width collar	1/4				6 1/2				
64.	Neck edge width	1/4				6 1/2				
66.	Neck edge width stretched	1/4				13				
68.	Neck base	1/4				7 1/2				
72.	Collar height	1/8				6				
73.	Collar band height	1/8				3/8				
122.	Side vent A. Height	1/4				2 1/2				
	B. Width rib	1/8				3/8				

COMMENTS:

The measured garment spec sheets are for ***illustrative purposes only*** and should not be used as industry standards

CHAPTER 5

Knit Skirts

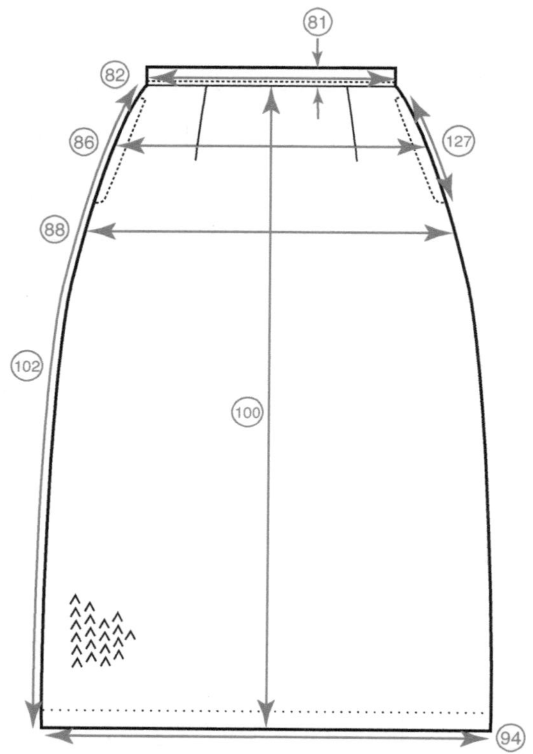

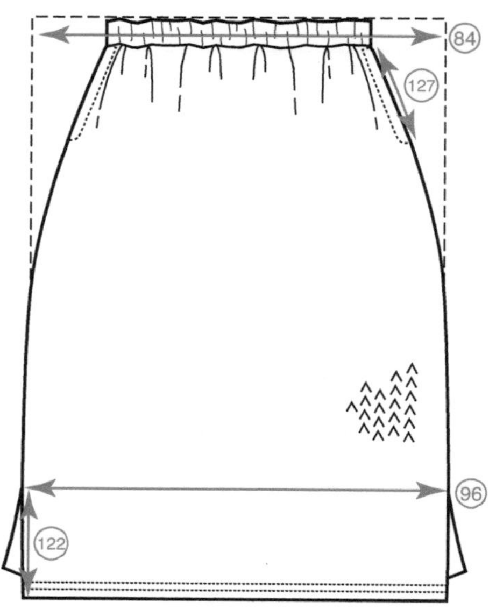

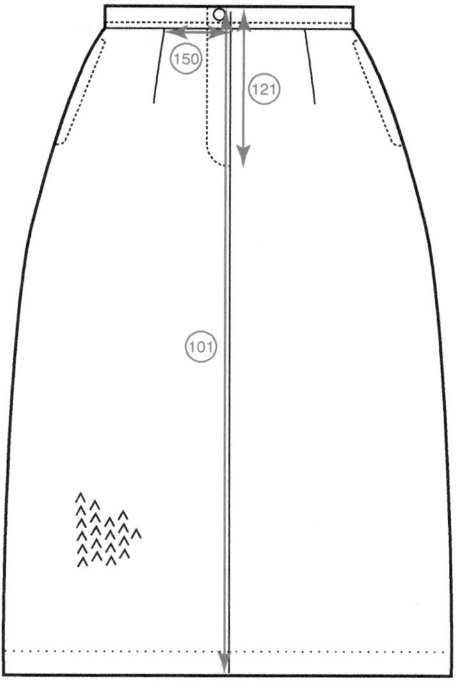

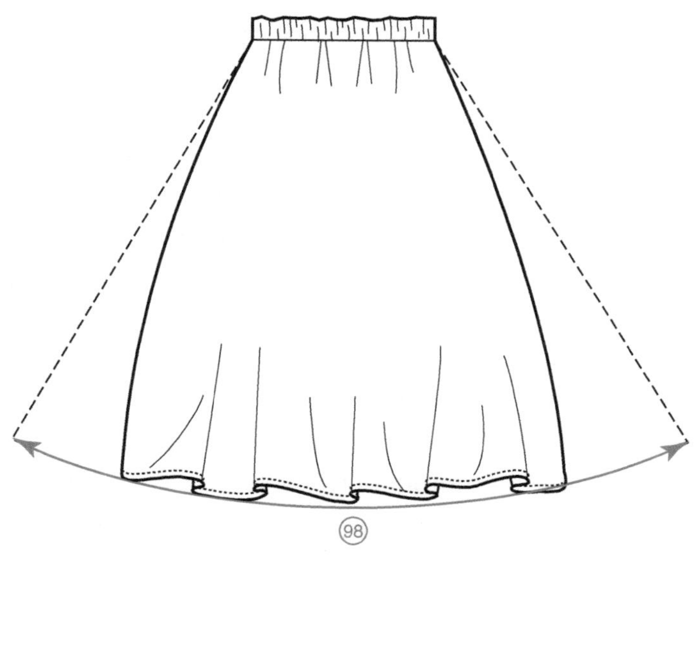

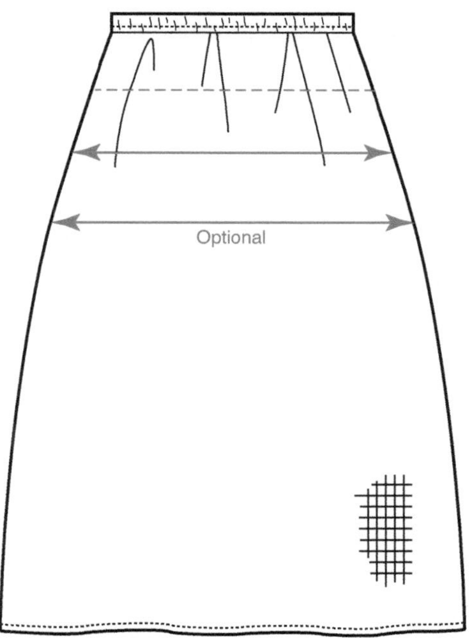

Figure 5.1 Choosing the best hip measurement point.

Measuring Knit Skirts

Knit skirts have become very popular over the last several years, in part due to increasing production costs and customer acceptance of elastic waistbands. Because styling is usually basic, knit skirts are one of the easiest garments to spec. However, there may be times when more than one method of measurement can be used for a measurement point (see Figure 5.1). As the technician, it is up to you to decide which measurement points are best suited to your garment style.

81. *Waistband Depth*—Measure from top of waistband edge straight down to bottom of waistband at waistband joining seam. [Note: If waistband is contoured, indicate measurement change on spec sheet.]

82. *Waistband Width (knit)*—Measure from side of bottom band to side of bottom band along center of band, following natural contour of waistband.

84. *Waistband Width, Stretched (knit)*—Measure from side of bottom band to side of bottom band straight across center of band in a fully extended position.

86. *High Hip Width (knit)*—Measure from edge of garment/side seam to edge of garment/side seam at a point 4" below bottom edge of waistband/seam, following contour of waist. [Note: The 4" point is for misses/women's wear only; adjust as needed ½" to 1" up or down for children's, petite's, junior's, or large/plus sizes. Indicate change on spec sheet.]

88. *Low Hip Width from Waist (knit)*—Measure from edge of garment/side seam to edge of garment/side seam at a point 7" below bottom edge of waistband/seam, following contour of waist. [Note: The 7" point is for misses/women's wear only; adjust as needed ½" to 1" up or down for children's, petite's, junior's, or large/plus sizes. Indicate change on spec sheet.]

94. *Bottom Opening/Sweep Width (knit skirt)*—Measure from edge of garment/side seam to edge of garment/side seam straight across garment at bottom opening. [Note: If sweep has pleats, measure with pleats closed or relaxed.]

96. *Vented Bottom Opening/Sweep Width (knit skirt)*—Measure from edge of garment/side seam to edge of garment/side seam straight across garment at top of side vents. [Note: Indicate on spec sheet if there is only one vent or if vent hits at a point other than sweep, e.g., thigh opening.]

98. *Circular Bottom Opening/Sweep Width (knit skirt)*—Measure from edge of garment/side seam to edge of garment/side seam, following natural contour of garment at bottom opening.

100. *Center Front Skirt Length*—Measure from bottom of waistband/seam (top edge if not banded, or stitching if self-elastic/drawstring casing) straight down to bottom of garment at center front. [Note: A fashion-forward skirt may have an asymmetrical waist. Indicate top point of measure on spec sheet.]

101. *Center Back Skirt Length*—Measure from bottom of waistband/seam (top edge if not banded, or stitching if self-elastic/drawstring casing) straight down to bottom of garment at center front. [Note: A fashion-forward skirt may have an asymmetrical waist. Indicate top point of measure on spec sheet.]

102. *Side Skirt Length*—Measure from bottom edge of waistband/seam (top edge if not banded, or stitching if self-elastic/drawstring casing) to bottom of garment along side seam/fold of garment, following any contour.

103. *Skirt/Pant Yoke Depth Front*—Measure from bottom of waistband/seam (top edge if not banded, or stitching if self-elastic/drawstring casing) straight down to bottom of yoke joining seam at center front. [Note: If yoke is contoured, indicate point of measure on spec sheet.]

104. *Skirt/Pant Yoke Depth Back*—Measure from bottom of waistband/seam (top edge if not banded, or stitching if self-elastic/drawstring casing) straight down to bottom of yoke joining seam at center back. [Note: If yoke is contoured, indicate point of measure on spec sheet.]

121. *Fly/Zipper*

A. *Length*—Measure from top of fly/zipper opening straight down to bottom of fly/zipper opening at zipper stop or bar tack.
B. *Fly/Zipper Width*—Measure top of fly/zipper at joining seam from edge/fold straight across to fly/zipper placket stitching.

122. *Vent/Slit*

A. *Height*—Measure from top of vent/slit straight down to bottom of vent/slit along edge of vent/slit.
B. *Width*—Measure top of vent/slit from edge/fold straight across to vent/slit placket stitching at a point parallel to garment hemline.

123. *Pleat Depth*—Measure from outer edge of pleat at fold/crease to inner fold of pleat. [Note 1: It is a good idea to indicate what type of pleat is being measured, e.g., box, inverted, knife, kick, kilt, or

envelope. Note 2: If pleats are not parallel or symmetrical, indicate any special instructions on spec sheet.]

124. *Distance Between Pleats*—Measure from start of pleat to start of pleat, excluding pleat depth at a point directly below pleat joining seam. [Note: If pleats are not parallel or symmetrical, indicate any special instructions on spec sheet.]

125. *Applied Pocket Height*—Measure from top edge of pocket to bottom edge of pocket along center of pocket. [Note: For contoured or irregularly shaped pockets, take a second measurement and indicate point of measure on spec sheet.]

126. *Applied Pocket Width*—Measure from side of pocket to side of pocket along top edge of pocket. [Note: For contoured or irregularly shaped pockets, take a second measurement and indicate point of measure on spec sheet.]

127. *Pocket Opening Within a Seam*—Measure from top of pocket to bottom of pocket along edge of pocket opening.

128. *Belt Length*

A. *Total*—Measure from end of belt at buckle along center of belt to opposite end of belt, following contour.
B. *Circumference*—Measure from end of belt at buckle along center of belt to middle hole at opposite end.

129. *Belt Width (or Height)*—Measure from edge of belt straight across to edge of belt. [Note: If belt is contoured, indicate points of measure on spec sheet.]

130. *Belt Loop Length*—Measure from top of belt loop straight down/vertically to bottom of belt loop along center of belt loop. [Note: Fashion-forward or irregularly shaped belt loops may require further spec instructions. Indicate points of measure on spec sheet.]

131. *Belt Loop Width*—Measure belt loop from edge of belt loop straight across/horizontally to edge of belt loop. [Note: Fashion-forward or irregularly shaped belt loops may require further spec instructions. Indicate points of measure on spec sheet.]

132. *Tie Length*—Measure from end of tie/joining seam straight down to tie end along center of tie.

133. *Tie Width*

A. *Straight*—Measure from edge of tie straight across to edge of tie.
B. *Contoured*—Measure from edge of tie straight across to edge of tie at widest point of tie.

134. *Flounce/Ruffle Width*—Measure from flounce/ruffle joining seam straight across to outer edge of flounce/ruffle. [Note: If flounce/ruffle is contoured, measure along narrowest and widest points if possible and indicate changes on spec sheet.]

146. *Pleats Placement*

C. *Front Pleat Skirt/Pant*—Measure the distance from center front of garment waistband joining seam/edge straight across to start of first pleat.

148. *Pocket Placement*

C. *Front Bottom Pocket Vertical*—Measure from waistband/joining seam/edge straight down to top edge of pocket.
D. *Front Bottom Pocket Horizontal*—Measure from center front straight across to side of pocket at top edge.
E. *Back Bottom Pocket Vertical*—Measure from waistband/joining seam/edge straight down to top edge of pocket.
F. *Back Bottom Pocket Horizontal*—Measure from center back straight across to side of pocket at top edge.
G. *Pocket from Side Seam*—Measure from side seam straight across to top of pocket. [Note: If pocket is contoured at sides, a top and bottom pocket size and placement must be measured and added to spec sheet.]

149. *Belt Loop Placement*

A. *Front*—Measure from center front of garment horizontally across to center of first front belt loop.
B. *Back*—Measure from center back of garment horizontally across to center of first back belt loop.
C. *Side Seam to Front*—Measure from center of side seam belt loop to center of front belt loop.
D. *Side Seam to Back*—Measure from center of side seam belt loop to center of back belt loop.

150. *Dart Placement*

F. *Center Front Skirt/Pant*—Measure from center front of garment at waistband joining seam/edge straight across to top of dart.
G. *Center Back Skirt/Pant*—Measure from center front of garment at waistband joining seam/edge straight across to top of dart.

CHAPTER 5 TERMS

When working with knit skirts, you may come across the following garment terms. If you are unfamiliar with any of them, please look up the definitions listed in the glossary at the end of this text.

Drawstring
Elastic waist

SPEC SHEET: Knit skirt

STYLE

SEASON:	DESCRIPTION:
LABEL: (SIZE CATEGORY)	
DATE:	
TECHNICAL SKETCH Pull on/elastic waist	SKETCH/PHOTO

81 84 84 127 88 102 100 94

CODE	POINT OF MEASURE	TOL. +/–	4	S/6	8	M/10	12	L/14	16	XL/18
81.	Waistband depth									
82.	Waistband width									
84.	Waistband width stretched									
88.	Low hip width									
94.	Bottom opening/sweep width									
96.	Vented bottom opening/sweep width									
98.	Circular bottom opening/sweep width									
100.	Center front skirt length									
101.	Center back skirt length									
102.	Side skirt length									
122.	Vent/slit A. Height									
	B. Width									
127.	Pocket opening									
COMMENTS:										

(Tolerance 1/2-3/4 S, M, L, XL = 3/8" 4-18 = 1/4")

The measured garment spec sheets are for ***illustrative purposes only*** and should not be used as industry standards

SPEC SHEET: Knit skirt

STYLE

SEASON: Summer

LABEL: (SIZE CATEGORY) Missy

DATE:

DESCRIPTION: Short elastic waist skirt with two front pockets and decorative trim stitch.

TECHNICAL SKETCH Pull on/elastic waist

SKETCH/PHOTO

CODE	POINT OF MEASURE	TOL. +/–	4	S/6	8	M/10	12	L/14	16	XL/18
81.	Waistband depth	1/8				1				
82.	Waistband width	1/4-3/8				14				
84.	Waistband width stretched	1/4-3/8				22				
88.	Low hip width	1/4-3/8				22				
94.	Bottom opening/sweep width	1/4-3/8				23				
96.	Vented bottom opening/sweep width	1/4-3/8								
98.	Circular bottom opening/sweep width	1/4-3/8								
100.	Center front skirt length	3/8				18				
101.	Center back skirt length	3/8				18				
102.	Side skirt length	3/8				19				
122.	Vent/slit A. Height	1/4								
	B. Width	1/8								
127.	Pocket opening	1/4				5				

COMMENTS:

(Tolerance 1/2-3/4 S, M, L, XL = 3/8" 4-18 = 1/4")

The measured garment spec sheets are for ***illustrative purposes only*** and should not be used as industry standards

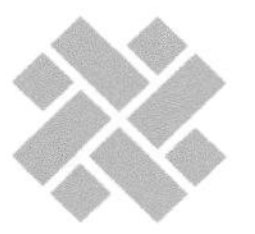

CHAPTER 6

Knit Pants

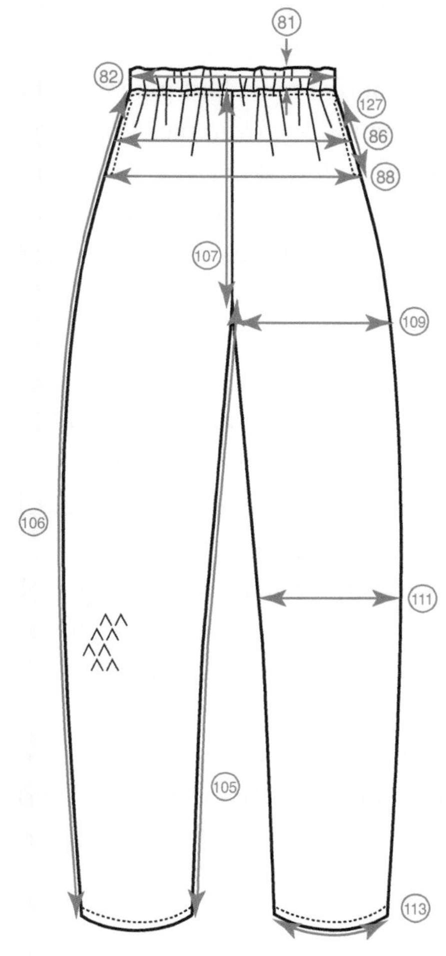

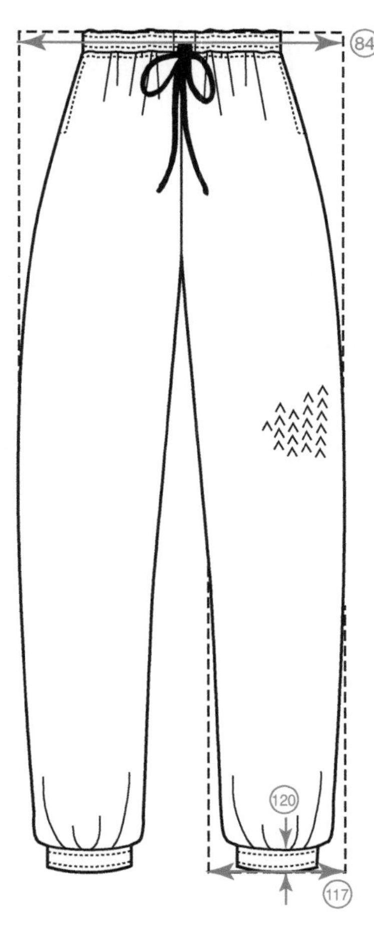

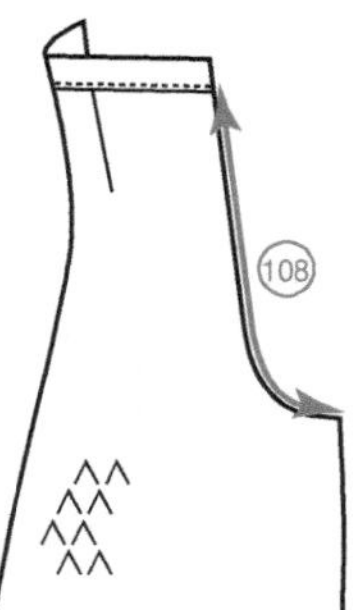

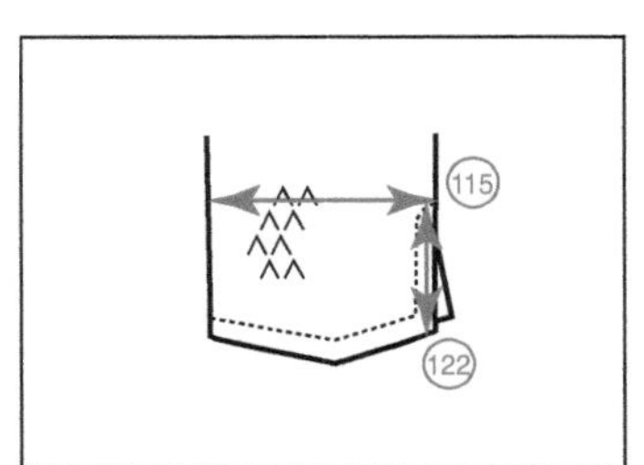

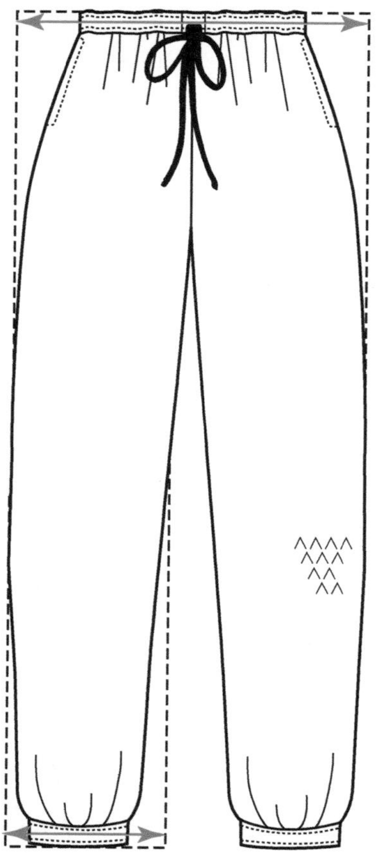

Figure 6.1 Waistband width, stretched, and leg opening width, stretched.

Measuring Knit Pants

Measuring knit pants is generally easier than measuring woven pants, in theory, because they often have fewer style features. However, knit pants can be difficult to measure because of bulk in the rise. When measuring the waist and hip areas, line up the waistband at the center front and center back top edges, unless otherwise designed. The crotch/rise curve will not lie flat; simply let it lie in a natural position. When measuring the pant leg, lay one leg flat on the table, gently pushing the other aside. It is not necessary to measure both legs, but an occasional spot-check will ensure continuity. The front and back rises are measured separately and will have to be manipulated slightly in order to measure in a flat relaxed position. Although most knit pants do not have the construction details of woven pants, all style instructions have been included for the rare constructed knit pant. Pull-on styling is common with knit pants, so stretch measurements must be added (see Figure 6.1).

81. *Waistband Depth*—Measure from top of waistband edge straight down to bottom of waistband at waistband joining seam. [Note: If waistband is contoured, indicate measurement change on spec sheet.]

82. *Waistband Width (knit)*—Measure from side of bottom band to side of bottom band along center of band, following natural contour of waistband.

84. *Waistband Width, Stretched (knit)*—Measure from side of bottom band to side of bottom band straight across center of band in a fully extended position.

86. *High Hip Width (knit)*—Measure from edge of garment/side seam to edge of garment/side seam at a point 4" below bottom edge of waistband/seam, following contour of waist. [Note: The 4" point is for misses/women's wear only; adjust as needed ½" to 1" up or down for children's, petite's, junior's, or large/plus sizes. Indicate change on spec sheet.]

88. *Low Hip Width from Waist (knit)*—Measure from edge of garment/side seam to edge of garment/side seam at a point 7" below bottom edge of waistband/seam, following contour of waist. [Note: The 7" point is for misses/women's wear only; adjust as needed ½" to 1" up or down for children's, petite's, junior's, or large/plus sizes. Indicate change on spec sheet.]

90. *Hip Width from High Point Shoulder (knit)*—Measure from edge of garment/side seam to edge of garment/side seam straight across at a point _____" below high point shoulder. [Note: You will have to estimate low hip point on garment if there is no waistband and fill in _____" from high point shoulder. This measurement will vary for children's, junior's, misses, and large/plus sizes.]

92. *Hip Seat Width (knit pant)*—Measure from edge of garment/side seam to edge of garment/side seam at a point _____" up from crotch seam, following contour of waist. [Note 1: This measurement is useful when waistband sits below natural waistline. Note 2: Adjust _____" up from crotch as needed for junior's and large/plus sizes. Note 3: A hip seat width of 2½" up for children's and 3" up for menswear can take place of low hip width.]

103. *Skirt/Pant Yoke Depth Front*—Measure from bottom of waistband/seam (top edge if not banded or stitching if self-elastic/drawstring casing) straight down to bottom of yoke joining seam at center front. [Note: If yoke is contoured, indicate point of measure on spec sheet.]

104. *Skirt/Pant Yoke Depth Back*—Measure from bottom of waistband/seam (top edge if not banded or stitching if self-elastic/drawstring casing) straight down to bottom of yoke joining seam at center back. [Note: If yoke is contoured, indicate point of measure on spec sheet.]

105. *Inseam*—Measure from crotch joining seam to bottom of leg opening, following inseam/inner fold.

106. *Outseam*—Measure from bottom edge of waistband/seam (top edge if not banded or stitching if self-elastic/drawstring casing) to bottom of garment along side seam/fold of garment.

107. *Front Rise*—Measure from bottom edge of waistband/seam (top edge if not banded or stitching if self-elastic/drawstring casing) to crotch joining seam, following curve of front rise seam. [Note: Measure over zipper if in front rise seam.]

108. *Back Rise*—Measure from bottom edge of waistband/seam (top edge if not banded or stitching if self-elastic/drawstring casing) to crotch joining seam, following curve of back rise seam. [Note: Measure over zipper if in front back seam.]

109. *Thigh Width (knit)*—Measure from pant leg edge/seam to pant leg edge/seam straight across pant leg at a point 1" below crotch and parallel to leg opening. [Note: If leg opening is asymmetrical, measure to a point that would be parallel to leg opening.]

111. *Knee Width (knit)*—Measure from pant leg edge/seam to pant leg edge/seam at a point one-half of inseam and parallel to leg opening. [Note 1: If leg opening is asymmetrical, measure to a point that would be parallel to leg opening. Note 2: If pant leg is three-quarter length, indicate point of measure on spec sheet. Note 3: A general knee measurement from crotch seam of misses 14", junior's 13", or large/plus women's size 15" can be used. Indicate change on spec sheet. For children's wear measure at one-half the inseam minus 1½", and for men's minus 2".]

113. *Leg Opening Width (knit)*—Measure from pant leg edge/seam to pant leg edge/seam straight across bottom edge of leg opening. [Note: If leg opening is contoured, follow contour and indicate measurement change on spec sheet.]

115. *Vented Leg Opening Width (knit)*—Measure from pant leg edge/seam to pant leg edge/seam straight across pant leg at top of side vents.

117. *Leg Opening Width, Stretched (knit)*—Measure from pant leg edge/seam to pant leg edge/seam straight across bottom edge of leg opening in a fully extended position.

119. *Cuff Height Pants*—Measure from top of cuff edge straight down to bottom of cuff fold and leg opening.

120. *Bottom Band/Ribbing Height Pants*—Measure from cuff joining seam or top of ribbing straight down to bottom edge of cuff or rib opening. [Note: For fashion-forward pants, you may want to include a cuff length. See point of measure 56, Cuff Length Sleeve, for measuring instructions and, if needed, indicate cuff length of pant on spec sheet.]

121. *Fly/Zipper*

A. *Length*—Measure from top of fly/zipper opening straight down to bottom of fly/zipper opening at zipper stop or bar tack.
B. *Fly/Zipper Width*—Measure top of fly/zipper at joining seam from edge/fold straight across to fly/zipper placket stitching.

122. *Vent/Slit*

A. *Height*—Measure from top of vent/slit straight down to bottom of vent/slit along edge of vent/slit.
B. *Width*—Measure top of vent/slit from edge/fold straight across to vent/slit placket stitching at a point parallel to garment hemline.

123. *Pleat Depth*—Measure from outer edge of pleat at fold/crease to inner fold of pleat. [Note 1: It is a good idea to indicate what type of pleat is being measured, e.g., box, inverted, knife, kick, kilt, or envelope. Note 2: If pleats are not parallel or symmetrical, indicate any special instructions on spec sheet.]

124. *Distance Between Pleats*—Measure from start of pleat to start of pleat, excluding pleat depth at a point directly below pleat joining seam. [Note: If pleats are not parallel or symmetrical, indicate any special instructions on spec sheet.]

125. *Applied Pocket Height*—Measure from top edge of pocket to bottom edge of pocket along center of pocket. [Note: For contoured or irregularly shaped pockets, take a second measurement and indicate point of measure on spec sheet.]

126. *Applied Pocket Width*—Measure from side of pocket to side of pocket along top edge of pocket. [Note: For contoured or irregularly shaped pockets, take a second measurement and indicate point of measure on spec sheet.]

127. *Pocket Opening Within a Seam*—Measure from top of pocket to bottom of pocket along edge of pocket opening.

128. *Belt Length*

A. *Total*—Measure from end of belt at buckle along center of belt to opposite end of belt, following contour.
B. *Circumference*—Measure from end of belt at buckle along center of belt to middle hole at opposite end.

129. *Belt Width (or Height)*—Measure from edge of belt straight across to edge of belt. [Note: If belt is contoured, indicate points of measure on spec sheet.]

130. *Belt Loop Length*—Measure from top of belt loop straight down/vertically to bottom of belt loop along center of belt loop. [Note: Fashion-forward or irregularly shaped belt loops may require further spec instructions. Indicate points of measure on spec sheet.]

131. *Belt Loop Width*—Measure belt loop from edge of belt loop straight across/horizontally to edge of belt loop. [Note: Fashion-forward or irregularly shaped belt loops may require further spec instructions. Indicate points of measure on spec sheet.]

132. *Tie Length*—Measure from end of tie/joining seam straight down to tie end along center of tie.

133. *Tie Width*

A. *Straight*—Measure from edge of tie straight across to edge of tie.

B. *Contoured*—Measure from edge of tie straight across to edge of tie at widest point of tie.

134. *Flounce/Ruffle Width*—Measure from flounce/ruffle joining seam straight across to outer edge of flounce/ruffle. [Note: If flounce/ruffle is contoured, measure along narrowest and widest points if possible and indicate changes on spec sheet.]

146. *Pleats Placement*

C. *Front Pleat Skirt/Pant*—Measure distance from center front of garment waistband joining seam/edge straight across to start of first pleat.

148. *Pocket Placement*

C. *Front Bottom Pocket Vertical*—Measure from waistband/joining seam/edge straight down to top edge of pocket.

D. *Front Bottom Pocket Horizontal*—Measure from center front straight across to side of pocket at top edge.

E. *Back Bottom Pocket Vertical*—Measure from waistband/joining seam/edge straight down to top edge of pocket.

F. *Back Bottom Pocket Horizontal*—Measure from center back straight across to side of pocket at top edge.

G. *Pocket from Side Seam*—Measure from side seam straight across to top of pocket. [Note: If pocket is contoured at sides, a top and bottom pocket size and placement must be measured and added to spec sheet.]

149. *Belt Loop Placement*

A. *Front*—Measure from center front of garment horizontally across to center of first front belt loop.

B. *Back*—Measure from center back of garment horizontally across to center of first back belt loop.

C. *Side Seam to Front*—Measure from center of side seam belt loop to center of front belt loop.

D. *Side Seam to Back*—Measure from center of side seam belt loop to center of back belt loop.

150. *Dart Placement*

F. *Center Front Skirt/Pant*—Measure from center front of garment at waistband joining seam/edge straight across to top of dart.

G. *Center Back Skirt/Pant*—Measure from center back of garment at waistband joining seam/edge straight across to top of dart.

CHAPTER 6 TERMS

When working with knit pants, you may come across the following garment terms. If you are unfamiliar with any of them, please look up the definition in the glossary at the end of this text.

Pull-on pant
Warm-up pant

SPEC SHEET Knit pant

STYLE

SEASON:	DESCRIPTION:
LABEL: (SIZE CATEGORY)	
DATE:	
TECHNICAL SKETCH Pull on pant	SKETCH/PHOTO

CODE	POINT OF MEASURE	TOL. +/–	4	S/6	8	M/10	12	L/14	16	XL/18
81.	Waistband depth	1/8								
82.	Waistband width	1/4-3/8								
84.	Waistband width stretched	1/4-3/8								
86.	High hip width	1/4-3/8								
88.	Low hip width	1/4-3/8								
105.	Inseam	3/8								
106.	Outseam	3/8								
107.	Front rise	3/8								
108.	Back rise	3/8								
109.	Thigh width	1/4								
111.	Knee width	1/4								
113.	Leg opening width	1/8								

(Tolerance 1/4-3/8 S, M, L, XL = 3/8" 4-18 = 1/4")

The measured garment spec sheets are for ***illustrative purposes only*** and should not be used as industry standards

CODE	POINT OF MEASURE	TOL. +/–	4	S/6	8	M/10	12	L/14	16	XL/18
120.	Bottom band/ribbing height	1/8								
127.	Pocket opening	1/4								

COMMENTS:

The measured garment spec sheets are for ***illustrative purposes only*** and should not be used as industry standards

SPEC SHEET Knit pant | **STYLE**

SEASON: Fall/winter	DESCRIPTION: Pull on wool pant with rib covered
LABEL: (SIZE CATEGORY) Missy	elastic waistband
DATE:	
TECHNICAL SKETCH Pull on pant	SKETCH/PHOTO

81 82 127 86 88 107 109 106 111 105 113

CODE	POINT OF MEASURE	TOL. +/–	4	S/6	8	M/10	12	L/14	16	XL/18
81.	Waistband depth	1/8				1				
82.	Waistband width	1/4-3/8				14				
84.	Waistband width stretched	1/4-3/8				19 1/2				
86.	High hip width	1/4-3/8				18 1/2				
88.	Low hip width	1/4-3/8				20 1/2				
105.	Inseam	3/8				28				
106.	Outseam	3/8				38 1/2				
107.	Front rise	3/8				11 1/2				
108.	Back rise	3/8				13 1/2				
109.	Thigh width	1/4				24				
111.	Knee width	1/4				10 1/4				
113.	Leg opening width	1/8				8				

(Tolerance 1/4-3/8 S, M, L, XL = 3/8" 4-18 = 1/4")

The measured garment spec sheets are for ***illustrative purposes only*** and should not be used as industry standards

CODE	POINT OF MEASURE	TOL. +/–	4	S/6	8	M/10	12	L/14	16	XL/18
120.	Bottom band/ribbing height	1/8				1/8				
127.	Pocket opening	1/4				-				

COMMENTS:

The measured garment spec sheets are for ***illustrative purposes only*** and should not be used as industry standards

CHAPTER 7

Knit Dresses

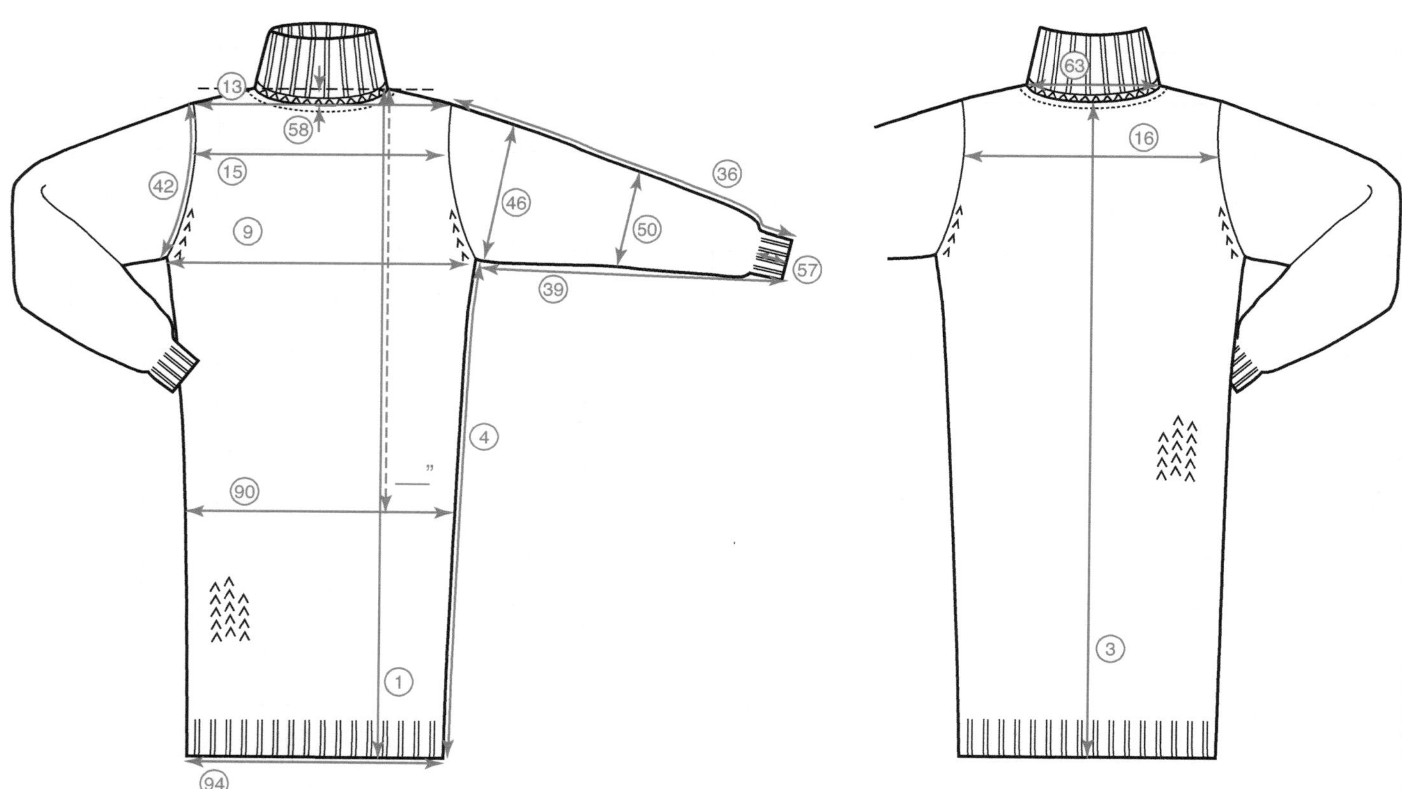

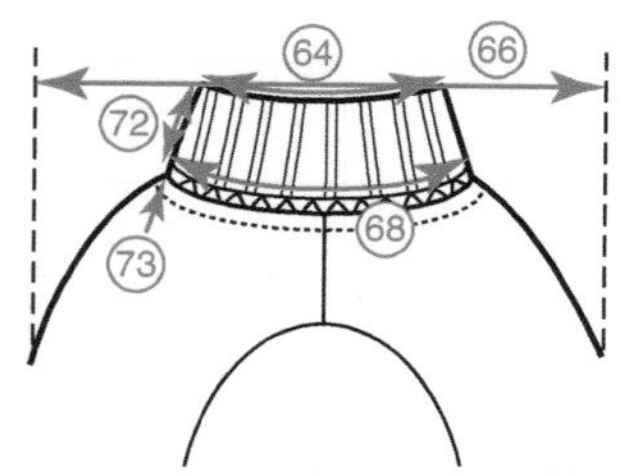

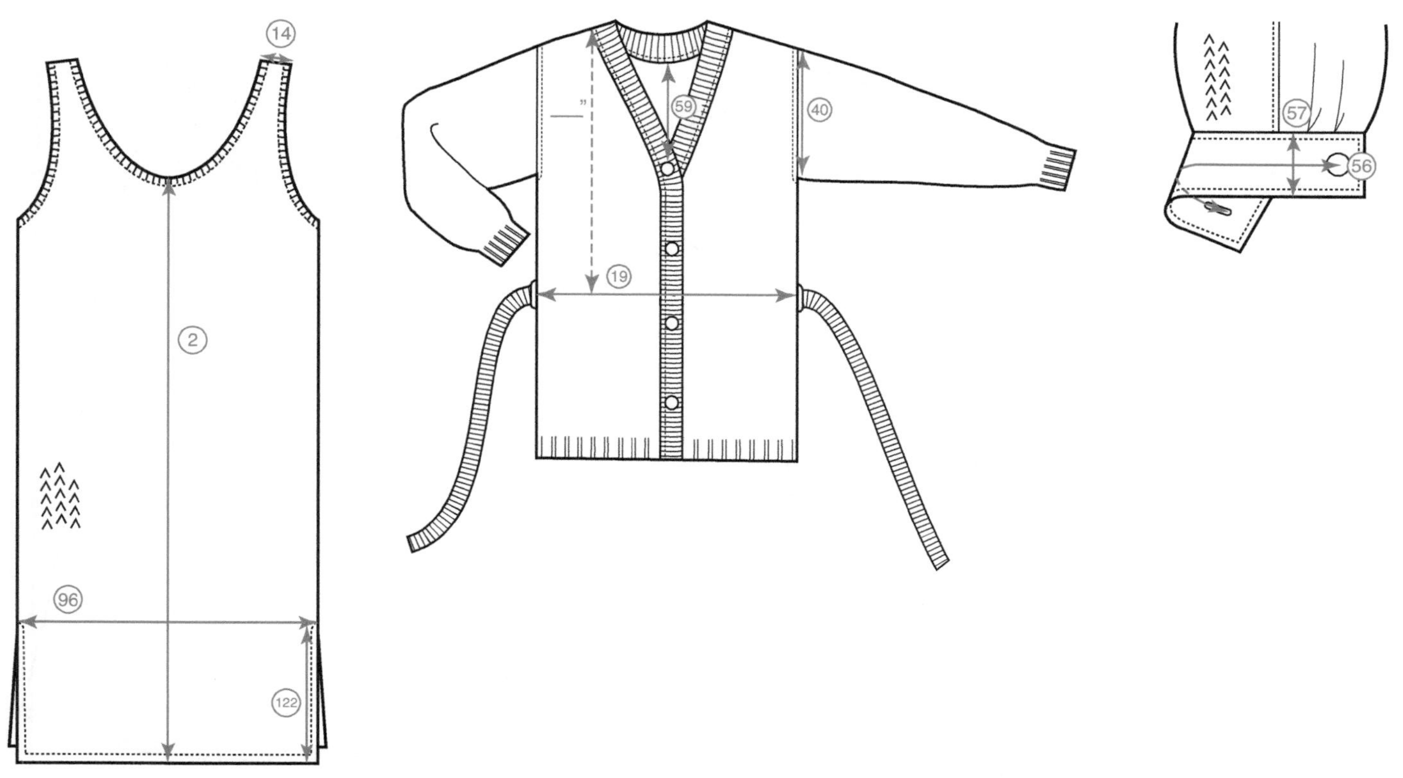
14
40
59
2
19
57
56
96
122

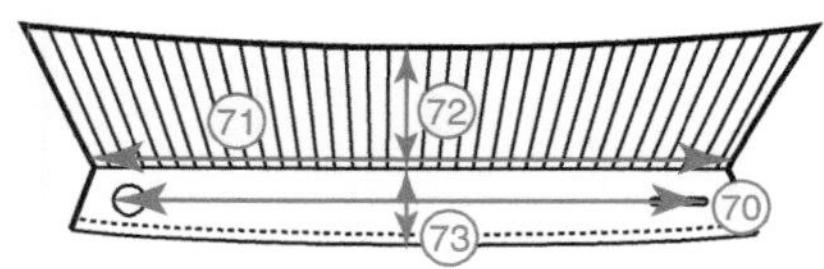
71
72
73
70

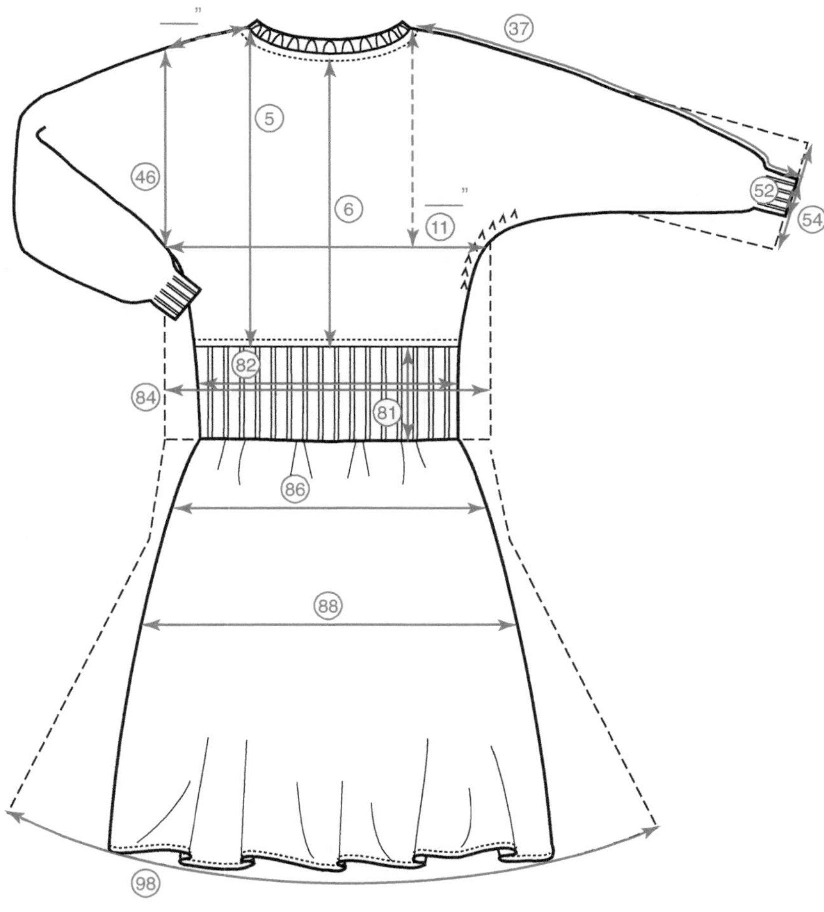
37
5
46
6
11
52
54
82
84
81
86
88
98

38
7
101
62
61
60
58
34
79
32
78
35
33
17
44

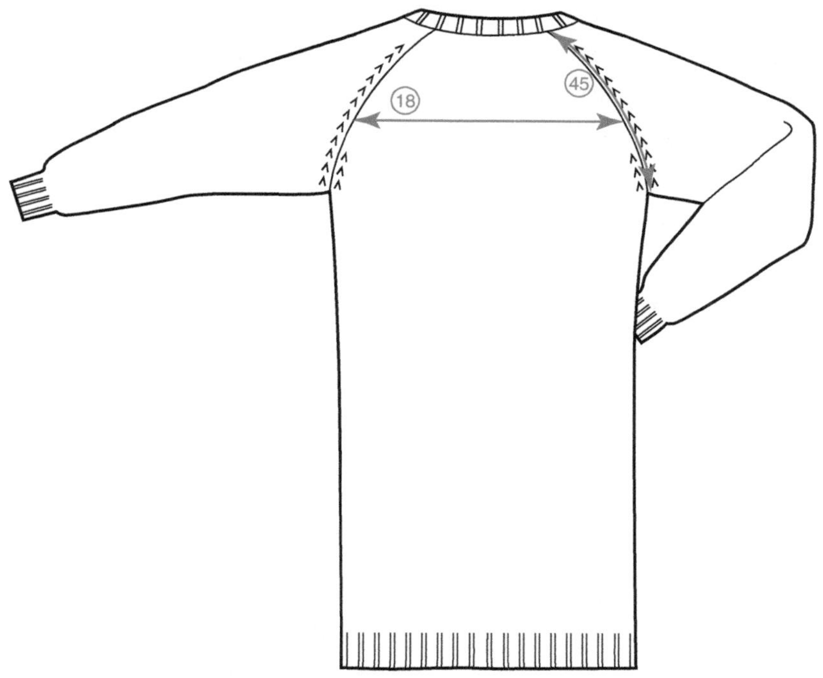

Measuring Knit Dresses

Many knit dresses are simply designed as long versions of T-shirts or sweaters, combining the measurements of a knit top and a knit skirt. For example the tank top dress, which is better measured from the center front rather than the high point shoulder (see Figure 7.1). Remember, the rules you learned for the knit top and knit skirt will be used here as well. If needed, look back over chapters 4 and 5.

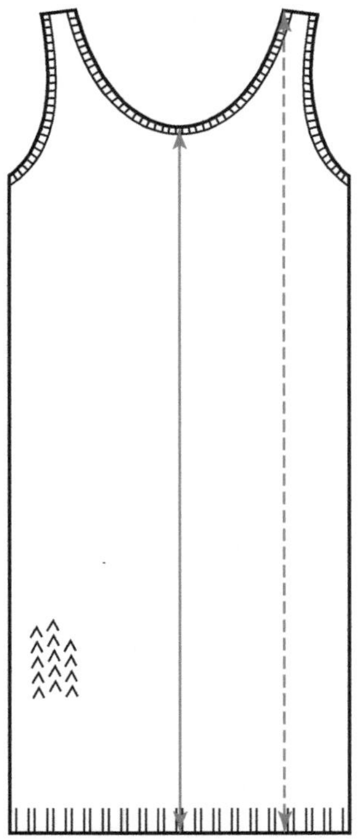

Figure 7.1 Choosing the best front length measurement point.

1. *Front Length (garments with a front opening)*—Measure from high point shoulder at neck straight down, parallel to center front, to bottom of garment at front. If garment has a collar, gently lift it away from shoulder-neck measuring point.

2. *Center Front Length (garments with a plain front; no front opening)*—Measure from center front neck joining seams straight down to bottom of garment at center front. [Note: A garment with a front opening may still require point of measure 1, Front Length, if neckline is unusual or is difficult to measure.]

3. *Center Back Length*—Measure from center back neck joining seams straight down to bottom of garment at center back. If needed, gently lift collar away from back neck to expose joining seam.

4. *Side Length*—Measure from bottom of armhole/side seam straight down to bottom of garment along side of garment. Do not follow natural curve of garment's side seam, unless otherwise indicated. If needed, gently lift sleeve away from armhole/side seam joining seam.

5. *Front Bodice Length (garments with a front opening)*—Measure from high point shoulder at neck straight down, parallel to center front, to top edge of waistband, joining seam, or rib. If garment has a collar, gently lift it away from shoulder-neck measuring point.

6. *Center Front Bodice Length (garments with a plain front; no front opening)*—Measure from center front neck joining seam straight down to top edge of waistband, joining seam, or rib. [Note: A garment with a center opening may still require point of measure 5, Front Bodice Length, if neckline is unusual or HPS is difficult to measure.]

7. *Center Back Bodice Length*—Measure from center back neck joining seams straight down to top edge of waistband, joining seam, or rib. If needed, gently lift collar away from back neck to expose joining seam.

8. *Side Seam Bodice Length*—Measure from bottom of armhole/side seam straight down to top edge of waistband, joining seam, or rib, along side of garment, following natural curve of garment's side seam, unless otherwise indicated. If needed, gently lift sleeve away from armhole/side seam joining seam. [Note: You can take side seam bodice measurement straight rather than contoured if joining seam/rib can be extended, but indicate change on spec sheet.]

9. *Chest Width (knit)*—Measure from edge of garment/side seam to edge of garment/side seam straight across garment at a point 1" below armhole.

11. *Chest Width/Raglan Sleeve (knit)*—Measure from edge of garment/side seam to edge of garment/side seam straight across garment at a point _____" below high point shoulder. [Note: You will have to determine number of inches down from high point shoulder for each raglan sleeve style based on depth of sleeve. Then indicate this number on spec sheet.]

13. *Across Shoulder*—Measure straight across front from armhole seam/edge to armhole seam/edge at shoulder seam or across natural shoulder fold line created if there is no seam.

14. *Shoulder Width*—Measure from neckband/collar/ribbing joining seam or neckline edge to top of armhole seam at shoulder, taken along shoulder seam or across natural shoulder fold line created if there is no seam.

15. *Across Chest*—Measure 2½" down from collar/rib joining seam at center front straight across front of garment from armhole seam/edge to armhole seam/edge. [Note: The 2½" measurement point is for misses/women's wear only and may need to be adjusted up or down ¼" to ½" accordingly for men's, children's, junior's, and large/plus sizes. Indicate any changes on spec sheet.]

16. *Across Back*—Measure 4" down from collar/rib joining seam at center back straight across back of garment from armhole seam/edge to armhole seam/edge. [Note: The 4" measurement point is for misses/women's wear only and may need to be adjusted up or down ¼" to ½" accordingly for men's, children's, junior's, and large/plus sizes. Indicate any changes on spec sheet.]

17. *Across Chest/Center Armhole*—Measure at one-half depth of armhole straight across front of garment from armhole seam/edge to armhole seam/edge.

18. *Across Back/Center Armhole*—Measure at one-half depth of armhole straight across back of garment from armhole seam/edge to armhole seam/edge.

19. *Waist Width (knit)*—Measure from edge of garment/side seam to edge of garment/side seam straight across garment on seam or at narrowest point of waist taper at a point _____" below high point shoulder. [Note: You will have to determine number of inches down from high point shoulder for each raglan sleeve style based on depth of sleeve. Then indicate this number on spec sheet.]

32. *Yoke Width Front*—Measure from armhole seam/edge to armhole seam/edge straight across front of garment, ignoring contours or points, at yoke-body joining seams. [Note: If yoke is asymmetrical, indicate changes in measuring as needed on spec sheet.]

33. *Yoke Width Back*—Measure from armhole seam/edge to armhole seam/edge straight across back of garment, ignoring contours or points, at yoke-body joining seams. [Note: If yoke is asymmetrical, indicate changes in measuring as needed on spec sheet.]

34. *Yoke Depth Front*—Measure from high point shoulder at neck straight down to bottom of front yoke-body joining seam. Be sure to gently lift collar away from shoulder-neck joining seam if needed.

35. *Yoke Back Depth*—Measure from center back neck joining seam straight down to bottom of back yoke-body joining seam. Gently lift collar away from back neck joining seam if needed.

36. *Sleeve Length Top Armhole*—Measure along top of sleeve/fold following contour of sleeve from armhole seam at shoulder to bottom of sleeve opening, including cuff.

37. *Sleeve Length Top Neck*—Measure along top of sleeve/fold following contour of sleeve from sleeve-neck joining seam/edge to edge of sleeve opening, including cuff. Gently lift away collar at sleeve-neck joining seam if needed.

38. *Sleeve Length Center Back*—Measure from center back neck joining seam or from a point above neck at an imaginary line, that of a joining seam, along top of sleeve/fold, following contour of sleeve to edge of sleeve opening, including cuff.

39. *Sleeve Length Underarm*—Measure straight from bottom of armhole along sleeve seam to edge of sleeve opening, including cuff.

40. *Straight Armhole Width (knit)*—Measure from top of shoulder joining seam/edge straight down to bottom of armhole.

42. *Curved Armhole Width (knit)*—Measure from top of shoulder joining seam/edge to bottom of armhole, following contour of armhole.

44. *Armhole Front*—Measure on front of garment from top of shoulder at neckline joining seam/edge to bottom of armhole, following contour of armhole. Gently lift collar away from neckline joining seam if needed.

45. *Armhole Back*—Measure on back of garment from top of shoulder at neck joining seam/edge to bottom of armhole, following contour of armhole. Gently lift collar away from neck joining seam if needed.

46. *Armhole Width Straight (knit)*—Measure from top of shoulder seam at a point _____" below neckline joining seam/edge straight down to bottom of armhole. [Note: Gently move collar from neck joining seam if needed when measuring down _____" to armhole start point. Indicate number of inches measured down on spec sheet.]

48. *Muscle Width (knit)*—Measure from inner sleeve edge/seam to outer sleeve edge/fold at a point 1" below armhole and parallel to sleeve opening.

50. *Elbow Width (knit)*—Measure from inner sleeve edge/seam to outer sleeve edge/fold straight across sleeve at a point one-half of underarm sleeve length and parallel to sleeve opening at wrist or cuff. [Note:

If sleeve is three-quarter length, indicate new point of measure on spec sheet.]

52. *Sleeve Opening Width (knit)*—Measure from inner sleeve edge/seam to outer sleeve edge/fold straight across bottom edge of sleeve opening.

54. *Sleeve Opening Width, Stretched (knit)*—Measure from inner sleeve edge/seam to outer sleeve edge/fold straight across bottom edge of sleeve opening in a fully extended position.

56. *Cuff Length Sleeve*—Measure from outside end of buttonhole to center of button straight along center of cuff. Open cuff out as flat as possible when measuring. [Note: If cuff length is contoured, measure along center-most point.]

57. *Cuff/Ribbing Height Sleeve*—Measure from cuff joining seam or top of ribbing straight down to bottom edge of cuff or rib opening. [Note: If cuff is contoured, indicate changes made to measurement on spec sheet.]

58. *Neck Depth Front (garments with a plain front/asymmetrical front opening)*—Measure from center back neck joining seam/edge straight down to center front neck joining seam/edge.

59. *Neck Depth Center Front (garments with a center front opening)*—Measure from center back neck joining seam/edge straight down to center of first button at center front of garment.

60. *Neck Drop Front*—Measure from an imaginary line connecting neckline edges straight down to center front neck opening edge. Use a ruler if needed to connect top neckline edges.

61. *Neck Drop Back*—Measure from an imaginary line connecting neckline edges straight down to center back neck opening edge. This measurement is taken with front of garment faceup. Use a ruler to connect top neckline edges if needed.

62. *Neck Width, No Collar*—Measure from inside neck edge/seam to inside neck edge/seam straight across back neck at widest point. This measurement is taken with front of garment faceup.

63. *Neck Width, Collar*—Measure straight across back neck from neck-shoulder joining seam to neck-shoulder joining seam or natural shoulder line if no seam. This measurement is taken with back of garment faceup.

64. *Neck Edge Width (knit)*—Measure from neck edge/seam/fold to neck edge/seam/fold along top opening edge, following natural contour of neck opening. Garment should be positioned with one shoulder on top of the other and with front and back neck edges meeting.

66. *Neck Edge Width, Stretched (knit)*—Measure from neck edge/seam/fold to neck edge/seam/fold along top opening edge in a fully extended position. Garment should be positioned with one shoulder on top of the other and with front and back neck edges meeting.

68. *Neck Base (knit)*—Measure from neck edge/seam to neck edge/seam along collar/rib joining seam or neckline edge, following natural contour of neck opening. Garment should be buttoned or zippered, if applicable, with one shoulder seam positioned on top of the other and with front and back neck edges meeting.

70. *Neckband Length*—Measure from outside end of buttonhole to center of buttonhole across neckband, following contour of neckband.

71. *Collar Length*—Measure from one end of collar to other end of collar along neck joining seam.

72. *Collar Height*—Measure from collar/rib joining seam at center back neck straight up to outer edge of collar/rib.

73. *Collar Band Height*—Measure from collar joining seam at center back straight up to neckband joining seam at center back.

74. *Collar Point Length*—Measure from collar joining seam to outer edge of collar along collar point edge. [Note: If collar is rounded, measure at a point parallel to center back and indicate change on spec sheet.]

75. *Collar Point Spread (pointed collars only)*—Measure, with collar band buttoned and collar in place, from collar point straight across collar edge to collar point.

76. *Lapel Width*

A. *Notched*—Measure from lower lapel notch straight across to lapel fold at a point perpendicular to garment center front.

B. *Without Notches*—Measure from lapel edge straight across widest point of lapel to lapel fold at a point _____" down from center back collar joining seam and perpendicular to front of garment.

77. *Center Front Extension*—Measure from an imaginary line at center front of garment horizontally to finished outer edge of front extended piece.

78. *Placket Length*—Measure from top edge of placket straight down to bottom of placket opening along center of placket.

79. *Placket Width*—Measure from placket joining seam straight across placket to placket edge at fold.

80. *Keyhole Length*—Measure from outer edge of neckline straight down to bottom of keyhole opening.

81. *Waistband Depth*—Measure from top of waistband edge straight down to bottom of waistband at waistband joining seam. [Note: If waistband is contoured, indicate measurement change on spec sheet.]

82. *Waistband Width (knit)*—Measure from side of bottom band to side of bottom band along center of band, following natural contour of waistband.

84. *Waistband Width, Stretched (knit)*—Measure from side of bottom band to side of bottom band straight across center of band in a fully extended position.

86. *High Hip Width (knit)*—Measure from edge of garment/side seam to edge of garment/side seam at a point 4" below bottom edge of waistband/seam, following contour of waist. [Note: The 4" point is for misses/women's wear only; adjust as needed ½" to 1" up or down for children's, petite's, junior's, or large/plus sizes. Indicate change on spec sheet.]

88. *Low Hip Width from Waist (knit)*—Measure from edge of garment/side seam to edge of garment/side seam at a point 7" below bottom edge of waistband/seam, following contour of waist. [Note: The 7" point is for misses/women's wear only; adjust as needed ½" to 1" up or down for children's, petite's, junior's, or large/plus sizes. Indicate change on spec sheet.]

90. *Hip Width from High Point Shoulder (knit)*—Measure from edge of garment/side seam to edge of garment/side seam straight across at a point _____" below high point shoulder. [Note: You will have to estimate low hip point on garment if there is no waistband and fill in _____" from high point shoulder. This measurement will vary for children's, junior's, misses, and large/plus sizes.]

94. *Bottom Opening/Sweep Width (knit skirt)*—Measure from edge of garment/side seam to edge of garment/side seam straight across garment at bottom opening. [Note: If sweep has pleats, measure with pleats closed or relaxed.]

96. *Vented Bottom Opening/Sweep Width (knit skirt)*—Measure from edge of garment/side seam to edge of garment/side seam straight across garment at top of side vents. [Note: Indicate on spec sheet if there is only one vent or if vent hits at a point other than sweep, e.g., thigh opening.]

98. *Circular Bottom Opening/Sweep Width (knit skirt)*—Measure from edge of garment/side seam to

edge of garment/side seam, following natural contour of garment at bottom opening.

100. *Center Front Skirt Length*—Measure from bottom of waistband/seam (top edge if not banded, or stitching if self-elastic/drawstring casing) straight down to bottom of garment at center front. [Note: A fashion-forward skirt may have an asymmetrical waist. Indicate top point of measure on spec sheet.]

101. *Center Back Skirt Length*—Measure from bottom of waistband/seam (top edge if not banded, or stitching if self-elastic/drawstring casing) straight down to bottom of garment at center front. [Note: A fashion-forward skirt may have an asymmetrical waist. Indicate top point of measure on spec sheet.]

102. *Side Skirt Length*—Measure from bottom edge of waistband/seam (top edge if not banded, or stitching if self-elastic/drawstring casing) to bottom of garment along side seam/fold of garment, following any contour.

103. *Skirt/Pant Yoke Depth Front*—Measure from bottom of waistband/seam (top edge if not banded, or stitching if self-elastic/drawstring casing) straight down to bottom of yoke joining seam at center front. [Note: If yoke is contoured, indicate point of measure on spec sheet.]

104. *Skirt/Pant Yoke Depth Back*—Measure from bottom of waistband/seam (top edge if not banded, or stitching if self-elastic/drawstring casing) straight down to bottom of yoke joining seam at center back. [Note: If yoke is contoured, indicate point of measure on spec sheet.]

121. *Fly/Zipper*

A. *Length*—Measure from top of fly/zipper opening straight down to bottom of fly/zipper opening at zipper stop or bar tack.

B. *Fly/Zipper Width*—Measure top of fly/zipper at joining seam from edge/fold straight across to fly/zipper placket stitching.

122. *Vent/Slit*

A. *Height*—Measure from top of vent/slit straight down to bottom of vent/slit along edge of vent/slit.

B. *Width*—Measure top of vent/slit from edge/fold straight across to vent/slit placket stitching at a point parallel to garment hemline.

123. *Pleat Depth*—Measure from outer edge of pleat at fold/crease to inner fold of pleat. [Note 1: It is a good idea to indicate what type of pleat is being measured, e.g., box, inverted, knife, kick, kilt, or envelope. Note 2: If pleats are not parallel or symmetrical, indicate any special instructions on spec sheet.]

124. *Distance Between Pleats*—Measure from start of pleat to start of pleat, excluding pleat depth at a point directly below pleat joining seam. [Note: If pleats are not parallel or symmetrical, indicate any special instructions on spec sheet.]

125. *Applied Pocket Height*—Measure from top edge of pocket to bottom edge of pocket along center of pocket. [Note: For contoured or irregularly shaped pockets, take a second measurement and indicate point of measure on spec sheet.]

126. *Applied Pocket Width*—Measure from side of pocket to side of pocket along top edge of pocket. [Note: For contoured or irregularly shaped pockets, take a second measurement and indicate point of measure on spec sheet.]

127. *Pocket Opening Within a Seam*—Measure from top of pocket to bottom of pocket along edge of pocket opening.

128. *Belt Length*

A. *Total*—Measure from end of belt at buckle along center of belt to opposite end of belt, following contour.

B. *Circumference*—Measure from end of belt at buckle along center of belt to middle hole at opposite end.

129. *Belt Width (or Height)*—Measure from edge of belt straight across to edge of belt. [Note: If belt is contoured, indicate points of measure on spec sheet.]

130. *Belt Loop Length*—Measure from top of belt loop straight down/vertically to bottom of belt loop along center of belt loop. [Note: Fashion-forward or irregularly shaped belt loops may require further spec instructions. Indicate points of measure on spec sheet.]

131. *Belt Loop Width*—Measure belt loop from edge of belt loop straight across/horizontally to edge of belt loop. [Note: Fashion-forward or irregularly shaped belt loops may require further spec instructions. Indicate points of measure on spec sheet.]

132. *Tie Length*—Measure from end of tie/joining seam straight down to tie end along center of tie.

133. *Tie Width*

A. *Straight*—Measure from edge of tie straight across to edge of tie.

B. *Contoured*—Measure from edge of tie straight across to edge of tie at widest point of tie.

134. *Flounce/Ruffle Width*—Measure from flounce/ruffle joining seam straight across to outer edge of flounce/ruffle. [Note: If flounce/ruffle is contoured, measure along narrowest and widest points if possible and indicate changes on spec sheet.]

135. *Strap Length*—Measure from strap joining seam along center of strap to end of strap. [Note: If strap is contoured or has a contoured edge, measure along center, approximating center end point, or indicate instructions as needed on spec sheet.]

136. *Strap Width*—Measure from edge of strap straight across to edge of strap. [Note: If strap is contoured, measure along narrowest and widest points if possible and indicate changes on spec sheet.]

137. *Front Hood Length*—Measure from top of hood to bottom of hood at center front joining seam along opening edge of hood.

138. *Back Hood Length*—Measure from top of hood at center front to bottom of hood at center back joining seam along outside curve of hood fold/seam.

139. *Hood Width*—Measure from front opening edge of hood straight across to back of hood along widest point of hood.

140. *Flange Depth*—Measure from center back neck joining seam straight down to bottom of flange at center back. [Note: If flange is contoured or asymmetrical, indicate point of measure on spec sheet.]

141. *Shoulder Pad Length*—Measure from edge of pad straight across to edge of pad along center of pad or natural shoulder line of pad.

142. *Shoulder Pad Width*—Measure from side of pad straight across to side of pad along edge of pad if straight, or at widest point of pad if curved.

143. *Straight Edge Shoulder Pad Height*—Measure from top of pad straight down to bottom of pad along center of pad.

144. *Curved Edge Shoulder Pad Height*—Stick a 1" straight pin into thickest part of shoulder pad. Push pin all way through pad until head of pin rests on top of pad. Be sure not to crush pad. Measure portion of pin sticking out of pad. Subtract this figure from 1" (length of pin) to get shoulder pad height.

145. *Shoulder Pad Placement*—Measure from neck edge or joining seam straight across shoulder seam or natural shoulder line to start of shoulder pad.

146. *Pleats Placement*

A. *Front Pleat Top*—Measure the distance from center front of garment straight across to start of first pleat at a point parallel to garment hem. [Note: You may need to use armhole or side seam as a starting point if there is no center front seam or placket.]

B. *Back Pleat Top*—Measure distance from armhole seam/side seam (depending on pleat placement) to first pleat at a point parallel to garment hem.
C. *Front Pleat Skirt/Pant*—Measure distance from center front of garment waistband joining seam/edge straight across to start of first pleat.

147. *Button Placement*—Refer to point of measure 59, Neck Depth Center Front, for placement of first button. Then measure distance of first button to second button. Be sure when measuring that button at bust point is lined up to apex of the bust. Adjust all buttons accordingly and respace as needed.

148. *Pocket Placement*
A. *Top Pocket Vertical*—Measure from shoulder-neck joining seam straight down to top edge of pocket.
B. *Top Pocket Horizontal*—Measure from center front straight across to side of pocket at top edge.
C. *Front Bottom Pocket Vertical*—Measure from waistband/joining seam/edge straight down to top edge of pocket.
D. *Front Bottom Pocket Horizontal*—Measure from center front straight across to side of pocket at top edge.
E. *Back Bottom Pocket Vertical*—Measure from waistband/joining seam/edge straight down to top edge of pocket.
F. *Back Bottom Pocket Horizontal*—Measure from center back straight across to side of pocket at top edge.
G. *Pocket from Side Seam*—Measure from side seam straight across to top of pocket. [Note: If pocket is contoured at sides, a top and bottom pocket size and placement must be measured and added to spec sheet.]

149. *Belt Loop Placement*
A. *Front*—Measure from center front of garment horizontally across to center of first front belt loop.
B. *Back*—Measure from center back of garment horizontally across to center of first back belt loop.
C. *Side Seam to Front*—Measure from center of side seam belt loop to center of front belt loop.
D. *Side Seam to Back*—Measure from center of side seam belt loop to center of back belt loop.

150. *Dart Placement*
A. *High Point Shoulder Bust Dart*—Measure from shoulder-neck joining seam or at a point _____" from shoulder-neck seam straight down, parallel to center front, to top of dart. [Note: The _____" from shoulder seam measurement is to be used for darts that are too short to be measured from high point shoulder. Be sure to indicate _____" measurement on spec sheet.]
B. *Center Front Bust Dart*—Measure from center front of garment straight across to top of dart.
C. *Side Seam Bust Dart*—Measure from underarm/side seam joining seam down along contour of side seam to bottom of dart.
D. *High Point Shoulder Princess Dart*—Measure from shoulder-neck joining seam straight down to top of dart.
E. *Center Front Princess Dart*—Measure from center front of garment straight across to top of dart.
F. *Center Front Skirt/Pant*—Measure from center front of garment at waistband joining seam/edge straight across to top of dart.
G. *Center Back Skirt/Pant*—Measure from center back of garment at waistband joining seam/edge straight across to top of dart.

CHAPTER 7 TERMS

When working with knit dresses, you may come across the following garment terms. If you are unfamiliar with any of them, please look up the definitions in the glossary at the end of this text.

Dress:
Cardigan
Polo shirt
Poor-boy shift
Sweater
T-shirt

ᴾEC SHEET: Knit dress | STYLE

:ASON: | DESCRIPTION:

ᴀBEL: (SIZE CATEGORY)

ᴀTE:

:CHNICAL SKETCH Turtleneck | SKETCH/PHOTO

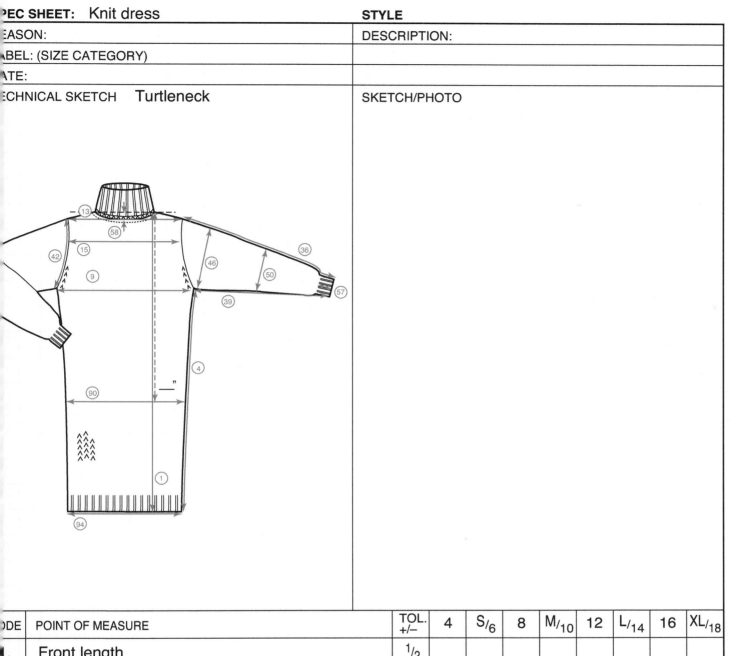

ᴅDE	POINT OF MEASURE	TOL. +/–	4	S/6	8	M/10	12	L/14	16	XL/18
1.	Front length	1/2								
3.	Center back length	1/2								
4.	Side length	1/4								
9.	Chest width	1/4-3/8								
3.	Across shoulder	1/4								
5.	Across chest	1/4								
6.	Across back	1/4								
5.	Bottom band/ribbing height	1/8								
6.	Sleeve length top armhole	3/8								
9.	Sleeve length underarm	3/8								
2.	Curved armhole width	1/4								
8.	Muscle width	1/8								

ırance 1/4-3/8 S, M, L, XL = 3/8" 4-18 = 1/4")

The measured garment spec sheets are for ***illustrative purposes only*** and should not be used as industry standards

CODE	POINT OF MEASURE	TOL. +/–	4	S/6	8	M/10	12	L/14	16	XL
50.	Elbow width	1/8								
52.	Sleeve opening width	1/8								
54.	Sleeve opening width stretched	1/8								
57.	Cuff/ribbing height sleeve	1/8								
58.	Neck depth front	1/8								
63.	Neck width collar	1/4								
64.	Neck edge width	1/4								
66.	Neck edge width stretched	1/4								
68.	Neck base	1/4								
72.	Collar height	1/8								
73.	Collar band height	1/8								
90.	Hip width from H.P.S. ______ "	1/4-3/8								
94.	Bottom opening sweep width	1/4-3/8								

COMMENTS:

The measured garment spec sheets are for ***illustrative purposes***
and should not be used as industry stand

ᴾEC SHEET: Knit dress	STYLE
ᴱASON: Fall	DESCRIPTION: Sleeveless Turtleneck Dress
ᴬBEL: (SIZE CATEGORY) Missy	
ᴬTE:	
ᴱCHNICAL SKETCH Turtleneck	SKETCH/PHOTO

ᴰDE	POINT OF MEASURE	TOL. +/–	4	S/6	8	M/10	12	L/14	16	XL/18
.	Front length	1/2				34				
3.	Center back length	1/2				32 3/4				
4.	Side length	1/4				25				
9.	Chest width	1/4-3/8				19				
3.	Across shoulder	1/4				14 3/4				
5.	Across chest	1/4				13 3/4				
6.	Across back	1/4				13 3/4				
5.	Bottom band/ribbing height	1/8				3/8				
6.	Sleeve length top armhole	3/8								
9.	Sleeve length underarm	3/8								
2.	Curved armhole width	1/4				9				
8.	Muscle width	1/8								

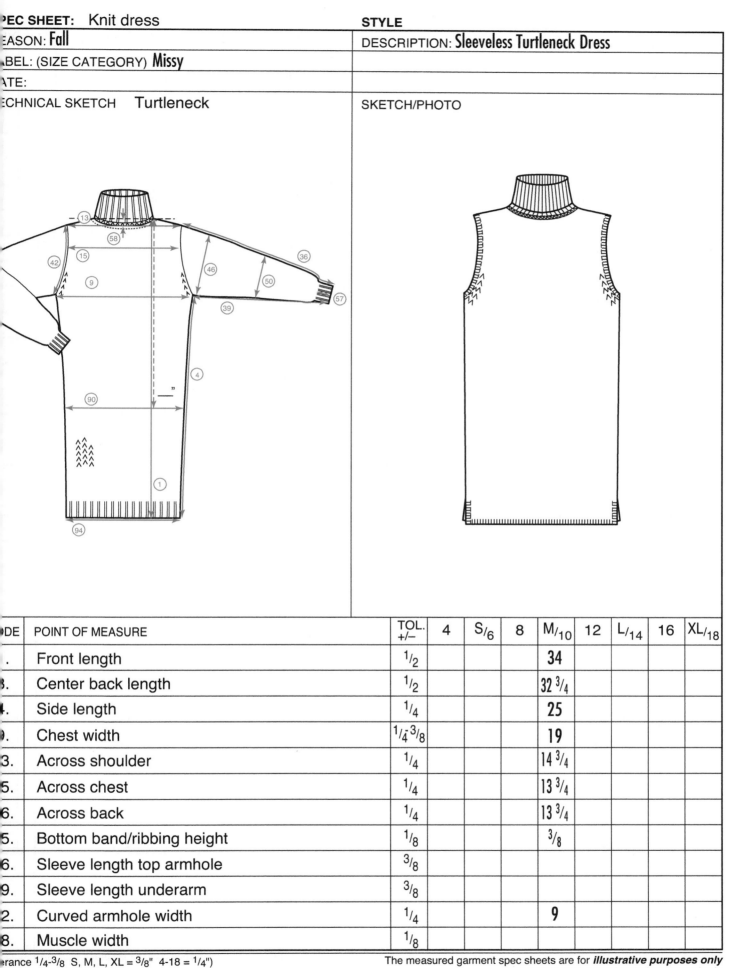

ᵉrance 1/4-3/8 S, M, L, XL = 3/8" 4-18 = 1/4")

The measured garment spec sheets are for ***illustrative purposes only*** and should not be used as industry standards

CODE	POINT OF MEASURE	TOL. +/–	4	S/6	8	M/10	12	L/14	16	XL
50.	Elbow width	1/8								
52.	Sleeve opening width	1/8								
54.	Sleeve opening width stretched	1/8								
57.	Cuff/ribbing height sleeve	1/8				3/8				
58.	Neck depth front	1/8				1				
63.	Neck width collar	1/4				6 1/2				
64.	Neck edge width	1/4				6 1/2				
66.	Neck edge width stretched	1/4				13				
68.	Neck base	1/4				7 1/2				
72.	Collar height	1/8				6				
73.	Collar band height	1/8				3/8				
90.	Hip width from H.P.S. 21 "	1/4-3/8				19				
94.	Bottom opening sweep width	1/4-3/8				18 1/2				

COMMENTS:

The measured garment spec sheets are for ***illustrative purposes*** and should not be used as industry stand

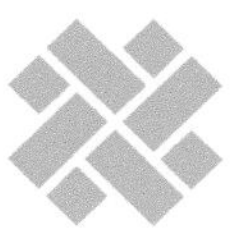

CHAPTER 8

Knit Jumpsuits and One-Piece Garments

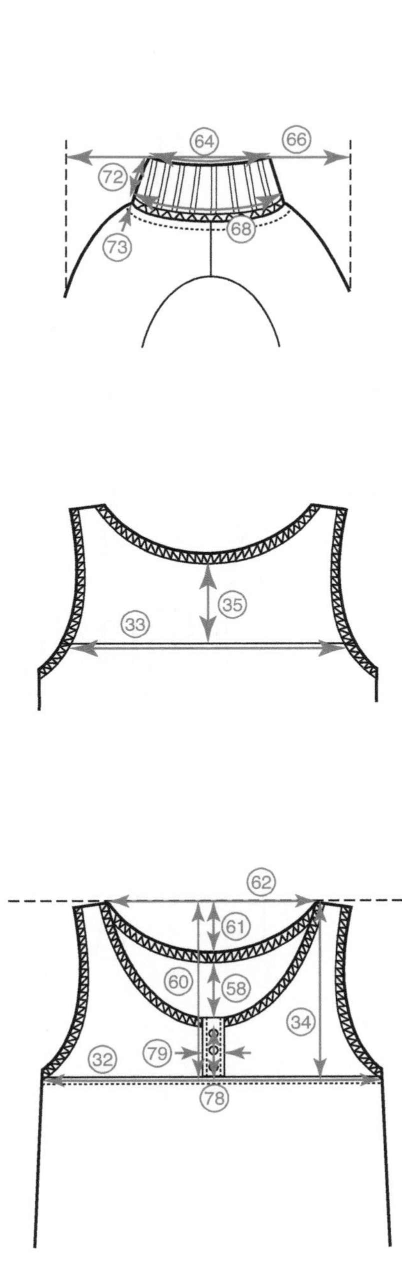

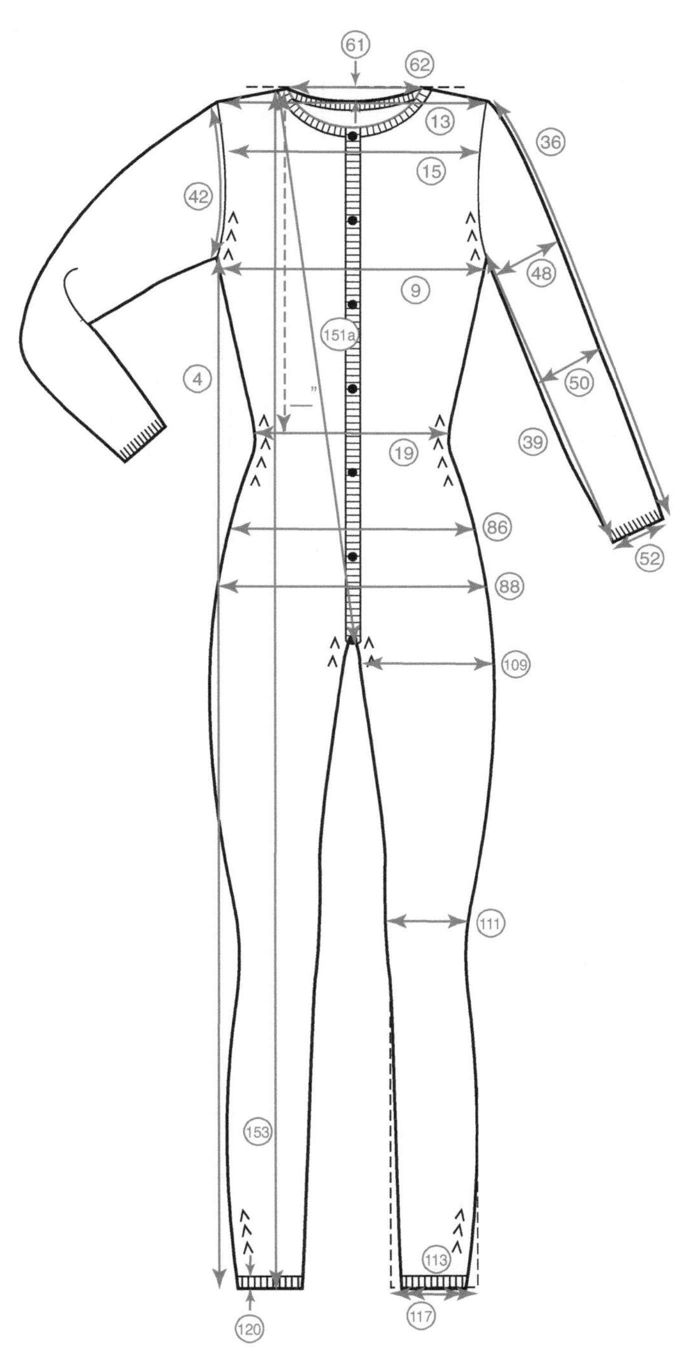

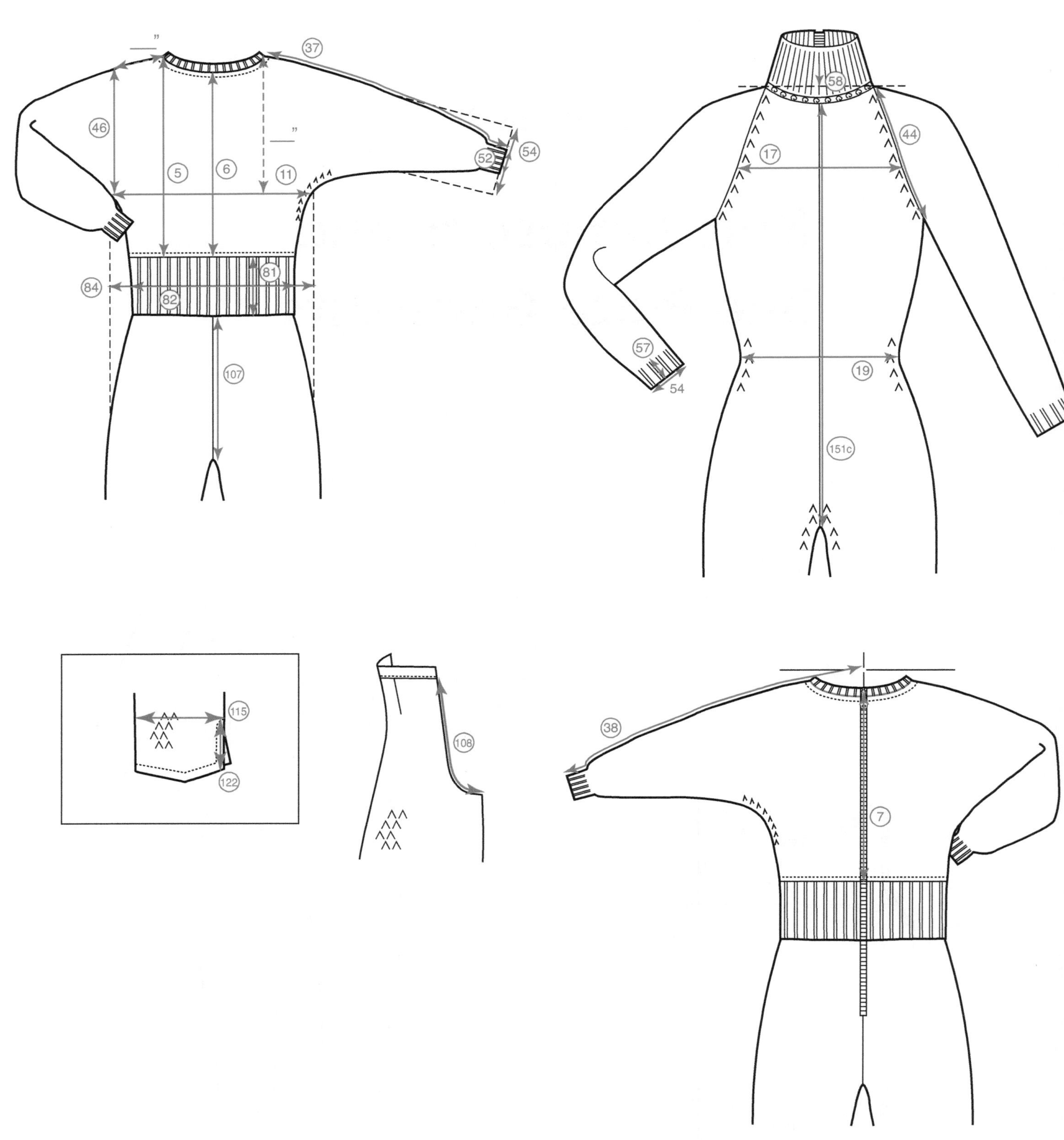
37
46
5
6
11
52
54
81
84
82
107
58
44
17
57
54
19
151c
115
122
108
38
7

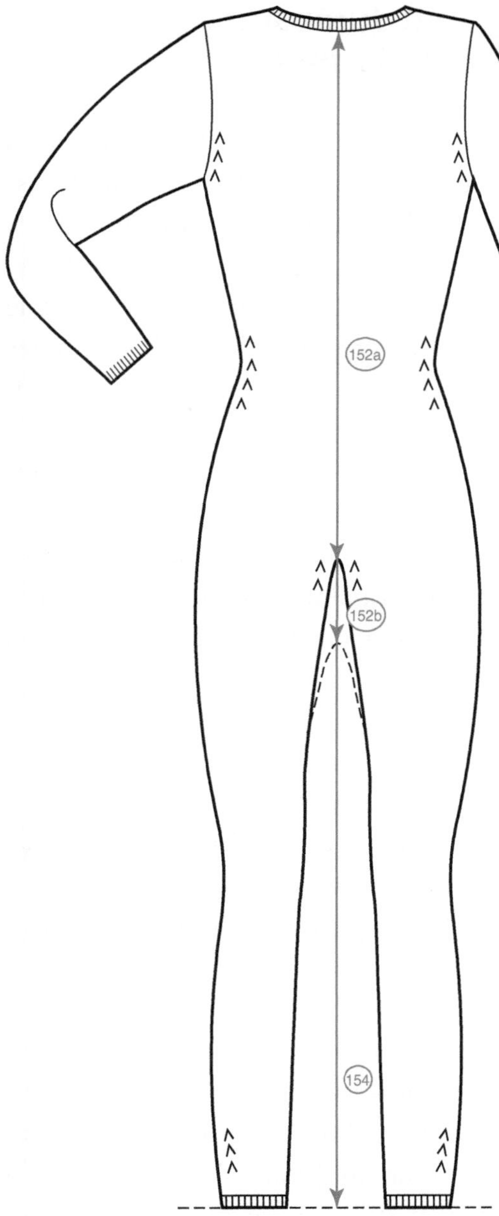

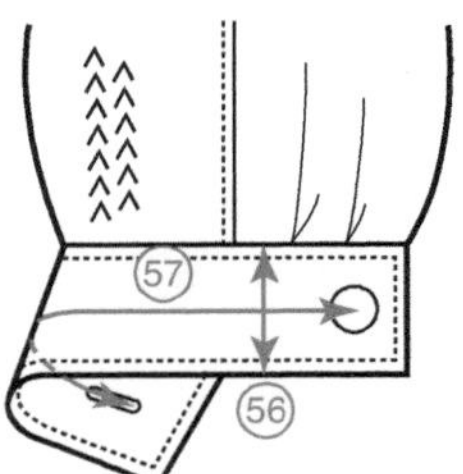
57
56

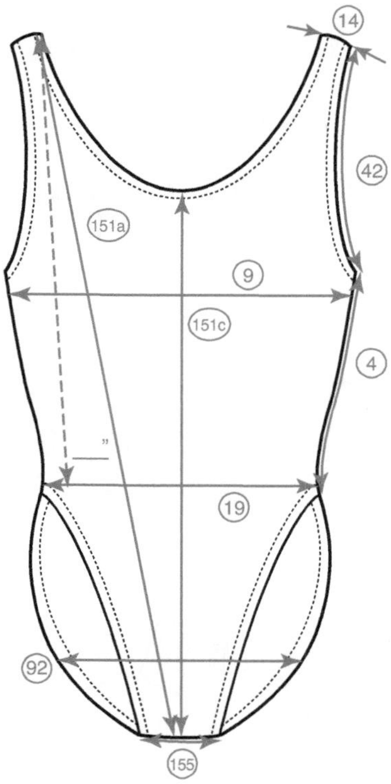

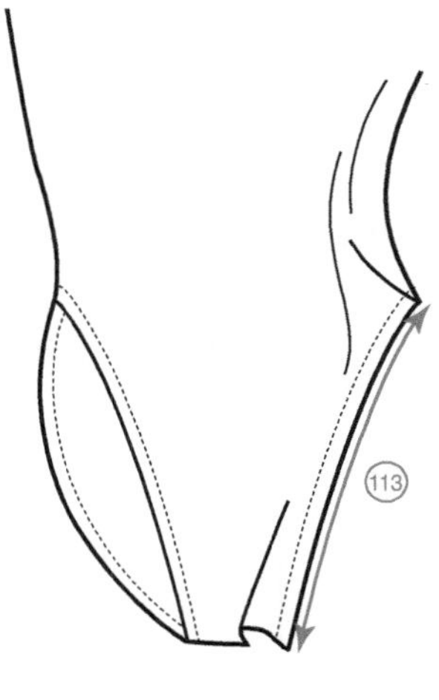

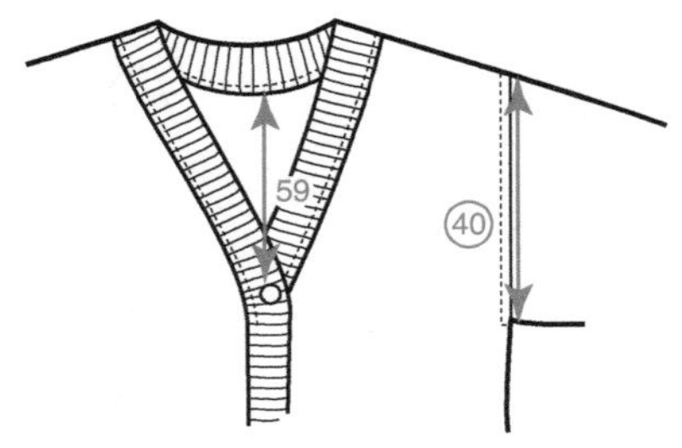

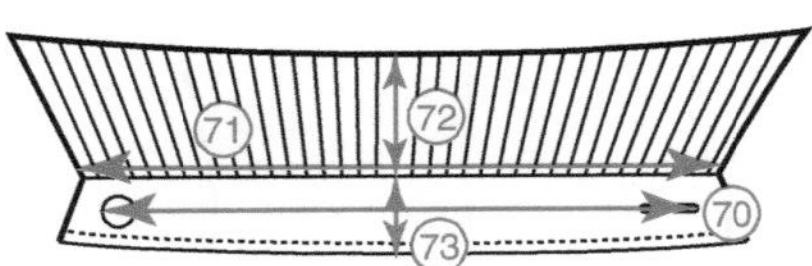

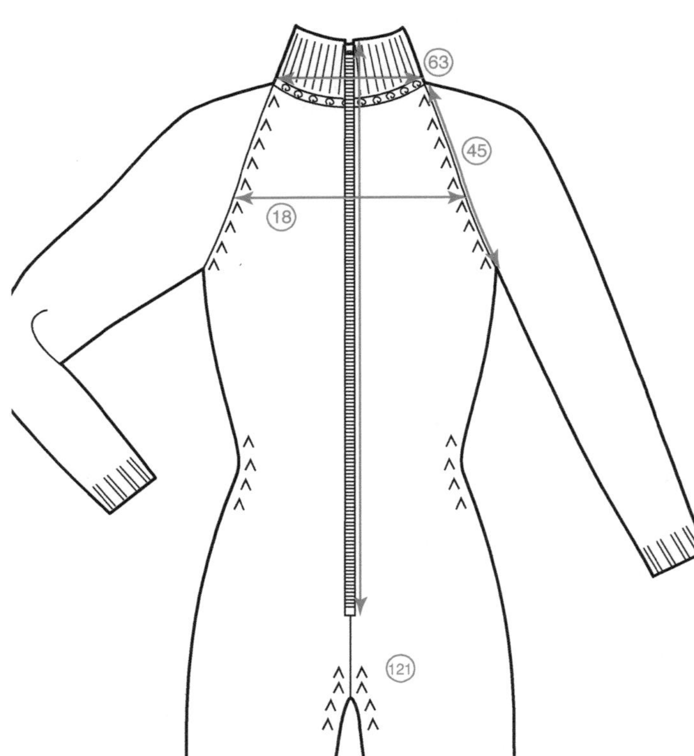

Measuring Knit Jumpsuits and One-Piece Garments

Knit jumpsuit and one-piece garment specification sheets are common in the children's wear industries, however this chapter is written for the misses market. Common one-piece garments include bodysuits, one-piece swimsuits, and rompers. Measuring a bodysuit or one-piece garment basically combines the measurement points of a knit top and a knit pant. Notice in the sketch (see Figure 8.1) that a one-piece swimsuit can be measured from point 151c, Front Torso Length, center front at neck to the crotch joining seam, or using point 151a, Front Torso Length, the high point shoulder to the crotch joining seam. Depending on styling, it may be a good idea to use both.

5. *Front Bodice Length (garments with a front opening)*—Measure from high point shoulder at neck straight down, parallel to center front, to top edge of waistband, joining seam, or rib. If garment has a collar, gently lift it away from shoulder-neck measuring point.

6. *Center Front Bodice Length (garments with a plain front; no front opening)*—Measure from center front neck joining seam straight down to top edge of waistband, joining seam, or rib. [Note: A garment with a center opening may still require point of measure 5, Front Bodice Length, if neckline is unusual or is difficult to measure.]

7. *Center Back Bodice Length*—Measure from center back neck joining seams straight down to top edge of waistband, joining seam, or rib. If needed, gently lift collar away from back neck to expose joining seam.

8. *Side Seam Bodice Length*—Measure from bottom of armhole/side seam straight down to top edge of waistband, joining seam, or rib, along side of garment, following natural curve of garment's side seam, unless otherwise indicated. If needed, gently lift sleeve away from armhole/side seam joining seam. [Note: You can

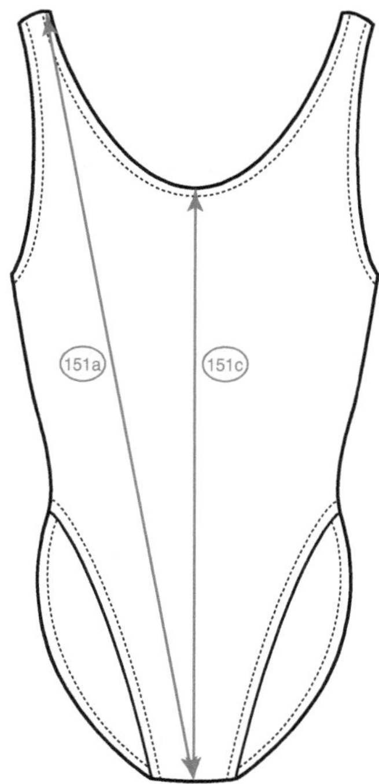

Figure 8.1 Choosing the best front length measurement point.

take side seam bodice measurement straight rather than contoured if joining seam/rib can be extended, but indicate change on spec sheet.]

9. *Chest Width (knit)*—Measure from edge of garment/ side seam to edge of garment/side seam straight across garment at a point 1" below armhole.

11. *Chest Width/Raglan Sleeve (knit)*—Measure from edge of garment/side seam to edge of garment/side seam straight across garment at a point _____" below high point shoulder. [Note: You will have to determine number of inches down from high point shoulder for each raglan sleeve style based on depth of sleeve. Then indicate this number on spec sheet.]

13. *Across Shoulder*—Measure straight across front from armhole seam/edge to armhole seam/edge at shoulder seam or across natural shoulder fold line created if there is no seam.

14. *Shoulder Width*—Measure from neckband/collar/ribbing joining seam or neckline edge to top of armhole seam at shoulder, taken along shoulder seam or across natural shoulder fold line created if there is no seam.

15. *Across Chest*—Measure 2½" down from collar/ rib joining seam at center front straight across front of garment from armhole seam/edge to armhole seam/edge. [Note: The 2½" measurement point is for misses/women's wear only and may need to be adjusted up or down ¼" to ½" accordingly for men's, children's, junior's, and large/plus sizes. Indicate any changes on spec sheet.]

16. *Across Back*—Measure 4" down from collar/rib joining seam at center back straight across back of garment from armhole seam/edge to armhole seam/ edge. [Note: The 4" measurement point is for misses/ women's wear only and may need to be adjusted up or down ¼" to ½" accordingly for men's, children's, junior's, and large/plus sizes. Indicate any changes on spec sheet.]

17. *Across Chest/Center Armhole*—Measure at one-half depth of armhole straight across front of garment from armhole seam/edge to armhole seam/edge.

18. *Across Back/Center Armhole*—Measure at one-half depth of armhole straight across back of garment from armhole seam/edge to armhole seam/edge.

19. *Waist Width (knit)*—Measure from edge of garment/side seam to edge of garment/side seam straight across garment on seam or at narrowest point of waist taper at a point _____" below high point shoulder. [Note: You will have to determine number of inches down from high point shoulder for each raglan sleeve style based on depth of sleeve. Then indicate this number on spec sheet.]

32. *Yoke Width Front*—Measure from armhole seam/ edge to armhole seam/edge straight across front of garment, ignoring contours or points, at yoke-body joining seams. [Note: If yoke is asymmetrical, indicate changes in measuring as needed on spec sheet.]

33. *Yoke Width Back*—Measure from armhole seam/edge to armhole seam/edge straight across back of garment, ignoring contours or points, at yoke-body joining seams. [Note: If yoke is asymmetrical, indicate changes in measuring as needed on spec sheet.]

34. *Yoke Depth Front*—Measure from high point shoulder at neck straight down to bottom of front yoke-body joining seam. Be sure to gently lift collar away from shoulder-neck joining seam if needed.

35. *Yoke Back Depth*—Measure from center back neck joining seam straight down to bottom of back yoke-body joining seam. Gently lift collar away from back neck joining seam if needed.

36. *Sleeve Length Top Armhole*—Measure along top of sleeve/fold following contour of sleeve from armhole seam at shoulder to bottom of sleeve opening, including cuff.

37. *Sleeve Length Top Neck*—Measure along top of sleeve/fold, following contour of sleeve from sleeve-neck joining seam/edge to edge of sleeve opening, including cuff. Gently lift collar at sleeve-neck joining seam if needed.

38. *Sleeve Length Center Back*—Measure from center back neck joining seam or from a point above neck at an imaginary line, that of a joining seam, along top of sleeve/fold, following contour of sleeve to edge of sleeve opening, including cuff.

39. *Sleeve Length Underarm*—Measure straight from bottom of armhole along sleeve seam to edge of sleeve opening, including cuff.

40. *Straight Armhole Width (knit)*—Measure from top of shoulder joining seam/edge straight down to bottom of armhole.

42. *Curved Armhole Width (knit)*—Measure from top of shoulder joining seam/edge to bottom of armhole, following contour of armhole.

44. *Armhole Front*—Measure on front of garment from top of shoulder at neckline joining seam/edge to bottom of armhole, following contour of armhole. Gently lift collar away from neckline joining seam if needed.

45. *Armhole Back*—Measure on back of garment from top of shoulder at neck joining seam/edge to bottom of armhole, following contour of armhole. Gently lift collar away from neck joining seam if needed.

46. *Armhole Width Straight (knit)*—Measure from top of shoulder seam at a point _____" below neckline joining seam/edge straight down to bottom of armhole. [Note: Gently move collar from neck joining seam if needed when measuring down _____" to armhole start point. Indicate number of inches measured down on spec sheet.]

48. *Muscle Width (knit)*—Measure from inner sleeve edge/seam to outer sleeve edge/fold at a point 1" below armhole and parallel to sleeve opening.

50. *Elbow Width (knit)*—Measure from inner sleeve edge/seam to outer sleeve edge/fold straight across sleeve at a point one-half of the underarm sleeve length and parallel to sleeve opening at wrist or cuff. [Note: If sleeve is three-quarter length, indicate new point of measure on spec sheet.]

52. *Sleeve Opening Width (knit)*—Measure from inner sleeve edge/seam to outer sleeve edge/fold straight across bottom edge of sleeve opening.

54. *Sleeve Opening Width, Stretched (knit)*—Measure from inner sleeve edge/seam to outer sleeve edge/fold straight across bottom edge of sleeve opening in a fully extended position.

56. *Cuff Length Sleeve*—Measure from outside end of buttonhole to center of button straight along center of cuff. Open cuff out as flat as possible when measuring. [Note: If cuff length is contoured, measure along center-most point.]

57. *Cuff/Ribbing Height Sleeve*—Measure from cuff joining seam or top of ribbing straight down to bottom edge of cuff or rib opening. [Note: If cuff is contoured, indicate changes made to measurement on spec sheet.]

58. *Neck Depth Front (garments with a plain front/ asymmetrical front opening)*—Measure from center back neck joining seam/edge straight down to center front neck joining seam/edge.

59. *Neck Depth Center Front (garments with a center front opening)*—Measure from center back neck joining seam/edge straight down to center of first button at center front of garment.

60. *Neck Drop Front*—Measure from an imaginary line connecting neckline edges straight down to center front neck opening edge. Use a ruler if needed to connect top neckline edges.

61. *Neck Drop Back*—Measure from an imaginary line connecting neckline edges straight down to center back neck opening edge. This measurement is taken with front of garment faceup. Use a ruler to connect top neckline edges if needed.

62. *Neck Width, No Collar*—Measure from inside neck edge/seam to inside neck edge/seam straight across back neck at widest point. This measurement is taken with front of garment faceup.

63. *Neck Width, Collar*—Measure straight across back neck from neck-shoulder joining seam to neck-shoulder joining seam or natural shoulder line if no seam. This measurement is taken with back of garment faceup.

64. *Neck Edge Width (knit)*—Measure from neck edge/seam/fold to neck edge/seam/fold along top opening edge, following natural contour of neck opening. Garment should be positioned with one shoulder on top of the other and with front and back neck edges meeting.

66. *Neck Edge Width, Stretched (knit)*—Measure from neck edge/seam/fold to neck edge/seam/fold along top opening edge in a fully extended position. Garment should be positioned with one shoulder on top of the other and with front and back neck edges meeting.

68. *Neck Base (knit)*—Measure from neck edge/seam to neck edge/seam along collar/rib joining seam or neckline edge, following natural contour of neck opening. Garment should be buttoned or zippered, if applicable, with one shoulder seam positioned on top of the other and with front and back neck edges meeting.

70. *Neckband Length*—Measure from outside end of buttonhole to center of buttonhole across neckband, following contour of neckband.

71. *Collar Length*—Measure from one end of collar to other end of collar along neck joining seam.

72. *Collar Height*—Measure from collar/rib joining seam at center back neck straight up to outer edge of collar/rib.

73. *Collar Band Height*—Measure from collar joining seam at center back straight up to neckband joining seam at center back.

74. *Collar Point Length*—Measure from collar joining seam to outer edge of collar along collar point edge. [Note: If collar is rounded, measure at a point parallel to center back and indicate change on spec sheet.]

75. *Collar Point Spread (pointed collars only)*—Measure, with collar band buttoned and collar in place, from collar point straight across collar edge to collar point.

76. *Lapel Width*

A. *Notched*—Measure from lower lapel notch straight across to lapel fold at a point perpendicular to garment center front.

B. *Without Notches*—Measure from lapel edge straight across widest point of lapel to lapel fold at a point ____" down from center back collar joining seam and perpendicular to front of garment.

77. *Center Front Extension*—Measure from an imaginary line at center front of garment horizontally to finished outer edge of front extended piece.

78. *Placket Length*—Measure from top edge of placket straight down to bottom of placket opening along center of placket.

79. *Placket Width*—Measure from placket joining seam straight across placket to placket edge at fold.

80. *Keyhole Length*—Measure from outer edge of neckline straight down to bottom of keyhole opening.

81. *Waistband Depth*—Measure from top of waistband edge straight down to bottom of waistband at waistband joining seam. [Note: If waistband is contoured, indicate measurement change on spec sheet.]

82. *Waistband Width (knit)*—Measure from side of bottom band to side of bottom band along center of band, following natural contour of waistband.

84. *Waistband Width, Stretched (knit)*—Measure from side of bottom band to side of bottom band straight across center of band in a fully extended position.

86. *High Hip Width (knit)*—Measure from edge of garment/side seam to edge of garment/side seam at a point 4" below bottom edge of waistband/seam, following contour of waist. [Note: The 4" point is for misses/women's wear only; adjust as needed ½" to 1" up or down for children's, petite's, junior's, or large/plus sizes. Indicate change on spec sheet.]

88. *Low Hip Width from Waist (knit)*—Measure from edge of garment/side seam to edge of garment/side seam at a point 7" below bottom edge of waistband/seam, following contour of waist. [Note: The 7" point is for misses/women's wear only; adjust as needed ½" to 1" up or down for children's, petite's, junior's, or large/plus sizes. Indicate change on spec sheet.]

90. *Hip Width from High Point Shoulder (knit)*—Measure from edge of garment/side seam to edge of garment/side seam straight across at a point _____" below high point of shoulder. [Note: You will have to estimate low hip point on garment if there is no waistband and fill in _____" from high point shoulder. This measurement will vary for children's, junior's, misses, and large/plus sizes.]

92. *Hip Seat Width (knit pant)*—Measure from edge of garment/side seam to edge of garment/side seam at a point _____" up from crotch seam, following contour of waist. [Note 1: This measurement is useful when waistband sits below natural waistline. Note 2: Adjust the _____" up from crotch as needed for junior's and large/plus sizes. Note 3: A hip seat width of 2½" up for children's and 3" up for menswear can take place of low hip width.]

103. *Skirt/Pant Yoke Depth Front*—Measure from bottom of waistband/seam (top edge if not banded or stitching if self-elastic/drawstring casing) straight down to bottom of yoke joining seam at center front. [Note: If yoke is contoured, indicate point of measure on spec sheet.]

104. *Skirt/Pant Yoke Depth Back*—Measure from bottom of waistband/seam (top edge if not banded or stitching if self-elastic/drawstring casing) straight down to bottom of yoke joining seam at center back. [Note: If yoke is contoured, indicate point of measure on spec sheet.]

105. *Inseam*—Measure from crotch joining seam to bottom of leg opening, following inseam/inner fold.

106. *Outseam*—Measure from bottom edge of waistband/seam (top edge if not banded or stitching if

self-elastic/drawstring casing) to bottom of garment along side seam/fold of garment.

107. *Front Rise*—Measure from bottom edge of waistband/seam (top edge if not banded or stitching if self-elastic/drawstring casing) to crotch joining seam, following curve of front rise seam. [Note: Measure over zipper if in front rise seam.]

108. *Back Rise*—Measure from bottom edge of waistband/seam (top edge if not banded or stitching if self-elastic/drawstring casing) to crotch joining seam, following curve of back rise seam. [Note: Measure over zipper if in front back seam.]

109. *Thigh Width (knit)*—Measure from pant leg edge/seam to pant leg edge/seam straight across pant leg at a point 1" below crotch and parallel to leg opening. [Note: If leg opening is asymmetrical, measure to a point that would be parallel to leg opening.]

111. *Knee Width (knit)*—Measure from pant leg edge/seam to pant leg edge/seam at a point one-half of inseam and parallel to leg opening. [Note 1: If leg opening is asymmetrical, measure to a point that would be parallel to leg opening. Note 2: If pant leg is three-quarter length, indicate point of measure on spec sheet. Note 3: A general knee measurement from crotch seam of misses 14", junior's 13", or large/plus women's size 15" can be used. Indicate change on spec sheet. For children's wear measure at one-half inseam minus 1½" and for men's minus 2".]

113. *Leg Opening Width (knit)*—Measure from pant leg edge/seam to pant leg edge/seam straight across bottom edge of leg opening. [Note: If leg opening is contoured, follow contour and indicate measurement change on spec sheet.]

115. *Vented Leg Opening Width (knit)*—Measure from pant leg edge/seam to pant leg edge/seam straight across pant leg at top of side vents.

117. *Leg Opening Width, Stretched (knit)*—Measure from pant leg edge/seam to pant leg edge/seam straight across bottom edge of leg opening in a fully extended position.

119. *Cuff Height Pants*—Measure from top of cuff edge straight down to bottom of cuff fold and leg opening.

120. *Bottom Band/Ribbing Height Pants*—Measure from cuff joining seam or top of ribbing straight down to bottom edge of cuff or rib opening. [Note: For fashion-forward pants, you may want to include a cuff length. See point of measure 56, Cuff Length Sleeve, for measuring instructions and, if needed, indicate cuff length of pant on spec sheet.]

121. *Fly/Zipper*

A. *Length*—Measure from top of fly/zipper opening straight down to bottom of fly/zipper opening at zipper stop or bar tack.
B. *Fly/Zipper Width*—Measure top of fly/zipper at joining seam from edge/fold straight across to fly/zipper placket stitching.

122. *Vent/Slit*

A. *Height*—Measure from top of vent/slit straight down to bottom of vent/slit along edge of vent/slit.
B. *Width*—Measure top of vent/slit from edge/fold straight across to vent/slit placket stitching at a point parallel to garment hemline.

123. *Pleat Depth*—Measure from outer edge of pleat at fold/crease to inner fold of pleat. [Note 1: It is a good idea to indicate what type of pleat is being measured, e.g., box, inverted, knife, kick, kilt, or envelope. Note 2: If pleats are not parallel or symmetrical, indicate any special instructions on spec sheet.]

124. *Distance Between Pleats*—Measure from start of pleat to start of pleat, excluding pleat depth at a point directly below pleat joining seam. [Note: If

pleats are not parallel or symmetrical, indicate any special instructions on spec sheet.]

125. *Applied Pocket Height*—Measure from top edge of pocket to bottom edge of pocket along center of pocket. [Note: For contoured or irregularly shaped pockets, take a second measurement and indicate point of measure on spec sheet.]

126. *Applied Pocket Width*—Measure from side of pocket to side of pocket along top edge of pocket. [Note: For contoured or irregularly shaped pockets, take a second measurement and indicate point of measure on spec sheet.]

127. *Pocket Opening Within a Seam*—Measure from top of pocket to bottom of pocket along edge of pocket opening.

128. *Belt Length*

A. *Total*—Measure from end of belt at buckle along center of belt to opposite end of belt, following contour.
B. *Circumference*—Measure from end of belt at buckle along center of belt to middle hole at opposite end.

129. *Belt Width (or Height)*—Measure from edge of belt straight across to edge of belt. [Note: If belt is contoured, indicate points of measure on spec sheet.]

130. *Belt Loop Length*—Measure from top of belt loop straight down/vertically to bottom of belt loop along center of belt loop. [Note: Fashion-forward or irregularly shaped belt loops may require further spec instructions. Indicate points of measure on spec sheet.]

131. *Belt Loop Width*—Measure belt loop from edge of belt loop straight across/horizontally to edge of belt loop. [Note: Fashion-forward or irregularly shaped belt loops may require further spec instructions. Indicate points of measure on spec sheet.]

132. *Tie Length*—Measure from end of tie/joining seam straight down to tie end along center of tie.

133. *Tie Width*

A. *Straight*—Measure from edge of tie straight across to edge of tie.
B. *Contoured*—Measure from edge of tie straight across to edge of tie at widest point of tie.

134. *Flounce/Ruffle Width*—Measure from flounce/ruffle joining seam straight across to outer edge of flounce/ruffle. [Note: If flounce/ruffle is contoured, measure along narrowest and widest points if possible and indicate changes on spec sheet.]

135. *Strap Length*—Measure from strap joining seam along center of strap to end of strap. [Note: If a strap is contoured or has a contoured edge, measure along center, approximating center end point, or indicate instructions as needed on spec sheet.]

136. *Strap Width*—Measure from edge of strap straight across to edge of strap. [Note: If strap is contoured, measure along narrowest and widest points if possible and indicate changes on spec sheet.]

137. *Front Hood Length*—Measure from top of hood to bottom of hood at center front joining seam along opening edge of hood.

138. *Back Hood Length*—Measure from top of hood at center front to bottom of hood at center back joining seam along outside curve of hood fold/seam.

139. *Hood Width*—Measure from front opening edge of hood straight across to back of hood at fold along widest point of hood.

140. *Flange Depth*—Measure from center back neck joining seam straight down to bottom of flange at center back. [Note: If flange is contoured or asymmetrical, indicate point of measure on spec sheet.]

141. *Shoulder Pad Length*—Measure from edge of pad straight across to edge of pad along center of pad or natural shoulder line of pad.

142. *Shoulder Pad Width*—Measure from side of pad straight across to side of pad along edge of pad if straight, or at widest point of pad if curved.

143. *Straight Edge Shoulder Pad Height*—Measure from top of pad straight down to bottom of pad along center of pad.

144. *Curved Edge Shoulder Pad Height*—Stick a 1" straight pin into thickest part of shoulder pad. Push pin all way through pad until head of pin rests on top of pad. Be sure not to crush pad. Measure portion of pin sticking out of pad. Subtract this figure from 1" (length of pin) to get shoulder pad height.

145. *Shoulder Pad Placement*—Measure from neck edge or joining seam straight across shoulder seam or natural shoulder line to start of shoulder pad.

146. *Pleats Placement*

A. *Front Pleat Top*—Measure distance from the center front of garment straight across to start of first pleat at a point parallel to garment hem. [Note: You may need to use armhole or side seam as a starting point if there is no center front seam or placket.]
B. *Back Pleat Top*—Measure distance from armhole seam/side seam (depending on pleat placement) to first pleat at a point parallel to garment hem.
C. *Front Pleat Skirt/Pant*—Measure distance from center front of garment waistband joining seam/edge straight across to start of first pleat.

147. *Button Placement*—Refer to point of measure 59, Neck Depth Center Front, for placement of first button. Then measure distance of first button to second button. Be sure when measuring that button at bust point is lined up to apex of bust. Adjust all buttons accordingly and respace as needed.

148. *Pocket Placement*

A. *Top Pocket Vertical*—Measure from shoulder-neck joining seam straight down to top edge of pocket.
B. *Top Pocket Horizontal*—Measure from center front straight across to side of pocket at top edge.
C. *Front Bottom Pocket Vertical*—Measure from waistband/joining seam/edge straight down to top edge of pocket.
D. *Front Bottom Pocket Horizontal*—Measure from center front straight across to side of pocket at top edge.
E. *Back Bottom Pocket Vertical*—Measure from waistband/joining seam/edge straight down to top edge of pocket.
F. *Back Bottom Pocket Horizontal*—Measure from center back straight across to side of pocket at top edge.
G. *Pocket from Side Seam*—Measure from side seam straight across to top of pocket. [Note: If pocket is contoured at sides, a top and bottom pocket size and placement must be measured and added to spec sheet.]

149. *Belt Loop Placement*

A. *Front*—Measure from center front of garment horizontally across to center of first front belt loop.
B. *Back*—Measure from center back of garment horizontally across to center of first back belt loop.
C. *Side Seam to Front*—Measure from center of side seam belt loop to center of front belt loop.
D. *Side Seam to Back*—Measure from center of side seam belt loop to center of back belt loop.

150. *Dart Placement*

A. *High Point Shoulder Bust Dart*—Measure from shoulder-neck joining seam or at a point _____" from shoulder-neck seam straight down, parallel to center front, to top of dart. [Note: The _____" from shoulder seam measurement is to be used for darts that are too short to be measured from high point shoulder. Be sure to indicate _____" measurement on spec sheet.]
B. *Center Front Bust Dart*—Measure from center front of garment straight across to top of dart.
C. *Side Seam Bust Dart*—Measure from underarm/side seam joining seam down along contour of side seam to bottom of dart.

D. *High Point Shoulder Princess Dart*—Measure from shoulder-neck joining seam straight down to top of dart.
E. *Center Front Princess Dart*—Measure from center front of garment straight across to top of dart.
F. *Center Front Skirt/Pant*—Measure from center front of garment at waistband joining seam/edge straight across to top of dart.
G. *Center Back Skirt/Pant*—Measure from center back of garment at waistband joining seam/edge straight across to top of dart.

151. *Front Torso Length (jumpsuits and one-piece garments)*
A. *Garments with a Front Opening, Relaxed*—Measure from high point shoulder at neck straight down to crotch joining seam with garment in a relaxed position.
B. *Garments with a Front Opening, Extended*—Measure from high point shoulder at neck straight down to crotch joining seam with garment in a fully extended position.
C. *Garments with a Plain Front, No Front Opening, Relaxed*—Measure from center front neck joining seam straight down to crotch joining seam with the garment in a relaxed position.
D. *Garments with a Plain Front, No Front Opening, Extended*—Measure from center front neck joining seam straight down to crotch joining seam with garment in a fully extended position.

152. *Back Torso Length (jumpsuits and one-piece garments)*
A. *Relaxed*—Measure from center back neck joining seam straight down to crotch joining seam with garment in a relaxed position.
B. *Extended*—Measure from center back neck joining seam straight down to crotch joining seam with garment in a fully extended position.

153. *High Point Shoulder Length (jumpsuits and one-piece garments)*—Measure from high point shoulder straight down to bottom/hem of garment.

154. *Center Back Garment Length (jumpsuits and one-piece garments)*—Measure from center back neckline seam/edge straight down to bottom hem of garment. [Note: For pantsuits this point will intersect at an imaginary line formed by hemlines of pant legs and center of garment.]

155. *Crotch Width*—Measure straight across crotch from side to side along seam/bottom edge/fold.

CHAPTER 8 TERMS

When working with knit jumpsuits and one-piece garments, you may come across the following garment terms. If you are unfamiliar with any of them, please look up the definitions in the glossary at the end of this text.

Body stocking
Bodysuit
Bunny suit
One-piece swimsuit (bathing suit)

SPEC SHEET: One-piece knit garment

STYLE

SEASON:	DESCRIPTION:
LABEL: (SIZE CATEGORY)	
DATE:	
TECHNICAL SKETCH One-piece swimsuit	SKETCH/PHOTO

14
42
151a
9
151c
4
___"
19
92
155

CODE	POINT OF MEASURE	TOL. +/–	4	S/6	8	M/10	12	L/14	16	XL/18
4.	Side length	1/4								
9.	Chest width	1/4-3/8								
14.	Shoulder width	1/4								
19.	Waist width	1/4-3/8								
42.	Curved armhole width	1/4								
60.	Neck drop front	1/8								
61.	Neck drop back	1/8								
62.	Neck width, no collar	1/4								
92.	Hip seat width _____ " up from crotch	1/4-3/8								
113.	Leg opening width	1/8								
117.	Leg opening width stretched	1/8								
151.	Front torso length A. H.P.S. to crotch	1/2								
	B. H.P.S. to crotch stretched	1/2								
	C. C.F. neck to crotch	1/2								
	D. C.F. neck stretched	1/2								
155.	Crotch width	1/8								
COMMENTS:										

(Tolerance 1/4-3/8 S, M, L, XL = 3/8" 4-18 = 1/4")

The measured garment spec sheets are for ***illustrative purposes only*** and should not be used as industry standards

SPEC SHEET: One-piece knit garment

STYLE

SEASON: Summer	DESCRIPTION: Updated tank style swimsuit with self binding
LABEL: (SIZE CATEGORY) Missy	
DATE:	
TECHNICAL SKETCH One-piece swimsuit	SKETCH/PHOTO

CODE	POINT OF MEASURE	TOL. +/–	4	S/6	8	M/10	12	L/14	16	XL/18
4.	Side length	1/4				12				
9.	Chest width	1/4-3/8				15 1/2				
19.	Waist width from C.F. neck 9 1/4 "	1/4-3/8				12				
42.	Curved armhole width Excluding strap	1/4				3 1/2				
60.	Neck drop front	1/8				5 1/2				
61.	Neck drop back	1/8				12 1/4				
62.	Neck width, no collar Strap to strap	1/4				9 1/4				
92.	Hip seat width 4 " up from crotch	1/4-3/8				11 1/2				
113.	Leg opening width	1/8				10 1/2				
151.	Front torso length A. H.P.S. to crotch	1/2								
	B. H.P.S. to crotch stretched	1/2								
	C. C.F. neck to crotch	1/2				21				
	D. C.F. neck stretched	1/2				25				
155.	Crotch width	1/8				3				
135.	Strap length Total front to back	1/4				12 3/4				
136.	Strap width	1/8				3/8				

COMMENTS:

(Tolerance 1/4-3/8 S, M, L, XL = 3/8" 4-18 = 1/4")

The measured garment spec sheets are for ***illustrative purposes only*** and should not be used as industry standards

PART III

WORKING WITH WOVENS

Wovens in Review

Weaving is one of the oldest arts known to humankind, dating back to ancient Egypt. Woven fabric is constructed by interlocking or interlacing two basic series of yarn, a warp and a weft, or filling. There are three basic weaves: plain, twill, and satin.

Basket weave—a variation of the plain weave construction by passing weft yarns over and under warp yarns, two or more warps up and two or more warps down, in alternating rows.

Plain weave—the construction of a woven fabric by passing weft yarns over and under warp yarns, one warp up and one warp down, in alternating rows.

Satin weave—the construction of a woven fabric by passing weft yarns over and under warp yarns; this weave is generally constructed with five warps up and one warp down, repeating, creating a smooth surface.

- Before starting Chapters 9 through 15, be sure to read the measurement preparation instructions listed in Chapter 3.
- Only those measurement points that are used when measuring basic garments are included in the respective chapters. Not every measurement point listed will be used on every garment; however, every measurement point for that type of garment has been listed in each chapter.
- Ignore any skipped numbers.
- You may want to try several different points of measure at first to see which one may yield the most accurate measurement. It takes time choosing the best point of measure for your garment, but it is imperative that you consistently use the same method each time you measure that garment.
- Measuring wovens will only include missy/women's wear sketches.
- A generic missy spec sheet has been added to each chapter for your use. [Note: some in the retail industry call their missy departments contemporary, misses or women's wear, the sizing is still considered missy; therefore, this terminology will be used on all spec sheets.]
- A completed example of a spec sheet has been added to each chapter for your reference.
- Basic garment illustrations and a blank spec sheet can be found in the croquis section of Appendix A, Basic Garment Croquis, at the back of this text. These can be used to create your own spec sheets.

Chapters 9 through 15 direct the user to measure wovens in the circumference to be consistent with many technicians in the industry. Measurements are to be taken flat, across the front, and then only doubled as indicated in the instructions that follow. There is no need to re-measure a circumference measurement from the back; it would be redundant. For those in the industry or in the classroom who prefer to measure all garments flat or singularly, you may simply ignore the instructions to double measurements and change your spec sheets accordingly.

CHAPTER 9

Woven Tops

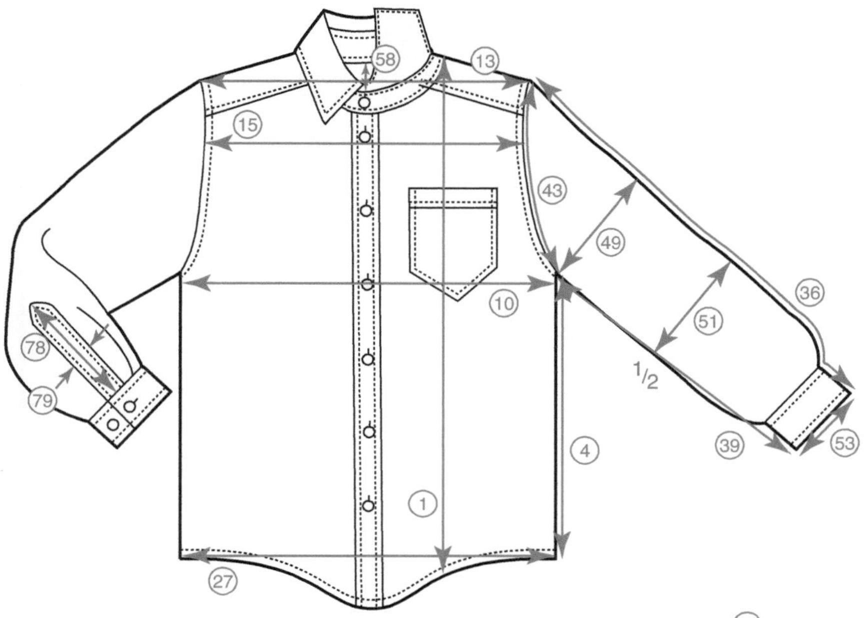

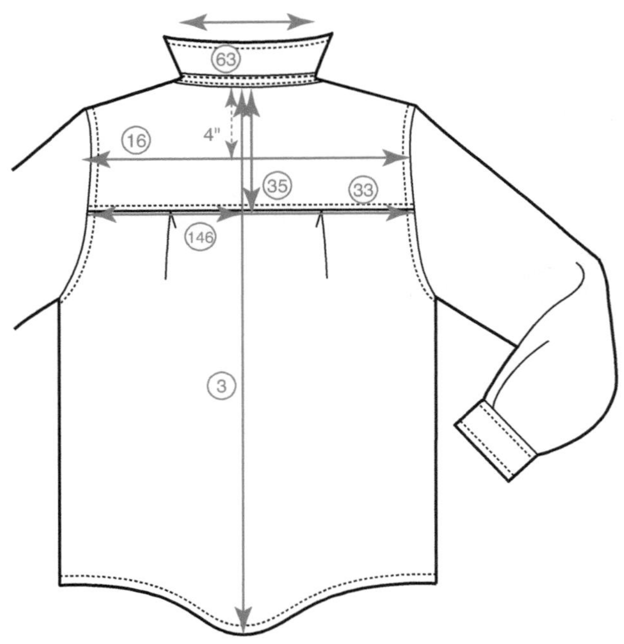
63
4"
16
35
33
146
3

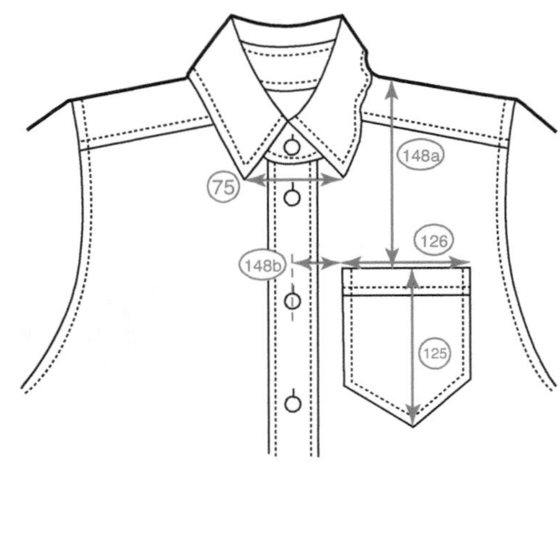
148a
75
126
148b
125

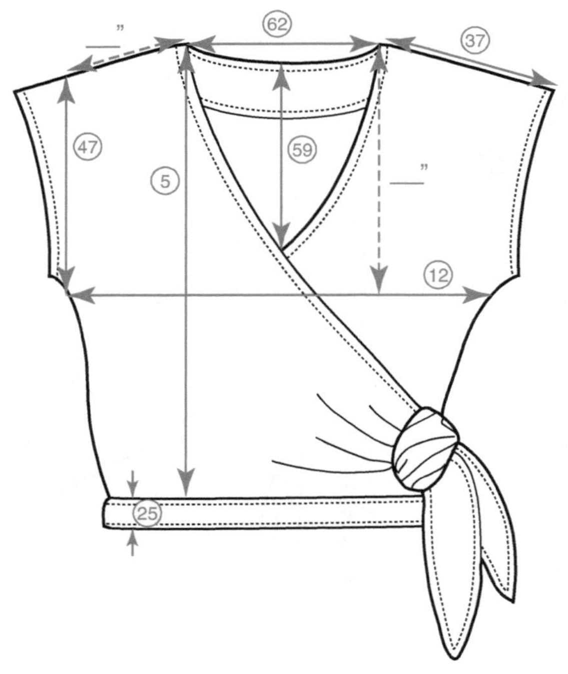
62
37
47
5
59
12
25

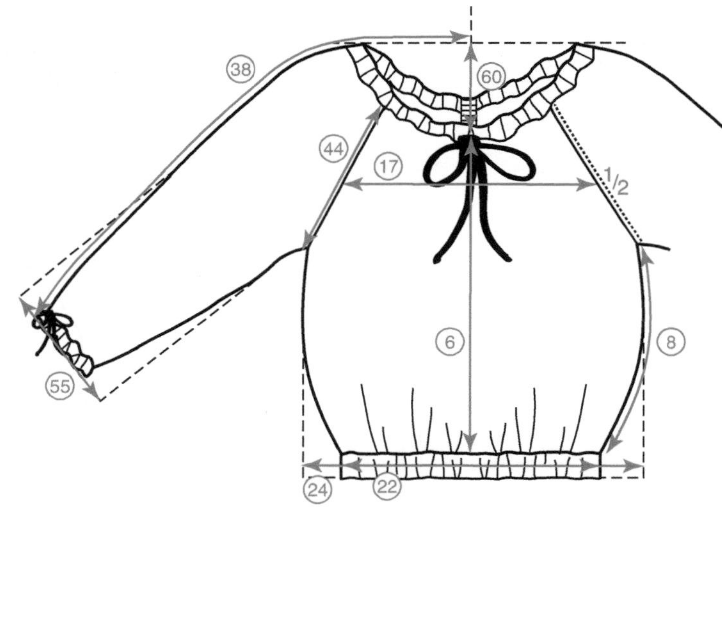
38
60
44
17
1/2
6
8
55
24
22

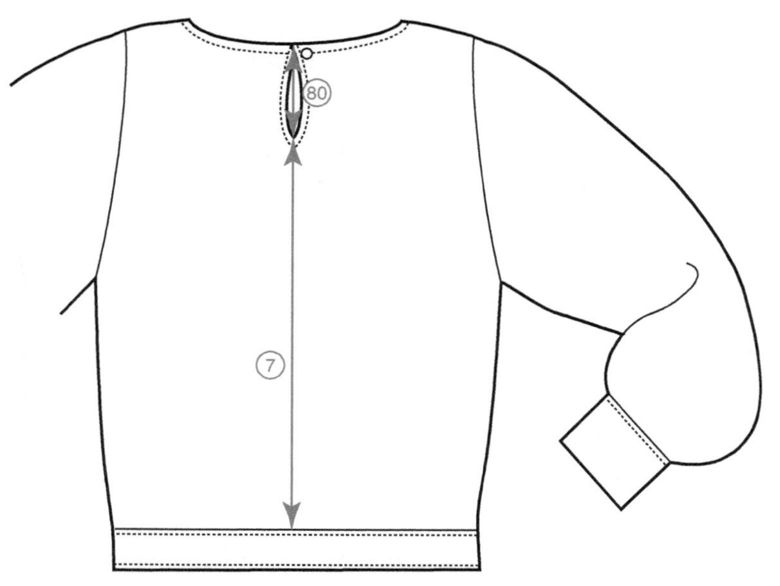
80
7

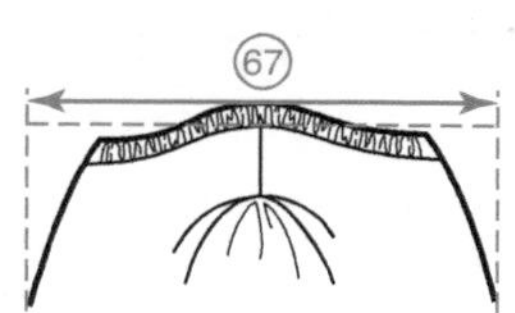
67

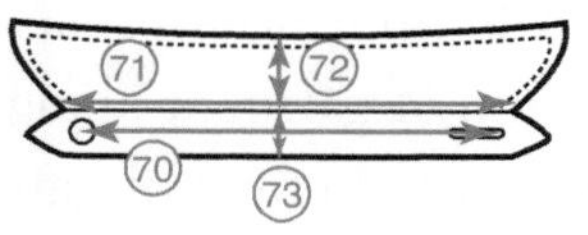
71
72
70
73

14
34
79
32
78
31

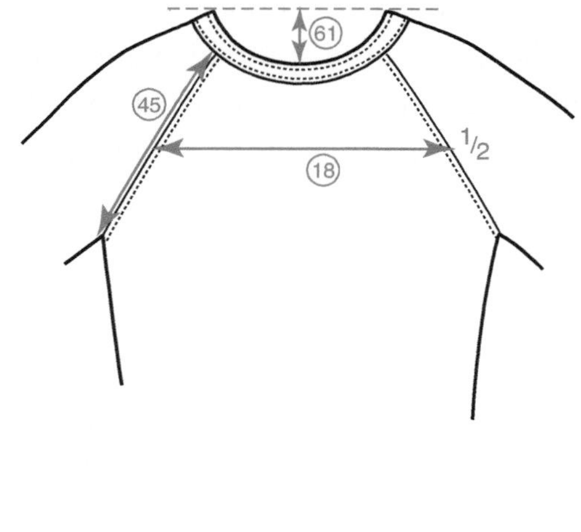
61
45
1/2
18

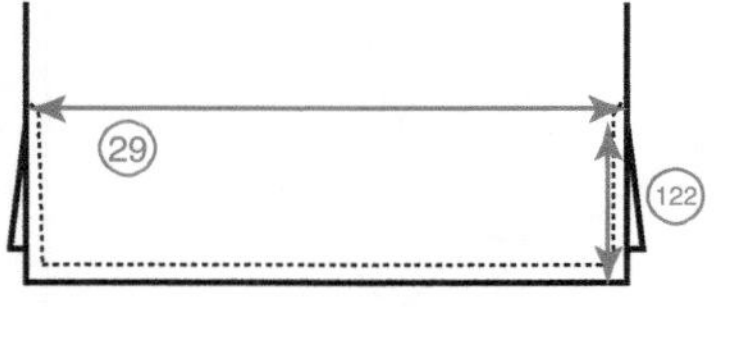
29
122

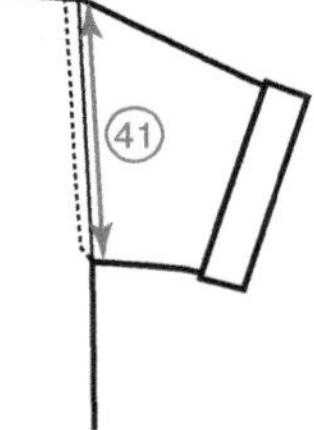
41

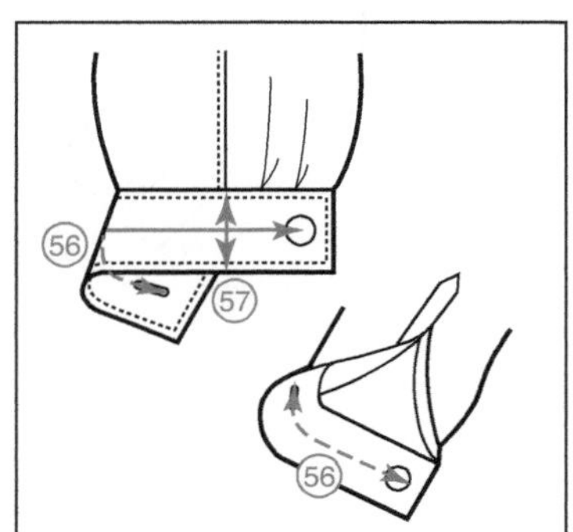
56
57
56

Measuring Woven Tops

Woven top spec sheets are used for woven garments, including blouses, shirts, and vests (although companies may have separate spec sheets for vests). As you measure, you will find instances when more than one method can be used for taking a measurement. You learned in Chapter 3 that the high point shoulder measurement is good for blouses with a front opening, and the center front measurement is used for blouses without one. However, a top with a loop closure on the center front opening falls between the two definitions. In this instance, it is difficult to accurately measure the front length at the center front; therefore, the high point shoulder would be a better measurement (see Figure 9.1). Conversely, if there is ruffling down the sides of the blouse, as shown in Figure 9.2, it would be better to measure using the center front point rather than measuring over the bulk of the ruffle at the high point shoulder. It is up to you the technician to decide which measurement method is better suited to your garment style.

1. *Front Length (garments with a front opening)*—Measure from high point shoulder at neck straight down, parallel to center front, to bottom of garment at front. If garment has a collar, gently lift it away from shoulder-neck measuring point.

2. *Center Front Length (garments with a plain front; no front opening)*—Measure from center front neck joining seams straight down to bottom of garment at center front. [Note: A garment with a front opening may still require point of measure 1, Front Length, if neckline is unusual or is difficult to measure.]

3. *Center Back Length*—Measure from center back neck joining seams straight down to bottom of garment at center back. If needed, gently lift collar away from back neck to expose joining seam.

4. *Side Length*—Measure from bottom of armhole/side seam straight down to bottom of garment along side of garment. Do not follow natural curve of garment's side seam, unless otherwise indicated. If

Figure 9.1 Selecting the high point shoulder measurement for front length.

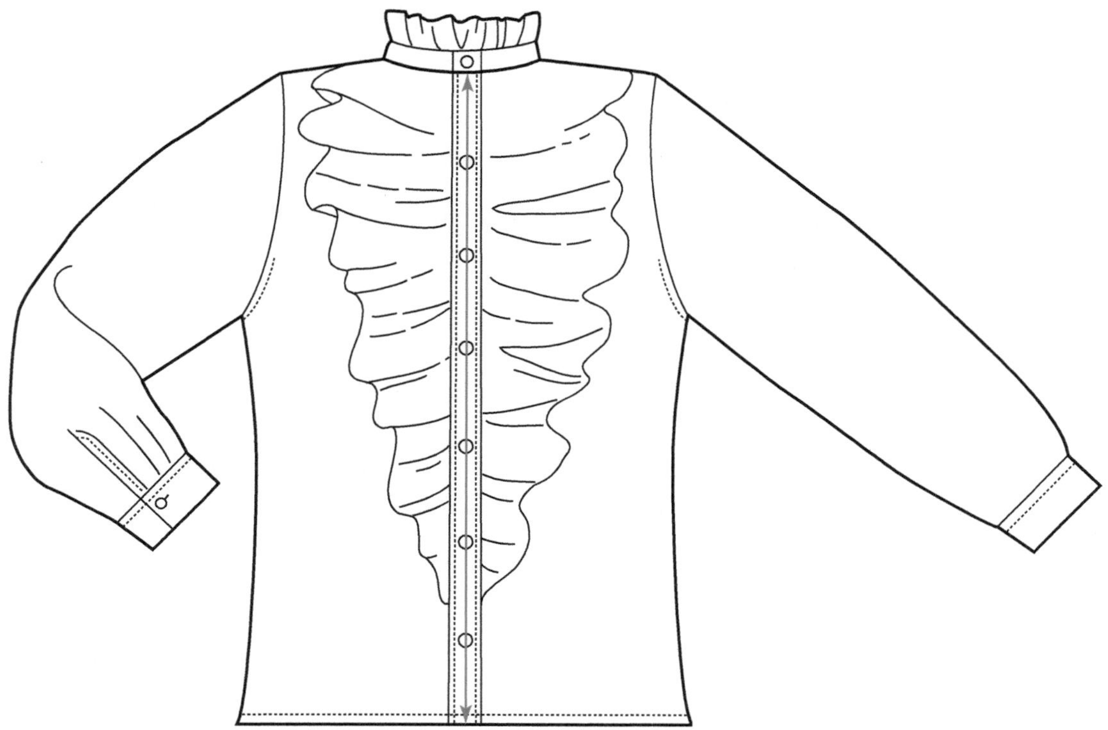

Figure 9.2 Selecting the center front measurement for front length.

needed, gently lift sleeve away from armhole/side seam joining seam.

5. *Front Bodice Length (garments with a front opening)*—Measure from high point shoulder at neck straight down, parallel to center front, to top edge of waistband, joining seam, or rib. If garment has a collar, gently lift it away from shoulder-neck measuring point.

6. *Center Front Bodice Length (garments with a plain front; no front opening)*—Measure from center front neck joining seam straight down to top edge of waistband, joining seam, or rib. [Note: A garment with a center opening may still require point of measure 5, Front Bodice Length, if neckline is unusual or is difficult to measure.]

7. *Center Back Bodice Length*—Measure from center back neck joining seam straight down to top edge of waistband, joining seam, or rib. If needed, gently lift collar away from back neck to expose joining seam.

8. *Side Seam Bodice Length*—Measure from bottom of armhole/side seam straight down to top edge of waistband, joining seam, or rib, along side of garment, following natural curve of garment's side seam, unless otherwise indicated. If needed, gently lift sleeve away from armhole/side seam joining seam. [Note: You can take side seam bodice measurement straight rather than contoured if joining seam/rib can be extended, but indicate change on spec sheet.]

10. *Chest Width Circumference (woven)*—Measure from edge of garment/side seam to edge of garment/side seam straight across garment at a point 1" below armhole. Double this measurement.

12. *Chest Width Circumference/Raglan Sleeve (woven)*—Measure from edge of garment/side seam to edge of garment/side seam straight across garment at a point _____" below high point shoulder. Double this measurement. [Note: You will have to determine number of inches down from high point shoulder for each raglan sleeve style based on depth of sleeve. Then indicate this number on spec sheet.]

13. *Across Shoulder*—Measure straight across front from armhole seam/edge to armhole seam/edge at shoulder seam or across natural shoulder fold line created if there is no seam.

14. *Shoulder Width*—Measure from neckband/collar/ribbing joining seam or neckline edge to top of armhole seam at shoulder, taken along shoulder seam or across natural shoulder fold line created if there is no seam.

15. *Across Chest*—Measure 2½" down from collar/rib joining seam at center front straight across front of garment from armhole seam/edge to armhole seam/edge. [Note: The 2½" measurement point is for misses/women's wear only and may need to be adjusted up or down ¼" to ½" accordingly for men's, children's, junior's, and large/plus sizes. Indicate any changes on spec sheet.]

16. *Across Back*—Measure 4" down from collar/rib joining seam at center back straight across back of garment from armhole seam/edge to armhole seam/edge. [Note: The 4" measurement point is for misses/women's wear only and may need to be adjusted up or down ¼" to ½" accordingly for men's, children's, junior's, and large/plus sizes. Indicate any changes on spec sheet.]

17. *Across Chest/Center Armhole*—Measure at one-half depth of armhole straight across front of garment from armhole seam/edge to armhole seam/edge.

18. *Across Back/Center Armhole*—Measure at one-half depth of armhole straight across back of garment from armhole seam/edge to armhole seam/edge.

20. *Waist Width Circumference (woven)*—Measure from edge of garment/side seam to edge of garment/side seam straight across garment on seam or at narrowest point of waist taper at a point _____" below high point shoulder. Double this measurement. [Note: You will have to determine number of inches down from high point shoulder for each raglan sleeve style based on depth of sleeve. Then indicate this number on spec sheet.]

22. *Bottom Band Circumference (woven top)*—Measure from side of bottom band to side of bottom band along center of band, following natural contour of waistband. Double this measurement.

24. *Bottom Band Width Circumference, Stretched (woven top)*—Measure from side of bottom band to side of bottom band straight across center of band in a fully extended position. Double this measurement.

25. *Bottom Band/Ribbing Height (knit or woven top)*—Measure from band/ribbing joining seam straight down to bottom edge of band/rib opening. [Note: If band is shaped or contoured, indicate special measurement instructions on spec sheet.]

27. *Bottom Opening/Sweep Width Circumference (woven top)*—Measure from edge of garment/side seam to edge of garment/side seam straight across garment at bottom opening. Double this measurement. [Note: If sweep has pleats, measure with pleats closed or relaxed.]

29. *Vented Bottom Opening/Sweep Width Circumference (woven top)*—Measure from edge of garment/side seam to edge of garment/side seam straight across garment at top of side vents. Do not follow natural curve of garment. Double this measurement. [Note: If vents are too high to measure sweep, indicate opening at appropriate position, e.g., midriff opening.]

31. *Circular Bottom Opening/Sweep Width Circumference (woven top)*—Measure from edge of garment/side seam to edge of garment/side seam, following natural contour of garment at bottom opening. Double this measurement.

32. *Yoke Width Front*—Measure from armhole seam/edge to armhole seam/edge straight across front of

garment, ignoring contours or points, at yoke-body joining seams. [Note: If yoke is asymmetrical, indicate changes in measuring as needed on spec sheet.]

33. *Yoke Width Back*—Measure from armhole seam/edge to armhole seam/edge straight across back of garment, ignoring contours or points, at yoke-body joining seam. [Note: If yoke is asymmetrical, indicate changes in measuring as needed on spec sheet.]

34. *Yoke Depth Front*—Measure from high point shoulder at neck straight down to bottom of front yoke-body joining seam. Gently lift collar away from shoulder-neck joining seam if needed.

35. *Yoke Back Depth*—Measure from center back neck joining seam straight down to bottom of back yoke-body joining seam. Gently lift collar away from back neck joining seam if needed.

36. *Sleeve Length Top Armhole*—Measure along top of sleeve/fold, following contour of sleeve from armhole seam at shoulder to bottom of sleeve opening, including cuff.

37. *Sleeve Length Top Neck*—Measure along top of sleeve/fold, following contour of sleeve from sleeve-neck joining seam/edge to edge of sleeve opening, including cuff. Gently lift collar at sleeve-neck joining seam if needed.

38. *Sleeve Length Center Back*—Measure from center back neck joining seam or from a point above neck at an imaginary line, that of a joining seam, along top of sleeve/fold, following contour of sleeve to edge of sleeve opening, including cuff.

39. *Sleeve Length Underarm*—Measure straight from the bottom of armhole along sleeve seam to edge of sleeve opening, including cuff.

41. *Straight Armhole Width Circumference (woven)*—Measure from top of shoulder joining seam/edge straight down to bottom of armhole. Double this measurement.

43. *Curved Armhole Width Circumference (woven)*—Measure from top of shoulder joining seam/edge to bottom of armhole, following contour of armhole. Double this measurement.

44. *Armhole Front*—Measure on front of garment from top of shoulder at neckline joining seam/edge to bottom of armhole, following contour of armhole. Gently lift collar away from neckline joining seam if needed.

45. *Armhole Back*—Measure on back of garment from top of shoulder at neck joining seam/edge to bottom of armhole, following contour of armhole. Gently lift collar away from neck joining seam if needed.

47. *Armhole Width Circumference Straight (woven)*—Measure from top of shoulder seam at a point _____" below neckline joining seam/edge straight down to bottom of armhole. Double this measurement. [Note: Gently move collar away from neck joining seam if needed when measuring down _____" to armhole start point. Indicate number of inches measured down on spec sheet.]

49. *Muscle Width Circumference (woven)*—Measure from inner sleeve edge/seam to outer sleeve edge/fold at a point 1" below armhole and parallel to sleeve opening. Double this measurement.

51. *Elbow Width Circumference (woven)*—Measure from inner sleeve edge/seam to outer sleeve edge/fold straight across sleeve at a point one-half of the underarm sleeve length and parallel to sleeve opening at wrist or cuff. Double this measurement. [Note: If sleeve is three-quarter length, indicate new point of measure on spec sheet.]

53. *Sleeve Opening Width Circumference (woven)*—Measure from inner sleeve edge/seam to outer sleeve

edge/fold straight across bottom edge of sleeve opening. Double this measurement.

55. *Sleeve Opening Width Circumference, Stretched (woven)*—Measure from inner sleeve edge/seam to outer sleeve edge/fold straight across bottom edge of sleeve opening in a fully extended position. Double this measurement.

56. *Cuff Length Sleeve*—Measure from outside end of buttonhole to center of button straight along center of cuff. Open cuff out as flat as possible when measuring. [Note: If cuff length is contoured, measure along center-most point.]

57. *Cuff/Ribbing Height Sleeve*—Measure from cuff joining seam or top of ribbing straight down to bottom edge of cuff or rib opening. [Note: If cuff is contoured, indicate changes made to measurement on spec sheet.]

58. *Neck Depth Front (garments with a plain front/asymmetrical front opening)*—Measure from center back neck joining seam/edge straight down to center front neck joining seam/edge.

59. *Neck Depth Center Front (garments with a center front opening)*—Measure from center back neck joining seam/edge straight down to center of first button at center front of garment.

60. *Neck Drop Front*—Measure from an imaginary line connecting neckline edges straight down to center front neck opening edge. Use a ruler if needed to connect top neckline edges.

61. *Neck Drop Back*—Measure from an imaginary line connecting neckline edges straight down to center back neck opening edge. This measurement is taken with front of garment faceup. Use a ruler to connect top neckline edges if needed.

62. *Neck Width, No Collar*—Measure from inside neck edge/seam to inside neck edge/seam straight across back neck at widest point. This measurement is taken with front of garment faceup.

63. *Neck Width, Collar*—Measure straight across back neck from neck-shoulder joining seam to neck-shoulder joining seam or natural shoulder line if no seam. This measurement is taken with back of garment faceup.

65. *Neck Edge Width Circumference (woven)*—Measure from neck edge/seam/fold to neck edge/seam/fold along top opening edge, following natural contour of neck opening. Garment should be positioned with one shoulder on top of the other and with front and back neck edges meeting. Double this measurement.

67. *Neck Edge Width Circumference, Stretched (woven)*—Measure from neck edge/seam/fold to neck edge/seam/fold along top opening edge in a fully extended position. Garment should be positioned with one shoulder on top of the other and with front and back neck edges meeting. Double this measurement.

69. *Neck Base Circumference (woven)*—Measure from neck edge/seam to neck edge/seam along collar/rib joining seam or neckline edge, following natural contour of neck opening. Garment should be buttoned or zippered, if applicable, with one shoulder seam positioned on top of the other and with front and back neck edges meeting. Double this measurement.

70. *Neckband Length*—Measure from outside end of buttonhole to center of buttonhole across neckband, following contour of neckband.

71. *Collar Length*—Measure from one end of collar to other end of collar along neck joining seam.

72. *Collar Height*—Measure from collar/rib joining seam at center back neck straight up to outer edge of collar/rib.

73. *Collar Band Height*—Measure from collar joining seam at center back straight up to neckband joining seam at center back.

74. *Collar Point Length*—Measure from collar joining seam to outer edge of collar along collar point edge. [Note: If collar is rounded, measure at a point parallel to center back and indicate change on spec sheet.]

75. *Collar Point Spread (pointed collars only)*—Measure, with collar band buttoned and collar in place, from collar point straight across collar edge to collar point.

76. *Lapel Width*

A. *Notched*—Measure from lower lapel notch straight across to lapel fold at a point perpendicular to garment center front.

B. *Without Notches*—Measure from lapel edge straight across widest point of lapel to lapel fold at a point _____" down from center back collar joining seam and perpendicular to front of garment.

77. *Center Front Extension*—Measure from an imaginary line at center front of garment horizontally to finished outer edge of front extended piece.

78. *Placket Length*—Measure from top edge of placket straight down to bottom of placket opening along center of placket.

79. *Placket Width*—Measure from placket joining seam straight across placket to placket edge at fold.

80. *Keyhole Length*—Measure from outer edge of neckline straight down to bottom of keyhole opening.

122. *Vent/Slit*

A. *Height*—Measure from top of vent/slit straight down to bottom of vent/slit along edge of vent/slit.

B. *Width*—Measure top of vent/slit from edge/fold straight across to vent/slit placket stitching at a point parallel to garment hemline.

123. *Pleat Depth*—Measure from outer edge of pleat at fold/crease to inner fold of pleat. [Note 1: It is a good idea to indicate what type of pleat is being measured, e.g., box, inverted, knife, kick, kilt, or envelope. Note 2: If pleats are not parallel or symmetrical, indicate any special instructions on spec sheet.]

124. *Distance Between Pleats*—Measure from start of pleat to start of pleat, excluding pleat depth at a point directly below pleat joining seam. [Note: If pleats are not parallel or symmetrical, indicate any special instructions on spec sheet.]

125. *Applied Pocket Height*—Measure from top edge of pocket to bottom edge of pocket along center of pocket. [Note: For contoured or irregularly shaped pockets, take a second measurement and indicate point of measure on spec sheet.]

126. *Applied Pocket Width*—Measure from side of pocket to side of pocket along top edge of pocket. [Note: For contoured or irregularly shaped pockets, take a second measurement and indicate point of measure on spec sheet.]

127. *Pocket Opening Within a Seam*—Measure from top of pocket to bottom of pocket along edge of pocket opening.

128. *Belt Length*

A. *Total*—Measure from end of belt at buckle along center of belt to opposite end of belt, following contour.

B. *Circumference*—Measure from end of belt at buckle along center of belt to middle hole at opposite end.

129. *Belt Width (or Height)*—Measure from edge of belt straight across to edge of belt. [Note: If belt is contoured, indicate points of measure on spec sheet.]

130. *Belt Loop Length*—Measure from top of belt loop straight down/vertically to bottom of belt loop along center of belt loop. [Note: Fashion-forward

or irregularly shaped belt loops may require further spec instructions. Indicate points of measure on spec sheet.]

131. *Belt Loop Width*—Measure belt loop from edge of belt loop straight across/horizontally to edge of belt loop. [Note: Fashion-forward or irregularly shaped belt loops may require further spec instructions. Indicate points of measure on spec sheet.]

132. *Tie Length*—Measure from end of tie/joining seam straight down to tie end along center of tie.

133. *Tie Width*

A. *Straight*—Measure from edge of tie straight across to edge of tie.
B. *Contoured*—Measure from edge of tie straight across to edge of tie at widest point of tie.

134. *Flounce/Ruffle Width*—Measure from flounce/ruffle joining seam straight across to outer edge of flounce/ruffle. [Note: If flounce/ruffle is contoured, measure along narrowest and widest points if possible and indicate changes on spec sheet.]

135. *Strap Length*—Measure from strap joining seam along center of strap to end of strap. [Note: If a strap is contoured or has a contoured edge, measure along center, approximating center end point, or indicate instructions as needed on spec sheet.]

136. *Strap Width*—Measure from edge of strap straight across to edge of strap. [Note: If strap is contoured, measure along narrowest and widest points if possible and indicate changes on spec sheet.]

137. *Front Hood Length*—Measure from top of hood to bottom of hood at center front joining seam along opening edge of hood.

138. *Back Hood Length*—Measure from top of hood at center front to bottom of hood at center back joining seam along outside curve of hood fold/seam.

139. *Hood Width*—Measure from front opening edge of hood straight across to back of hood at fold along widest point of hood.

140. *Flange Depth*—Measure from center back neck joining seam straight down to bottom of flange at center back. [Note: If flange is contoured or asymmetrical, indicate point of measure on spec sheet.]

141. *Shoulder Pad Length*—Measure from edge of pad straight across to edge of pad along center of pad or natural shoulder line of pad.

142. *Shoulder Pad Width*—Measure from side of pad straight across to side of pad along edge of pad if straight, or at widest point of pad if curved.

143. *Straight Edge Shoulder Pad Height*—Measure from top of pad straight down to bottom of pad along center of pad.

144. *Curved Edge Shoulder Pad Height*—Stick a 1" straight pin into thickest part of shoulder pad. Push pin all way through pad until head of pin rests on top of pad. Be sure not to crush pad. Measure portion of pin sticking out of pad. Subtract this figure from 1" (length of pin) to get shoulder pad height.

145. *Shoulder Pad Placement*—Measure from neck edge or joining seam straight across shoulder seam or natural shoulder line to start of shoulder pad.

146. *Pleats Placement*

A. *Front Pleat Top*—Measure distance from center front of garment straight across to start of first pleat at a point parallel to garment hem. [Note: You may need to use armhole or side seam as a starting point if there is no center front seam or placket.]
B. *Back Pleat Top*—Measure distance from armhole seam/side seam (depending on pleat placement) to first pleat at a point parallel to garment hem.

147. *Button Placement*—Refer to point of measure 59, Neck Depth Center Front, for placement of first

button. Then measure distance of first button to second button. Be sure when measuring that button at bust point is lined up to apex of bust. Adjust all buttons accordingly and respace as needed.

148. *Pocket Placement*

A. *Top Pocket Vertical*—Measure from shoulder-neck joining seam straight down to top edge of pocket.
B. *Top Pocket Horizontal*—Measure from center front straight across to side of pocket at top edge.
C. *Front Bottom Pocket Vertical*—Measure from waistband/joining seam/edge straight down to top edge of pocket.
D. *Front Bottom Pocket Horizontal*—Measure from center front straight across to side of pocket at top edge.
E. *Back Bottom Pocket Vertical*—Measure from waistband/joining seam/edge straight down to top edge of pocket.
F. *Back Bottom Pocket Horizontal*—Measure from center back straight across to side of pocket at top edge.
G. *Pocket from Side Seam*—Measure from side seam straight across to top of pocket. [Note: If pocket is contoured at sides, a top and bottom pocket size and placement must be measured and added to spec sheet.]

149. *Belt Loop Placement*

A. *Front*—Measure from center front of garment horizontally across to center of first front belt loop.
B. *Back*—Measure from center back of garment horizontally across to center of first back belt loop.
C. *Side Seam to Front*—Measure from center of side seam belt loop to center of front belt loop.
D. *Side Seam to Back*—Measure from center of side seam belt loop to center of back belt loop.

150. *Dart Placement*

A. *High Point Shoulder Bust Dart*—Measure from shoulder-neck joining seam or at a point _____" from shoulder-neck seam straight down, parallel to center front, to top of dart. [Note: The _____" from shoulder seam measurement is to be used for darts that are too short to be measured from high point shoulder. Be sure to indicate _____" measurement on spec sheet.]
B. *Center Front Bust Dart*—Measure from center front of garment straight across to top of dart.
C. *Side Seam Bust Dart*—Measure from underarm/side seam joining seam down along contour of side seam to bottom of dart.
D. *High Point Shoulder Princess Dart*—Measure from shoulder-neck joining seam straight down to top of dart.
E. *Center Front Princess Dart*—Measure from center front of garment straight across to top of dart.

CHAPTER 9 TERMS

When working with woven tops, you may come across the following garment terms. If you are unfamiliar with any of them, please look up the definitions listed in the glossary at the end of this text.

Blouse:

Basic or front buttoning
Body shirt or fitted
Bow
Cossack
Cowboy (Western)
Drawstring
Dress Shirt
Epaulet
Guayabera
Hawaiian
Jabot
Nautical/Middy
Oversized
Peasant
Stock-tie
Tunic
Wrap

SPEC SHEET: Woven top | **STYLE**

SEASON:	DESCRIPTION:
LABEL: (SIZE CATEGORY)	
DATE:	
TECHNICAL SKETCH Basic blouse	SKETCH/PHOTO

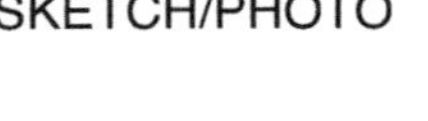

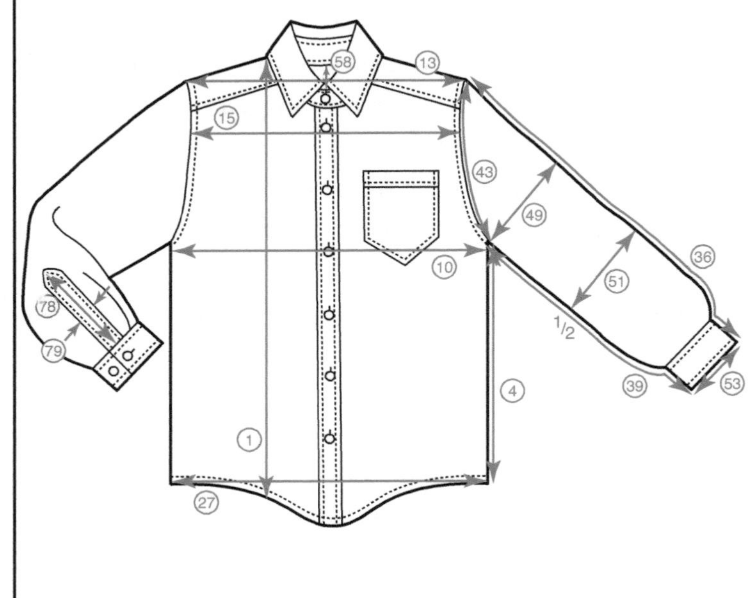

CODE	POINT OF MEASURE	TOL. +/–	4	S/6	8	M/10	12	L/14	16	XL/18
1.	Front length	1/2								
2.	Center front length	1/2								
3.	Center back length	1/2								
4.	Side length	1/4								
10.	Chest width circumference	1/2								
13.	Across shoulder	1/4								
15.	Across chest	1/4								
16.	Across back	1/4								
27.	Bottom opening/sweep width circumference	1/2-3/4								
32.	Yoke width front	1/4								
33.	Yoke width back	1/4								
34.	Yoke depth front	1/8								
35.	Yoke depth back	1/8								
36.	Sleeve length top armhole	3/8								
39.	Sleeve length underarm	3/8								
43.	Curved armhole width circumference	3/8								
49.	Muscle width circumference	1/4								
51.	Elbow width circumference	1/4								

(Tolerance 1/4-3/8 S, M, L, XL = 3/8" 4-18 = 1/4")

The measured garment spec sheets are for ***illustrative purposes only*** and should not be used as industry standards

CODE	POINT OF MEASURE		TOL. +/–	4	S/6	8	M/10	12	L/14	16	XL/18
53.	Sleeve opening width circumference		1/4								
56.	Cuff length sleeve		1/4								
57	Cuff/ribbing height sleeve		1/8								
58.	Neck depth front		1/8								
63.	Neck width collar		1/8								
69.	Neck base circumference		1/4								
70.	Neckband length		1/4								
71.	Collar length		1/4								
72.	Collar height		1/8								
73.	Collar band height		1/16								
74.	Collar point length		1/8								
75.	Collar point spread		1/4								
77.	Center front extension		1/8								
78.	Placket length		1/4								
79.	Placket width		1/8								
123.	Pleat depth		1/8								
124.	Distance between pleats		1/16								
125.	Applied pocket height		1/4								
126.	Applied pocket width		1/4								
146.	Pleats placement	A. Front pleat top	1/4								
		B. Back pleat top	1/4								
147.	Button placement		1/8								
148.	Pocket placement	A. Top pocket vertical	1/8								
		B. Top pocket horizontal	1/8								
		C. Pocket from side seam	1/8								

COMMENTS:

The measured garment spec sheets are for ***illustrative purposes only*** and should not be used as industry standards

SPEC SHEET: Woven top | **STYLE**

SEASON: Spring	DESCRIPTION: Oversized Blouse
LABEL: (SIZE CATEGORY) Missy	
DATE:	
TECHNICAL SKETCH Basic blouse	SKETCH/PHOTO

CODE	POINT OF MEASURE	TOL. +/–	4	S/6	8	M/10	12	L/14	16	XL/18
1.	Front length	1/2				30 1/2				
2.	Center front length	1/2								
3.	Center back length	1/2				30 1/2				
4.	Side length	1/4				20				
10.	Chest width circumference	1/2				48 1/2				
13.	Across shoulder	1/4				18 1/4				
15.	Across chest 6" from H.P.S.	1/4				17 1/4				
16.	Across back	1/4								
27.	Bottom opening/sweep width circumference	1/2-3/4				48 1/2				
32.	Yoke width front	1/4				6 1/4				
33.	Yoke width back	1/4				19				
34.	Yoke depth front	1/8				3 1/2				
35.	Yoke depth back	1/8				1/2				
36.	Sleeve length top armhole	3/8				23 1/2				
39.	Sleeve length underarm	3/8				19				
43.	Curved armhole width circumference	3/8				20 1/4				
49.	Muscle width circumference	1/4				17 3/4				
51.	Elbow width circumference	1/4				15 1/2				

(Tolerance 1/4-3/8 S, M, L, XL = 3/8" 4-18 = 1/4")

The measured garment spec sheets are for ***illustrative purposes only*** and should not be used as industry standards

SPEC SHEET: Woven top **STYLE**

CODE	POINT OF MEASURE	TOL. +/–	4	S/6	8	M/10	12	L/14	16	XL/18
53.	Sleeve opening width circumference	1/4				8				
56.	Cuff length sleeve	1/4				8 1/2				
57.	Cuff/ribbing height sleeve	1/8				2 3/4				
58.	Neck depth front	1/8				1 1/8				
63.	Neck width collar	1/8				7				
69.	Neck base circumference	1/4				18				
70.	Neckband length	1/4				17				
71.	Collar length	1/4				15 3/4				
72.	Collar height	1/8				2 1/8				
73.	Collar band height	1/8				1 1/8				
74.	Collar point length	1/8				3				
75.	Collar point spread	1/4				3				
77.	Center front extension	1/8				5/8				
78.	Placket length	1/4				4 1/4				
79.	Placket width	1/8				1				
123.	Pleat depth **(2 pleats, sleeve)**	1/8				3/4				
124.	Distance between pleats	1/8				1				
125.	Applied pocket width	1/8								
126.	Applied pocket height	1/8								
146.	Pleats placement A. Front pleat top	1/4								
	B. Back pleat top	1/4								
147.	Button placement	1/8				3 3/4				
148.	Pocket placement A. Top pocket vertical	1/8								
	B. Top pocket horizontal	1/8								
	G. Pocket from side seam	1/8								
122.	**Vent/slit A. Height**	1/4				10				
123.	**Pleat depth (back yoke box pleat)**	1/8				3/4				
124.	**Distance between pleats (back yoke box pleat)**	1/8				2				

COMMENTS: **All topstiching is 1/16" from edge/seams**
hem depth rolled and stitched is 1/2" wide

The measured garment spec sheets are for ***illustrative purposes only*** and should not be used as industry standards

CHAPTER 10

Woven Skirts

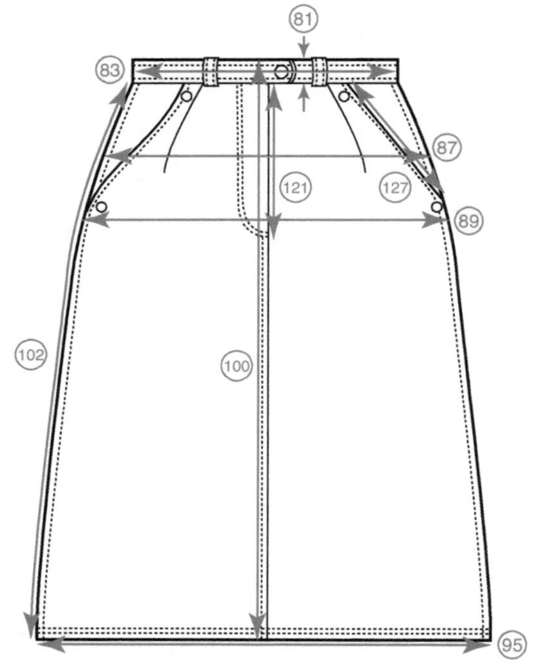

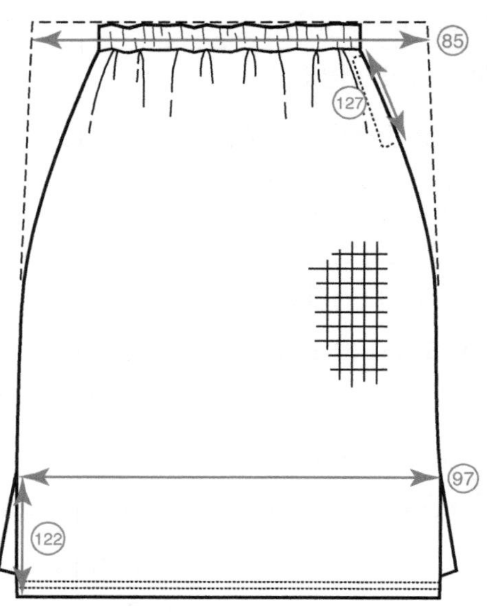

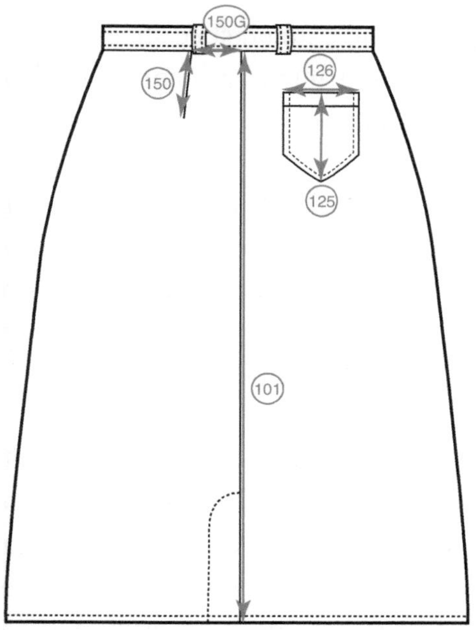

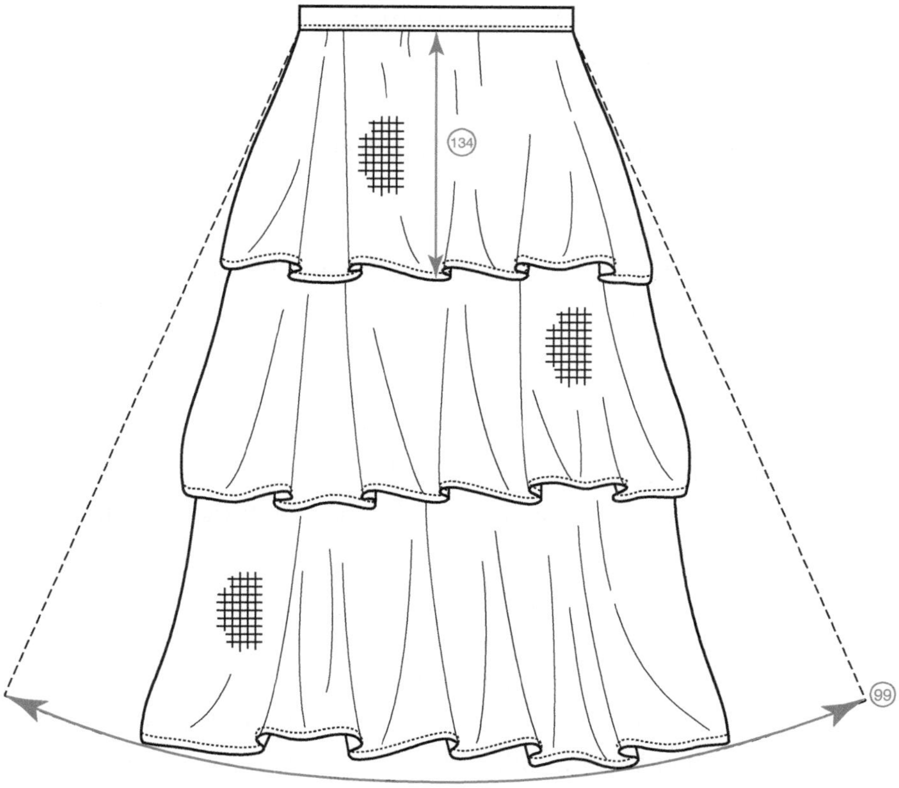

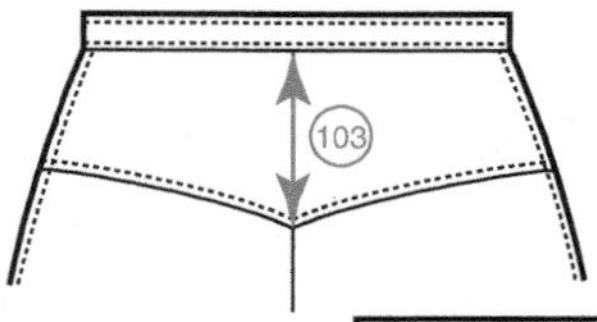

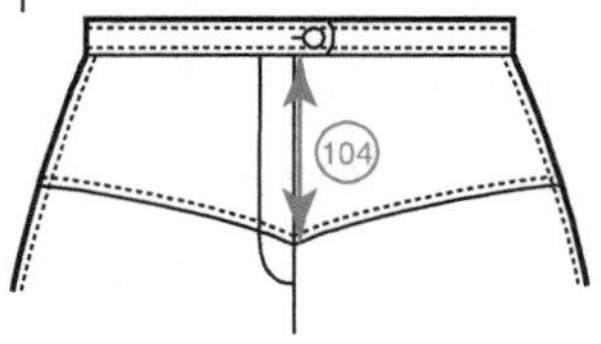

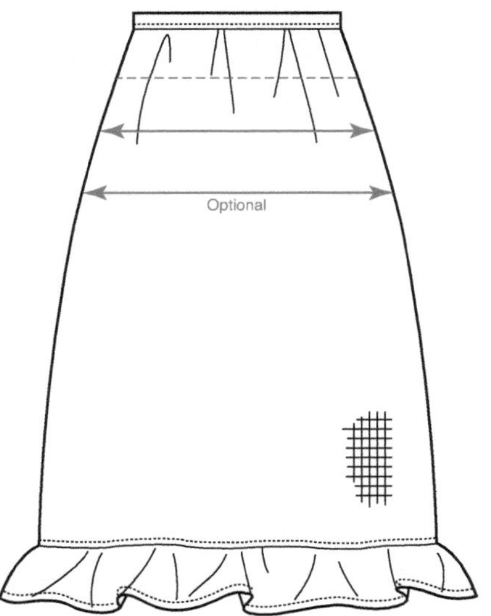

Figure 10.1 Choosing the best hip measurement point.

Measuring Woven Skirts

A-line, kick-pleat, straight, and wrap are just a few of the types of woven skirt that can be evaluated using the woven skirt spec sheet. Just like measuring a top, there are times when more than one method of measurement can be used for a measurement point. For example, most skirts are measured at both the high and low hip points. If you are measuring a granny skirt with a large amount of shirring at the waist (see Figure 10.1), the high point measurement will be difficult to obtain accurately. In that situation, as the technician, you may choose to eliminate the high hip measurement and add an additional low hip or across thigh measurement.

81. *Waistband Depth*—Measure from top of waistband edge straight down to bottom of waistband at waistband joining seam. [Note: If waistband is contoured, indicate measurement change on spec sheet.]

83. *Waistband Width Circumference (woven)*—Measure from side of bottom band to side of bottom band along center of band, following natural contour of waistband. Double this measurement.

85. *Waistband Width Circumference, Stretched (woven)*—Measure from side of bottom band to side of bottom band straight across center of band in a fully extended position. Double this measurement.

87. *High Hip Width Circumference (woven)*—Measure from edge of garment/side seam to edge of garment/side seam at a point 4" below bottom edge of waistband/seam, following contour of waist. Double this measurement. [Note: The 4" point is for misses/women's wear only; adjust as needed ½" to 1" up or down for children's, petite's, junior's, or large/plus sizes. Indicate change on spec sheet.]

89. *Low Hip Width Circumference from Waist d(woven)*—Measure from edge of garment/side seam to edge of garment/side seam at a point 7" below bottom edge of waistband/seam, following contour of waist. Double this measurement. [Note: The 7" point is for misses/women's wear only; adjust as needed ½" to 1" up or down for children's, petite's, junior's, or large/plus sizes. Indicate change on spec sheet.]

95. *Bottom Opening/Sweep Width Circumference (woven skirt)*—Measure from edge of garment/side seam to edge of garment/side seam straight across garment at bottom opening. Double this measurement. [Note: If sweep has pleats, measure with pleats closed or relaxed.]

97. *Vented Bottom Opening/Sweep Width Circumference (woven skirt)*—Measure from edge of garment/side seam to edge of garment/side seam straight across garment at top of side vents. Double this measurement. [Note: Indicate on spec sheet if there is only one vent or if vent hits at a point other than sweep, e.g., thigh opening.]

99. *Circular Bottom Opening/Sweep Width Circumference (woven skirt)*—Measure from edge of garment/side seam to edge of garment/side seam, following natural contour of garment at bottom opening. Double this measurement.

100. *Center Front Skirt Length*—Measure from bottom of waistband/seam (top edge if not banded, or stitching if self-elastic/drawstring casing) straight down to bottom of garment at center front. [Note: A fashion-forward skirt may have an asymmetrical waist. Indicate top point of measure on spec sheet.]

101. *Center Back Skirt Length*—Measure from the bottom of the waistband/seam (top edge if not banded, or stitching if self-elastic/drawstring casing) straight down to the bottom of garment at center front. [Note: A fashion-forward skirt may have an asymmetrical waist. Indicate top point of measure on spec sheet.]

102. *Side Skirt Length*—Measure from bottom edge of waistband/seam (top edge if not banded, or stitching if self-elastic/drawstring casing) to bottom of garment along side seam/fold of garment, following any contour.

103. *Skirt/Pant Yoke Depth Front*—Measure from bottom of waistband/seam (top edge if not banded, or stitching if self-elastic/drawstring casing) straight down to bottom of yoke joining seam at center front. [Note: If yoke is contoured, indicate point of measure on spec sheet.]

104. *Skirt/Pant Yoke Depth Back*—Measure from bottom of waistband/seam (top edge if not banded, or stitching if self-elastic/drawstring casing) straight down to bottom of yoke joining seam at center back. [Note: If yoke is contoured, indicate point of measure on spec sheet.]

121. *Fly/Zipper*

A. *Length*—Measure from top of fly/zipper opening straight down to bottom of fly/zipper opening at zipper stop or bar tack.

B. *Fly/Zipper Width*—Measure top of fly/zipper at joining seam from edge/fold straight across to fly/zipper placket stitching.

122. *Vent/Slit*

A. *Height*—Measure from top of vent/slit straight down to bottom of vent/slit along edge of vent/slit.

B. *Width*—Measure top of vent/slit from edge/fold straight across to vent/slit placket stitching at a point parallel to garment hemline.

123. *Pleat Depth*—Measure from outer edge of pleat at fold/crease to inner fold of pleat. [Note 1: It is a good idea to indicate what type of pleat is being measured, e.g., box, inverted, knife, kick, kilt, or envelope. Note 2: If pleats are not parallel or symmetrical, indicate any special instructions on spec sheet.]

124. *Distance Between Pleats*—Measure from start of pleat to start of pleat, excluding pleat depth at a point directly below pleat joining seam. [Note: If pleats are not parallel or symmetrical, indicate any special instructions on spec sheet.]

125. *Applied Pocket Height*—Measure from top edge of pocket to bottom edge of pocket along center of pocket. [Note: For contoured or irregularly shaped pockets, take a second measurement and indicate point of measure on spec sheet.]

126. *Applied Pocket Width*—Measure from side of pocket to side of pocket along top edge of pocket. [Note: For contoured or irregularly shaped pockets, take a second measurement and indicate point of measure on spec sheet.]

127. *Pocket Opening Within a Seam*—Measure from top of pocket to bottom of pocket along edge of pocket opening.

128. *Belt Length*

A. *Total*—Measure from end of belt at buckle along center of belt to opposite end of belt, following contour.

B. *Circumference*—Measure from end of belt at buckle along center of belt to middle hole at opposite end.

129. *Belt Width (or Height)*—Measure from edge of belt straight across to edge of belt. [Note: If belt is contoured, indicate points of measure on spec sheet.]

130. *Belt Loop Length*—Measure from top of belt loop straight down/vertically to bottom of belt loop along center of belt loop. [Note: Fashion-forward or irregularly shaped belt loops may require further spec instructions. Indicate points of measure on spec sheet.]

131. *Belt Loop Width*—Measure belt loop from edge of belt loop straight across/horizontally to edge of belt loop. [Note: Fashion-forward or irregularly shaped belt loops may require further spec instructions. Indicate points of measure on spec sheet.]

132. *Tie Length*—Measure from end of tie/joining seam straight down to tie end along center of tie.

133. *Tie Width*

A. *Straight*—Measure from edge of tie straight across to edge of tie.

B. *Contoured*—Measure from edge of tie straight across to edge of tie at widest point of tie.

134. *Flounce/Ruffle Width*—Measure from flounce/ruffle joining seam straight across to outer edge of flounce/ruffle. [Note: If flounce/ruffle is contoured, measure along narrowest and widest points if possible and indicate changes on spec sheet.]

146. *Pleats Placement*

C. *Front Pleat Skirt/Pant*—Measure distance from center front of garment waistband joining seam/edge straight across to start of first pleat.

148. *Pocket Placement*

C. *Front Bottom Pocket Vertical*—Measure from waistband/joining seam/edge straight down to top edge of pocket.

D. *Front Bottom Pocket Horizontal*—Measure from center front straight across to side of pocket at top edge.

E. *Back Bottom Pocket Vertical*—Measure from waistband/joining seam/edge straight down to top edge of pocket.

F. *Back Bottom Pocket Horizontal*—Measure from center back straight across to side of pocket at top edge.

G. *Pocket from Side Seam*—Measure from side seam straight across to top of pocket. [Note: If pocket is contoured at sides, a top and bottom pocket size and placement must be measured and added to spec sheet.]

149. *Belt Loop Placement*

A. *Front*—Measure from center front of garment horizontally across to center of first front belt loop.

B. *Back*—Measure from center back of garment horizontally across to center of first back belt loop.

C. *Side Seam to Front*—Measure from center of side seam belt loop to center of front belt loop.

D. *Side Seam to Back*—Measure from center of side seam belt loop to center of back belt loop.

150. *Dart Placement*

F. *Center Front Skirt/Pant*—Measure from center front of garment at waistband joining seam/edge straight across to top of dart.

G. *Center Back Skirt/Pant*—Measure from center back of garment at waistband joining seam/edge straight across to top of dart.

CHAPTER 10 TERMS

When working with woven skirts, you may come across the following garment terms. If you are unfamiliar with any of them, please look up the definitions in the glossary at the end of this text.

Skirt:

A-line
Asymmetric
Fitted (straight)
Gored
Granny
Jean/Denim
Kick pleated
Layered/Tiered
Pleated
Slit
Wrap
Yoke

SPEC SHEET: Woven skirt

STYLE

SEASON:	DESCRIPTION:
LABEL: (SIZE CATEGORY)	
DATE:	
TECHNICAL SKETCH Basic skirt	SKETCH/PHOTO

CODE	POINT OF MEASURE	TOL. +/–	4	S/6	8	M/10	12	L/14	16	XL/18
81.	Waistband depth	1/8								
83.	Waistband width circumference	1/2-3/4								
87.	High hip width circumference	1/2-3/4								
89.	Low hip width circumference	1/2-3/4								
95.	Bottom opening/sweep width circumference	1/2-3/4								
100.	Center front skirt length	3/8								
101.	Center back skirt length	3/8								
102.	Side length skirt	3/8								
121.	Fly/zipper A. Length	1/4								
	B. Width	1/8								
122.	Vent/slit A. Height	1/4								
	B. Width	1/8								
123.	Pleat depth	1/8								
125.	Applied pocket height	1/8								
126.	Applied pocket width	1/8								
127.	Pocket opening	1/4								
146.	Pleats placement C. Front pleat skirt	1/4								
148.	Pocket placement C. Front vertical	1/8								

(Tolerance 1/2-3/4 S, M, L, XL = 3/4" 4-18 = 1/2")

The measured garment spec sheets are for ***illustrative purposes only*** and should not be used as industry standards

CODE	POINT OF MEASURE	TOL. +/–	4	S/6	8	M/10	12	L/14	16	XL/18
	D. Front horizontal	1/8								
	E. Back vertical	1/8								
	F. Back horizontal	1/8								
	G. From side seam	1/8								
149.	Belt loop A. Length	1/8								
	B. Width	1/8								
	C. Placement C.F.	1/8								
	D. Placement C.B.	1/8								
150.	Dart length front	1/8								
	Back	1/8								
	F. Placement C.F.	1/8								
	G. Placement C.B.	1/8								

COMMENTS:

The measured garment spec sheets are for ***illustrative purposes only*** and should not be used as industry standards

SPEC SHEET: Woven skirt

STYLE

SEASON: Early fall	DESCRIPTION: Knee length skirt with a tailored buttonhole
LABEL: (SIZE CATEGORY) Missy	pocket side zipper opening and back kick vent.
DATE:	
TECHNICAL SKETCH Basic skirt	SKETCH/PHOTO

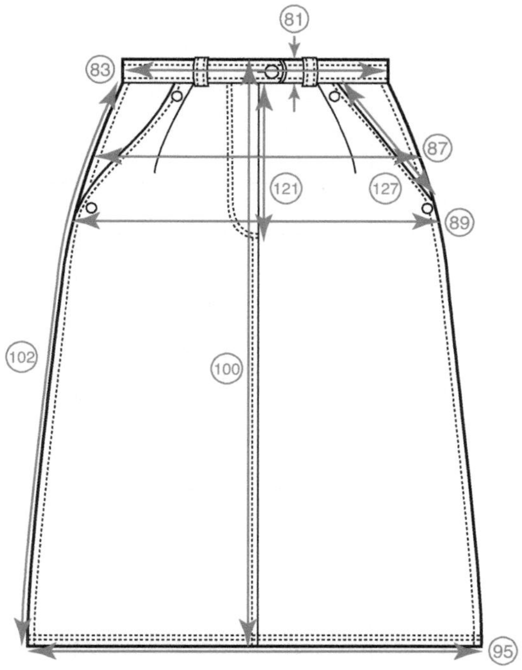

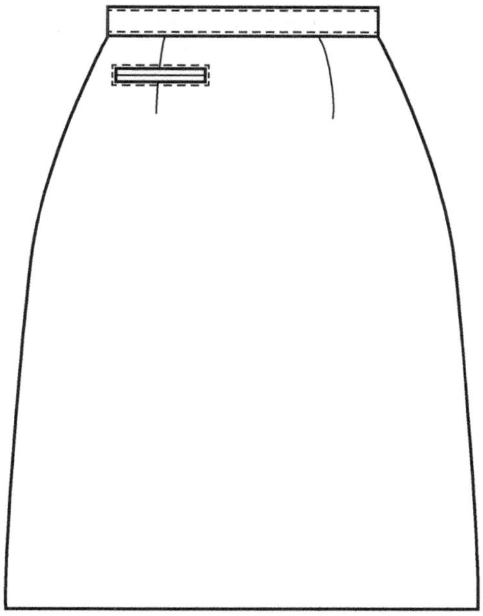

CODE	POINT OF MEASURE	TOL. +/–	4	S/6	8	M/10	12	L/14	16	XL/18
81.	Waistband depth	1/8				1				
83.	Waistband width circumference	1/2-3/4				29				
87.	High hip width circumference	1/2-3/4				36				
89.	Low hip width circumference	1/2-3/4				40				
95.	Bottom opening/sweep width circumference	1/2-3/4				39				
100.	Center front skirt length	3/8				20				
101.	Center back skirt length	3/8				20				
102.	Side length skirt	3/8				20				
121.	Fly/zipper A. Length	1/4				7				
	B. Width **(invisible)**	1/8				-				
122.	Vent/slit A. Height	1/4				7				
	B. Width	1/8				1 1/2				
123.	Pleat depth	1/8								
125.	Applied pocket height **(buttonhole)**	1/8				1/2				
126.	Applied pocket width	1/8								
127.	Pocket opening	1/4				4 1/2				
146.	Pleats placement C. Front pleat skirt	1/4								
148.	Pocket placement C. Front vertical	1/8				1 1/4				

(Tolerance 1/2-3/4 S, M, L, XL = 1/2" 4-18 = 3/4")

The measured garment spec sheets are for ***illustrative purposes only*** and should not be used as industry standards

CODE	POINT OF MEASURE	TOL. +/–	4	S/6	8	M/10	12	L/14	16	XL/18
	D. Front horizontal	1/8								
	E. Back vertical	1/8								
	F. Back horizontal	1/8								
	G. From side seam	1/8				1/2				
149.	Belt loop A. Length	1/8								
	B. Width	1/8								
	C. Placement C.F.	1/8								
	D. Placement C.B.	1/8								
150.	Dart length front	1/8				4 1/2				
	Back **(2 back darts)**	1/8				4				
	F. Placement C.F.	1/8				6 1/2				
	G. Placement C.B.	1/8				4 5/8				
	Distance between back darts	1/8				1 3/8				

COMMENTS:

The measured garment spec sheets are for ***illustrative purposes only*** and should not be used as industry standards

CHAPTER 11

Woven Pants

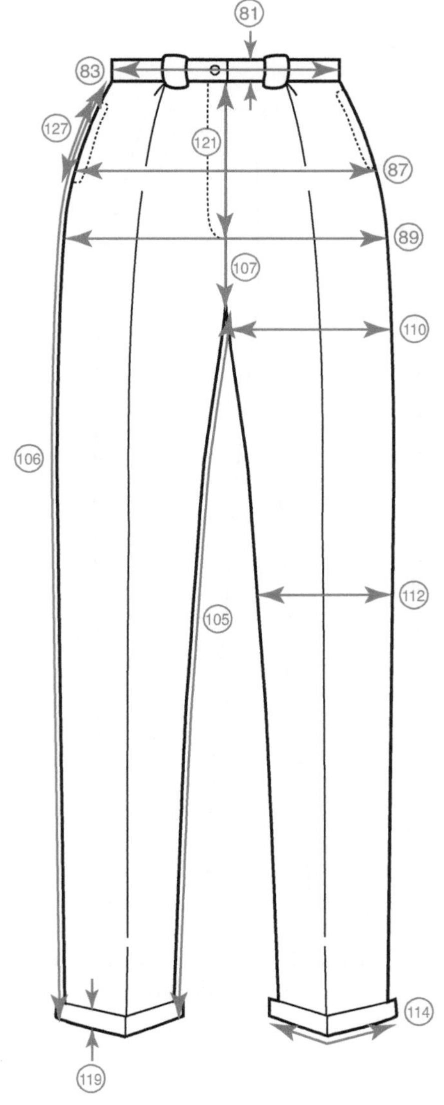

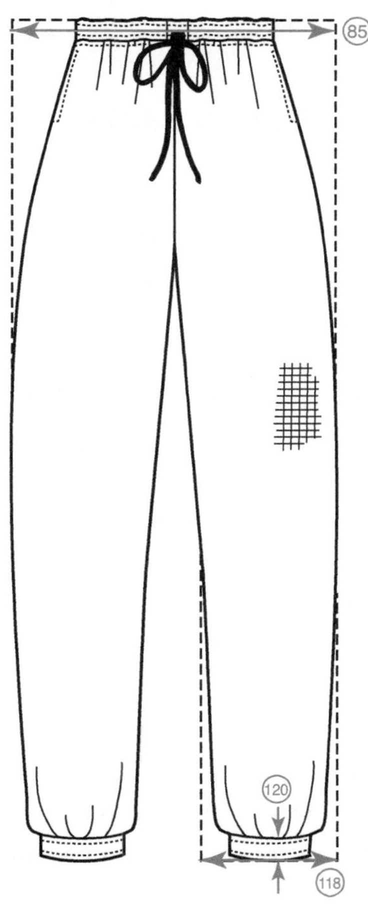

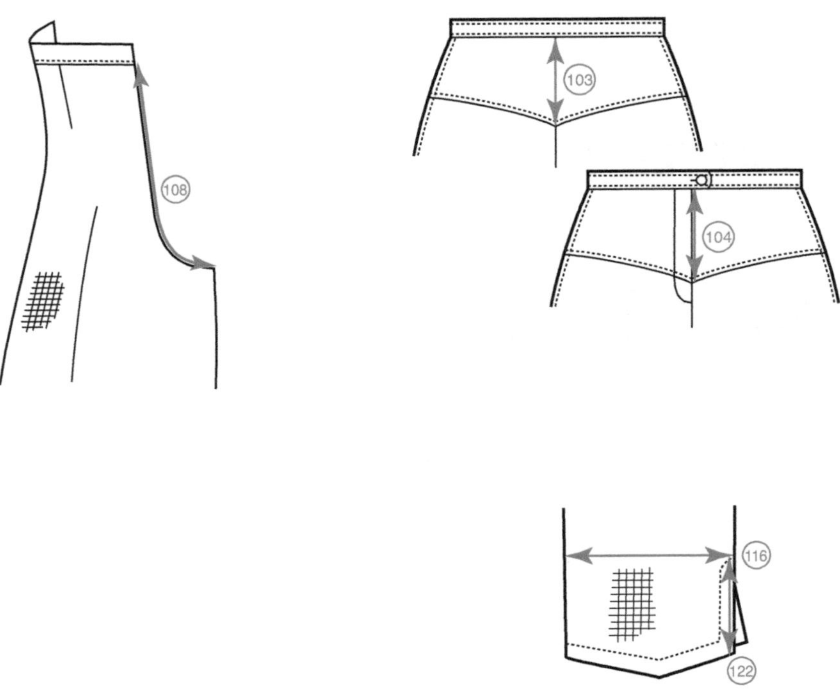

Measuring Woven Pants

The three most common types of woven pant construction are pleated, darted, and flat front. The waistlines may be high, low, or anywhere in between. Leg widths may be anywhere from slim/stovepipe to full palazzo. Because of such variety there will be instances when more than one point of measurement can be used when evaluating a woven pant. For example, the woven pant shown in Figure 11.1 should be measured at the low hip and seat rather than at the high hip and low hip, because of the low-rise design. As always, you will need to pick the measurement point that best represents a specific garment's features.

Unless otherwise stated, woven pants are measured flat, and then the measurement is doubled. When measuring the waist and hip areas, the waistband should line up at the center front and center back top edges, unless the design prohibits that. Pants can be difficult to measure because of the rise. The crotch/rise curve will not lie flat; let it lie

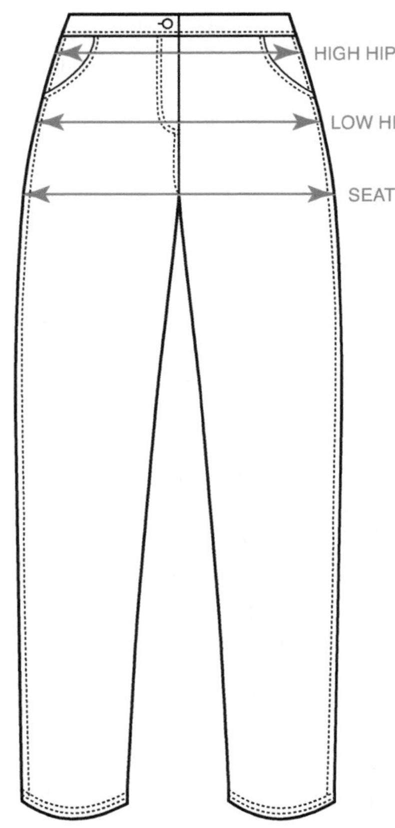

Figure 11.1 Choose the best measurement point based on garment design.

in a natural position. When measuring the pant leg, lay one flat, gently pushing the other aside. It is not necessary to measure both legs; however, an occasional spot-check will ensure continuity. Front and back rises are measured separately and will have to be manipulated slightly in order to measure them in a flat relaxed position.

81. *Waistband Depth*—Measure from top of waistband edge straight down to bottom of waistband at waistband joining seam. [Note: If waistband is contoured, indicate measurement change on spec sheet.]

83. *Waistband Width Circumference (woven)*—Measure from side of bottom band to side of bottom band along center of band, following natural contour of waistband. Double this measurement.

85. *Waistband Width Circumference, Stretched (woven)*—Measure from side of bottom band to side of bottom band straight across center of band in a fully extended position. Double this measurement.

87. *High Hip Width Circumference (woven)*—Measure from edge of garment/side seam to edge of garment/side seam at a point 4" below bottom edge of waistband/seam, following contour of waist. Double this measurement. [Note: The 4" point is for misses/women's wear only; adjust as needed ½" to 1" up or down for children's, petite's, junior's, or large/plus sizes. Indicate change on spec sheet.]

89. *Low Hip Width Circumference from Waist* (woven)—Measure from edge of garment/side seam to edge of garment/side seam at a point 7" below bottom edge of waistband/seam, following contour of waist. Double this measurement. [Note: The 7" point is for misses/women's wear only; adjust as needed ½" to 1" up or down for children's, petite's, junior's, or large/plus sizes. Indicate change on spec sheet.]

91. *Hip Width from High Point Shoulder Circumference (woven)*—Measure from edge of garment/side seam to edge of garment/side seam straight across at a point _____" below high point shoulder. Double this measurement. [Note: You will have to estimate low hip point on garment if there is no waistband and fill in _____" from high point shoulder. This measurement will vary for children's, junior's, misses, and large/plus sizes.]

93. *Hip Seat Width Circumference (woven pant)*—Measure from edge of garment/side seam to edge of garment/side seam at a point _____" up from crotch seam, following contour of waist. Double this measurement. [Note 1: This measurement is useful when waistband sits below natural waistline. Note 2: Adjust _____" up from crotch as needed for junior's and large/plus sizes. Note 3: A hip seat width of 2½" up for children's and 3" up for menswear can take the place of low hip width.]

103. *Skirt/Pant Yoke Depth Front*—Measure from bottom of waistband/seam (top edge if not banded, or stitching if self-elastic/drawstring casing) straight down to bottom of yoke joining seam at center front. [Note: If yoke is contoured, indicate point of measure on spec sheet.]

104. *Skirt/Pant Yoke Depth Back*—Measure from bottom of waistband/seam (top edge if not banded, or stitching if self-elastic/drawstring casing) straight down to bottom of yoke joining seam at center back. [Note: If yoke is contoured, indicate point of measure on spec sheet.]

105. *Inseam*—Measure from crotch joining seam to bottom of leg opening, following inseam/inner fold.

106. *Outseam*—Measure from bottom edge of waistband/seam (top edge if not banded, or stitching if self-elastic/drawstring casing) to bottom of garment along side seam/fold of garment.

107. *Front Rise*—Measure from bottom edge of waistband/seam (top edge if not banded, or stitching if self-elastic/drawstring casing) to crotch joining seam,

following curve of front rise seam. [Note: Measure over zipper if in front rise seam.]

108. *Back Rise*—Measure from bottom edge of waistband/seam (top edge if not banded, or stitching if self-elastic/drawstring casing) to crotch joining seam, following curve of back rise seam. [Note: Measure over zipper if in front back seam.]

110. *Thigh Width Circumference (woven)*—Measure from pant leg edge/seam to pant leg edge/seam straight across pant leg at a point 1" below crotch and parallel to leg opening. Double this measurement. [Note: If leg opening is asymmetrical, measure to a point that would be parallel to leg opening.]

112. *Knee Width Circumference (woven)*—Measure from pant leg edge/seam to pant leg edge/seam at a point one-half of the inseam and parallel to leg opening. Double this measurement. [Note 1: If leg opening is asymmetrical, measure to a point that would be parallel to leg opening. Note 2: If pant leg is three-quarter length, indicate point of measure on spec sheet. Note 3: A general knee measurement from crotch seam of misses/women's 14", junior's 13", large/plus sizes 15" can be used. Indicate change on spec sheet. Measure children's at one-half inseam minus 1½", and for men's minus 2".]

114. *Leg Opening Width Circumference (woven)*—Measure from pant leg edge/seam to pant leg edge/seam straight across bottom edge of leg opening. Double this measurement. [Note: If leg opening is contoured, follow contour and indicate measurement change on spec sheet.]

116. *Vented Leg Opening Circumference (woven)*—Measure from pant leg edge/seam to pant leg edge/seam straight across pant leg at top of side vents. Double this measurement.

118. *Leg Opening Width Circumference, Stretched (woven)*—Measure from pant leg edge/seam to pant leg edge/seam straight across bottom edge of leg opening in a fully extended position. Double this measurement.

119. *Cuff Height Pants*—Measure from top of cuff edge straight down to bottom of cuff fold and leg opening.

120. *Bottom Band/Ribbing Height Pants*—Measure from cuff joining seam or top of ribbing straight down to bottom edge of cuff or rib opening. [Note: For fashion-forward pants, you may want to include a cuff length. See point of measure 56, Cuff Length Sleeve, for measuring instructions and, if needed, indicate cuff length of pant on spec sheet.]

121. *Fly/Zipper*

A. *Length*—Measure from top of fly/zipper opening straight down to bottom of fly/zipper opening at zipper stop or bar tack.
B. *Fly/Zipper Width*—Measure top of fly/zipper at joining seam from edge/fold straight across to fly/zipper placket stitching.

122. *Vent/Slit*

A. *Height*—Measure from top of vent/slit straight down to bottom of vent/slit along edge of vent/slit.
B. *Width*—Measure top of vent/slit from edge/fold straight across to vent/slit placket stitching at a point parallel to garment hemline.

123. *Pleat Depth*—Measure from outer edge of pleat at fold/crease to inner fold of pleat. [Note 1: It is a good idea to indicate what type of pleat is being measured, e.g., box, inverted, knife, kick, kilt, or envelope. Note 2: If pleats are not parallel or symmetrical, indicate any special instructions on spec sheet.]

124. *Distance Between Pleats*—Measure from start of pleat to start of pleat, excluding pleat depth at a point directly below pleat joining seam. [Note: If pleats are not parallel or symmetrical, indicate any special instructions on spec sheet.]

125. *Applied Pocket Height*—Measure from top edge of pocket to bottom edge of pocket along center of pocket. [Note: For contoured or irregularly shaped pockets, take a second measurement and indicate point of measure on spec sheet.]

126. *Applied Pocket Width*—Measure from side of pocket to side of pocket along top edge of pocket. [Note: For contoured or irregularly shaped pockets, take a second measurement and indicate point of measure on spec sheet.]

127. *Pocket Opening Within a Seam*—Measure from top of pocket to bottom of pocket along edge of pocket opening.

128. *Belt Length*

A. *Total*—Measure from end of belt at buckle along center of belt to opposite end of belt, following contour.

B. *Circumference*—Measure from end of belt at buckle along center of belt to middle hole at opposite end.

129. *Belt Width (or Height)*—Measure from edge of belt straight across to edge of belt. [Note: If belt is contoured, indicate points of measure on spec sheet.]

130. *Belt Loop Length*—Measure from top of belt loop straight down/vertically to bottom of belt loop along center of belt loop. [Note: Fashion-forward or irregularly shaped belt loops may require further spec instructions. Indicate points of measure on spec sheet.]

131. *Belt Loop Width*—Measure belt loop from edge of belt loop straight across/horizontally to edge of belt loop. [Note: Fashion-forward or irregularly shaped belt loops may require further spec instructions. Indicate points of measure on spec sheet.]

132. *Tie Length*—Measure from end of tie/joining seam straight down to tie end along center of tie.

133. *Tie Width*

A. *Straight*—Measure from edge of tie straight across to edge of tie.

B. *Contoured*—Measure from edge of tie straight across to edge of tie at widest point of tie.

134. *Flounce/Ruffle Width*—Measure from flounce/ruffle joining seam straight across to outer edge of flounce/ruffle. [Note: If flounce/ruffle is contoured, measure along narrowest and widest points if possible and indicate changes on spec sheet.]

146. *Pleats Placement*

A. *Front Pleat Top*—Measure distance from center front of garment straight across to start of first pleat at a point parallel to garment hem. [Note: You may need to use armhole or side seam as a starting point if there is no center front seam or placket.]

B. *Back Pleat Top*—Measure distance from armhole seam/side seam (depending on pleat placement) to first pleat at a point parallel to garment hem.

C. *Front Pleat Skirt/Pant*—Measure distance from center front of garment waistband joining seam/edge straight across to start of first pleat.

148. *Pocket Placement*

C. *Front Bottom Pocket Vertical*—Measure from waistband/joining seam/edge straight down to top edge of pocket.

D. *Front Bottom Pocket Horizontal*—Measure from center front straight across to side of pocket at top edge.

E. *Back Bottom Pocket Vertical*—Measure from waistband/joining seam/edge straight down to top edge of pocket.

F. *Back Bottom Pocket Horizontal*—Measure from center back straight across to side of pocket at top edge.

G. *Pocket from Side Seam*—Measure from side seam straight across to top of pocket. [Note: If pocket is contoured at sides, a top and bottom pocket size and placement must be measured and added to spec sheet.]

149. *Belt Loop Placement*

A. *Front*—Measure from center front of garment horizontally across to center of first front belt loop.

B. *Back*—Measure from center back of garment horizontally across to center of first back belt loop.

C. *Side Seam to Front*—Measure from center of side seam belt loop to center of front belt loop.

D. *Side Seam to Back*—Measure from center of side seam belt loop to center of back belt loop.

150. *Dart Placement*

F. *Center Front Skirt/Pant*—Measure from center front of garment at waistband joining seam/edge straight across to top of dart.

G. *Center Back Skirt/Pant*—Measure from center back of garment at waistband joining seam/edge straight across to top of dart.

CHAPTER 11 TERMS

When working with woven pants, you may come across the following garment terms. If you are unfamiliar with any of them, please look up the definitions in the glossary at the end of this text.

Pants:

Baggy (baggies)
Bell-bottom (bell-bottoms)
Continental
Cropped
Hip-hugger (low rise)
Oxford
Palazzo
Sailor
Stovepipe
Western
Seat

SPEC SHEET Woven pant

STYLE

SEASON:	DESCRIPTION:
LABEL: (SIZE CATEGORY)	
DATE:	
TECHNICAL SKETCH Classic cuffed pant	SKETCH/PHOTO

CODE	POINT OF MEASURE	TOL. +/–	4	S/6	8	M/10	12	L/14	16	XL/18
81.	Waistband depth	1/8								
83.	Waistband width circumference	1/2-3/4								
85.	Waistband circumference stretched	1/2-3/4								
87.	High hip width	1/2-3/4								
89.	Low hip width	1/2-3/4								
105.	Inseam	3/8								
106.	Outseam	3/8								
107.	Front rise	3/8								
108.	Back rise	3/8								
110.	Thigh width circumference	3/8								
112.	Knee width circumference	3/8								
114.	Leg opening width circumference	1/4								

(Tolerance 1/2-3/4 S, M, L, XL = 3/4" 4-18 = 1/2")

The measured garment spec sheets are for ***illustrative purposes only*** and should not be used as industry standards

CODE	POINT OF MEASURE	TOL. +/–	4	S/6	8	M/10	12	L/14	16	XL/18
119.	Cuff height pants	1/8								
121.	Fly/zipper A. Length	1/4								
	B. Width	1/8								
123.	Pleat depth	1/8								
124.	Distance between pleats	1/8								
127.	Pocket opening	1/4								
130.	Belt loop length	1/8								
131.	Belt loop width	1/8								
150.	Dart length	1/8								

COMMENTS:

The measured garment spec sheets are for ***illustrative purposes only*** and should not be used as industry standards

SPEC SHEET Woven pant	STYLE
SEASON: Early fall	DESCRIPTION: Updated classic pant with cuff, front dart,
LABEL: (SIZE CATEGORY) Missy	and pleat back buttoned vent pocket
DATE:	
TECHNICAL SKETCH Classic cuffed pant	SKETCH/PHOTO

CODE	POINT OF MEASURE		TOL. +/–	4	S/6	8	M/10	12	L/14	16	XL/18
81.	Waistband depth	To stitching	1/8			1 1/2					
83.	Waistband width circumference		1/2-3/4			30					
85.	Waistband circumference stretched		1/2-3/4								
87.	High hip width	Below stitching	1/2-3/4			38 1/4					
89.	Low hip width	Below stitching	1/2-3/4			43					
105.	Inseam		3/8			31					
106.	Outseam	Below stitching	3/8			41					
107.	Front rise	Below stitching	3/8			12 1/2					
108.	Back rise	Below stitching	3/8			14 3/4					
110.	Thigh width circumference		3/8			28					
112.	Knee width circumference		3/8			22					
114.	Leg opening width circumference		1/4			18 1/2					

(Tolerance 1/2-3/4 S, M, L, XL = 3/4" 4-18 = 1/2")

The measured garment spec sheets are for ***illustrative purposes only*** and should not be used as industry standards

CODE	POINT OF MEASURE	TOL. +/–	4	S/6	8	M/10	12	L/14	16	XL/18
119.	Cuff height pants	1/8			1 1/2					
121.	Fly/zipper A. Length **Below stitching**	1/2-3/4			7					
	B. Width	1/2-3/4			1 1/8					
123.	Pleat depth	1/2-3/4			1 1/8					
124.	Distance between pleats	1/2-3/4								
127.	Pocket opening **Side seam**	1/4			6					
130.	Belt loop length	1/8			2					
131.	Belt loop width	1/8			3/8					
150.	Dart length **Front below stitching**	1/8			4					
	Back below stitching	1/8			4 1/8					
127.	**Pocket opening back vent height**	1/4			3/8					
	Length/width	1/8			4 1/2					
146.	**Pleats placement from C.F.**	1/4			4 1/8					
148.	**Pocket placement E. Back vertical**	1/8			2 3/8					
	F. Back horizontal	1/8			1 3/8					
149.	**Belt loop placement A. C.F. to loop**	1/8			4 1/8					
	B. C.B. to loop	1/8			3/4					
	Distance between back darts	1/8			1 3/4					
150.	**Dart placement F. C.F. to dart**	1/8			5 3/4					
	G. C.B. to 1st dart	1/8			2 1/2					

COMMENTS:

The measured garment spec sheets are for ***illustrative purposes only*** and should not be used as industry standards

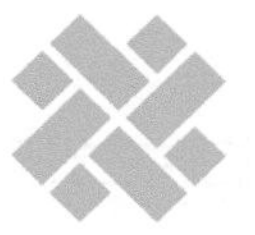

CHAPTER 12

Woven Dresses

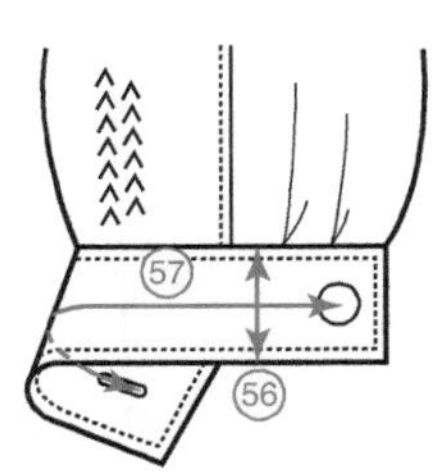

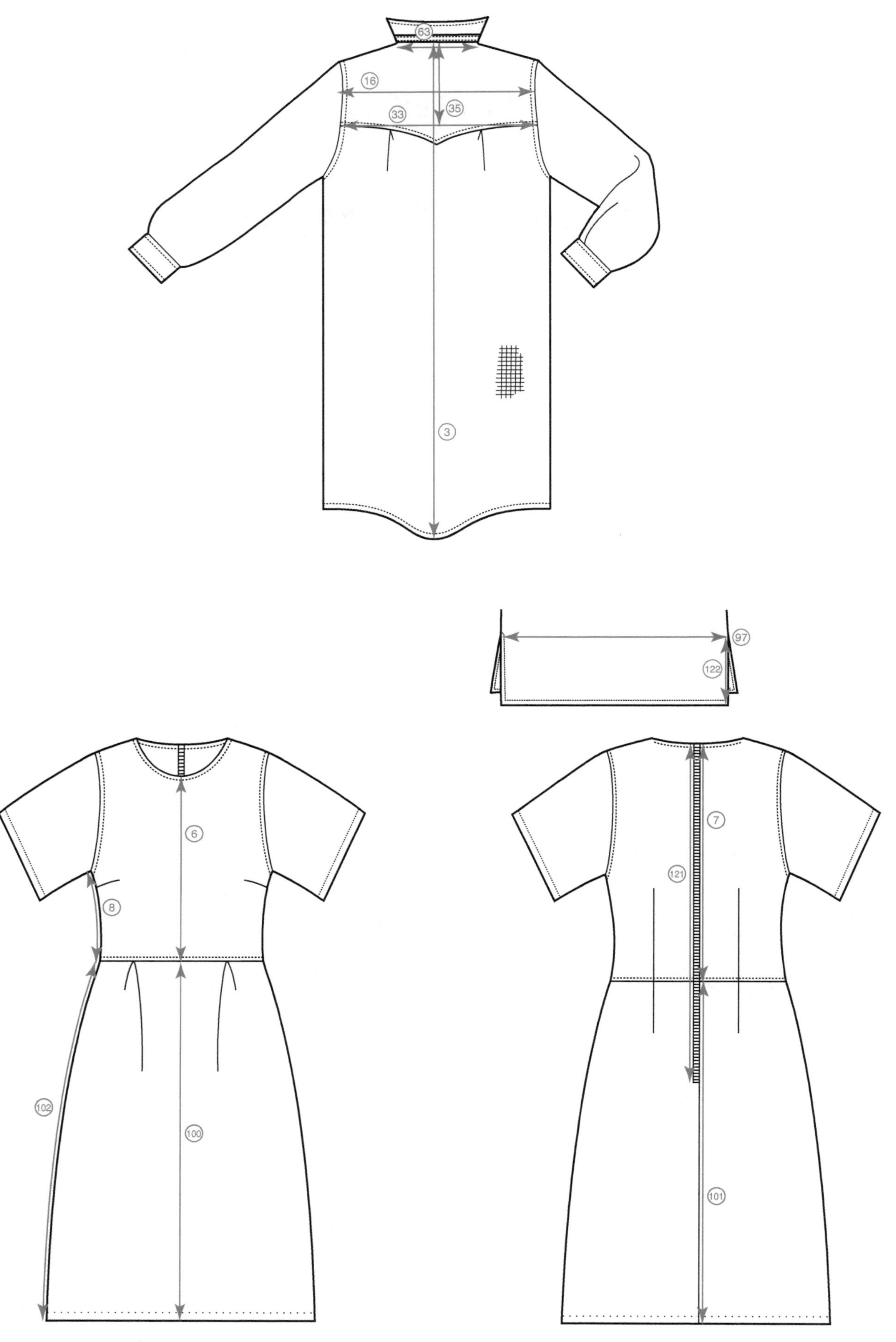
63
16
35
33
3
97
122
6
8
102
100
7
121
101

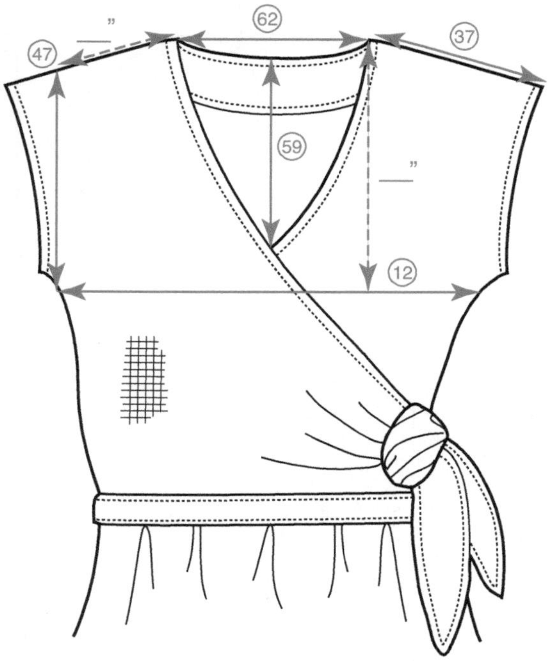

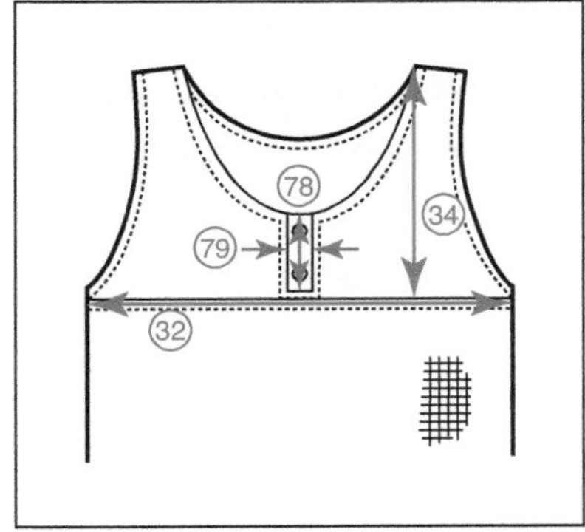
78
79
34
32

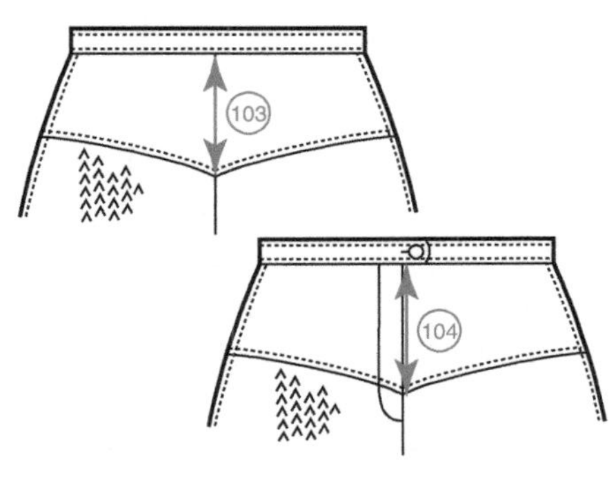
103
104

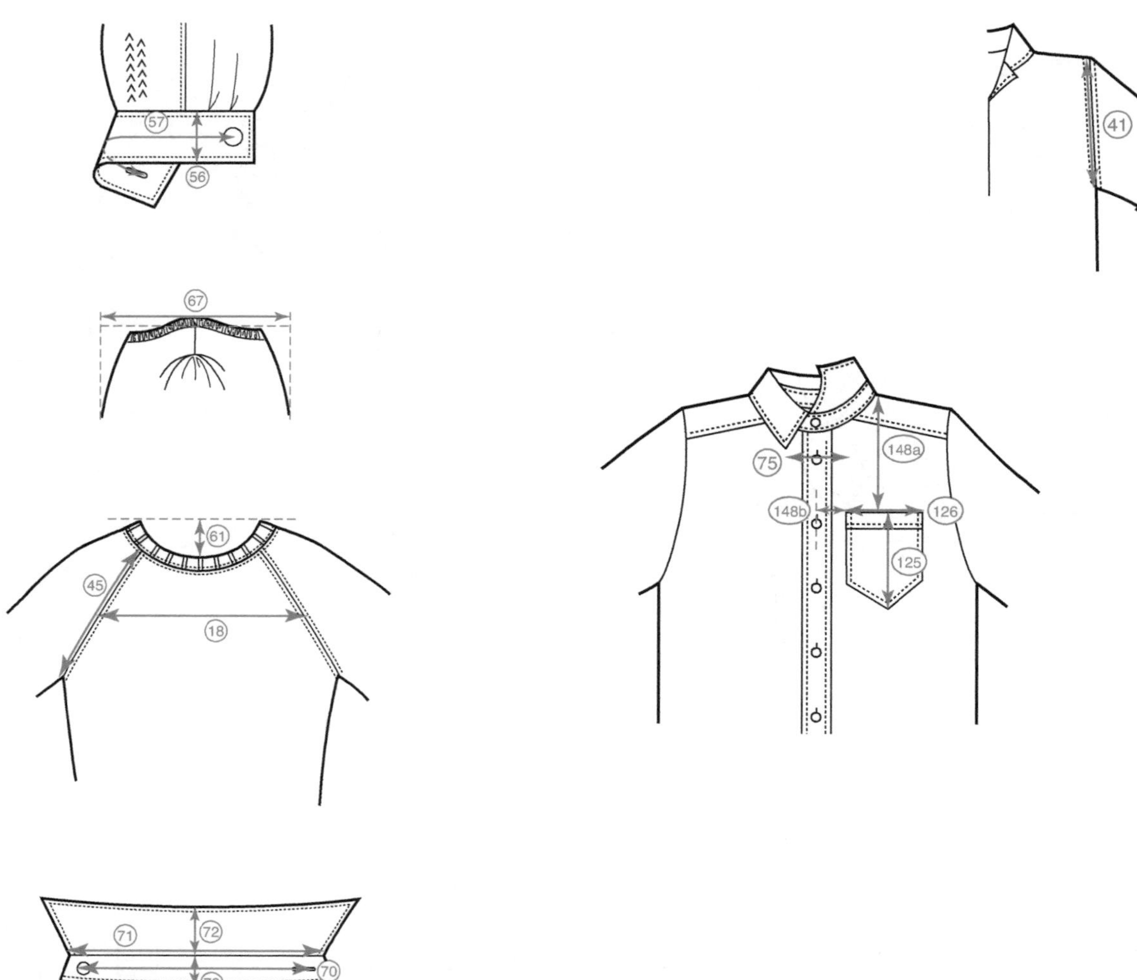

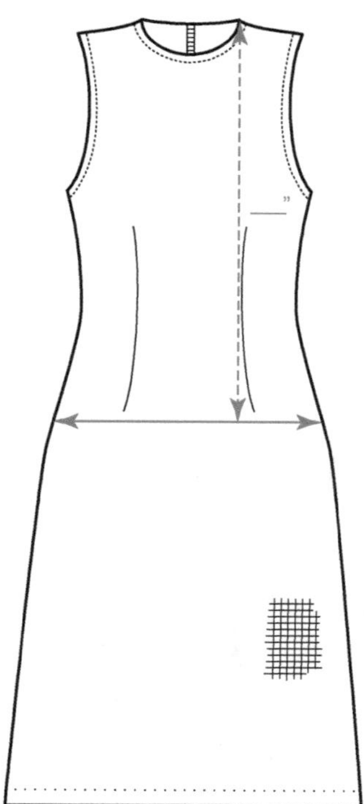

Figure 12.1 Measuring hip width circumference from high point shoulder.

Measuring Woven Dresses

Measuring a woven dress basically combines the measurements of a woven top and a woven skirt; therefore, the rules you learned for each of those styles will be used here as well. If needed, look back over Chapters 9 and 10. However, there will be measurement points unique to dresses that are not covered in those chapters; measurement point 91, Hip Width Circumference from High Point Shoulder is an example (see Figure 12.1). As the technician, be sure to decide which measurements are best suited to the garment under evaluation.

1. *Front Length (garments with a front opening)*—Measure from high point shoulder at neck straight down, parallel to center front, to bottom of garment at front. If garment has a collar, gently lift it away from shoulder-neck measuring point.

2. *Center Front Length (garments with a plain front; no front opening)*—Measure from center front neck joining seams straight down to bottom of garment at center front. [Note: A garment with a front opening may still require point of measure 1, Front Length, if neckline is unusual or is difficult to measure.]

3. *Center Back Length*—Measure from center back neck joining seams straight down to bottom of garment at center back. If needed, gently lift the collar away from back neck to expose joining seam.

4. *Side Length*—Measure from bottom of armhole/side seam straight down to bottom of garment along side of garment. Do not follow natural curve of garment's side seam, unless otherwise indicated. If needed, gently lift sleeve away from armhole/side seam joining seam.

5. *Front Bodice Length (garments with a front opening)*—Measure from high point shoulder at neck straight down, parallel to center front, to top edge of waistband, joining seam, or rib. If garment has a collar, gently lift it away from shoulder-neck measuring point.

6. *Center Front Bodice Length (garments with a plain front; no front opening)*—Measure from center front neck joining seam straight down to top edge of waistband, joining seam, or rib. [Note: A garment with a center opening may still require point of measure 5, Front Bodice Length, if neckline is unusual or is difficult to measure.]

7. *Center Back Bodice Length*—Measure from center back neck joining seams straight down to top edge of waistband, joining seam, or rib. If needed, gently lift collar away from back neck to expose joining seam.

8. *Side Seam Bodice Length*—Measure from bottom of armhole/side seam straight down to top edge of waistband, joining seam, or rib, along side of garment, following natural curve of garment's side seam, unless otherwise indicated. If needed, gently lift sleeve away from armhole/side seam joining seam. [Note: You can take side seam bodice measurement straight rather than contoured if joining seam/rib can be extended, but indicate change on spec sheet.]

10. *Chest Width Circumference (woven)*—Measure from edge of garment/side seam to edge of garment/side seam straight across garment at a point 1" below armhole. Double this measurement.

12. *Chest Width Circumference/Raglan Sleeve (woven)*—Measure from edge of garment/side seam to edge of garment/side seam straight across garment at a point _____" below high point shoulder. Double this measurement. [Note: You will have to determine number of inches down from high point shoulder for each raglan sleeve style based on depth of sleeve. Then indicate this number on spec sheet.]

13. *Across Shoulder*—Measure straight across front from armhole seam/edge to armhole seam/edge at shoulder seam or across natural shoulder fold line created if there is no seam.

14. *Shoulder Width*—Measure from neckband/collar/ribbing joining seam or neckline edge to top of armhole seam at shoulder, taken along shoulder seam or across natural shoulder fold line created if there is no seam.

15. *Across Chest*—Measure 2½" down from collar/rib joining seam at center front straight across front of garment from armhole seam/edge to armhole seam/edge. [Note: The 2½" measurement point is for misses/women's wear only and may need to be adjusted up or down ¼" to ½" accordingly for men's, children's, junior's, and large/plus sizes. Indicate any changes on spec sheet.]

16. *Across Back*—Measure 4" down from collar/rib joining seam at center back straight across back of garment from armhole seam/edge to armhole seam/edge. [Note: The 4" measurement point is for misses/women's wear only and may need to be adjusted up or down ¼" to ½" accordingly for men's, children's, junior's, and large/plus sizes. Indicate any changes on spec sheet.]

17. *Across Chest/Center Armhole*—Measure at one-half depth of armhole straight across front of garment from armhole seam/edge to armhole seam/edge.

18. *Across Back/Center Armhole*—Measure at one-half depth of armhole straight across back of garment from armhole seam/edge to armhole seam/edge.

20. *Waist Width Circumference (woven)*—Measure from edge of garment/side seam to edge of garment/side seam straight across garment on seam or at narrowest point of waist taper at a point _____" below high point shoulder. Double this measurement. [Note: You will have to determine number of inches down from high point shoulder for each raglan sleeve style based on depth of sleeve. Then indicate this number on spec sheet.]

32. *Yoke Width Front*—Measure from armhole seam/edge to armhole seam/edge straight across front of garment, ignoring contours or points, at yoke-body joining seams. [Note: If yoke is asymmetrical, indicate changes in measuring as needed on spec sheet.]

33. *Yoke Width Back*—Measure from armhole seam/edge to armhole seam/edge straight across back of garment, ignoring contours or points, at yoke-body joining seams. [Note: If yoke is asymmetrical, indicate changes in measuring as needed on spec sheet.]

34. *Yoke Depth Front*—Measure from high point shoulder at neck straight down to bottom of front yoke-body joining seam. Gently lift collar away from shoulder-neck joining seam if needed.

35. *Yoke Back Depth*—Measure from center back neck joining seam straight down to bottom of back yoke-body joining seam. Gently lift collar away from back neck joining seam if needed.

36. *Sleeve Length Top Armhole*—Measure along top of sleeve/fold, following contour of sleeve from armhole seam at shoulder to bottom of sleeve opening, including cuff.

37. *Sleeve Length Top Neck*—Measure along top of sleeve/fold, following contour of sleeve from sleeve-neck joining seam/edge to edge of sleeve opening, including cuff. Gently lift collar at sleeve-neck joining seam if needed.

38. *Sleeve Length Center Back*—Measure from center back neck joining seam or from a point above neck at an imaginary line, that of a joining seam, along top of sleeve/fold, following contour of sleeve to edge of sleeve opening, including cuff.

39. *Sleeve Length Underarm*—Measure straight from bottom of armhole along sleeve seam to edge of sleeve opening, including cuff.

41. *Straight Armhole Width Circumference (woven)*—Measure from top of shoulder joining seam/edge straight down to bottom of armhole. Double this measurement.

43. *Curved Armhole Width Circumference (woven)*—Measure from top of shoulder joining seam/edge to bottom of armhole, following contour of armhole. Double this measurement.

44. *Armhole Front*—Measure on front of garment from top of shoulder at neckline joining seam/edge to bottom of armhole, following contour of armhole. Gently lift collar away from neckline joining seam if needed.

45. *Armhole Back*—Measure on back of garment from top of shoulder at neck joining seam/edge to bottom

of armhole, following contour of armhole. Gently lift collar away from neck joining seam if needed.

47. *Armhole Width Circumference Straight (woven)*—Measure from top of shoulder seam at a point _____" below neckline joining seam/edge straight down to bottom of armhole. Double this measurement. [Note: Gently move collar away from neck joining seam if needed when measuring down _____" to armhole start point. Indicate number of inches measured down on spec sheet.]

49. *Muscle Width Circumference (woven)*—Measure from inner sleeve edge/seam to outer sleeve edge/fold at a point 1" below armhole and parallel to sleeve opening. Double this measurement.

51. *Elbow Width Circumference (woven)*—Measure from inner sleeve edge/seam to outer sleeve edge/fold straight across sleeve at a point one-half of underarm sleeve length and parallel to sleeve opening at wrist or cuff. Double this measurement. [Note: If sleeve is three-quarter length, indicate new point of measure on spec sheet.]

53. *Sleeve Opening Width Circumference (woven)*—Measure from inner sleeve edge/seam to outer sleeve edge/fold straight across bottom edge of sleeve opening. Double this measurement.

55. *Sleeve Opening Width Circumference, Stretched (woven)*—Measure from inner sleeve edge/seam to outer sleeve edge/fold straight across bottom edge of sleeve opening in a fully extended position. Double this measurement.

56. *Cuff Length Sleeve*—Measure from outside end of buttonhole to center of button straight along center of cuff. Open cuff out as flat as possible when measuring. [Note: If cuff length is contoured, measure along center-most point.]

57. *Cuff/Ribbing Height Sleeve*—Measure from cuff joining seam or top of ribbing straight down to bottom edge of cuff or rib opening. [Note: If cuff is contoured, indicate changes made to measurement on spec sheet.]

58. *Neck Depth Front (garments with a plain front/ asymmetrical front opening)*—Measure from center back neck joining seam/edge straight down to center front neck joining seam/edge.

59. *Neck Depth Center Front (garments with a center front opening)*—Measure from center back neck joining seam/edge straight down to center of first button at center front of garment.

60. *Neck Drop Front*—Measure from an imaginary line connecting neckline edges straight down to center front neck opening edge. Use a ruler if needed to connect top neckline edges.

61. *Neck Drop Back*—Measure from an imaginary line connecting neckline edges straight down to center back neck opening edge. This measurement is taken with front of garment faceup. Use a ruler to connect top neckline edges if needed.

62. *Neck Width, No Collar*—Measure from inside neck edge/seam to inside neck edge/seam straight across back neck at widest point. This measurement is taken with front of garment faceup.

63. *Neck Width, Collar*—Measure straight across back neck from neck-shoulder joining seam to neck-shoulder joining seam or natural shoulder line if no seam. This measurement is taken with back of garment faceup.

65. *Neck Edge Width Circumference (woven)*—Measure from neck edge/seam/fold to neck edge/ seam/ fold along top opening edge, following natural contour of neck opening. Garment should be positioned with one shoulder on top of the other and with front and back neck edges meeting. Double this measurement.

67. *Neck Edge Width Circumference, Stretched (woven)*—Measure from neck edge/seam/fold to

neck edge/seam/fold along top opening edge in a fully extended position. Garment should be positioned with one shoulder on top of the other and with front and back neck edges meeting. Double this measurement.

69. *Neck Base Circumference (woven)*—Measure from neck edge/seam to neck edge/seam along collar/rib joining seam or neckline edge, following natural contour of neck opening. Garment should be buttoned or zippered, if applicable, with one shoulder seam positioned on top of the other and with front and back neck edges meeting. Double this measurement.

70. *Neckband Length*—Measure from outside end of buttonhole to center of buttonhole across neckband, following contour of neckband.

71. *Collar Length*—Measure from one end of collar to other end of collar along neck joining seam.

72. *Collar Height*—Measure from collar/rib joining seam at center back neck straight up to outer edge of collar/rib.

73. *Collar Band Height*—Measure from collar joining seam at center back straight up to neckband joining seam at center back.

74. *Collar Point Length*—Measure from collar joining seam to outer edge of collar along collar point edge. [Note: If collar is rounded, measure at a point parallel to center back and indicate change on spec sheet.]

75. *Collar Point Spread (pointed collars only)*—Measure, with collar band buttoned and collar in place, from collar point straight across collar edge to collar point.

76. *Lapel Width*

A. *Notched*—Measure from lower lapel notch straight across to lapel fold at a point perpendicular to garment center front.

B. *Without Notches*—Measure from lapel edge straight across widest point of lapel to lapel fold at a point _____" down from center back collar joining seam and perpendicular to front of garment.

77. *Center Front Extension*—Measure from an imaginary line at center front of garment horizontally to finished outer edge of front extended piece.

78. *Placket Length*—Measure from top edge of placket straight down to bottom of placket opening along center of placket.

79. *Placket Width*—Measure from placket joining seam straight across placket to placket edge at fold.

80. *Keyhole Length*—Measure from outer edge of neckline straight down to bottom of keyhole opening.

81. *Waistband Depth*—Measure from top of waistband edge straight down to bottom of waistband at waistband joining seam. [Note: If waistband is contoured, indicate measurement change on spec sheet.]

83. *Waistband Width Circumference (woven)*—Measure from side of bottom band to side of bottom band along center of band, following natural contour of waistband. Double this measurement.

85. *Waistband Width Circumference, Stretched (woven)*—Measure from side of bottom band to side of bottom band straight across center of band in a fully extended position. Double this measurement.

87. *High Hip Width Circumference (woven)*—Measure from edge of garment/side seam to edge of garment/side seam at a point 4" below bottom edge of waistband/seam, following contour of waist. Double this measurement. [Note: The 4" point is for misses/women's wear only; adjust as needed ½" to 1" up or down for children's, petite's, junior's, or large/plus sizes. Indicate change on spec sheet.]

89. *Low Hip Width Circumference from Waist (woven)*—Measure from edge of garment/side seam to edge of garment/side seam at a point 7" below bottom edge of waistband/seam, following contour of waist. Double this measurement. [Note: The 7" point is for misses/women's wear only; adjust as needed ½" to 1" up or down for children's, petite's, junior's, or large/plus sizes. Indicate change on spec sheet.]

91. *Hip Width from High Point Shoulder Circumference (woven)*—Measure from edge of garment/side seam to edge of garment/side seam straight across at a point _____" below high point shoulder. Double this measurement. [Note: You will have to estimate low hip point on garment if there is no waistband and fill in _____" from high point shoulder. This measurement will vary for children's, junior's, misses, and large/plus sizes.]

95. *Bottom Opening/Sweep Width Circumference (woven skirt)*—Measure from edge of garment/side seam to edge of garment/side seam straight across garment at bottom opening. Double this measurement. [Note: If sweep has pleats, measure with pleats closed or relaxed.]

97. *Vented Bottom Opening/Sweep Width Circumference (woven skirt)*—Measure from edge of garment/side seam to edge of garment/side seam straight across garment at top of side vents. Double this measurement. [Note: Indicate on spec sheet if there is only one vent or if vent hits at a point other than sweep, e.g., thigh opening.]

99. *Circular Bottom Opening/Sweep Width Circumference (woven skirt)*—Measure from edge of garment/side seam to edge of garment/side seam, following natural contour of garment at bottom opening. Double this measurement.

100. *Center Front Skirt Length*—Measure from bottom of waistband/seam (top edge if not banded, or stitching if self-elastic/drawstring casing) straight down to bottom of garment at center front. [Note: A fashion-forward skirt may have an asymmetrical waist. Indicate top point of measure on spec sheet.]

101. *Center Back Skirt Length*—Measure from bottom of waistband/seam (top edge if not banded, or stitching if self-elastic/drawstring casing) straight down to bottom of garment at center front. [Note: A fashion-forward skirt may have an asymmetrical waist. Indicate top point of measure on spec sheet.]

102. *Side Skirt Length*—Measure from bottom edge of waistband/seam (top edge if not banded, or stitching if self-elastic/drawstring casing) to bottom of garment along side seam/fold of garment, following any contour.

103. *Skirt/Pant Yoke Depth Front*—Measure from bottom of waistband/seam (top edge if not banded, or stitching if self-elastic/drawstring casing) straight down to bottom of yoke joining seam at center front. [Note: If yoke is contoured, indicate point of measure on spec sheet.]

104. *Skirt/Pant Yoke Depth Back*—Measure from bottom of waistband/seam (top edge if not banded, or stitching if self-elastic/drawstring casing) straight down to bottom of yoke joining seam at center back. [Note: If yoke is contoured, indicate point of measure on spec sheet.]

121. *Fly/Zipper*

A. *Length*—Measure from top of fly/zipper opening straight down to bottom of fly/zipper opening at zipper stop or bar tack.

B. *Fly/Zipper Width*—Measure top of fly/zipper at joining seam from edge/fold straight across to fly/zipper placket stitching.

122. *Vent/Slit*

A. *Height*—Measure from top of vent/slit straight down to bottom of vent/slit along edge of vent/slit.

B. *Width*—Measure top of vent/slit from edge/fold straight across to vent/slit placket stitching at a point parallel to garment hemline.

123. *Pleat Depth*—Measure from outer edge of pleat at fold/crease to inner fold of pleat. [Note 1: It is a good idea to indicate what type of pleat is being measured, e.g., box, inverted, knife, kick, kilt, or envelope. Note 2: If pleats are not parallel or symmetrical, indicate any special instructions on spec sheet.]

124. *Distance Between Pleats*—Measure from start of pleat to start of pleat, excluding pleat depth at a point directly below pleat joining seam. [Note: If pleats are not parallel or symmetrical, indicate any special instructions on spec sheet.]

125. *Applied Pocket Height*—Measure from top edge of pocket to bottom edge of pocket along center of pocket. [Note: For contoured or irregularly shaped pockets, take a second measurement and indicate point of measure on spec sheet.]

126. *Applied Pocket Width*—Measure from side of pocket to side of pocket along top edge of pocket. [Note: For contoured or irregularly shaped pockets, take a second measurement and indicate point of measure on spec sheet.]

127. *Pocket Opening Within a Seam*—Measure from top of pocket to bottom of pocket along edge of pocket opening.

128. *Belt Length*

A. *Total*—Measure from end of belt at buckle along center of belt to opposite end of belt, following contour.

B. *Circumference*—Measure from end of belt at buckle along center of belt to middle hole at opposite end.

129. *Belt Width (or Height)*—Measure from edge of belt straight across to edge of belt. [Note: If belt is contoured, indicate points of measure on spec sheet.]

130. *Belt Loop Length*—Measure from top of belt loop straight down/vertically to bottom of belt loop along center of belt loop. [Note: Fashion-forward or irregularly shaped belt loops may require further spec instructions. Indicate points of measure on spec sheet.]

131. *Belt Loop Width*—Measure belt loop from edge of belt loop straight across/horizontally to edge of belt loop. [Note: Fashion-forward or irregularly shaped belt loops may require further spec instructions. Indicate points of measure on spec sheet.]

132. *Tie Length*—Measure from end of tie/joining seam straight down to tie end along center of tie.

133. *Tie Width*

A. *Straight*—Measure from edge of tie straight across to edge of tie.

B. *Contoured*—Measure from edge of tie straight across to edge of tie at widest point of tie.

134. *Flounce/Ruffle Width*—Measure from flounce/ruffle joining seam straight across to outer edge of flounce/ruffle. [Note: If flounce/ruffle is contoured, measure along narrowest and widest points if possible and indicate changes on spec sheet.]

135. *Strap Length*—Measure from strap joining seam along center of strap to end of strap. [Note: If a strap is contoured or has a contoured edge, measure along center, approximating center end point, or indicate instructions as needed on spec sheet.]

136. *Strap Width*—Measure from edge of strap straight across to edge of strap. [Note: If strap is contoured, measure along narrowest and widest points if possible and indicate changes on spec sheet.]

137. *Front Hood Length*—Measure from top of hood to bottom of hood at center front joining seam along opening edge of hood.

138. *Back Hood Length*—Measure from top of hood at center front to bottom of hood at center back joining seam along outside curve of hood fold/seam.

139. *Hood Width*—Measure from front opening edge of hood straight across to back of hood at fold along widest point of hood.

140. *Flange Depth*—Measure from center back neck joining seam straight down to bottom of flange at center back. [Note: If flange is contoured or asymmetrical, indicate point of measure on spec sheet.]

141. *Shoulder Pad Length*—Measure from edge of pad straight across to edge of pad along center of pad or natural shoulder line of pad.

142. *Shoulder Pad Width*—Measure from side of pad straight across to side of pad along edge of pad if straight, or at widest point of pad if curved.

143. *Straight Edge Shoulder Pad Height*—Measure from top of pad straight down to bottom of pad along center of pad.

144. *Curved Edge Shoulder Pad Height*—Stick a 1" straight pin into thickest part of shoulder pad. Push pin all the way through pad until head of pin rests on top of pad. Be sure not to crush pad. Measure portion of pin sticking out of pad. Subtract this figure from 1" (length of pin) to get shoulder pad height.

145. *Shoulder Pad Placement*—Measure from neck edge or joining seam straight across shoulder seam or natural shoulder line to start of shoulder pad.

146. *Pleats Placement*

A. *Front Pleat Top*—Measure distance from center front of garment straight across to start of first pleat at a point parallel to garment hem. [Note: You may need to use armhole or side seam as a starting point if there is no center front seam or placket.]

B. *Back Pleat Top*—Measure distance from armhole seam/side seam (depending on pleat placement) to first pleat at a point parallel to garment hem.

C. *Front Pleat Skirt/Pant*—Measure distance from center front of garment waistband joining seam/edge straight across to start of first pleat.

147. *Button Placement*—Refer to point of measure 59, Neck Depth Center Front, for placement of first button. Then measure distance of first button to second button. Be sure when measuring that button at bust point is lined up to apex of bust. Adjust all buttons accordingly and respace as needed.

148. *Pocket Placement*

A. *Top Pocket Vertical*—Measure from shoulder-neck joining seam straight down to top edge of pocket.

B. *Top Pocket Horizontal*—Measure from center front straight across to side of pocket at top edge.

C. *Front Bottom Pocket Vertical*—Measure from waistband/joining seam/edge straight down to top edge of pocket.

D. *Front Bottom Pocket Horizontal*—Measure from center front straight across to side of pocket at top edge.

E. *Back Bottom Pocket Vertical*—Measure from waistband/joining seam/edge straight down to top edge of pocket.

G. *Back Bottom Pocket Horizontal*—Measure from center back straight across to side of pocket at top edge.

H. *Pocket from Side Seam*—Measure from side seam straight across to top of pocket. [Note: If pocket is contoured at sides, a top and bottom pocket size and placement must be measured and added to spec sheet.]

149. *Belt Loop Placement*

A. *Front*—Measure from center front of garment horizontally across to center of first front belt loop.

B. *Back*—Measure from center back of garment horizontally across to center of first back belt loop.

C. *Side Seam to Front*—Measure from center of side seam belt loop to center of front belt loop.
D. *Side Seam to Back*—Measure from center of side seam belt loop to center of back belt loop.

150. *Dart Placement*
A. *High Point Shoulder Bust Dart*—Measure from shoulder-neck joining seam or at a point _____" from shoulder-neck seam straight down, parallel to center front, to top of dart. [Note: The _____" from shoulder seam measurement is to be used for darts that are too short to be measured from high point shoulder. Be sure to indicate _____" measurement on spec sheet.]
B. *Center Front Bust Dart*—Measure from center front of garment straight across to top of dart.
C. *Side Seam Bust Dart*—Measure from underarm/side seam joining seam down along contour of side seam to bottom of dart.
D. *High Point Shoulder Princess Dart*—Measure from shoulder-neck joining seam straight down to top of dart.
E. *Center Front Princess Dart*—Measure from center front of garment straight across to top of dart.
F. *Center Front Skirt/Pant*—Measure from center front of garment at waistband joining seam/edge straight across to top of dart.
G. *Center Back Skirt/Pant*—Measure from center back of garment at waistband joining seam/edge straight across to top of dart.

CHAPTER 12 TERMS

When working with woven dresses, you may come across the following garment terms. If you are unfamiliar with any of them, please look up the definitions in the glossary at the end of this text.

Dress:

Basic A-line (shift)
Caftan
Coat
Safari
Sheath
Shirt (shirtdress)
Slip
Wedge
Wrap

SPEC SHEET Woven dress | **STYLE**

SEASON:	DESCRIPTION:
LABEL: (SIZE CATEGORY)	
DATE:	
TECHNICAL SKETCH Basic/shift dress	SKETCH/PHOTO

CODE	POINT OF MEASURE	TOL. +/–	4	S/6	8	M/10	12	L/14	16	XL/18
1.	Front length	1/2								
2.	Center front length	1/2								
3.	Center back length	1/2								
4.	Side length	1/4								
10.	Chest width circumference	1/2-3/4								
13.	Across shoulder	1/4								
14.	Shoulder width	1/8								
15.	Across chest	1/4								
16.	Across back	1/4								
20.	Waist width circumference	1/2-3/4								
43.	Curved arm hole width circumference	3/8								
60.	Neck drop front	1/8								

(Tolerance 1/2-3/4 S, M, L, XL = 3/4" 4-18 = 1/2")

The measured garment spec sheets are for ***illustrative purposes only*** and should not be used as industry standards

CODE	POINT OF MEASURE	TOL. +/–	4	S/6	8	M/10	12	L/14	16	XL/18
61.	Neck drop back	1/8								
62.	Neck width, no collar	1/4								
91.	Hip width from H.P.S. circumference ______	1/2-3/4								
95.	Bottom opening sweep width circumference	1/2-3/4								
121.	Fly/zipper A. Length	1/8								
122.	Vent/slit A. Height	1/4								
	B. Width	1/8								
150.	Dart length	1/8								

COMMENTS:

The measured garment spec sheets are for ***illustrative purposes only*** and should not be used as industry standards

SPEC SHEET Woven dress **STYLE**

SEASON: Summer	DESCRIPTION: Floral print shift with lace inset hem.
LABEL: (SIZE CATEGORY) Missy	
DATE:	
TECHNICAL SKETCH Basic/shift dress	SKETCH/PHOTO

CODE	POINT OF MEASURE	TOL. +/–	4	S/6	8	M/10	12	L/14	16	XL/18
1.	Front length	1/2			37					
2.	Center front length	1/2			30 3/4					
3.	Center back length	1/2			36 1/2					
4.	Side length	1/4			29 1/2					
10.	Chest width circumference	1/2-3/4			38					
13.	Across shoulder	1/4								
14.	Shoulder width	1/8			1 1/8					
15.	Across chest * 5" from HPS	1/4			13 1/2					
16.	Across back	1/4			35					
20.	Waist width circumference * 14" from HPS	1/2-3/4			20					
43.	Curved arm hole width circumference	3/8			7 1/2					
60.	Neck drop front	1/8			1 1/2					

(Tolerance 1/2-3/4 S, M, L, XL = 3/4" 4-18 = 1/2")

The measured garment spec sheets are for ***illustrative purposes only*** and should not be used as industry standards

CODE	POINT OF MEASURE	TOL. +/–	4	S/6	8	M/10	12	L/14	16	XL/18
61.	Neck drop back	1/8			1 1/2					
62.	Neck width, no collar	1/4			12					
91.	Hip width from H.P.S. circumference 21 "	1/2-3/4			41					
95.	Bottom opening sweep width circumference	1/2-3/4			45					
121.	Fly/zipper A. Length	1/8			20					
122.	Vent/slit A. Height	1/4								
	B. Width	1/8								
150.	Dart length Front bust	1/8			5					
	Front princess	1/8			10					
	Back princess	1/8			11 1/2					
150.	Dart placement A. H.P.S. to bust dart	1/8			9 3/4					
	D. H.P.S. to front princess	1/8			11					
	H.P.S. to back princess	1/8			9 5/8					
	E. C.F. to front princess	1/8			4					
	C.B. to back princess	1/8			4					
	Distance from hem to lace insert	1/8			1 5/8					

COMMENTS:

The measured garment spec sheets are for illustrative purposes only and should not be used as industry standards

CHAPTER 13

Woven Jumpsuits and One-Piece Garments

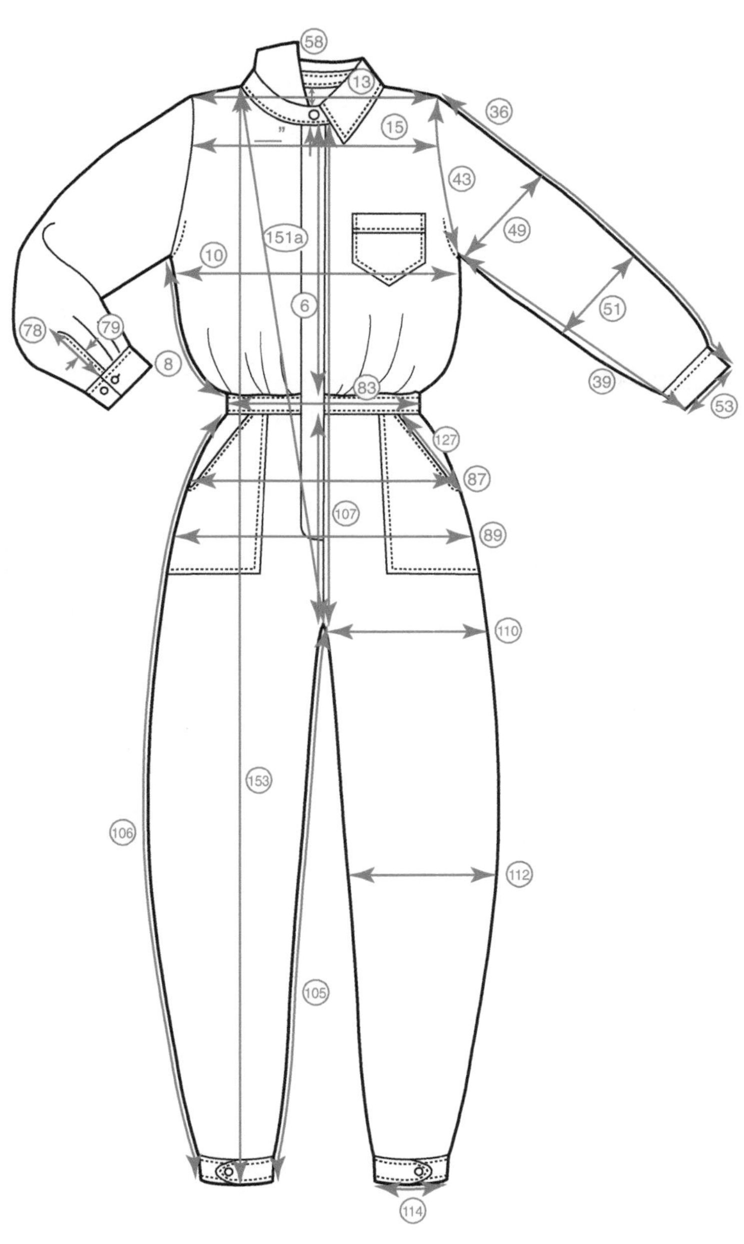

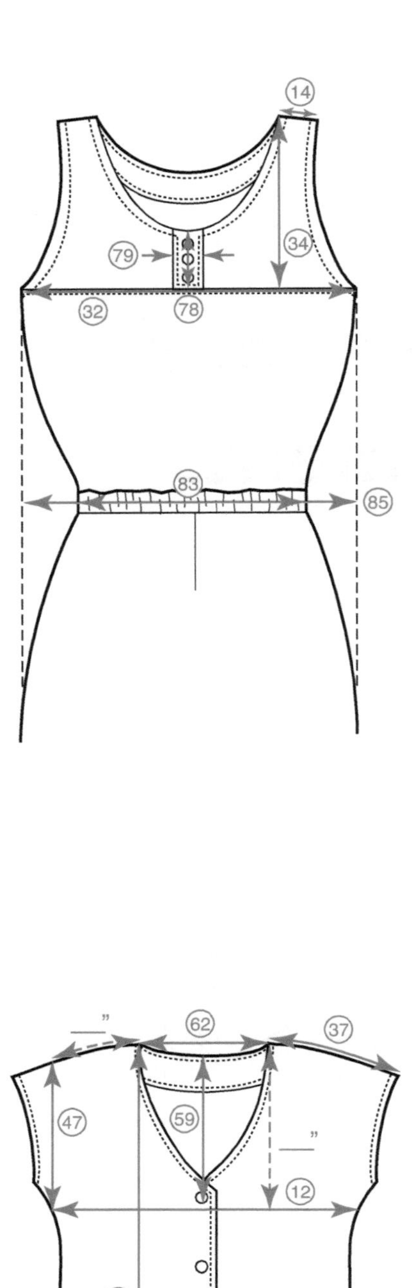
14
79
34
32
78
83
85

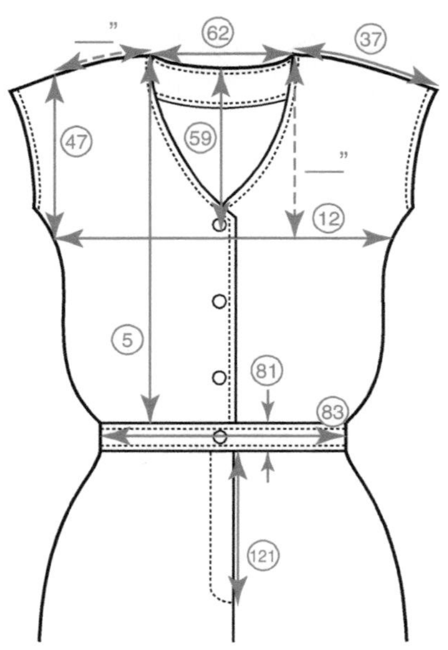
62
37
47
59
12
5
81
83
121

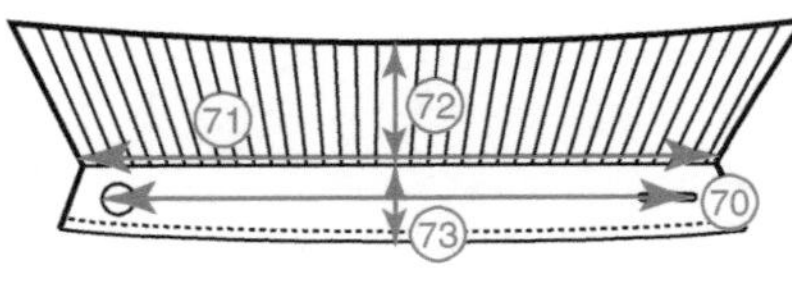
71
72
70
73

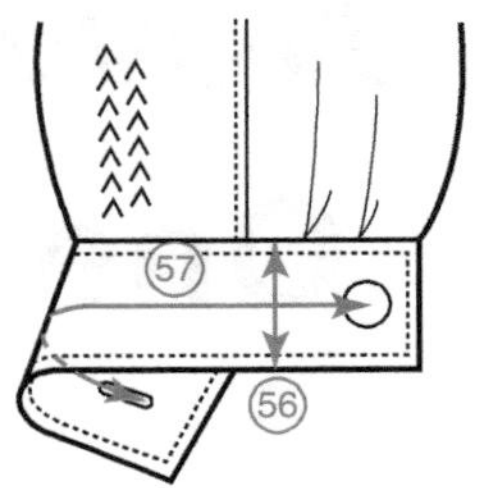
57
56

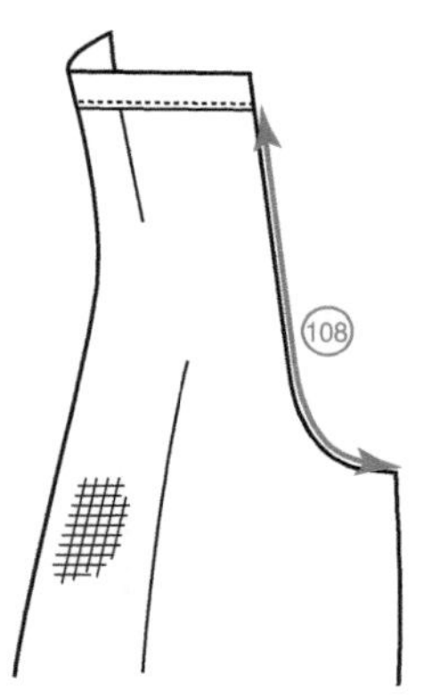
108

75
148a
148b
126
125

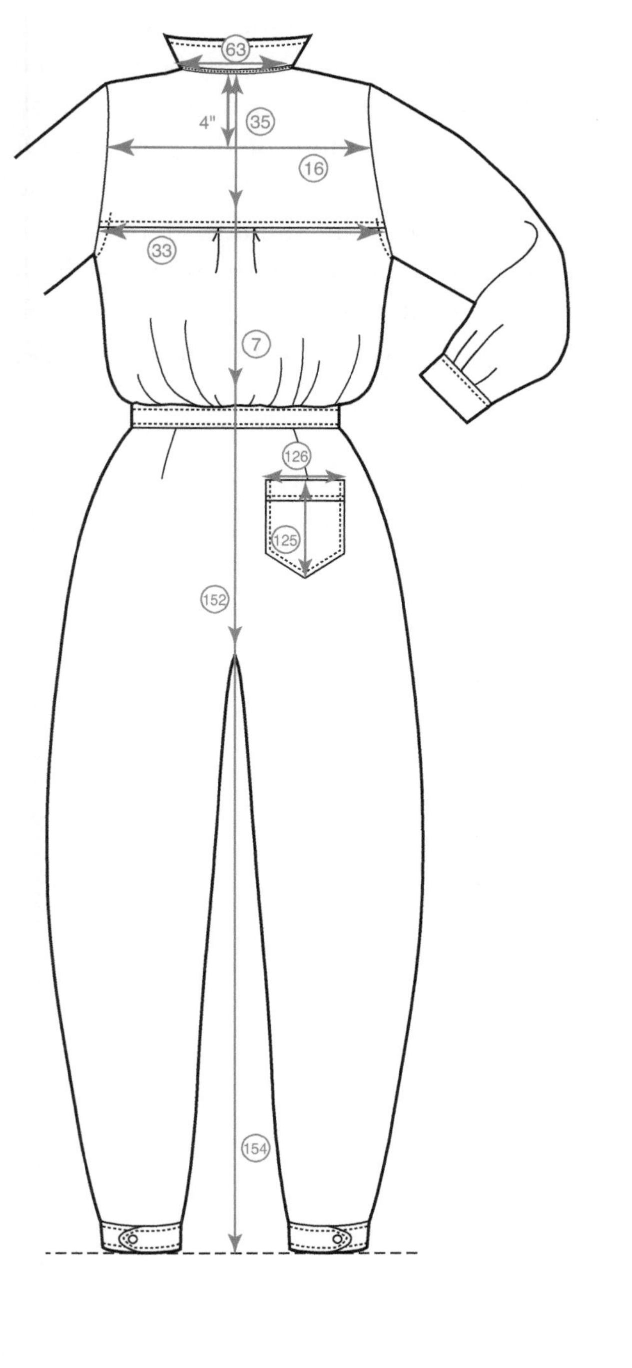

63
4"
35
16
33
7
126
125
152
154

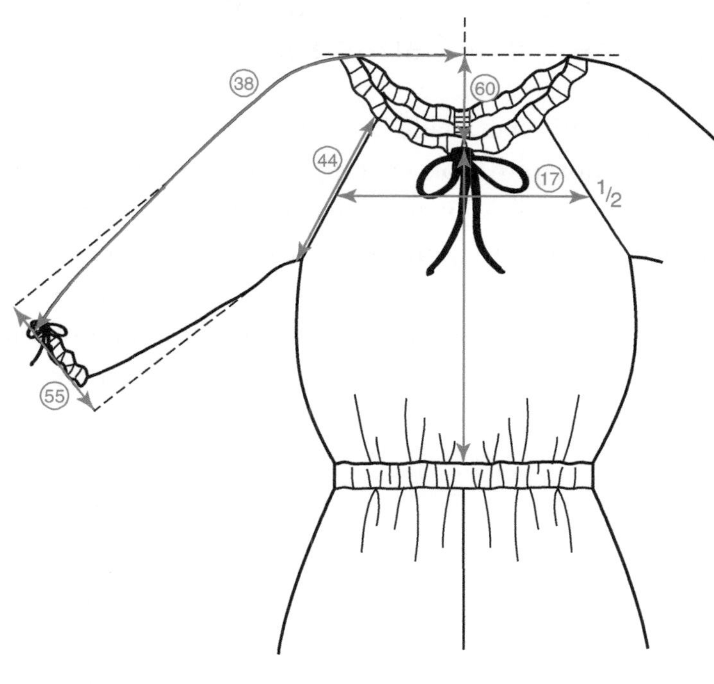

38
60
44
17
1/2
55

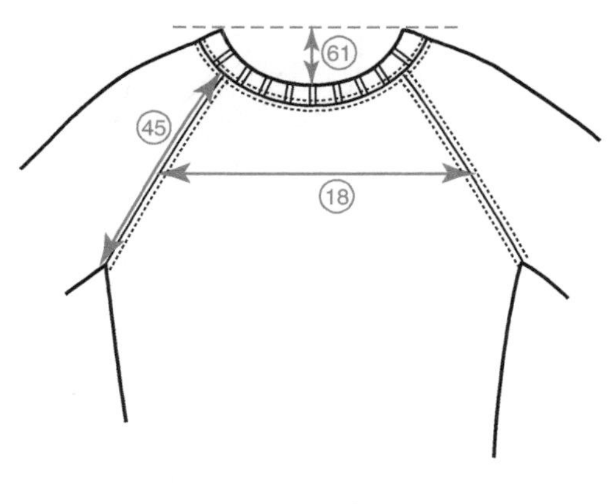

61
45
18

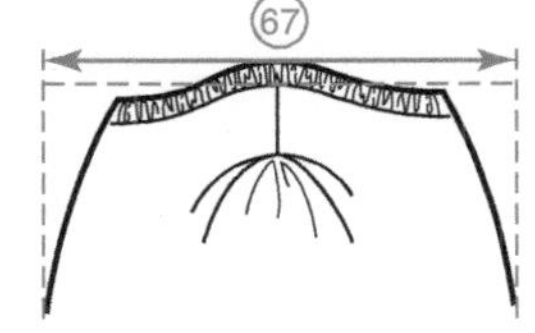

67

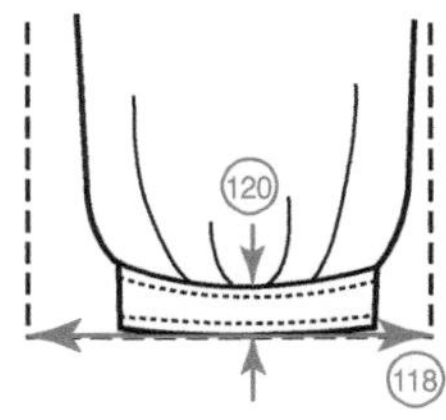

120
118

41

Measuring Woven Jumpsuits and One-Piece Garments

The jumpsuit has made a comeback in women's fashion, not only for eveningwear, but daytime and work wear as well. Measuring woven one-piece garments or jumpsuits basically combines the measurements of a woven top and a woven pant. Therefore, the rules you learned for each of those styles will be used here as well. You may want to look back over Chapters 9 and 11. Figure 13.1 shows that a jumpsuit can be measured from point 153, Front Torso Length, from the high point shoulder to the bottom of the garment. Or it can be measured from point 151a, Front Torso Length, from the high point shoulder to the crotch joining seam. Some technicians choose to use both measurements. As always, you will decide which measurement points work best for the style under evaluation.

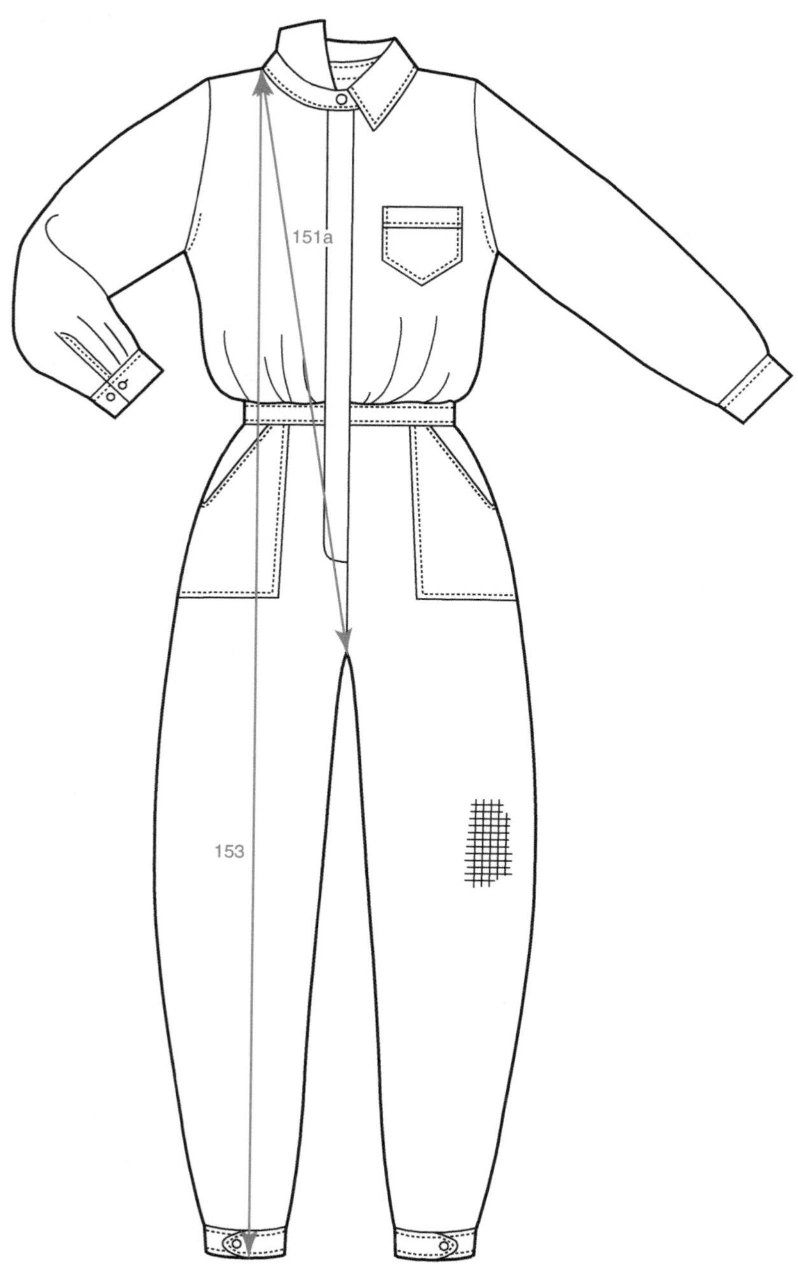

Figure 13.1 Choose the best measuring point based on garment design.

5. *Front Bodice Length (garments with a front opening)*—Measure from high point shoulder at neck straight down, parallel to center front, to top edge of waistband, joining seam, or rib. If garment has a collar, gently lift it away from shoulder-neck measuring point.

6. *Center Front Bodice Length (garments with a plain front; no front opening)*—Measure from center front neck joining seam straight down to top edge of waistband, joining seam, or rib. [Note: A garment with a center opening may still require point of measure 5, Front Bodice Length, if neckline is unusual or is difficult to measure.]

7. *Center Back Bodice Length*—Measure from center back neck joining seams straight down to top edge of waistband, joining seam, or rib. If needed, gently lift collar away from back neck to expose joining seam.

8. *Side Seam Bodice Length*—Measure from bottom of armhole/side seam straight down to top edge of waistband, joining seam, or rib, along side of garment, following natural curve of garment's side seam, unless otherwise indicated. If needed, gently lift sleeve away from armhole/side seam joining seam. [Note: You can take side seam bodice measurement straight rather than contoured if joining seam/rib can be extended, but indicate change on spec sheet.]

10. *Chest Width Circumference (woven)*—Measure from edge of garment/side seam to edge of garment/side seam straight across garment at a point 1" below armhole. Double this measurement.

12. *Chest Width Circumference/Raglan Sleeve (woven)*—Measure from edge of garment/side seam to edge of garment/side seam straight across garment at a point _____" below high point shoulder. Double this measurement. [Note: You will have to determine number of inches down from high point shoulder for each raglan sleeve style based on depth of sleeve. Then indicate this number on spec sheet.]

13. *Across Shoulder*—Measure straight across front from armhole seam/edge to armhole seam/edge at shoulder seam or across natural shoulder fold line created if there is no seam.

14. *Shoulder Width*—Measure from neckband/collar/ribbing joining seam or neckline edge to top of armhole seam at shoulder, taken along shoulder seam or across natural shoulder fold line created if there is no seam.

15. *Across Chest*—Measure 2½" down from collar/rib joining seam at center front straight across front of garment from armhole seam/edge to armhole seam/edge. [Note: The 2½" measurement point is for misses/women's wear only and may need to be adjusted up or down ¼" to ½" accordingly for men's, children's, junior's, and large/plus sizes. Indicate any changes on spec sheet.]

16. *Across Back*—Measure 4" down from collar/rib joining seam at center back straight across back of garment from armhole seam/edge to armhole seam/edge. [Note: The 4" measurement point is for misses/women's wear only and may need to be adjusted up or down ¼" to ½" accordingly for men's, children's, junior's, and large/plus sizes. Indicate any changes on the spec sheet.]

17. *Across Chest/Center Armhole*—Measure at one-half depth of armhole straight across front of garment from armhole seam/edge to armhole seam/edge.

18. *Across Back/Center Armhole*—Measure at one-half depth of armhole straight across back of garment from armhole seam/edge to armhole seam/edge.

20. *Waist Width Circumference (woven)*—Measure from edge of garment/side seam to edge of garment/side seam straight across garment on seam or at narrowest point of waist taper at a point _____" below high point shoulder. Double this measurement. [Note: You will have to determine number of inches down from high point shoulder for each raglan sleeve

style based on depth of sleeve. Then indicate this number on spec sheet.]

32. *Yoke Width Front*—Measure from armhole seam/edge to armhole seam/edge straight across front of garment, ignoring contours or points, at yoke-body joining seams. [Note: If yoke is asymmetrical, indicate changes in measuring as needed on spec sheet.]

33. *Yoke Width Back*—Measure from armhole seam/edge to armhole seam/edge straight across back of garment, ignoring contours or points, at yoke-body joining seams. [Note: If yoke is asymmetrical, indicate changes in measuring as needed on spec sheet.]

34. *Yoke Depth Front*—Measure from high point shoulder at neck straight down to bottom of front yoke-body joining seam. Gently lift collar away from shoulder-neck joining seam if needed.

35. *Yoke Back Depth*—Measure from center back neck joining seam straight down to bottom of back yoke-body joining seam. Gently lift collar away from back neck joining seam if needed.

36. *Sleeve Length Top Armhole*—Measure along top of sleeve/fold, following contour of sleeve from armhole seam at shoulder to bottom of sleeve opening, including cuff.

37. *Sleeve Length Top Neck*—Measure along top of sleeve/fold, following contour of sleeve from sleeve-neck joining seam/edge to edge of sleeve opening, including cuff. Gently lift collar at sleeve-neck joining seam if needed.

38. *Sleeve Length Center Back*—Measure from center back neck joining seam or from a point above neck at an imaginary line, that of a joining seam, along top of sleeve/fold, following contour of sleeve to edge of sleeve opening, including cuff.

39. *Sleeve Length Underarm*—Measure straight from bottom of armhole along sleeve seam to edge of sleeve opening, including cuff.

41. *Straight Armhole Width Circumference (woven)*—Measure from top of shoulder joining seam/edge straight down to bottom of armhole. Double this measurement.

43. *Curved Armhole Width Circumference (woven)*—Measure from top of shoulder joining seam/edge to bottom of armhole, following contour of armhole. Double this measurement.

44. *Armhole Front*—Measure on front of garment from top of shoulder at neckline joining seam/edge to bottom of armhole, following contour of armhole. Gently lift collar away from neckline joining seam if needed.

45. *Armhole Back*—Measure on back of garment from top of shoulder at neck joining seam/edge to bottom of armhole, following contour of armhole. Gently lift collar away from neck joining seam if needed.

47. *Armhole Width Circumference Straight (woven)*—Measure from top of shoulder seam at a point _____" below neckline joining seam/edge straight down to bottom of armhole. Double this measurement. [Note: Gently move collar away from neck joining seam if needed when measuring down _____" to armhole start point. Indicate the number of inches measured down on spec sheet.]

49. *Muscle Width Circumference (woven)*—Measure from inner sleeve edge/seam to outer sleeve edge/fold at a point 1" below armhole and parallel to sleeve opening. Double this measurement.

51. *Elbow Width Circumference (woven)*—Measure from inner sleeve edge/seam to outer sleeve edge/fold straight across sleeve at a point one-half of underarm sleeve length and parallel to sleeve opening at wrist

or cuff. Double this measurement. [Note: If sleeve is three-quarter length, indicate new point of measure on spec sheet.]

53. *Sleeve Opening Width Circumference (woven)*—Measure from inner sleeve edge/seam to outer sleeve edge/fold straight across bottom edge of sleeve opening. Double this measurement.

55. *Sleeve Opening Width Circumference, Stretched (woven)*—Measure from inner sleeve edge/seam to outer sleeve edge/fold straight across bottom edge of sleeve opening in a fully extended position. Double this measurement.

56. *Cuff Length Sleeve*—Measure from outside end of buttonhole to center of button straight along center of cuff. Open cuff out as flat as possible when measuring. [Note: If cuff length is contoured, measure along center-most point.]

57. *Cuff/Ribbing Height Sleeve*—Measure from cuff joining seam or top of ribbing straight down to bottom edge of cuff or rib opening. [Note: If cuff is contoured, indicate changes made to measurement on spec sheet.]

58. *Neck Depth Front (garments with a plain front/asymmetrical front opening)*—Measure from center back neck joining seam/edge straight down to center front neck joining seam/edge.

59. *Neck Depth Center Front (garments with a center front opening)*—Measure from center back neck joining seam/edge straight down to center of first button at center front of garment.

60. *Neck Drop Front*—Measure from an imaginary line connecting neckline edges straight down to center front neck opening edge. Use a ruler if needed to connect top neckline edges.

61. *Neck Drop Back*—Measure from an imaginary line connecting neckline edges straight down to center back neck opening edge. This measurement is taken with front of garment faceup. Use a ruler to connect top neckline edges if needed.

62. *Neck Width, No Collar*—Measure from inside neck edge/seam to inside neck edge/seam straight across back neck at widest point. This measurement is taken with front of garment faceup.

63. *Neck Width, Collar*—Measure straight across back neck from neck-shoulder joining seam to neck-shoulder joining seam or natural shoulder line if no seam. This measurement is taken with back of garment faceup.

65. *Neck Edge Width Circumference (woven)*—Measure from neck edge/seam/fold to neck edge/seam/fold along top opening edge, following natural contour of neck opening. Garment should be positioned with one shoulder on top of the other and with front and back neck edges meeting. Double this measurement.

67. *Neck Edge Width Circumference, Stretched (woven)*—Measure from neck edge/seam/fold to neck edge/seam/fold along top opening edge in a fully extended position. Garment should be positioned with one shoulder on top of the other and with front and back neck edges meeting. Double this measurement.

69. *Neck Base Circumference (woven)*—Measure from neck edge/seam to neck edge/seam along collar/rib joining seam or neckline edge, following natural contour of neck opening. Garment should be buttoned or zippered, if applicable, with one shoulder seam positioned on top of the other and with front and back neck edges meeting. Double this measurement.

70. *Neckband Length*—Measure from outside end of buttonhole to center of buttonhole across neckband, following contour of neckband.

71. *Collar Length*—Measure from one end of collar to other end of collar along neck joining seam.

72. *Collar Height*—Measure from collar/rib joining seam at center back neck straight up to outer edge of collar/rib.

73. *Collar Band Height*—Measure from collar joining seam at center back straight up to neckband joining seam at center back.

74. *Collar Point Length*—Measure from collar joining seam to outer edge of collar along collar point edge. [Note: If collar is rounded, measure at a point parallel to center back and indicate change on spec sheet.]

75. *Collar Point Spread (pointed collars only)*—Measure, with collar band buttoned and collar in place, from collar point straight across collar edge to collar point.

76. *Lapel Width*

A. *Notched*—Measure from lower lapel notch straight across to lapel fold at a point perpendicular to garment center front.

B. *Without Notches*—Measure from lapel edge straight across widest point of lapel to lapel fold at a point _____" down from center back collar joining seam and perpendicular to front of garment.

77. *Center Front Extension*—Measure from an imaginary line at center front of garment horizontally to finished outer edge of front extended piece.

78. *Placket Length*—Measure from top edge of placket straight down to bottom of placket opening along center of placket.

79. *Placket Width*—Measure from placket joining seam straight across placket to placket edge at fold.

80. *Keyhole Length*—Measure from outer edge of neckline straight down to bottom of keyhole opening.

81. *Waistband Depth*—Measure from top of waistband edge straight down to bottom of waistband at waistband joining seam. [Note: If waistband is contoured, indicate measurement change on spec sheet.]

83. *Waistband Width Circumference (woven)*—Measure from side of bottom band to side of bottom band along center of band, following natural contour of waistband. Double this measurement.

85. *Waistband Width Circumference, Stretched (woven)*—Measure from side of bottom band to side of bottom band straight across center of band in a fully extended position. Double this measurement.

87. *High Hip Width Circumference (woven)*—Measure from edge of garment/side seam to edge of garment/side seam at a point 4" below bottom edge of waistband/seam, following contour of waist. Double this measurement. [Note: The 4" point is for misses/women's wear only; adjust as needed ½" to 1" up or down for children's, petite's, junior's, or large/plus sizes. Indicate change on spec sheet.]

89. *Low Hip Width Circumference from Waist (woven)*—Measure from edge of garment/side seam to edge of garment/side seam at a point 7" below bottom edge of waistband/seam, following contour of waist. Double this measurement. [Note: The 7" point is for misses/women's wear only; adjust as needed ½" to 1" up or down for children's, petite's, junior's, or large/plus sizes. Indicate change on spec sheet.]

91. *Hip Width from High Point Shoulder Circumference (woven)*—Measure from edge of garment/side seam to edge of garment/side seam straight across at a point _____" below high point shoulder. Double this measurement. [Note: You will have to estimate low hip point on garment if there is no waistband and fill in _____" from high point shoulder. This measurement will vary for children's, junior's, misses, and large/plus sizes.]

93. *Hip Seat Width Circumference (woven pant)*—Measure from edge of garment/side seam to edge of garment/side seam at a point _____" up from

crotch seam, following contour of waist. Double this measurement. [Note 1: This measurement is useful when the waistband sits below the natural waistline. Note 2: Adjust _____" up from crotch as needed for junior's and large/plus sizes. Note 3: A hip seat width of 2½" up for children's and 3" up for menswear can take place of low hip width.]

103. *Skirt/Pant Yoke Depth Front*—Measure from bottom of waistband/seam (top edge if not banded, or stitching if self-elastic/drawstring casing) straight down to bottom of yoke joining seam at center front. [Note: If yoke is contoured, indicate point of measure on spec sheet.]

104. *Skirt/Pant Yoke Depth Back*—Measure from bottom of waistband/seam (top edge if not banded, or stitching if self-elastic/drawstring casing) straight down to bottom of yoke joining seam at center back. [Note: If yoke is contoured, indicate point of measure on spec sheet.]

105. *Inseam*—Measure from crotch joining seam to bottom of leg opening, following inseam/inner fold.

106. *Outseam*—Measure from bottom edge of waistband/seam (top edge if not banded, or stitching if self-elastic/drawstring casing) to bottom of garment along side seam/fold of garment.

107. *Front Rise*—Measure from bottom edge of waistband/seam (top edge if not banded, or stitching if self-elastic/drawstring casing) to crotch joining seam, following curve of front rise seam. [Note: Measure over zipper if in front rise seam.]

108. *Back Rise*—Measure from bottom edge of waistband/seam (top edge if not banded, or stitching if self-elastic/drawstring casing) to crotch joining seam, following curve of back rise seam. [Note: Measure over zipper if in front back seam.]

110. *Thigh Width Circumference (woven)*—Measure from pant leg edge/seam to pant leg edge/seam straight across pant leg at a point 1" below crotch and parallel to leg opening. Double this measurement. [Note: If leg opening is asymmetrical, measure to a point that would be parallel to leg opening.]

112. *Knee Width Circumference (woven)*—Measure from pant leg edge/seam to pant leg edge/seam at a point one-half of the inseam and parallel to leg opening. Double this measurement. [Note 1: If leg opening is asymmetrical, measure to a point that would be parallel to leg opening. Note 2: If pant leg is three-quarter length, indicate point of measure on spec sheet. Note 3: A general knee measurement from crotch seam of misses 14", junior's 13", large/plus women's 15" can be used. Indicate change on spec sheet. Measure children's at one-half inseam minus 1½", and for men's minus 2".]

114. *Leg Opening Width Circumference (woven)*—Measure from pant leg edge/seam to pant leg edge/seam straight across bottom edge of leg opening. Double this measurement. [Note: If leg opening is contoured, follow contour and indicate measurement change on spec sheet.]

116. *Vented Leg Opening Circumference (woven)*—Measure from pant leg edge/seam to pant leg edge/seam straight across pant leg at top of side vents. Double this measurement.

118. *Leg Opening Width Circumference, Stretched (woven)*—Measure from pant leg edge/seam to pant leg edge/seam straight across bottom edge of leg opening in a fully extended position. Double this measurement.

119. *Cuff Height Pants*—Measure from top of cuff edge straight down to bottom of cuff fold and leg opening.

120. *Bottom Band/Ribbing Height Pants*—Measure from cuff joining seam or top of ribbing straight down to bottom edge of cuff or rib opening. [Note: For fashion-forward pants, you may want to include a

cuff length. See point of measure 56, Cuff Length Sleeve, for measuring instructions and, if needed, indicate cuff length of pant on spec sheet.]

121. *Fly/Zipper*
A. *Length*—Measure from top of fly/zipper opening straight down to bottom of fly/zipper opening at zipper stop or bar tack.
B. *Fly/Zipper Width*—Measure top of fly/zipper at joining seam from edge/fold straight across to fly/zipper placket stitching.

122. *Vent/Slit*
A. *Height*—Measure from top of vent/slit straight down to bottom of vent/slit along edge of vent/slit.
B. *Width*—Measure top of vent/slit from edge/fold straight across to vent/slit placket stitching at a point parallel to garment hemline.

123. *Pleat Depth*—Measure from outer edge of pleat at fold/crease to inner fold of pleat. [Note 1: It is a good idea to indicate what type of pleat is being measured, e.g., box, inverted, knife, kick, kilt, or envelope. Note 2: If pleats are not parallel or symmetrical, indicate any special instructions on spec sheet.]

124. *Distance Between Pleats*—Measure from start of pleat to start of pleat, excluding pleat depth at a point directly below pleat joining seam. [Note: If pleats are not parallel or symmetrical, indicate any special instructions on spec sheet.]

125. *Applied Pocket Height*—Measure from top edge of pocket to bottom edge of pocket along center of pocket. [Note: For contoured or irregularly shaped pockets, take a second measurement and indicate point of measure on spec sheet.]

126. *Applied Pocket Width*—Measure from side of pocket to side of pocket along top edge of pocket. [Note: For contoured or irregularly shaped pockets, take a second measurement and indicate point of measure on spec sheet.]

127. *Pocket Opening Within a Seam*—Measure from top of pocket to bottom of pocket along edge of pocket opening.

128. *Belt Length*
A. *Total*—Measure from end of belt at buckle along center of belt to opposite end of belt, following contour.
B. *Circumference*—Measure from end of belt at buckle along center of belt to middle hole at opposite end.

129. *Belt Width (or Height)*—Measure from edge of belt straight across to edge of belt. [Note: If belt is contoured, indicate points of measure on spec sheet.]

130. *Belt Loop Length*—Measure from top of belt loop straight down/vertically to bottom of belt loop along center of belt loop. [Note: Fashion-forward or irregularly shaped belt loops may require further spec instructions. Indicate points of measure on spec sheet.]

131. *Belt Loop Width*—Measure belt loop from edge of belt loop straight across/horizontally to edge of belt loop. [Note: Fashion-forward or irregularly shaped belt loops may require further spec instructions. Indicate points of measure on spec sheet.]

132. *Tie Length*—Measure from end of tie/joining seam straight down to tie end along center of tie.

133. *Tie Width*
A. *Straight*—Measure from edge of tie straight across to edge of tie.
B. *Contoured*—Measure from edge of tie straight across to edge of tie at widest point of tie.

134. *Flounce/Ruffle Width*—Measure from flounce/ruffle joining seam straight across to outer edge of flounce/ruffle. [Note: If flounce/ruffle is contoured, measure along narrowest and widest points if possible and indicate changes on spec sheet.]

135. *Strap Length*—Measure from strap joining seam along center of strap to end of strap. [Note: If a strap

is contoured or has a contoured edge, measure along center, approximating center end point, or indicate instructions as needed on spec sheet.]

136. *Strap Width*—Measure from edge of strap straight across to edge of strap. [Note: If strap is contoured, measure along narrowest and widest points if possible and indicate changes on spec sheet.]

137. *Front Hood Length*—Measure from top of hood to bottom of hood at center front joining seam along opening edge of hood.

138. *Back Hood Length*—Measure from top of hood at center front to bottom of hood at center back joining seam along outside curve of hood fold/seam.

139. *Hood Width*—Measure from front opening edge of hood straight across to back of hood at fold along widest point of hood.

140. *Flange Depth*—Measure from center back neck joining seam straight down to bottom of flange at center back. [Note: If flange is contoured or asymmetrical, indicate point of measure on spec sheet.]

141. *Shoulder Pad Length*—Measure from edge of pad straight across to edge of pad along center of pad or natural shoulder line of pad.

142. *Shoulder Pad Width*—Measure from side of pad straight across to side of pad along edge of pad if straight or at widest point of pad if curved.

143. *Straight Edge Shoulder Pad Height*—Measure from top of pad straight down to bottom of pad along center of pad.

144. *Curved Edge Shoulder Pad Height*—Stick a 1" straight pin into the thickest part of shoulder pad. Push pin all the way through pad until head of pin rests on top of pad. Be sure not to crush pad. Measure portion of pin sticking out of pad. Subtract this figure from 1" (length of pin) to get shoulder pad height.

145. *Shoulder Pad Placement*—Measure from neck edge or joining seam straight across shoulder seam or natural shoulder line to start of shoulder pad.

146. *Pleats Placement*

A. *Front Pleat Top*—Measure distance from center front of garment straight across to start of first pleat at a point parallel to garment hem. [Note: You may need to use armhole or side seam as a starting point if there is no center front seam or placket.]
B. *Back Pleat Top*—Measure distance from armhole seam/side seam (depending on pleat placement) to first pleat at a point parallel to garment hem.
C. *Front Pleat Skirt/Pant*—Measure distance from center front of garment waistband joining seam/edge straight across to start of first pleat.

147. *Button Placement*—Refer to point of measure 59, Neck Depth Center Front, for placement of first button. Then measure distance of first button to second button. Be sure when measuring that button at bust point is lined up to apex of bust. Adjust all buttons accordingly and respace as needed.

148. *Pocket Placement*

A. *Top Pocket Vertical*—Measure from shoulder-neck joining seam straight down to top edge of pocket.
B. *Top Pocket Horizontal*—Measure from center front straight across to side of pocket at top edge.
C. *Front Bottom Pocket Vertical*—Measure from waistband/joining seam/edge straight down to top edge of pocket.
D. *Front Bottom Pocket Horizontal*—Measure from center front straight across to side of pocket at top edge.
E. *Back Bottom Pocket Vertical*—Measure from waistband/joining seam/edge straight down to top edge of pocket.
F. *Back Bottom Pocket Horizontal*—Measure from center back straight across to side of pocket at top edge.
G. *Pocket from Side Seam*—Measure from side seam straight across to top of pocket. [Note: If pocket is contoured at sides, a top and bottom pocket size and placement must be measured and added to spec sheet.]

149. *Belt Loop Placement*

A. *Front*—Measure from center front of garment horizontally across to center of first front belt loop.
B. *Back*—Measure from center back of garment horizontally across to center of first back belt loop.
C. *Side Seam to Front*—Measure from center of side seam belt loop to center of front belt loop.
D. *Side Seam to Back*—Measure from center of side seam belt loop to center of back belt loop.

150. *Dart Placement*

A. *High Point Shoulder Bust Dart*—Measure from shoulder-neck joining seam or at a point _____" from shoulder-neck seam straight down, parallel to center front, to top of dart. [Note: The _____" from shoulder seam measurement is to be used for darts that are too short to be measured from high point shoulder. Be sure to indicate _____" measurement on spec sheet.]
B. *Center Front Bust Dart*—Measure from center front of garment straight across to top of dart.
C. *Side Seam Bust Dart*—Measure from underarm/side seam joining seam down along contour of side seam to bottom of dart.
D. *High Point Shoulder Princess Dart*—Measure from shoulder-neck joining seam straight down to top of dart.
E. *Center Front Princess Dart*—Measure from center front of garment straight across to top of dart.
F. *Center Front Skirt/Pant*—Measure from the center front of the garment at waistband joining seam/edge straight across to top of dart.
G. *Center Back Skirt/Pant*—Measure from center back of garment at waistband joining seam/edge straight across to top of dart.

151. *Front Torso Length (jumpsuits and one-piece garments)*

A. *Garments with a Front Opening, Relaxed*—Measure from high point shoulder at neck straight down to crotch joining seam with garment in a relaxed position.
B. *Garments with a Front Opening, Extended*—Measure from high point shoulder at neck straight down to crotch joining seam with garment in a fully extended position.
C. *Garments with a Plain Front, No Front Opening, Relaxed*—Measure from center front neck joining seam straight down to crotch joining seam with garment in a relaxed position.
D. *Garments with a Plain Front, No Front Opening, Extended*—Measure from center front neck joining seam straight down to crotch joining seam with garment in a fully extended position.

152. *Back Torso Length (jumpsuits and one-piece garments)*

A. *Relaxed*—Measure from center back neck joining seam straight down to crotch joining seam with garment in a relaxed position.
B. *Extended*—Measure from center back neck joining seam straight down to crotch joining seam with garment in a fully extended position.

153. *High Point Shoulder Length (jumpsuits and one-piece garments)*—Measure from high point shoulder straight down to bottom/hem of garment.

154. *Center Back Garment Length (jumpsuits and one-piece garments)*—Measure from center back neckline seam/edge, straight down to bottom hem of garment. [Note: For pantsuits this point will intersect at an imaginary line formed by hemlines of pant legs and the center of garment.]

155. *Crotch Width*—Measure straight across crotch from side to side along seam/bottom edge/fold.

CHAPTER 13 TERMS

When working with woven jumpsuits and one-piece garments, you may come across the following garment terms. If you are unfamiliar with any of them, please look up the definitions in the glossary at the end of this text.

Bib overalls
Body shirt
Jumpsuit
Overalls
Pant jumper

SPEC SHEET: One-piece woven jumpsuit	**STYLE**
SEASON:	DESCRIPTION:
LABEL: (SIZE CATEGORY)	
DATE:	
TECHNICAL SKETCH	SKETCH/PHOTO

58 13 15 36 43 49 151a 10 6 51 78 79 8 39 83 53 127 87 107 89 110 153 106 112 105 114

CODE	POINT OF MEASURE	TOL. +/–	4	S/6	8	M/10	12	L/14	16	XL/18
5.	Front bodice length	3/8								
6.	Center front bodice length	3/8								
7.	Center back bodice length	3/8								
8.	Side seam bodice length	3/8								
10.	Chest width circumference	1/2-3/4								
13.	Across shoulder	1/4								
15.	Across chest	1/4								
16.	Across back	1/4								
32.	Yoke width front	1/4								
33.	Yoke width back	1/4								
34.	Yoke depth front	1/8								
35.	Yoke depth back	1/8								

(Tolerance 1/2-3/4 S, M, L, XL = 3/4" 4-18 = 1/2")

The measured garment spec sheets are for ***illustrative purposes only*** and should not be used as industry standards

CODE	POINT OF MEASURE	TOL. +/–	4	S/6	8	M/10	12	L/14	16	XL/18
36.	Sleeve length top armhole	3/8								
39.	Sleeve length underarm	3/8								
43.	Curved armhole width circumference	3/8								
49.	Muscle width circumference	1/4								
51.	Elbow width circumference	1/4								
53.	Sleeve opening width circumference	1/4								
56.	Cuff length sleeve	1/4								
57.	Cuff/ribbing height sleeve	1/8								
58.	Neck depth front	1/8								
63.	Neck width collar	1/4								
70.	Neckband length	1/4								
71.	Collar length	1/4								
72.	Collar height	1/8								
73.	Collar band height	1/8								
74.	Collar point length	1/8								
75.	Collar point spread	1/4								
81.	Waistband depth	1/8								
83.	Waistband width circumference	1/2-3/4								
85.	Waistband width circumference stretched	1/2-3/4								
87.	High hip width circumference	1/2-3/4								
89.	Low hip width circumference	1/2-3/4								
105.	Inseam	3/8								
106.	Outseam	3/8								
107.	Front rise	3/8								
108.	Back rise	3/8								
110.	Thigh width circumference	3/8								
112.	Knee width circumference	3/8								
114.	Leg opening width circumference	1/8								
121.	Fly/zipper A. Length	1/4								
	B. Width	1/8								
125.	Applied pocket height	1/8								

COMMENTS:

The measured garment spec sheets are for ***illustrative purposes only*** and should not be used as industry standards

CODE	POINT OF MEASURE	TOL. +/–	4	S/6	8	M/10	12	L/14	16	XL/18
126.	Applied pocket width	1/8								
127.	Pocket opening	1/8								
151.	Front torso length A. Front opening relaxed	1/2								
152.	Back torso length	1/2								
153.	Total garment length front	3/4								
154.	Total garment length back	3/4								

COMMENTS:

The measured garment spec sheets are for ***illustrative purposes only*** and should not be used as industry standards

SPEC SHEET One-piece woven jumpsuit	STYLE
SEASON: Spring/summer	DESCRIPTION: One-piece madris plaid bathing suit
LABEL: (SIZE CATEGORY) Missy	cover-up with contrast piping and back elastic waist
DATE:	
TECHNICAL SKETCH	SKETCH/PHOTO

CODE	POINT OF MEASURE	TOL. +/–	4	S/6	8	M/10	12	L/14	16	XL/18
5.	Front bodice length	3/8				16 1/2				
6.	Center front bodice length	3/8				10 1/2				
7.	Center back bodice length	3/8				15				
8.	Side seam bodice length	3/8				8 1/2				
10.	Chest width circumference	1/2-3/4				38				
13.	Across shoulder	1/4				14				
15.	Across chest 5" from HPS	1/4				13 1/2				
16.	Across back	1/4				13				
32.	Yoke width front	1/4								
33.	Yoke width back	1/4								
34.	Yoke depth front	1/8								
35.	Yoke depth back	1/8								

(Tolerance 1/2-3/4 S, M, L, XL = 3/4" 4-18 = 1/2")

The measured garment spec sheets are for ***illustrative purposes only*** and should not be used as industry standards

CODE	POINT OF MEASURE	TOL. +/–	4	S/6	8	M/10	12	L/14	16	XL/18
36.	Sleeve length top armhole	3/8				8				
39.	Sleeve length underarm	3/8				3				
43.	Curved armhole width circumference	3/8				19				
49.	Muscle width circumference	1/4				15				
51.	Elbow width circumference	1/4								
53.	Sleeve opening width circumference	1/4				14				
56.	Cuff length sleeve	1/4								
57.	Cuff/ribbing height sleeve	1/8								
58.	Neck depth front	1/8								
63.	Neck width collar	1/4								
70.	Neckband length	1/4								
71.	Collar length	1/4								
72.	Collar height	1/8								
73.	Collar band height	1/8								
74.	Collar point length	1/8								
75.	Collar point spread	1/4								
81.	Waistband depth	1/8								
83.	Waistband width circumference	1/2-3/4				30				
85.	Waistband width circumference stretched	1/2-3/4				35				
87.	High hip width circumference	1/2-3/4				40				
89.	Low hip width circumference	1/2-3/4				43				
105.	Inseam	3/8				6				
106.	Outseam	3/8				17				
107.	Front rise	3/8				12 1/2				
108.	Back rise	3/8				15				
110.	Thigh width circumference	3/8				27				
112.	Knee width circumference	3/8								
114.	Leg opening width circumference	1/8				25				
121.	Fly/zipper A. Length	1/4								
	B. Width	1/8								
125.	Applied pocket height	1/8								

COMMENTS:

The measured garment spec sheets are for ***illustrative purposes only*** and should not be used as industry standards

CODE	POINT OF MEASURE	TOL. +/–	4	S/6	8	M/10	12	L/14	16	XL/18
126.	Applied pocket width	1/8								
127.	Pocket opening	1/8				7				
151.	Front torso length A. Front opening relaxed	1/2				30 1/4				
152.	Back torso length Straight, do not follow curve	1/2				31				
153.	Total garment length front	3/4				35				
154.	Total garment length back	3/4				33 1/2				
60.	Neck drop front	1/8				6				
61.	Neck drop back	1/8				1 3/4				
62.	Neck width, no collar	1/4				7 1/2				
78.	Placket length	1/4				20				
79.	Placket width	1/8				1 1/2				
150.	Dart length front princess	1/8				4 1/2				
150.	Dart placement E. C.F. to princess	1/8				4				
	Piping width	-				1/8				

COMMENTS:

The measured garment spec sheets are for illustrative purposes only and should not be used as industry standards

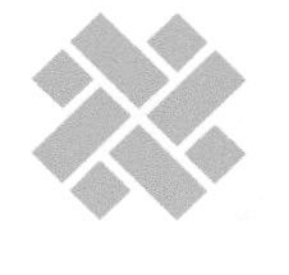

CHAPTER 14

Blazers and Unconstructed Jackets

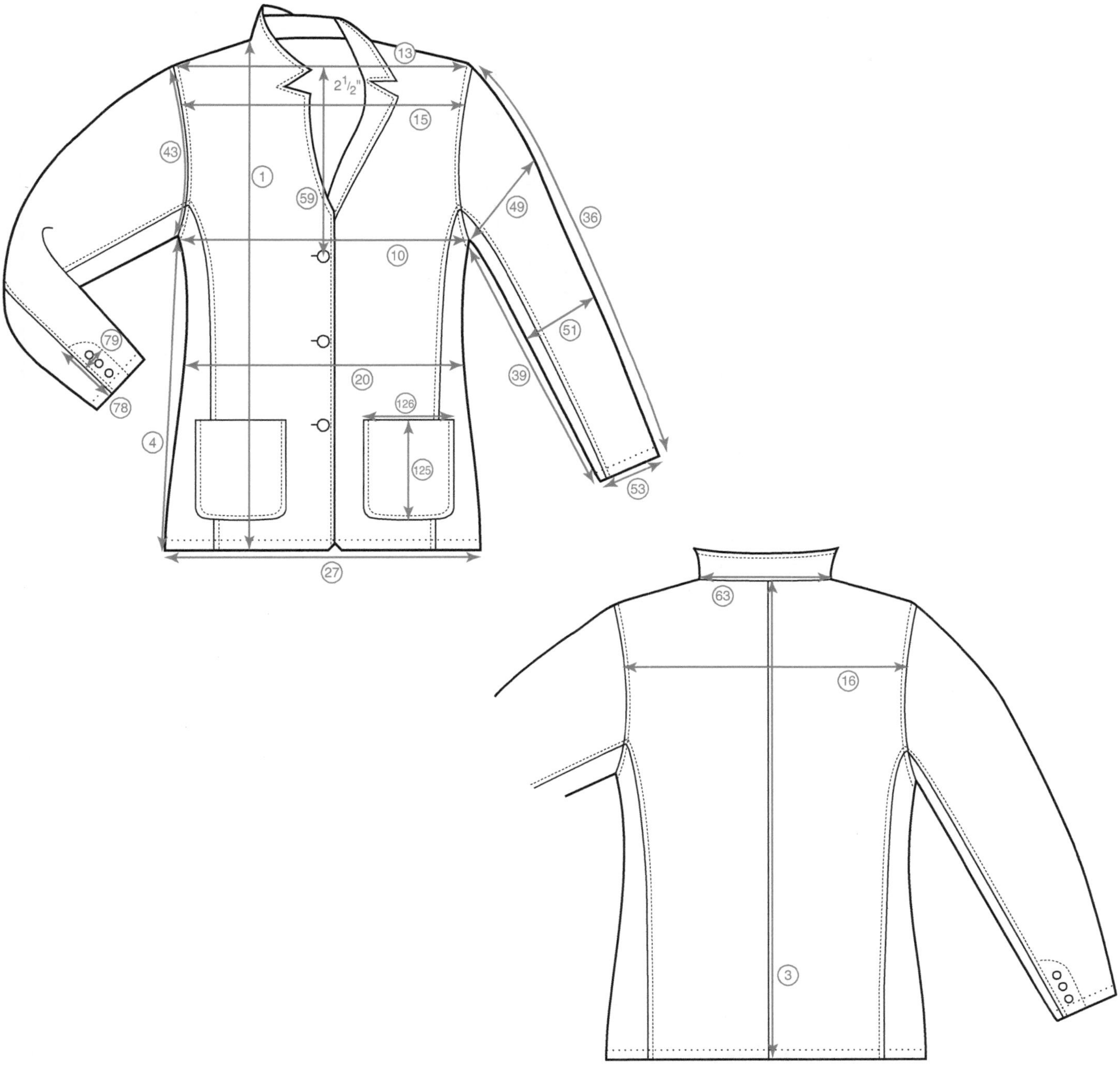

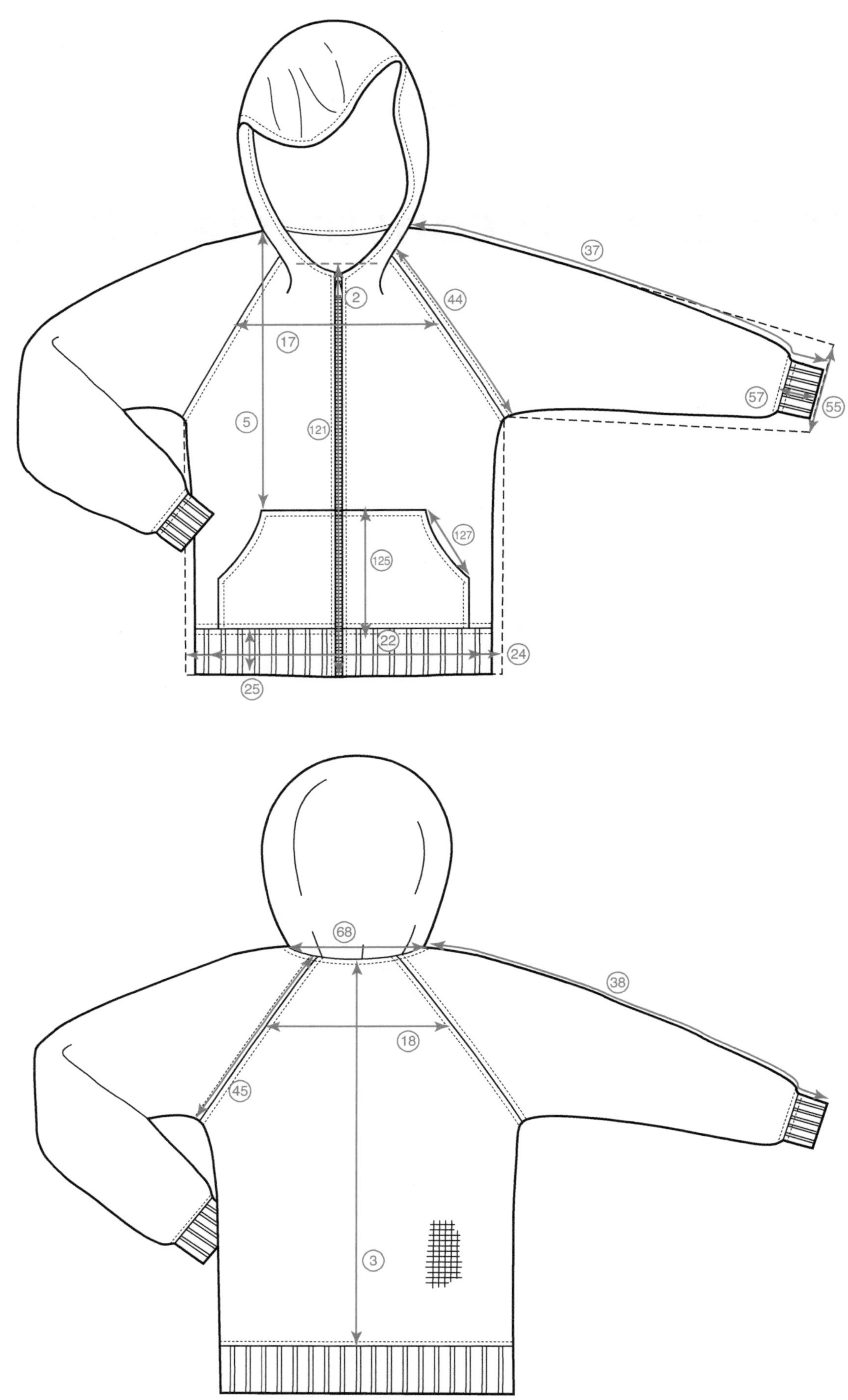

37
2
44
17
57
55
5
121
127
125
22
24
25
68
38
18
45
3

138
139
137
29
122
57
56
41
65
69
34
32
78
79
127
24
25
63
35
33
71
72
70
73

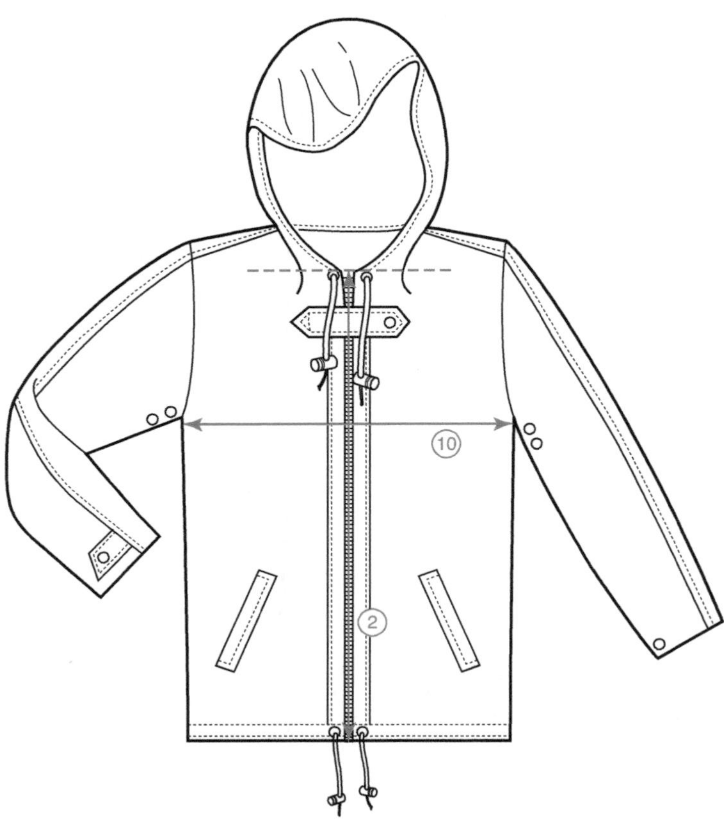

Figure 14.1 Choosing the best measurement points based on style features.

Measuring Blazers and Unconstructed Jackets

Blazers and unconstructed jackets, either knitted or woven, are treated as wovens when measuring due to garment construction. Unconstructed knitted jackets are either classified as jackets—thus using this category—or as cardigans, therefore using the knit top category. As always it is important to look at style features when choosing which measurement points are best for individual garments (see Figure 14.1).

1. *Front Length (garments with a front opening)*—Measure from high point shoulder at neck straight down, parallel to center front, to the bottom of garment at front. If the garment has a collar, gently lift it away from the shoulder-neck measuring point.

2. *Center Front Length (garments with a plain front; no front opening)*—Measure from center front neck joining seams straight down to bottom of garment at center front. [Note: A garment with a front opening may still require point of measure 1, Front Length, if neckline is unusual or is difficult to measure.]

3. *Center Back Length*—Measure from center back neck joining seams straight down to bottom of garment at center back. If needed, gently lift collar away from back neck to expose joining seam.

4. *Side Length*—Measure from bottom of armhole/side seam straight down to bottom of garment along side of garment. Do not follow natural curve of garment's side seam, unless otherwise indicated. If needed, gently lift the sleeve away from armhole/side seam joining seam.

5. *Front Bodice Length (garments with a front opening)*—Measure from high point shoulder at neck straight down, parallel to center front, to top edge of waistband, joining seam, or rib. If garment has a collar, gently lift it away from shoulder-neck measuring point.

6. *Center Front Bodice Length (garments with a plain front; no front opening)*—Measure from center front neck joining seam straight down to top edge of waistband, joining seam, or rib. [Note: A garment with a center opening may still require point of measure 5, Front Bodice Length, if neckline is unusual or is difficult to measure]

7. *Center Back Bodice Length*—Measure from center back neck joining seams straight down to top edge of waistband, joining seam, or rib. If needed, gently lift collar away from back neck to expose joining seam.

8. *Side Seam Bodice Length*—Measure from bottom of armhole/side seam straight down to top edge of waistband, joining seam, or rib, along side of garment, following natural curve of garment's side seam, unless otherwise indicated. If needed, gently lift sleeve away from armhole/side seam joining seam. [Note: You can take side seam bodice measurement straight rather than contoured if joining seam/rib can be extended, but indicate change on spec sheet.]

10. *Chest Width Circumference (woven)*—Measure from edge of garment/side seam to edge of garment/side seam straight across garment at a point 1" below armhole. Double this measurement.

12. *Chest Width Circumference Raglan Sleeve (woven)*—Measure from edge of garment/side seam to edge of garment/side seam straight across garment at a point _____" below high point shoulder. Double this measurement. [Note: You will have to determine number of inches down from high point shoulder for each raglan sleeve style based on depth of sleeve. Then indicate this number on spec sheet.]

13. *Across Shoulder*—Measure straight across front from armhole seam/edge to armhole seam/edge at shoulder seam or across natural shoulder fold line created if there is no seam.

14. *Shoulder Width*—Measure from neckband/collar/ribbing joining seam or neckline edge to top of armhole seam at shoulder, taken along shoulder seam or across natural shoulder fold line created if there is no seam.

15. *Across Chest*—Measure 2½" down from collar/rib joining seam at center front straight across front of garment from armhole seam/edge to armhole seam/edge. [Note: The 2½" measurement point is for misses/women's wear only and may need to be adjusted up or down ¼" to ½" accordingly for men's, children's, junior's, and large/plus sizes. Indicate any changes on spec sheet.]

16. *Across Back*—Measure 4" down from collar/rib joining seam at center back straight across back of garment from armhole seam/edge to armhole seam/edge. [Note: The 4" measurement point is for misses/women's wear only and may need to be adjusted up or down ¼" to ½" accordingly for men's, children's, junior's, and large/plus sizes. Indicate any changes on spec sheet.]

17. *Across Chest/Center Armhole*—Measure at one-half depth of armhole straight across front of garment from armhole seam/edge to armhole seam/edge.

18. *Across Back/Center Armhole*—Measure at one-half depth of armhole straight across back of garment from armhole seam/edge to armhole seam/edge.

20. *Waist Width Circumference (woven)*—Measure from edge of garment/side seam to edge of garment/side seam straight across garment on seam or at narrowest point of waist taper at a point _____" below high point shoulder. Double this measurement. [Note: You will have to determine the number of inches down from high point shoulder for each raglan sleeve style based on depth of sleeve. Then indicate this number on spec sheet.]

22. *Bottom Band Circumference (woven top/jacket)*—Measure from side of bottom band to side of bottom band along center of band, following natural contour of waistband. Double this measurement.

24. *Bottom Band Width Circumference, Stretched (woven top/jacket)*—Measure from side of bottom band to side of bottom band straight across center of band in a fully extended position. Double this measurement.

25. *Bottom Band/Ribbing Height (knit or woven top/jacket)*—Measure from band/ribbing joining seam straight down to bottom edge of band/rib opening. [Note: If band is shaped or contoured, indicate special measurement instructions on spec sheet.]

27. *Bottom Opening/Sweep Width Circumference (woven top/jacket)*—Measure from edge of garment/side seam to edge of garment/side seam straight across garment at bottom opening. Double this measurement. [Note: If sweep has pleats, measure with pleats closed or relaxed.]

29. *Vented Bottom Opening/Sweep Width Circumference (woven top/jacket)*—Measure from edge of garment/side seam to edge of garment/side seam straight across garment at top of side vents. Do not follow natural curve of garment. Double this measurement. [Note: If vents are too high to measure sweep, indicate opening at appropriate position, e.g., midriff opening.]

31. *Circular Bottom Opening/Sweep Width Circumference (woven top/jacket)*—Measure from edge of garment/side seam to edge of garment/side seam, following natural contour of garment at bottom opening. Double this measurement.

32. *Yoke Width Front*—Measure from armhole seam/edge to armhole seam/edge straight across front of garment, ignoring contours or points, at yoke-body joining seams. [Note: If yoke is asymmetrical, indicate changes in measuring as needed on spec sheet.]

33. *Yoke Width Back*—Measure from armhole seam/edge to armhole seam/edge straight across back of garment, ignoring contours or points, at yoke-body joining seams. [Note: If yoke is asymmetrical, indicate changes in measuring as needed on spec sheet.]

34. *Yoke Depth Front*—Measure from high point shoulder at neck straight down to bottom of front yoke-body joining seam. Gently lift collar away from shoulder-neck joining seam if needed.

35. *Yoke Back Depth*—Measure from center back neck joining seam straight down to bottom of back yoke-body joining seam. Gently lift collar away from back neck joining seam if needed.

36. *Sleeve Length Top Armhole*—Measure along top of sleeve/fold, following contour of sleeve from armhole seam at shoulder to bottom of sleeve opening, including cuff.

37. *Sleeve Length Top Neck*—Measure along top of sleeve/fold, following contour of sleeve from sleeve-neck joining seam/edge to edge of sleeve opening, including cuff. Gently lift collar away at sleeve-neck joining seam if needed.

38. *Sleeve Length Center Back*—Measure from center back neck joining seam or from a point above neck at an imaginary line, that of a joining seam, along top of sleeve/fold, following contour of sleeve to edge of sleeve opening, including cuff.

39. *Sleeve Length Underarm*—Measure straight from bottom of armhole along sleeve seam to edge of sleeve opening, including cuff.

41. *Straight Armhole Width Circumference (woven)*—Measure from top of shoulder joining seam/edge straight down to bottom of armhole. Double this measurement.

42. *Curved Armhole Width (knit)*—Measure from top of shoulder joining seam/edge to bottom of armhole, following contour of armhole.

44. *Armhole Front*—Measure on front of garment from top of shoulder at neckline joining seam/edge to bottom of armhole, following contour of armhole. Gently lift collar away from neckline joining seam if needed.

45. *Armhole Back*—Measure on back of garment from top of shoulder at neck joining seam/edge to bottom of armhole, following contour of armhole. Gently lift collar away from neck joining seam if needed.

47. *Armhole Width Circumference Straight (woven)*—Measure from top of shoulder seam at a point _____" below neckline joining seam/edge straight down to bottom of armhole. Double this measurement. [Note: Gently move collar away from neck joining seam if needed when measuring down _____" to armhole start point. Indicate number of inches measured down on spec sheet.]

49. *Muscle Width Circumference (woven)*—Measure from inner sleeve edge/seam to outer sleeve edge/fold at a point 1" below armhole and parallel to sleeve opening. Double this measurement.

51. *Elbow Width Circumference (woven)*—Measure from inner sleeve edge/seam to outer sleeve edge/fold straight across sleeve at a point one-half of underarm sleeve length and parallel to sleeve opening at wrist or cuff. Double this measurement. [Note: If sleeve is three-quarter length, indicate new point of measure on spec sheet.]

53. *Sleeve Opening Width Circumference (woven)*—Measure from inner sleeve edge/seam to outer sleeve edge/fold straight across bottom edge of sleeve opening. Double this measurement.

55. *Sleeve Opening Width Circumference, Stretched (woven)*—Measure from inner sleeve edge/seam to outer sleeve edge/fold straight across bottom edge of sleeve opening in a fully extended position. Double this measurement.

56. *Cuff Length Sleeve*—Measure from outside end of buttonhole to center of button straight along center of cuff. Open cuff out as flat as possible when measuring. [Note: If cuff length is contoured, measure along center-most point.]

57. *Cuff/Ribbing Height Sleeve*—Measure from cuff joining seam or top of ribbing straight down to bottom edge of cuff or rib opening. [Note: If cuff is contoured, indicate changes made to measurement on spec sheet.]

58. *Neck Depth Front (garments with a plain front/asymmetrical front opening)*—Measure from center back neck joining seam/edge straight down to center front neck joining seam/edge.

59. *Neck Depth Center Front (garments with a center front opening)*—Measure from center back neck joining seam/edge straight down to center of first button at center front of garment.

60. *Neck Drop Front*—Measure from an imaginary line connecting neckline edges straight down to center front neck opening edge. Use a ruler if needed to connect top neckline edges.

61. *Neck Drop Back*—Measure from an imaginary line connecting neckline edges straight down to center back neck opening edge. This measurement is taken with front of garment faceup. Use a ruler to connect top neckline edges if needed.

62. *Neck Width, No Collar*—Measure from inside neck edge/seam to inside neck edge/seam straight across back neck at widest point. This measurement is taken with front of garment faceup.

63. *Neck Width, Collar*—Measure straight across back neck from neck-shoulder joining seam to neck-shoulder joining seam or natural shoulder line if no seam. This measurement is taken with back of garment faceup.

64. *Neck Edge Width (knit)*—Measure from neck edge/seam/fold to neck edge/seam/fold along top

opening edge, following natural contour of neck opening. Garment should be positioned with one shoulder on top of the other and with front and back neck edges meeting. [Note: Occasionally, a knit collar or edge will be put on a woven jacket. You may use this measurement, but measure it in circumference for jacket continuity, noting correction on spec sheet.]

65. *Neck Edge Width Circumference (woven)*—Measure from neck edge/seam/fold to neck edge/seam/fold along top opening edge, following natural contour of neck opening. Garment should be positioned with one shoulder on top of the other and with front and back neck edges meeting. Double this measurement.

66. *Neck Edge Width, Stretched (knit)*—Measure from neck edge/seam/fold to neck edge/seam/fold along top opening edge in a fully extended position. Garment should be positioned with one shoulder on top of the other and with front and back neck edges meeting. [Note: Occasionally, a knit collar or edge will be put on a woven jacket. You may use this measurement, but measure it in circumference for jacket continuity, noting correction on spec sheet.]

67. *Neck Edge Width Circumference, Stretched (woven)*—Measure from neck edge/seam/fold to neck edge/seam/fold along top opening edge in a fully extended position. Garment should be positioned with one shoulder on top of the other and with front and back neck edges meeting. Double this measurement.

68. *Neck Base (knit)*—Measure from neck edge/seam to neck edge/seam along collar/rib joining seam or neckline edge, following natural contour of neck opening. Garment should be buttoned or zippered, if applicable, with one shoulder seam positioned on top of the other and with front and back neck edges meeting. [Note: Occasionally, a knit collar or edge will be put on a woven jacket. You may use this measurement, but measure it in circumference for jacket continuity, noting correction on spec sheet.]

69. *Neck Base Circumference (woven)*—Measure from neck edge/seam to neck edge/seam along collar/rib joining seam or neckline edge, following natural contour of neck opening. Garment should be buttoned or zippered, if applicable, with one shoulder seam positioned on top of the other and with front and back neck edges meeting. Double this measurement.

70. *Neckband Length*—Measure from outside end of buttonhole to center of buttonhole across neckband, following contour of neckband.

71. *Collar Length*—Measure from one end of collar to other end of collar along neck joining seam.

72. *Collar Height*—Measure from collar/rib joining seam at center back neck straight up to outer edge of collar/rib.

73. *Collar Band Height*—Measure from collar joining seam at center back straight up to neckband joining seam at center back.

74. *Collar Point Length*—Measure from collar joining seam to outer edge of collar along collar point edge. [Note: If collar is rounded, measure at a point parallel to center back and indicate change on spec sheet.]

75. *Collar Point Spread (pointed collars only)*—Measure, with collar band buttoned and collar in place, from collar point straight across collar edge to collar point.

76. *Lapel Width*

A. *Notched*—Measure from lower lapel notch straight across to lapel fold at a point perpendicular to garment center front.

B. *Without Notches*—Measure from lapel edge straight across the widest point of lapel to lapel fold at a point _____" down from center back collar joining seam and perpendicular to front of garment.

77. *Center Front Extension*—Measure from an imaginary line at center front of garment horizontally to finished outer edge of front extended piece.

78. *Placket Length*—Measure from top edge of placket straight down to bottom of placket opening along center of placket.

79. *Placket Width*—Measure from placket joining seam straight across placket to placket edge at fold.

121. *Fly/Zipper*

A. *Length*—Measure from top of fly/zipper opening straight down to bottom of fly/zipper opening at zipper stop or bar tack.
B. *Fly/Zipper Width*—Measure top of fly/zipper at joining seam from edge/fold straight across to fly/zipper placket stitching.

122. *Vent/Slit*

A. *Height*—Measure from top of vent/slit straight down to bottom of vent/slit along edge of vent/slit.
B. *Width*—Measure top of vent/slit from edge/fold straight across to vent/slit placket stitching at a point parallel to garment hemline.

123. *Pleat Depth*—Measure from outer edge of pleat at fold/crease to inner fold of pleat. [Note 1: It is a good idea to indicate what type of pleat is being measured, e.g., box, inverted, knife, kick, kilt, or envelope. Note 2: If pleats are not parallel or symmetrical, indicate any special instructions on spec sheet.]

124. *Distance Between Pleats*—Measure from start of pleat to start of pleat, excluding pleat depth at a point directly below pleat joining seam. [Note: If pleats are not parallel or symmetrical, indicate any special instructions on spec sheet.]

125. *Applied Pocket Height*—Measure from top edge of pocket to bottom edge of pocket along center of pocket. [Note: For contoured or irregularly shaped pockets, take a second measurement and indicate point of measure on spec sheet.]

126. *Applied Pocket Width*—Measure from side of pocket to side of pocket along top edge of pocket. [Note: For contoured or irregularly shaped pockets, take a second measurement and indicate point of measure on spec sheet.]

127. *Pocket Opening Within a Seam*—Measure from top of pocket to bottom of pocket along edge of pocket opening.

128. *Belt Length*

A. *Total*—Measure from end of belt at buckle along center of belt to opposite end of belt, following contour.
B. *Circumference*—Measure from end of belt at buckle along center of belt to middle hole at opposite end.

129. *Belt Width (or Height)*—Measure from edge of belt straight across to edge of belt. [Note: If belt is contoured, indicate points of measure on spec sheet.]

130. *Belt Loop Length*—Measure from top of belt loop straight down/vertically to bottom of belt loop along center of belt loop. [Note: Fashion-forward or irregularly shaped belt loops may require further spec instructions. Indicate points of measure on spec sheet.]

131. *Belt Loop Width*—Measure belt loop from edge of belt loop straight across/horizontally to edge of belt loop. [Note: Fashion-forward or irregularly shaped belt loops may require further spec instructions. Indicate points of measure on spec sheet.]

132. *Tie Length*—Measure from end of tie/joining seam straight down to tie end along center of tie.

133. *Tie Width*

A. *Straight*—Measure from edge of tie straight across to edge of tie.

B. *Contoured*—Measure from edge of tie straight across to edge of tie at widest point of tie.

137. *Front Hood Length*—Measure from top of hood to bottom of hood at center front joining seam along opening edge of hood.

138. *Back Hood Length*—Measure from top of hood at center front to bottom of hood at center back joining seam along outside curve of hood fold/seam.

139. *Hood Width*—Measure from front opening edge of hood straight across to back of hood along widest point of hood.

140. *Flange Depth*—Measure from center back neck joining seam straight down to bottom of flange at center back. [Note: If flange is contoured or asymmetrical, indicate point of measure on spec sheet.]

141. *Shoulder Pad Length*—Measure from edge of pad straight across to edge of pad along center of pad or natural shoulder line of pad.

142. *Shoulder Pad Width*—Measure from side of pad straight across to side of pad along edge of pad if straight, or at widest point of pad if curved.

143. *Straight Edge Shoulder Pad Height*—Measure from top of pad straight down to bottom of pad along center of pad.

144. *Curved Edge Shoulder Pad Height*—Stick a 1"straight pin into thickest part of shoulder pad. Push pin all the way through pad until head of pin rests on top of pad. Be sure not to crush pad. Measure portion of pin sticking out of pad. Subtract this figure from 1" (length of pin) to get shoulder pad height.

145. *Shoulder Pad Placement*—Measure from neck edge or joining seam straight across shoulder seam or natural shoulder line to start of shoulder pad.

146. *Pleats Placement*

A. *Front Pleat Top/Jacket*—Measure distance from center front of garment straight across to start of first pleat at a point parallel to garment hem. [Note: You may need to use armhole or side seam as a starting point if there is no center front seam or placket.]
B. *Back Pleat Top/Jacket*—Measure distance from armhole seam/side seam (depending on pleat placement) to first pleat at a point parallel to garment hem.

147. *Button Placement*—Refer to point of measure 59, Neck Depth Center Front, for placement of first button. Then measure distance of first button to second button. Be sure when measuring that button at bust point is lined up to apex of bust. Adjust all buttons accordingly and respace as needed.

148. *Pocket Placement*

A. *Top Pocket Vertical*—Measure from shoulder-neck joining seam straight down to top edge of pocket.
B. *Top Pocket Horizontal*—Measure from center front straight across to side of pocket at top edge.
C. *Front Bottom Pocket Vertical*—Measure from waistband/joining seam/edge straight down to top edge of pocket. [Note: The bottom pocket on a blazer or unconstructed jacket may use this measurement code, but it is measured from bottom of garment up to bottom of pocket. Make this correction on spec sheet.]
D. *Front Bottom Pocket Horizontal*—Measure from center front straight across to side of pocket at top edge.

149. *Belt Loop Placement*

A. *Front*—Measure from center front of garment horizontally across to center of first front belt loop.
B. *Back*—Measure from center back of garment horizontally across to center of first back belt loop.
C. *Side Seam to Front*—Measure from center of side seam belt loop to center of front belt loop.

D. *Side Seam to Back*—Measure from center of side seam belt loop to center of back belt loop.

150. *Dart Placement*

A. *High Point Shoulder Bust Dart*—Measure from shoulder-neck joining seam or at a point _____" from shoulder-neck seam straight down, parallel to center front, to top of dart. [Note: The _____" from shoulder seam measurement is to be used for darts that are too short to be measured from high point shoulder. Be sure to indicate _____" measurement on spec sheet.]
B. *Center Front Bust Dart*—Measure from center front of garment straight across to top of dart.
C. *Side Seam Bust Dart*—Measure from underarm/ side seam joining seam down along contour of side seam to bottom of dart.
D. *High Point Shoulder Princess Dart*—Measure from shoulder-neck joining seam straight down to top of dart.
E. *Center Front Princess Dart*—Measure from center front of garment straight across to top of dart.

CHAPTER 14 TERMS

When working with blazers and unconstructed jackets, you may come across the following garment terms. If you are unfamiliar with any of them, please look up the definitions in the glossary at the end of this text.

Basic blazer
Double-breasted blazer
Jacket:
- *Baseball*
- *Bike*
- *Denim*
- *Karate*
- *Safari*
- *Sweat*
- *Unconstructed*
- *Windbreaker*

SPEC SHEET: Blazer

STYLE

SEASON:	DESCRIPTION:
LABEL: (SIZE CATEGORY)	
DATE:	
TECHNICAL SKETCH Basic blazer	SKETCH/PHOTO

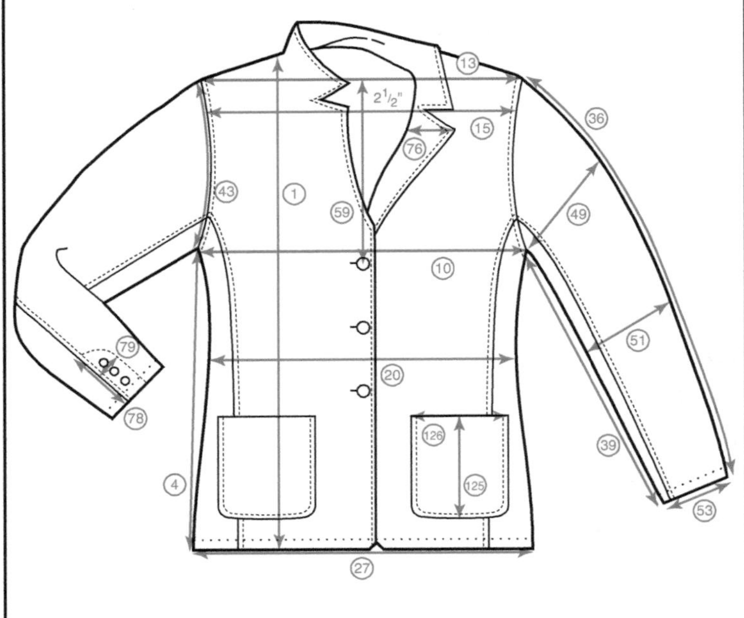

CODE	POINT OF MEASURE	TOL. +/–	4	S/6	8	M/10	12	L/14	16	XL/18
1.	Front length	1/2								
3.	Center back length	1/2								
4.	Side length	1/4								
10.	Chest width circumference	1/2-3/4								
13.	Across shoulder	1/4								
15.	Across chest _____" below H.P.S.	1/4								
16.	Across back	1/4								
20.	Waist width circumference _____" from H.P.S.	1/2-3/4								
27.	Bottom opening/sweep width circumference	1/2-3/4								
36.	Sleeve length top armhole	3/8								
39.	Sleeve length underarm	3/8								
43.	Curved armhole width circumference	3/2								
49.	Muscle width circumference	1/4								
51.	Elbow width circumference	1/4								
53.	Sleeve opening width circumference	1/4								
59.	Neck depth center front	1/8								
71.	Collar length	1/4								
72.	Collar height	1/8								

(Tolerance 1/2-3/4 S, M, L, XL = 3/4" 4-18 = 1/2")

The measured garment spec sheets are for ***illustrative purposes only*** and should not be used as industry standards

CODE	POINT OF MEASURE	TOL. +/–	4	S/6	8	M/10	12	L/14	16	XL/18
76.	Lapel width A. Notched	1/8								
	B. Without notches	1/8								
77.	Center front extension	1/8								
78.	Placket length	1/4								
79.	Placket width	1/8								
122.	Vent/slit A. Height	1/4								
	B. Width	1/8								
125.	Applied pocket height	1/8								
126.	Applied pocket width	1/8								
141.	Shoulder pad length	1/8								
142.	Shoulder pad width	1/8								
143.	Straight edge, shoulder pad height	1/8								
144.	Curved edge, shoulder pad height	1/8								
145.	Shoulder pad placement	1/8								
147.	Button placement (Distance between)	1/8								
148.	Pocket placement A. Top pocket vertical	1/8								
	B. Top pocket horizontal	1/8								
	C. Bottom pocket vertical	1/8								
	D. Bottom pocket horizontal	1/8								
150.	Dart length bust dart	1/8								
	Princess dart	1/8								
150.	Dart placement A. H.P.S. to bust dart	1/8								
	B. C.F. to bust dart	1/8								
	C. Underarm to bust dart	1/8								
	D. H.P.S. to princess dart	1/8								
	E. C.F. to princess dart	1/8								

COMMENTS:

The measured garment spec sheets are for ***illustrative purposes only*** and should not be used as industry standards

SPEC SHEET: Blazer

STYLE

SEASON: Early fall

DESCRIPTION: Classic blazer with pocket flaps

LABEL: (SIZE CATEGORY) Missy

DATE:

TECHNICAL SKETCH Basic blazer

SKETCH/PHOTO

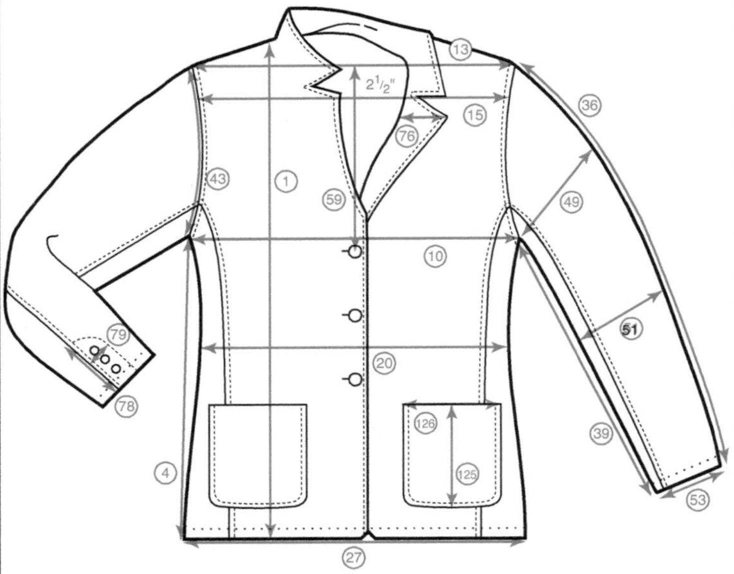

CODE	POINT OF MEASURE	TOL. +/–	4	S/6	8	M/10	12	L/14	16	XL/18
1.	Front length	1/2				30				
3.	Center back length	1/2				29 3/4				
4.	Side length	1/4				20 1/8				
10.	Chest width circumference	1/2-3/4				39 1/4				
13.	Across shoulder	1/4				16 1/4				
15.	Across chest 5 " below H.P.S.	1/4				4 1/4				
16.	Across back	1/4				16 1/2				
20.	Waist width circumference 16 " from H.P.S.	1/2-3/4				35 1/2				
27.	Bottom opening/sweep width circumference	1/2-3/4				41 1/2				
36.	Sleeve length top armhole	3/8				24 3/4				
39.	Sleeve length underarm	3/8				17				
43.	Curved armhole width circumference	3/2				21				
49.	Muscle width circumference	1/4				14 1/4				
51.	Elbow width circumference	1/4				13 1/4				
53.	Sleeve opening width circumference	1/4				10 1/2				
59.	Neck depth center front	1/8				10 1/2				
71.	Collar length Follow seam	1/4				17				
72.	Collar height	1/8				2 7/8				

(Tolerance 1/2-3/4 S, M, L, XL = 3/4" 4-18 = 1/2")

The measured garment spec sheets are for ***illustrative purposes only*** and should not be used as industry standards

CODE	POINT OF MEASURE	TOL. +/–	4	S/6	8	M/10	12	L/14	16	XL/18
76.	Lapel width A. Notched	1/8				3				
	B. Without notches	1/8								
77.	Center front extension	1/8				7/8				
78.	Placket length	1/4				3 1/2				
79.	Placket width	1/8				1 1/8				
122.	Vent/slit A. Height	1/4				1 7/8				
	B. Width	1/8								
125.	Applied pocket height **Pocket flap**	1/8								
126.	Applied pocket width **Pocket flap**	1/8				5 5/8				
141.	Shoulder pad length	1/8				4 1/2				
142.	Shoulder pad width	1/8				7				
143.	Straight edge, shoulder pad height	1/8				3/8				
144.	Curved edge, shoulder pad height	1/8								
145.	Shoulder pad placement	1/8				1/2				
147.	Button placement (Distance between)	1/8				5 7/8				
148.	Pocket placement A. Top pocket vertical	1/8								
	B. Top pocket horizontal	1/8								
	C. Bottom pocket vertical	1/8				18 1/8				
	D. Bottom pocket horizontal	1/8				2 3/4				
150.	Dart length bust dart	1/8								
	Princess dart	1/8								
150.	Dart placement A. H.P.S. to bust dart	1/8								
	B. C.F. to bust dart	1/8								
	C. Underarm to bust dart	1/8								
	D. H.P.S. to princess dart	1/8								
	E. C.F. to princess dart	1/8								
	Button hole pocket binding width	1/8				3/16				
	Distance between front princess seams armhole					14				
	Waist	1/4				8 3/4				
	Hem	1/4				9 5/8				
	Distance between back princess seams armhole					16 1/2				
	Waist	1/4				10 5/8				
	Hem	1/4				12 1/2				

COMMENTS:

The measured garment spec sheets are for ***illustrative purposes only*** and should not be used as industry standards

CHAPTER 15

Outerwear/Coats

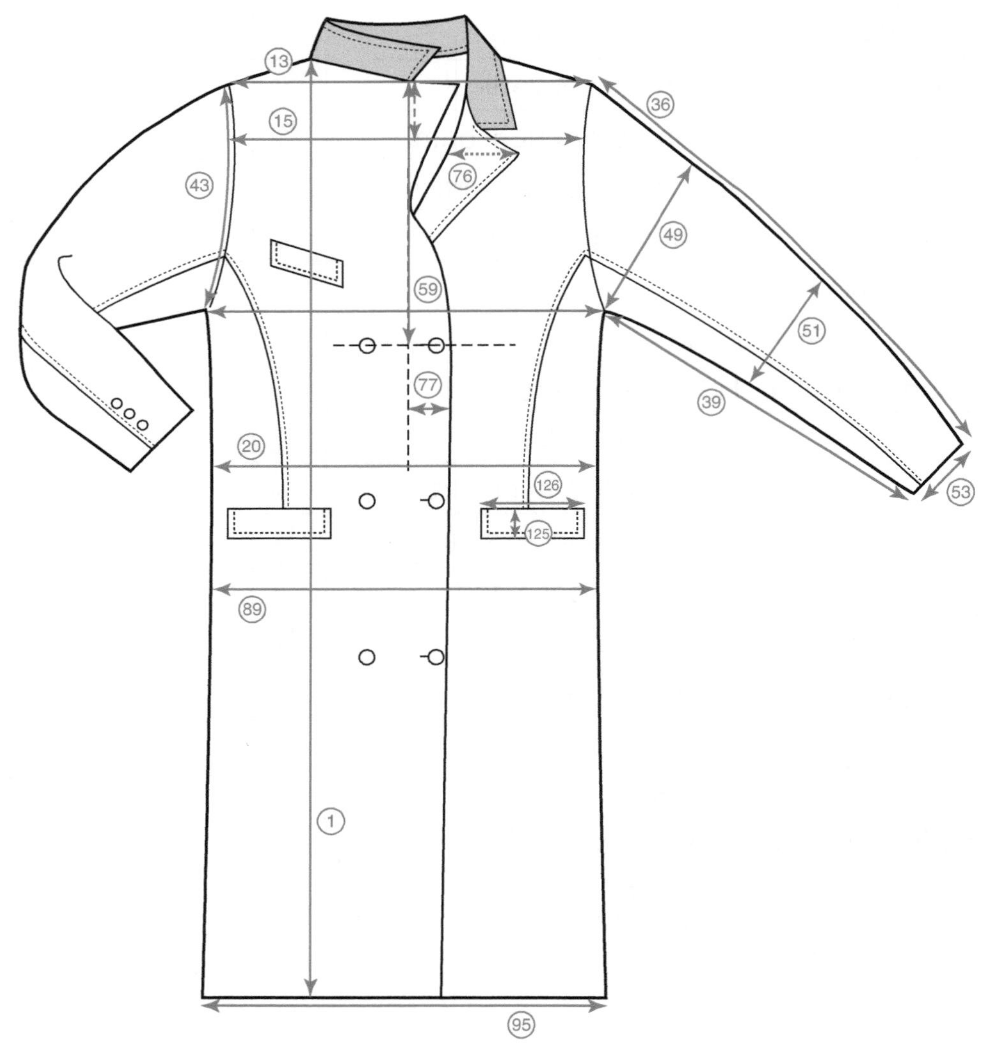

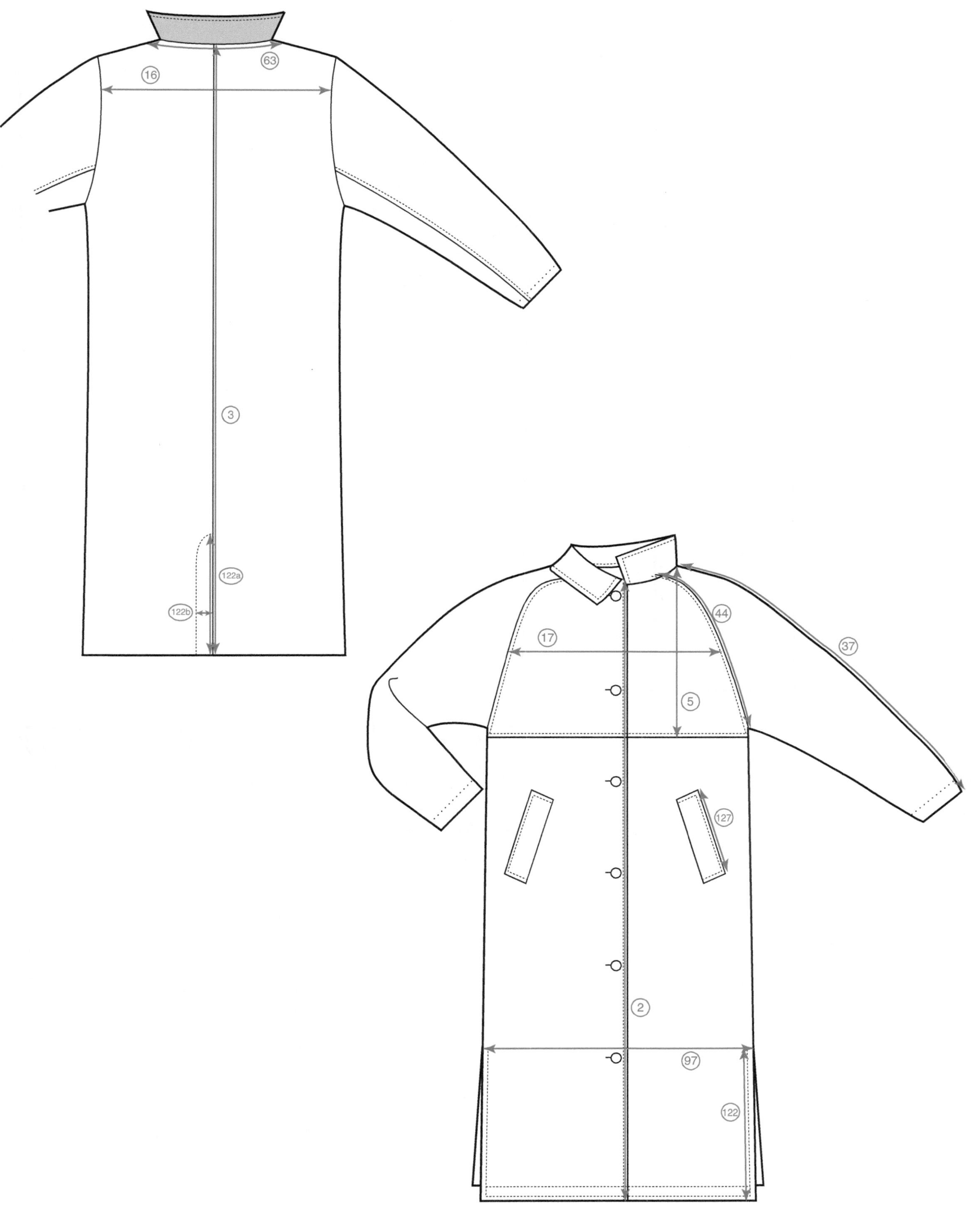
16
63
3
122a
122b
17
44
37
5
127
2
97
122

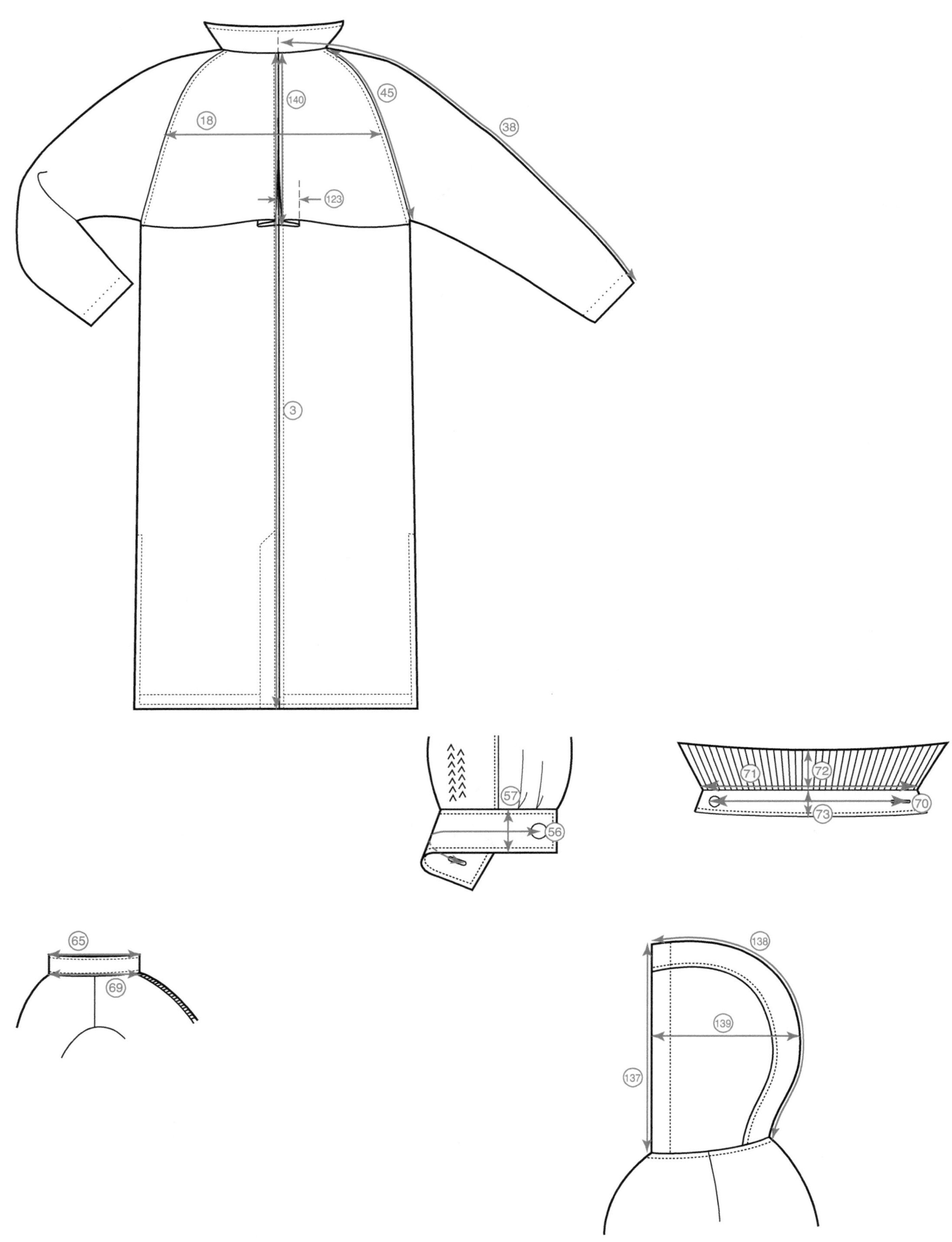

140
45
38
18
123
3
57
56
71
72
70
73
65
69
138
139
137

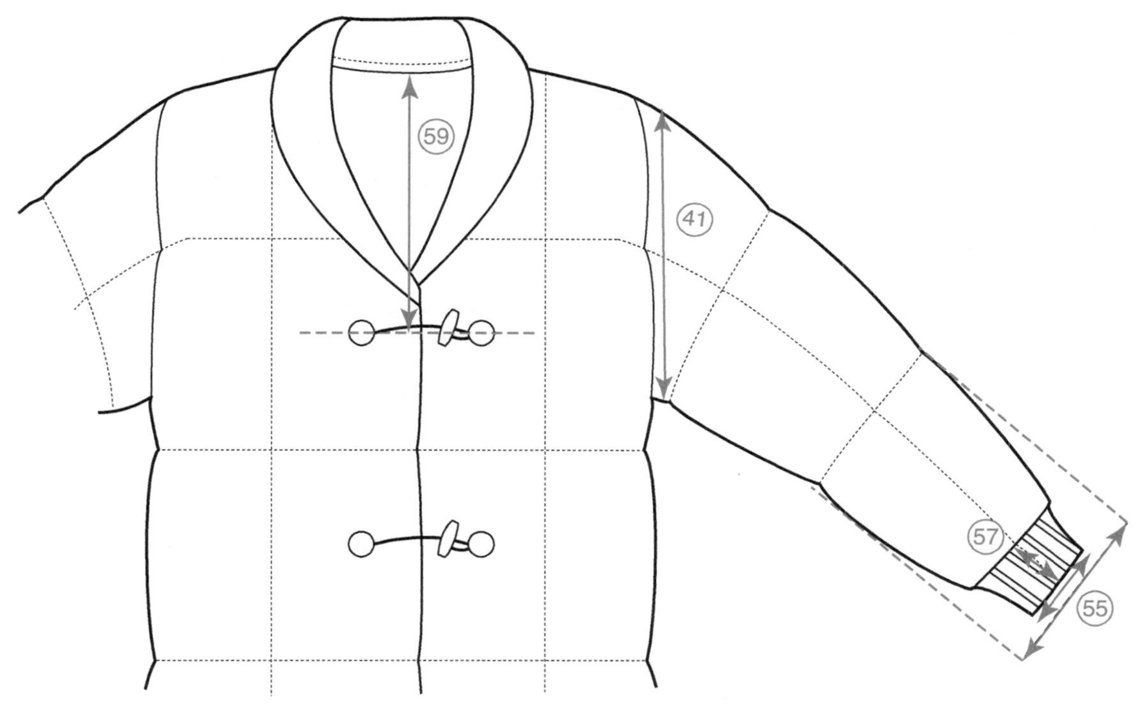

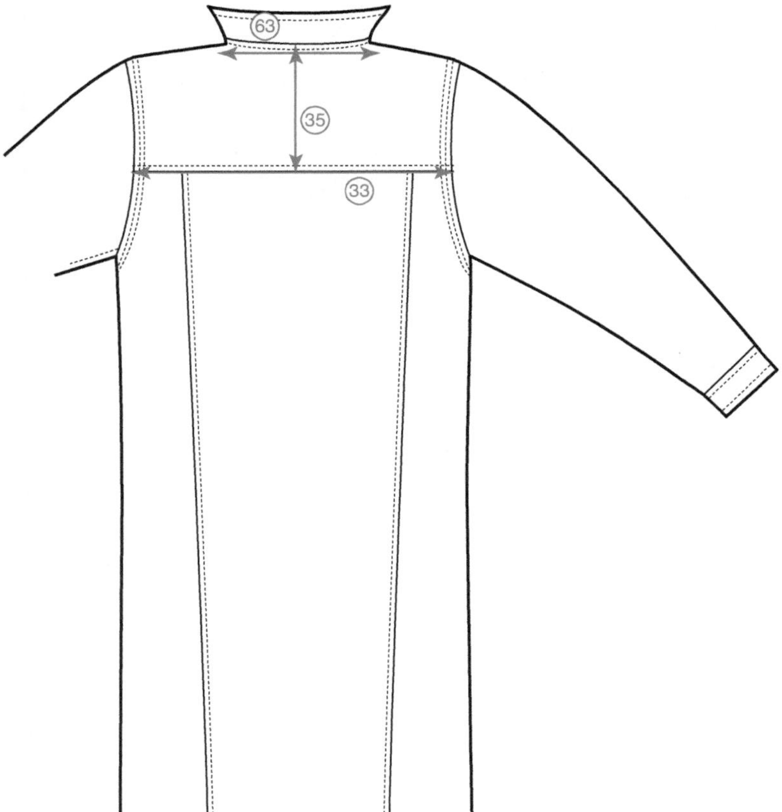

63
35
33

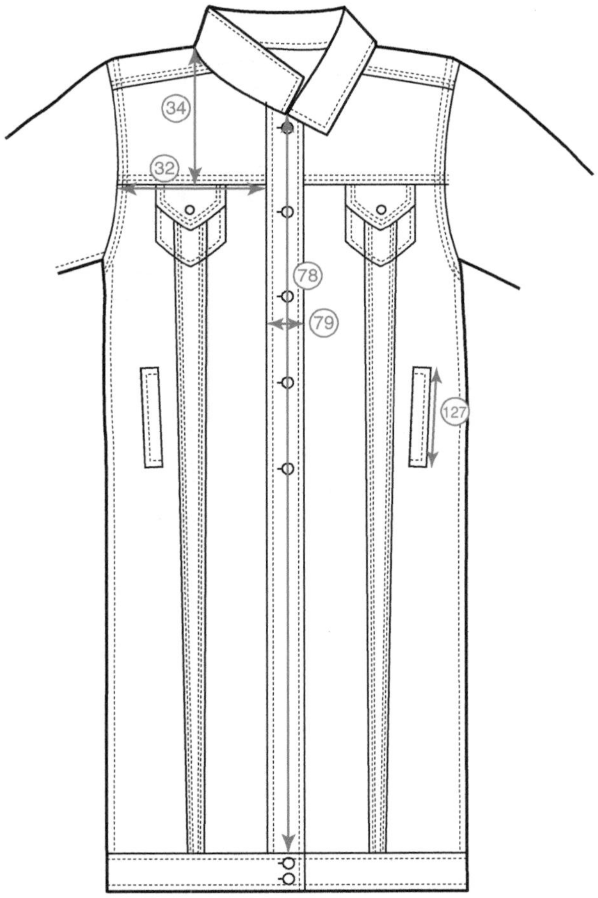

34
32
78
79
127

Measuring Outerwear/Coats

Outerwear and coats, either knitted or woven, are treated as wovens when measuring, due to the garment's construction. When measuring a cardigan coat, one should use the knit dress spec sheet if the cardigan coat is not lined, and the outerwear/coat spec sheet if it is lined. Short, unlined jackets are usually spec'd on the blazer and unconstructed jacket spec sheets, while lined jackets are usually spec'd on the outerwear/coat spec sheets. As you measure these garments, you will have to make that decision based on style features and details. The short pea coat shown in Figure 15.1 is a good example of a coat that should be spec'd with the outerwear/coat spec sheet—not the blazer and jacket spec sheet—because it is lined. This section does not contain measurement points for facings, inside pockets, and linings. If you choose to detail these measurements, simply add them to the spec sheet.

Figure 15.1 Pea coat with chest measurement point.

1. *Front Length (garments with a front opening)*—Measure from high point shoulder at neck straight down, parallel to center front, to bottom of garment at front. If garment has a collar, gently lift it away from shoulder-neck measuring point.

2. *Center Front Length (garments with a plain front; no front opening)*—Measure from center front neck joining seams straight down to bottom of garment at center front. [Note: A garment with a front opening may still require point of measure 1, Front Length, if neckline is unusual or is difficult to measure.]

3. *Center Back Length*—Measure from center back neck joining seams straight down to bottom of garment at center back. If needed, gently lift collar away from back neck to expose joining seam.

4. *Side Length*—Measure from bottom of armhole/side seam straight down to bottom of garment along side of garment. Do not follow natural curve of garment's side seam, unless otherwise indicated. If needed, gently lift sleeve away from armhole/side seam joining seam.

5. *Front Bodice Length (garments with a front opening)*—Measure from high point shoulder at neck straight down, parallel to center front, to top edge of waistband, joining seam, or rib. If garment has a collar, gently lift it away from shoulder-neck measuring point.

6. *Center Front Bodice Length (garments with a plain front; no front opening)*—Measure from center front neck joining seam straight down to top edge of waistband, joining seam, or rib. [Note: A garment with a center opening may still require point of measure 5, Front Bodice Length, if neckline is unusual or is difficult to measure.]

7. *Center Back Bodice Length*—Measure from center back neck joining seams straight down to top edge of waistband, joining seam, or rib. If needed, gently lift collar away from back neck to expose joining seam.

8. *Side Seam Bodice Length*—Measure from bottom of armhole/side seam straight down to top edge of waistband, joining seam, or rib, along side of garment, following natural curve of garment's side seam, unless otherwise indicated. If needed, gently lift sleeve away from armhole/side seam joining seam. [Note: You can take side seam bodice measurement straight rather than contoured if joining seam/rib can be extended, but indicate change on spec sheet.]

10. *Chest Width Circumference (woven)*—Measure from edge of garment/side seam to edge of garment/side seam straight across garment at a point 1" below armhole. Double this measurement.

12. *Chest Width Circumference Raglan Sleeve (woven)*—Measure from edge of garment/side seam to edge of garment/side seam straight across garment at a point _____" below high point shoulder. Double this measurement. [Note: You will have to determine number of inches down from high point shoulder for each raglan sleeve style based on depth of sleeve. Then indicate this number on spec sheet.]

13. *Across Shoulder*—Measure straight across front from armhole seam/edge to armhole seam/edge at shoulder seam or across natural shoulder fold line created if there is no seam.

14. *Shoulder Width*—Measure from neckband/collar/ribbing joining seam or neckline edge to top of armhole seam at shoulder, taken along shoulder seam or across natural shoulder fold line created if there is no seam.

15. *Across Chest*—Measure 2½" down from collar/rib joining seam at center front straight across front of garment from armhole seam/edge to armhole seam/edge. [Note: The 2½" measurement point is for misses/women's wear only and may need to be adjusted up or down ¼" to ½" accordingly for men's, children's, junior's, and large/plus sizes. Indicate any changes on spec sheet.]

16. *Across Back*—Measure 4" down from collar/rib joining seam at center back straight across back of garment from armhole seam/edge to armhole seam/edge. [Note: The 4" measurement point is for misses/women's wear only and may need to be adjusted up or down ¼" to ½" accordingly for men's, children's, junior's, and large/plus sizes. Indicate any changes on spec sheet.]

17. *Across Chest/Center Armhole*—Measure at one-half depth of armhole straight across front of garment from armhole seam/edge to armhole seam/edge.

18. *Across Back/Center Armhole*—Measure at one-half depth of armhole straight across back of garment from armhole seam/edge to armhole seam/edge.

20. *Waist Width Circumference (woven)*—Measure from edge of garment/side seam to edge of garment/side seam straight across garment on seam or at narrowest point of waist taper at a point _____" below high point shoulder. Double this measurement. [Note: You will have to determine number of inches down from high point shoulder for each raglan sleeve style based on depth of sleeve. Then indicate this number on spec sheet.]

22. *Bottom Band Circumference (woven top/jacket)*—Measure from side of bottom band to side of bottom band along center of band, following natural contour of waistband. Double this measurement.

24. *Bottom Band Width Circumference, Stretched (woven top/jacket)*—Measure from side of bottom band to side of bottom band straight across center of band in a fully extended position. Double this measurement.

25. *Bottom Band/Ribbing Height (knit or woven top/jacket)*—Measure from band/ribbing joining seam straight down to bottom edge of band/rib opening. [Note: If band is shaped or contoured, indicate special measurement instructions on spec sheet.]

27. *Bottom Opening/Sweep Width Circumference (woven top/jacket)*—Measure from edge of garment/side seam to edge of garment/side seam straight across garment at bottom opening. Double this measurement. [Note: If sweep has pleats, measure with pleats closed or relaxed.]

29. *Vented Bottom Opening/Sweep Width Circumference (woven top/jacket)*—Measure from edge of garment/side seam to edge of garment/side seam straight across garment at top of side vents. Do not follow the natural curve of the garment. Double this measurement. [Note: If vents are too high to measure sweep, indicate opening at appropriate position, e.g., midriff opening.]

31. *Circular Bottom Opening/Sweep Width Circumference (woven top/jacket)*—Measure from edge of garment/side seam to edge of garment/side seam, following natural contour of garment at bottom opening. Double this measurement.

32. *Yoke Width Front*—Measure from armhole seam/edge to armhole seam/edge straight across front of garment, ignoring contours or points, at yoke-body joining seams. [Note: If yoke is asymmetrical, indicate changes in measuring as needed on spec sheet.]

33. *Yoke Width Back*—Measure from armhole seam/edge to armhole seam/edge straight across back of garment, ignoring contours or points, at yoke-body joining seams. [Note: If yoke is asymmetrical, indicate changes in measuring as needed on spec sheet.]

34. *Yoke Depth Front*—Measure from high point shoulder at neck straight down to bottom of front yoke-body joining seam. Gently lift collar away from shoulder-neck joining seam if needed.

35. *Yoke Back Depth*—Measure from center back neck joining seam straight down to bottom of back yoke-body joining seam. Gently lift collar away from back neck joining seam if needed.

36. *Sleeve Length Top Armhole*—Measure along top of sleeve/fold, following contour of sleeve from armhole seam at shoulder to bottom of sleeve opening, including cuff.

37. *Sleeve Length Top Neck*—Measure along top of sleeve/fold, following contour of sleeve from sleeve-neck joining seam/edge to edge of sleeve opening, including cuff. Gently lift collar at sleeve-neck joining seam if needed.

38. *Sleeve Length Center Back*—Measure from center back neck joining seam or from a point above neck at an imaginary line, that of a joining seam, along top of sleeve/fold, following contour of sleeve to edge of sleeve opening, including cuff.

39. *Sleeve Length Underarm*—Measure straight from bottom of armhole along sleeve seam to edge of sleeve opening, including cuff.

41. *Straight Armhole Width Circumference (woven)*—Measure from top of shoulder joining seam/edge straight down to bottom of armhole. Double this measurement.

43. *Curved Armhole Width Circumference (woven)*—Measure from top of shoulder joining seam/edge to bottom of armhole, following contour of armhole. Double this measurement.

44. *Armhole Front*—Measure on front of garment from top of shoulder at neckline joining seam/edge to bottom of armhole, following contour of armhole. Gently lift collar away from neckline joining seam if needed.

45. *Armhole Back*—Measure on back of garment from top of shoulder at neck joining seam/edge to bottom of armhole, following contour of armhole. Gently lift collar away from neck joining seam if needed.

47. *Armhole Width Circumference Straight (woven)*—Measure from top of shoulder seam at a point _____" below neckline joining seam/edge straight down to bottom of armhole. Double this measurement. [Note: Gently move collar away from neck joining seam if needed when measuring down _____" to armhole start point. Indicate number of inches measured down on spec sheet.]

49. *Muscle Width Circumference (woven)*—Measure from inner sleeve edge/seam to outer sleeve edge/fold at a point 1" below armhole and parallel to sleeve opening. Double this measurement.

51. *Elbow Width Circumference (woven)*—Measure from inner sleeve edge/seam to outer sleeve edge/fold straight across sleeve at a point one-half of the underarm sleeve length and parallel to sleeve opening at wrist or cuff. Double this measurement. [Note: If sleeve is three-quarter length, indicate new point of measure on spec sheet.]

53. *Sleeve Opening Width Circumference (woven)*—Measure from inner sleeve edge/seam to outer sleeve edge/fold straight across bottom edge of sleeve opening. Double this measurement.

55. *Sleeve Opening Width Circumference, Stretched (woven)*—Measure from inner sleeve edge/seam to outer sleeve edge/fold straight across bottom edge of sleeve opening in a fully extended position. Double this measurement.

56. *Cuff Length Sleeve*—Measure from outside end of buttonhole to center of button straight along center of cuff. Open cuff out as flat as possible when measuring. [Note: If cuff length is contoured, measure along center-most point.]

57. *Cuff/Ribbing Height Sleeve*—Measure from cuff joining seam or top of ribbing straight down to bottom edge of cuff or rib opening. [Note: If cuff is contoured, indicate changes made to measurement on spec sheet.]

58. *Neck Depth Front (garments with a plain front/asymmetrical front opening)*—Measure from center

back neck joining seam/edge straight down to center front neck joining seam/edge.

59. *Neck Depth Center Front (garments with a center front opening)*—Measure from center back neck joining seam/edge straight down to center of first button at center front of garment.

60. *Neck Drop Front*—Measure from an imaginary line connecting neckline edges straight down to center front neck opening edge. Use a ruler if needed to connect top neckline edges.

61. *Neck Drop Back*—Measure from an imaginary line connecting neckline edges straight down to center back neck opening edge. This measurement is taken with front of garment faceup. Use a ruler to connect top neckline edges if needed.

62. *Neck Width, No Collar*—Measure from inside neck edge/seam to inside neck edge/seam straight across back neck at widest point. This measurement is taken with front of garment faceup.

63. *Neck Width, Collar*—Measure straight across back neck from neck-shoulder joining seam to neck-shoulder joining seam or natural shoulder line if no seam. This measurement is taken with back of garment faceup.

64. *Neck Edge Width (knit)*—Measure from neck edge/seam/fold to neck edge/seam/fold along top opening edge, following natural contour of neck opening. Garment should be positioned with one shoulder on top of the other and with front and back neck edges meeting. [Note: Occasionally, a knit collar or edge will be put on a woven jacket. You may use this measurement, but measure it in circumference for jacket continuity, noting correction on spec sheet.]

65. *Neck Edge Width Circumference (woven)*—Measure from neck edge/seam/fold to neck edge/seam/fold along top opening edge, following natural contour of neck opening. Garment should be positioned with one shoulder on top of the other and with front and back neck edges meeting. Double this measurement.

66. *Neck Edge Width, Stretched (knit)*—Measure from neck edge/seam/fold to neck edge/seam/fold along top opening edge in a fully extended position. Garment should be positioned with one shoulder on top of the other and with front and back neck edges meeting. [Note: Occasionally, a knit collar or edge will be put on a woven jacket. You may use this measurement, but measure it in circumference for jacket continuity, noting correction on spec sheet.]

67. *Neck Edge Width Circumference, Stretched (woven)*—Measure from neck edge/seam/fold to neck edge/seam/fold along top opening edge in a fully extended position. Garment should be positioned with one shoulder on top of the other and with front and back neck edges meeting. Double this measurement.

68. *Neck Base (knit)*—Measure from neck edge/seam to neck edge/seam along collar/rib joining seam or neckline edge, following natural contour of neck opening. Garment should be buttoned or zippered, if applicable, with one shoulder seam positioned on top of the other and with front and back neck edges meeting. [Note: Occasionally, a knit collar or edge will be put on a woven jacket. You may use this measurement, but measure it in circumference for jacket continuity, noting correction on spec sheet.]

69. *Neck Base Circumference (woven)*—Measure from neck edge/seam to neck edge/seam along collar/rib joining seam or neckline edge, following natural contour of neck opening. Garment should be buttoned or zippered, if applicable, with one shoulder seam positioned on top of the other and with front and back neck edges meeting. Double this measurement.

70. *Neckband Length*—Measure from outside end of buttonhole to center of buttonhole across neckband, following contour of neckband.

71. *Collar Length*—Measure from one end of collar to other end of collar along neck joining seam.

72. *Collar Height*—Measure from collar/rib joining seam at center back neck straight up to outer edge of collar/rib.

73. *Collar Band Height*—Measure from collar joining seam at center back straight up to neckband joining seam at center back.

74. *Collar Point Length*—Measure from collar joining seam to outer edge of collar along collar point edge. [Note: If collar is rounded, measure at a point parallel to center back and indicate change on spec sheet.]

75. *Collar Point Spread (pointed collars only)*—Measure, with collar band buttoned and collar in place, from collar point straight across collar edge to collar point.

76. *Lapel Width*

A. *Notched*—Measure from lower lapel notch straight across to lapel fold at a point perpendicular to garment center front.

B. *Without Notches*—Measure from lapel edge straight across the widest point of lapel to lapel fold at a point _____" down from center back collar joining seam and perpendicular to front of garment.

77. *Center Front Extension*—Measure from an imaginary line at center front of garment horizontally to finished outer edge of front extended piece.

78. *Placket Length*—Measure from top edge of placket straight down to bottom of placket opening along center of placket.

79. *Placket Width*—Measure from placket joining seam straight across placket to placket edge at fold.

87. *High Hip Width Circumference (woven)*—Measure from edge of garment/side seam to edge of garment/side seam at a point 4" below bottom edge of waistband/seam following contour of waist. Double this measurement. [Note: The 4" point is for misses/women's wear only; adjust as needed ½" to 1" up or down for children's, petite's, junior's, or large/plus sizes. Indicate change on spec sheet.]

89. *Low Hip Width Circumference from Waist (woven)*—Measure from edge of garment/side seam to edge of garment/side seam at a point 7" below bottom edge of waistband/seam, following contour of waist. Double this measurement. [Note: The 7" point is for misses/women's wear only; adjust as needed ½" to 1" up or down for children's, petite's, junior's, or large/plus sizes. Indicate change on spec sheet.]

91. *Hip Width from High Point Shoulder Circumference (woven)*—Measure from edge of garment/side seam to edge of garment/side seam straight across at a point _____" below high point shoulder. Double this measurement. [Note: You will have to estimate low hip point on garment if there is no waistband and fill in the _____" from high point shoulder. This measurement will vary for children's, junior's, misses, and large/plus sizes.]

95. *Bottom Opening/Sweep Width Circumference (woven skirt)*—Measure from edge of garment/side seam to edge of garment/side seam straight across garment at bottom opening. Double this measurement. [Note: If sweep has pleats, measure with pleats closed or relaxed.]

97. *Vented Bottom Opening/Sweep Width Circumference (woven skirt)*—Measure from edge of garment/side seam to edge of garment/side seam straight across garment at top of side vents. Double this measurement. [Note: Indicate on spec sheet if there is only one vent or if vent hits at a point other than sweep, e.g., thigh opening.]

99. *Circular Bottom Opening/Sweep Width Circumference (woven skirt)*—Measure from edge of garment/side seam to edge of garment/side seam,

following natural contour of garment at bottom opening. Double this measurement.

100. *Center Front Skirt Length*—Measure from bottom of waistband/seam (top edge if not banded, or stitching if self-elastic/drawstring casing) straight down to bottom of garment at center front. [Note: A fashion-forward skirt may have an asymmetrical waist. Indicate top point of measure on spec sheet.]

101. *Center Back Skirt Length*—Measure from bottom of waistband/seam (top edge if not banded, or stitching if self-elastic/drawstring casing) straight down to bottom of garment at center front. [Note: A fashion-forward skirt may have an asymmetrical waist. Indicate top point of measure on spec sheet.]

102. *Side Skirt Length*—Measure from bottom edge of waistband/seam (top edge if not banded, or stitching if self-elastic/drawstring casing) to bottom of garment along side seam/fold of garment, following any contour.

121. *Fly/Zipper*

A. *Length*—Measure from top of fly/zipper opening straight down to bottom of fly/zipper opening at zipper stop or bar tack.

B. *Fly/Zipper Width*—Measure top of fly/zipper at joining seam from edge/fold straight across to fly/zipper placket stitching.

122. *Vent/Slit*

A. *Height*—Measure from top of vent/slit straight down to bottom of vent/slit along edge of vent/slit.

B. *Width*—Measure top of vent/slit from edge/fold straight across to vent/slit placket stitching at a point parallel to garment hemline.

123. *Pleat Depth*—Measure from outer edge of pleat at fold/crease to inner fold of pleat. [Note 1: It is a good idea to indicate what type of pleat is being measured, e.g., box, inverted, knife, kick, kilt, or envelope. Note 2: If pleats are not parallel or symmetrical, indicate any special instructions on spec sheet.]

124. *Distance Between Pleats*—Measure from start of pleat to start of pleat, excluding pleat depth at a point directly below pleat joining seam. [Note: If pleats are not parallel or symmetrical, indicate any special instructions on spec sheet.]

125. *Applied Pocket Height*—Measure from top edge of pocket to bottom edge of pocket along center of pocket. [Note: For contoured or irregularly shaped pockets, take a second measurement and indicate point of measure on spec sheet.]

126. *Applied Pocket Width*—Measure from side of pocket to side of pocket along top edge of pocket. [Note: For contoured or irregularly shaped pockets, take a second measurement and indicate point of measure on spec sheet.]

127. *Pocket Opening Within a Seam*—Measure from top of pocket to bottom of pocket along edge of pocket opening.

128. *Belt Length*

A. *Total*—Measure from end of belt at buckle along center of belt to opposite end of belt, following contour.

B. *Circumference*—Measure from end of belt at buckle along center of belt to middle hole at opposite end.

129. *Belt Width (or Height)*—Measure from edge of belt straight across to edge of belt. [Note: If belt is contoured, indicate points of measure on spec sheet.]

130. *Belt Loop Length*—Measure from top of belt loop straight down/vertically to bottom of belt loop along center of belt loop. [Note: Fashion-forward or irregularly shaped belt loops may require further spec instructions. Indicate points of measure on spec sheet.]

131. *Belt Loop Width*—Measure belt loop from edge of belt loop straight across/horizontally to edge of belt loop. [Note: Fashion-forward or irregularly shaped

belt loops may require further spec instructions. Indicate points of measure on spec sheet.]

132. *Tie Length*—Measure from end of tie/joining seam straight down to tie end along center of tie.

133. *Tie Width*

A. *Straight*—Measure from edge of tie straight across to edge of tie.
B. *Contoured*—Measure from edge of tie straight across to edge of tie at widest point of tie.

137. *Front Hood Length*—Measure from top of hood to bottom of hood at center front joining seam along opening edge of hood.

138. *Back Hood Length*—Measure from top of hood at center front to bottom of hood at center back joining seam along outside curve of hood fold/seam.

139. *Hood Width*—Measure from front opening edge of hood straight across to back of hood at fold along widest point of hood.

140. *Flange Depth*—Measure from center back neck joining seam straight down to bottom of flange at center back. [Note: If flange is contoured or asymmetrical, indicate point of measure on spec sheet.]

141. *Shoulder Pad Length*—Measure from edge of pad straight across to edge of pad along center of pad or natural shoulder line of pad.

142. *Shoulder Pad Width*—Measure from side of pad straight across to side of pad along edge of pad if straight, or at widest point of pad if curved.

143. *Straight Edge Shoulder Pad Height*—Measure from top of pad straight down to bottom of pad along center of pad.

144. *Curved Edge Shoulder Pad Height*—Stick a 1" straight pin into thickest part of shoulder pad. Push pin all the way through pad until head of pin rests on top of pad. Be sure not to crush pad. Measure portion of pin sticking out of pad. Subtract this figure from 1" (length of pin) to get shoulder pad height.

145. *Shoulder Pad Placement*—Measure from neck edge or joining seam straight across shoulder seam or natural shoulder line to start of shoulder pad.

146. *Pleats Placement*

A. *Front Pleat Top/Coat*—Measure distance from center front of garment straight across to start of first pleat at a point parallel to garment hem. [Note: You may need to use armhole or side seam as a starting point if there is no center front seam or placket.]
B. *Back Pleat Top/Coat*—Measure distance from armhole seam/side seam (depending on pleat placement) to first pleat at a point parallel to garment hem.

147. *Button Placement*—Refer to point of measure 59, Neck Depth Center Front, for placement of first button. Then measure distance of first button to second button. Be sure when measuring that button at bust point is lined up to apex of bust. Adjust all buttons accordingly and respace as needed.

148. *Pocket Placement*

A. *Top Pocket Vertical*—Measure from shoulder-neck joining seam straight down to top edge of pocket.
B. *Top Pocket Horizontal*—Measure from center front straight across to side of pocket at top edge.
C. *Front Bottom Pocket Vertical*—Measure from waistband/joining seam/edge straight down to top edge of pocket. [Note: Bottom pocket on a coat can use this measurement code, but it is measured from bottom of garment up to bottom of pocket. Make correction on spec sheet.]
D. *Front Bottom Pocket Horizontal*—Measure from center front straight across to side of pocket at top edge.

149. *Belt Loop Placement*

A. *Front*—Measure from center front of garment horizontally across to center of first front belt loop.

B. *Back*—Measure from center back of garment horizontally across to center of first back belt loop.
C. *Side Seam to Front*—Measure from center of side seam belt loop to center of front belt loop.
D. *Side Seam to Back*—Measure from center of side seam belt loop to center of back belt loop.

150. *Dart Placement*

A. *High Point Shoulder Bust Dart*—Measure from shoulder-neck joining seam or at a point _____" from shoulder-neck seam straight down, parallel to center front, to top of dart. [Note: The _____" from shoulder seam measurement is to be used for darts that are too short to be measured from high point shoulder. Be sure to indicate _____" measurement on spec sheet.]
B. *Center Front Bust Dart*—Measure from center front of garment straight across to top of dart.
C. *Side Seam Bust Dart*—Measure from underarm/side seam joining seam down along contour of side seam to bottom of dart.
D. *High Point Shoulder Princess Dart*—Measure from shoulder-neck joining seam straight down to top of dart.
E. *Center Front Princess Dart*—Measure from center front of garment straight across to top of dart.

CHAPTER 15 TERMS

When working with outerwear and coats, you may come across the following garment terms. If you are unfamiliar with any of them, please look up the definitions in the glossary at the end of this text.

Coat:
- *Balmacaan*
- *Car*
- *Chesterfield*
- *Classic*
- *Clutch*
- *Duster*
- *Military*
- *Pea*
- *Peasant*
- *Princess*
- *Raglan*
- *Stadium/Storm*
- *Tent*
- *Toggle*
- *Wrap*

Outerwear

SPEC SHEET Outerwear

	STYLE
SEASON:	DESCRIPTION:
LABEL: (SIZE CATEGORY)	
DATE:	
TECHNICAL SKETCH Chesterfield coat	SKETCH/PHOTO

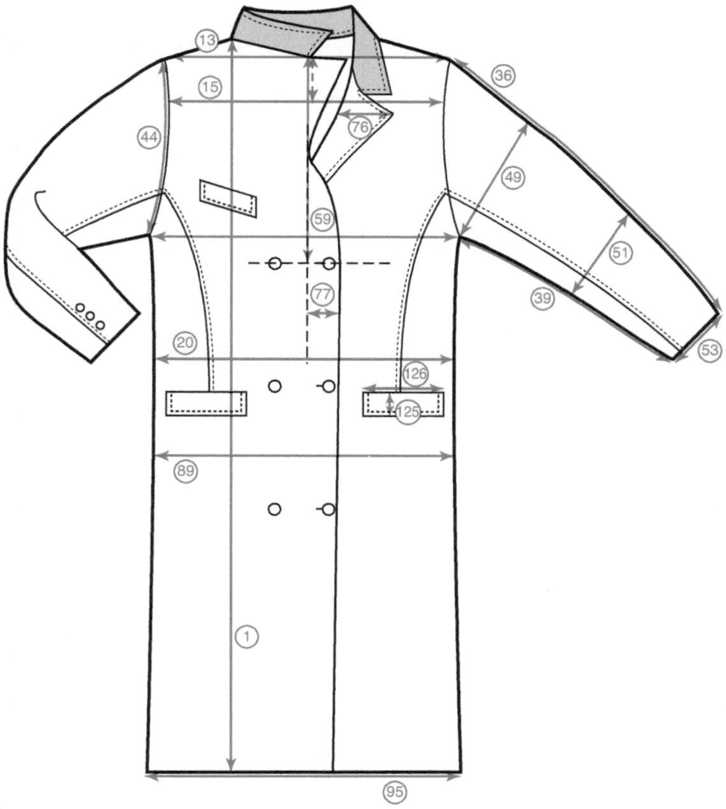

CODE	POINT OF MEASURE	TOL. +/–	4	S/6	8	M/10	12	L/14	16	XL/18
1.	Front length	1/2								
3.	Center back length	1/2								
4.	Side length	1/4								
10.	Chest width circumference	1/2-3/4								
13.	Across shoulder	1/4								
15.	Across chest _____" below H.P.S.	1/4								
16.	Across back	1/4								
20.	Waist width circumference _____" from H.P.S.	1/2-3/4								
36.	Sleeve length top armhole	3/8								
39.	Sleeve length underarm	3/8								
43.	Curved armhole width circumference	3/8								
49.	Muscle width circumference	1/4								

The measured garment spec sheets are for ***illustrative purposes only*** and should not be used as industry standards

CODE	POINT OF MEASURE	TOL. +/–	4	S/6	8	M/10	12	L/14	16	XL/18
51.	Elbow width circumference	1/4								
53.	Sleeve opening width circumference	1/4								
59.	Neck depth center front	1/8								
71.	Collar length	1/4								
72.	Collar height	1/8								
76.	Lapel width A. With notches	1/8								
	B. Without notches	1/8								
77.	Center front extension	1/8								
78.	Placket length	1/4								
79.	Placket width	1/8								
91.	Hip width from H.P.S. circumference _____ "	1/2-3/4								
95.	Bottom opening/sweep width circumference	1/2-3/4								
122.	Vent/slit A. Height	1/4								
	B. Width	1/8								
125.	Applied pocket height	1/8								
126.	Applied pocket width	1/8								
141.	Shoulder pad length	1/8								
142.	Shoulder pad width	1/8								
143.	Straight edge, shoulder pad height	1/8								
144.	Curved edge, shoulder pad height	1/8								
147.	Button placement (Distance between)	1/8								
148.	Pocket placement A. Top pocket vertical	1/8								
	B. Top pocket horizontal	1/8								
	C. Bottom pocket vertical	1/8								
	D. Bottom pocket horizontal	1/8								
150.	Dart length princess	1/8								
150.	Dart placement princess D. H.P.S.	1/8								
	E. C.F.	1/8								

COMMENTS:

The measured garment spec sheets are for ***illustrative purposes only*** and should not be used as industry standards

SPEC SHEET Outerwear | **STYLE**

SEASON: Winter	DESCRIPTION: Updated Chesterfield with turned up
LABEL: (SIZE CATEGORY) Missy	cuffs on sleeve and velvet collar
DATE:	
TECHNICAL SKETCH Chesterfield coat	SKETCH/PHOTO

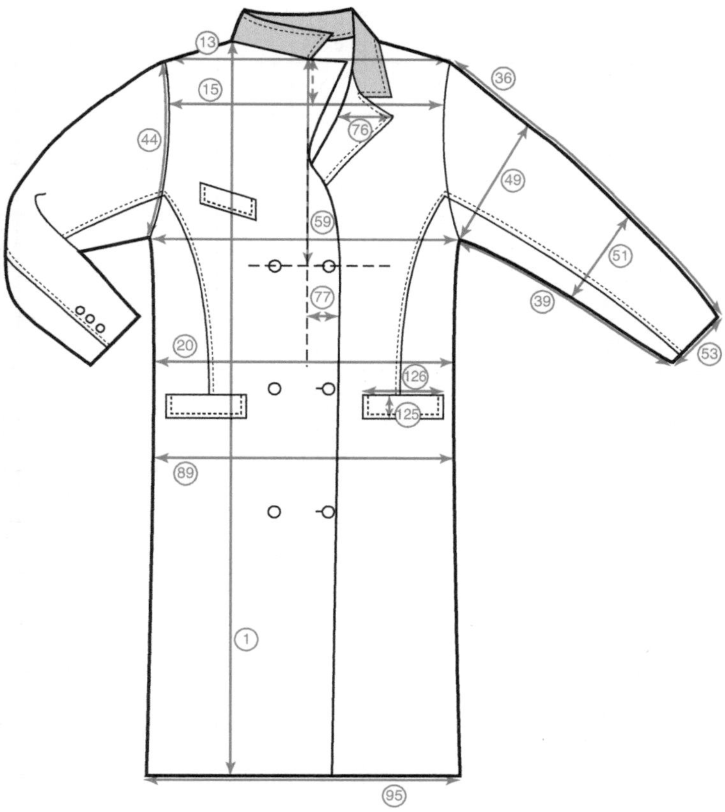

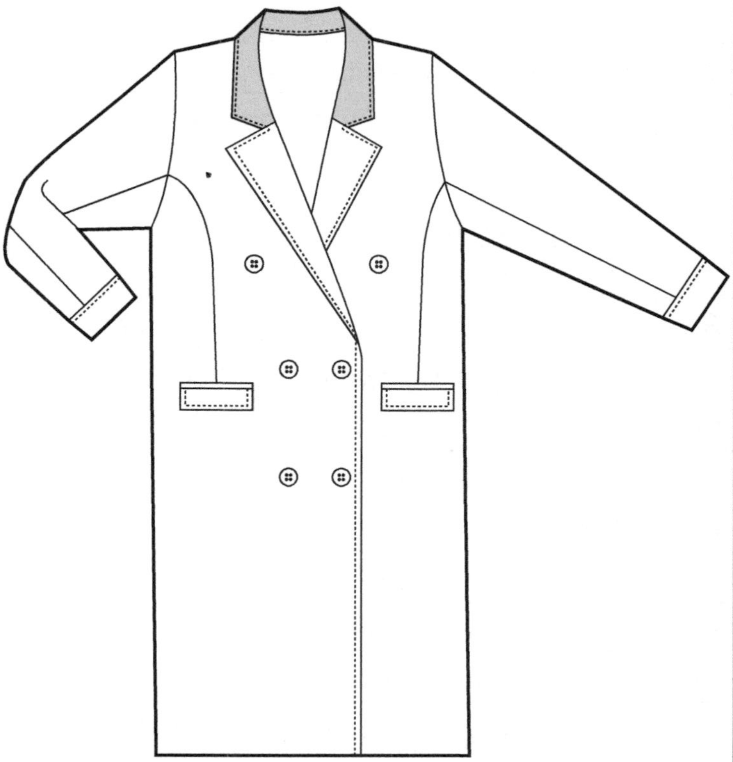

CODE	POINT OF MEASURE	TOL. +/–	4	S/6	8	M/10	12	L/14	16	XL/18
1.	Front length	1/2				49 1/2				
3.	Center back length	1/2				49 1/2				
4.	Side length	1/4				34				
10.	Chest width circumference	1/2-3/4				46				
13.	Across shoulder	1/4				18 1/2				
15.	Across chest 7 " below H.P.S.	1/2-3/4				18				
16.	Across back	1/4				18 1/2				
20.	Waist width circumference 22 " from H.P.S.	1/4				44				
36.	Sleeve length top armhole	3/8				21				
39.	Sleeve length underarm	3/8				17 1/2				
43.	Curved armhole width circumference	3/8				24				
49.	Muscle width circumference	1/4				19				

The measured garment spec sheets are for ***illustrative purposes only*** and should not be used as industry standards

CODE	POINT OF MEASURE	TOL. +/–	4	S/6	8	M/10	12	L/14	16	XL/18
51.	Elbow width circumference	1/4				18				
53.	Sleeve opening width circumference	1/4				16				
59.	Neck depth center front	1/8				19				
71.	Collar length	1/4				22				
72.	Collar height	1/8				3 3/4				
76.	Lapel width A. With notches	1/8				5				
	B. Without notches	1/8								
77.	Center front extension	1/8				2 3/4				
78.	Placket length	1/4								
79.	Placket width	1/8								
91.	Hip width from H.P.S. circumference 25 "	1/2-3/4				44				
95.	Bottom opening/sweep width circumference	1/2-3/4				44				
122.	Vent/slit A. Height	1/4				21 1/2				
	B. Width	1/8				1 3/4				
125.	Applied pocket height Flap	1/8				2 1/2				
126.	Applied pocket width Flap	1/8				5 1/2				
141.	Shoulder pad length	1/8				7				
142.	Shoulder pad width	1/8				4				
143.	Straight edge, shoulder pad height	1/8								
144.	Curved edge, shoulder pad height	1/8				1/2				
147.	Button placement (Distance between)	1/8				6 1/2				
148.	Pocket placement A. Top pocket vertical	1/8								
	B. Top pocket horizontal	1/8								
	C. Bottom pocket vertical	1/8				20 3/4				
	D. Bottom pocket horizontal	1/8				4 1/4				
150.	Dart length princess	1/8				12				
150.	Dart placement princess D. H.P.S.	1/8				-				
	E. C.F.	1/8				4 1/4				
57	Cuff height	1/8				2				

COMMENTS:

The measured garment spec sheets are for ***illustrative purposes only*** and should not be used as industry standards

PART IV

CHILDREN'S WEAR AND MENSWEAR

A look into children's wear and menswear garments is to further the advanced student's or technical designer's interests. However, once again the novice can use this section to get an overview of the processes involved. Chapter 16 looks at basic children's wear garments from newborn to junior sizes. It explains how to measure them and how to use what you learned from misses/women's wear to know which measurement points are needed for each garment. A basic garment sheet has been added for practical application and sample spec sheets for referencing. Chapter 17 looks at menswear, also offering measuring points for basic garments. Several spec sheets have been added in various style options for referencing.

CHAPTER 16

Children's Wear Garments

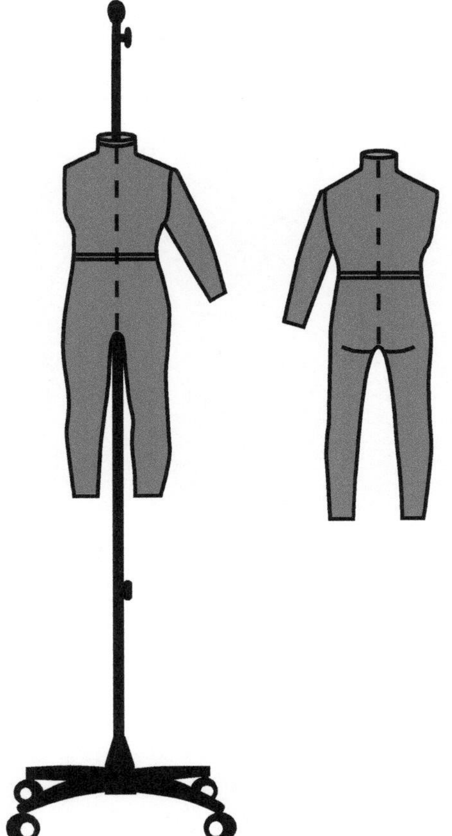

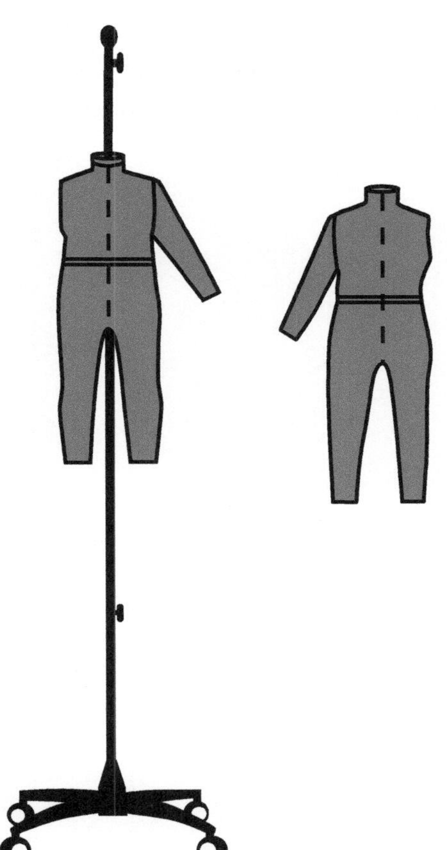

Measuring Children's Wear

Measuring children's wear garments is very much like measuring misses/women's wear garments. Therefore most of what you have learned up to this point will be applied to measuring garments in this chapter; for that reason, the points of measure have not been repeated. What you will find are examples for practical application. A basic garment has been chosen for each size category, newborn through junior.

You may notice when looking at the children's wear spec sheets that many garments resemble smaller versions of the misses sheets. While the garments look alike in styling, proportions are vastly different.

To make your own spec sheets, a girls/boys 4 to 6x/7 and toddler dress form for proportioning has been provided in this chapter. (Other forms are available on the online STUDIO.) Use the generic spec sheet and adapt the misses/women's wear templates found in Appendix A for style ideas.

CHAPTER 16 TERMS

The terms used for measuring children's wear are the same as misses/women's wear; additional terms follow. If you are unfamiliar with any of them, please look up the definitions in the glossary at the end of this text.

Children's wear
Boy's wear
Girl's wear
Junior's
Newborn
Toddler

GENERIC SPEC SHEET | **STYLE**

SEASON: Spring	DESCRIPTION: Knit onesie with yoke and ruffles at sleeve openings
LABEL: (SIZE CATEGORY) Newborn/Infant	
DATE:	
TECHNICAL SKETCH	SKETCH/PHOTO

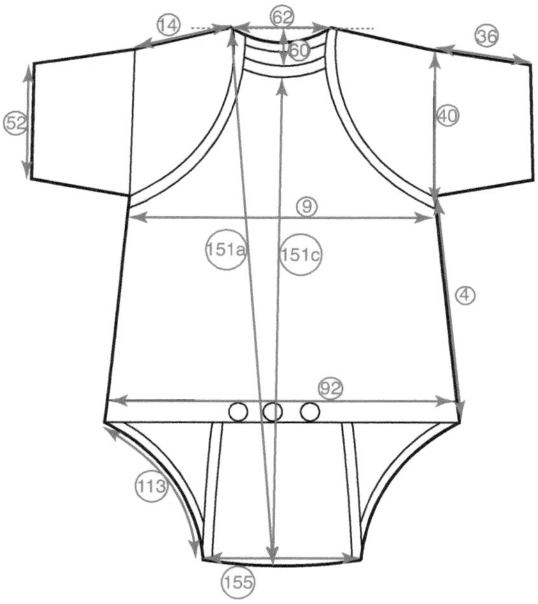

14 62 36 60 52 40 9 151a 151c 4 92 113 155

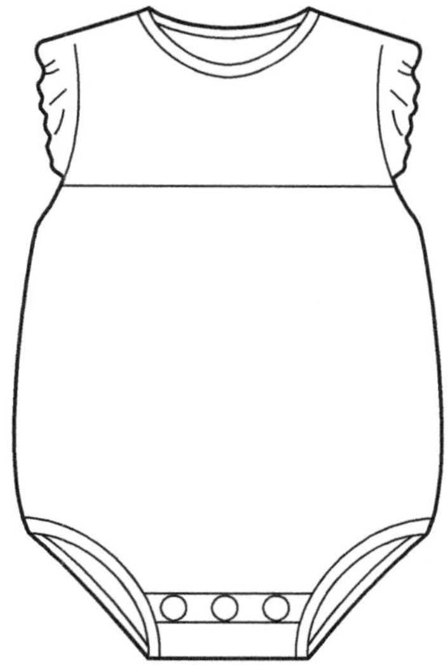

CODE	POINT OF MEASURE	TOL. +/–	PM	NB	3M	6M	9M	12M	18M	24M
4.	Side seam length	1/4			8 3/4			9 1/2		
9.	Chest width	1/2			8 1/2			11 1/2		
14.	Shoulder width	1/8			1 1/4			1 1/2		
19.	Waist width (4" down from yoke)	1/2			10			13		
34.	Yoke depth front				4			4 1/4		
35.	Yoke depth back				3 1/4			3 1/2		
42.	Curved armhole width	1/8			4 1/2			5 3/4		
60.	Neck drop front	1/8			1 1/4			1 3/4		
61.	Neck back drop	1/8			3/4			3/4		
62.	Neck width, no collar	1/8			4 1/4			4 1/4		
78.	Placket length (back neck)				4 1/2			5		
79.	Placket width (back neck)				1			1		
	Distance between snaps on placket				1 3/4			1 3/4		
92	Hip seat width 3.25" up from crotch	1/2			9 1/2			12 1/2		
113.	Leg opening width	1/4			5 1/4			5 3/4		
117.	Leg opening width stretched	1/4			7 1/2			8		
134.	Ruffle height at shoulder/sleeve opening				1			1		
	Length of ruffle on sleeve opening				6 1/4			7 3/4		

(Tolerance 1/4-3/8 S, M, L, XL = 3/8" 4-18 = 1/4")

The measured garment spec sheets are for ***illustrative purposes only*** and should not be used as industry standards

CODE	POINT OF MEASURE		TOL. +/–	PM	NB	3M	6M	9M	12M	18M	24M
151.	Front torso length	a. H.P.S. to crotch	1/2			15			18		
		d. C.F. neck stretched	1/2			13			16		
155.	Crotch width		1/8			3 1/2			3 1/2		
	Distance bottom of crotch to crotch opening					1			1		
	Distance between crotch snaps					3/4			3/4		
	Width binding neck opening					3/8			3/8		

COMMENTS:

(Tolerance 1/4-3/8 S, M, L, XL = 3/8" 4-18 = 1/4")

The measured garment spec sheets are for ***illustrative purposes only*** and should not be used as industry standards

GENERIC SPEC SHEET **STYLE**

SEASON: Spring	DESCRIPTION: Denim overall with metal buttons closure
LABEL: (SIZE CATEGORY) Toddler	
DATE:	
TECHNICAL SKETCH Toddler	SKETCH/PHOTO

CODE	POINT OF MEASURE	TOL. +/–		T2		T3		T4		
6.	Center front bodice length (bib)	1/4				7				
8.	Side seam bodice length (bib)	1/4				7				
15.	Across chest (top of bib)	1/4				5 1/2				
33.	Yoke width back	1/8				6 1/4				
35.	Yoke depth back	1/8				4				
81.	Waistband depth	1/8				1 1/8				
83.	Waistband width ~~circumference~~ (front only)	1/4				11				
87.	High hip width circumference (3" down from natural waist)	1/4				13				
105.	Inseam	1/2				2 1/2				
106.	Outseam	1/2				9				
107.	Front rise	1/4				6 3/4				
108.	Back rise	1/4				10 1/4				
110.	Thigh width circumference	1/4				8 1/2				
114.	Leg opening width circumference	1/4				8				
121.	Fly/zipper A. Length	1/4				3 1/4				
	B. Width					1				
125.	Applied pocket height (on bib at CF)	1/8				3 1/2				
126.	Applied pocket width (on bib across top)	1/8				4 5/8				
127.	Pocket opening (pant)	1/8				4 3/8				

(Tolerance 1/4-3/8 S, M, L, XL = 3/8" 4-18 = 1/4")

The measured garment spec sheets are for ***illustrative purposes only*** and should not be used as industry standards

CODE	POINT OF MEASURE	TOL. +/–		T2		T3		T4		
	Applied pocket height back hip (center point)	1/8				3 1/2				
	Applied pocket width back hip (across top)	1/8				3 1/2				
130.	Belt loop length					1 5/8				
131.	Belt loop width					1/2				
135.	Strap length	1/4				9 1/4				
136.	Strap width (front)					1 1/4				
	Strap width back					3				
151.	Front torso length	1/2				18				

COMMENTS:

(Tolerance 1/4-3/8 S, M, L, XL = 3/8" 4-18 = 1/4")

The measured garment spec sheets are for ***illustrative purposes only*** and should not be used as industry standards

GENERIC SPEC SHEET

STYLE

SEASON: Spring	DESCRIPTION: Sundress with ribbon tie at waist
LABEL: (SIZE CATEGORY) Girls 4–6x	
DATE:	
TECHNICAL SKETCH	SKETCH/PHOTO

62 14 60 43 34 6 8 32 20 87 102 100 99

CODE	POINT OF MEASURE	TOL. +/–		4		5		6x		
6.	Center front bodice length	1/4				5 1/4				
7.	Center back bodice length	1/4				8 1/2				
8.	Side length	1/4				4				
14.	Across shoulder	1/4				1 3/4				
20.	Waist width circumference	1/2				23				
43.	Curved armhole width circumference	1/4				13				
60.	Neck depth front	1/4				4 3/4				
61.	Neck depth back	1/4				1				
62.	Neck width, no collar	1/4				5 1/2				
89.	Low hip width circumference (5" down)	1/2				40				
99.	Bottom opening sweep width circumference	1/2				50				
121.	Back fly zipper length					12 1/2				
	Ribbon width					1 1/2				
	Length of each ribbon tie at back					22				

COMMENTS:

(Tolerance 1/4-3/8 S, M, L, XL = 3/8" 4-18 = 1/4")

The measured garment spec sheets are for ***illustrative purposes only*** and should not be used as industry standards

GENERIC SPEC SHEET | **STYLE**

SEASON: Spring	DESCRIPTION: Short Sleeve Polo
LABEL: (SIZE CATEGORY) Boys 4-7X	
DATE:	
TECHNICAL SKETCH	SKETCH/PHOTO

CODE	POINT OF MEASURE	TOL. +/–		S/4		M/5		L/6		XL/7–7x
1.	Front length	1/2				19				
3.	Center back length	1/2				19 1/2				
4.	Side length	1/2				12 1/2				
9.	Chest width	1/2				13 1/2				
13.	Across shoulder	1/4				11 1/2				
15.	Across chest (2" down)	1/4				11				
16.	Across back (3" down)	1/4				11 1/2				
26.	Bottom sweep opening (at top of vent)	1/2				13 1/12				
36.	Sleeve length	1/4				6				
42.	Curved armhole width	1/4				6 1/4				
52.	Sleeve opening width	1/4				4 1/4				
57.	Cuff/ribbing height					5/8				
59.	Neck depth front	1/4				1				
63.	Neck width collar	1/4				7				
71.	Collar length	1/4				13 1/4				
72.	Collar height					2 1/2				
78.	Placket length					4 1/2				
79.	Placket width					4 1/4				
122.	Vent/slit height					2				

COMMENTS:

(Tolerance 1/4-3/8 S, M, L, XL = 3/8" 4-18 = 1/4")

The measured garment spec sheets are for ***illustrative purposes only*** and should not be used as industry standards

GENERIC SPEC SHEET | **STYLE**

SEASON: Spring	DESCRIPTION:
LABEL: (SIZE CATEGORY) Girls 4-18	Woven Skirt with Box Pleats
DATE:	
TECHNICAL SKETCH	SKETCH/PHOTO

CODE	POINT OF MEASURE	TOL. +/–	4	S/6	8	M/10	12	L/14	16	XL/18
81.	Waistband depth (front)	1/8				2				
81.	Waistband depth (back elastic casing)	1/8				1 1/4				
83.	Waistband width circumference	1/2				24				
85.	Waistband width circumference, stretched	1/2				29				
87.	High hip width circumference (2 1/2" below waist seam)	1/2				31				
89.	Low hip width circumference (5" below waist seam)	1/2				34				
95.	Bottom opening/sweep width circumference	1/2				38				
100.	Center front skirt length	3/8				13 1/2				
101.	Center back skirt length	3/8				14 1/2				
102.	Side length skirt	3/8				13 1/2				
123.	Pleat depth	1/8				1				
124.	Distance between pleats	1/8				2				
	Length of pleat topstitching from top bottom of waist					2 1/2				
149.	Faux belt loop/tab A. Length	1/8				2				
	B. Width	1/8				3 1/2				

COMMENTS:

(Tolerance 1/4-3/8 S, M, L, XL = 3/8" 4-18 = 1/4")

The measured garment spec sheets are for ***illustrative purposes only*** and should not be used as industry standards

GENERIC SPEC SHEET **STYLE**

SEASON: Spring	DESCRIPTION: Technical jacket/rain coat
LABEL: (SIZE CATEGORY) Boys 8-20	
DATE:	
TECHNICAL SKETCH	SKETCH/PHOTO

13 58 14 43 36 10 49 1 51 39 127 2 4 53 27

XRTFN

CODE	POINT OF MEASURE	TOL. +/–	8	S/9	10	M/12	14	L/16	18	XL/20
1.	Front length	1/2				22 1/2				
3.	Center back length	1/2				22 1/2				
4.	Side length	1/4				14				
10.	Chest width circumference	1/2				36				
13.	Across shoulder	1/4				14				
15.	Across chest 6" below H.P.S (at yoke seam)	1/4				13 3/4				
16.	Across back 5 1/5" below CB (at yoke seam)	1/4				11 1/2				
27.	Bottom opening/sweep width circumference	1/2				32				
	Bottom opening/sweep width circumference stretched	1/2				38				
	Elastic height, bottom band					1				
32.	Yoke trim across chest (center measure)	1/4				14 1/2				
33.	Yoke trim across back (center measure)	1/4				15				
34.	Yoke depth from HPS to yoke trim	1/4				6				
35.	Yoke depth from CB to yoke trim					5 1/2				
	Height of yoke trim (across chest)					3				
	Height of yoke trim (across chest)					3				
36.	Sleeve length top armhole	3/8				12				
39.	Sleeve length underarm	3/8				17 1/2				
43.	Curved armhole width circumference	3/2				14				

(Tolerance 1/4-3/8 S, M, L, XL = 3/8" 4-18 = 1/4")

The measured garment spec sheets are for ***illustrative purposes only*** and should not be used as industry standards

CODE	POINT OF MEASURE	TOL. +/–	8	S/9	10	M/12	14	L/16	18	XL/20
49.	Muscle width circumference	1/8				14				
51.	Elbow width circumference	1/8				12				
53.	Sleeve opening width circumference	1/2				7.5				
55.	Sleeve opening width circumference stretched	1/2				10				
	Elastic height cuff band	3/4				1				
	Width of yoke/trim on sleeve (total underarm)	3/4				6				
125.	Applied pocket height					5				
126.	Applied pocket width					1				
137.	Front hood length					11				
138.	Back hood length					16 1/2				
139.	Hood width					9				
	Width of trim on center of hood					3				

COMMENTS:

(Tolerance 1/4-3/8 S, M, L, XL = 3/8" 4-18 = 1/4")

The measured garment spec sheets are for ***illustrative purposes only*** and should not be used as industry standards

GENERIC SPEC SHEET | **STYLE**

SEASON: Spring | DESCRIPTION: Criss-Cross Razor Back Dress

LABEL: (SIZE CATEGORY) Juniors

DATE:

TECHNICAL SKETCH | SKETCH/PHOTO

CODE	POINT OF MEASURE	TOL. +/–	XS/1	S/3/5	M/7/9	L/11/13	XL/15
1.	Front length	1/2			35		
5.	Front bodice length	1/4			9		
8.	Side seam bodice length	1/4			7		
9.	Chest width	1/4–3/8			14 1/4		
36.	Sleeve length top armhole	3/8			7		
39.	Sleeve length underarm	3/8			2		
44.	Armhole front	1/4			6		
45.	Armhole back	1/4			8		
52.	Sleeve opening width	1/8			6		
57.	Binding/ribbing height sleeve (and all bindings)				3/8		
58.	Neck depth front	1/8			6		
61.	Neck drop back				7		
64.	Neck edge width	1/4			7 1/2		
81.	Back elastic waistband depth	1/8			3/4		
83.	Back elastic waistband width	1/4			11 1/2		
84.	Back elastic waistband width stretched	1/4			17		
90.	Hip width from H.P.S. 19"	1/4–3/8			18		
94.	Bottom opening sweep width	1/4–3/8			40		
100.	Center back skirt length	3/8			17		
102.	Side skirt length	3/8			19		
	Height of racer back at side seam	1/8			6 1/4		

(Tolerance 1/4-3/8 S, M, L, XL = 3/8" 4-18 = 1/4")

The measured garment spec sheets are for ***illustrative purposes only*** and should not be used as industry standards

CODE	POINT OF MEASURE	TOL. +/–	XS/1	S/3/5	M/7/9	L/11/13	XL/15
49.	Length of racer back measured along center from armhole to side seam	1/4			13		

COMMENTS:

(Tolerance 1/4-3/8 S, M, L, XL = 3/8" 4-18 = 1/4")

The measured garment spec sheets are for ***illustrative purposes only*** and should not be used as industry standards

CHAPTER 17

Menswear Garments

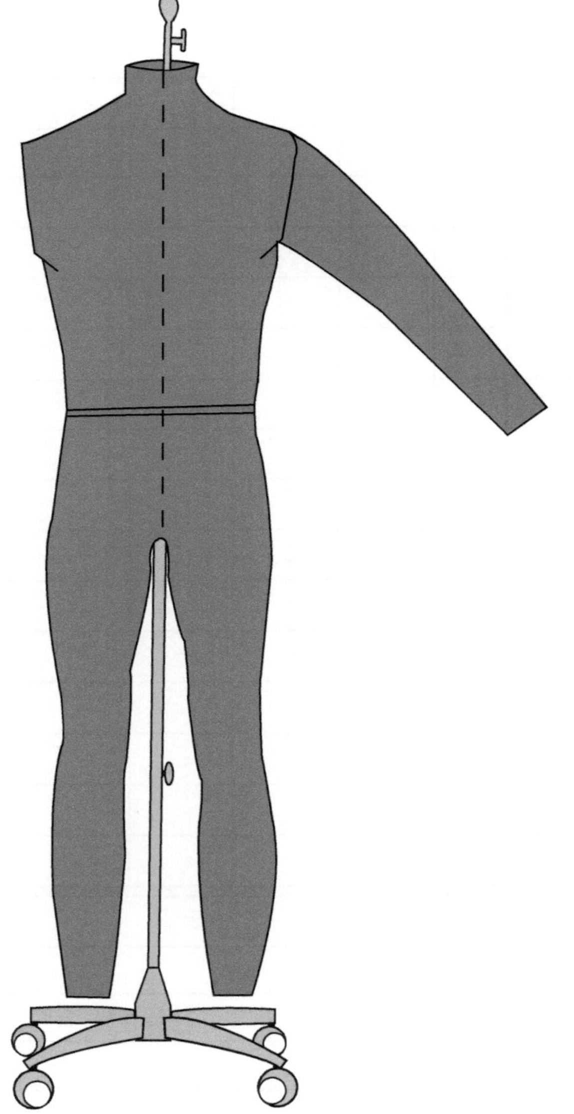

Measuring Menswear

Measuring menswear garments is very much like measuring misses/women's wear garments. Although there are a few measurement points that vary, most of what you have learned up to this point may be applied to measuring menswear garments; for that reason, the points of measure have not been repeated in this chapter. What you will find are examples for practical application. Eight of the most classic menswear garments are shown in spec form with basic points of measure and general specifications. The numeric specifications listed are based on classic styling and are offered as a guide. These specifications are not to be used as industry standards, but are an average of several popular industry brands.

You may notice when looking at the menswear sheets that the two major points of measure that differ from misses wear are (1) sleeve length and (2) hip seat. Most men's sleeve length measurements are taken from the center back neck, down to the sleeve opening, and most hip measurements are taken from the seat—either at a point 3" up from the crotch or 7" down from the waist. It is easy to make these corrections on the spec sheet. In fact, any time a technician has a spec that he or she would like to deviate from on the general points of measure, it is acceptable to simply change or write them in on the spec sheet. The menswear industry has its own computerized templates for technicians to use, making the measuring process much easier. Take a look at the specs that follow. Try to spec out a garment of your own.

If you would like to add sketches to your specs, a body form is added to this chapter for men's proportioning. You can use some of the basic styles on the spec sheets as templates, and use the generic spec sheet and style templates in Appendix A for ideas.

Menswear sizing may be foreign to some as it does not follow traditional women's wear sizing. Men's shirts are generally sized by neck measurements, hence sizes 14 through 17½. They are then further broken down by sleeve length, generally 32–34" on smaller sizes and 34–36" for larger sizes. Trousers are sized by waist measurements, 28–42", and then have inseam of 30–34". Jackets and coats are sized by chest measurements: sizes 34 through 48. They are sold in short (S), regular (R), long (L), and extra long (XL) which denotes sleeve and body proportions. (See Table 17.1 for further explanation of the correlating sizes.)

CHAPTER 17 TERMS

The terms used for measuring menswear are the same as misses/women's; additional terms follow. If you are unfamiliar with any of them, please look up the definitions in the glossary at the end of this text.

Menswear
Template

Table 17.1 MENSWEAR SIZE RANGE CONVERSION CHART

Size	**S**		**M**		**L**		**XL**	
Dress shirt	14	14½	15	15½	16	16½	17	17½
Trouser	28	30	32	34	36	38	40	42
Jacket/Coat	34R	36R	38R	40R	42R	44R	46R	48R

GENERIC SPEC SHEET **STYLE**

SEASON: SPRING	DESCRIPTION: BASIC T-SHIRT W/ POCKET
LABEL: (SIZE CATEGORY) MENSWEAR	
DATE:	
TECHNICAL SKETCH	SKETCH/PHOTO

CODE	POINT OF MEASURE	TOL. +/–	14	S $14^1/_2$	15	M $15^1/_2$	16	L $16^1/_2$	17	XL $17^1/_2$
1.	Front length	1/2				28				
3.	Center back length	1/2				28 1/2				
4.	Side length	1/4				18				
9.	Chest width	1/2				21				
13.	Across shoulder	1/4				20				
15.	Across chest (2 1/2 down)	1/4				19 1/2				
16.	Across back (4" down)	1/4				19				
26.	Bottom sweep opening	1/2				21				
42.	Curved armhole width	3/8				10				
48.	Muscle width	1/4				9				
52.	Sleeve opening width	1/8				7 1/2				
60.	Neck drop back	1/8				1 1/4				
62.	Neck width no collar	1/8				7 1/4				
67.	Neck edge width circumference	1/4				26				
125.	Applied pocket height	-				5 5/8				
126.	Applied pocket width	-				5 3/8				
148A.	Top pocket placement vertical (from H.P.S.)	-				7 1/4				
148G.	(Bottom) pocket placement from side seam	-				2 3/4				

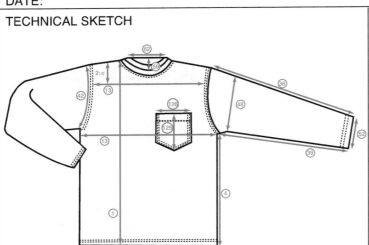

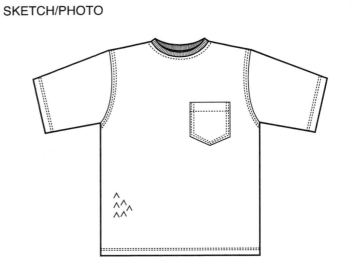

COMMENTS:

(Tolerance 1/4-3/8 S, M, L, XL = 3/8" 4-18 = 1/4")

The measured garment spec sheets are for ***illustrative purposes only*** and should not be used as industry standards

GENERIC SPEC SHEET **STYLE**

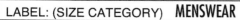

SEASON: **FALL** DESCRIPTION: **MOCK–NECK SWEATER**

LABEL: (SIZE CATEGORY) **MENSWEAR**

DATE:

TECHNICAL SKETCH

SKETCH/PHOTO

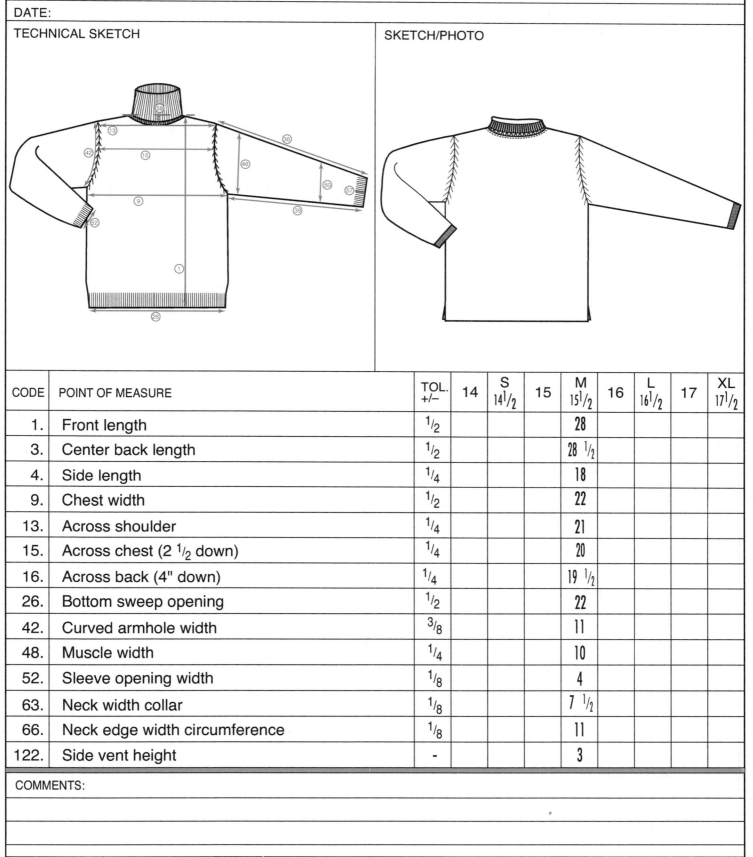

CODE	POINT OF MEASURE	TOL. +/–	14	S 14 1/2	15	M 15 1/2	16	L 16 1/2	17	XL 17 1/2
1.	Front length	1/2				28				
3.	Center back length	1/2				28 1/2				
4.	Side length	1/4				18				
9.	Chest width	1/2				22				
13.	Across shoulder	1/4				21				
15.	Across chest (2 1/2 down)	1/4				20				
16.	Across back (4" down)	1/4				19 1/2				
26.	Bottom sweep opening	1/2				22				
42.	Curved armhole width	3/8				11				
48.	Muscle width	1/4				10				
52.	Sleeve opening width	1/8				4				
63.	Neck width collar	1/8				7 1/2				
66.	Neck edge width circumference	1/8				11				
122.	Side vent height	-				3				

COMMENTS:

(Tolerance 1/4-3/8 S, M, L, XL = 3/8" 4-18 = 1/4")

The measured garment spec sheets are for ***illustrative purposes only*** and should not be used as industry standards

GENERIC SPEC SHEET | **STYLE**

SEASON: SUMMER | DESCRIPTION: SHORT SLEEVE POLO SHIRT

LABEL: (SIZE CATEGORY) MENSWEAR

DATE:

TECHNICAL SKETCH | SKETCH/PHOTO

CODE	POINT OF MEASURE	TOL. +/–	14	S 14 1/2	15	M 15 1/2	16	L 16 1/2	17	XL 17 1/2
1.	Front length	1/2				28				
3.	Center back length	1/2				28 1/2				
4.	Side length	1/4				18				
9.	Chest width	1/2				22				
13.	Across shoulder	1/4				21				
15.	Across chest (2 1/2 down)	1/4				20				
16.	Across back (4" down)	1/4				20				
26.	Bottom sweep opening	1/2				22				
42.	Curved armhole width	3/8				10 1/2				
48.	Muscle width	1/4				10				
52.	Sleeve opening width	1/8				6 3/4				
57.	Cuff/ribbing height	-				5/8				
58.	Neck depth front	1/8				2				
63.	Neck width collar	1/8				7				
71.	Collar length	1/4				17 1/2				
72.	Collar height	-				2 3/4				
78.	Placket length	-				6 1/4				
79.	Placket width	-				1 3/8				
122.	Vent/slit height	-				3				

COMMENTS:

(Tolerance 1/4-3/8 S, M, L, XL = 3/8" 4-18 = 1/4")

The measured garment spec sheets are for ***illustrative purposes only*** and should not be used as industry standards

GENERIC SPEC SHEET

STYLE

SEASON: FALL	DESCRIPTION: KNIT JOG PANT
LABEL: (SIZE CATEGORY) MENSWEAR	
DATE:	
TECHNICAL SKETCH	SKETCH/PHOTO

82 81 127 107 97 109 106 105 111 113

CODE	POINT OF MEASURE	TOL. +/–	28	S 30	32	M 34	36	L 38	40	XL 42
81.	Waistband depth	-				2				
82.	Waistband width	1/2				14				
84.	Waistband width stretched	1/2				42				
92.	Seat width (3" up from crotch)	1/2				22 1/2				
105.	Inseam	3/8				32				
106.	Outseam	3/8				39				
107.	Front rise	3/8				11 1/8				
108.	Back rise	3/8				14 3/4				

(Tolerance 1/4-3/8 S, M, L, XL = 3/8" 4-18 = 1/4")

The measured garment spec sheets are for ***illustrative purposes only*** and should not be used as industry standards

CODE	POINT OF MEASURE	TOL. +/–	28	S/30	32	M/32	34	L/38	40	XL/42
109.	Thigh width	1/4				14				
111.	Knee width	1/8				11				
113.	Leg width	1/8				9				
122.	Zipper vent/slit height	-				8				
127.	Pocket opening	1/4				9				

COMMENTS:

The measured garment spec sheets are for ***illustrative purposes only*** and should not be used as industry standards

GENERIC SPEC SHEET | **STYLE**

SEASON: SUMMER	DESCRIPTION: SHORT SLEEVE LINEN SHIRT
LABEL: (SIZE CATEGORY) MENSWEAR	
DATE:	
TECHNICAL SKETCH	SKETCH/PHOTO

CODE	POINT OF MEASURE	TOL. +/–	14	S $14^1/_2$	15	M $15^1/_2$	16	L $16^1/_2$	17	XL $17^1/_2$
1.	Front length	$^1/_2$				31				
4.	Side length	$^1/_4$				20				
10.	Chest width circumference	1				46				
13.	Across shoulder	$^1/_4$				19				
15.	Across chest 6" from H.P.S.	$^1/_4$				17				
16.	Across back 2 $^1/_2$" from CB neck	$^1/_2$				18 $^1/_2$				
27.	Bottom opening/sweep width circumference	1				46				
32.	Yoke width front	$^1/_4$				6 $^1/_2$				

(Tolerance $^1/_4$-$^3/_8$ S, M, L, XL = $^3/_8$" 4-18 = $^1/_4$")

The measured garment spec sheets are for ***illustrative purposes only*** and should not be used as industry standards

CODE	POINT OF MEASURE		14	S/14½	15	M/15½	16	L/16½	17	XL/17½
33.	Yoke width back	1/2				18 1/2				
34.	Yoke depth front	1/8				1 1/4				
35.	Yoke width back	1/8				2 1/2				
36.	Sleeve length top armhole	1/2				10				
39.	Sleeve length underarm	1/2				6				
43.	Curved armhole width circumference	1/4				22				
49.	Muscle width circumference	1/4				20				
53.	Sleeve opening circumference	1/8				16				
58.	Neck depth front	1/8				2				
63.	Neck width collar	1/8				7 3/8				
69.	Neck base circumference	1/4				16				
70.	Neck band length	1/4				15 1/2				
72.	Collar height (CB)	1/8				2				
73.	Collar band height	1/16				1 3/8				
74.	Collar point length	1/8				2 5/8				
75.	Collar point spread	1/4				3				
122.	Vent/slit height	-				3 1/2				
125.	Applied pocket length	1/8				5 5/8				
126.	Applied pocket width	1/8				5				
148.	Pocket placement A. Top pocket H.P.S.	1/8				8 5/8				
	B. Top pocket horizontal	1/8				1 3/4				

COMMENTS:

The measured garment spec sheets are for ***illustrative purposes only*** and should not be used as industry standards

GENERIC SPEC SHEET **STYLE**

SEASON: SUMMER	DESCRIPTION: LINEN TROUSER
LABEL: (SIZE CATEGORY) MENSWEAR	
DATE:	
TECHNICAL SKETCH	SKETCH/PHOTO

81 83 127 121 93 107 106 110 112 105 114

CODE	POINT OF MEASURE	TOL. +/–	28	S 30	32	M 34	36	L 38	40	XL 42
81.	Waistband depth	-				1 1/2				
83.	Waistband circumference	1				32				
93.	Hip seat width circumference	1				44				
105.	Inseam	3/8				VARY				
106.	Outseam	3/8				VARY BASED ON INSEAM				
107.	Front rise	3/8				10 3/8				
108.	Back rise	3/8				13 5/8				
110.	Thigh width circumference	1/2				26				

(Tolerance 1/4-3/8 S, M, L, XL = 3/8" 4-18 = 1/4")

The measured garment spec sheets are for ***illustrative purposes only*** and should not be used as industry standards

CODE	POINT OF MEASURE	TOL. +/–	28	S/30	32	M/34	36	L/38	40	XL/42
112.	Knee width circumference	3/8				20				
114.	Leg opening width circumference	1/4				18				
119.	Cuff height pants	-				1 1/4				
121.	Fly/zipper A. Length	-				7				
	B. Width	-				1 3/8				
125.	Back pocket (applied vented) height	-				1/2				
126.	Back pocket (applied vented) width	-				5 3/8				
127.	Pocket opening (side seam)	-				6 3/4				
130.	Belt loop length	-				2 1/4				
131.	Belt loop width	-				1/2				
148.	Back pocket placement E. From waist	-				2 1/2				
	F. From CB seam	-				1 3/4				

COMMENTS:

The measured garment spec sheets are for ***illustrative purposes only*** and should not be used as industry standards

GENERIC SPEC SHEET

STYLE

SEASON: FALL	DESCRIPTION: WOOL SPORTCOAT
LABEL: (SIZE CATEGORY) MENSWEAR	
DATE:	
TECHNICAL SKETCH	SKETCH/PHOTO

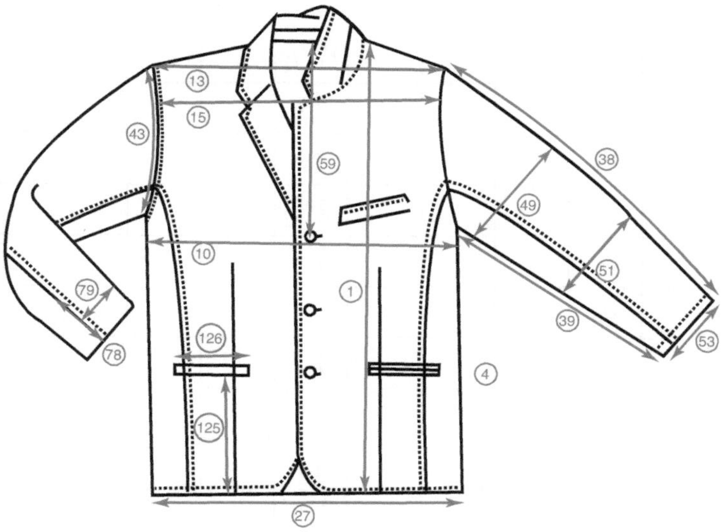

CODE	POINT OF MEASURE	TOL. +/–	34R	S 36R	38R	M 40R	42R	L 44R	46R	XL 48R
1.	Front length	1/2				31				
3.	Center back length	1/2				31				
4.	Side length	1/4				19				
10.	Chest circumference	1				44				
13.	Across shoulder	1/4				19				
15.	Across chest 5" below HPS	1/4				16 1/2				
20.	Waist width circumference 16" from HPS	1				42				
27.	Bottom opening sweep circumference	1				44				

(Tolerance 1/4-3/8 S, M, L, XL = 3/8" 4-18 = 1/4")

The measured garment spec sheets are for ***illustrative purposes only*** and should not be used as industry standards

CODE	POINT OF MEASURE		TOL. +/–	34R	S 36R	38R	M/40R	42R	L 44R	46R	XL/48R
36.	Sleeve length top armhole		1/2				25				
36a.	Sleeve length from CB neck to cuff		3/4				35				
39.	Sleeve length underarm on seam		1/2				15 1/2				
43.	Curved armhole width circumference		1/2				27				
49.	Muscle width circumference		1/4				16				
51.	Elbow width circumference		1/4				14 1/2				
53.	Sleeve width circumference		1/4				11 1/2				
59.	Neck depth center front		1/8				13				
71.	Collar length (follow seam)		1/4				19				
72.	Collar height		1/8				2 1/2				
76.	Lapel width notched		-				3 1/2				
77.	Center front extension		1/8				1				
78.	Placket length		1/4				3 1/2				
79.	Placket width		1/8				1 1/4				
122.	Back vent/slit	A. Height	-				10				
		B. Width	-				1 1/2				
125a.	Applied pocket height (chest)		1/8				1 1/8				
	Applied pocket width (chest)		1/8				4 3/8				
125b.	Applied pocket height (hip)		1/8				1/2				
	Applied pocket width (hip)		1/8				6 1/2				
141.	Shoulder pad length		1/8				5 1/2				
142.	Shoulder pad width		1/8				9				
144.	Curved edge shoulder pad height		1/16				3/8				
145.	Shoulder pad placement		1/8				1				
148a.	Pocket placement	A. Top pocket vertical	-				9 3/4				
		B. Top pocket horizontal	1/8				3 1/2				
148b.	Pocket placement	A. Bottom pocket vertical	-				20				
		B. Bottom pocket horizontal	1/8				4 3/4				

COMMENTS:

The measured garment spec sheets are for ***illustrative purposes only***
and should not be used as industry standards

SPEC SHEET GENERIC SPEC SHEET

STYLE

SEASON: **FALL**	DESCRIPTION: **WOOL COAT**
LABEL: (SIZE CATEGORY) **MENSWEAR**	
DATE:	
TECHNICAL SKETCH	SKETCH/PHOTO

CODE	POINT OF MEASURE	TOL. +/–	34R	S 36R	38R	M 40R	42R	L 44R	46R	XL 48R
1.	Front length	1/2				32				
3.	Center back length	1/2				32				
4.	Side length	1/4				19				
10.	Chest circumference	1				50				
13.	Across shoulder	1/4				20				
15.	Across chest (7" below HPS)	1/4				18 1/2				
16.	Across back (6" below CB neck)	1/4				19 1/2				
32.	Yoke width front	1/4				19				

(Tolerance 1/4-3/8 S, M, L, XL = 3/8" 4-18 = 1/4")

The measured garment spec sheets are for ***illustrative purposes only*** and should not be used as industry standards

CODE	POINT OF MEASURE	TOL. +/–	34R	S36R	38R	M/40R	42R	L44R	46R	XL/48R
33.	Yoke width back	1/4				19 1/2				
34.	Yoke depth front	1/8				9 1/2				
35.	Yoke width back	1/8				6				
36.	Sleeve length	1/2				25				
36a.	Sleeve length CB neck	3/4				35 1/2				
39.	Sleeve length underarm	1/2				19 1/2				
43.	Curved armhole width circumference	1/2				25				
49.	Muscle width circumference	1/4				20				
51.	Elbow width circumference	1/4				16 1/2				
53.	Sleeve opening width circumference	1/4				11				
57.	Cuff height	1/8				2				
59.	Neck depth center front	1/8				5				
71.	Collar length	1/4				19 1/2				
72.	Collar height	1/8				4				
77.	Center front extension	1/8				1 1/2				
78.	Placket length	1/4				5				
79.	Placket width	1/8				1/4				
95.	Bottom opening/sweep width circumference	1				44				
125.	Applied pocket height	1/8				6 1/2				
126.	Applied pocket width	1/8				1 1/2				
147.	Button placement (Distance between)	1/8				6 1/2				
148.	Pocket placement A. Pocket vertical H.P.S.	1/8				18				
	B. Pocket vertical C.F.	1/8				6				

COMMENTS:

The measured garment spec sheets are for ***illustrative purposes only*** and should not be used as industry standards

PART V

FITTING AND GRADING

Fitting and grading are for the advanced student or technical designer. However, the novice can use this section to get an overview of the processes involved. A comprehensive understanding of good fit is needed before one tries to evaluate garments and make the necessary adjustments. Instructions are given for fitting a garment on a fit-model or dress form, evaluating that fit, and making the proper fit corrections as needed.

A comprehensive understanding of patternmaking, pattern adjustments, and alterations and grading patterns is also imperative. Technology has taken much of the workload out of grading on a technical design level, as many computer programs have automatized this process; however, knowing how to grade rules, how to grade a pattern, and how to adjust grades if needed are all tools a good technician keeps in her arsenal.

CHAPTER 18

Achieving the Perfect Fit

Fit Evaluation Sequencing and Procedures

Fit is a very important aspect of technical design. Measurements only tell part of the story, as it is possible for garment measurements to be accurate, but for pattern shapes and slopers to be incorrect. Therefore, every garment that is given numerical specification must also be looked at on a fit-model or dress form. Achieving the perfect fit is sometimes in the eyes of the designer; she or he will look for lines that flatter the figure and camouflage or balance body flaws. However, there are a few hard-and-fast rules that must be followed for proper movement and comfort.

- A perfect-fitting garment begins with accurate measurements.
- A perfect-fitting garment requires proper garment ease for movement.
- A perfect-fitting garment does not have wrinkles, sagging, gaping, or rippling.
- A perfect-fitting garment enhances the wearer's attractiveness.

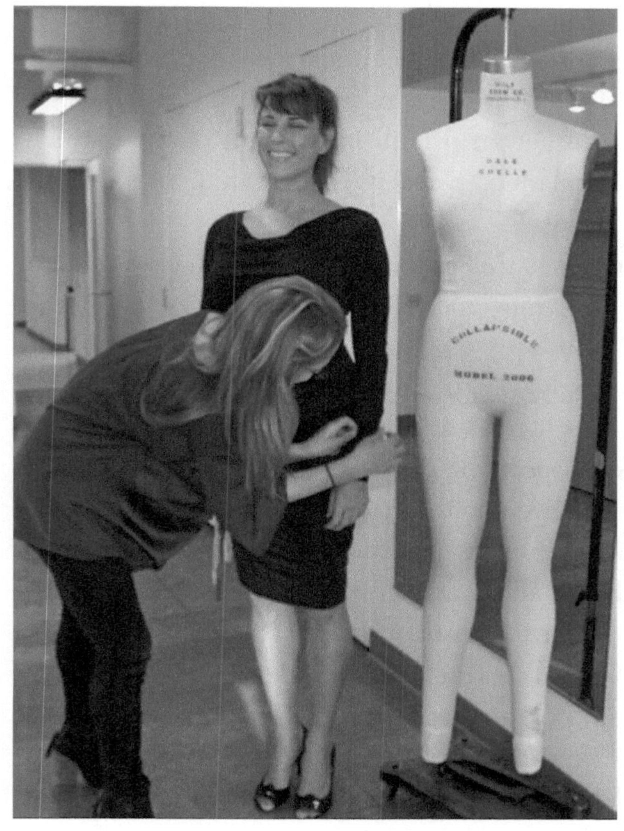

Figure 18.1 A garment being evaluated on fit model.
(Dale Noelle, TRUE Model Management, and Meredith Sherwood, Designer)

Judgment will be your first tool when evaluating a garment for fit. Fashion and styling characteristics, as well as garment function, must be considered when evaluating the appearance and fit elements of a garment. You will use the rules just listed when systematically scrutinizing a garment. Any discrepancies should be conveyed to the manufacturing plant or an overseas agent. The following sequence is suggested when evaluating a garment.

Procedures for Conducting a Fit Session

1. Garment Appearance Inadequacies
   a. Inspect the garment when it's lying flat, looking for such things as uneven collars, pockets, or hems. Also look for fabric or sewing defects that affect the quality of the garment.
2. Fit-Model or Form Observations
   a. Place the garment on your fit-model or form correctly. Close any openings/closures. Fit the garment to be evaluated over any garments that might be worn with it; for example, fit a coat over a dress or pants outfit.
   b. A garment that cannot be placed on the body because it is too tight or that appears very big once on the body may not be the correct size. Check your spec measurements.
   c. View the garment from the front and the back to get an overall impression of the garment balance. Does it bind, catch, or hang too loose?
   d. Does the garment have enough ease to allow for movement? (See Table 18.1 for more on body ease.) Note: Live model fitting is the only way to truly check the ease of a garment as it relates to allowances for movement.
   e. Inspect the garment again for such things as uneven collars, pockets, or hems that may not have been seen when the garment was lying flat.
   f. Do all seams lie either parallel or perpendicular to the floor, as designed?
3. Casual Garment Observation
   a. Look at the front view, from top to bottom, for any fit problems.
   b. Look at both side views, from top to bottom, for any fit problems.
   c. Look at the back view, from top to bottom, for any fit problems.
4. Concentrated Garment Observations
   a. Look at the upper front half, including the neck, shoulders, arms, bust, midriff, waist, and trim details for any fit problems.
   b. Look at the upper back half, including the neck, shoulders, arms, across the back, waist, and trim details for any fit problems.
   c. Look at the lower front half, including the hips, rise or sweep, hemline, and any style details for fit problems.
   d. Look at the lower back half, including the hips, rise or sweep, hemline, and any style details for fit problems.
5. Fit-model's Expertise
   a. Take advantage of your fit-model's expertise. During each stage of the fitting ask how the garment feels. This cannot be done on a form or avatar.
   b. Have the model bend and flex, moving his or her arms and legs as needed to check the ease areas of each garment.

Note: If you are evaluating a dress, long coat, or one-piece garment, you may want to evaluate the front top and bottom before moving to the back.

For practical application, you may use any of the measured garment spec sheets generated so far. Start by putting a measured garment on a body form and use the corresponding spec sheet to evaluate each measurement point one by one. Use the sequencing tips and rules that follow for a good fit. Remember that judgment is your first tool. If a measurement is incorrect, too big or too small, simply cross out the number and place the new number next to it. At first, you may not know how to correct the measurement points. That is why practice and apprenticing under a qualified technician are so important. In the industry, the corrected spec sheet is rewritten and sent back to the manufacturing plant or to the overseas agent with instructions for corrections. When you are ready to begin, look at the fit example (see Figure 18.23) at the end of this chapter.

Rules for a Good Fit

Good-fitting garments start with a good understanding of how garments should fit. This section contains more than 30 basic rules for good-fitting garments.

Table 18.1 MISSES EASE ALLOWANCE

	Close fitting	Fitted	Semifitted	Loose fitting	Oversized
Bust	½"–2"	2"–4"	4"–5"	5"–8"	over 8"
Waist/Hip	½"–2"	2"–3"	3"–4"	4"–6"	over 6"
Waistband	¼"–½"	½"–¾"	¾"–1"	1"–2"	over 2"
Crotch Depth	¾"–1"	1"–1½"	1½"–2"	2"–2½"	over 2½"
Armhole	1"–2"	2"–3"	3"–4"	4"–5"	over 5"
Upper Arm/Sleeve	1"–2"	2"–3"	3"–4"	4"–5"	over 5"
Elbow	½"–1"	1"–2"	2"–3"	3"–4"	over 4"
Wrist	½"	½"–1"	1"–2"	2"–3"	over 3"
Thigh/Knee/Leg Opening	1"–2"	2"–3"	3"–4"	4"–5"	over 5"
Shoulder Seams	0"–½"	¼"–½"	½"–1"	1"–1½"	over 1½"
Across Back	½"–¾"	¾"–1½"	1½"– 2½"	2½"–3½"	over 3½"

Note: For most blazer/suit jacket ease minimums, use the semifitted measurements, and for most coat/outwear ease minimums, use the loose-fitting measurements.

Be sure to read and understand all of them before trying to evaluate a garment for fit. Further information relating to specific garment types is listed in the Common Fit Problems and How to Correct Them section that follows.

Necklines—The neckline should always lie nicely around the curve of the base of the neck, unless otherwise designed. The garment should not cut into the neck, wrinkle, pull, or gape. Necklines designed to be wide or lowered should lie flat, but not too snug on the body, unless otherwise designed.

Neckbands—Neckbands and collars must fit the neck comfortably. Check the fit by inserting one finger into the neckband/collar, buttoned. Unless otherwise designed, only one finger should fit easily between the body and the garment.

Lapels—Lapels must lie symmetrical and flat, unless otherwise designed. Lapels should not gape open.

Center Front Seams—Center front seams must be centered on the front of the body and should lie straight from the center front neck down to the bottom of the garment/seam, perpendicular to the floor. They should not pull or shift to either side or buckle at the neck.

Center Back Seams—Center back seams must be centered on the back of the body and should lie straight from the center back neck down to the bottom of the garment/seam, perpendicular to the floor. They should not pull or shift to either side or buckle at the neck.

Center Front and Center Back Closures—Center front and center back closures must hang straight and smooth, without any pulling, puckers, wrinkles, and gaps. A garment top with a full front button/snap/Velcro® opening should always have a closure parallel to the bust apex. A garment bottom with a full front button/snap/Velcro® opening should always have a closure parallel to the fullest part of the abdomen.

Shoulder Seams—Shoulder seams are to lie on top of the shoulder at a point bisecting the shoulder bone and the side neck, unless otherwise designed.

Shoulder Pads—Shoulder pads should be placed on the shoulder seam at a point that appears natural. Generally, the center of the shoulder pads will be placed parallel on the shoulder seam and may extend lengthwise into the sleeve cap ¼" to ½", depending on the design.

Front and Back Armhole Seams—The front armhole seams should cross the body at the end of the shoulder joint (collarbone) but before the end of the shoulder bone, depending on the styling. The back armhole seams should appear to line up with the back arm crease. Jacket seams often extend ½" to 1" beyond this point and coats may extend 1" to 1½" depending on the styling.

Armholes—Armholes must be large enough to allow for easy movement without cutting into the arm/underarm, gaping, or pulling. The lowest point of the armhole should lie approximately 1" to 2" below the armpit, unless otherwise designed.

Sleeve Caps—Sleeve caps should lie smoothly on the end of the shoulders and curve nicely around the armhole without any puckers or wrinkles, unless otherwise designed. Fullness added as a design feature should be evenly distributed and should not extend below a point perpendicular to across front chest and across back. The sleeve must be able to lift with the arm without any pulling of the sleeve cap or the garment.

Sleeves—Sleeves must be large enough to hang smoothly around the arm with approximately 2" of ease, unless designed to fit snugly and fabric allows for movement. The elbow must be able to completely bend without binding, wrinkling, or stretching the fabric. If sleeves contain darts or fullness at the elbow, they must be centered over the end of the bone when the arm is bent.

Sleeve Opening—Sleeve openings must be large enough for at least one finger to be easily inserted into hems or cuffs.

Sleeve Length—Sleeve lengths will vary with the design. Short sleeves should be in proportion to the garment and total arm length. Three-quarter-length sleeves should extend below the elbow bone and not rise above the bone when the elbow is bent. Long sleeves should not extend below the bend of the wrist, unless otherwise designed; they should not rise above the wrist bone when the elbow is bent, unless otherwise designed.

Across Chest—Across chest areas and seams should lie smooth, without wrinkles or gaping fabric. There should be no diagonal wrinkling or bulging between the neck and the armhole.

Across Back—Across back areas and seams must lie smooth, without wrinkles or bulges. There should be no wrinkling or bulging below the neckline or between the neck and armholes. The upper back area must have enough ease to allow for movement of the armhole seams when arms are forward, without pulling or straining the seams/fabric.

Darts—Darts should point toward the fullest part of the body. Bust darts should end approximately 1" to 2" from the apex of the bust, depending on the styling. Back darts should end approximately 1" to 1½" from the fullest part of the back, again depending on the styling. Skirt darts should end approximately 1" to 1½" from the fullest part of the abdomen or back, depending on the styling. Darts should always be pressed in an outward or downward position, without wrinkles or bubbles at the dart tip.

Center Front Seams—Center front seams must be centered on the front of the body and should lie straight from the center front neck joining seam to the hem (for tops and dresses) or the waist joining seam down to the bottom of the garment/seam (for skirts), perpendicular to the floor. They should not pull or shift to either side or buckle at the waist.

Center Back Seams—Center back seams must be centered on the back of the body and should lie straight from the center back neck joining seam (for tops and dresses) or the waist joining seam down to the bottom of the garment/seam (for skirts), perpendicular to the floor. They should not pull or shift to either side or buckle at the waist.

Side Seams (top/blouse)—Side seams should always lie straight on the body from the center of the underarm down to the bottom of the garment/seam, perpendicular to the floor. Side seams should never pull to the front or the back of the body.

Grain Lines/Knitted Courses—Grain lines/knitted courses must hang straight on the desired grain, as designed. Lengthwise grain lines/knitted courses should hang straight down the center front and back of the garment, perpendicular to the floor and down the center of the sleeve. Horizontal grain lines/knitted courses should lay at a point parallel to the floor at the shoulders, chest, across back, and hemline. Diagonal/bias grain lines/knitted courses are rare with knits, as extra stretch is generally not needed; however, for styling they may be used and should lie at a 45-degree angle to the shoulders, chest, across back, and hem.

Pockets—Pockets must be sewn on straight in a horizontal, vertical, or biased position and should lie flat to the garment without gaping open, unless otherwise designed.

Slits and Vents—Slits and vents should hang straight on the body and should lie smooth without pulling or gaping open when standing. The slit/vent should be large/long enough to allow for ease of movement when walking, sitting, and climbing stairs.

Pleats—Pleats and tucks should hang flat and straight on the body, without any pulling or gaping, except during movement.

Gathers—Gathers should be small and evenly spaced without any puckering or bulges.

Bottom Bands—Bottom bands on tops should fit comfortably around the body without pulling, gaping, and wrinkling during movement. Two fingers should be able to be easily inserted into the bottom band.

Waistbands—Waistbands should fit comfortably around the waist while standing and sitting without pulling, cutting, or gaping. Two fingers should fit easily between the body and the waistband.

Hems—Hems should always be straight and even, lying parallel to the shoulders, chest, and across back (for tops), or waist and hips (for skirts, dresses, coats, and pants), unless otherwise designed. Classic skirt hemlines are: ultra-mini 14", mini 16", short skirt 18" to 20", knee-length 22", traditional 26" to 28" or 2" to 2½" below the knee, maxi 36", and floor-length 42" below the waistline. Lengths longer or shorter should be styled in proportion to body figures and fabric types. Hems crossing at the widest part of the calf will make the leg look heavier and the woman appear shorter.

Skirts—Skirts should fit comfortably on the body and lie in a smooth, relaxed position. There should be a minimum of 2" ease at the abdomen, hips, and thighs, unless designed to fit snugly and fabric allows for movement. The skirt fabric should not fall into horizontal folds, wrinkles, or creases at the waist, hips, and thighs, nor should it cup under the stomach, thighs, or buttocks.

Across Front Hip—Across front hip areas and seams should lie smooth, without pulling or fabric gaping. There should be no diagonal pulls or bulging between the waist and the thighs, especially when sitting.

Across Back Hip—Across back hip areas and seams must lie smooth, without wrinkles or bulges. There should be no pulling or bulging between the waist and the thighs, especially when sitting.

Side seams (skirt/pant)—Side seams should always lie straight on the body from the side of the waist joining seam down to the bottom of the garment/ seam, perpendicular to the floor. Side seams should never pull to the front or the back of the body.

Rise—The rise of a pant must be long enough to be comfortable when standing, sitting, and moving without cutting into the crotch area. A well-sloped rise will not wrinkle or fold around the waist, or wrinkle or pull at the crotch or into the thigh area.

Linings—Linings must fit smoothly under any garments and must follow the same ease rules that apply to that garment for comfort.

Generalized Garment Fitting Tips

As previously stated, fitting garments can be a very difficult process; many assistant technicians apprentice for several years before conducting a fitting without supervision. One of the reasons behind ill-fitting ready-to-wear in the past few years is a general lack of understanding of pattern construction. When a fit problem is not corrected on a sample garment, it will be repeated as the pattern is graded into a full size range. Unfortunately, ill-fitting patterns are often sent into production to save costs as well. More pattern pieces will fit on a sloper if the rises are long and shallow than if they have a generous curve. Cost aside, a good technician will always strive to achieve a perfect fit.

Designers, buyers, and consumers may have different ideas of what that perfect fit is, how tight or loose a blouse or top should be. However, a top should never be as snug as to pull the weave or knitted loops/yarns beyond their natural relaxed position. For example, a top pulling across the apex of the bust may indicate that there is not enough ease in that area. A knit top generally lacks the darts or seams of a woven top; therefore, bust ease is often gained by increasing the chest width. As a result, the sweep of that garment is often increased as well.

Full skirts with ample shirring at the waist generally only need to be adjusted at the waist because the fullness is very forgiving for many body types. However, formfitting skirts can be very difficult to fit. Some women have fuller hips, stomachs, buttocks, and thighs. A woven skirt pulling across the stomach may indicate that there is not enough ease in that area. It can also signal improper dart placement. Most designers will have their customer's ideal figure type and fit to it. For example, a designer fitting a junior's skirt generally fits to a straighter waist and hip, while designers fitting a women's wear skirt generally have to accommodate a protruding stomach or hips.

Knit skirts are usually the easiest garments to fit. The stretch property of the knit allows for ease of movement. However, a woman with fuller hips, stomach, buttocks, and thighs may find that the knit fabric unwittingly clings to her body. A knit skirt pulling across the stomach may indicate that there is not enough ease in that area or that the fabric has been knitted with a different degree of stretch than the designer anticipated.

Knit pants are generally easier to fit than woven pants because they are often less constructed; however, most of the fit rules are the same. Women with fuller hips, stomachs, buttocks, and thighs may find knit and woven pants too tight in these areas if an ample amount of ease has not been added. Designers, buyers, and consumers have a different idea of how tight or loose a pant should be, and many popular designers fit to a taller, slimmer figure. It is important that the pant is comfortable and easy to move in no matter what body prototype is used. A pant should never be so snug as to pull the fabric or side seams. Pleats, rarely used in knits, should lie flat to the body in a natural relaxed position. Pleats are added for garment contouring, not body ease. A pant pulling across the stomach area may indicate that there is not enough ease in that area. Increasing the stomach or hip area does not necessarily mean increasing the thigh as well.

When fitting knit and woven dresses, the fit rules and solutions to fitting tops and skirts should be combined. In many instances, a dress will not have a waistband, but the skirt portions of the dress will follow the skirt rules.

When fitting a jumpsuit or a one-piece garment, the fit rules and problem solutions for a top and pant should be combined. Additional rules that should be taken into consideration during the fitting process are:

1. There should be enough ease in the bodice length to allow for ease of sitting, without pulling up the bottom portion of the garment.
2. There should be enough ease and/or rise length to allow for movement of the bottom portion of the garment without pulling down on the bodice or top of the garment.

The same techniques for fitting tops and fixing common fitting problems apply to blazers and unconstructed jackets. Keep in mind that the ease allowances must now compensate for the blazer or jacket to fit over a blouse or sweater. Note these differences.

1. The shoulder pad should extend ½" to ¾" into the sleeve cap.
2. The lowest point of the armhole should lie approximately 2" to 3" below the armpit, unless otherwise designed.

When fitting outerwear/coats, the fitting rules and solutions to problems for tops and dresses should be applied. Keep in mind that the ease allowances must now compensate for the coat to fit over a blouse or sweater and blazer. Note these differences.

1. The shoulder pad should extend ¾" to 1" into the sleeve cap.
2. The lowest point of the armhole should lie approximately 3" to 4" below the armpit, unless otherwise designed.
3. A minimum of 4" ease is required at the abdomen, hips, and thighs.

Common Fit Problems and How to Correct Them

Technical designers often face common fit issues when evaluating garments. Solutions for these corrections must be sent along with the spec sheet to the manufacturing plant or overseas agent. This section addresses some of those issues with suggestions for correction. [Note: For some students, prior patternmaking classes may be helpful.] On occasion, it is necessary to take the garment apart to check the pattern slope. Do not assume you know what the problem is or that you have the correct solution. For those in the industry using this text, it is always a good idea to check with your patternmaker when advising a pattern correction.

Tops and Blouses

Problem Area 1—Chest width. The top pulls across the chest (Figures 18.1a and b).

Solution A—Check the chest width measurement. Is there enough ease allowed in this garment? If not, add the required amount of ease, depending on the results you desire (Figure 18.1c).

Solution B—Check the dart placement. Does the dart fall at the proper point on or below the apex? If the dart is too high or too low or too long, adjust it accordingly.

Solution C—Check the apex button placement. (This is a common problem with woven blouses. With knits, it is often a combination of too little ease and improper button placement.) The blouse

Figure 18.1a Fitting problem: blouse pulls across chest.

Figure 18.1b Fitting problem: sweater pulls across chest.

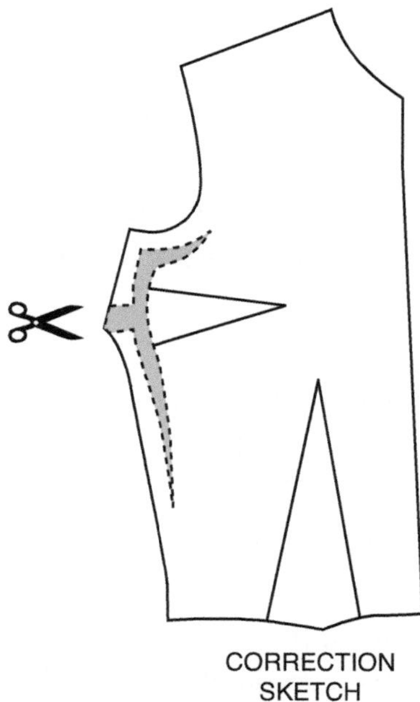

Figure 18.1c Pattern alteration: slash and spread pattern at bust adding ease.

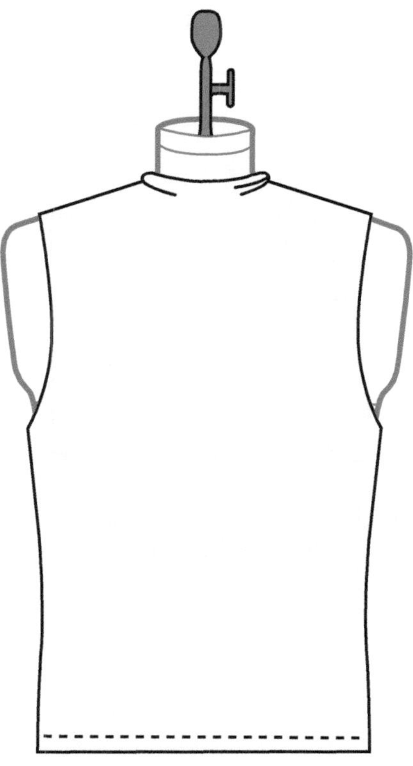

Figure 18.2a Fitting problem: neck opening is too tight.

may have enough ease, and the darts placement may be correct, but the button at the bust does not fall parallel to the bust apex. When the bust button is too high or too low, gaping may result, giving the appearance of a garment that is too tight. Align the buttons so that the bust button is aligned with the apex of the bust, and then adjust all the other buttons accordingly.

[Note: If the chest width is too large/small, other width measurements may be affected as well. Be sure to make all corrections as needed.]

Problem Area 2—Neck opening circumference is too tight/ too loose (Figures 18.2a and b).

Solution A—Often, adding or subtracting to the spec circumference is all that is needed to fix this problem. However, if the neck depth or neck width is not correct, then further investigation is needed. With knits, it is important to check the stretch as well. Knits do not often have buttoned vent openings or zippers; therefore, it is important that the neck-opening circumference is large enough to get over the head, yet still looks good on the neck.

Solution B—Check the front and back neck depth measurements. Does the neck opening or joining seam fall at a point that is comfortable for the wearer? If it is too high or too low, adjust it accordingly. Again, check the stretch as stated above.

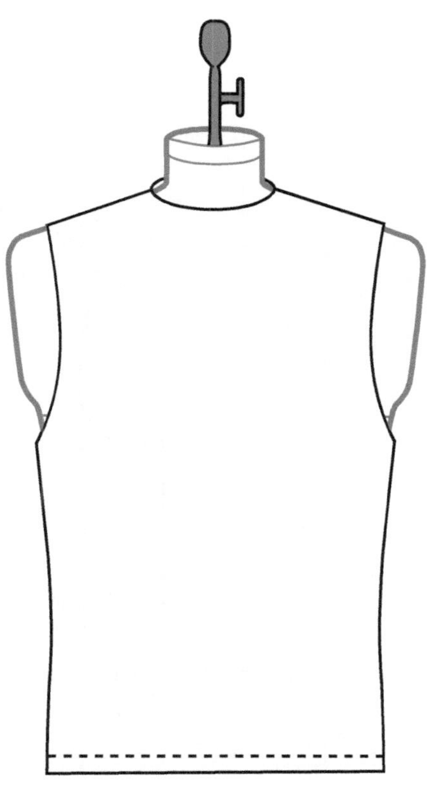

Figure 18.2b Fitting problem: neck opening is too loose.

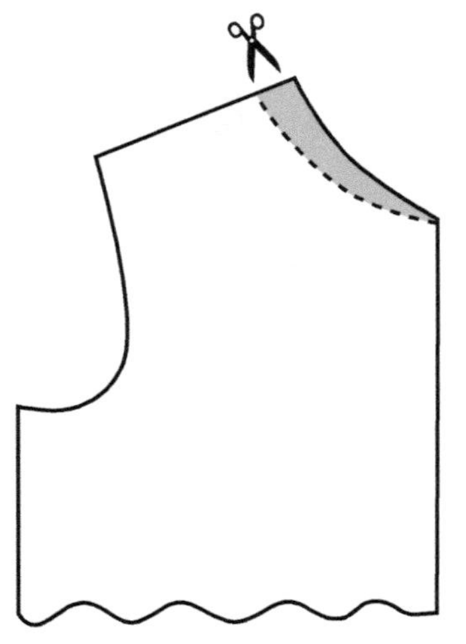

Figure 18.2c Pattern alteration: open up the neck width from shoulder seam.

Solution C—Check the neck width. If the neck width is too narrow, it will draw the shoulders and sleeve cap up. It probably will not fit over the head well. If the neck width is too wide, the neck opening or joining seam will gape along the sides of the neck and look stretched out. Adjust the measurement accordingly—there are two ways to correct each (Figures 18.2c and d).

Problem Area 3—Shoulder seams do not lie smoothly on the shoulder (Figures 18.3a, b, and c).

Solution A—The slope of the shoulder seam may be too severe. Check the garment off of the form while it's lying flat. Does the shoulder seam appear to be too straight or too sloped? If so, correct the slope accordingly (Figure 18.3d).

Solution B—The shoulder seam width may be too long or too short. If the shoulder seam is too short, it may pull the sleeve cap up, giving the garment the appearance of being too tight. If the seam is too long, the shoulder cap can droop, giving the garment the appearance of being too big. Sometimes, a shoulder seam is long on purpose for styling reasons. Be sure not to shorten a shoulder seam if, for example, the armhole seam is straight rather than curved (Figures 18.3e and f).

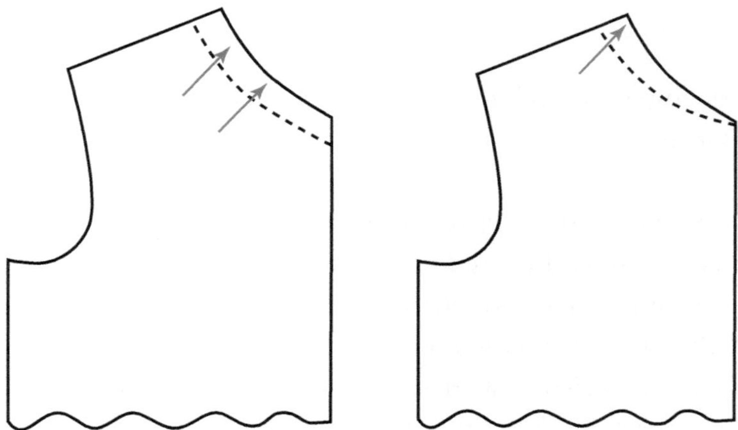

Figure 18.2d Pattern alteration: add to neck pattern at shoulder seam or entire neck opening.

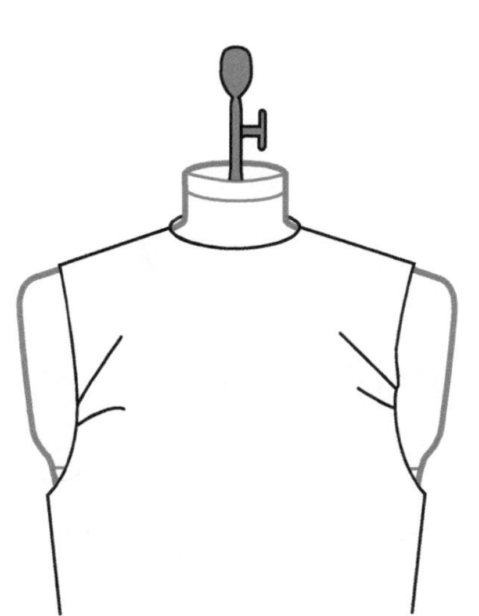

Figure 18.3a Fitting problem: shoulder seams do not lie properly causing ripples at arms eye.

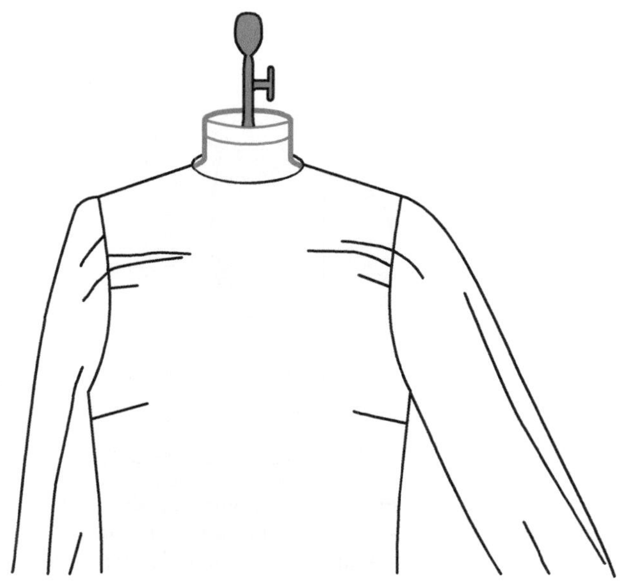

Figure 18.3b Fitting problem: shoulder seams do not lie properly causing ripples at arms eye and sleeve.

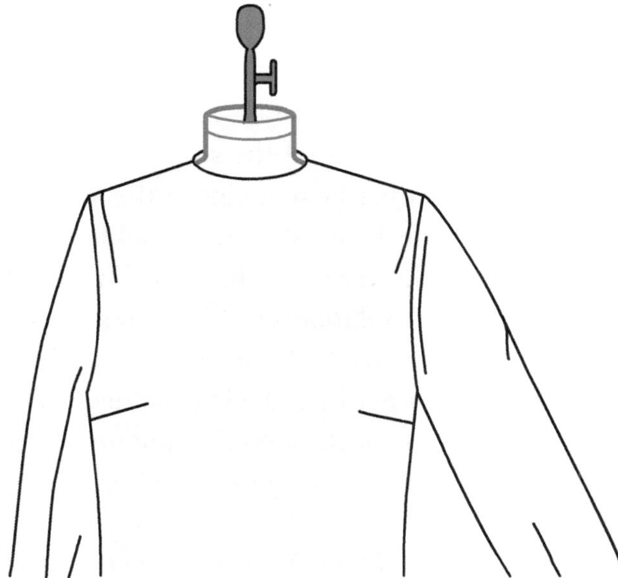

Figure 18.3c Fitting problem: shoulder seams do not lie properly causing ripples at shoulder and sleeve.

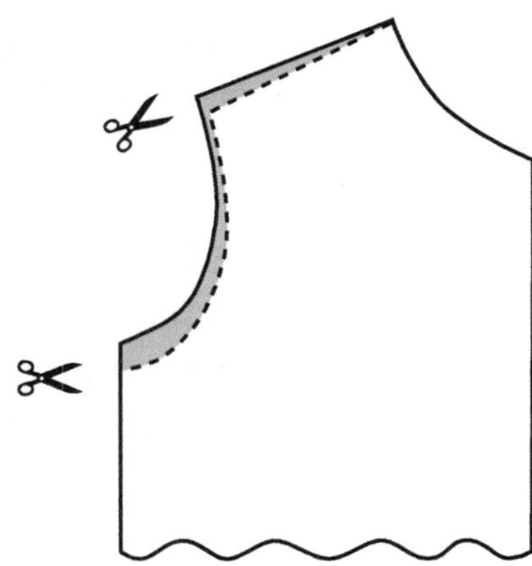

Figure 18.3d Pattern alteration: correct slope of pattern by removing excess at shoulder and armhole.

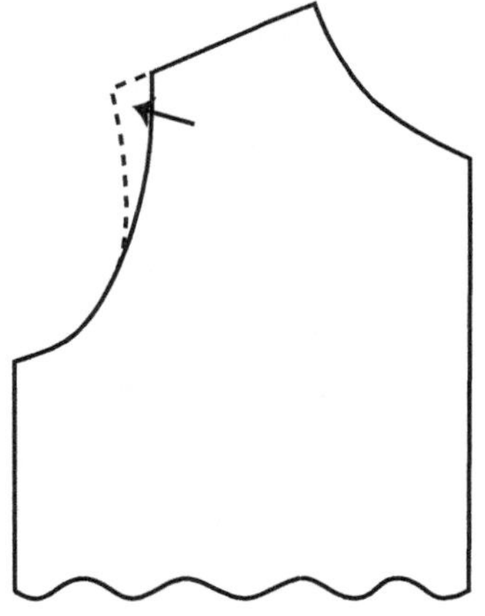

Figure 18.3e Pattern alteration: add to pattern with narrow shoulder seam.

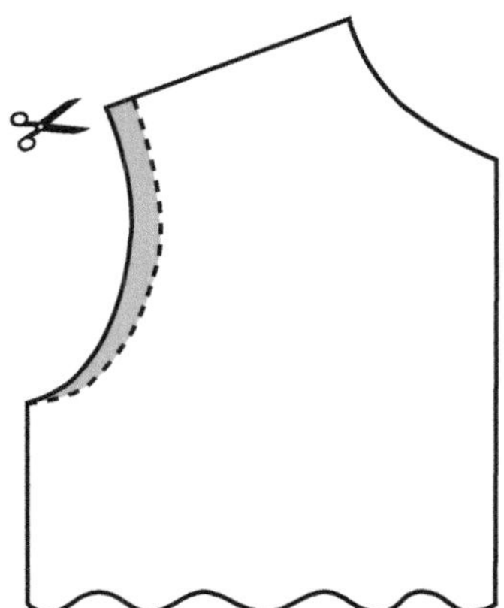

Figure 18.3f Pattern alteration: remove excess from pattern with wide shoulder seam.

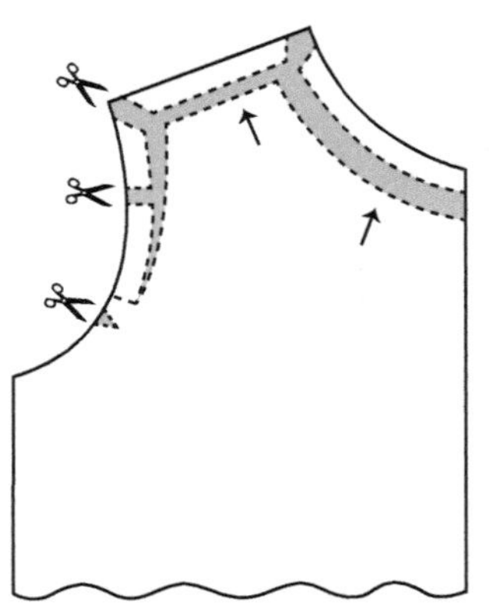

Figure 18.3g Pattern alteration: reduce pattern at armseye adding back at shoulder and neck.

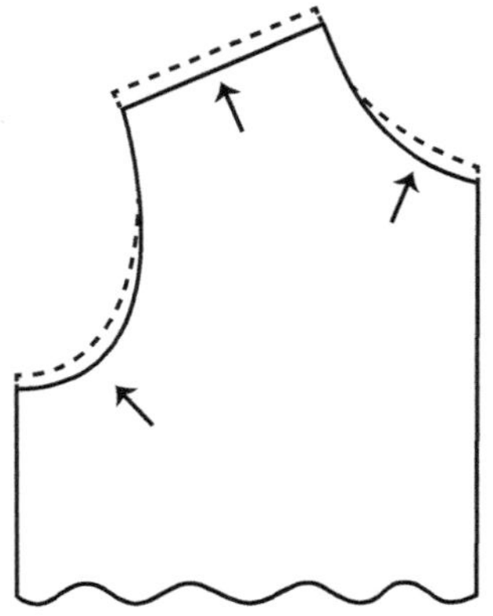

Figure 18.3h Pattern alteration: add to pattern at shoulder, neck, and armhole.

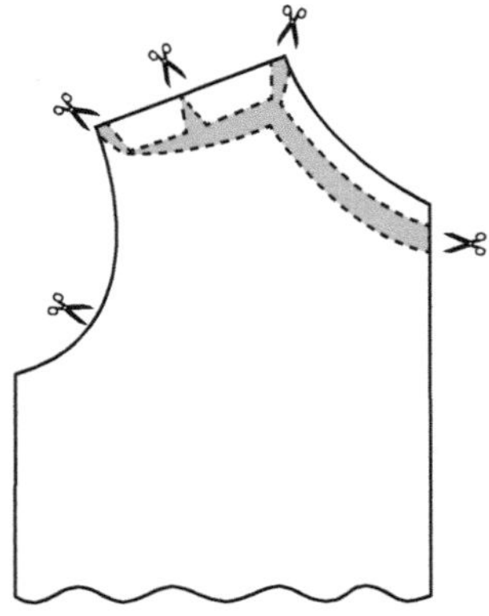

Figure 18.3i Pattern alteration: reduce pattern at shoulder and neck.

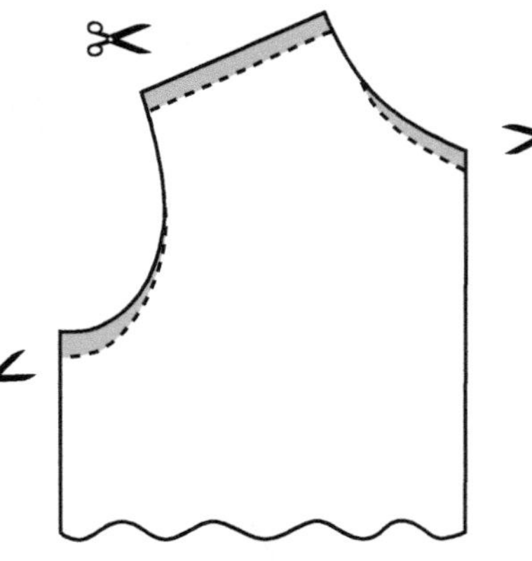

Figure 18.3j Pattern alteration: reduce pattern at shoulder, neck, and armhole.

Solution C—The shoulder seam may actually lie too far to the front of the shoulder. Add to the pattern one of two ways, either by reducing at the armhole and then adding back at the neck and shoulder or adding to all three points, depending on the garment's fit issue (Figures 18.3g and h).

Solution D—The shoulder seam may actually lie too far to the back of the shoulder. Reduce the pattern one of two ways, either by reducing the neck and shoulder only or by reducing the neck, shoulder, and underarm, depending on the garment's fit issue (Figures 18.3i and j).

Problem Area 4—Waist or bottom opening/sweep is pulling or gaping open (Figures 18.4a and b).

Solution A—Check the waist and bottom opening/sweep width measurements. Is there enough ease allowed in this garment? If not, add the required amount of ease depending on the results you desire (Figures 18.4c).

[Note: Occasionally, the front opening will be pulling, but the sides or back are loose. This indicates a problem in the bust area. Perhaps not enough ease was allowed or the dart placement is incorrect. Sometimes, diagnosing one problem area leads to a different area or solution.]

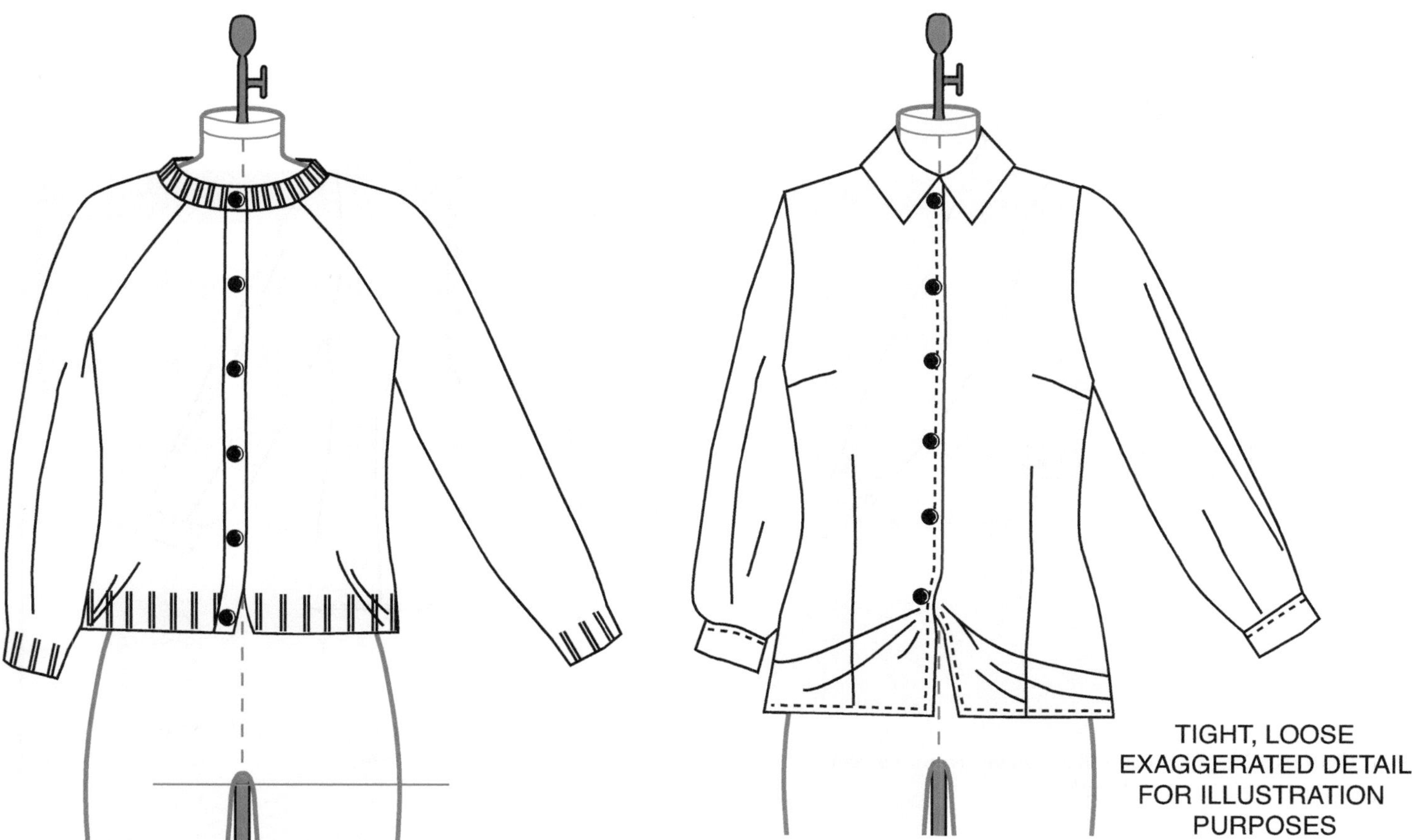

Figure 18.4a Fitting problem: Sweater pulls at bottom opening.

Figure 18.4b Fitting problem: blouse pulls at sweep.

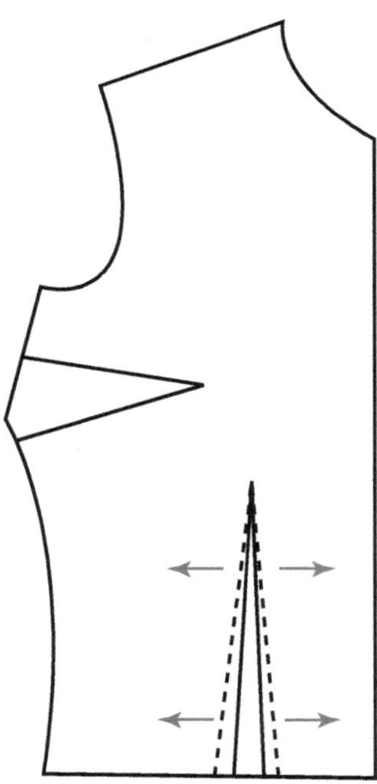

Figure 18.4c Pattern alteration: add to dart or slash and spread pattern, gaining ease.

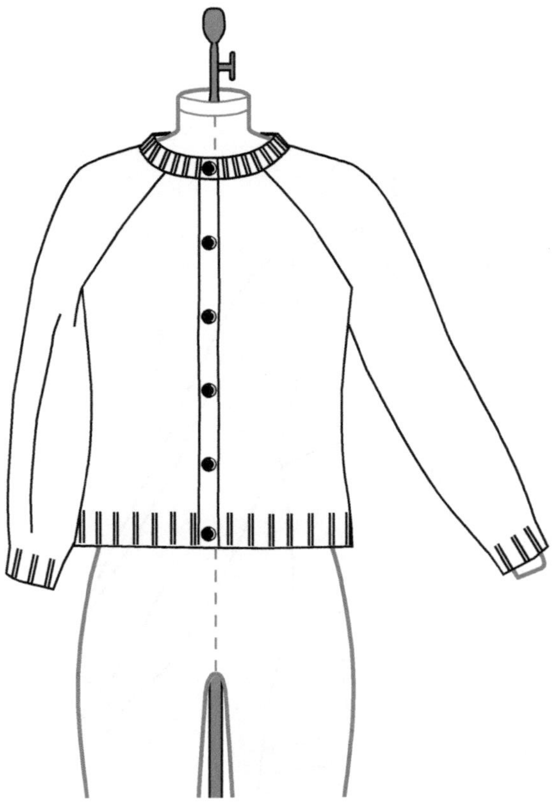

Figure 18.5a Fitting problem: sleeve is not correct length.

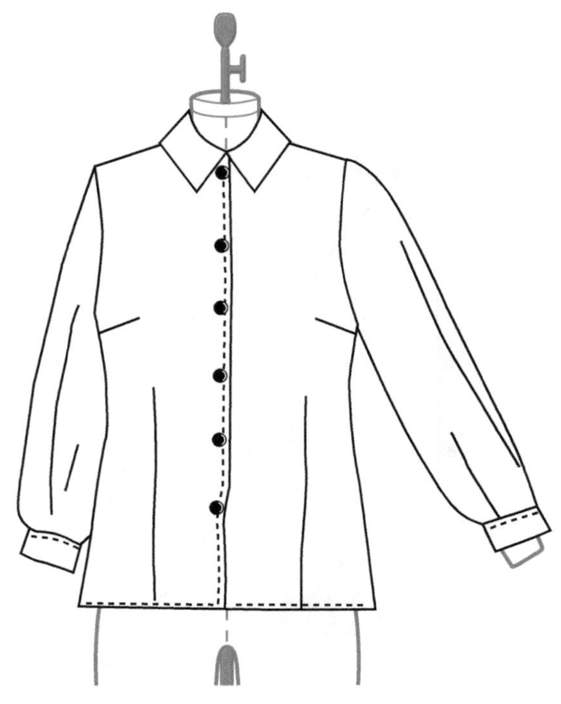

Figure 18.5b Fitting problem: sleeve is pulling up at underarm.

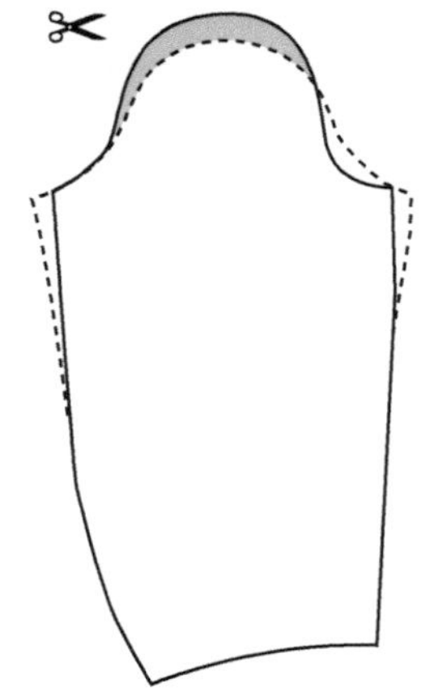

Figure 18.5c Pattern alteration: shorten the sleeve cap and adjust pattern accordingly.

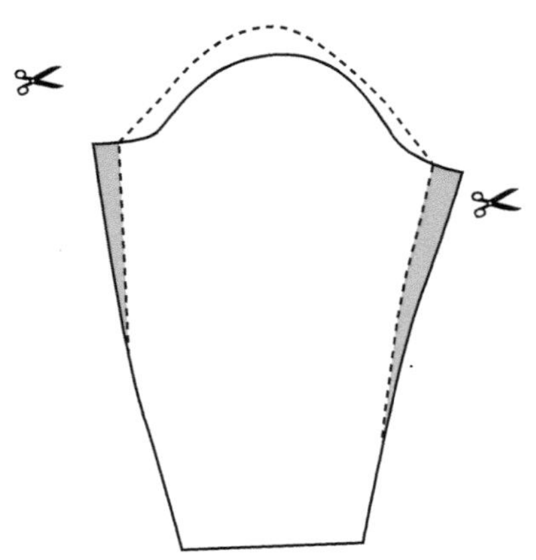

Figure 18.5d Pattern alteration: lengthen the sleeve cap and adjust pattern accordingly.

Problem Area 5—Sleeve length is too long/short (Figures 18.5a and b).

Solution A—The problem may be simply that the sleeve length needs to be lengthened or shortened.

Solution B—The sleeve length is longer on either the outer or inner seams or the sleeve opening does not lie parallel on the hand/wrist. Either of these problems is due to an improperly sloped sleeve cap. If the sleeve cap is too long, the sleeve length will pull up on the underarm seam (Figure 18.5c). If the sleeve cap is too short, the sleeve will droop along the outer edge (Figure 18.5d). Remove the sleeve from the garment and look at the sleeve cap slope, then adjust accordingly.

Solution C—The shoulder seam may be too short, pulling the sleeve up, or it may be too long, making the sleeve appear too long. Check the shoulder width. Does it lie properly? If not, adjust accordingly.

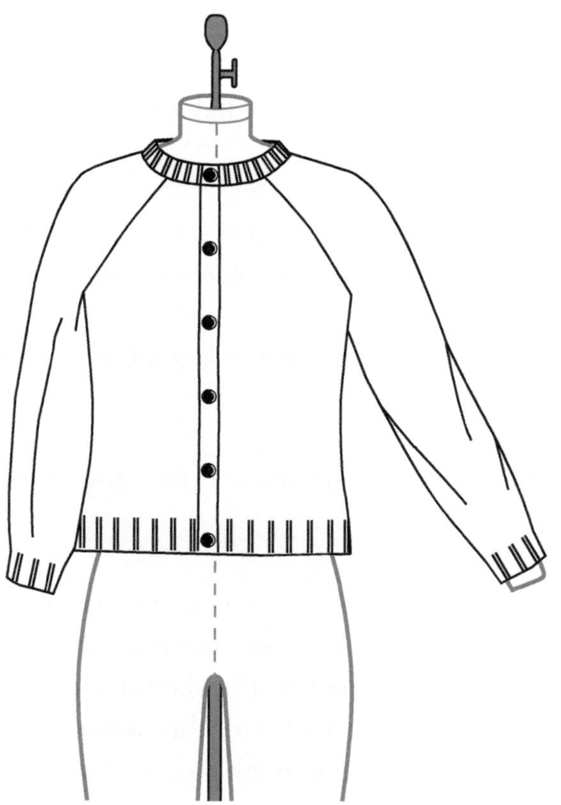

Figure 18.6a Fitting problem: sleeve is too tight on upper arm of sweater.

Figure 18.6b Fitting problem: sleeve is too loose on upper arm of blouse.

Problem Area 6—Sleeve is too tight or too loose on the upper arm (Figures 18.6a and b).

Solution A—Rule out the possibility that there is not enough ease in the sleeve. If this is the case, adjust the entire sleeve width (Figure 18.6c).

Solution B—A more common problem is the sleeve cap slope. If the sleeve cap has not been cut with the proper curve, the underarm seam may ride too high under the arm causing the sleeve to pull and appear to be too small. A good way to check this problem without removing the sleeve from the garment is to lift the arm. If the sleeve pulls across the upper arm and pulls across the chest, the sleeve cap is definitely cut with too long a cap. Some manufacturers will often cut sleeve caps this way to save fabric on the width of the sleeve without affecting any of the other measurements (Figure 18.6d).

Solution C—If the sleeve is too loose, check the specs and adjust accordingly. A pattern alteration opposite to that of Figure 18.6c may be necessary.

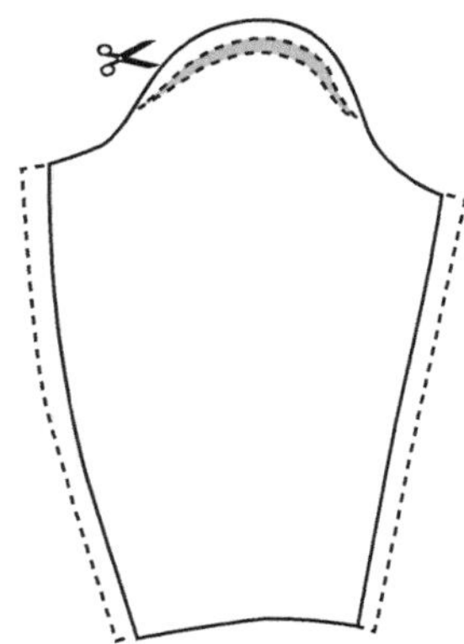

Figure 18.6c Pattern alteration: add to sleeve width and adjust sleeve cap accordingly.

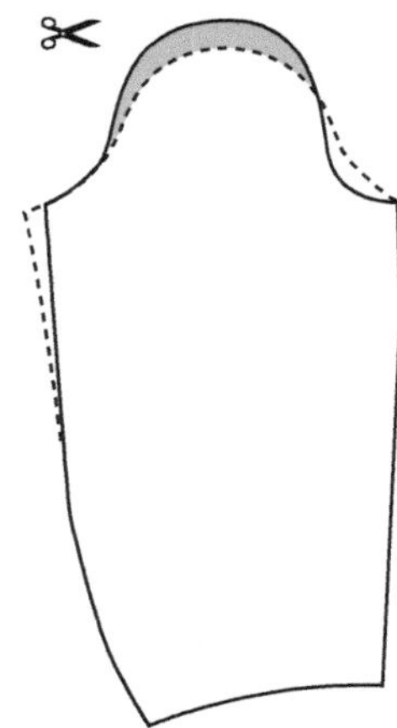

Figure 18.6d Pattern alteration: reduce sleeve cap adjusting armhole and sleeve width accordingly.

Problem Area 7—Armhole is too tight/too loose (Figures 18.7a and b).

Solution A—Simply check the spec measurement. Is the armhole too small? Make the necessary adjustments (Figure 18.7c).

Solution B—If the curve is too large, add to the pattern as needed (Figure 18.7d).

Problem Area 8—The front bodice does not lie flat and pulls up (Figure 18.8a).

Solution A—The pattern needs to be slashed and spread adding more at the bust area down to the waist and under the arm (Figure 18.8b). Lying flat, the shoulder seam may appear to fall toward the back; however, this will give a little extra fabric to the front of the garment to accommodate the chest.

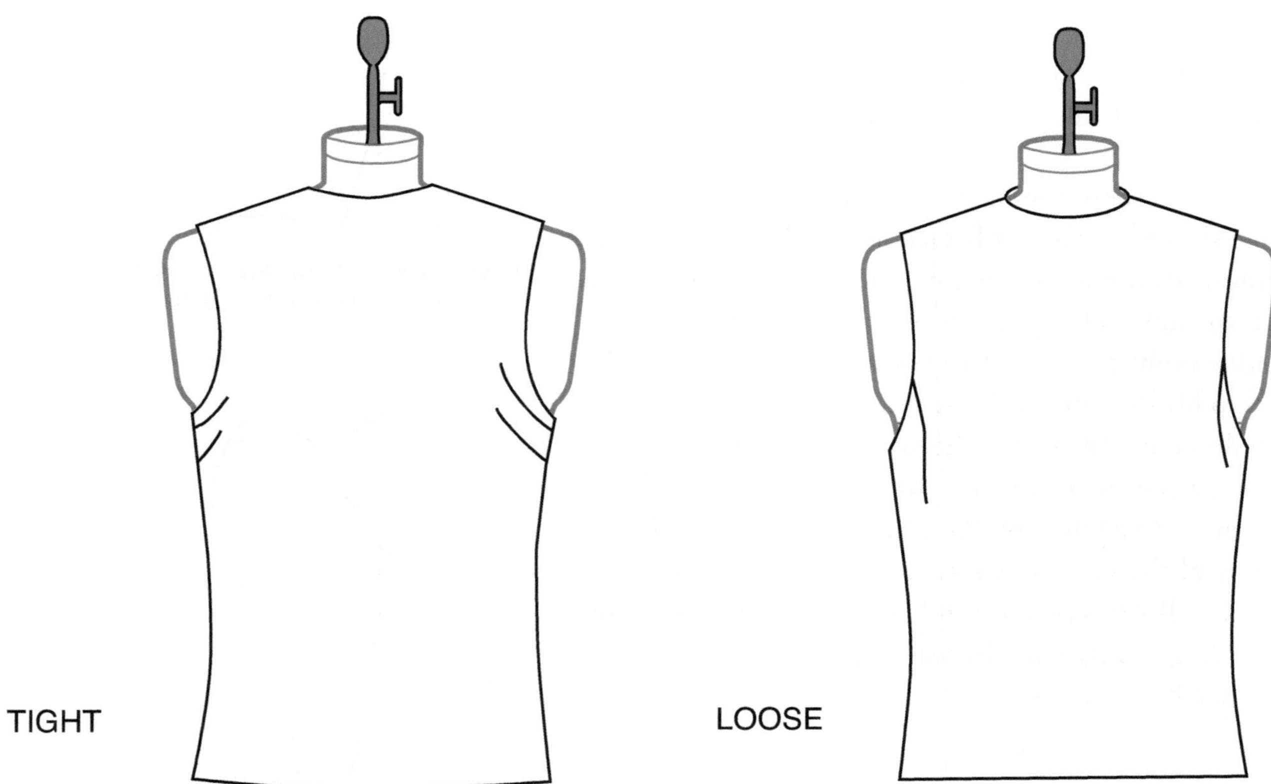

Figure 18.7a Fitting problem: armhole is too tight.

Figure 18.7b Fitting problem: armhole is too loose.

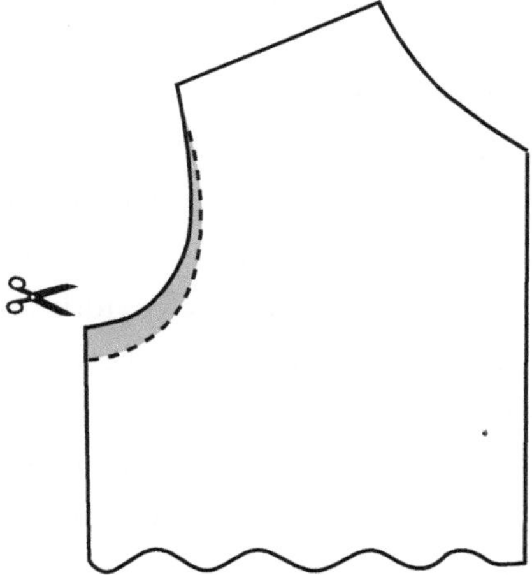

Figure 18.7c Pattern alteration: cut armhole larger accordingly.

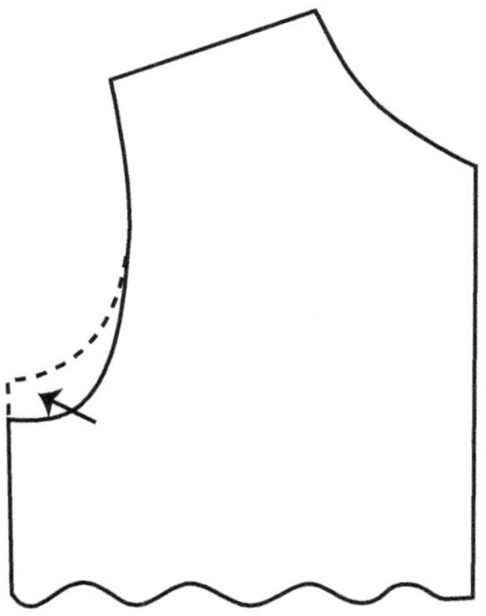

Figure 18.7d Pattern alteration: reduce pattern, making armhole smaller accordingly.

Figure 18.8a Fitting problem: the front bodice pulls up at hem.

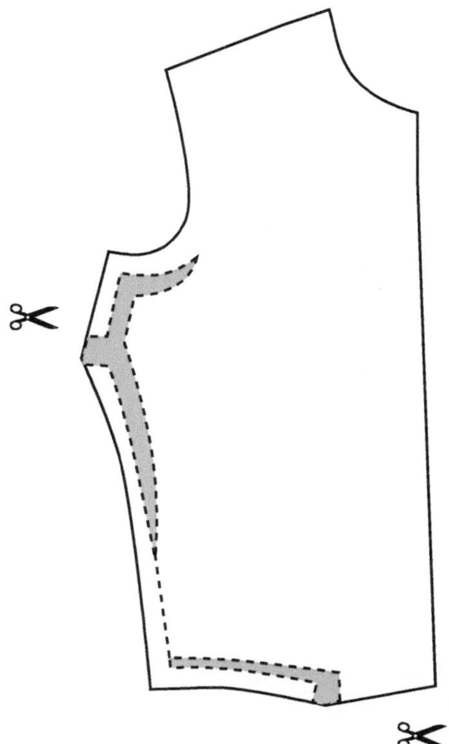

Figure 18.8b Pattern alteration: slash and spread pattern adding ease as indicated.

Figure 18.9a Fitting problem: knit skirt pulls across abdomen.

Problem Area 9—The garment does not fit over the head.

Solution A—A majority of knit tops are designed without buttoned or zippered neck openings. As a result, it is imperative that there is enough stretch in the neck opening to allow the garment to be slipped over the head. This is especially crucial for turtleneck styles. Double-check the neck width and neck drop measurements to make sure they are correct.

Solution B—If the spec measurements are correct and the neck opening is still too tight, the manufacturer may have to be notified. They may have to adjust their knitting machines to allow for more stretch.

Solution C—On rare occasions, the specs are correct and the knitting cannot be adjusted without adversely affecting the garment in other fit areas. In this case, the neck shape of the garment will have to be redesigned.

Skirts

Problem Area 1—Skirt pulls across the abdomen (Figures 18.9a and b).

Solution A—This is a common problem for knit skirts since few of them have darts, pleating, or shirring. If the skirt is full fashioned, meaning that the shape is achieved by adding or removing stitches, then the actual knitting process must be looked at and stitches must be added as needed. This process is common in flat-knit weft knitting. Check with the pattern-maker and make corrections in construction.

Solution B—If the side seam is too narrow, adjust the curve accordingly (Figure 18.9c).

Solution C—Does the hemline also pull up? If so, slash and spread the pattern horizontally at the waist, over but not through the waist at the side seam. Add the required ease (Figure 18.9d).

Figure 18.9b Fitting problem: woven skirt pulls across abdomen.

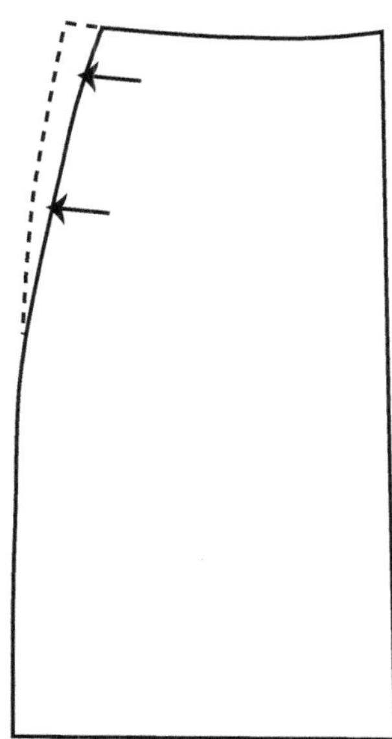

Figure 18.9c Pattern alteration: add to side seam at waist.

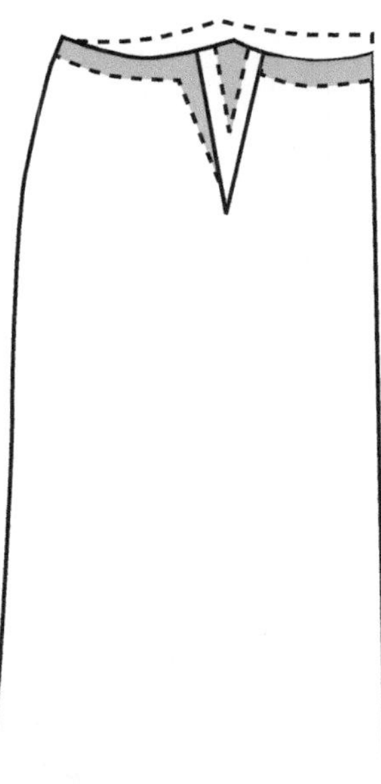

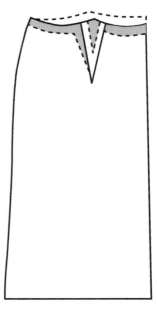

Figure 18.9d Pattern alteration: slash and spread pattern at waist and adjust accordingly.

Figure 18.10a Fitting problem: knit skirt sags across abdomen.

Figure 18.10b Fitting problem: woven skirt sags across abdomen.

Problem Area 2—The skirt is too big, sags across the abdomen (Figures 18.10a and b).

Solution A—This is a common problem for fitted skirts when there is too much ease added across the abdomen. If the skirt is full fashioned, meaning that the shape is achieved by adding/removing stitches, then the actual knitting process must be looked at and stitches must be removed as needed. This process is common in flat-knit weft knitting. Corrections are made in construction.

Solution B—For woven skirts, if the skirt has darts, simply add more depth to the dart curve (Figure 18.10c). If it has princess seams, reduce the ease at the princess joining seam. If it has gathers, add width to the pattern in the shirring area.

Solution B—If the dart, princess seam, pleat, or shirred area depths are correct, then check the side seam hip curve. If the side seam is too full, reduce the curve accordingly (Figure 18.10d).

Solution C—There may be too much length in the abdomen. Does the hemline also sag at the center front? If so, reduce excess from the top waist or slash and pinch or fold the pattern horizontally at the center front waist, over but not through the waist at the side seam. Reduce the ease accordingly (Figures 18.10e and f).

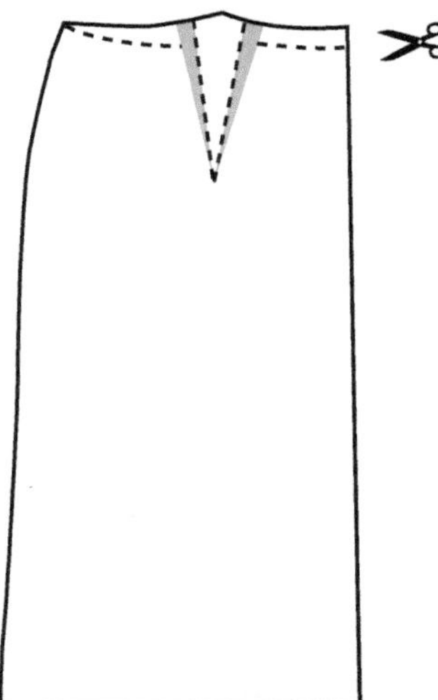

Figure 18.10c Pattern alteration: reduce dart, adjust pattern accordingly.

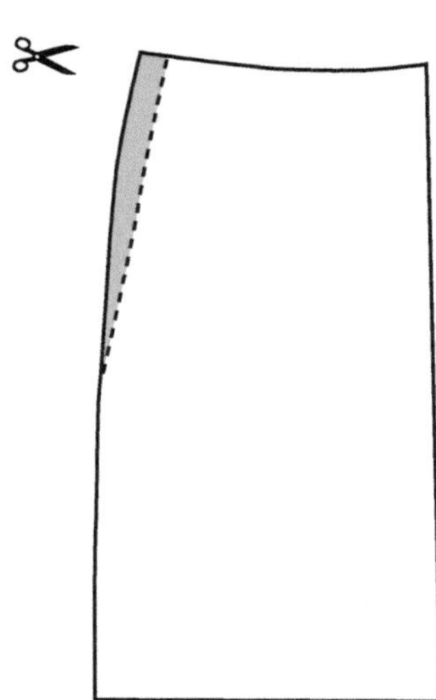

Figure 18.10d Pattern alteration: reduce pattern at side seam.

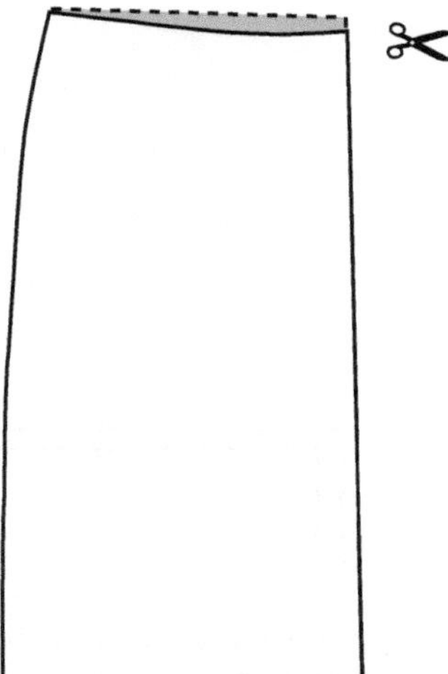

Figure 18.10e Pattern alteration: reduce pattern at top waist.

Figure 18.10f Pattern alteration: reduce pattern by slashing, pinching, and folding at abdomen.

Problem Area 3—Fabric at the side seam, and hip areas bulge either because the skirt is too tight or too loose (Figure 18.11).

Solution A—The ease has been placed at the side seam and not distributed evenly throughout the body. See skirts solutions A and B in Problem Area 1 or solutions A and C in Problem Area 2 and adjust accordingly.

Problem Area 4—There is horizontal folding below the back waist and above the buttocks (Figures 18.12a and b).

Solution A—The skirt needs less fabric in the length between the waist and hip area. Reduce excess from the top waist or tuck the pattern horizontally at the center back, without distorting the side seam length (Figures 18.12c and d).

Solution B—The back darts are too long; shorten accordingly (Figure 18.12e).

Figure 18.11 Fitting problem: side seams bulge.

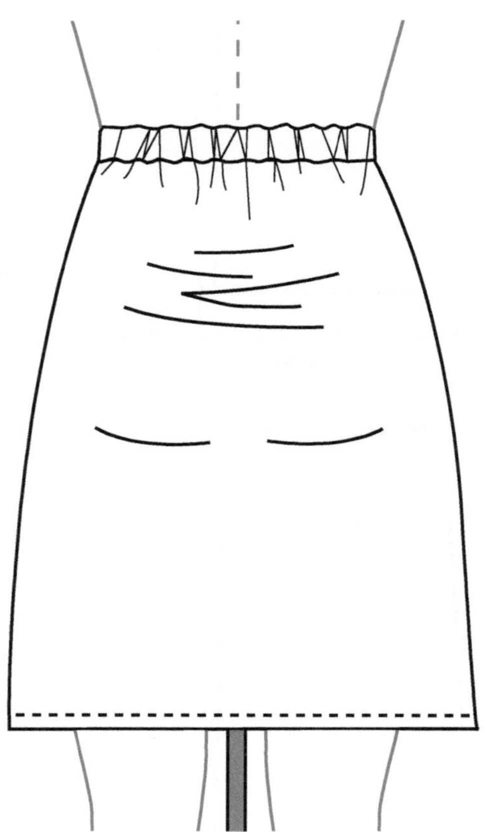

Figure 18.12a Fitting problem: excess fabric folds above buttocks on knit skirt.

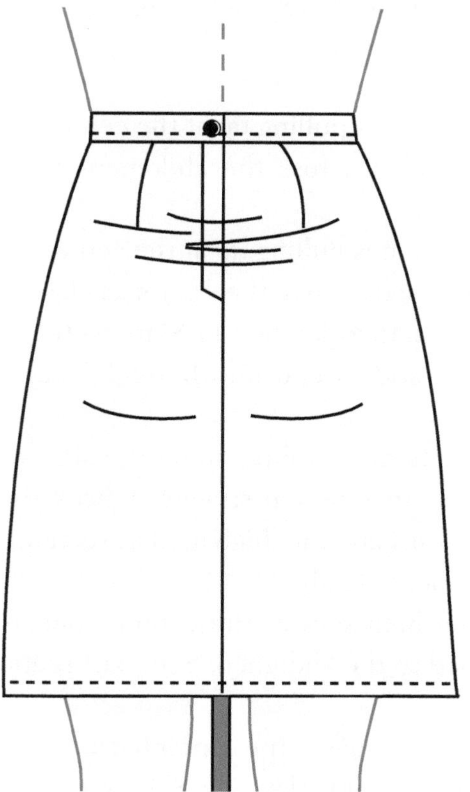

Figure 18.12b Fitting problem: excess fabric folds above buttocks on woven skirt.

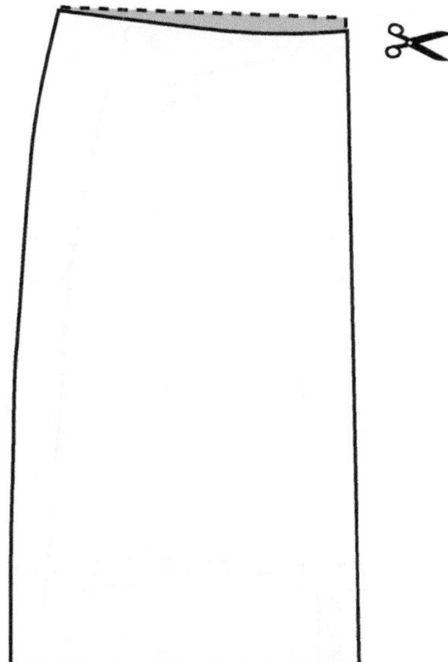

Figure 18.12c Pattern alteration: reduce pattern at center top waist tapering to side.

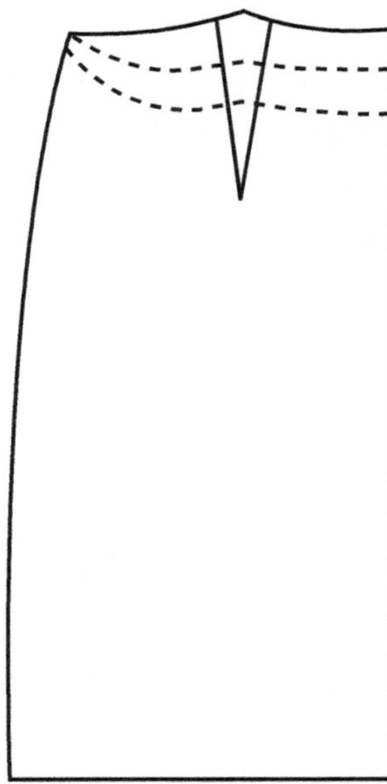

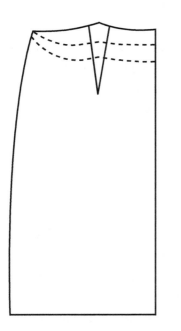

Figure 18.12d Pattern alteration: reduce pattern by slashing, pinching, and folding at back below waist.

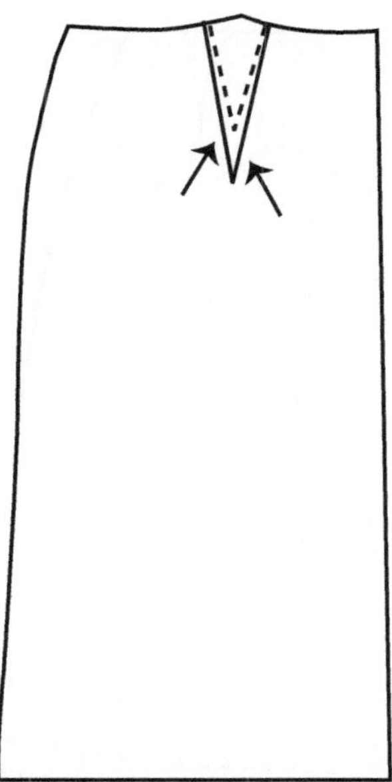

Figure 18.12e Pattern alteration: shorten back darts.

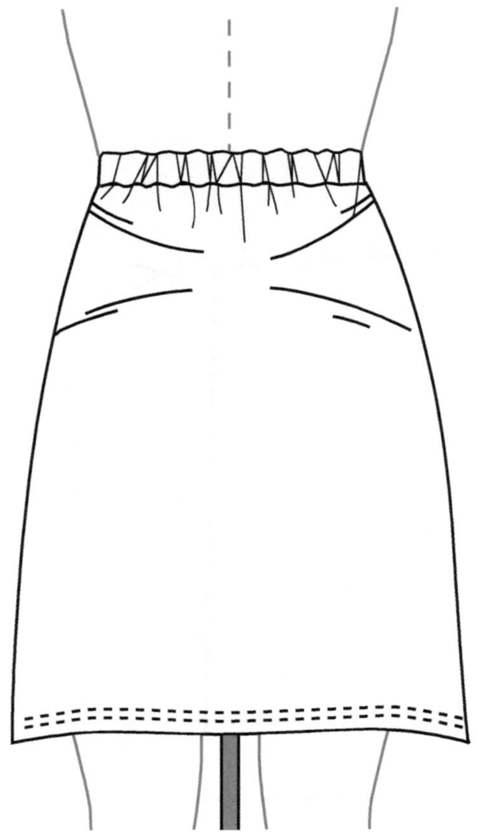

Figure 18.13a Fitting problem: hemline pulls up.

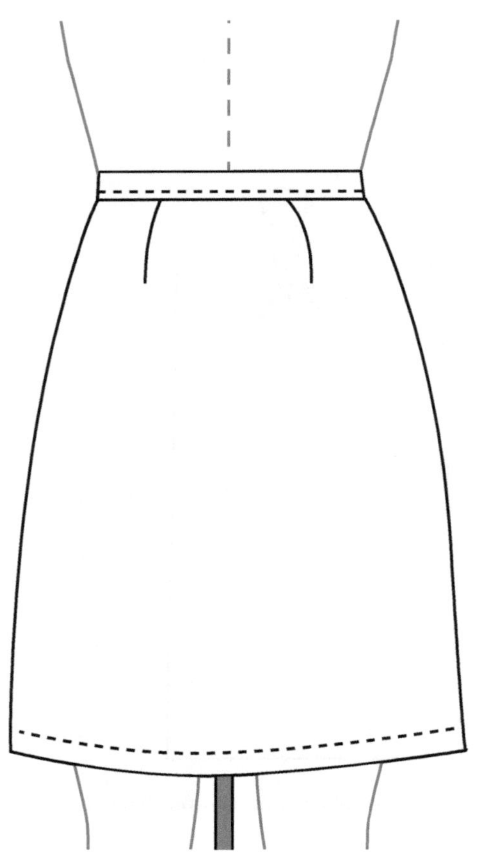

Figure 18.13b Fitting problem: hemline sags down.

Problem Area 5—Hemline does not hang straight (Figures 18.13a and b).

Solution A—The hem is pulling up at the center front; more ease needs to be added across the abdomen. See Problem Area 1 in Skirt section.

Solution B—The hem is pulling up at the center back; more ease needs to be added across the buttocks. Use the slash and spread pattern method learned in Skirt section, Problem Area 1, Solution B, and extend into buttocks, adjusting the pattern as needed.

Solution C—The hem is pulling up on the side seams; the side seam at the hip may be too straight. Check the pattern curve between the waist and the thigh in Skirt section, Problem Area 1, and adjust accordingly.

Solution D—The hem sags at the center front; too much ease has been added to the abdomen. See Skirt section, Problem Area 2.

Solution E—The hem sags at the center back; too much ease has been added to the buttocks. See Skirt section, Problem Area 4, Solution 2; however, rather than reducing the pattern above the buttock area, reduce it across the buttocks where there is too much ease.

Solution F—The hem is sagging at the side seams; the side seam curve at the hip may be round, making the seam long. See Skirt section, Problem Area 2, Solution B, and adjust accordingly.

Solution G—The hem is simply not straight. Check the pattern. If the hemline is straight on the pattern, and none of the problems exist in solutions A through F, then the garment may have been cut or sewn unevenly.

Pants

Problem Area 1—Pant pulls across the abdomen (Figures 18.14a and b).

Solution A—This is a common problem for knit pants since few of them have darts or pleating. If the pant is full fashioned, meaning that the shape is achieved by adding or removing stitches, then the actual knitting process must be looked at and stitches must be added as needed. This process is common in flat-knit weft knitting. Corrections are made in construction.

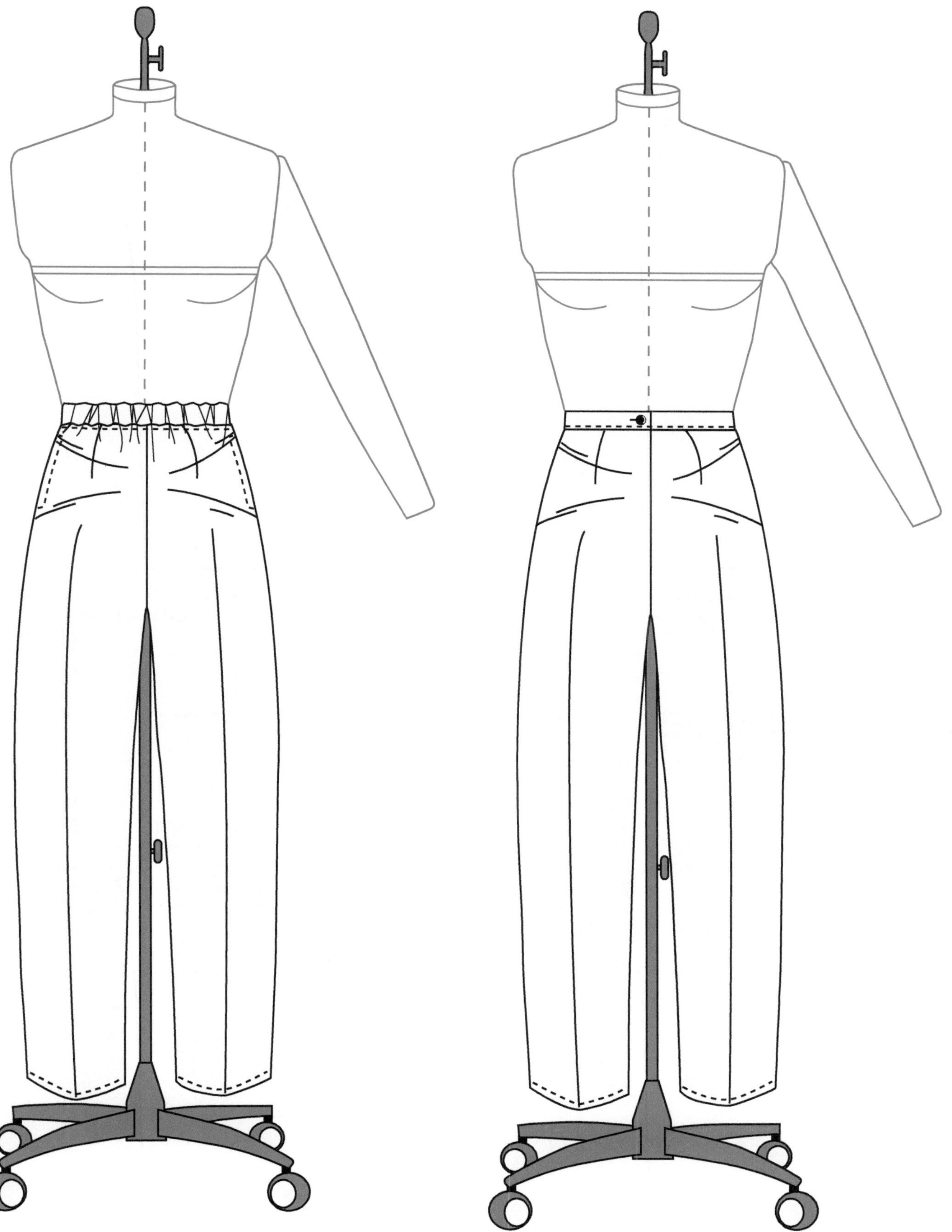

Figure 18.14a Fitting problem: knit pant pulls across abdomen.

Figure 18.14b Fitting problem: woven pant pulls across abdomen.

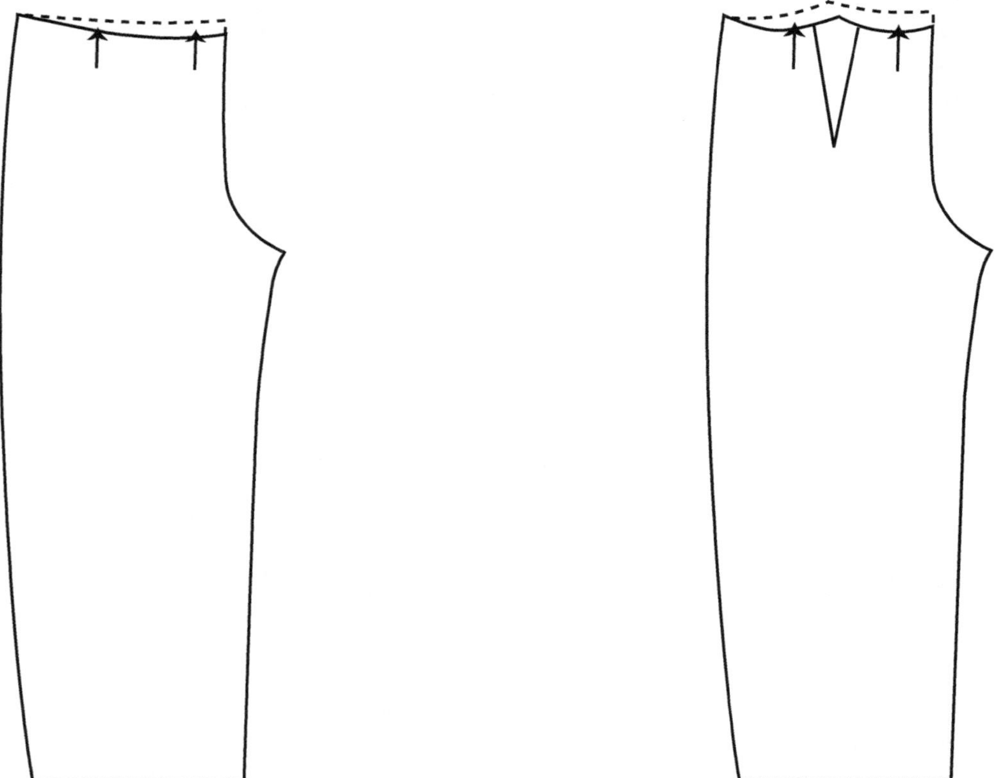

Figure 18.14c Pattern alteration: add to waist at center front, tapering to side seam.

Figure 18.14d Pattern alteration: add to waist at dart, tapering accordingly center front and to side seam.

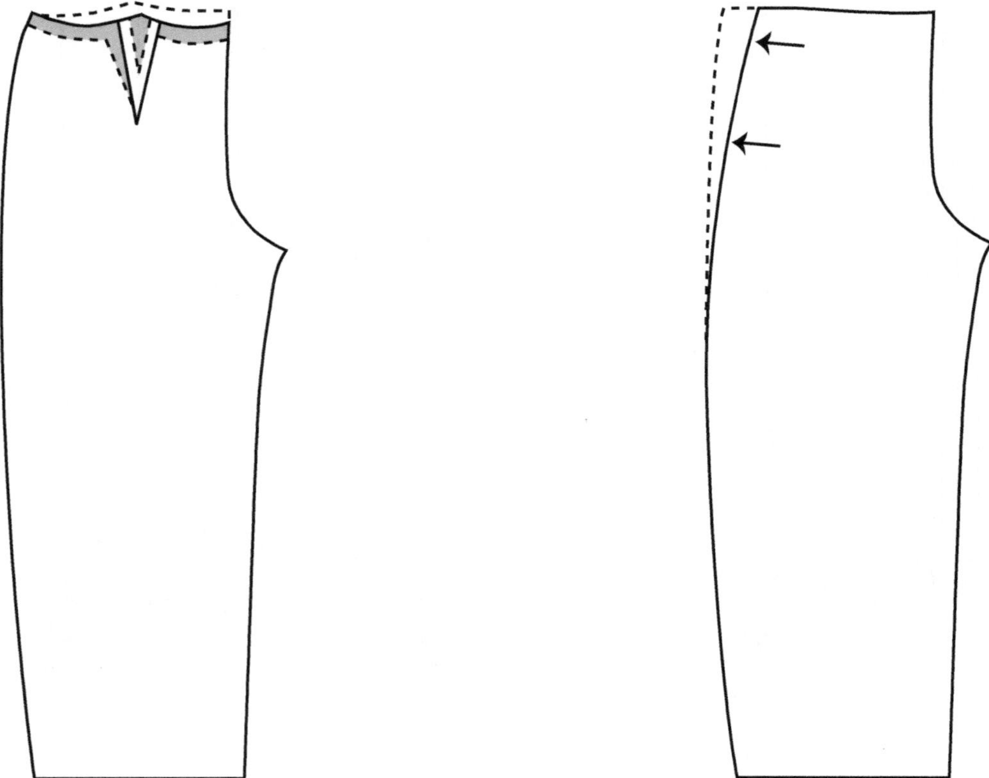

Figure 18.14e Pattern alteration: add depth to dart curve and adjust pattern accordingly.

Figure 18.14f Pattern alteration: add depth to side seam at waist and adjust pattern accordingly.

Solution B—The front rise may not be long enough. The garment may need more length and/or width at the abdomen. Lengthen or raise the garment at the center front waist tapering back to the side seam (Figures 18.14c and 18.14d).

Solution C—If the pant has darts, simply add more depth to the dart curve and adjust the pattern accordingly (Figures 18.14e).

Solution D—If the dart, or pleat, areas seem to have enough depth, then check the side seam hip curve. If the side seam is too narrow, adjust the curve accordingly (Figure 18.14f).

Problem Area 2—The pant is too big, sagging across the abdomen (Figures 18.15a and b).

Solution A—This is a common problem for knit pants when there is too much ease for the abdomen. Since few knitted pants have darts or pleating, the pant construction must be looked at very closely. If the pant is full fashioned, then the actual knitting process must be looked at and stitches must be reduced as needed. This process is common in flat-knit weft knitting. Check with the patternmaker and adjust in production accordingly.

Solution B—The front rise may be too long. The garment may need less length at the abdomen. Shorten by reducing excess from the top waist, or slash and pinch or fold the pattern horizontally at the center front waist, over but not through the waist at the side seam (Figures 18.15c and d).

Solution C—If the pant has darts, simply reduce the depth of the dart curve, and adjust pattern accordingly (Figure 18.15e).

Solution D—If the dart and pleat depths are correct, then check the side seam hip curve. If the side seam is too full, reduce the hip curve accordingly (Figure 18.15f).

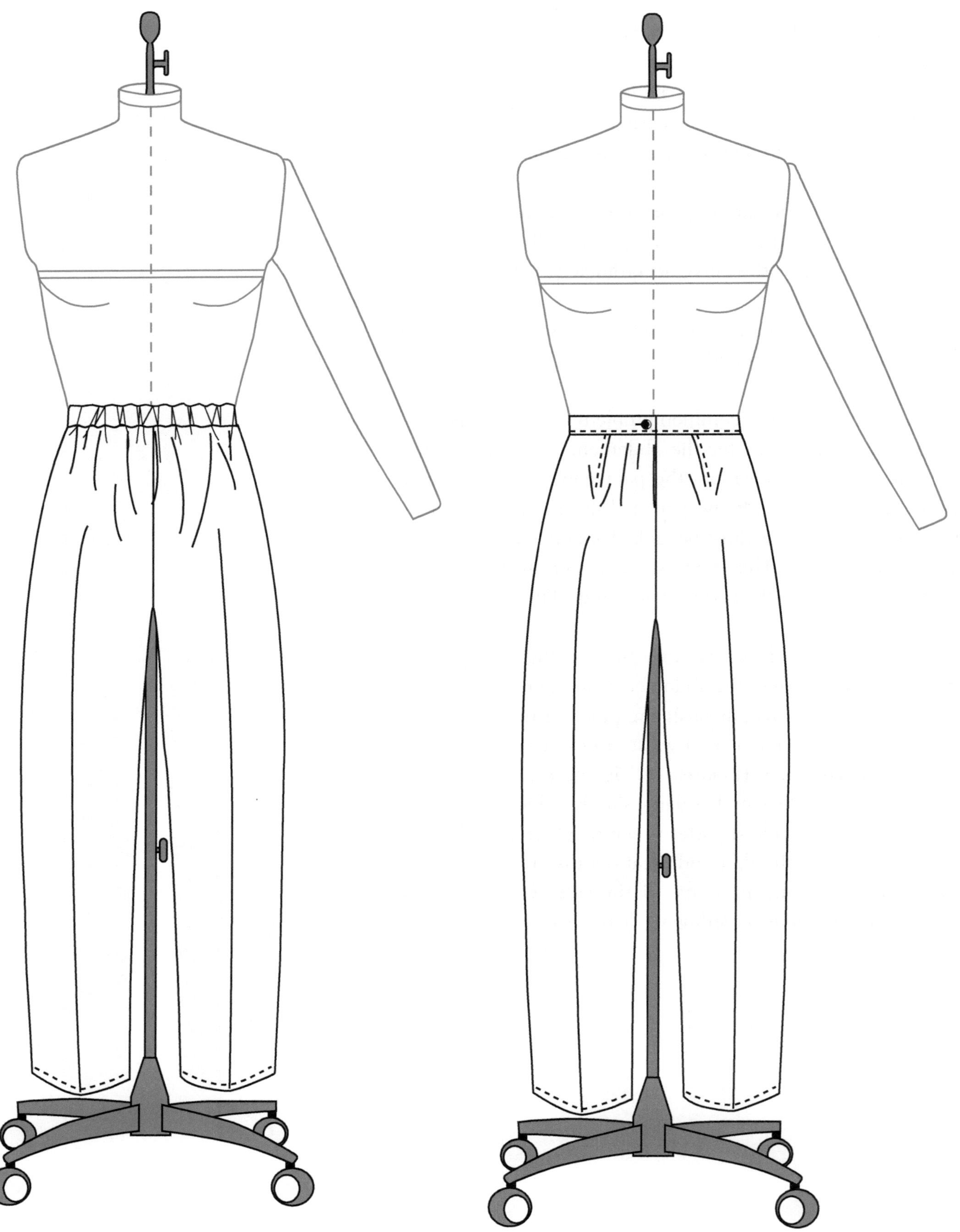

Figure 18.15a Fitting problem: knit pant sags at abdomen.

Figure 18.15b Fitting problem: woven pant sags at abdomen.

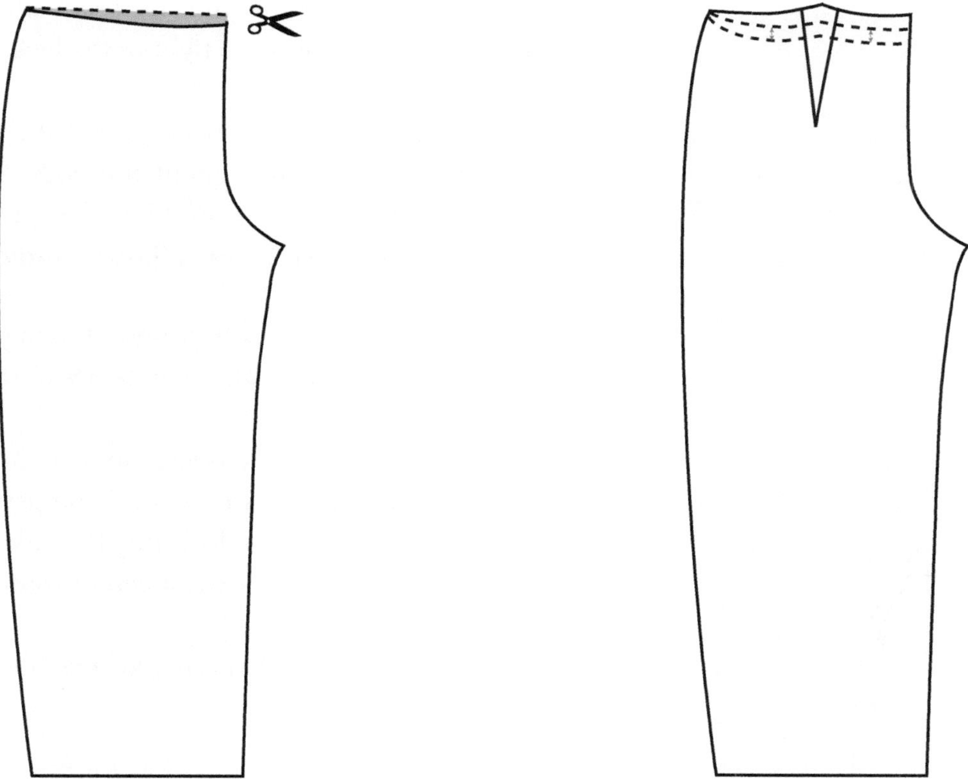

Figure 18.15c Pattern alteration: reduce pattern at center top waist, tapering to side.

Figure 18.15d Pattern alteration: reduce pattern by slashing, pinching, and folding at back below waist.

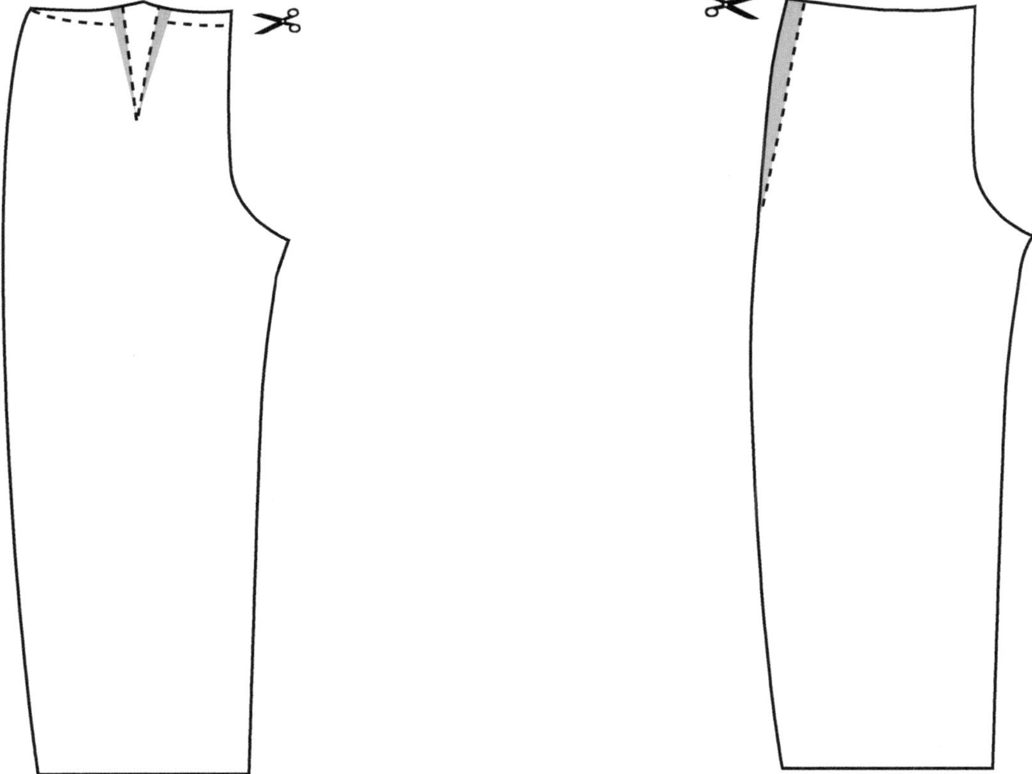

Figure 18.15e Pattern alteration: shorten back darts and adjust pattern accordingly.

Figure 18.15f Pattern alteration: reduce pattern at side seam.

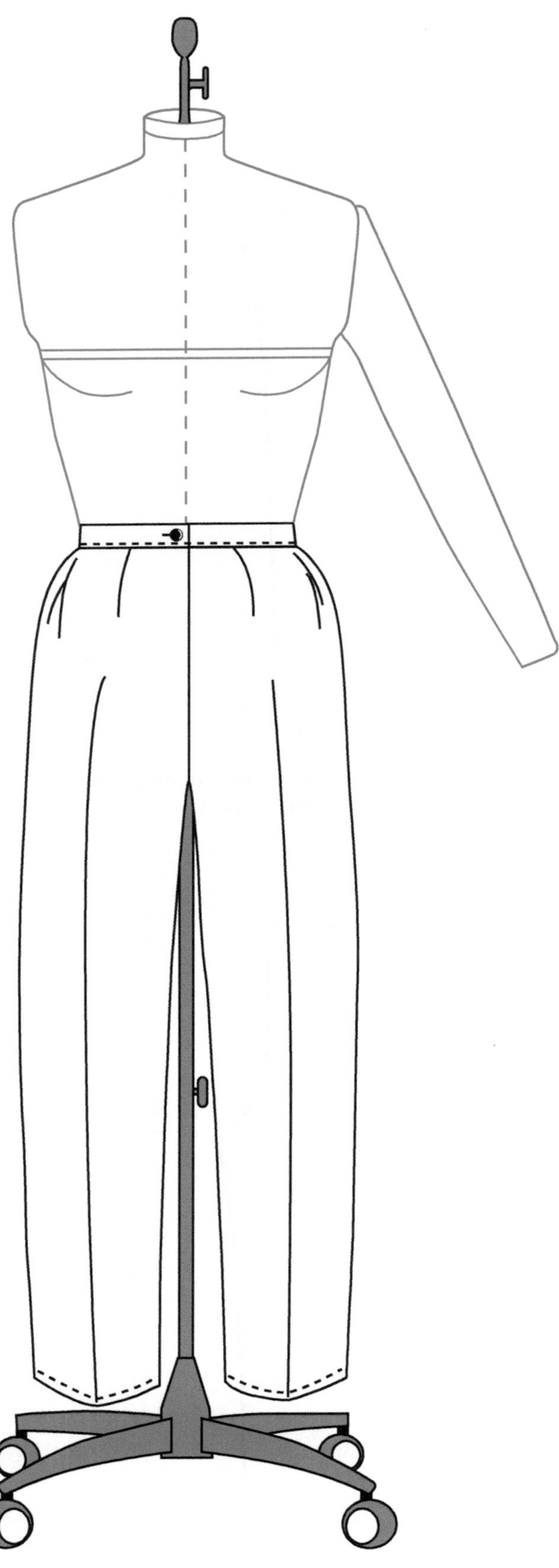

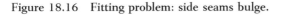

Figure 18.16 Fitting problem: side seams bulge.

***Problem Area* 3**—Fabric at the side seam and hip areas bulge either because the pant is too tight or too loose (Figure 18.16).

Solution A—The ease has been placed at the side seam and not distributed evenly throughout the body. See Solutions C and D in the Pants section, Problem Area 1, or Solutions D and E in Problem Area 2, and adjust accordingly.

Problem Area 4—There is horizontal folding below the back waist and above the buttocks (Figure 18.17a).

Solution A—The pant needs less fabric in the length between the waist and hip area. Slash and tuck the pattern horizontally at the center back, without distorting the side seam length, or reduce the pattern height at waist center front tapering to side seam (Figures 18.17b and c).

Solution B—The back darts are too long. Shorten accordingly (Figure 18.17d).

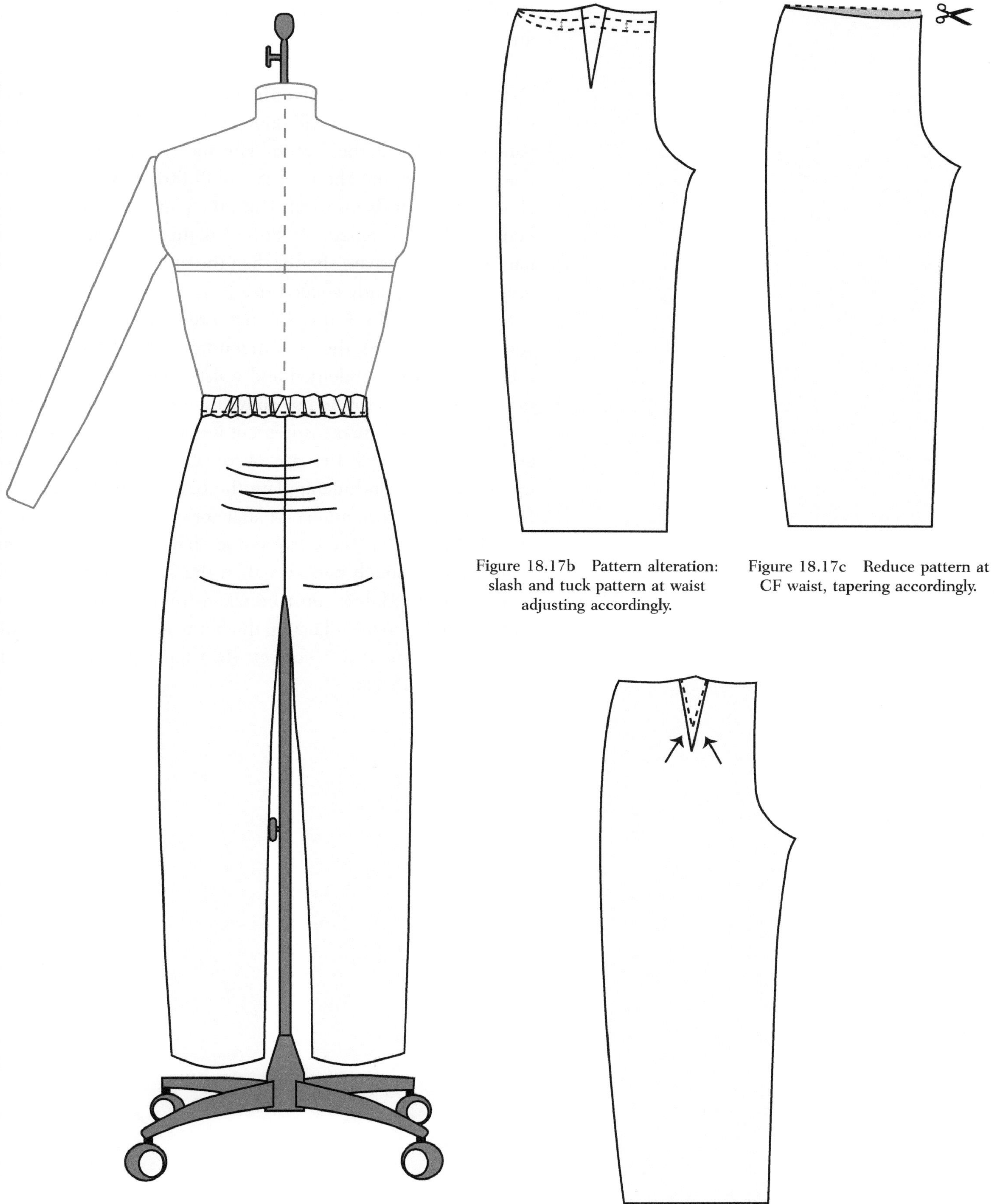

Figure 18.17a Fitting problem: horizontal folds at waist.

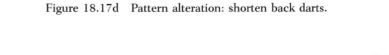

Figure 18.17b Pattern alteration: slash and tuck pattern at waist adjusting accordingly.

Figure 18.17c Reduce pattern at CF waist, tapering accordingly.

Figure 18.17d Pattern alteration: shorten back darts.

***Problem Area* 5**—The front rise does not fit well; it sags (Figure 18.18a).

[Note: Rises are the most difficult area to fit. Always check the rise curve first. You will know if the rise is ill fitting if the pant hangs flat at the crotch. The measurement of the rise may be to spec, but the pant is still ill fitting. An easy way to check for a poor rise is to sit. Does the pant leg pull up on the body to allow movement for sitting? Is the thigh measurement narrow? Is the inseam shorter than the outseam? These are all indicators of a poorly shaped rise.]

Solution A—Check the rise measurement first. If the measurement is too big, then too much fabric has been added to the pattern at the abdomen and waist. Does the garment sag in this area? Shorten the rise above the curve (Figure 18.18b).

Solution B—If the measurement is correct, yet the pant sags at the crotch, check the rise curve. Lay the pant front side up on the table and manipulate the curve so that it lays flat. Does the curve turn at a good angle or is it mostly straight? A good indicator that the curve is too shallow is that the front thigh width is much narrower than the back thigh width. To correct the rise, fabric must be taken from the top waist and added into the curve, adjusting thigh if needed. Also if the side seam measurement was correct, than taper pattern into side seam (Figure 18.18c).

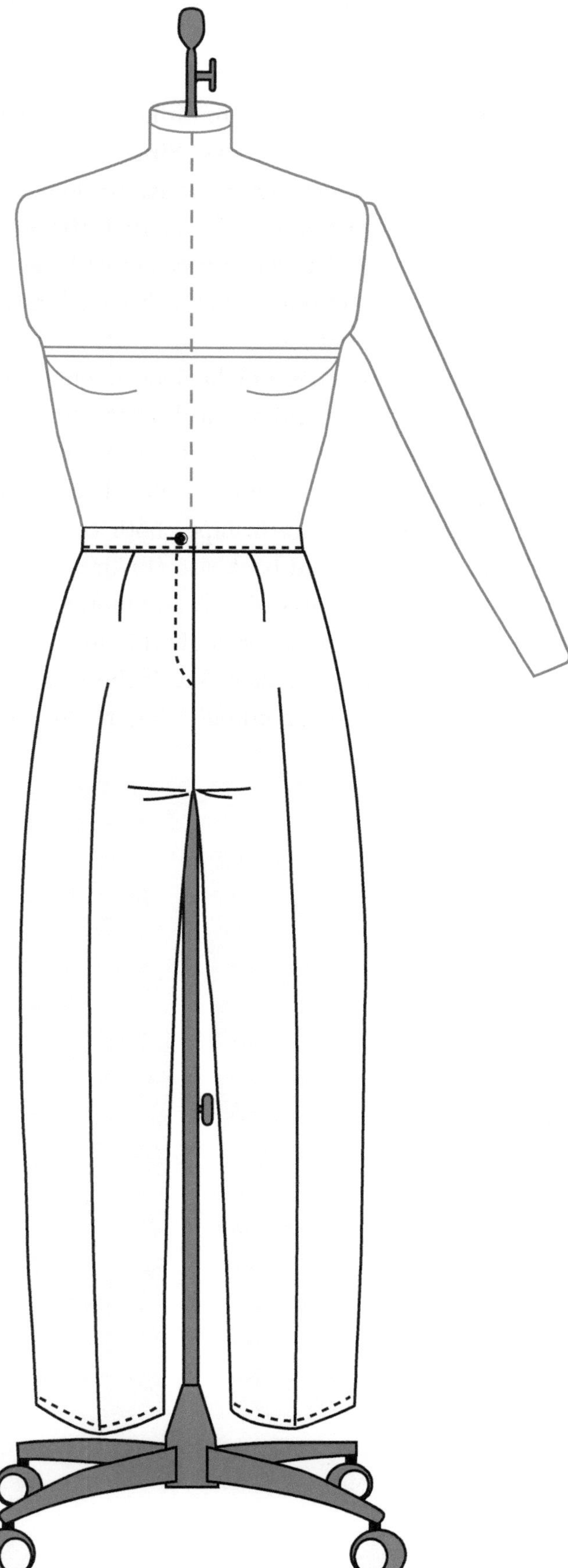

Figure 18.18a Fitting problem: front rise sags.

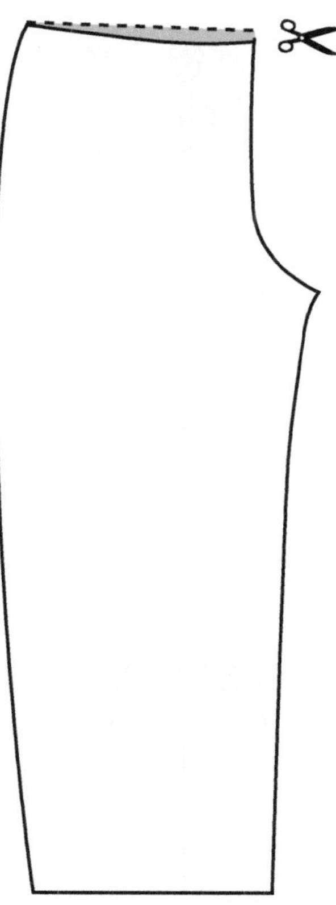

Figure 18.18b Pattern alteration: shorten the rise at waist.

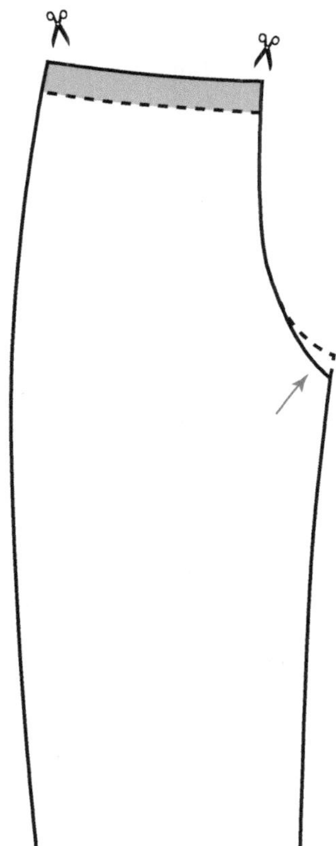

Figure 18.18c Pattern alteration: reduce the rise at waist and add to bottom curve.

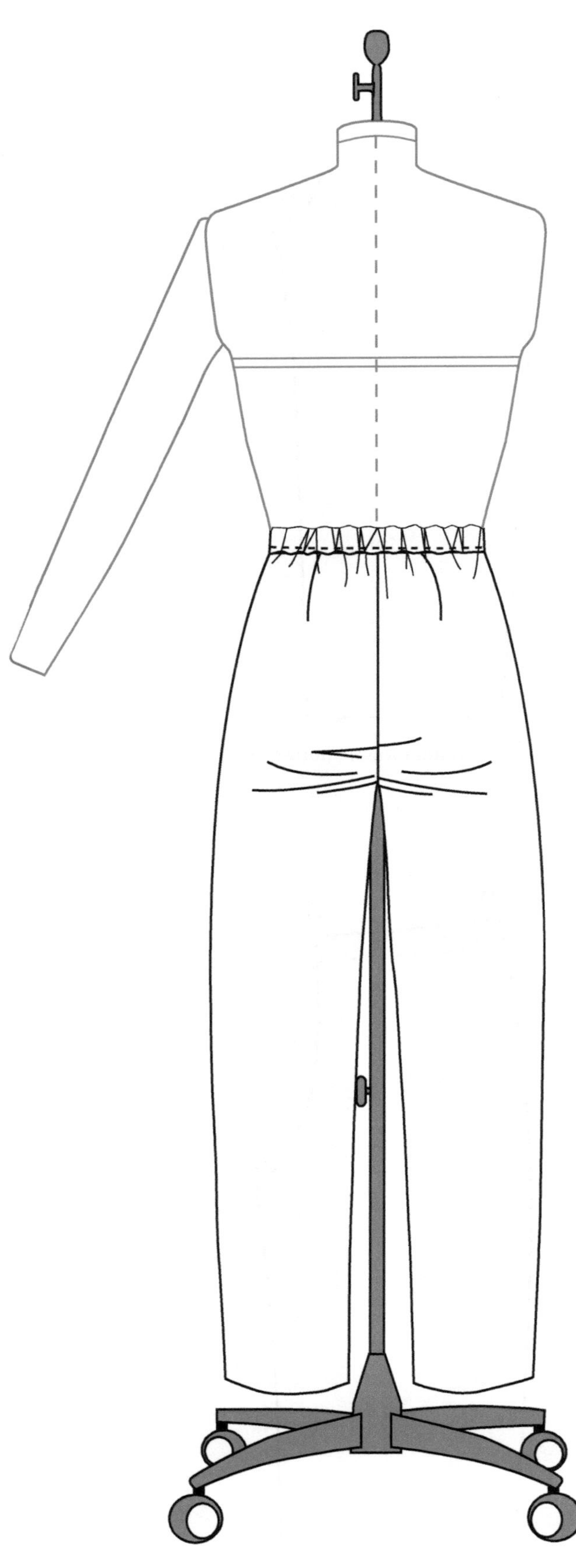

Figure 18.19a Fitting problem: pant is too tight at buttocks.

Problem Area 6—The pant is too tight across the buttocks (Figure 18.19a).

Solution A—This is a common problem for knit pants when there is not enough ease for the buttocks. Since few knitted pants have darts, the pant construction must be looked at very closely. Is the pant full fashioned? If it is, then the actual knitting process must be looked at and stitches must be added as needed. This process is common in flat-knit weft knitting. Adjust accordingly in production.

Solution B—The back rise may not be long enough. The garment may need more length and/or width at the buttocks. Slash and spread pattern raising the garment at the back waist, and widen or move out the garment at the center back; adjust thigh at inseam if needed. Be sure to taper both corrections back to the original side seam and back rise (Figure 18.19b).

Solution C—If the pant has darts, simply add more depth to the dart curve and adjust pattern accordingly (Figure 18.19c).

Solution D—If the dart depth is okay, see if the side seam is too narrow. Add to the curve accordingly (Figure 18.19d).

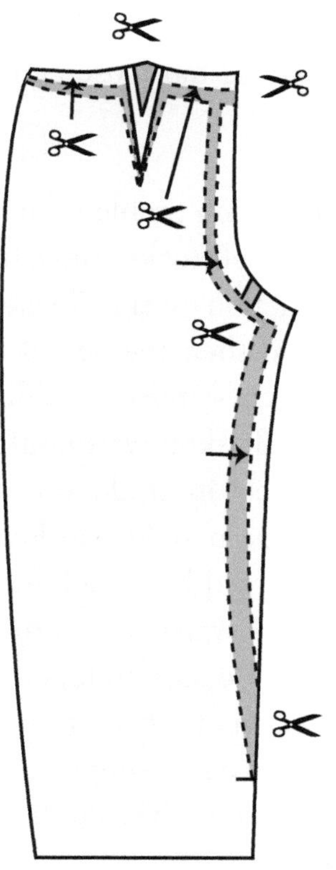

Figure 18.19b Pattern alteration: slash and spread pattern adding width to waist, crotch, and thigh as needed.

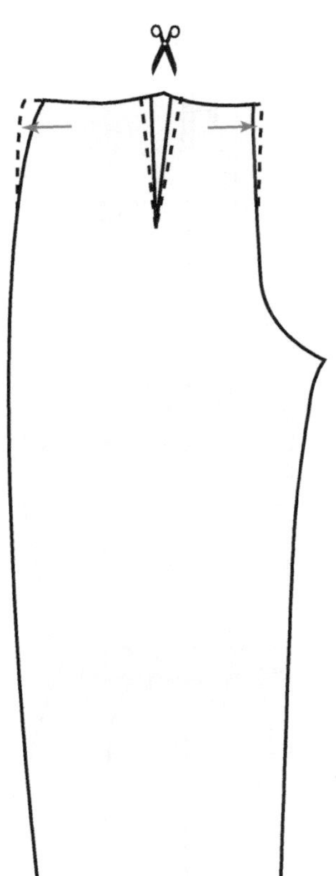

Figure 18.19c Pattern alteration: add to pattern at dart, waist, and crotch seams as needed.

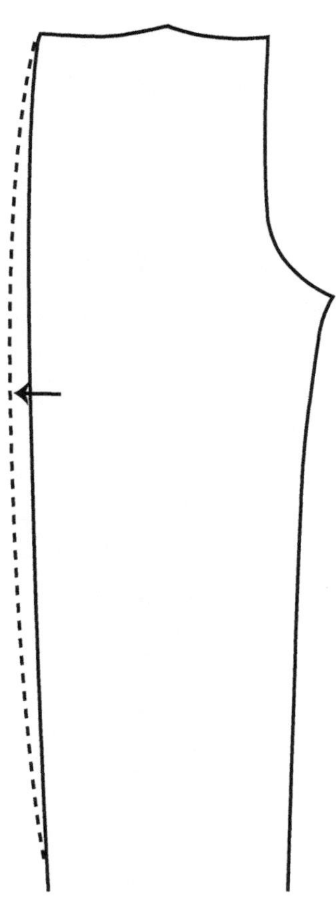

Figure 18.19d Pattern alteration: add more curve at hip and thigh.

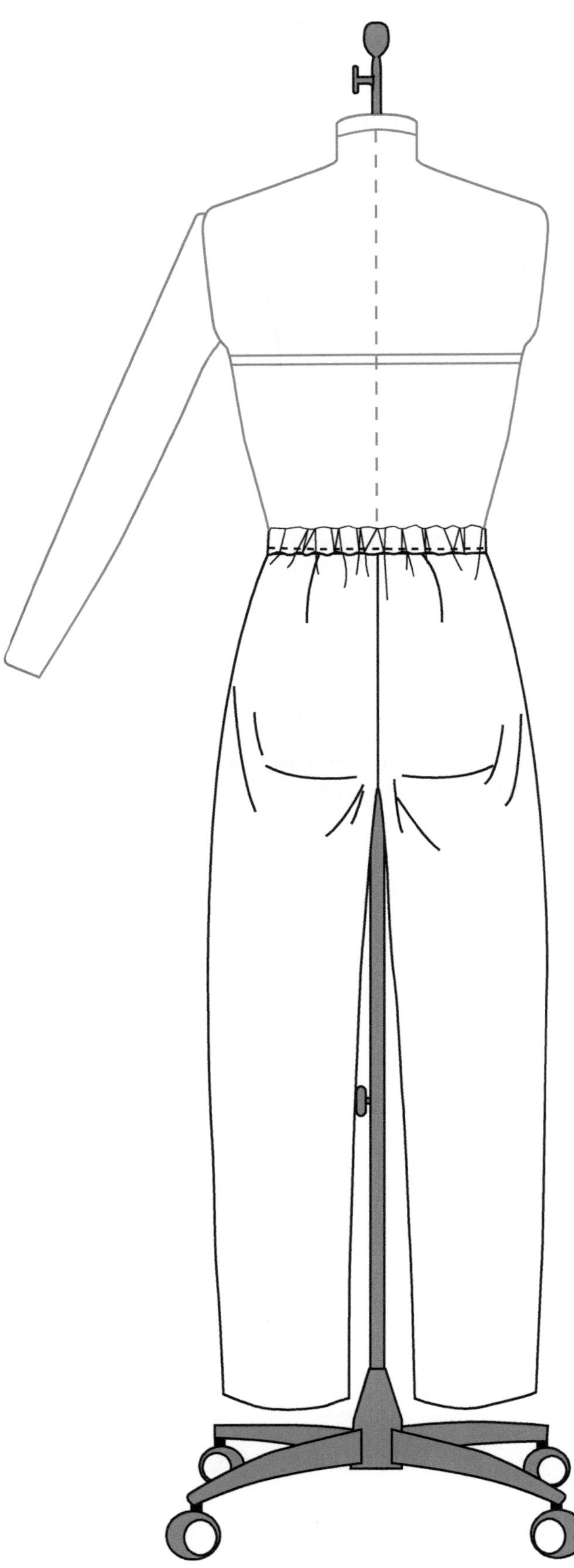

Figure 18.20a Fitting problem: pant is too loose at buttocks.

Problem Area 7—The pant is too loose across the buttocks and sags (Figure 18.20a).

Solution A—This is a common problem for knit pants when there is too much ease for the buttocks. Since few knitted pants have darts, the pant construction must be looked at very closely. If the pant is full fashioned then the actual knitting process must be looked at and stitches must be reduced as needed. This process is common in flat-knit weft knitting. Check with your patternmaker and correct in production.

Solution B—The back rise may be too long. The garment may need less length and/or width at the buttocks. Shorten or lower the garment at the back waist and narrow or move in the garment at the center back. Be sure to taper both corrections back to the original side seam and back rise (Figure 18.20b).

Solution C—If the pant has darts, simply reduce the depth of the dart, side seam, and back crotch seam needed by adjusting pattern accordingly (Figure 18.20c).

Solution D—If the dart depth is okay, see if the side seam is too wide. Reduce the curve accordingly (Figure 18.20d).

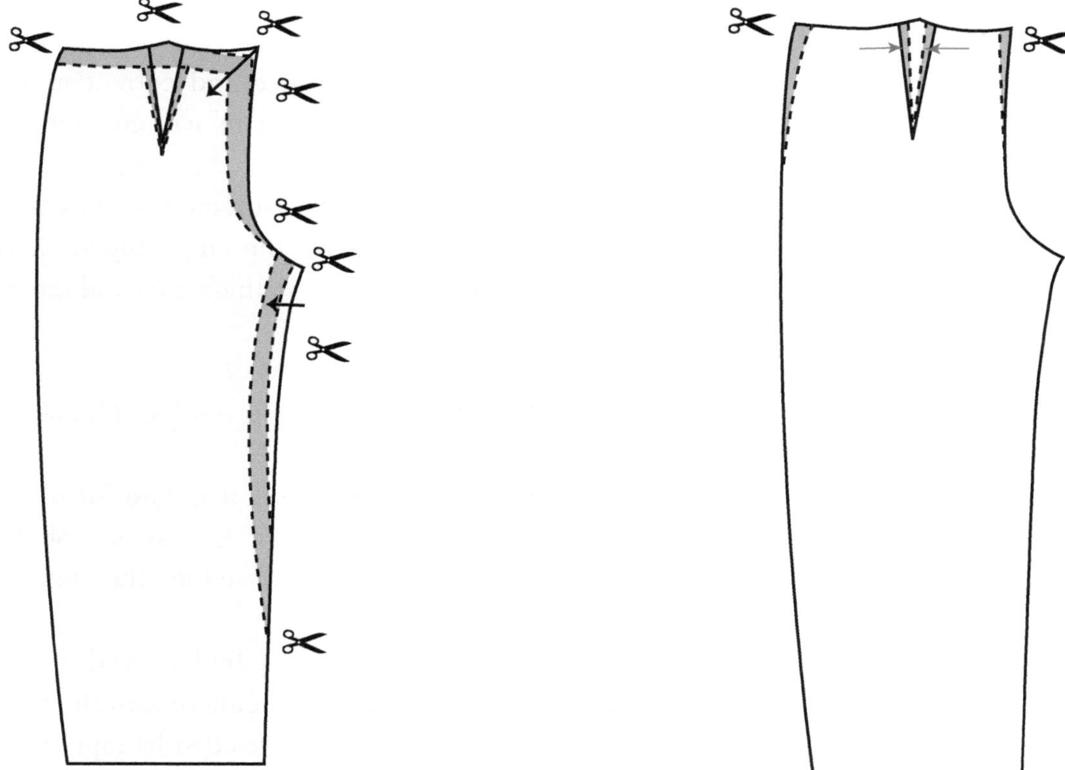

Figure 18.20b Pattern alteration: slash and spread pattern, reducing width at waist, crotch, and thigh.

Figure 18.20c Pattern alteration: reduce pattern at dart, waist, and crotch seams as needed.

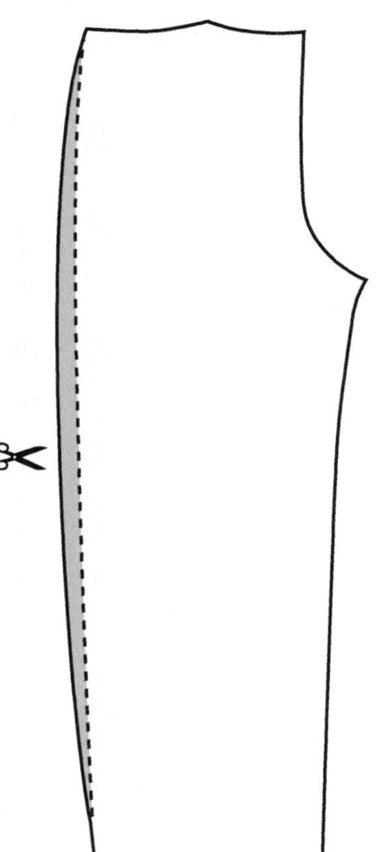

Figure 18.20d Pattern alteration: reduce curve at hip and thigh.

Problem Area 8—Thigh area is too tight (Figure 18.21a).

Solution A—Check the rise and correct as instructed in Problem Area 5, Solution B. This will give more ease to the thigh area.

Solution B—If the rise measurement is correct, you can still add more ease by adjusting the curve slightly and by adding width to the side seams at the thigh area and tapering into the hip and leg (Figure 18.21b).

Problem Area 9—Thigh area is too big (Figure 18.22a).

Solution A—Check the rise. It is rare for too much curve to be added to the rise, but it is possible. Shorten the rise curve at the crotch, which will reduce the width of the thigh (Figure 18.22b).

Solution B—Rise curve may be long and wide. Correct by adjusting at the waist and reducing the width of the inseam at the thigh area; adjust pattern needed by tapering into the hip and leg. Also reduce the outseam as necessary (Figure 18.22c).

Over the course of your career, you may encounter these and many other fit issues.

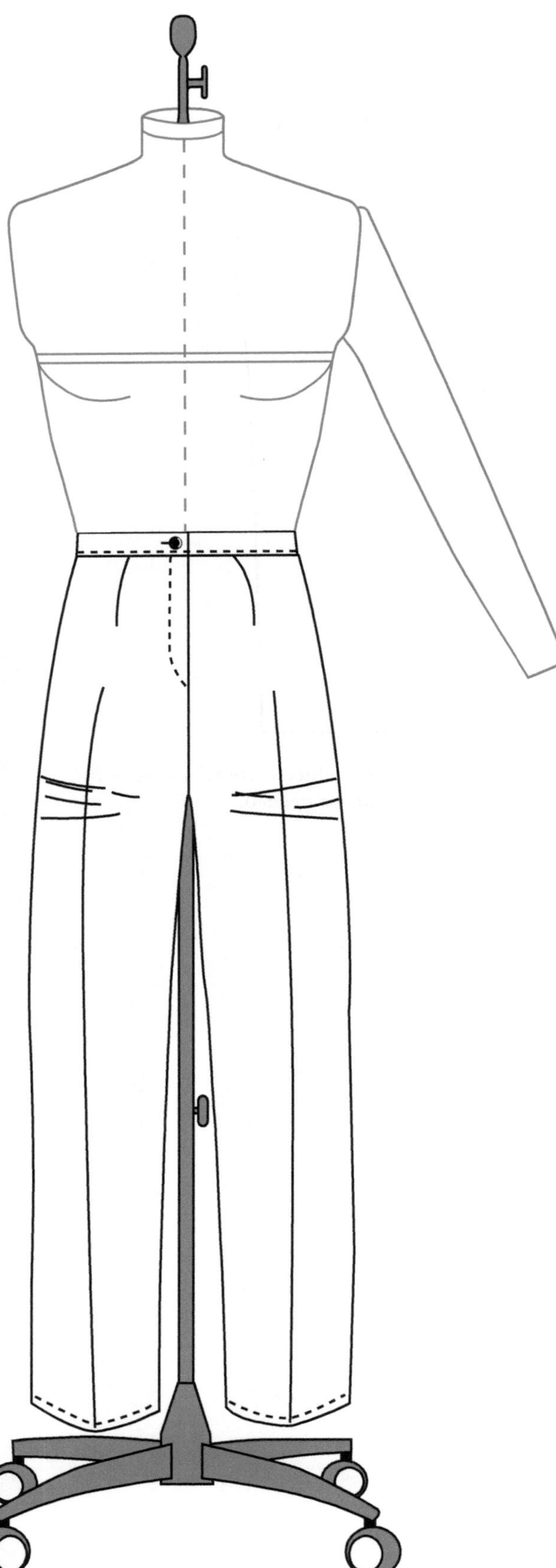

Figure 18.21a Fitting problem: thigh is too tight.

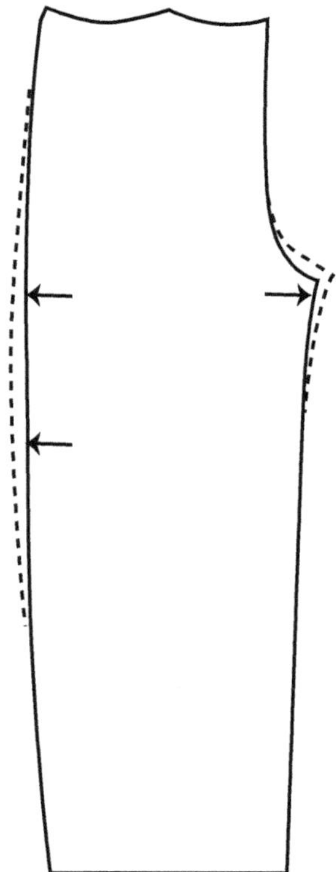

Figure 18.21b Add to pattern at hip and crotch curve.

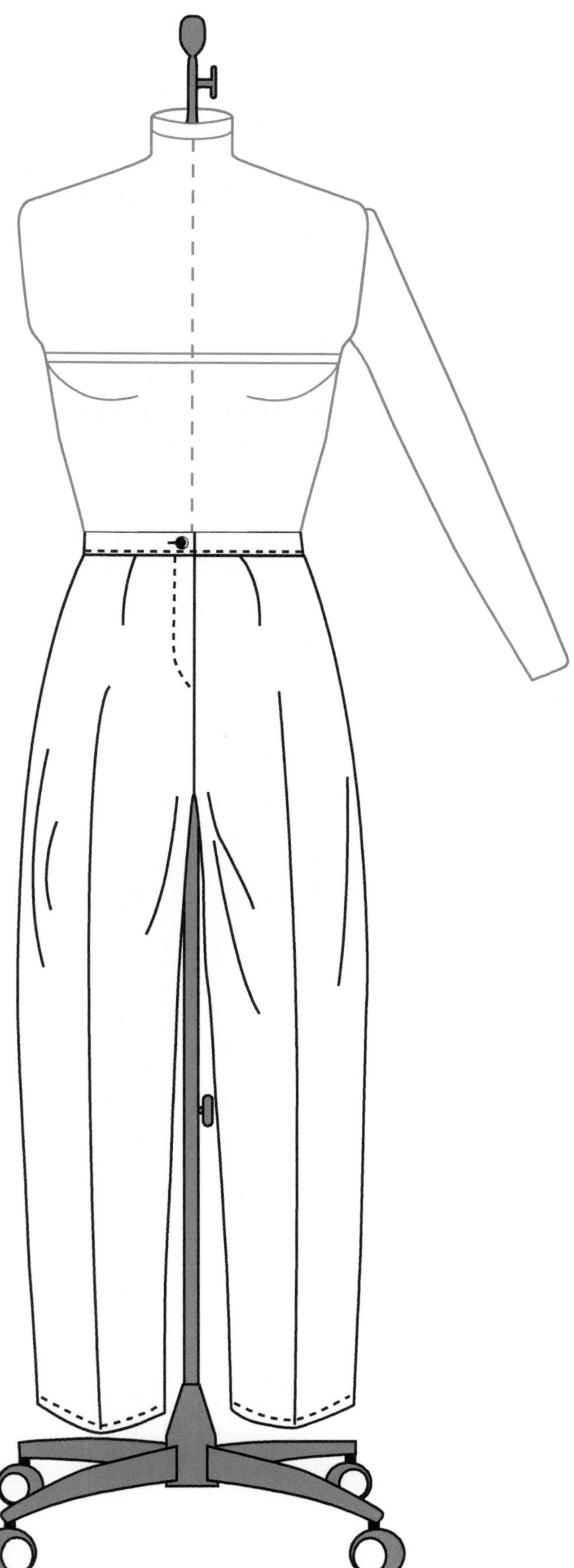

Figure 18.22a Fitting problem: thigh is too loose.

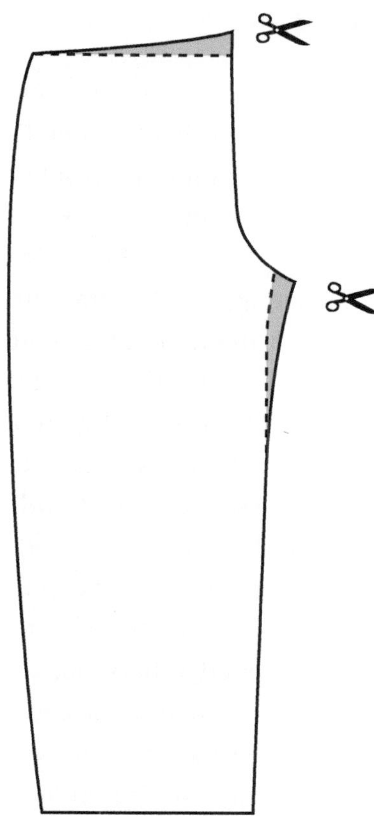

Figure 18.22b Pattern alteration: shorten rise curve to reduce thigh width.

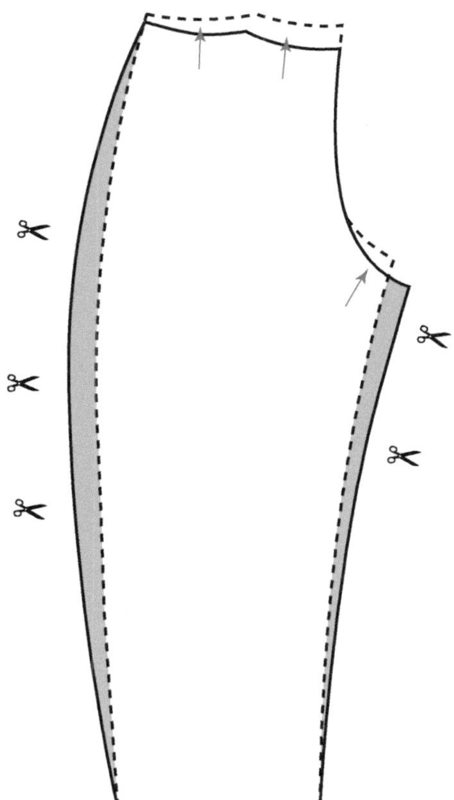

Figure 18.22c Pattern alteration: correct rise curve adjusting pattern; reduce inseam and outseam as needed.

Conducting a Fit Session

Once you know the fit evaluation sequence, all the rules for a good fitting garment, generalized garment fitting tips, plus the common fit problems and solutions, it is time to conduct a fit session.

Each point of measure (POM) is taken on the sample and checked against the measurements previously given to the manufacturer; many technical designers use a fit sheet for this (see Figure 18.23). Next the garment is tried on a live model or dress form. The garment is looked at for overall fit, then again following all the sequencing, fit rules, etc. Each POM is looked at individually and evaluated. It's important to clearly communicate any fit issues to your patternmaker. Photos, if possible, are helpful if such communication is needed; otherwise, add comments such as, "Front rise is too straight causing garment to droop at crotch; be sure to check crotch curve and correct accordingly," or "Front neckline is too deep; raise ½" as indicated on spec." If the garment requires minor or no corrections, it is approved for production. However when a garment requires major corrections, then second samples are requested. Factories are not happy when production is held up, so maintaining a good working relationship is important and solving problems quickly is imperative.

CHAPTER 18 TERMS

When working with fitting and grading, you may come across the following garment terms. If you are unfamiliar with any of them, please look up the definitions in the glossary at the end of this text.

Balance
Ease
Fit
Slope
Sloper

Fit Sheet

COMPANY NAME:	STYLE # 1234
ADDRESS:	GROUP NAME: Basics
	CLASSIFICATION: Woman — SEASON: Fall
PHONE:	LABEL:
FAX:	COLORWAY:
TECHNICAL SKETCH	SKETCH/PHOTO

CODE	POINT OF MEASURE	TOL.+/-	M/10-12 Measurements		1st Fit		Approved Spec
1	Front length	1/2	23		23		23
3	Center back length	1/2	21 1/2		21 1/2		21 1/2
4	Side length	1/4	14		14		14
9	Chest width	1/4-3/8	18 1/2		18 1/2		18/12
13	Across shoulder	1/4	15		14 3/4		15
15	Across chest	1/4	14		13 3/4		14
16	Across back	1/4	14		14		14
25	Bottom band/ribbing height	1/8	3/8		3/8		3/8
26	Bottom opening/sweep	1/4-3/8	18 1/2		18 1/2		18 1/2
42	Curved armhole width (opening)	1/8	9		9		9
57	Cuff/ribbing height sleeve (armhole)	1/4-3/8	3/8		3/8		3/8
58	Neck depth front	1/8	1		1		1
63	Neck width collar	1/4	6 1/2		6 1/2		6 1/2
64	Neck width edge	1/4	6 1/2		6 1/2		6 1/2
66	Neck edge width stretched	1/4	13		13		13
68	Neck base	1/4	7 1/2		7 1/2		7 1/2
72	Collar height	1/8	6		6		6
73	Collar band height	1/8	3/8		3/8		3/8
122	Side vent						
	A.	1/4	2 1/2		2 1/2		2 1/2
	B.	1/8	3/8		3/8		3/8

Comments: Garment looks great, all measurements are with-in tolerance. Style is approved for production.

DATE CREATED:	DATE MODIFIED:	DATE RELEASED:

Figure 18.23 Fit Sheet

CHAPTER 19

Grading

How to Grade a Spec Sheet

A sample garment, once approved for production, is graded or converted into all of the other sizes that will be produced. In other words, each piece of the approved pattern is made either smaller or larger (graded) to achieve the rest of the patterns in that size range. Every point is given a grade rule. For example, a top evaluated and approved in a size medium must then be converted to sizes small, large, and extra large, the points of measure are marked, the grade rules are applied, and then measurements are converted by hand or through popular CAD systems (see Figure 19.1).

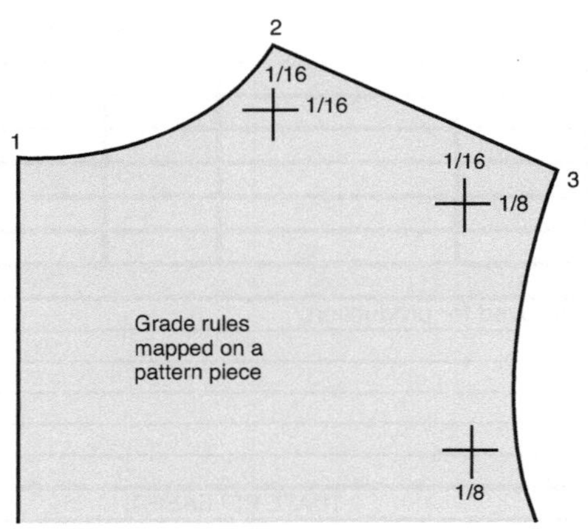

Figure 19.1 Incremental grading using mapped points.
(Style Cad by Cathleen Fasannella, Fashion Incubator)

Many private labels and most merchandising companies send their patterns out to jobbers to be produced. In order to get the exact size conversions desired, it is imperative for the spec sheet to contain grading information. This information sheet is called a Fully Graded Specification. If the pattern is not converted hand computer systems such as Lectra's Modaris V7, Gerber AccuScan, Telestia Creator, StyleCAD or Opitex PDS to name a few, allows the operators to do size customizations (see Figure19.2). Regardless of the system used, the operator/grader needs to know the desired proportions to use, which he or she will get from your graded spec sheet (see Figure19.3)

As you might guess, garment grading is another one of those difficult processes, most graders apprentice as patternmakers for several years before grading their own patterns. Many companies have set up or purchased mathematical formulas for grading and computers do most of it; however, there are occasions when the numbers will not convert correctly. It takes years of trial and error, plus working closely with a grading expert, for the technician to be able to troubleshoot these instances. For now, simply use the charts provided for practice.

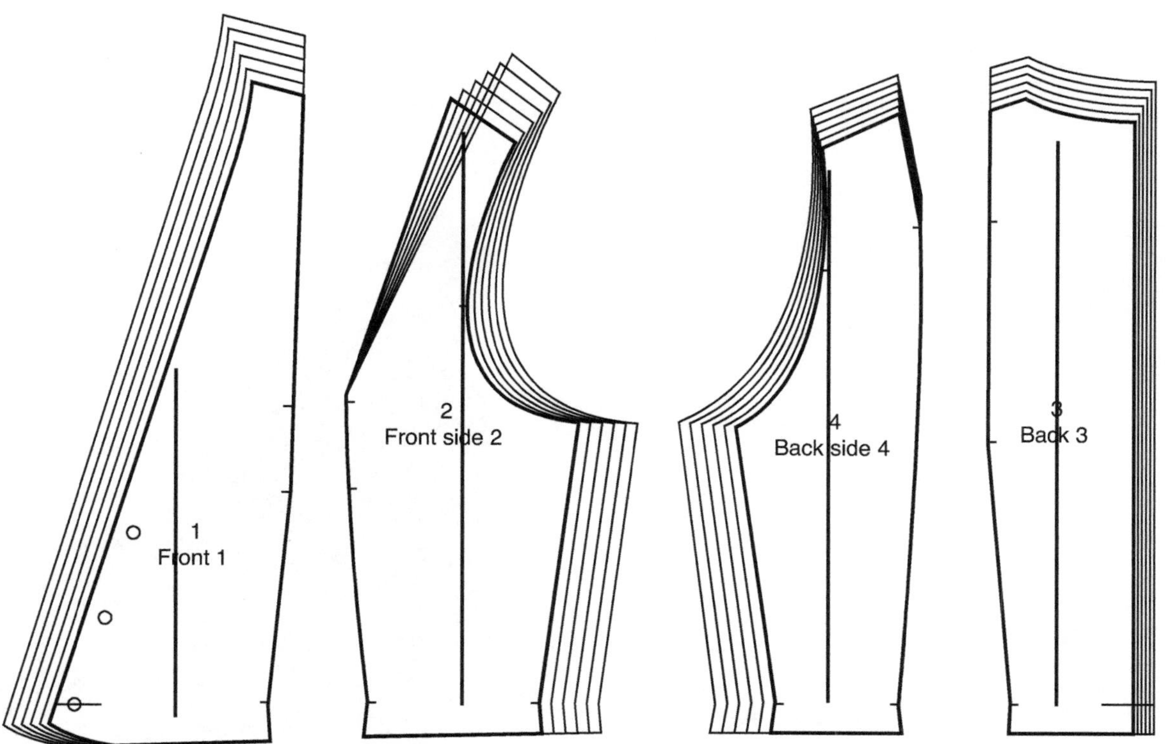

Figure 19.2 Grading with CAD systems.
(Anastasia Vouyouka for Telestia Creator, Automatic Grading Module)

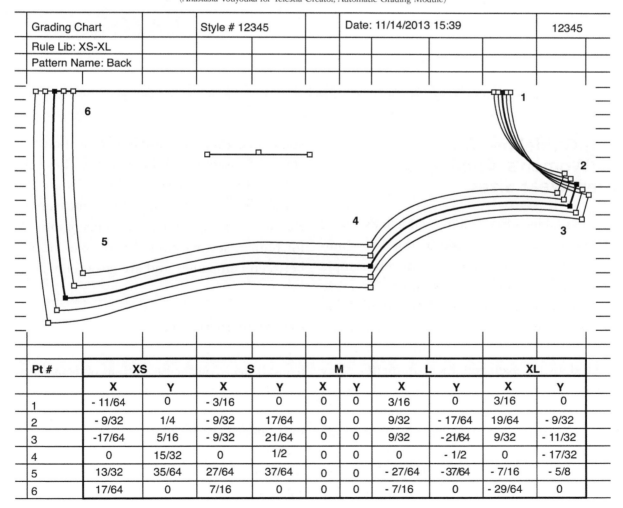

Grading Chart	Style # 12345	Date: 11/14/2013 15:39	12345
Rule Lib: XS-XL			
Pattern Name: Back			

Pt #	XS		S		M		L		XL	
	X	Y	X	Y	X	Y	X	Y	X	Y
1	- 11/64	0	- 3/16	0	0	0	3/16	0	3/16	0
2	- 9/32	1/4	- 9/32	17/64	0	0	9/32	- 17/64	19/64	- 9/32
3	-17/64	5/16	- 9/32	21/64	0	0	9/32	-21/64	9/32	- 11/32
4	0	15/32	0	1/2	0	0	0	- 1/2	0	- 17/32
5	13/32	35/64	27/64	37/64	0	0	- 27/64	-37/64	- 7/16	- 5/8
6	17/64	0	7/16	0	0	0	- 7/16	0	- 29/64	0

Figure 19.3 Grade rules chart from specs.
(Alejandro Esparza P. for Smart Pattern Making)

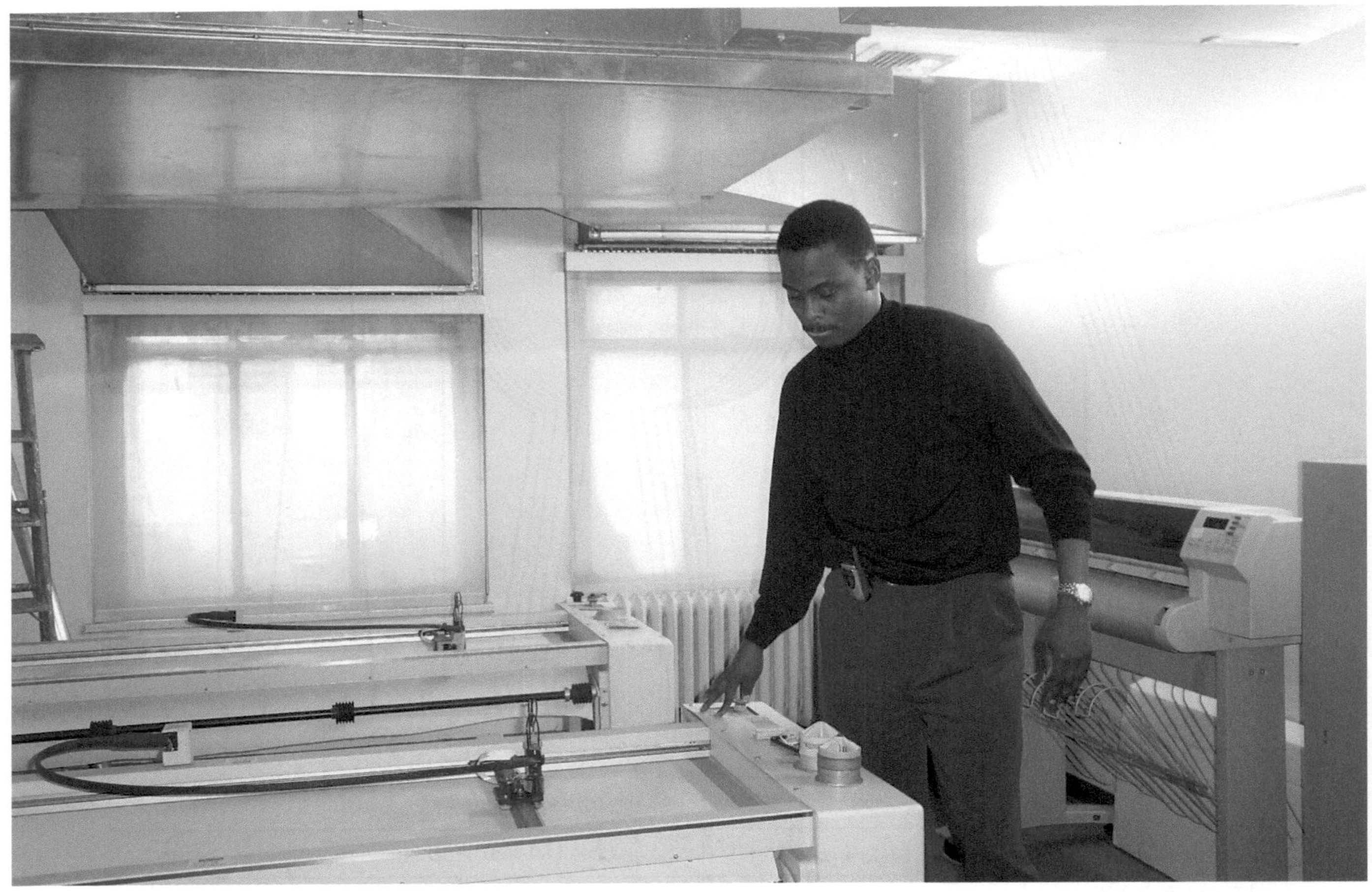

Figure 19.4 Patternmaker using Gerber™ plotter to grade and print patterns.

Grading Guidelines for Misses/Women's, Children's, and Menswear Sizes

The following tables offer grading guidelines for all of the measurement points used in this text. Simply add or subtract measurements from your sample size, as shown on the chart. Please note that these guidelines, set forth by the ASTM Standard Table of Body Measurements, are an average of popular industry grades. Because these grading guidelines were created using averaged measurements, they will not work for everyone. Most technical designers round grades to the closest eighth or quarter of an inch; however, many graders will grade as precisely as one-sixteenth to one thirty-second of an inch. Therefore, I would like to caution the reader not to presume that the measurements given are industry standards; they are simply a reflection of popular standards used within the industry. These charts also include tolerance levels. Tolerances are the differential allowed between a given measurement and the actual measurement, an acceptable allowance for human sewing error. Again, tolerances will vary between companies and are given only as a guide.

CHAPTER 19 TERMS

When grading a garment, you may come across the following terms. If you are unfamiliar with any of them, please look up the definitions listed in the glossary at the end of this text.

Fully graded specification
Grade rule
Grading
Tolerance

Table 19.1 GRADING CHART FOR NEWBORNS AND INFANTS

Codes and Terms		Premie	NB/ 0–3 mo	3 mo and 3–6 mo	6 mo and 6–9 mo	9 mo and 9–12 mo	12 mo	18 mo	24 mo	Tol +/–
1.	Front Length	½ – 1	½ – 1	½ – 1	x	½ – 1	½ – 1	x	1 – 2	½
4.	Side Length	¼ – ½	¼ – ½	¼ – ½	x	¼ – ½	¼ – ½	x	½ – 1	¼ – ½
9.	Chest Width (knit)	½	½	½	x	½	½	x	½ – 1	½
10.	Chest Width Circumference (woven)	1	1	1	x	1	1	x	2	½
11.	Chest Width (raglan sleeve, knit)	½	½	½	x	½	½	x	1	½
12.	Chest Width Circumference (raglan sleeve, woven)	1	1	1	x	1	1	x	2	½
14.	Shoulder Width	0	0	0	x	⅛	⅛	x	¼	⅛
26.	Bottom Opening/Sweep (knit top)	½	½	½	x	½	½	x	1	½
27.	Bottom Opening/Sweep Circumference (woven top)	1	1	1	x	1	1	x	2	½
36.	Sleeve Length Top Armhole (short sleeve to long sleeve)	⅛ – ¼	⅛ – ¼	⅛ – ¼	x	⅛ – ¼	⅛ – ¼	x	¼ – ½	¼
37.	Sleeve Length Top Neck (short sleeve to long sleeve)	¼ – ⅜	¼ – ⅜	¼ – ⅜	x	¼ – ⅜	¼ – ⅜	x	⅜ – ⅝	¼
40.	Straight Armhole Width (knit)	⅛	⅛	⅛	x	⅛	⅛	x	¼ – ½	⅛
41.	Straight Armhole Width Circumference (woven)	¼	¼	¼	x	¼	¼	x	½	¼
42.	Curved Armhole Width (knit)	⅛	⅛	⅛	x	⅛	⅛	x	¼	⅛
43.	Curved Armhole Width Circumference (woven)	¼	¼	¼	x	¼	¼	x	¼	¼
50.	Elbow Width (knit)	⅛	⅛	⅛	x	⅛	⅛	x	¼	⅛
51.	Elbow Width Circumference (woven)	¼	¼	¼	x	¼	¼	x	½	¼
52.	Sleeve Opening Width (knit) (long sleeve to short & capped)	⅛	⅛	⅛	x	⅛	⅛	x	¼	⅛
53.	Sleeve Opening Width Circumference (woven) (long sleeve to short & capped)	¼	¼	¼	x	¼	¼	x	½	¼
62.	Neck Width, No Collar	0	0	⅛	x	⅛	⅛	x	¼	⅛
63.	Neck Width, Collar	0	0	⅛	x	⅛	⅛	x	¼	⅛
64.	Neck Edge Width (knit)	0	0	⅛	x	⅛	⅛	x	¼	⅛
65.	Neck Edge Width Circumference (woven)	⅛	⅛	⅛	x	¼	¼	x	¼	¼
82.	Waistband Width (knit)	½	½	½	x	½	½	x	1	½
83.	Waistband Width Circumference (woven)	1	1	1	x	1	1	x	2	½

(continued)

Table 19.1 GRADING CHART FOR NEWBORNS AND INFANTS *(continued)*

Codes and Terms	Premie	NB/ 0–3 mo	3 mo and 3–6 mo	6 mo and 6–9 mo	9 mo and 9–12 mo	12 mo	18 mo	24 mo	Tol +/–
90. Hip Width From HPS (knit)	½	½	½	x	½	½	x	1	½
91. Hip Width from HPS Circumference (woven)	1	1	1	x	1	1	x	2	½
92. Hip Seat Width (knit pant)	½	½	½	x	½	½	x	1	½
93. Hip Seat Width Circumference (woven pant)	1	1	1	x	1	1	x	2	½
105. Inseam *(or grade accordingly if an inseam length grade is desired)*	1	1	1	x	1	1½	x	1½	½
106. Outseam *(or grade accordingly if an inseam length grade is desired and add that measurement to this one)*	1	1	1	x	1	1½	x	1½	½
109. Thigh Width (knit)	⅛	⅛	¼	x	¼	½	x	¾	¼
110. Thigh Width Circumference (woven)	¼	¼	½	x	½	1	x	1½	¼
113. Leg Opening Width (knit)	⅛	⅛	¼	x	¼	¼	x	¼	¼
114. Leg Opening Width Circumference (woven)	¼	¼	½	x	½	½	x	½	¼
151. Front Torso Length (jumpsuits and one-piece garments)									
A. Garments with a Front Opening Relaxed *(or use "adjust accordingly" if other length measurements have already been given)*	¾	¾	¾	x	1	1	x	2	½
B. Garments with a Front Opening Extended *(or use "adjust accordingly" if other length measurements have already been given)*	¾	¾	¾	x	1	1	x	2	½
C. Garments with a Plain Front, No Front Opening, Relaxed *(or use "adjust accordingly" if other length measurements have already been given)*	¾	¾	¾	x	1	1	x	2	½
D. Garments with a Plain Front, No Front Opening, Relaxed *(or use "adjust accordingly" if other length measurements have already been given)*	¾	¾	¾	x	1	1	x	2	½
153. Total Garment Length Front	¾	¾	¾	x	1	1	x	2	½
154. Total Garment Length Back	¾	¾	¾	x	1	1	x	2	½
155. Crotch Width	⅛	⅛	⅛	x	⅛	¼	x	¼	⅛

Table 9.2 GRADING CHARTS FOR TODDLERS

Codes and Terms	2T	3T	4T	Tol +/–
1. Front Length	½ – 1	x	½ – 1	½
9. Chest Width (knit)	½	x	½	½
10. Chest Width Circumference (woven)	1	x	1	½
14. Shoulder Width	¼	x	¼	⅛
26. Bottom Opening/Sweep (knit top)	½	x	½	½
27. Bottom Opening/Sweep Circumference (woven top)	1	x	1	½
37. Sleeve Length Top Neck (short sleeve to long sleeve)	⅜ – ⅝	x	⅜ – ⅝	¼
42. Curved Armhole Width (knit)	¼	x	¼	⅛
43. Curved Armhole Width Circumference (woven)	½	x	½	¼
52. Sleeve Opening Width (knit) (long sleeve to short & capped)	⅛	x	⅛	⅛
53. Sleeve Opening Width Circumference (woven) (long sleeve to short & capped)	¼	x	¼	¼
82. Waistband Width (knit)	½	x	½	½
83. Waistband Width Circumference (woven)	1	x	1	½
90. Hip Width from HPS (knit)	½	x	½	½
91. Hip Width from HPS Circumference (woven)	1	x	1	½
105. Inseam *(or grade accordingly if an inseam length grade is desired)*	1½	x	1½	½
107. Front Rise	½	x	¾	¼
108. Back Rise	½	x	¾	¼
109. Thigh Width (knit)	⅜	x	⅜	¼
110. Thigh Width Circumference (woven)	⅝	x	⅝	¼
113. Leg Opening Width (knit)	⅛	x	⅛	¼
114. Leg Opening Width Circumference (woven)	¼	x	¼	¼
151. Front Torso Length (jumpsuits and one-piece garments)				
A. Garments with a Front Opening Relaxed *(or use "adjust accordingly" if other length measurements have already been given)*	1	x	1	½
C. Garments with a Plain Front, No Front Opening, Relaxed *(or use "adjust accordingly" if other length measurements have already been given)*	1	x	1	½
153. Total Garment Length Front	1	x	1	½
154. Total Garment Length Back	1	x	1	½
155. Crotch Width	¼	x	¼	¼

Table 19.3 GRADING CHART FOR GIRLS 4–6X AND BOYS 4–7X

Codes and Terms		S	M	L	Tol +/–
1.	Front Length (shirts, top of girls dresses)	¾	x	¾	½
2.	Front Length (dresses, girls only)	2	x	2	½
4.	Side Length (shirts, top of dresses)	¾	x	¾	½
9.	Chest Width (knit)	¾	x	¾	½
10.	Chest Width Circumference (woven)	1½	x	1½	½
11.	Chest Width (raglan sleeve, knit)	¾	x	¾	½
12.	Chest Width Circumference (raglan sleeve, woven)	1½	x	1½	½
14.	Shoulder Width	¼	x	¼	¼
19.	Waist Width (woven shirts, girls knit dresses)	¾	x	¾	½
20.	Waist Width Circumference (woven shirts, girls woven dresses)	1½	x	1½	½
26.	Bottom Opening/Sweep (knit top)	¾	x	¾	½
27.	Bottom Opening/Sweep Circumference (woven top)	1½	x	1½	½
36.	Sleeve Length Top Armhole (short sleeve to long sleeve)	1⅝	x	1⅝	¼
37.	Sleeve Length Top Neck (short sleeve to long sleeve)	1¾	x	1¾	¼
40.	Straight Armhole Width (knit)	⅜	x	⅜	¼
41.	Straight Armhole Width Circumference (woven)	¾	x	¾	¼
42.	Curved Armhole Width (knit)	⅜	x	⅜	¼
43.	Curved Armhole Width Circumference (woven)	¾	x	¾	¼
50.	Elbow Width (knit)	¼	x	¼	¼
51.	Elbow Width Circumference (woven)	⅜	x	⅜	¼
52.	Sleeve Opening Width (knit) (long sleeve to short & capped)	⅛	x	⅛	¼
53.	Sleeve Opening Width Circumference (woven) (long sleeve to short & capped)	¼	x	¼	¼
62.	Neck Width, No Collar	¼	x	¼	¼
63.	Neck Width, Collar	½	x	½	¼
64.	Neck Edge Width (knit)	¼	x	¼	¼
65.	Neck Edge Width Circumference (woven)	½	x	½	¼
82.	Waistband Width (knit)	½	x	½	½
83.	Waistband Width Circumference (woven)	1	x	1	½
90.	Hip Width from HPS (knit)	¾	x	¾	½
91.	Hip Width from HPS Circumference (woven)	1½	x	1½	½
92.	Hip Seat Width (knit pant)	¾	x	¾	½
93.	Hip Seat Width Circumference (woven pant)	1½	x	1½	½
94.	Bottom Opening/Sweep Width (girls knit skirt only)	¾	x	¾	½
95.	Bottom Opening/Sweep Width Circumference (girls knit skirt only)	1½	x	1½	½

Table 19.3 GRADING CHART FOR GIRLS 4–6X AND BOYS 4–7X *(continued)*

Codes and Terms	S	M	L	Tol +/–
105. Inseam *(or grade accordingly if an inseam length grade is desired)*	1¾	x	1¾	½
106. Outseam *(or grade accordingly if an inseam length grade is desired and add that measurement to this one)*	1¾	x	1¾	½
107. Front Rise	¾	x	¾	¼
108. Back Rise	¾	x	¾	¼
109. Thigh Width (knit)	½	x	½	¼
110. Thigh Width Circumference (woven)	1	x	1	¼
113. Leg Opening Width (knit)	⅛	x	⅛	¼
114. Leg Opening Width Circumference (woven)	¼	x	¼	¼

Table 19.4 GRADING CHART FOR GIRLS 4–6X AND BOYS 4–7X

Codes and Terms	4	5	6	Girls 6x and Boys 7	Boys 7x	Tol +/–
1. Front Length (shirts, top of girls dresses)	½	x	½	½	½	½
2. Front Length (dresses, girls only)	1¾	x	1¾	1¾	n/a	½
4. Side Length (shirts, top of dresses)	½	x	½	½	½	½
9. Chest Width (knit)	½	x	½	1	1	½
10. Chest Width Circumference (woven)	1	x	1	2	2	½
11. Chest Width (raglan sleeve, knit)	½	x	½	1	1	½
12. Chest Width Circumference (raglan sleeve, woven)	1	x	1	2	2	½
14. Shoulder Width	⅛	x	⅛	⅛	¼	¼
19. Waist Width (woven shirts, girls knit dresses)	½	x	½	1	1	½
20. Waist Width Circumference (woven shirts, girls woven dresses)	1	x	1	2	2	½
26. Bottom Opening/Sweep (knit top)	½	x	½	1	1	½
27. Bottom Opening/Sweep Circumference (woven top)	1	x	1	2	2	½
36. Sleeve Length Top Armhole (short sleeve to long sleeve)	1¼	x	1	1	½	½
37. Sleeve Length Top Neck (short sleeve to long sleeve)	1½	x	1¼	1¼	½	½
40. Straight Armhole Width (knit)	¼	x	¼	¼	¼	¼
41. Straight Armhole Width Circumference (woven)	½	x	½	½	¼	¼
42. Curved Armhole Width (knit)	⅜	x	⅜	⅜	¼	¼
43. Curved Armhole Width Circumference (woven)	¾	x	¾	¾	¼	¼
50. Elbow Width (knit)	⅛	x	⅛	⅛	¼	¼
51. Elbow Width Circumference (woven)	¼	x	¼	¼	¼	¼

(continued)

Table 19.4 GRADING CHART FOR GIRLS 4–6X AND BOYS 4–7X *(continued)*

Codes and Terms	4	5	6	Girls 6x and Boys 7	Boys 7x	Tol +/–
52. Sleeve Opening Width (knit) (long sleeve to short & capped)	1/8	x	1/8	1/8	1/4	1/4
53. Sleeve Opening Width Circumference (woven) (long sleeve to short & capped)	1/4	x	1/4	1/4	1/4	1/4
62. Neck Width, No Collar	1/4	x	1/4	1/4	1/4	1/4
63. Neck Width, Collar	1/2	x	1/2	1/4	1/4	1/4
64. Neck Edge Width (knit)	1/4	x	1/4	1/8	1/4	1/4
65. Neck Edge Width Circumference (woven)	3/8	x	3/8	1/4	1/4	1/4
82. Waistband Width (knit)	1/2	x	1/2	1	1	1/2
83. Waistband Width Circumference (woven)	1	x	1	2	2	1/2
90. Hip Width From HPS (knit)	1/2	x	1/2	1	1	1/2
91. Hip Width from HPS Circumference (woven)	1	x	1	2	2	1/2
92. Hip Seat Width (knit pant)	1/2	x	1/2	1	1	1/2
93. Hip Seat Width Circumference (woven pant)	1	x	1	2	2	1/2
94. Bottom Opening/Sweep Width (girls knit skirt only)	1/2	x	1/2	1	n/a	1/2
95. Bottom Opening/Sweep Width Circumference (girls knit skirt only)	1	x	1	2	n/a	1/2
105. Inseam *(or grade accordingly if an inseam length grade is desired)*	1 1/2	x	1	1 1/2	1 1/2	1/2
106. Outseam *(or grade accordingly if an inseam length grade is desired and add that measurement to this one)*	1 1/2	x	1	1 1/2	1 1/2	1/2
107. Front Rise	3/4	x	3/8	3/4	3/4	1/4
108. Back Rise	3/4	x	3/8	3/4	3/4	1/4
109. Thigh Width (knit)	3/8	x	3/8	3/8	3/8	1/4
110. Thigh Width Circumference (woven)	5/8	x	5/8	5/8	5/8	1/4
113. Leg Opening Width (knit)	1/4	x	1/4	1/4	1/4	1/4
114. Leg Opening Width Circumference (woven)	3/8	x	3/8	3/8	3/8	1/4

Table 19.5 GRADING CHART FOR GIRLS 7–16					
Codes and Terms	**S**	**M**	**L**	**XL**	**Tol +/–**
1. Front Length	1	x	1	1	½
4. Side Length	¾	x	¾	¾	½
9. Chest Width (knit)	1	x	1	1	½
10. Chest Width Circumference (woven)	2	x	2	2	½
11. Chest Width (raglan sleeve, knit)	¾	x	¾	¾	½
12. Chest Width Circumference (raglan sleeve, woven)	1½	x	1½	1½	½
14. Shoulder Width	¼	x	¼	¼	¼
19. Waist Width	1	x	1	1	½
20. Waist Width Circumference	2	x	2	2	½
26. Bottom Opening/Sweep (knit top)	1	x	1	1	½
27. Bottom Opening/Sweep Circumference (woven top)	2	x	2	2	½
36. Sleeve Length Top Armhole (short sleeve to long sleeve)	¼ – ½	x	¼ – ½	¼ – ½	¼
37. Sleeve Length Top Neck (short sleeve to long sleeve)	⅜ – ⅝	x	⅜ – ⅝	⅜ – ⅝	¼
40. Straight Armhole Width (knit)	½	x	½	½	¼
41. Straight Armhole Width Circumference (woven)	1	x	1	1	¼
42. Curved Armhole Width (knit)	½	x	½	½	¼
43. Curved Armhole Width Circumference (woven)	1	x	1	1	¼
50. Elbow Width (knit)	⅜	x	⅜	⅜	¼
51. Elbow Width Circumference (woven)	⅝	x	⅝	⅝	¼
52. Sleeve Opening Width (knit) (long sleeve to short & capped)	⅛	x	⅛	¼	¼
53. Sleeve Opening Width Circumference (woven) (long sleeve to short & capped)	¼	x	¼	¼	¼
62. Neck Width, No Collar	¼	x	¼	¼	¼
63. Neck Width, Collar	½	x	½	¼	¼
64. Neck Edge Width (knit)	¼	x	¼	¼	¼
65. Neck Edge Width Circumference (woven)	½	x	½	¼	¼
82. Waistband Width (knit)	1	x	1	1	½
83. Waistband Width Circumference (woven)	2	x	2	2	½
88. Low Hip Width from Waist (knit)	1	x	1	1	½
89. Low Hip Width Circumference from Waist (woven)	2	x	2	2	½
90. Hip Width from HPS (knit)	1	x	1	1	½
91. Hip Width from HPS Circumference (woven)	2	x	2	2	½
94. Bottom Opening/Sweep Width	1	x	1	1	½
95. Bottom Opening/Sweep Width Circumference	2	x	2	2	½

(continued)

Table 19.5 GRADING CHART FOR GIRLS 7–16 *(continued)*

Codes and Terms	S	M	L	XL	Tol +/–
105. Inseam *(or grade accordingly if an inseam length grade is desired)*	2½	x	3	3	½
106. Outseam *(or grade accordingly if an inseam length grade is desired and add that measurement to this one)*	2½	x	3	3	½
107. Front Rise	¾	x	¾	¾	¼
108. Back Rise	¾	x	¾	¾	¼
109. Thigh Width (knit)	¾	x	¾	¾	¼
110. Thigh Width Circumference (woven)	1½	x	1½	1½	¼
113. Leg Opening Width (knit)	⅜	x	⅜	⅜	¼
114. Leg Opening Width Circumference (woven)	¾	x	¾	¾	¼

Table 19.6 GRADING CHART FOR GIRLS 7–16

Codes and Terms	7	8	10	12	14	16	Tol +/–
1. Front Length	½	½	x	½	½	½	½
4. Side Length	⅜	⅜	x	⅜	⅜	⅜	½
9. Chest Width (knit)	½	½	x	½	½	½	½
10. Chest Width Circumference (woven)	1	1	x	1	1	1	½
11. Chest Width (raglan sleeve, knit)	⅜	⅜	x	⅜	⅜	⅜	½
12. Chest Width Circumference (raglan sleeve, woven)	¾	¾	x	¾	¾	¾	½
14. Shoulder Width	⅛	⅛	x	⅛	⅛	⅛	¼
19. Waist Width	½	½	x	½	½	½	½
20. Waist Width Circumference	1	1	x	1	1	1	½
26. Bottom Opening/Sweep (knit top)	½	½	x	½	½	½	½
27. Bottom Opening/Sweep Circumference (woven top)	1	1	x	1	1	1	½
36. Sleeve Length Top Armhole (short sleeve to long sleeve)	⅛ – ¼	⅛ – ¼	x	⅛ – ¼	⅛ – ¼	⅛ – ¼	¼
37. Sleeve Length Top Neck (short sleeve to long sleeve)	¼ – ½	¼ – ½	x	¼ – ½	¼ – ½	¼ – ½	¼
40. Straight Armhole Width (knit)	¼	¼	x	¼	¼	¼	¼
41. Straight Armhole Width Circumference (woven)	½	½	x	½	½	½	¼
42. Curved Armhole Width (knit)	¼	¼	x	¼	¼	¼	¼
43. Curved Armhole Width Circumference (woven)	½	½	x	½	½	½	¼
50. Elbow Width (knit)	¼	¼	x	¼	¼	¼	¼
51. Elbow Width Circumference (woven)	½	½	x	½	½	½	¼
52. Sleeve Opening Width (knit) (long sleeve to short & capped)	⅛	⅛	x	⅛	⅛	¼	¼
53. Sleeve Opening Width Circumference (woven) (long sleeve to short & capped)	¼	¼	x	¼	¼	¼	¼
62. Neck Width, No Collar	⅛	⅛	x	⅛	⅛	⅛	¼

Table 19.6 GRADING CHART FOR GIRLS 7–16 *(continued)*							
Codes and Terms	**7**	**8**	**10**	**12**	**14**	**16**	**Tol +/–**
65. Neck Edge Width Circumference (woven)	¼	¼	x	¼	¼	¼	¼
82. Waistband Width (knit)	½	½	x	½	½	½	½
83. Waistband Width Circumference (woven)	1	1	x	1	1	1	½
88. Low Hip Width from Waist (knit)	½	½	x	½	½	½	½
89. Low Hip Width Circumference from Waist (woven)	1	1	x	1	1	1	½
90. Hip Width from HPS (knit)	½	½	x	½	½	½	½
91. Hip Width from HPS Circumference (woven)	1	1	x	1	1	1	½
94. Bottom Opening/Sweep Width	½	½	x	½	½	½	½
95. Bottom Opening/Sweep Width Circumference	1	1	x	1	1	1	½
105. Inseam *(or grade accordingly if an inseam length grade is desired)*	1¼	1¼	x	2	2	2	½
106. Outseam *(or grade accordingly if an inseam length grade is desired and add that measurement to this one)*	1¼	1¼	x	2	2	2	½
107. Front Rise	⅜	⅜	x	⅜	⅜	⅜	¼
108. Back Rise	⅜	⅜	x	⅜	⅜	⅜	¼
109. Thigh Width (knit)	⅜	⅜	x	⅜	⅜	⅜	¼
110. Thigh Width Circumference (woven)	¾	¾	x	¾	¾	¾	¼
113. Leg Opening Width (knit)	⅛	⅛	x	⅛	⅛	⅛	¼
114. Leg Opening Width Circumference (woven)	⅛	⅜	x	⅜	⅜	⅜	¼

Table 19.7 GRADING CHART FOR BOYS 8–20								
Codes and Terms	**S 8**	**10**	**M 12**	**14**	**L 16**	**18**	**XL 20**	**Tol +/–**
1. Front Length	1, ½	½	x	½	1, ½	½	1, ½	½
4. Side Length	1, ½	½	x	½	1, ½	½	1, ½	½
9. Chest Width (knit)	1, ½	½	x	½	1½, ¾	1	2, 1	½
10. Chest Width Circumference (woven)	2, 1	1	x	1	3, 1½	2	4, 2	½
11. Chest Width (raglan sleeve, knit)	1, ½	½	x	½	1½, ¾	1	2, 1	½
12. Chest Width Circumference (raglan sleeve, woven)	2, 1	1	x	1	3, 1½	2	4, 2	½
14. Shoulder Width	¼, ⅛	⅛	x	⅛	¼, ⅛	⅛	¼, ⅛	¼
19. Waist Width	1, ½	½	x	½	1½, ¾	1	2, 1	½
20. Waist Width Circumference	2, 1	1	x	1	3, 1½	2	4, 2	½
26. Bottom Opening/Sweep (knit top)	1, ½	½	x	½	1½, ¾	1	2, 1	½
27. Bottom Opening/Sweep Circumference (woven top)	2, 1	1	x	1	3, 1½	2	4, 2	½
36. Sleeve Length Top Armhole (short sleeve to long sleeve)	¼ – ½ ⅛ – ¼	⅛ – ¼	x	⅛ – ¼	¼ – ½ ⅛ – ¼	⅛ – ¼	¼ – ½ ⅛ – /¼	½
37. Sleeve Length Top Neck (short sleeve to long sleeve)	⅜ – ⅝ ¼ – ½	¼ – ½	x	¼ – ½	⅜ – ⅝ ¼ – ½	¼ – ½	⅜ – ⅝ ½ – ½	½

(continued)

Table 19.7 GRADING CHART FOR BOYS 8–20 *(continued)*

Codes and Terms	S 8	10	M 12	14	L 16	18	XL 20	Tol +/–
40. Straight Armhole Width (knit)	½, ¼	¼	x	¼	½, ¼	¼	½, ¼	¼
41. Straight Armhole Width Circumference (woven)	1, ½	½	x	½	1, ½	½	1, ½	¼
42. Curved Armhole Width (knit)	¾, ⅜	⅜	x	⅜	¾, ⅜	⅜	¾, ⅜	¼
43. Curved Armhole Width Circumference (woven)	1½, ¾	¾	x	¾	1½, ¾	¾	1½, ¾	¼
50. Elbow Width (knit)	¼, ⅛	⅛	x	⅛	¼, ⅛	⅛	¼, ⅛	¼
51. Elbow Width Circumference (woven)	½, ¼	¼	x	¼	½, ¼	¼	½, ¼	¼
52. Sleeve Opening Width (knit) (long sleeve to short & capped)	¼, ⅛	⅛	x	⅛	¼, ⅛	⅛	¼, ⅛	¼
53. Sleeve Opening Width Circumference (woven) (long sleeve to short & capped)	½, ¼	¼	x	¼	½, ¼	¼	½, ¼	¼
62. Neck Width, No Collar	½, ¼	¼	x	¼	¾, 3/8	¼	½, ¼	¼
65. Neck Edge Width Circumference (woven)	¾, ⅜	⅜	x	¼	¾, ⅜	¼	¾, ⅜	¼
82. Waistband Width (knit)	1, ½	½	x	¾	1½, ¾	1	2, 1	½
83. Waistband Width Circumference (woven)	2, 1	1	x	1½	3, 1½	2	4, 2	½
92. Hip Seat Width (knit pant)	1, ½	½	x	1	1, ½	1	2, 1	½
93. Hip Seat Width Circumference (woven pant)	2, 1	1	x	1½	3, 1½	2	4, 2	½
105. Inseam (or grade accordingly if an inseam length grade is desired)	2½, 1¼	1¼	x	1½	3, 1½	1½	4, 2	½
106. Outseam (or grade accordingly if an inseam length grade is desired and add that measurement to this one)	2½, 1¼	1¼	x	1½	3, 1½	1½	4, 2	½
107. Front Rise	¾, ⅜	⅜	x	⅜	¾, ⅜	⅜	¾, ⅜	¼
108. Back Rise	¾, ⅜	¾	x	⅜	¾, ⅜	⅜	¾, ⅜	¼
109. Thigh Width (knit)	¾, ⅜	⅜	x	⅜	¾, ⅜	⅜	¾, ⅜	¼
110. Thigh Width Circumference (woven)	1½, ¾	¾	x	¾	1½, ¾	¾	1½, ¾	¼
113. Leg Opening Width (knit)	½, ¼	¼	x	¼	½, ¼	¼	½, ¼	¼
114. Leg Opening Width Circumference (woven)	¾, ⅜	⅜	x	⅜	¾, ⅜	⅜	¾, ⅜	¼

When grading junior sizes use the misses/women's wear grade rules.

CODE AND TERM	4	6	8	10	12	14	16	18	TOL. +/–
1. Front Length	–1/4	–1/4	–1/4	X	+1/4	+1/4	+1/4	+1/4	1/2
2. Center Front Length	–1/4	–1/4	–1/4	X	+1/4	+1/4	+1/4	+1/4	1/2
3. Center Back Length	–1/4	–1/4	–1/4	X	+1/4	+1/4	+1/4	+1/4	1/2
4. Side Length	–1/4	–1/4	–1/4	X	+1/4	+1/4	+1/4	+1/4	1/4
5. Front Bodice Length	–1/4	–1/4	–1/4	X	+1/4	+1/4	+1/4	+1/4	1/4
6. Center Front Bodice length	–1/4	–1/4	–1/4	X	+1/4	+1/4	+1/4	+1/4	1/4
7. Center Back Bodice length	–1/4	–1/4	–1/4	X	+1/4	+1/4	+1/4	+1/4	1/4
8. Side Seam Bodice Length	–1/4	–1/4	–1/4	X	+1/4	+1/4	+1/4	+1/4	1/4
9. Chest Width (knit)	–1/2	–1/2	–1/2	X	+3/4	+3/4	+3/4	+1	1/4
10. Chest Width Circumference (woven)	–1	–1	–1	X	+1 1/2	+1 1/2	+1 1/2	+2	1/2
11. Chest Width (raglan sleeve, knit)	–1/2	–1/2	–1/2	X	+3/4	+3/4	+3/4	+1	1/4
12. Chest Width Circumference (raglan sleeve, woven)	–1	–1	–1	X	+1 1/2	+1 1/2	+1 1/2	+2	1/2
13. Across Shoulder	–1/4	–1/4	–1/4	X	+3/8	+3/8	+3/8	+1/2	1/4
14. Shoulder Width	–0	–1/8	–0	X	+1/8	+1/8	+1/8	+1/4	1/4
15. Across Chest	–1/4	–1/4	–1/4	X	+3/8	+3/8	+3/8	+1/2	1/4
16. Across Back	–1/4	–1/4	–1/4	X	+3/8	+3/8	+3/8	+1/2	1/4
17. Across Chest Center Armhole	–1/4	–1/4	–1/4	X	+3/8	+3/8	+3/8	+1/2	1/4
18. Across Back Center Armhole	–1/4	–1/4	–1/4	X	+3/8	+3/8	+3/8	+1/2	1/4
19. Waist Width (knit)	–1/2	–1/2	–1/2	X	+3/4	+3/4	+3/4	+1	1/4
20. Waist Width Circumference (woven)	–1	–1	–1	X	1 1/2	1 1/2	1 1/2	2	1/2
21. Bottom Band Width (knit top)	–1/2	–1/2	–1/2	X	+3/4	+3/4	+3/4	+1	1/4
22. Bottom Band Circumference (woven top)	–1	–1	–1	X	+1 1/2	+1 1/2	+1 1/2	+2	1/2
23. Bottom Band Width Stretched (knit top)	–1/2	–1/2	–1/2	X	+3/4	+3/4	+3/4	+1	1/4
24. Bottom Band Width Circumference Stretched (woven top)	–1	–1	–1	X	+1 1/2	+1 1/2	+1 1/2	+2	1/2
25. Bottom Band/Ribbing Height (knit or woven top)	–0	–0	–0	X	+0	+0	+0	+0	1/8
26. Bottom Opening/Sweep (knit top)	–1/2	–1/2	–1/2	X	+3/4	+3/4	+3/4	+1	1/4
27. Bottom Opening/Sweep Width Circumference (woven top)	–1	–1	–1	X	+1 1/2	+1 1/2	+1 1/2	+2	1/2

(continued)

Table 19.8 GRADING CHART FOR JUNIORS AND MISSY/WOMAN *(continued)*

CODE AND TERM	4	6	8	10	12	14	16	18	TOL. +/–
28. Vented Bottom Opening/Sweep Width (knit top)	–1/2	–1/2	–1/2	X	+3/4	+3/4	+3/4	+1	1/4
29. Vented Bottom Opening/Sweep Width Circumference (woven top)	–1	–1	–1	X	+1 1/2	+1 1/2	+1 1/2	+2	1/2
30. Circular Bottom Opening/Sweep Width (knit top)	–1/2	–1/2	–1/2	X	+3/4	+3/4	+3/4	+1	1/4
31. Circular Bottom Opening/Sweep Width Circumference (woven top)	–1	–1	–1	X	+1 1/2	+1 1/2	+1 1/2	+2	1/2
32. Yoke Width Front	–1/4	–1/4	–1/4	X	+3/8	+3/8	+3/8	+1/2	1/4
33. Yoke Width Back	–1/4	–1/4	–1/4	X	+3/8	+3/8	+3/8	+1/2	1/4
34. Yoke Depth Front	–0	–0	–0	X	+0	+0	+0	+0	1/8
35. Yoke Back Depth	–0	–0	–0	X	+0	+0	+0	+0	1/8
36. Sleeve Length Top Armhole (Short Sleeve to Long Sleeve)	–1/8-1/4	–1/8-1/4	–1/8-1/4	X	–1/8-1/4	–1/8-1/4	–1/8-1/4	–1/8-1/4	3/8
37. Sleeve Length Top Neck (Short Sleeve to Long Sleeve)	–1/4-1/2	–1/4-1/2	–1/4-1/2	X	–1/4-1/2	–1/4-1/2	–1/4-1/2	–1/4-1/2	3/8
38. Sleeve Length Center Back (Short Sleeve to Long Sleeve)	–1/4-1/2	–1/4-1/2	–1/4-1/2	X	–1/4-1/2	–1/4-1/2	–1/4-1/2	–1/4-1/2	3/8
39. Sleeve Length Underarm (Short Sleeve to Long Sleeve)	–1/8-1/4	–1/8-1/4	–1/8-1/4	X	–1/8-1/4	–1/8-1/4	–1/8-1/4	–1/8-1/4	3/8
40. Straight Armhole Width (knit)	–1/4	–1/4	–1/4	X	+3/8	+3/8	+3/8	+1/2	1/4
41. Straight Armhole Width Circumference (woven)	–1/2	–1/2	–1/2	X	+5/8	+5/8	+5/8	+3/4	3/8
42. Curved Armhole Width (knit)	–1/4	–1/4	–1/4	X	+3/8	+3/8	+3/8	+1/2	1/4
43. Curved Armhole Width Circumference (woven)	–1/2	–1/2	–1/2	X	+5/8	+5/8	+5/8	+3/4	3/8
44. Armhole Front *(Or Use: Grade Accordingly)*	–1/4	–1/4	–1/4	X	+1/4	+1/4	+1/4	+1/4	1/4
45. Armhole Back *(Or Use: Grade Accordingly)*	–1/4	–1/4	–1/4	X	+1/4	+1/4	+1/4	+1/4	1/4
46. Armhole Width Straight (knit)	–1/4	–1/4	–1/4	X	+3/8	+3/8	+3/8	+1/2	1/4
47. Armhole Width Circumference Straight (woven)	–1/2	–1/2	–1/2	X	+5/8	+5/8	+5/8	+3/4	3/8
48. Muscle Width (knit) (Regular Sleeve vs Dolman Sleeve)	–1/8-1/4	–1/8-1/4	–1/8-1/4	X	+1/4-3/8	+1/4-3/8	+1/4-3/8	+3/8-1/2	1/8
49. Muscle Width Circumference (woven) (Regular Sleeve vs Dolman Sleeve)	–1/8-1/4	–1/8-1/4	–1/8-1/4	X	+1/4-3/8	+1/4-3/8	+1/4-3/8	+3/8-1/2	1/4
50. Elbow Width (knit)	–1/8	–1/8	–1/8	X	+1/8	+1/8	+1/8	+1/4	1/8
51. Elbow Width Circumference (woven)	–1/4	–1/4	–1/4	X	+3/8	+3/8	+3/8	+1/2	1/4
52. Sleeve Opening Width (knit) (Long Sleeve to Short & Capped)	–1/8-1/4	–1/8-1/4	–1/8-1/4	X	+1/8-1/4	+1/8-1/4	+1/8-1/4	+1/4-3/8	1/8
53. Sleeve Opening Width Circumference (woven) (Long Sleeve to Short & Capped)	–1/4-1/2	–1/4-1/2	–1/4-1/2	X	+1/4-1/2	+1/4-1/2	+1/4-1/2	+1/2-5/8	1/4
54. Sleeve Opening Width Stretched (knit) (Long Sleeve to Short & Capped)	–1/8-1/4	–1/8-1/4	–1/8-1/4	X	+1/8-1/4	+1/8-1/4	+1/8-1/4	+1/4-3/8	1/8

CODE AND TERM	4	6	8	10	12	14	16	18	TOL. +/–
55. Sleeve Opening Width Circumference Stretched (woven) (Long Sleeve to Short & Capped)	–1/4-1/2	–1/4-1/2	–1/4-1/2	X	–1/4-1/2	–1/4-1/2	–1/4-1/2	–1/2-3/4	1/4
56. Cuff Length Sleeve	–1/4	–1/4	–1/4	X	+1/4	+1/4	+1/4	+1/4	1/4
57. Cuff/Ribbing Height Sleeve	–0	–0	–0	X	+0	+0	+0	+0	1/8
58. Neck Depth Front (garments with a plain front/asymmetrical front opening)	-0-1/4	-0-1/4	-0-1/4	X	-0-1/4	-0-1/4	-0-1/4	-0-1/4	1/8
59. Neck Depth Center Front (garments with a center front opening)	-0-1/4	-0-1/4	-0-1/4	X	-0-1/4	-0-1/4	-0-1/4	-0-1/4	1/8
60. Neck Drop Front	-0-1/4	-0-1/4	-0-1/4	X	-0-1/4	-0-1/4	-0-1/4	-0-1/4	1/8
61. Neck Drop Back *Depending on Style*	-0-1/4	-0-1/4	-0-1/4	X	-0-1/4	-0-1/4	-0-1/4	-0-1/4	1/8
62. Neck Width, No Collar	–1/8	–1/8	–1/8	X	+1/4	+1/4	+1/4	+1/4	1/8
63. Neck Width, Collar	–1/8	–1/8	–1/8	X	+1/4	+1/4	+1/4	+1/4	1/8
64. Neck Edge Width (knit)	–1/8	–1/8	–1/8	X	+1/4	+1/4	+1/4	+1/4	1/8
65. Neck Edge Width Circumference (woven)	–1/4	–1/4	–1/4	X	+3/8	+3/8	+3/8	+3/8	1/4
66. Neck Edge Width, Stretched (knit)	–1/8	–1/8	–1/8	X	+1/4	+1/4	+1/4	+1/4	1/8
67. Neck Edge Width Circumference, Stretched (woven)	–1/4	–1/4	–1/4	X	+3/8	+3/8	+3/8	+3/8	1/4
68. Neck Base (knit)	–1/8	–1/8	–1/8	X	+1/4	+1/4	+1/4	+1/4	1/8
69. Neck Base Circumference (woven)	–1/4	–1/4	–1/4	X	+3/8	+3/8	+3/8	+3/8	1/4
70. Neckband Length	–1/4	–1/4	–1/4	X	+3/8	+3/8	+3/8	+3/8	1/4
71. Collar Length	–1/4	–1/4	–1/4	X	+3/8	+3/8	+3/8	+3/8	1/4
72. Collar Height	–0	–0	–0	X	+0	+0	+0	+0	1/8
73. Collar Band Height	–0	–0	–0	X	+0	+0	+0	+0	1/16
74. Collar Point Length	–0	–0	–0	X	+0	+0	+0	+0	1/8
75. Collar Point Spread (pointed collars only) *(Or Use: Grade Accordingly)*	–1/16	–1/16	–1/16	X	+1/16	+1/16	+1/16	+1/16	1/4
76. Lapel Width	–	–	–	X	–	–	–	–	–
A. Notched	–0	–0	–0	X	+0	+0	+0	+0	1/8
B. Without Notches	–0	–0	–0	X	+0	+0	+0	+0	1/8
77. Center Front Extension *(Or Use: Grade Accordingly)*	–0	–0	–0	X	+0	+0	+0	+0	1/8
78. Placket Length *(Or Use: Grade Accordingly)*	–0	–0	–0	X	+0	+0	+0	+0	1/4
79. Placket Width	–0	–0	–0	X	+0	+0	+0	+0	1/8

(continued)

Table 19.8 GRADING CHART FOR JUNIORS AND MISSY/WOMAN *(continued)*

CODE AND TERM	4	6	8	10	12	14	16	18	TOL. +/–
80. Keyhole Length *(Or Use: Grade Accordingly)*	–0	–0	–0	X	+0	+0	+0	+0	1/8
81. Waistband Depth	–0	–0	–0	X	+0	+0	+0	+0	1/8
82. Waistband Width (knit)	–1/2	–1/2	–1/2	X	+3/4	+3/4	+3/4	+1	1/4
83. Waistband Width Circumference (woven)	–1	–1	–1	X	+1 1/2	+1 1/2	+1 1/2	+2	1/2
84. Waistband Width Stretched (knit)	–1/2	–1/2	–1/2	X	+3/4	+3/4	+3/4	+1	1/4
85. Waistband Width Circumference Stretched (woven)	–1	–1	–1	X	+1 1/2	+1 1/2	+1 1/2	+2	1/2
86. High Hip Width (knit)	–1/2	–1/2	–1/2	X	+3/4	+3/4	+3/4	+1	1/4
87. High Hip Width Circumference (woven)	–1	–1	–1	X	+1 1/2	+1 1/2	+1 1/2	+2	1/2
88. Low Hip Width From Waist (knit)	–1/2	–1/2	–1/2	X	+3/4	+3/4	+3/4	+1	1/4
89. Low Hip Width Circumference From Waist (woven)	–1	–1	–1	X	+1 1/2	+1 1/2	+1 1/2	+2	1/2
90. Hip Width From HPS (knit)	–1/2	–1/2	–1/2	X	+3/4	+3/4	+3/4	+1	1/4
91. Hip Width From HPS Circumference (woven)	–1	–1	–1	X	+1 1/2	+1 1/2	+1 1/2	+2	1/2
92. Hip Seat Width (knit pant)	–1/2	–1/2	–1/2	X	+3/4	+3/4	+3/4	+1	1/4
93. Hip Seat Width Circumference (woven pant)	–1	–1	–1	X	+1 1/2	+1 1/2	+1 1/2	+2	1/2
94. Bottom Opening/Sweep Width (knit skirt)	–1/2	–1/2	–1/2	X	+3/4	+3/4	+3/4	+1	1/4
95. Bottom Opening/Sweep Width Circumference (woven skirt)	–1	–1	–1	X	+1 1/2	+1 1/2	+1 1/2	+2	1/2
96. Vented Bottom Opening/Sweep Width (knit skirt)	–1/2	–1/2	–1/2	X	+3/4	+3/4	+3/4	+1	1/4
97. Vented Bottom Opening/Sweep Width Circumference (woven skirt)	–1	–1	–1	X	+1 1/2	+1 1/2	+1 1/2	+2	1/2
98. Circular Bottom Opening/Sweep Width (knit skirt)	–1/2	–1/2	–1/2	X	+3/4	+3/4	+3/4	+1	1/4
99. Circular Bottom Opening/Sweep Width Circumference (woven skirt)	–1	–1	–1	X	+1 1/2	+1 1/2	+1 1/2	+2	1/2
100. Center Front Skirt Length	–0	–0	–0	X	+0	+0	+0	+0	3/8
101. Center Back Skirt Length	–0	–0	–0	X	+0	+0	+0	+0	3/8
102. Side Skirt Length	–0	–0	–0	X	+0	+0	+0	+0	3/8
103. Skirt/Pant Yoke Depth Front	–0	–0	–0	X	+0	+0	+0	+0	1/4
104. Skirt/Pant Yoke Depth Back	–0	–0	–0	X	+0	+0	+0	+0	1/4
105. Inseam — Or grade accordingly if an inseam length grade is desired (add above length to this meadurement	–0	–0	–0	X	+0	+0	+0	+0	3/8
106. Outseam	–1/8	–1/4	–1/4	X	+1/4	+1/4	+1/4	+3/8	3/8

CODE AND TERM	4	6	8	10	12	14	16	18	TOL. +/–
107. Front Rise	–1/4	–3/8	–3/8	X	+3/8	+3/8	+3/8	+1/2	3/8
108. Back Rise	–1/4	–3/8	–3/8	X	+3/8	+3/8	+3/8	+3/8	3/8
109. Thigh Width (knit)	–1/4	–3/8	–3/8	X	+1/2	+1/2	+1/2	+1/2	1/4
110. Thigh Width Circumference (woven)	–1/2	–3/4	–3/4	X	+1	+1	+1	+1 1/4	3/8
111. Knee Width (knit) *(Or use: Grade accordingly)*	–1/4	–1/4	–1/4	X	+3/8	+3/8	+3/8	+1/2	1/4
112. Knee Width Circumference (woven) *(Or use: Grade accordingly)*	–3/8	–1/2	–1/2	X	+3/4	+3/4	+3/4	+1	3/8
113. Leg Opening Width (knit)	–1/8	–1/8	–1/8	X	+1/4	+1/4	+1/4	+1/4	1/8
114. Leg Opening Width Circumference (woven)	–1/4	–1/4	–1/4	X	+3/8	+3/8	+3/8	+3/8	1/4
115. Vented Leg Opening Width (knit)	–1/8	–1/8	–1/8	X	+1/4	+1/4	+1/4	+1/4	1/8
116. Vented Leg Opening Circumference (woven)	–1/4	–1/4	–1/4	X	+3/8	+3/8	+3/8	+3/8	1/4
117. Leg Opening Width Stretched (knit)	–1/8	–1/8	–1/8	X	+1/4	+1/4	+1/4	+1/4	1/8
118. Leg Opening Width Stretched Circumference (woven)	–1/4	–1/4	–1/4	X	+3/8	+3/8	+3/8	+3/8	1/4
119. Cuff Height Pants	–0	–0	–0	X	+0	+0	+0	+0	1/8
120. Bottom Band/Ribbing Height pants	–0	–0	–0	X	+0	+0	+0	+0	1/8
121. Fly/Zipper	—	—	—	X	—	—	—	—	—
A. Length *(Or use: Grade accordingly)*	–0	–0	–0	X	+0	+0	+0	+0	1/4
B. Fly/Zipper width	–0	–0	–0	X	+0	+0	+0	+0	1/8
122. Vent/Slit	—	—	—	X	—	—	—	—	—
A. Height *(Or use: Grade accordingly)*	–0	–0	–0	X	+0	+0	+0	+0	1/4
B. Width	–0	–0	–0	X	+0	+0	+0	+0	1/8
123. Pleat Depth	–0	–0	–0	X	+0	+0	+0	+0	1/8
124. Distance Between Pleats	*	*	*	X	*	*	*	*	1/16
125. Applied Pocket Height	–0	–0	–0	X	+0	+0	+0	+0	1/8
126. Applied Pocket Width	–0	–0	–0	X	+0	+0	+0	+0	1/8
127. Pocket Opening	–0	–0	–0	X	+0	+0	+0	+0	1/4
128. Belt Length	—	—	—	X	—	—	—	—	—
A. Total	-1	-1	-1	X	+1 1/2	+1 1/2	+1 1/2	+2	1/2

* *Grade Accordingly*

(continued)

Table 19.8 GRADING CHART FOR JUNIORS AND MISSY/WOMAN *(continued)*

CODE AND TERM		4	6	8	10	12	14	16	18	TOL. +/–
B. Circumference		–1	–1	–1	X	+1 1/2	+1 1/2	+1 1/2	+2	1/2
129. Belt Width (or height)		–0	–0	–0	X	+0	+0	+0	+0	1/8
130. Belt Loop Length		–0	–0	–0	X	+0	+0	+0	+0	1/8
131. Belt Loop Width		–0	–0	–0	X	+0	+0	+0	+0	1/8
132. Tie Length		*	*	*	X	*	*	*	*	1/4
133. Tie Width		—	—	—	—	—	—	—	—	—
A. Straight		–0	–0	–0	X	+0	+0	+0	+0	1/8
B. Contoured		–0	–0	–0	X	+0	+0	+0	+0	1/8
134. Flounce/Ruffle Width		–0	–0	–0	X	+0	+0	+0	+0	1/8
135. Strap Length		*	*	*	X	*	*	*	*	1/4
136. Strap Width		–0	–0	–0	X	+0	+0	+0	+0	1/8
137. Front Hood Length		–0	–0	–0	X	+0	+0	+0	+0	1/4
138. Back Hood Length		–0	–0	–0	X	+0	+0	+0	+0	1/4
139. Hood Width		*	*	*	X	*	*	*	*	1/4
140. Flange Depth		*	*	*	X	*	*	*	*	1/8
141. Shoulder Pad Length	*(May use: Grade accordingly or give a spec grade if a certain size is desired)*	–0	–0	–0	X	+0	+0	+0	+0	1/8
142. Shoulder Pad Width		–0	–0	–0	X	+0	+0	+0	+0	1/8
143. Straight Edge Shoulder Pad Height		–0	–0	–0	X	+0	+0	+0	+0	1/16
144. Curved Edge Shoulder Pad Height		–0	–0	–0	X	+0	+0	+0	+0	1/16
145. Shoulder Pad Placement		*	*	*	X	*	*	*	*	1/8
146. Pleats Placement		—	—	—	—	—	—	—	—	—
A. Front Pleat Top		*	*	*	X	*	*	*	*	1/4
B. Back Pleat Top		*	*	*	X	*	*	*	*	1/4
C. Front Pleat Skirt/Pant		*	*	*	X	*	*	*	*	1/4
147. Button Placement		*	*	*	X	*	*	*	*	1/8
148. Pocket Placement		—	—	—	—	—	—	—	—	—
A. Top Pocket Vertical		*	*	*	X	*	*	*	*	1/8

* Grade accordingly

CODE AND TERM	4	6	8	10	12	14	16	18	TOL. +/–
B. Top Pocket Horizontal	*	*	*	X	*	*	*	*	1/8
C. Front Bottom Pocket Vertical	*	*	*	X	*	*	*	*	1/8
D. Front Bottom Pocket Horizontal	*	*	*	X	*	*	*	*	1/8
E. Back Bottom Pocket Vertical	*	*	*	X	*	*	*	*	1/8
F. Back Bottom Pocket Horizontal	*	*	*	X	*	*	*	*	1/8
G. Pocket From Side Seam	*	*	*	X	*	*	*	*	1/8
149. Belt Loop	—	—	—	—	—	—	—	—	—
A. Length	–0	–0	–0	X	+0	+0	+0	+0	1/8
B. Width	–0	–0	–0	X	+0	+0	+0	+0	1/8
C. Placement C.F.	*	*	*	X	*	*	*	*	1/8
D. Placement C.B.	*	*	*	X	*	*	*	*	1/8
150. Dart Length Front	*	*	*	X	*	*	*	*	1/8
Dart Placement: Center Front & Center Back	*	*	*	X	*	*	*	*	1/8
A. High Point Shoulder Bust Dart	*	*	*	X	*	*	*	*	1/8
B. Center Front Bust Dart	*	*	*	X	*	*	*	*	1/8
C. Side Seam Bust Dart	*	*	*	X	*	*	*	*	1/8
D. High Point Shoulder Princess Dart	*	*	*	X	*	*	*	*	1/8
E. Center Front Princess Dart	*	*	*	X	*	*	*	*	1/8
F. Center Front Skirt/Pant	*	*	*	X	*	*	*	*	1/8
G. Center Back Skirt/Pant	*	*	*	X	*	*	*	*	1/8
151. Front Torso Length (Jumpsuits and One-Piece Garments)	—	—	—	—	—	—	—	—	—
A. Garments With a Front Opening Relaxed *(Or use "adjust accordingly" if other length measurements have already been given.)*	–1/2	–1/2	–1/2	X	+1	+1	+1	+1	5/8
B. Garments With a Front Opening Extended	–1/2	–1/2	–1/2	X	+1	+1	+1	+1	5/8
C. Garments With a Plain Front, No front Opening, Relaxed	–1/2	–1/2	–1/2	X	+1	+1	+1	+1	5/8
D. Garments With a Plain Front, No Front Opening, Extended	–1/2	–1/2	–1/2	X	+1	+1	+1	+1	5/8
152. Back Torso Length (Jumpsuits and One-Piece Garments)	—	—	—	—	—	—	—	—	—
A. Relaxed *(Or use "adjust accordingly" if other length measurements have already been given.)*	–1/2	–1/2	–1/2	X	+1	+1	+1	+1	5/8

* *Grade accordingly*

(continued)

Table 19.8 GRADING CHART FOR JUNIORS AND MISSY/WOMAN *(continued)*

CODE AND TERM	4	6	8	10	12	14	16	18	TOL. +/–
B. Extended *(Or use "adjust accordingly" if other length measurements have already been given.)*	–1/2	–1/2	–1/2	X	+1	+1	+1	+1	5/8
153. Total Garment Length Front	–1/2	–1/2	–1/2	X	+1	+1	+1	+1	7/8
154. Total Garment Length Back	–1/2	–1/2	–1/2	X	+1	+1	+1	+1	7/8
155. Crotch Width	–1/8	–1/8	–1/8	X	+1/8	+1/8	+1/8	+1/8	1/8

(continued)

CODE AND TERM	S	M	L	XL	TOL. +/–
1. Front Length	–1/2	X	+1/2	+1/2	1/2
2. Center Front Length	–1/2	X	+1/2	+1/2	1/2
3. Center Back Length	–1/2	X	+1/2	+1/2	1/2
4. Side Length	–1/2	X	+1/2	+1/2	1/4
5. Front Bodice Length	–1/2	X	+1/2	+1/2	1/4
6. Center Front Bodice length	–1/2	X	+1/2	+1/2	1/4
7. Center Back Bodice length	–1/2	X	+1/2	+1/2	1/4
8. Side Seam Bodice Length	–1/2	X	+1/2	+1/2	1/4
9. Chest Width (knit)	–1	X	+1 1/2	+2	3/8
10. Chest Width Circumference (woven)	–2	X	+3	+4	3/4
11. Chest Width (raglan sleeve, knit)	–1	X	+1 1/2	+2	3/8
12. Chest Width Circumference (raglan sleeve, woven)	–2	X	+3	+4	3/4
13. Across Shoulder	–1/2	X	+3/4	+1	1/4
14. Shoulder Width	–1/8	X	+1/4	+1/2	1/4
15. Across Chest	–1/2	X	+3/4	+1	1/4
16. Across Back	–1/2	X	+3/4	+1	1/4
17. Across Chest Center Armhole	–1/2	X	+3/4	+1	1/4
18. Across Back Center Armhole	–1/2	X	+3/4	+1	1/4
19. Waist Width (knit)	–1	X	+1 1/2	+2	3/8
20. Waist Width Circumference (woven)	–2	X	+3	+4	3/4
21. Bottom Band Width (knit top)	–1	X	+1 1/2	+2	3/8
22. Bottom Band Circumference (woven top)	–2	X	+3	+4	3/4
23. Bottom Band Width Stretched (knit top)	–1	X	+1 1/2	+2	3/8
24. Bottom Band Width Circumference Stretched (woven top)	–2	X	+3	+4	3/4
25. Bottom Band/Ribbing Height (knit or woven top)	–0	X	+0	+0	1/8
26. Bottom Opening/Sweep (knit top)	–1	X	+1 1/2	+2	3/8
27. Bottom Opening/Sweep Width Circumference (woven top)	–2	X	+3	+4	3/4

(continued)

Table 19.8 GRADING CHART FOR JUNIORS AND MISSY/WOMAN *(continued)*

CODE AND TERM	S	M	L	XL	TOL. +/–
28. Vented Bottom Opening/Sweep Width (knit top)	–1	X	+1 1/2	+2	3/8
29. Vented Bottom Opening/Sweep Width Circumference (woven top)	–2	X	+3	+4	3/4
30. Circular Bottom Opening/Sweep Width (knit top)	–1	X	+1 1/2	+2	3/8
31. Circular Bottom Opening/Sweep Width Circumference (woven top)	–2	X	+3	+4	3/4
32. Yoke width Front	–1/2	X	+3/4	+1	1/4
33. Yoke Width Back	–1/2	X	+3/4	+1	1/4
34. Yoke Depth Front	–0	X	+0	+0	1/8
35. Yoke Back Depth	–0	X	+0	+0	1/8
36. Sleeve Length Top Armhole (Short Sleeve to Long Sleeve)	–1/4-1/2	X	+1/4-1/2	+1/2-5/8	3/8
37. Sleeve Length Top Neck (Short Sleeve to Long Sleeve)	–3/8-5/8	X	+3/8-5/8	+5/8-3/4	3/8
38. Sleeve Length Center Back (Short Sleeve to Long Sleeve)	–3/8-5/8	X	+3/8-5/8	+5/8-3/4	3/8
39. Sleeve Length Underarm	–1/4-1/2	X	+1/4-1/2	+1/2-5/8	3/8
40. Straight Armhole Width (knit)	–1/2	X	+3/4	+1	1/4
41. Straight Armhole Width Circumference (woven)	–1	X	+1 1/4	+2	3/8
42. Curved Armhole Width (knit)	–1/2	X	+3/4	+1	1/4
43. Curved Armhole Width Circumference (woven)	–1	X	+1 1/4	+1 3/4	3/8
44. Armhole Front *(Or Use: Grade Accordingly)*	–1/2	X	+1/2	+3/4	1/4
45. Armhole Back *(Or Use: Grade Accordingly)*	–1/2	X	+1/2	+3/4	1/4
46. Armhole Width Straight (knit)	–1/2	X	+3/4	+1	1/4
47. Armhole Width Circumference Straight (woven)	–1	X	+1 1/4	+1 1/2	3/8
48. Muscle Width (knit) (Regular Sleeve vs Dolman Sleeve)	–1/4-1/2	X	+3/8-5/8	+3/4-1	1/8
49. Muscle Width Circumference (woven) (Regular Sleeve vs Dolman Sleeve)	–1/4-1/2	X	+3/8-5/8	+3/4-1	1/4
50. Elbow Width (knit)	–1/4	X	+1/2	+3/4	1/8
51. Elbow Width Circumference (woven)	–1/2	X	+3/4	+1	1/4
52. Sleeve Opening Width (knit) (Long Sleeve to Short & Capped)	–1/4-1/2	X	+1/4-1/2	+1/2-3/4	1/8
53. Sleeve Opening Width Circumference (woven) (Long Sleeve to Short & Capped)	–1/2-1	X	+1/2-1	+3/4-1	1/4
54. Sleeve Opening Width Stretched (knit) (Long Sleeve to Short & Capped)	–1/4-1/2	X	+1/4-1/2	+1/2-3/4	1/8

CODE AND TERM	S	M	L	XL	TOL. +/–
55. Sleeve Opening Width Circumference Stretched (woven) (Long Sleeve to Short & Capped)	–1/2-1	X	+1/2-1	+3/4-1	1/4
56. Cuff Length Sleeve	–1/2	X	+1/2	+1/2	1/4
57. Cuff/Ribbing Height Sleeve	–0	X	+0	+0	1/8
58. Neck Depth Front (garments with a plain front/asymmetrical front opening)	–0-1/4	X	+0-1/4	+0-1/4	1/8
59. Neck Depth Center Front (garments with a center front opening)	–0-1/4	X	+0-1/4	+0-1/4	1/8
60. Neck Drop Front	–0-1/4	X	+0-1/4	+0-1/4	1/8
61. Neck Drop Back *Depending on Style*	–0-1/4	X	+0-1/4	+0-1/4	1/8
62. Neck Width, No Collar	–3/8	X	+3/8	+1/2	1/8
63. Neck Width, Collar	–3/8	X	+3/8	+1/2	1/8
64. Neck Edge Width (knit)	–3/8	X	+3/8	+1/2	1/8
65. Neck Edge Width Circumference (woven)	–3/4	X	+3/4	+1	1/8
66. Neck Edge Width, Stretched (knit)	–3/8	X	+3/8	+1	1/8
67. Neck Edge Width Circumference, Stretched (woven)	–3/4	X	+3/4	+1	1/4
68. Neck Base (knit)	–3/8	X	+3/8	+1/2	1/8
69. Neck Base Circumference (woven)	–3/4	X	+3/4	+1	1/4
70. Neckband Length	–3/4	X	+3/4	+1	1/4
71. Collar Length	–3/4	X	+3/4	+1	1/4
72. Collar Height	–0	X	+0	+0	1/8
73. Collar Band Height	–0	X	+0	+0	1/16
74. Collar Point Length	–0	X	+0	+0	1/8
75. Collar Point Spread (pointed collars only) *(Or Use: Grade Accordingly)*	–1/8	X	+1/8	+1/8	1/4
76. Lapel Width	—	—	—	—	—
A. Notched	–0	X	+0	+0	1/8
B. Without Notches	–0	X	+0	+0	1/8
77. Center Front Extension *(Or Use: Grade Accordingly)*	–0	X	+0	+0	1/8
78. Placket Length *(Or Use: Grade Accordingly)*	–0	X	+0	+0	1/4
79. Placket Width	–0	X	+0	+0	1/8

(continued)

Table 19.8 GRADING CHART FOR JUNIORS AND MISSY/WOMAN *(continued)*

CODE AND TERM	S	M	L	XL	TOL. +/–
80. Keyhole Length *(Or Use: Grade Accordingly)*	–0	X	+0	+0	1/8
81. Waistband Depth	–0	X	+0	+0	1/8
82. Waistband Width (knit)	–1	X	+1 1/2	+2	3/8
83. Waistband Circumference (woven)	–2	X	+3	+4	3/4
84. Waistband Width Stretched (knit)	–1	X	+1 1/2	+2	3/8
85. Waistband Width Circumference Stretched (woven)	–2	X	+3	+4	3/4
86. High Hip Width (knit)	–1	X	+1 1/2	+2	3/8
87. High Hip Width Circumference (woven)	–2	X	+3	+4	3/4
88. Low Hip Width From Waist (knit)	–1	X	+1 1/2	+2	3/8
89. Low Hip Width Circumference From Waist (woven)	–2	X	+3	+4	3/4
90. Hip Width From HPS (knit)	–1	X	+1 1/2	+2	3/8
91. Hip Width From HPS Circumference (woven)	–2	X	+3	+4	3/4
92. Hip Seat Width (knit pant)	–1	X	+1 1/2	+2	3/8
93. Hip Seat Width Circumference (woven pant)	–2	X	+3	+4	3/4
94. Bottom Opening/Sweep Width (knit skirt)	–1	X	+1 1/2	+2	3/8
95. Bottom Opening/Sweep Width Circumference (woven skirt)	–2	X	+3	+4	3/4
96. Vented Bottom Opening/Sweep Width (knit skirt)	–1	X	+1 1/2	+2	3/8
97. Vented Bottom Opening/Sweep Width Circumference (woven skirt)	–2	X	+3	+4	3/4
98. Circular Bottom Opening/Sweep Width (knit skirt)	–1	X	+1 1/2	+2	3/8
99. Circular Bottom Opening/Sweep Width Circumference (woven skirt)	–2	X	+3	+4	3/4
100. Center Front Skirt Length	–0	X	+0	+0	3/8
101. Center Back Skirt Length	–0		+0	+0	3/8
102. Side Skirt Length	–0	X	+0	+0	3/8
103. Skirt/Pant Yoke Depth Front	–0	X	+0	+0	1/4
104. Skirt/Pant Yoke Depth Back	–0	X	+0	+0	1/4
105. Inseam — Or grade accordingly if an inseam length grade is desired (add above length to this meadurement	–0	X	+0	+0	3/8
106. Outseam	–1/2	X	+1/2	+3/4	3/8

CODE AND TERM	S	M	L	XL	TOL. +/–
107. Front Rise	–3/4	X	+3/4	+3/4	3/8
108. Back Rise	–3/4	X	+3/4	+3/4	3/8
109. Thigh Width (knit)	–3/4	X	+1	+1	1/4
110. Thigh Width Circumference (woven)	–1 1/2	X	+2	+2 1/2	3/8
111. Knee Width (knit) *(Or use: Grade accordingly)*	–3/8	X	+3/4	+1	1/4
112. Knee Width Circumference (woven) *(Or use: Grade accordingly)*	–1	X	+1 1/2	+2	3/8
113. Leg Opening Width (knit)	–1/4	X	+3/8	+3/8	1/8
114. Leg Opening Width Circumference (woven)	–1/2	X	+3/4	+3/4	1/4
115. Vented Leg Opening Width (knit)	–1/4	X	+3/8	+3/8	1/8
116. Vented Leg Opening Circumference (woven)	–1/2	X	+3/4	+3/4	1/4
117. Leg Opening Width Stretched (knit)	–1/4	X	+3/8	+3/8	1/8
118. Leg Opening Width Stretched Circumference (woven)	–1/2	X	+3/4	+3/4	1/4
119. Cuff Height Pants	–0	X	+0	+0	1/8
120. Bottom Band/Ribbing Height pants	–0	X	+0	+0	1/8
121. Fly/Zipper	—	—	—	—	—
A. Length *(Or use: Grade accordingly)*	–0	X	+0	+0	1/4
B. Fly/Zipper width	–0	X	+0	+0	1/8
122. Vent/Slit	—	—	—	—	—
A. Height *(Or use: Grade accordingly)*	–0	X	+0	+0	1/4
B. Width	–0	X	+0	+0	1/8
123. Pleat Depth	–0	X	+0	+0	1/8
124. Distance Between Pleats	*	*	*	*	1/16
125. Applied Pocket Height	–0	X	+0	+0	1/8
126. Applied Pocket Width	–0	X	+0	+0	1/8
127. Pocket Opening	–0	X	+0	+0	1/4
128. Belt Length	—	—	—	—	—
A. Total	–2	X	+3	+4	3/4

** Grade Accordingly*

(continued)

Table 19.8 GRADING CHART FOR JUNIORS AND MISSY/WOMAN *(continued)*

CODE AND TERM		S	M	L	XL	TOL. +/–
B. Circumference		–2	X	+3	+4	3/4
129. Belt Width (or height)		–0	X	+0	+0	1/8
130. Belt Loop Length		–0	X	+0	+0	1/8
131. Belt Loop Width		–0	X	+0	+0	1/8
132. Tie Length		*	X	*	*	1/4
133. Tie Width		—	—	—	—	—
A. Straight		–0	X	+0	+0	1/8
B. Contoured		–0	X	+0	+0	1/8
134. Flounce/Ruffle Width		–0	X	+0	+0	1/8
135. Strap Length		*	X	*	*	1/4
136. Strap Width		–0	X	+0	+0	1/8
137. Front Hood Length		–0	X	+0	+0	1/4
138. Back Hood Length		–0	X	+0	+0	1/4
139. Hood Width		*	X	*	*	1/4
140. Flange Depth		*	X	*	*	1/8
141. Shoulder Pad Length	(May use: Grade accordingly or give a spec grade if a certain size is desired)	–0	X	+0	+0	1/8
142. Shoulder Pad Width		–0	X	+0	+0	1/8
143. Straight Edge Shoulder Pad Height		–0		+0	+0	1/16
144. Curved Edge Shoulder Pad Height		–0	X	+0	+0	1/16
145. Shoulder Pad Placement		*	X	*	*	1/8
146. Pleats Placement		—	—	—	—	—
A. Front Pleat Top		*	X	*	*	1/4
B. Back Pleat Top		*	X	*	*	1/4
C. Front Pleat Skirt/Pant		*	X	*	*	1/4
147. Button Placement		*	X	*	*	1/8
148. Pocket Placement		—	—	—	—	—
A. Top Pocket Vertical		*	X	*	*	1/8

CODE AND TERM	S	M	L	XL	TOL. +/–
B. Top Pocket Horizontal	*	X	*	*	1/8
C. Front Bottom Pocket Vertical	*	X	*	*	1/8
D. Front Bottom Pocket Horizontal	*	X	*	*	1/8
E. Back Bottom Pocket Vertical	*	X	*	*	1/8
F. Back Bottom Pocket Horizontal	*	X	*	*	1/8
G. Pocket From Side Seam	*	X	*	*	1/8
149. Belt Loop	—	—	—	—	—
A. Length	–0	X	+0	+0	1/8
B. Width	–0	X	+0	+0	1/8
C. Placement C.F.	*	X	*	*	1/8
D. Placement C.B.	*	X	*	*	1/8
150. Dart Length Front	*	X	*	*	1/8
Dart Placement: Center Front & Center Back	*	X	*	*	1/8
A. High Point Shoulder Bust Dart	*	X	*	*	1/8
B. Center Front Bust Dart	*	X	*	*	1/8
C. Side Seam Bust Dart	*	X	*	*	1/8
D. High Point Shoulder Princess Dart	*	X	*	*	1/8
E. Center Front Princess Dart	*	X	*	*	1/8
F. Center Front Skirt/Pant	*	X	*	*	1/8
G. Center Back Skirt/Pant	*	X	*	*	1/8
151. Front Torso Length (Jumpsuits and One-Piece Garments)	—	—	—	—	—
A. Garments With a Front Opening Relaxed	–1		+2	+2	5/8
B. Garments With a Front Opening Extended *(Or use "adjust accordingly" if other length measurements have already been given.)*	–1	X	+2	+2	5/8
C. Garments With a Plain Front, No front Opening, Relaxed	–1	X	+2	+2	5/8
D. Garments With a Plain Front, No Front Opening, Extended	–1	X	+2	+2	5/8
152. Back Torso Length (Jumpsuits and One-Piece Garments)	—	—	—	—	—
A. Relaxed *(Or use "adjust accordingly" if other length measurements have already been given.)*	–1	X	+2	+2	5/8

* *Grade accordingly*

(continued)

Table 19.8 GRADING CHART FOR JUNIORS AND MISSY/WOMAN *(continued)*

CODE AND TERM	S	M	L	XL	TOL. +/–
B. Extended *(Or use "adjust accordingly" if other length measurements have already been given.)*	–1	X	+2	+2	5/8
153. Total Garment Length Front	–1	X	+2	+2	7/8
154. Total Garment Length Back	–1	X	+2	+2	7/8
155. Crotch Width	–1/4	X	+1/4	+1/4	1/8

Table 19.9 GRADING CHART FOR MEN'S SIZES

Codes and Terms	14	14½	15	15½	16	16½	17	17½	Tol +/–
1. Front Length	–¼	–¼	–¼	X	+¼	+¼	+¼	+¼	½
9. Chest Width (knit)	–1	–1	–1	X	+1	+1	+1	+1	½
10. Chest Width Circumference (woven)	–2	–2	–2	X	+2	+2	+2	+2	1
13. Across Shoulder	–½	–½	–½	X	+½	+½	+½	+½	¼
14. Shoulder Width	–⅛	–⅛	–⅛	X	+⅛	+⅛	+⅛	+⅛	⅛
15. Across Front	–½	–½	–½	X	+½	+½	+½	+½	¼
16. Across Back	–½	–½	–½	X	+½	+½	+½	+½	¼
26. Bottom Opening/Sweep (knit)	–1	–1	–1	X	+1	+1	+1	+1	½
27. Bottom Opening/Sweep Circumference (woven)	–2	–2	–2	X	+2	+2	+2	+2	1
28. Vented Bottom Opening/Sweep (knit)	–1	–1	–1	X	+1	+1	+1	+1	½
29. Vented Bottom Opening/Sweep Circumference (woven)	–2	–2	–2	X	+2	+2	+2	+2	1
36. Sleeve Length Top Armhole (short sleeve to long sleeve)	–¼ – ½	–¼ – ½	–¼ – ½	X	+¼ – ½	+¼ – ½	+¼ – ½	+¼ – ½	½
37. Sleeve Length Top Neck (short sleeve to long sleeve)	–½ – ¾	–½ – ¾	–½ – ¾	X	+½ – ¾	+½ – ¾	+½ – ¾	+½ – ¾	¾
38. Sleeve Length Center Back (short sleeve to long sleeve)	–½ – ¾	–½ – ¾	–½ – ¾	X	+½ – ¾	+½ – ¾	+½ – ¾	+½ – ¾	¾
39. Sleeve Length Underarm (short sleeve to long sleeve)	–¼ – ½	–¼ – ½	–¼ – ½	X	+¼ – ½	+¼ – ½	+¼ – ½	+¼ – ½	½
40. Straight Armhole Width (knit)	–⅜	–⅜	–⅜	X	+½	+½	+½	+½	⅜
41. Straight Armhole Width Circumference (woven)	–¾	–¾	–¾	X	+1	+1	+1	+1	½
42. Curved Armhole Width (knit)	–⅜	–⅜	–⅜	X	+½	+½	+½	+½	⅜
43. Curved Armhole Width Circumference (woven)	–¾	–¾	–¾	X	+1	+1	+1	+1	½
48. Muscle Width (knit) (regular sleeve vs. dolman sleeve)	–¼	–¼	–¼	X	+¼ – ½	+¼ – ½	+¼ – ½	+¼ – ½	¼
49. Muscle Width Circumference (woven) (regular vs. dolman)	–¼ – ½	–¼ – ½	–¼ – ½	X	+¼ – ½	+¼ – ½	+¼ – ½	+¼ – ½	¼
50. Elbow Width (knit)	–¼	–¼	–¼	X	+¼ – ⅜	+¼ – ⅜	+¼ – ⅜	+¼ – ⅜	¼
51. Elbow Width (Circumference)	–⅜	–⅜	–⅜	X	+⅜	+⅜	+⅜	+⅜	¼
52. Sleeve Opening Width (knit) (long to short sleeve)	–⅛ – ¼	–⅛ – ¼	–⅛ – ¼	X	+⅛ – ¼	+⅛ – ¼	+⅛ – ¼	+⅛ – ¼	⅛
53. Sleeve Opening Width Circumference (Woven) (long to short)	–¼ – ½	–¼ – ½	–¼ – ½	X	+¼ – ½	+¼ – ½	+¼ – ½	+¼ – ½	¼
62. Neck Width, No Collar	–¼	–¼	–¼	X	+¼	+¼	+¼	+¼	⅛
63. Neck Width, Collar	–¼	–¼	–¼	X	+¼	+¼	+¼	+¼	⅛
64. Neck Edge Width (knit)	–¼	–¼	–¼	X	+¼	+¼	+¼	+¼	⅛
65. Neck Edge Width Circumference (woven)	–½	–½	–½	X	+½	+½	+½	+½	¼
68. Neck Base (knit)	–¼	–¼	–¼	X	+¼	+¼	+¼	+¼	⅛

(continued)

Table 19.9 GRADING CHART FOR MEN'S SIZES *(continued)*

Codes and Terms	14	14½	15	15½	16	16½	17	17½	Tol +/–
69. Neck Base Circumference (woven)	–½	–½	–½	X	+½	+½	+½	+½	¼
82. Waistband Width (knit)	–1	–1	–1	X	+1	+1	+1	+1	½
83. Waistband Width (circumference)	–2	–2	–2	X	+2	+2	+2	+2	1
92. Hip Seat Width (knit pant)	–1	–1	–1	X	+1	+1	+1	+1	½
93. Hip Seat Width Circumference (woven pant)	–2	–2	–2	X	+2	+2	+2	+2	1
107. Front Rise	–⅜	–⅜	–⅜	X	+⅜	+⅜	+⅜	+⅜	⅜
108. Back Rise	–⅜	–⅜	–⅜	X	+⅜	+⅜	+⅜	+⅜	⅜
109. Thigh Width (knit)	–¼	–¼	–¼	X	+½	+½	+½	+½	¼
110. Thigh Width Circumference (woven)	–½	–½	–½	X	+1	+1	+1	+1	½
111. Knee Width (knit) (or use: Grade accordingly)	–¼	–¼	–¼	X	+¼	+¼	+¼	+¼	⅛
112. Knee Width Circumference (woven) (Or use: Grade accordingly)	–⅜	–⅜	–⅜	X	+½	+½	+½	+½	⅜
113. Leg Opening Width Circumference (knit)	–⅛	–⅛	–⅛	X	+¼	+¼	+¼	+¼	⅛
114. Leg Opening Width Circumference (woven)	–¼	–¼	–¼	X	+⅜	+⅜	+⅜	+⅜	¼
153. Total Garment Length Front	–1½	–1½	–1½	X	+1½	+1½	+1½	+1½	1
154. Total Garment Length Back	–1½	–1½	–1½	X	+1½	+1½	+1½	+1½	

Table 19.9 GRADING CHART FOR MEN'S SIZES

Codes and Terms	S	M	L	XL	Tol +/–
1. Front Length	–½	X	+½	+½	½
9. Chest Width (knit)	–2	X	+2	+2	½
10. Chest Width Circumference (woven)	–4	X	+4	+4	1
13. Across Shoulder	–1	X	+1	+1	¼
14. Shoulder Width	–¼	X	+¼	+¼	⅛
15. Across Front	–1	X	+1	+1	¼
16. Across Back	–1	X	+1	+1	¼
26. Bottom Opening/Sweep (knit)	–2	X	+2	+2	½
27. Bottom Opening/Sweep Circumference (woven)	–4	X	+4	+4	1
28. Vented Bottom Opening/Sweep (knit)	–2	X	+2	+2	½
29. Vented Bottom Opening/Sweep Circumference (woven)	–4	X	+4	+4	1
36. Sleeve Length Top Armhole (short sleeve to long sleeve)	–½ – 1	X	+½ – 1	+½ – 1	½
37. Sleeve Length Top Neck (short sleeve to long sleeve)	–1 – 1½	X	+1 – 1½	+1 – 1½	¾
38. Sleeve Length Center Back (short sleeve to long sleeve)	–1 – 1½	X	+1 – 1½	+1 – 1½	¾
39. Sleeve Length Underarm (short sleeve to long sleeve)	–½ – 1	X	+½ – 1	+½ – 1	½
40. Straight Armhole Width (knit)	–¾	X	+1	+1	⅜

Table 19.9 GRADING CHART FOR MEN'S SIZES *(continued)*					
Codes and Terms	**S**	**M**	**L**	**XL**	**Tol +/–**
41. Straight Armhole Width Circumference (woven)	–1½	X	+2	+2	½
42. Curved Armhole Width (knit)	–¾	X	+1	+1	⅜
43. Curved Armhole Width Circumference (woven)	–1½	X	+2	+2	½
48. Muscle Width (knit) (regular sleeve vs. dolman sleeve)	–½	X	+½ – 1	+½ – 1	¼
49. Muscle Width Circumference (woven) (regular vs. dolman)	–½ – 1	X	+½ – 1	+½ – 1	¼
50. Elbow Width (knit)	–½	X	+½ – ¾	+½ – ¾	¼
51. Elbow Width (Circumference)	–¾	X	+¾	+¾	¼
52. Sleeve Opening Width (knit) (long to short sleeve)	–¼ – ½	X	+¼ – ½	+¼ – ½	⅛
53. Sleeve Opening Width Circumference (woven) (long to short)	–½ – 1	X	+½ – 1	+½ – 1	¼
62. Neck Width, No Collar	–½	X	+½	+½	⅛
63. Neck Width, Collar	–½	X	+½	+½	⅛
64. Neck Edge Width (knit)	–½	X	+½	+½	⅛
65. Neck Edge Width Circumference (woven)	–1	X	+1	+1	¼
68. Neck Base (knit)	–½	X	+½	+½	⅛
69. Neck Base Circumference (woven)	–1	X	+1	+1	¼
82. Waistband Width (knit)	–2	X	+2	+2	½
83. Waistband Width (circumference)	–4	X	+4	+4	1
92. Hip Seat Width (knit pant)	–2	X	+2	+2	½
93. Hip Seat Width Circumference (woven pant)	–4	X	+4	+4	1
107. Front Rise	–¾	X	+¾	+¾	⅜
108. Back Rise	–¾	X	+¾	+¾	⅜
109. Thigh Width (knit)	–½	X	+1	+1	¼
110. Thigh Width Circumference (woven)	–1	X	+2	+2	½
111. Knee Width (knit) (Or use: Grade accordingly)	–½	X	+½	+½	⅛
112. Knee Width Circumference (woven) (Or use: Grade accordingly)	–¾	X	+1	+1	⅜
113. Leg Opening Width Circumference (knit)	–¼	X	+½	+½	⅛
114. Leg Opening Width Circumference (woven)	–½	X	+¾	+¾	¼
153. Total Garment Length Front	–3	X	+3	+3	1
154. Total Garment Length Back	–3	X	+3	+3	1

APPENDIX A

Basic Garment Croquis

How to Use a Garment Croquis

When many people think of a fashion illustration, they think of the creative sketches often seen in magazines. Technical sketches are not those. Technical sketches must be drawn in a format called flat, in other words, without dimension. Every detail from a collar, placket, pocket, button, and topstitch must be illustrated in order to ensure garment accuracy. When creating sketches for size specification and technical design, detail is very important. First garment samples may be drafted from size specifications where the only references are the sketch and the measurements. This section contains 162 flat sketches of the most commonly designed garments. They are classic styles that may be found in the stores at anytime. The garments do not reflect any particular trends in the market and are classic in their fit, not oversized or formfitting. They are all uniform in misses/women's wear proportion, size 8/10 or medium, so the user can trace or copy the garment body to be used as needed. Practical application of the croquis can be expedited as follows:

- They may be used as a guide for illustrating garments under evaluation. Simply trace the croquis that is closest to your garment into the sketch/photo section of your spec sheet, changing style features as needed. Keep in mind your proportions may vary. Adjust, alter, or combine the croquis as needed.
- They may be used to set up a new spec sheet. Trace the croquis into the technical sketch section of your spec sheet. Add the appropriate measurement arrows, fill in the points of measure, and you have a custom-made spec sheet. A blank spec sheet has been added to this section for your use (Figure A.1).

GENERIC SPEC SHEET	STYLE
SEASON:	DESCRIPTION:
LABEL: (SIZE CATEGORY)	
DATE:	
TECHNICAL SKETCH	SKETCH/PHOTO

CODE	POINT OF MEASURE	TOL. +/–								

Figure A.1

GENERIC SPEC SHEET **STYLE**

CODE	POINT OF MEASURE	TOL. +/–								

COMMENTS:

Figure A.1 Continued

Woven Tops

Basic or front buttoning
Bat wing
Body shirt or fitted
Bow
Camisole
Cossack
Cowboy (Western)
Drawstring
Dress
Epaulet
Guayabera
Hawaiian
Ruffle Front
Jabot
Nautical or Middy
Peasant
Peplum
Princess
Stock tie
Tunic
Tuxedo
Oversized
Wrap

Basic or front-buttoning

Bat wing

Body shirt or fitted

Bow

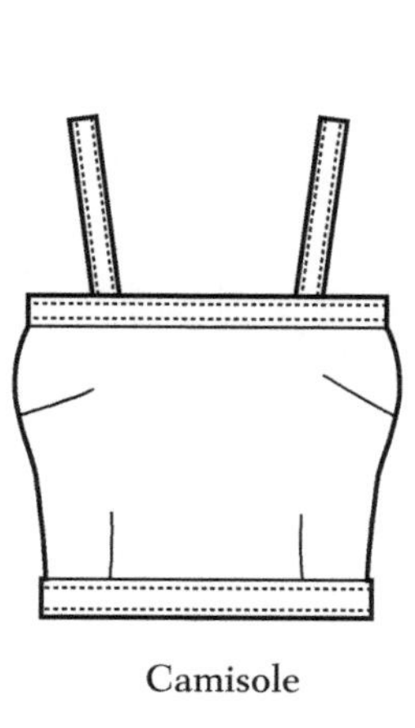
Camisole

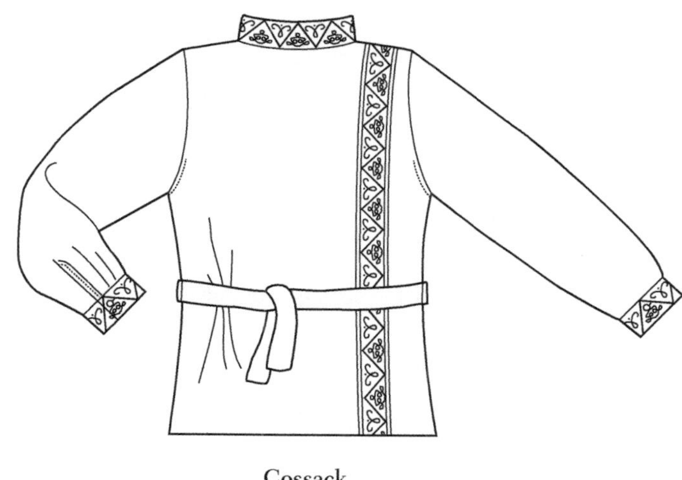
Cossack

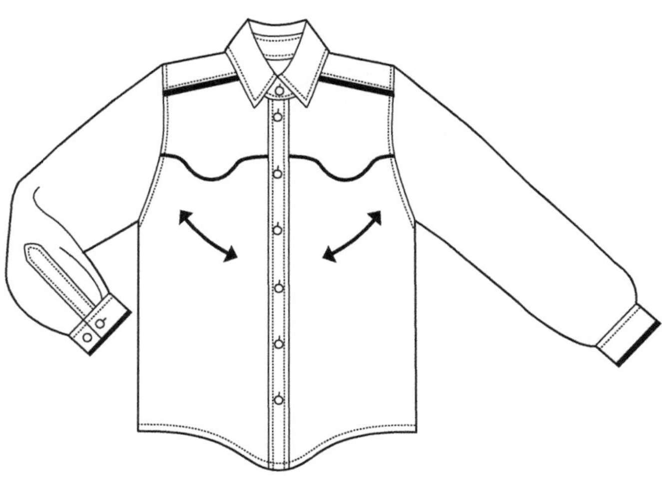
Cowboy (Western)

Drawstring

Dress

Epaulet

Guayabera

Hawaiian

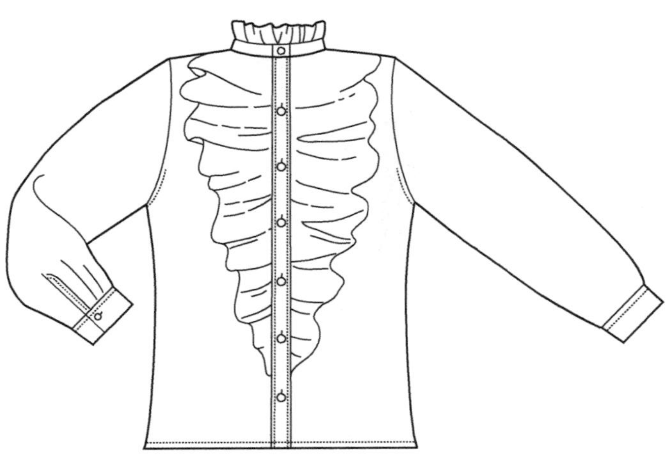

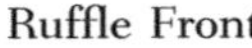

Ruffle Front

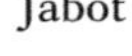

Jabot

Nautical or Middy

Peasant

Peplum
Princess
Stock-tie
Tunic
Tuxedo
Oversized

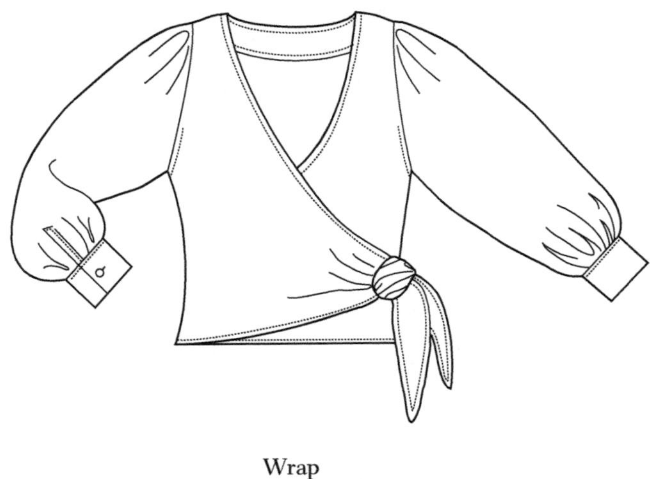

Wrap

Knit Tops

Bat wing
Belted cardigan
Boat neck sweater
Boat neck T-shirt
Capped sleeve
Classic cardigan
Crew neck sweater
Crew neck T-shirt
Cropped
Cowl neck
Dolman sleeve
Flashdance
Golf shirt
Henley
Hoodie
Mock turtleneck
Oversized T-shirt
Sweatshirt
Tank top
Turtleneck
V-neck sweater
V-neck T-shirt
V-neck cardigan
Vest
Wrapped
Wide-banded/shrink

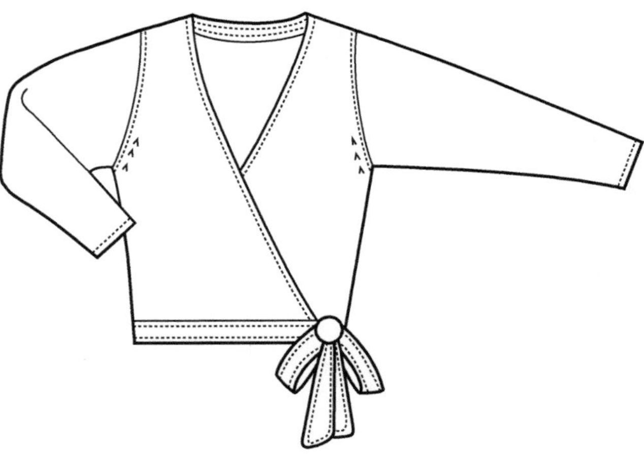

Bat wing

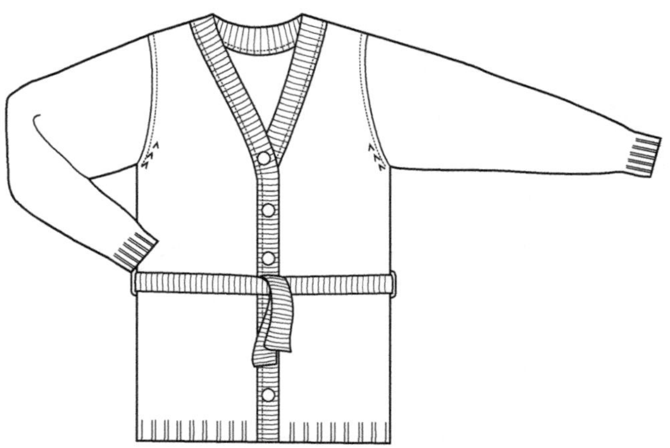

Belted cardigan

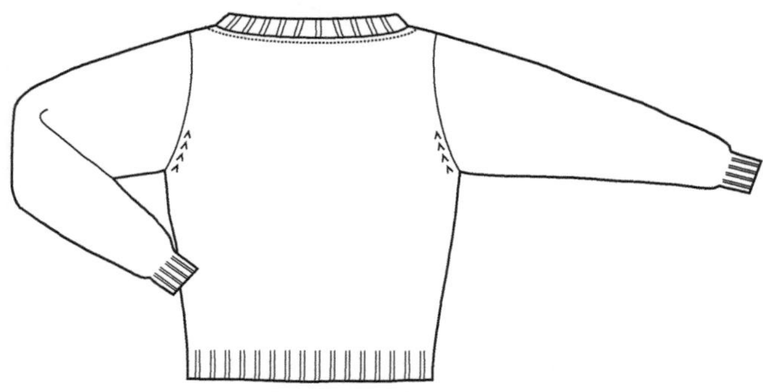

Boat neck sweater

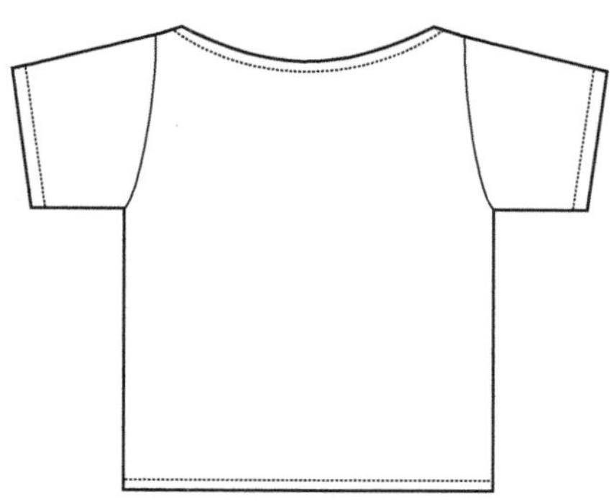

Boat neck T-shirt

Capped sleeve

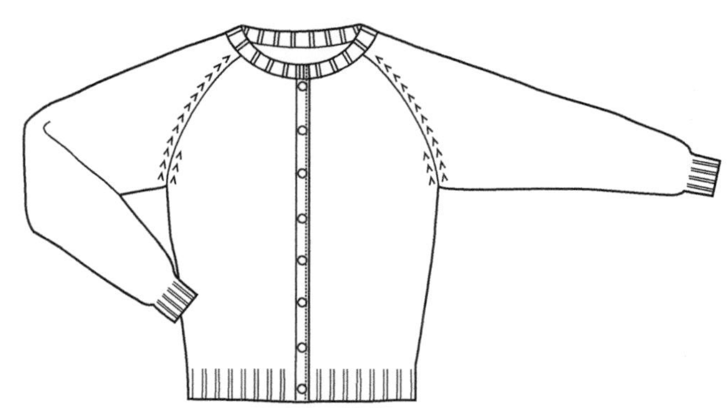

Classic cardigan

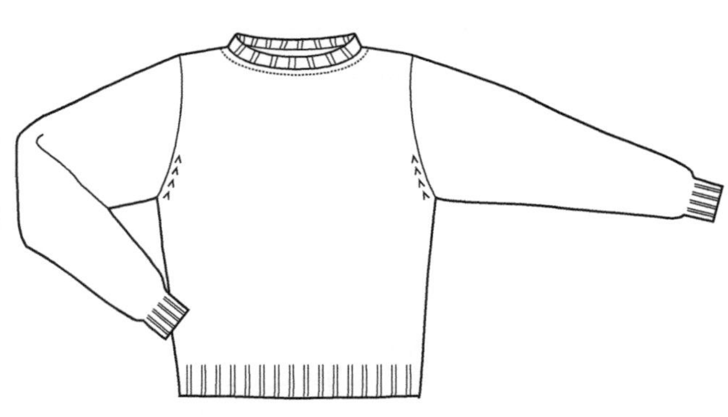

Crew neck sweater

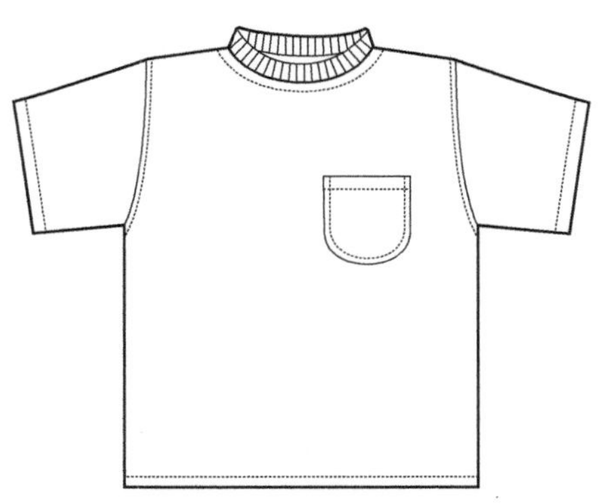

Crew neck T-shirt

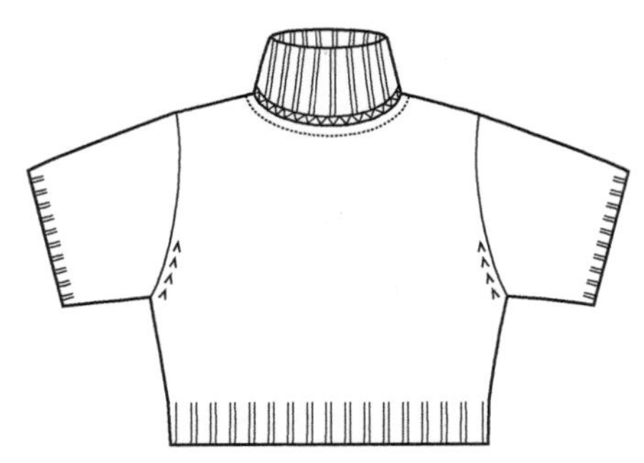

Cropped

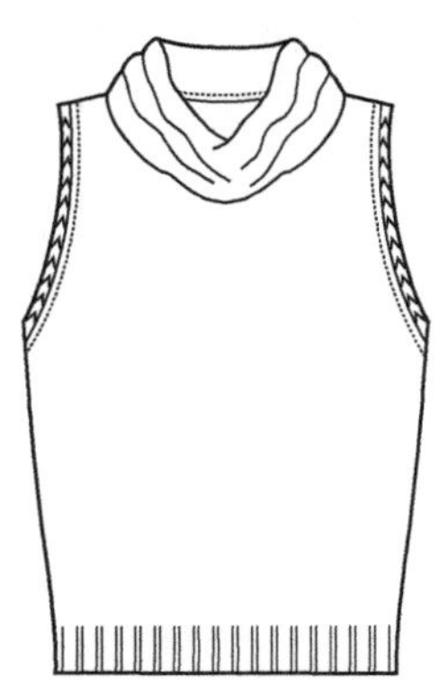

Cowl neck

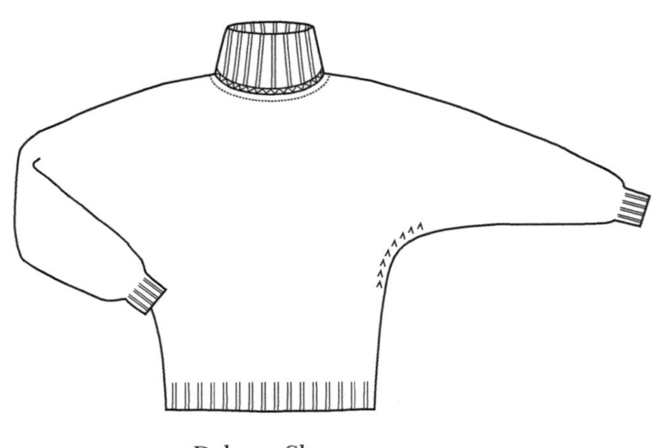

Dolman Sleeve

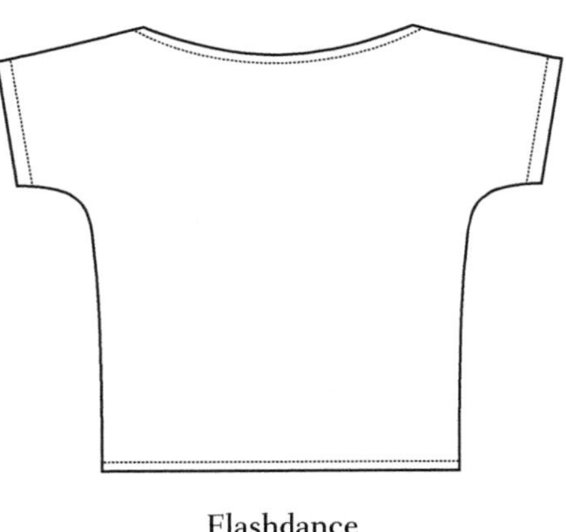

Flashdance

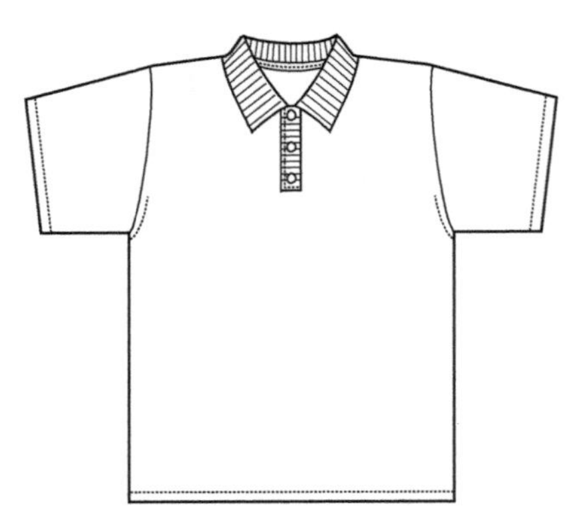

Golf shirt

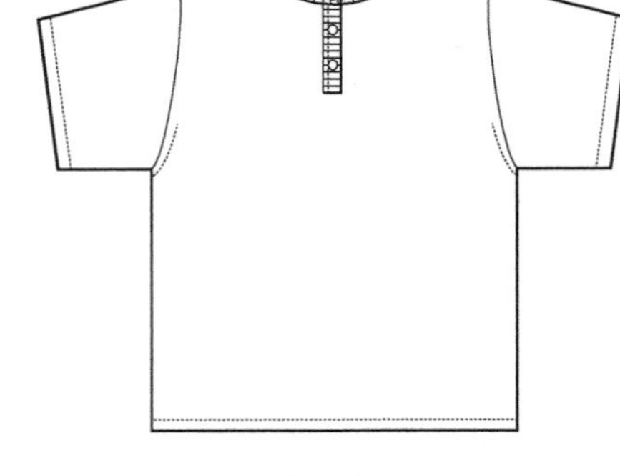

Henley

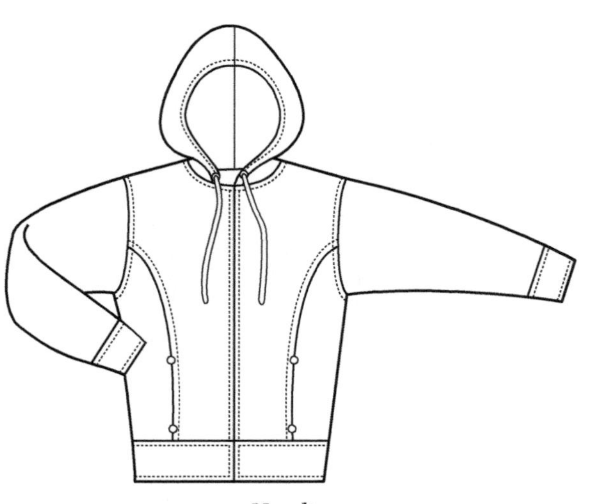

Hoodie

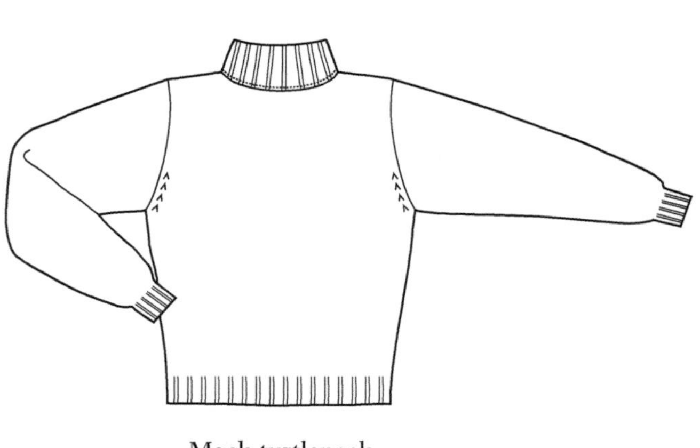

Mock turtleneck

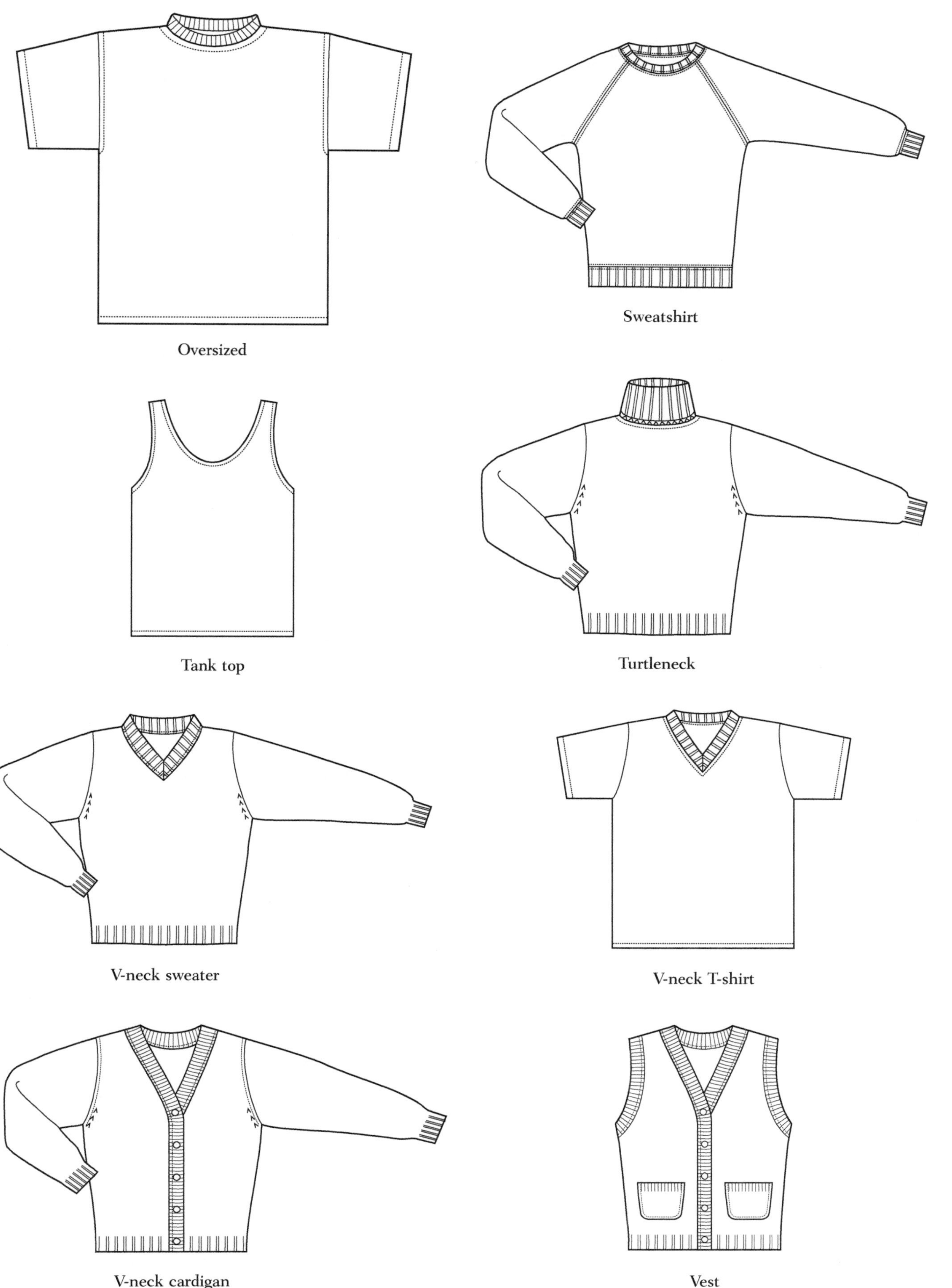
Oversized
Sweatshirt
Tank top
Turtleneck
V-neck sweater
V-neck T-shirt
V-neck cardigan
Vest

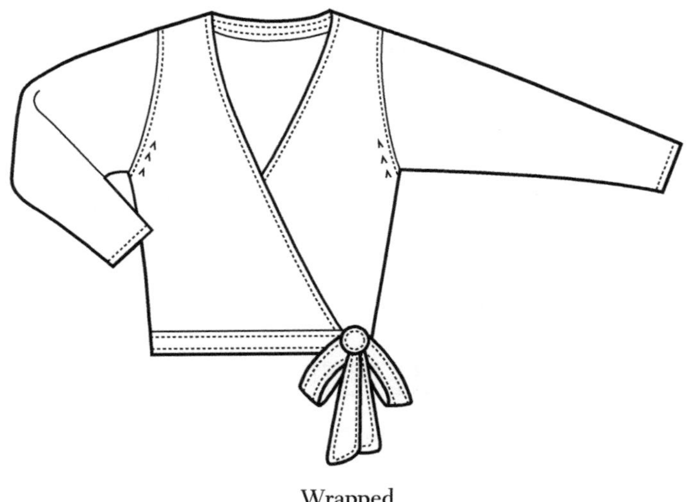
Wrapped

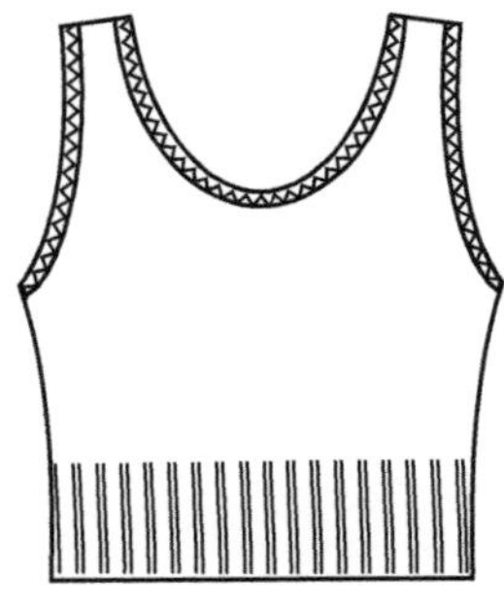
Wide-banded/shrink

Skirts

A-line
Asymmetric
Bubble
Denim
Drawstring
Granny
Gored
High-low
Handkerchief
Kick pleated
Layered/tiered
Pegged
Pleated
Pleated waist
Pull-on
Skirt lengths
Sarong
Slit
Straight
Trumpet
Wrap
Yoke

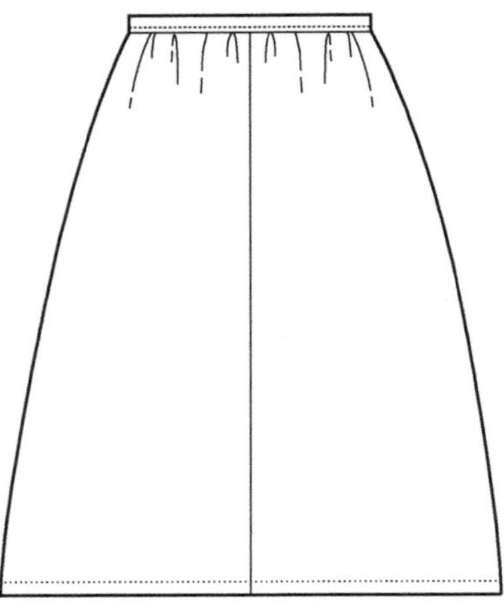
A-line

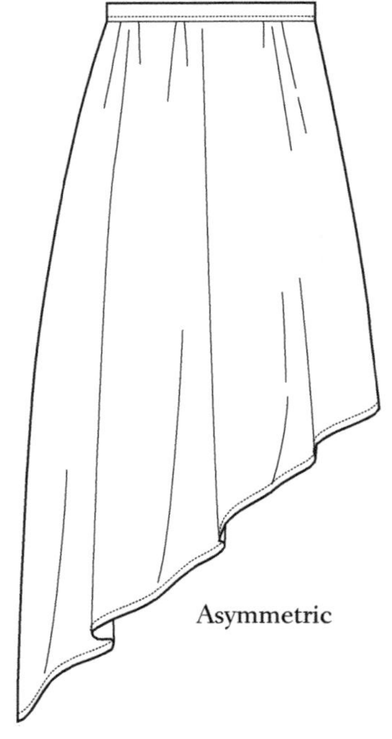
Asymmetric

Bubble
Denim
Drawstring
Granny
Gored
High-low
Handkerchief
Kick pleated
Layered/tiered

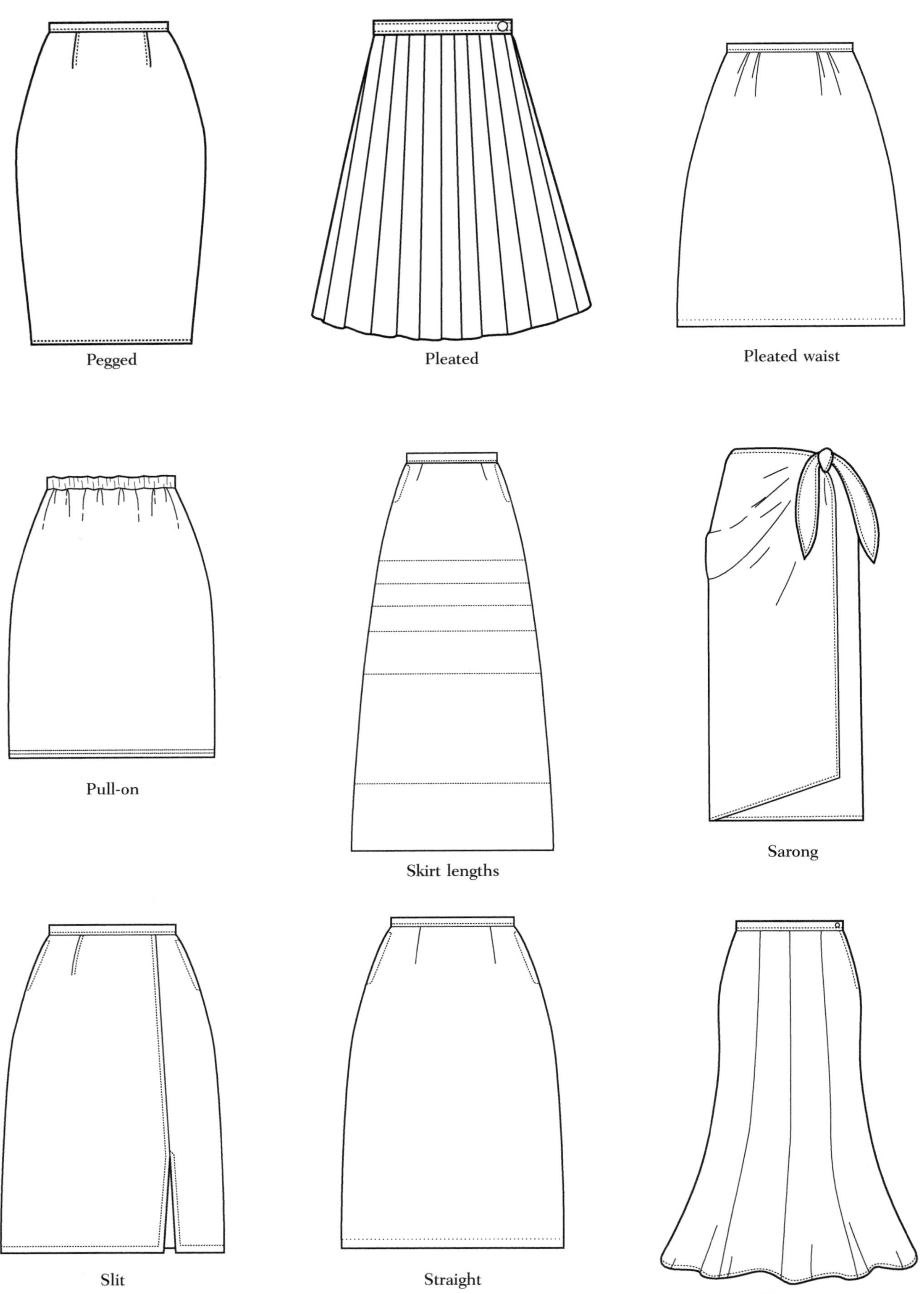
Pegged
Pleated
Pleated waist
Pull-on
Skirt lengths
Sarong
Slit
Straight
Trumpet

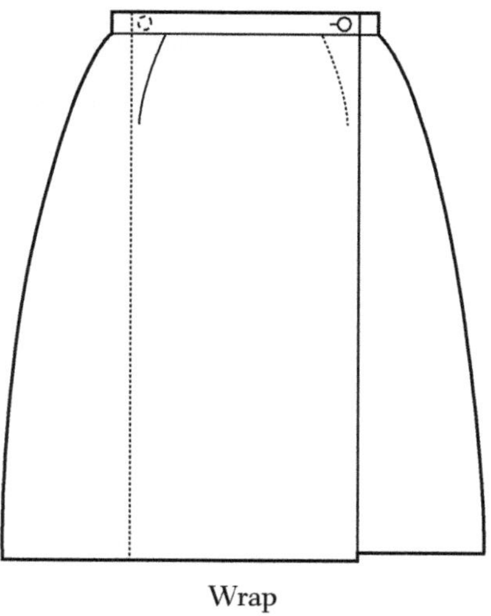
Wrap

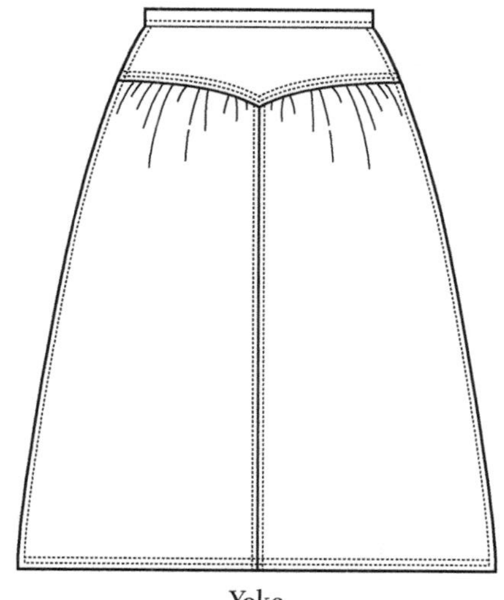
Yoke

Pants

Baggy
Bell-bottoms/flares
Blue jean/denim
Cargo
Continental
Cropped
Cuffed
Drawstring
Harem/dhoti
Hip-hugger
Jodhpur
Knickers
Oxford
Palazzo
Parachute/zippered
Pull-on, elastic/warm-up
Sailor
Skinny
Stirrup
Stovepipe/tapered
Surfer/biker
Western/boot cut

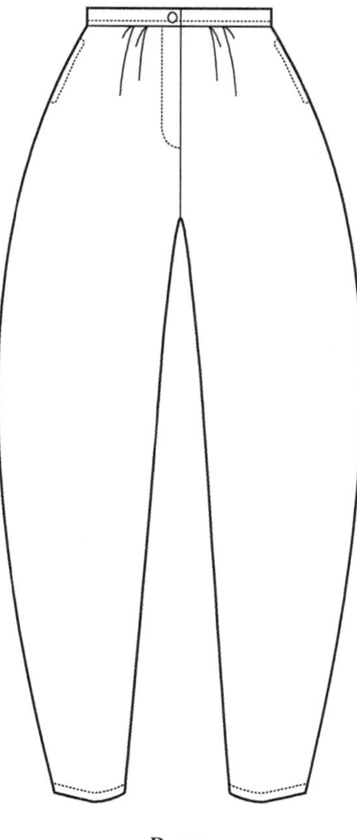
Baggy

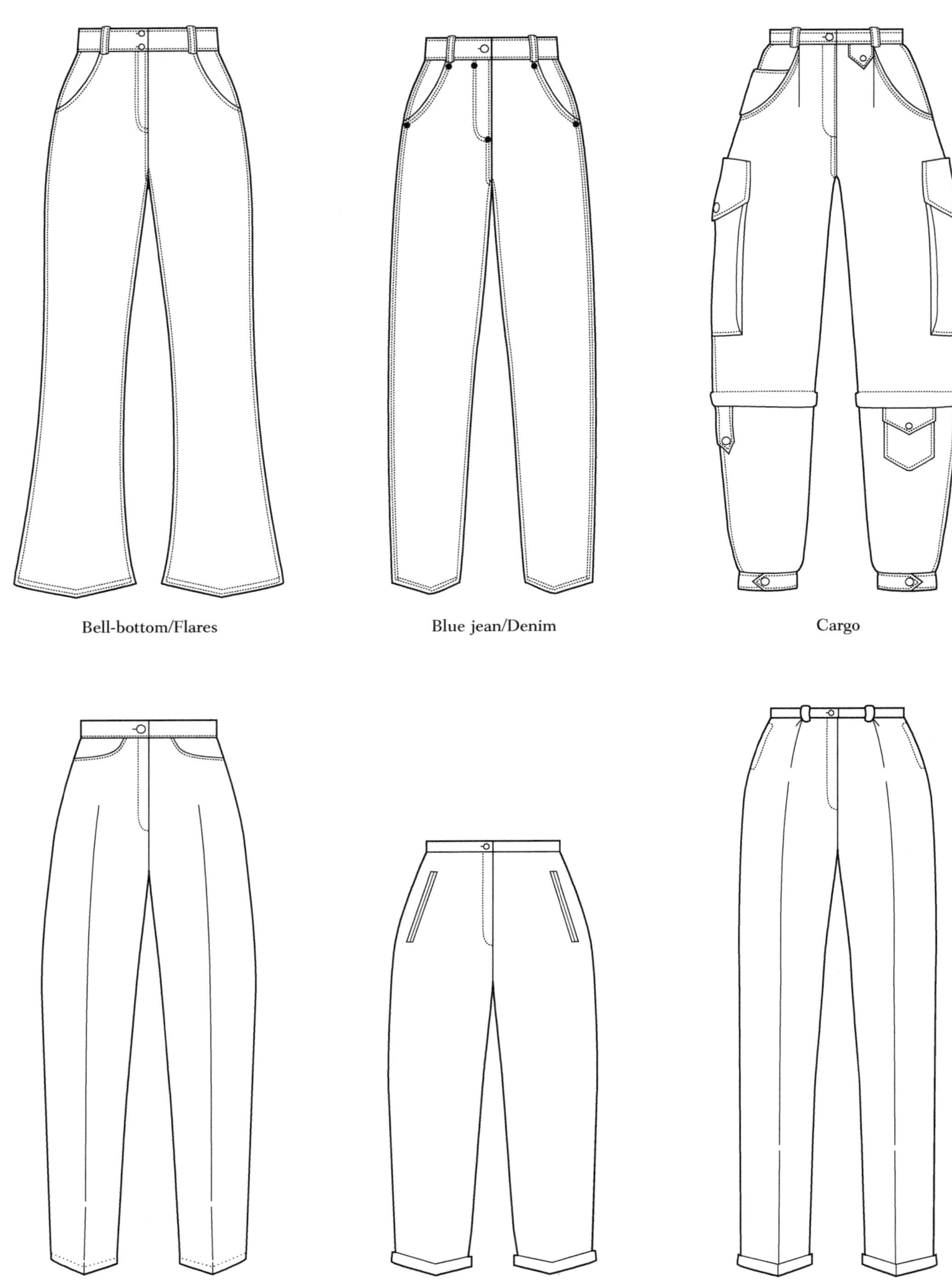
Bell-bottom/Flares
Blue jean/Denim
Cargo
Continental
Cropped
Cuffed

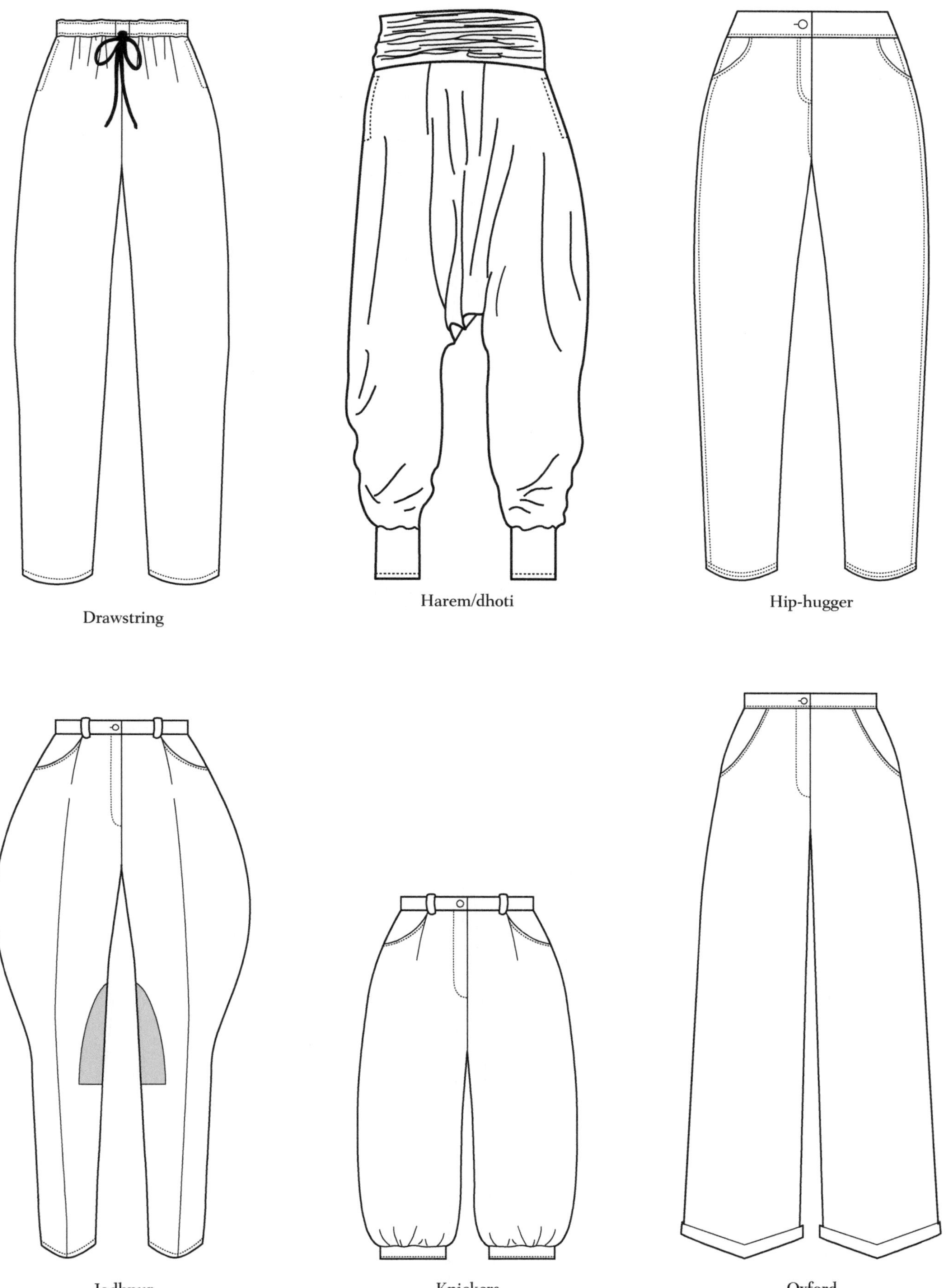
Drawstring
Harem/dhoti
Hip-hugger
Jodhpur
Knickers
Oxford

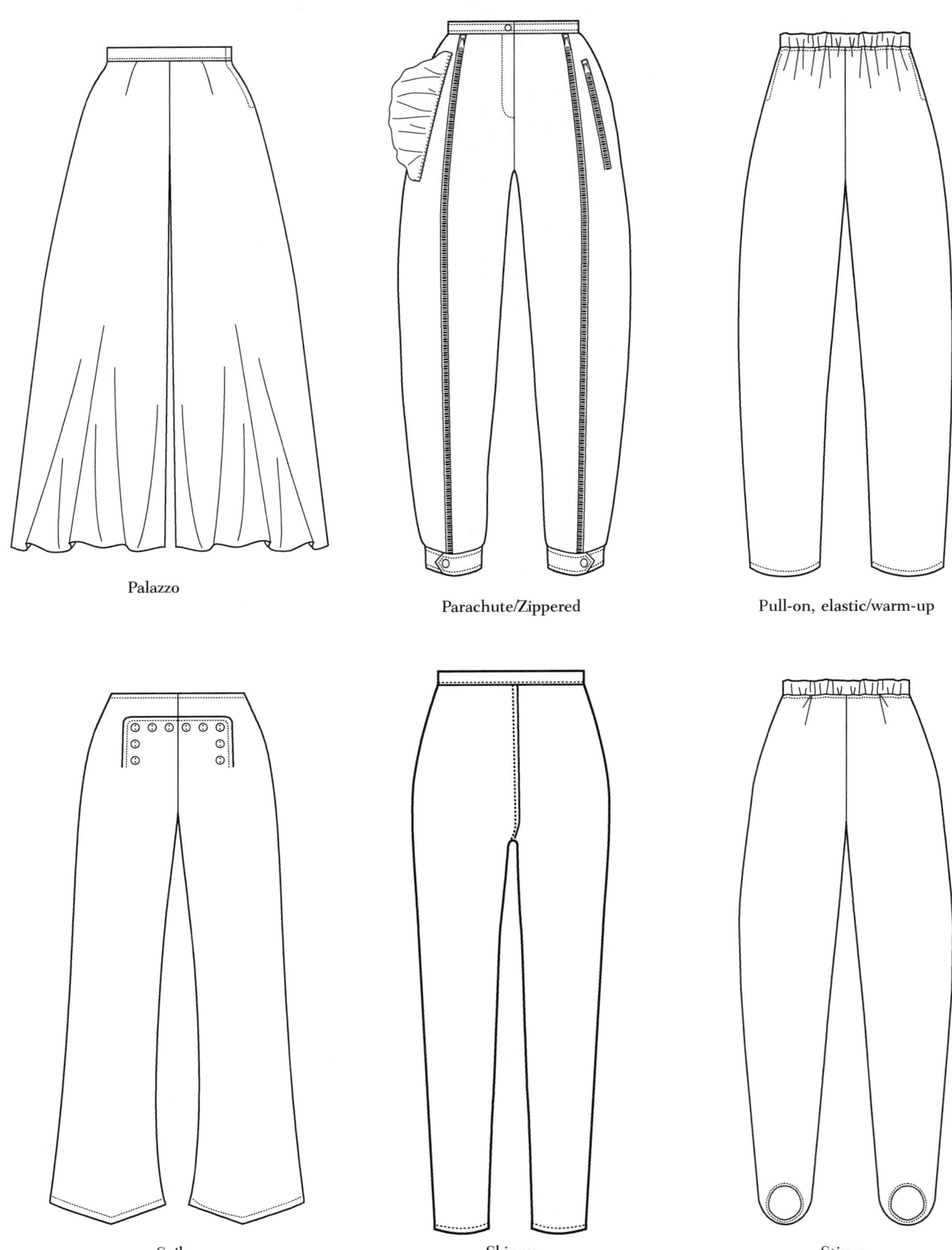
Palazzo
Parachute/Zippered
Pull-on, elastic/warm-up
Sailor
Skinny
Stirrup

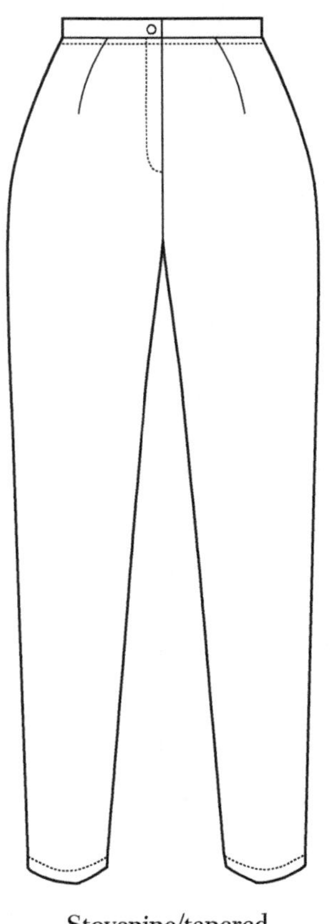

Stovepipe/tapered

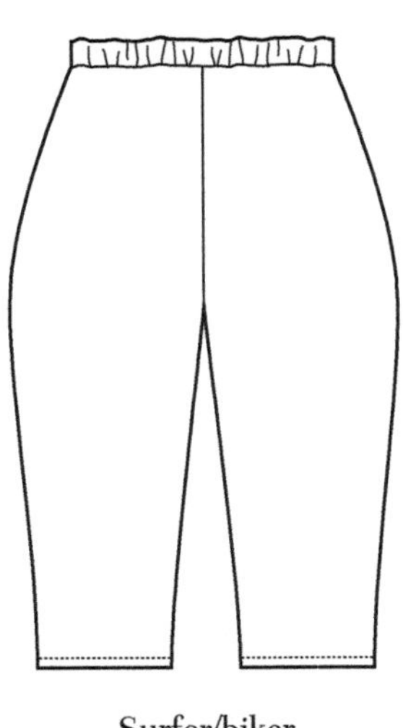

Surfer/biker

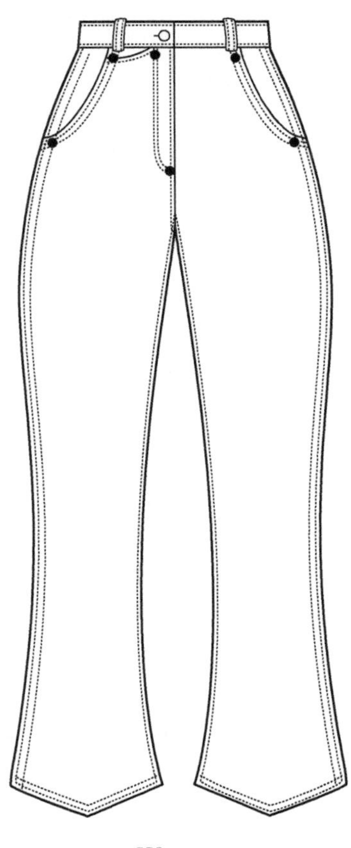

Western

Dresses

- A-line jumper
- Basic shift
- Bra top
- Caftan
- Cardigan
- Coat
- Draped
- Empire
- Full circular skirt
- Granny
- One-shoulder
- Princess
- Plunging neckline
- Safari
- Shirt
- Slip
- Sheath
- Sundress
- Sweater
- T-shirt
- Tank
- Trumpet
- Torso
- Wrap Dress
- Wedge Dress

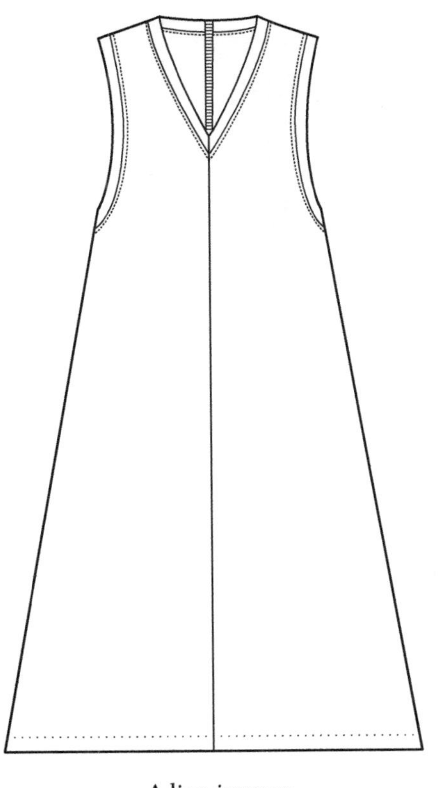

A-line jumper

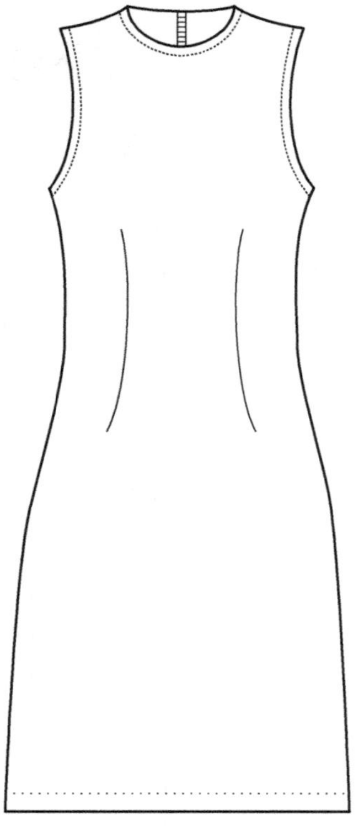
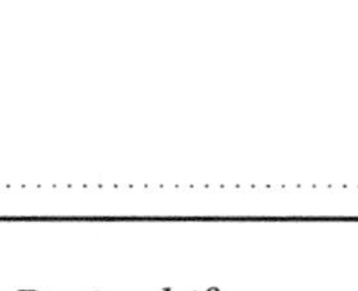

Basic shift

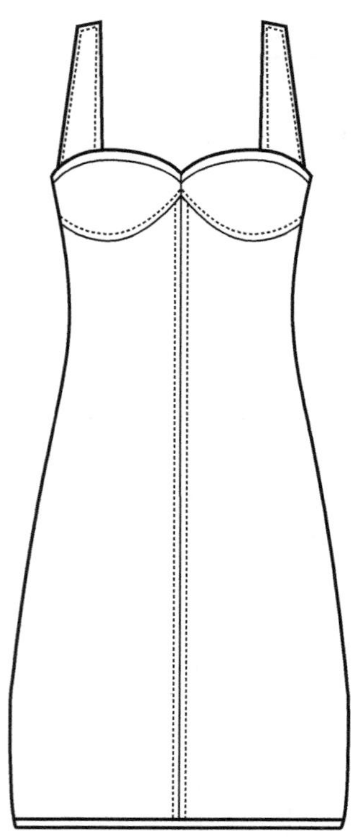

Bra top

Caftan

Cardigan

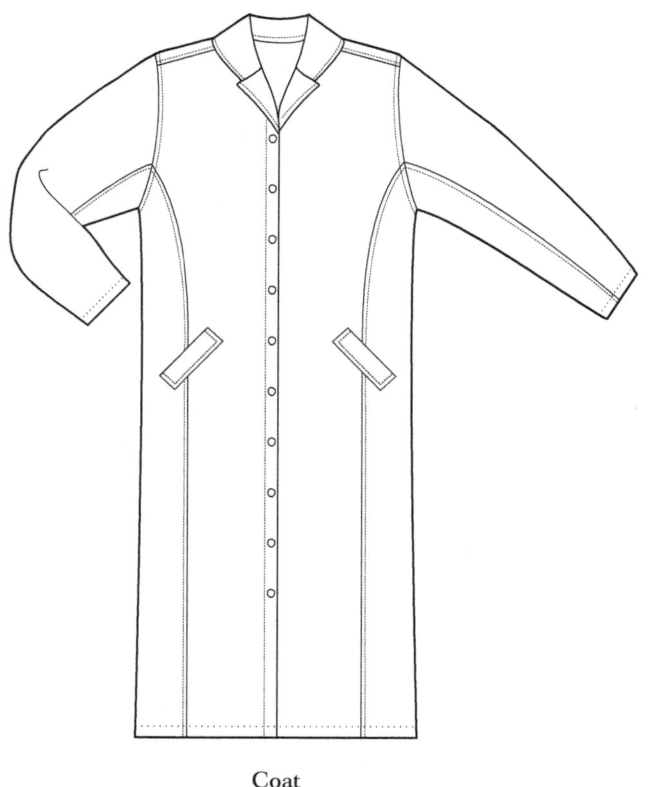
Coat

Draped

Empire

Full circular skirt

Granny

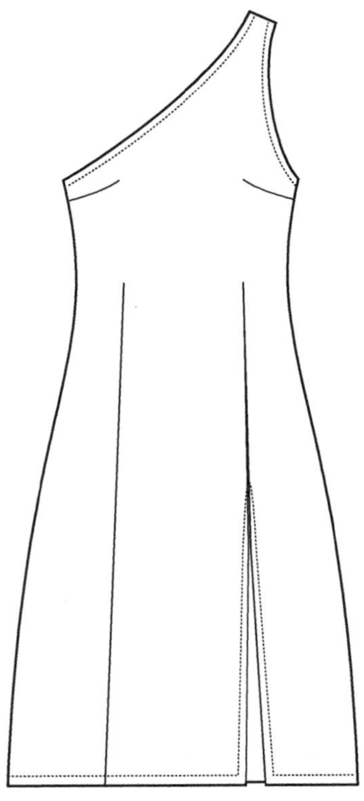
One-shoulder

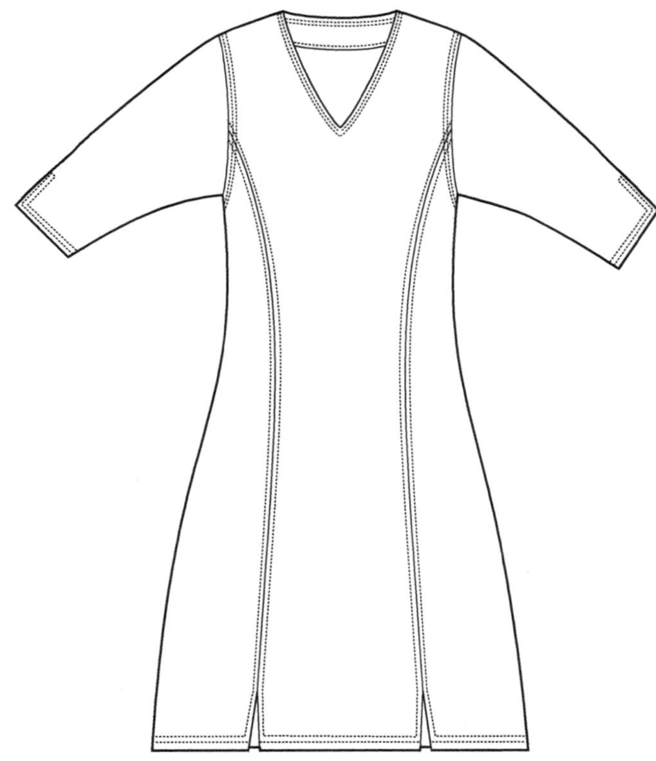
Princess

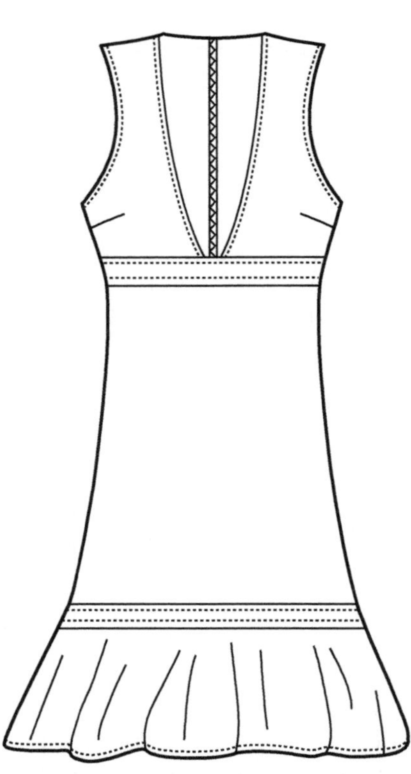
Plunging neckline

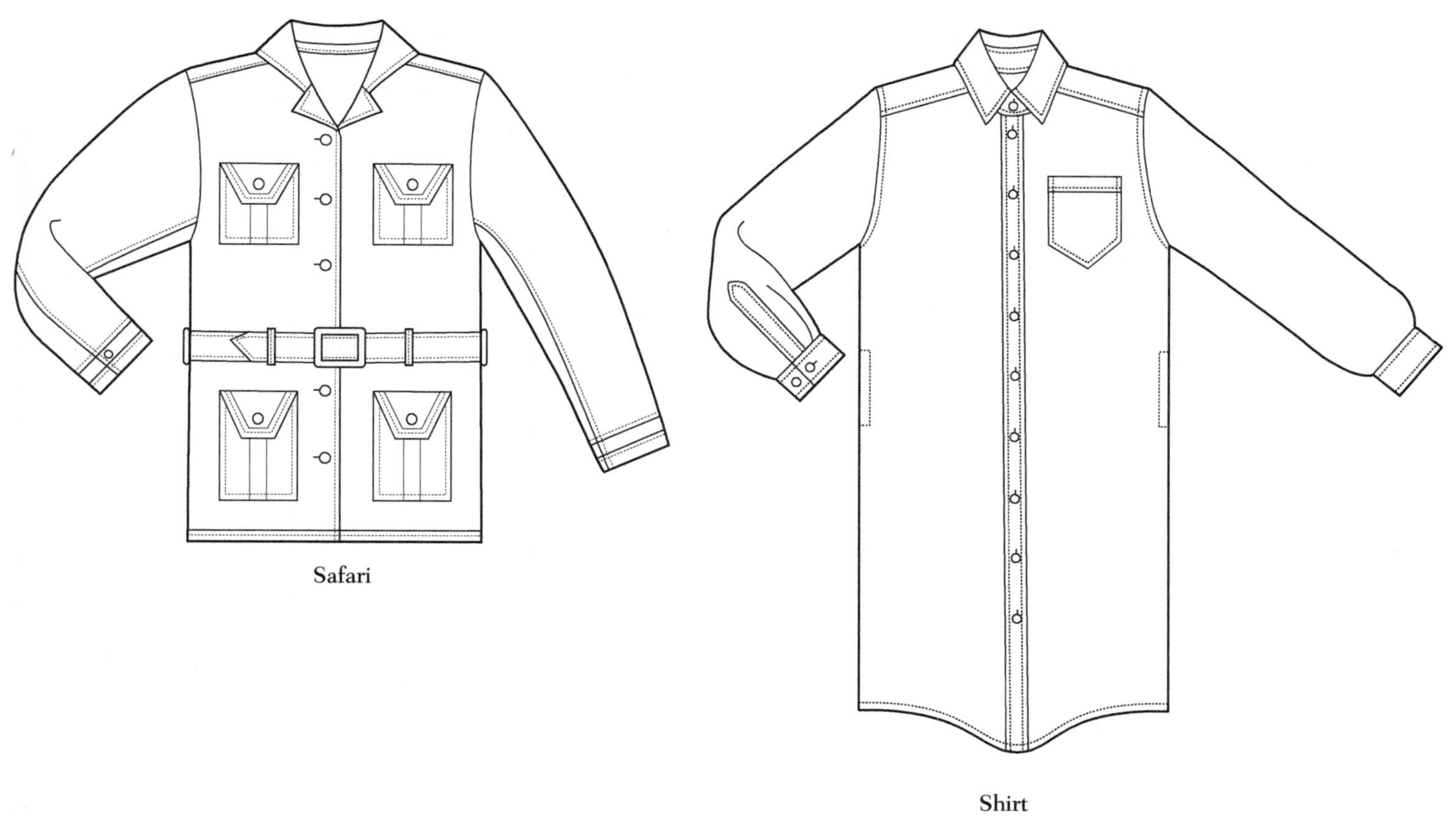

Safari

Shirt

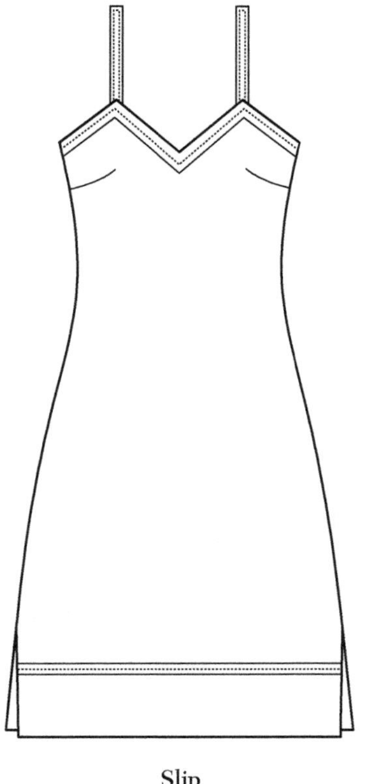

Slip

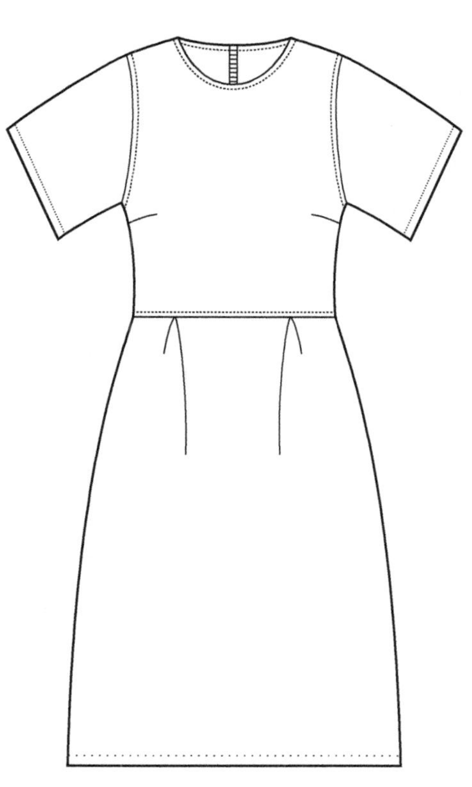

Sheath

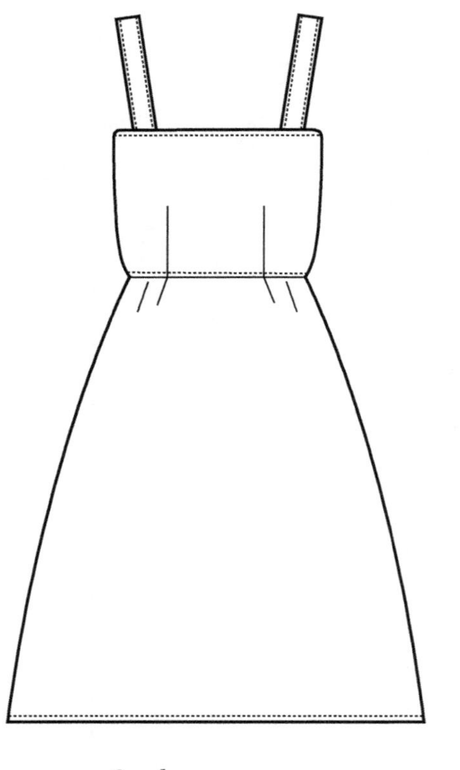

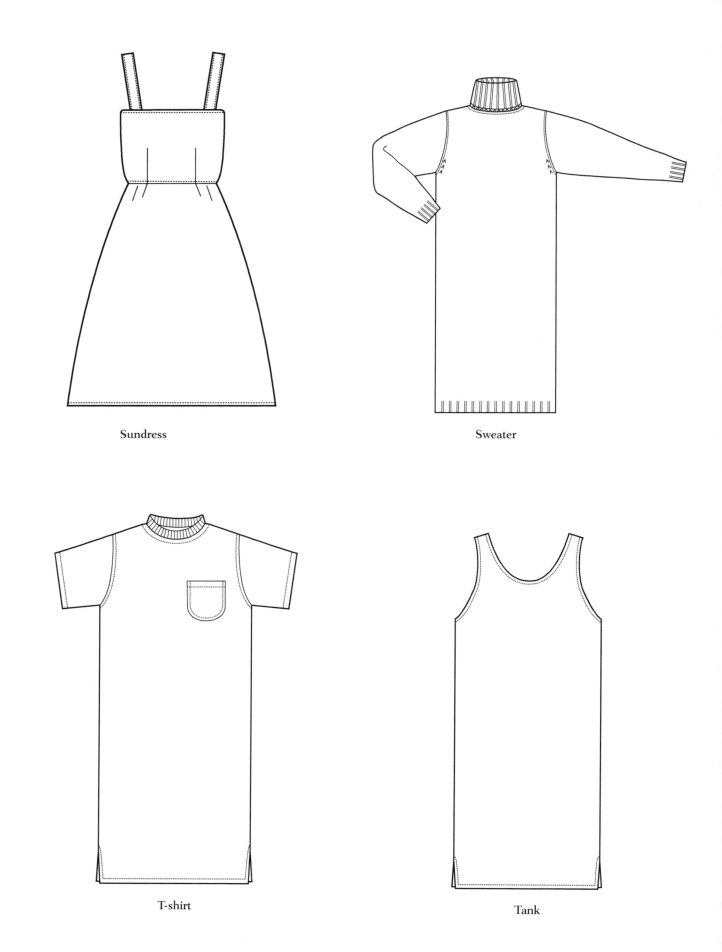

Sundress

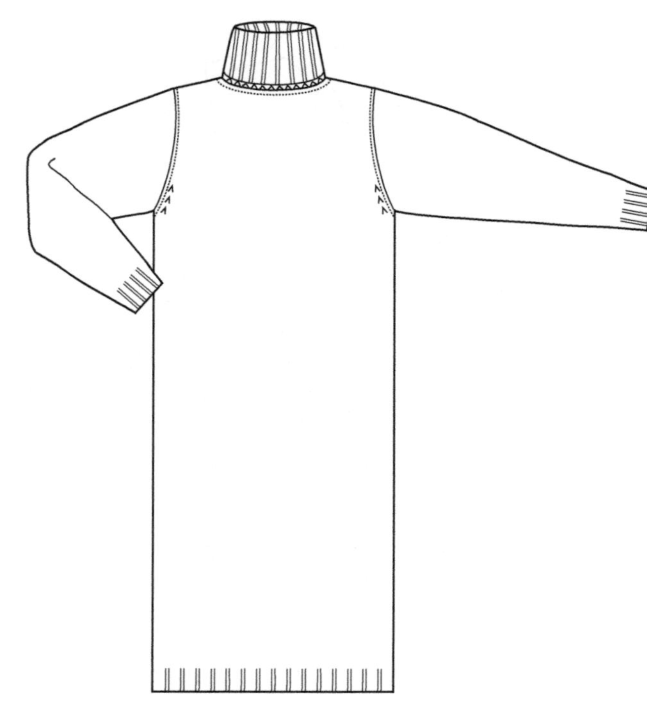

Sweater

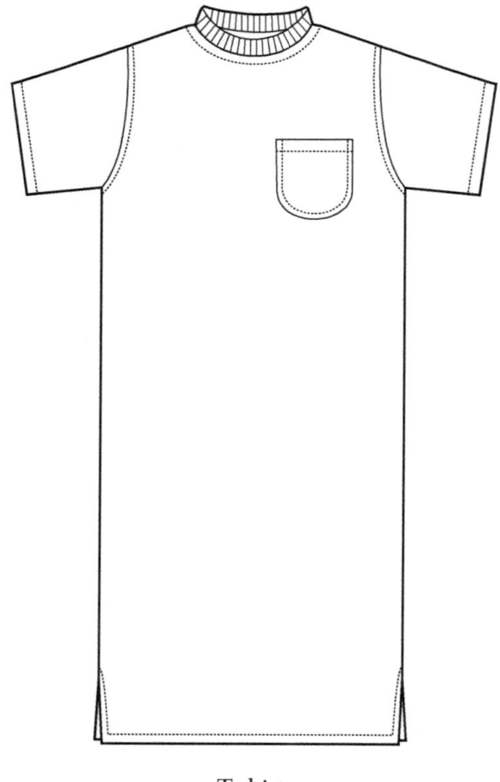

T-shirt

Tank

Trumpet

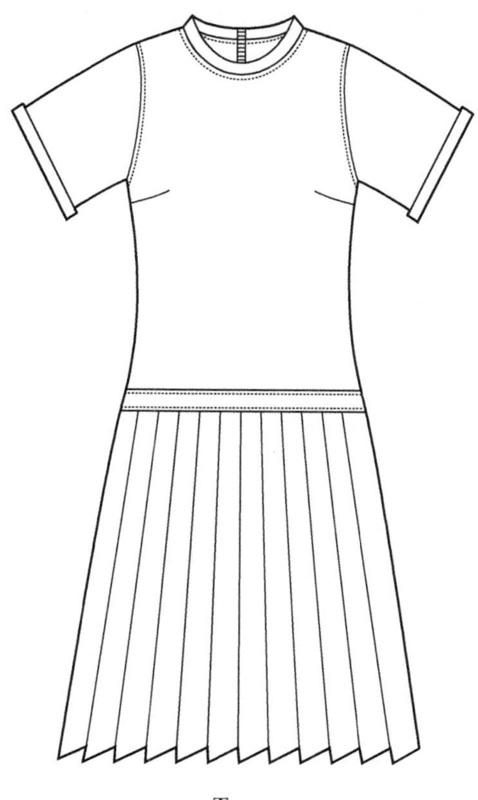

Torso

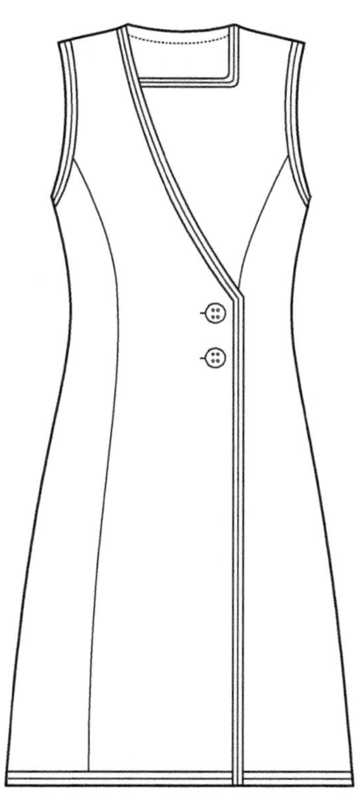

Wrap Dress

Wedge Dress

One-Piece Outfits/Jumpsuits

Bib-overall
Body shirt
Body stocking
Bodysuit
Bunny suit
Cargo long
Cargo short
Jumpsuit
One-piece swimsuit
Jumper
Teddy

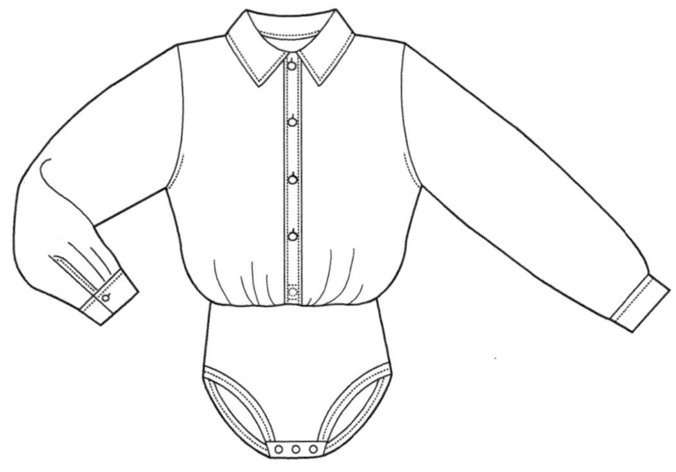

Bodyshirt

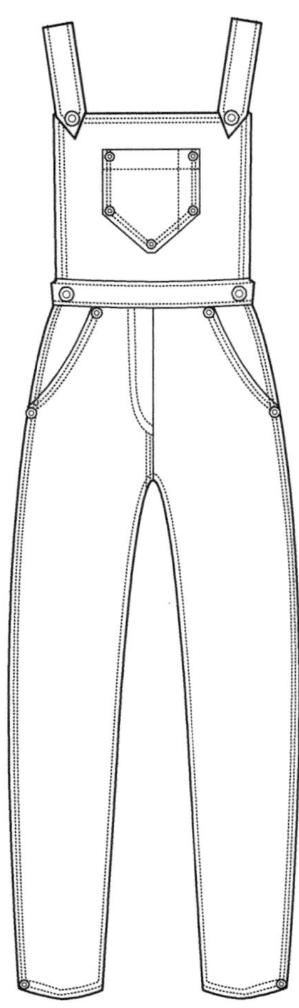

Bib-overall

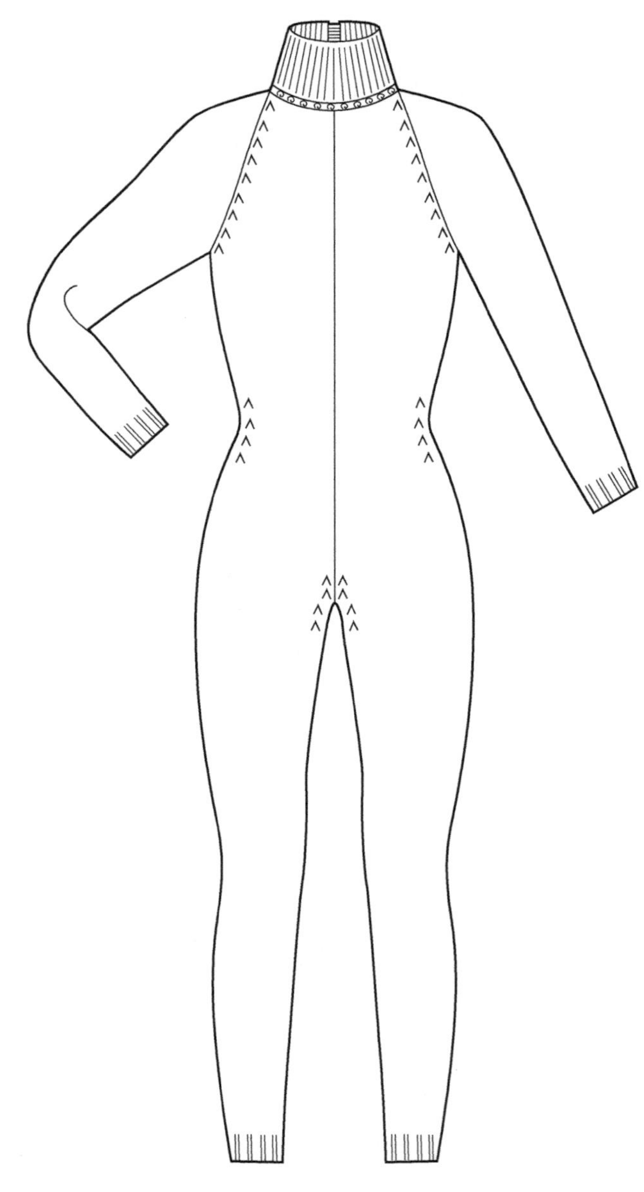

Body stocking

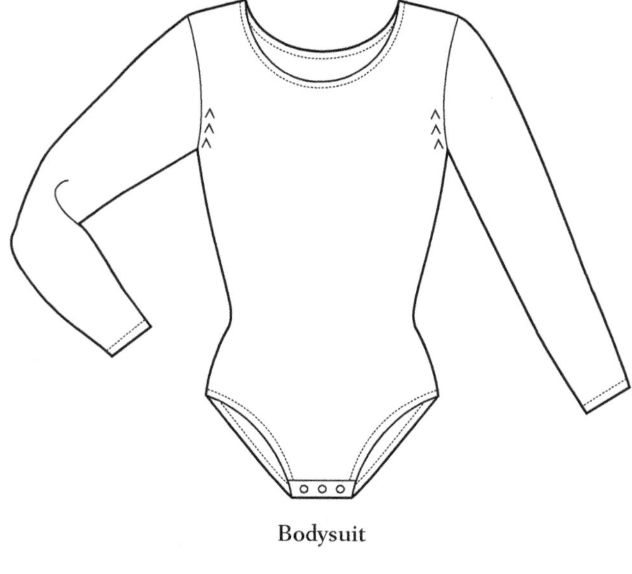
Bodysuit

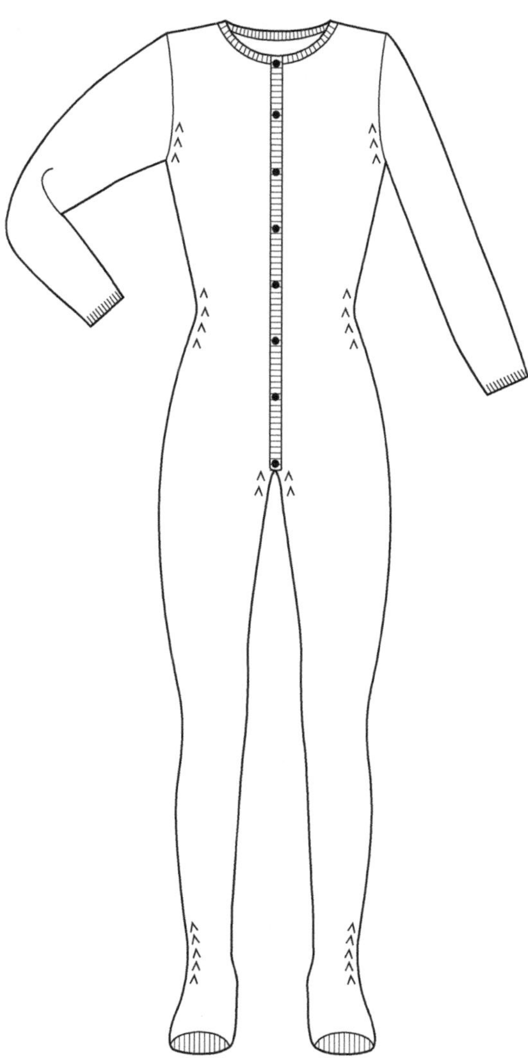
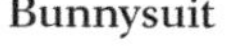
Bunnysuit

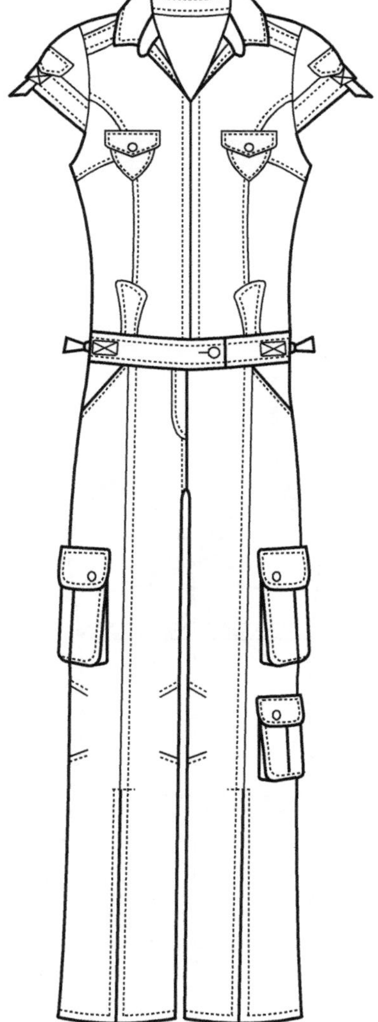
Cargo long

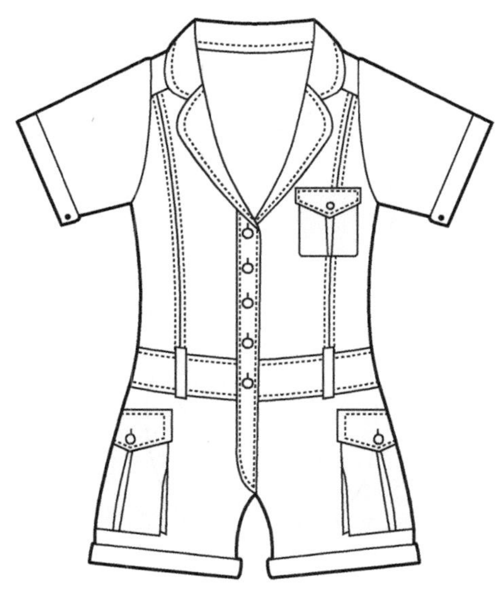
Cargo short

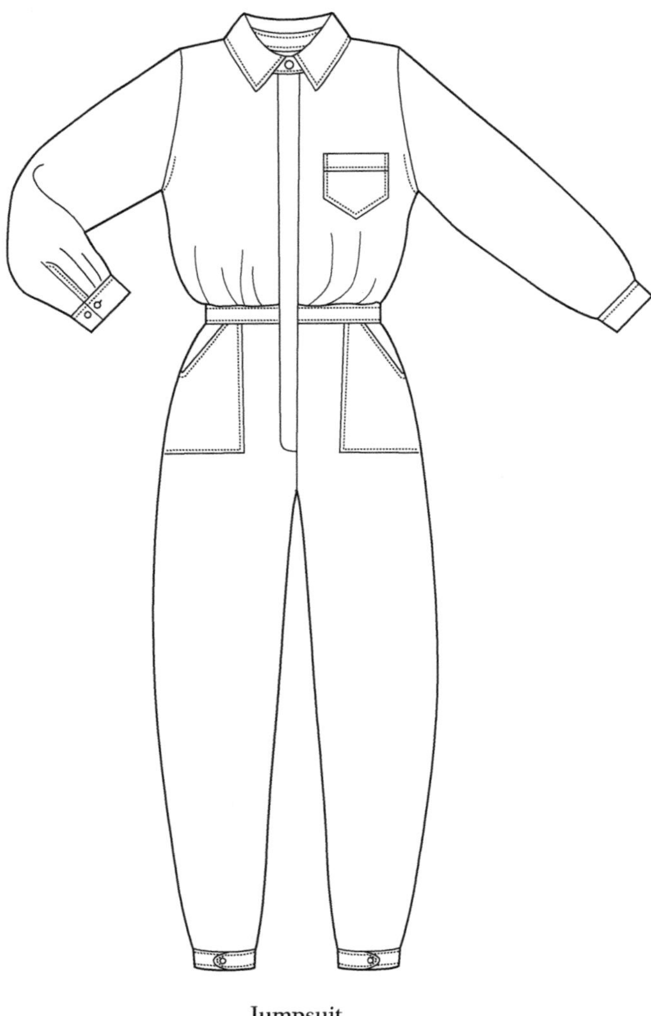

Jumpsuit

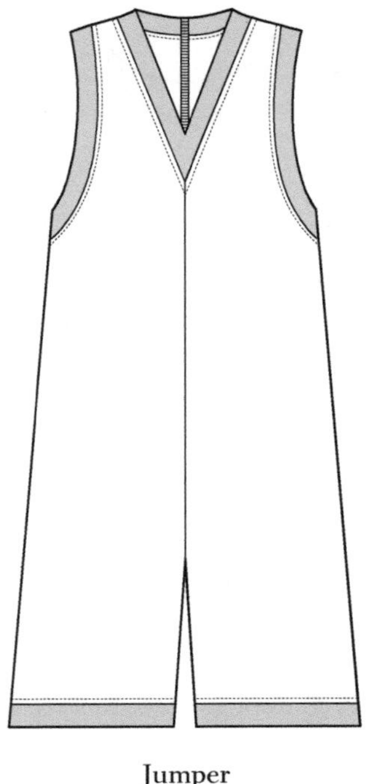

Jumper

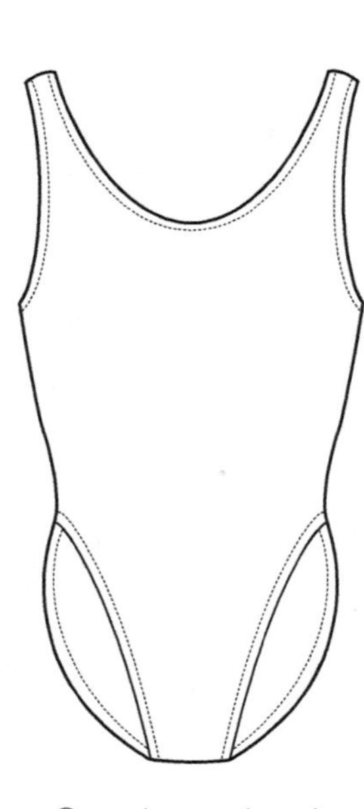

One-piece swimsuit

Teddy

Blazers and Unconstructed Jackets

- Baseball
- Basic blazer
- Bike
- Bolero
- Box
- Chanel
- Denim
- Double-breasted
- Golf
- Fly-away
- Karate
- Nehru
- Safari
- Sweat jacket/Hoodie
- Tyrolean
- Windbreaker

Baseball

Basic Blazer

Bike

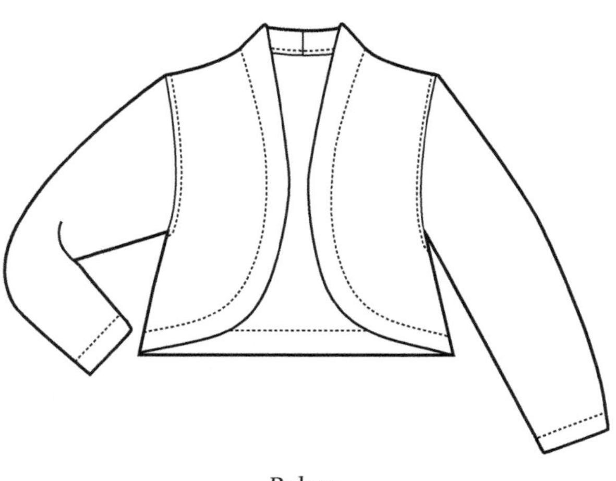

Bolero

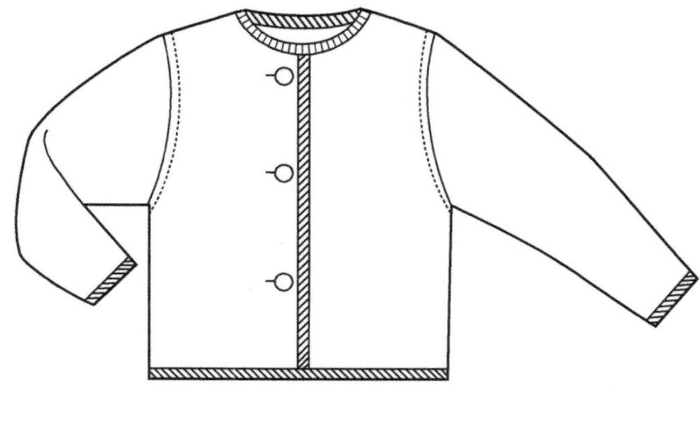

Box

Chanel

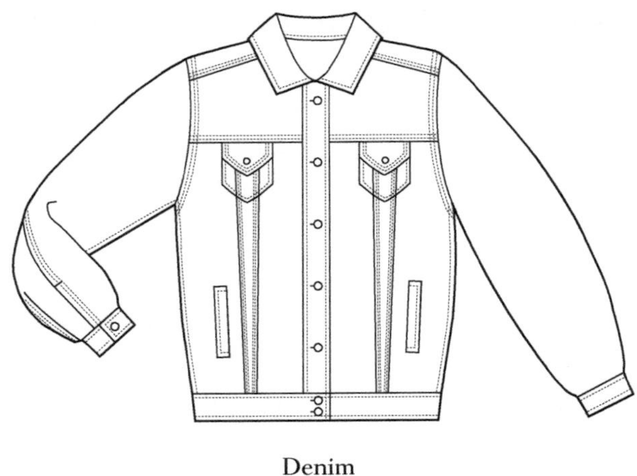
Denim

Double-breasted

Golf

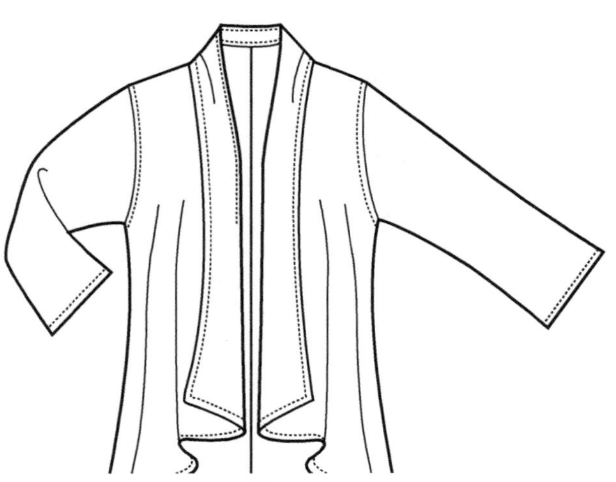
Fly-away

Karate

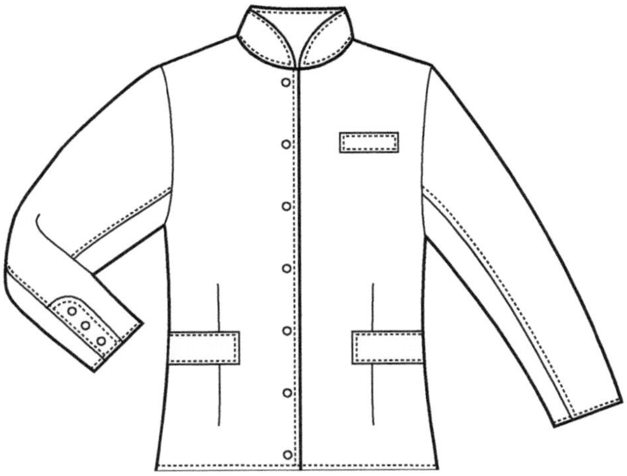

Nehru

Safari

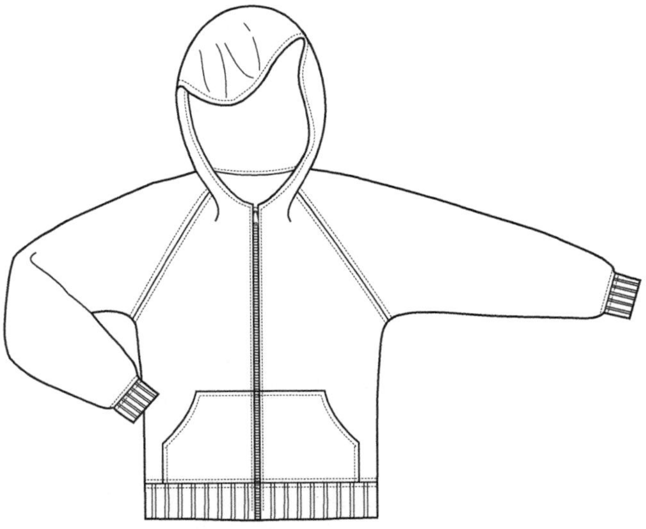

Sweat jacket/Hoodie

Tyrolean

Windbreaker

Coats

- Balmacaan
- Basic coat lengths
- Bomber
- Chesterfield
- Clutch
- Duster
- Mackinaw
- Military/pea
- Cape
- Parka
- Peasant
- Princess
- Raglan
- Stadium/Storm
- Technical
- Tent
- Toggle
- Wrap

Balmacaan

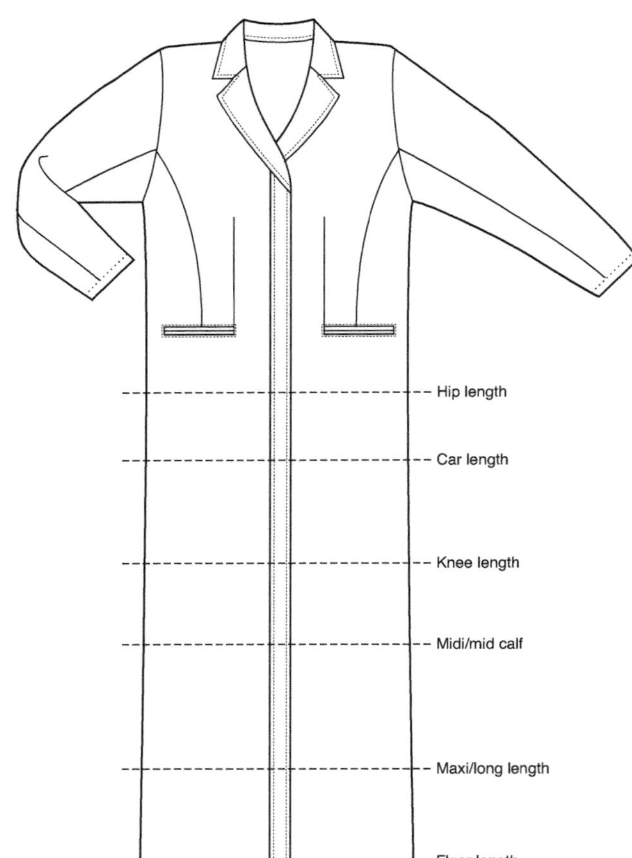

Basic coat lengths

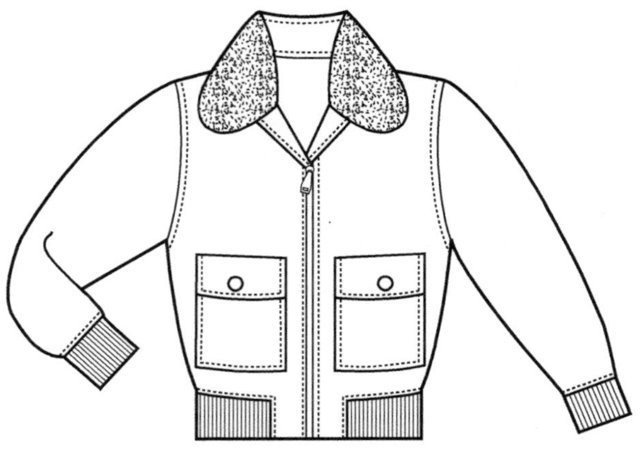

Bomber

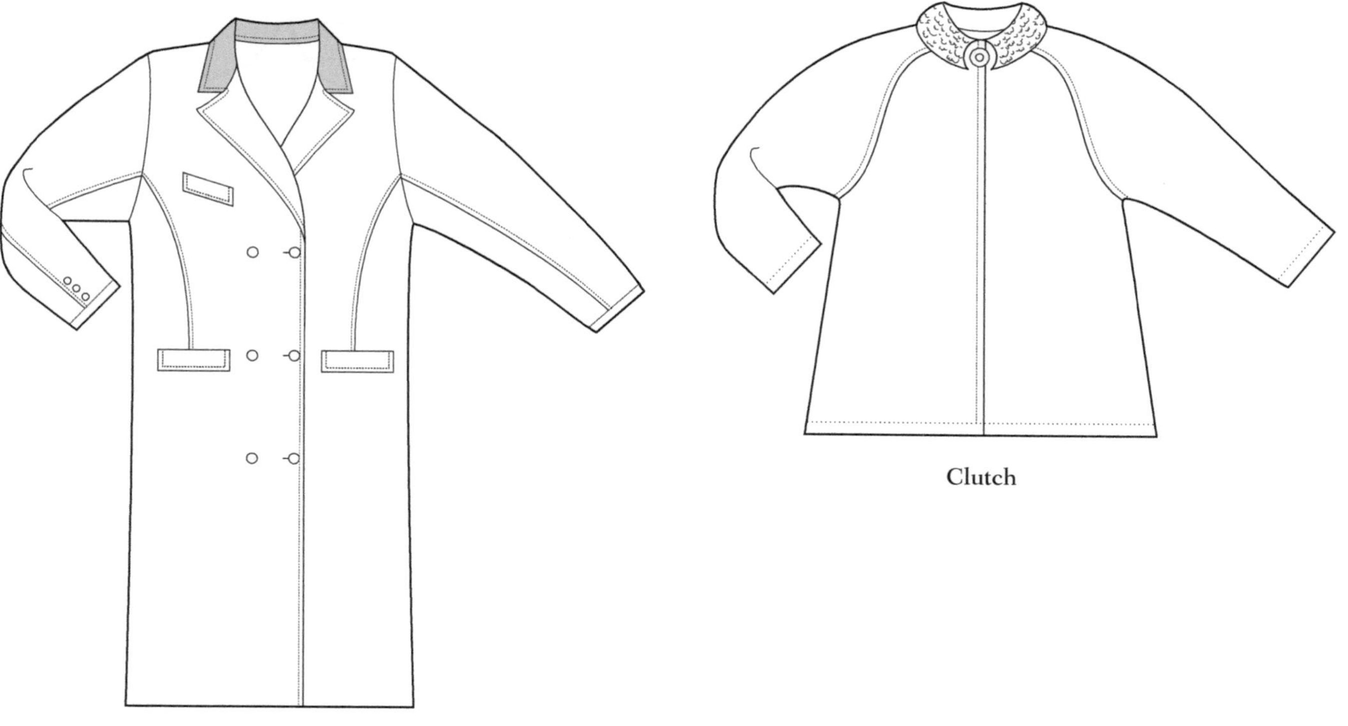

Chesterfield

Clutch

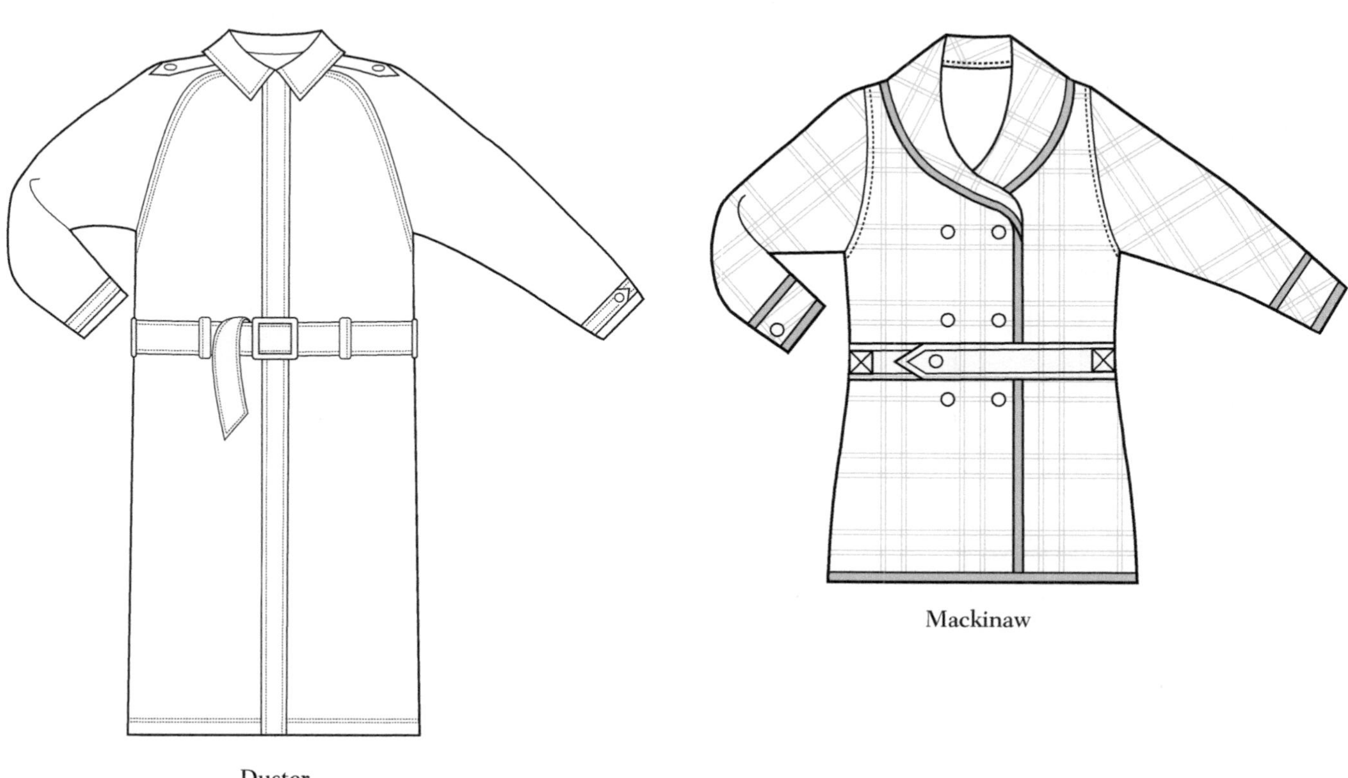

Mackinaw

Duster

Military/pea

Cape

Parka

Peasant

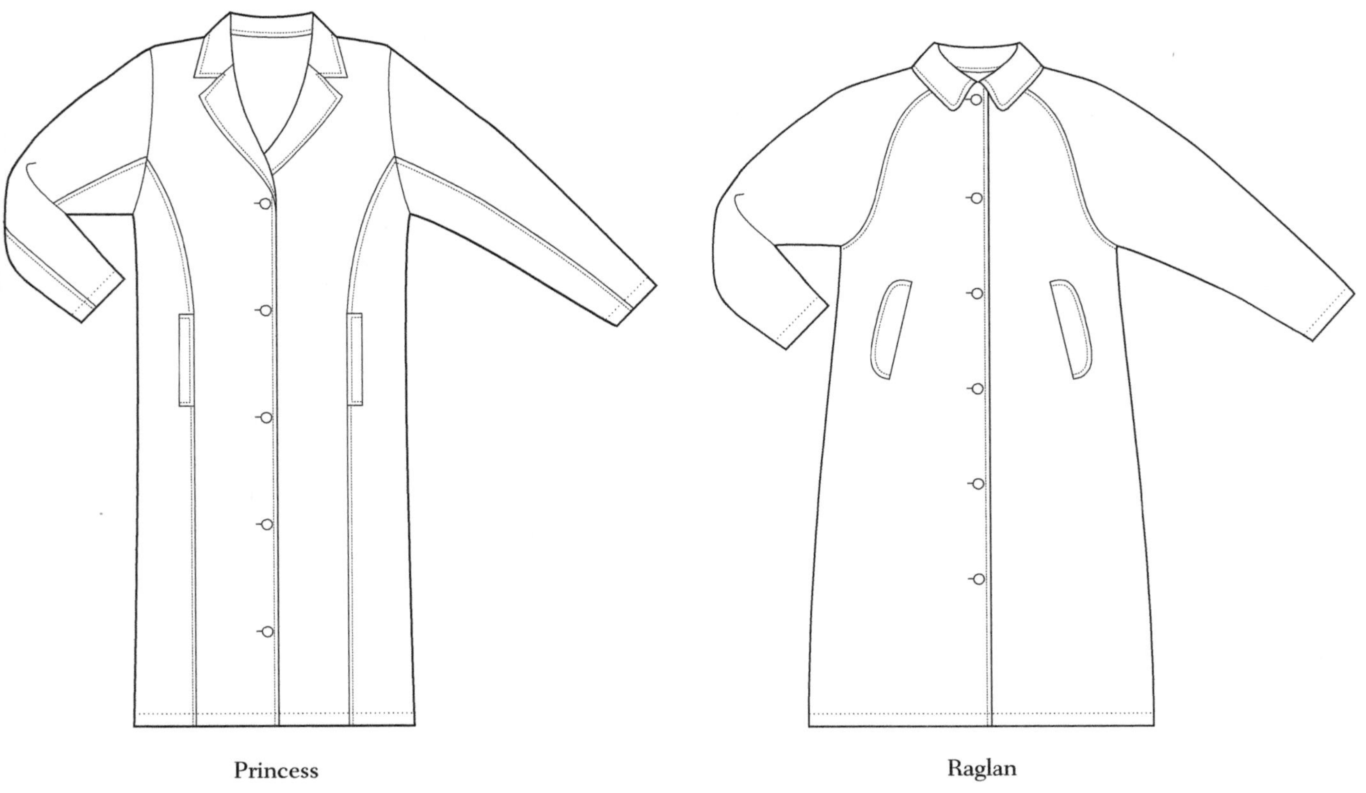

Princess

Raglan

Stadium/Storm

Technical

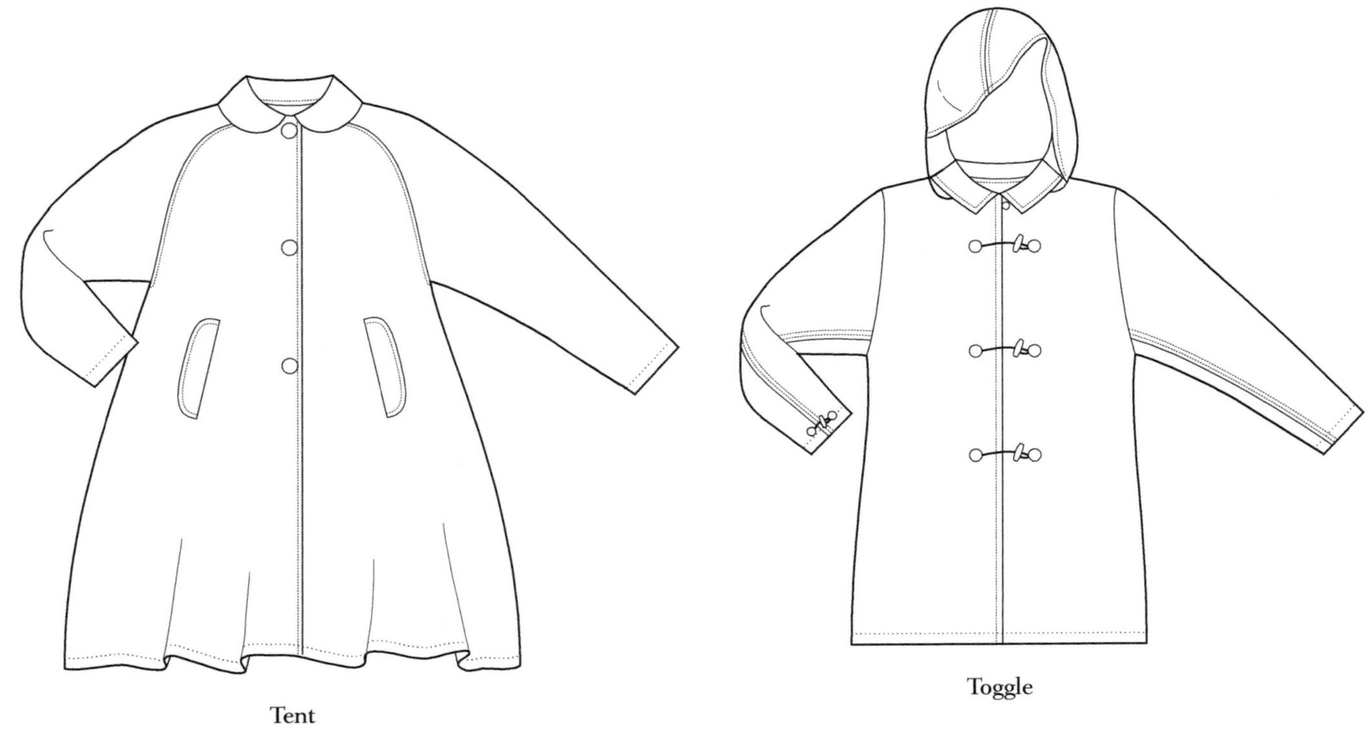
Tent
Toggle

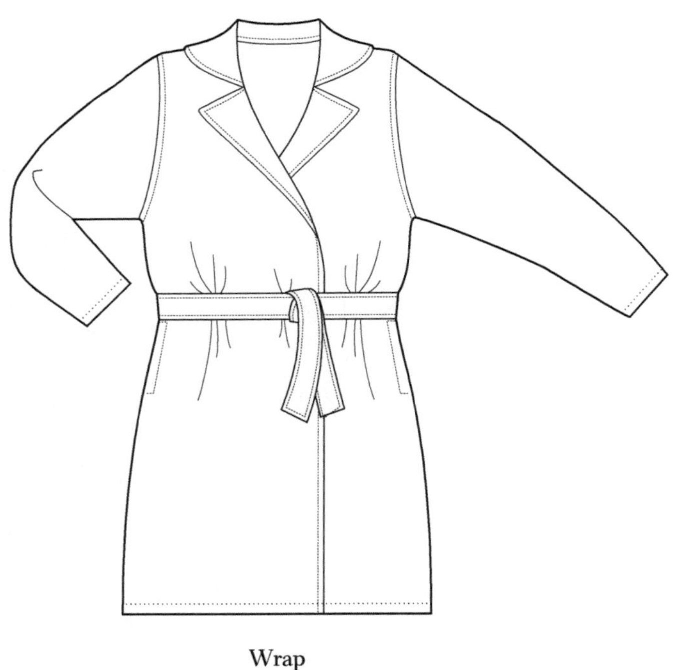
Wrap

APPENDIX B

Metric to Imperial Conversion

How to Convert

One inch (in.) in the imperial system, which is used in the United States, equals .039 millimeters or 2.54 centimeters; therefore, the formula for conversion is "in. × 2.54 = cm." Conversely, use the formula "cm × 0.39 = in." to convert from centimeters to inches. To find fractions, a simple method of converting is to divide the top fraction by the bottom. For example ¾ is 3 ÷ 4 = .75.

The following table has been provided for your reference. The first two columns show conversions between millimeters and inches. Use the middle columns for inches to decimal and millimeter conversions. The last two columns show inches to centimeter conversions.

CONVERSION CHART

MM	Inches	Inches	Decimal	MM	Inches	CM
1	.039	1/16"	.06125	1.59	1	2.54
2	.079				2	5.08
3	.118	1/8"	.125	3.18	3	7.62
4	.157				4	10.16
5	.197	3/16"	.1875	4.47	5	12.70
6	.236	¼"	.250	6.35	6	15.24
7	.276				7	17.78
8	.315	5/16"	.3124	7.94	8	20.32
9	.354				9	22.86
10	.394	3/8"	.375	9.53	10	25.40
11	.433	7/16"	.4373	11.11	11	27.94

(continued)

CONVERSION CHART *(continued)*

MM	Inches	Inches	Decimal	MM	Inches	CM
12	.472				12	30.48
13	.512	½"	.500	12.70	13	33.02
14	.551	9/16"	.5625	14.29	14	35.56
15	.591				15	38.10
16	.630	5/8"	.626	15.88	16	40.64
17	.669	11/16"	.6875	17.46	17	43.18
18	.709				18	45.72
19	.748	¾"	.750	19.05	19	48.26
20	.787				20	50.80
21	.827	13/16"	.8125	20.64	21	53.34
22	.888	7/8"	.875	22.23	22	55.88
23	.906				23	58.42
24	.945	15/16"	.9375	23.81	24	60.96
25	.984	1"	1.00	25.40	25	63.50
26	1.024				26	66.04
27	1.063				27	68.58
28	1.102	1 1/8"	1.13	28.70	28	71.12
29	1.142				29	73.66
30	1.181	1¼"	1.25	31.75	30	76.20
35	1.378	1 3/8"	1.375	34.93	31	78.74
40	1.575	1½'	1.50	38.10	32	81.28
45	1.772	1¾"	1.75	44.45	33	83.82
50	1.969	2"	2.00	50.80	34	86.36
55	2.165				35	88.90
60	2.362				36	91.44
65	2.559	2½"	2.50	63.50	37	93.98
70	2.756				38	96.52
75	2.953				39	99.06
80	3.150	3"	3.00	76.20	40	101.60

GLOSSARY

Important Terms and Definitions

Apex The highest or culminating point of the bust.

Apparel A general or blanket term that applies to all men's, women's, and children's clothing.

Apparel manufacturer A broad spectrum of fashion industry companies that may develop, produce, and sell garments.

Applied pocket Any pocket stitched or applied onto the garment, e.g., a patch pocket.

Assistant designer A person who assists in interpreting the designer's creations.

Assistant merchandiser A person working for a merchandiser who is primarily responsible for clerical duties.

Assistant product developer/manager A person who helps develop and manage private label and/or brand merchandise within the sales and business plans.

Assistant size specification analyst A person who performs clerical duties for a specification analyst. This person knows how to measure and is apprenticing in fit analysis.

Assistant technical designer A person who performs clerical duties for the technician. This person knows how to measure and is apprenticing in fit analysis and design.

Baby/Infant Clothing designed to be worn by babies, generally sold in sizes 3–6m to 24m.

Balance A visual weight in design, or the concept of visual equilibrium; it must be pleasing as it relates to our physical sense. Balance can be achieved in one of two ways: symmetrically or asymmetrically.

Basic blazer A slightly fitted, single-breasted sport jacket.

Basket weave A variation of the plain weave construction accomplished by passing filling yarns over and under warp yarns, two or more warp yarns up and two or more warp yarns down, in alternating rows.

Bat wing A sleeve on a blouse or sweater cut with a deep armhole almost to the waist often made tight at the arm, elbow or wrist opening giving a wing-like appearance.

Belted cardigan A slightly fitted hip-length jacket or sweater that may or may not button, worn with a matching belt. See *Cardigan*.

Bib overalls A pant with a piece of cloth attached to the waistline/band, often held in place by shoulder straps. See *Overalls*.

Bifurcated body form A form that is divided by branches or parts. The best forms are solid and bifurcated with twill tape.

Blazer A single-breasted sport jacket.

Blouse

Basic or front buttoning A traditional front-buttoning garment or top often styled after a man's dress shirt, and may or may not have a separate placket, chest pocket, or shoulder yoke.

Body shirt or fitted See *Body shirt or Fitted* under their alphabetical listing.

Bow A blouse generally having a band around the neck with two long ends attached that tie in a bow formation at the front of the neck.

Camisole A short bodice garment with straps that is often worn alone or under a blouse. Also called a chemise, some versions are made as lingerie.

Cossack A long blouse or over blouse often made with an embroidered high-standing collar, cuffs, and asymmetrical front placket, secured with a belt.

Cowboy (Western) A version of the basic blouse often styled with curved or V-shaped yokes, fancy buttonhole pockets, and piping trim; a look that is synonymous with Western United States cowboys.

Drawstring A blouse with a drawstring closure at the neckline. See *Drawstring* under its alphabetical listing.

Dress shirt Traditional front buttoning shirt with conservative menswear details.

Epaulet A blouse with shoulder epaulets and patch pockets.

Guayabera A shirt with pin tucks running down the front from the shoulder to the yoked hem, patch pockets, and button-trimmed shoulder yokes; often associated with Cuba.

Hawaiian A floral-patterned shirt associated with Hawaii. It usually has two patch chest pockets.

Jabot A front or back-buttoning blouse with jabot-styled ruffles at the neck or front placket.

Nautical/Middy An over-the-head or slip-on blouse of traditional U.S. Navy/sailor styling. It has a large collar, neckerchief, and two or three rows of trim on the collar and cuffs.

Oversized A blouse that generally fits loosely on the body and may give the appearance of being sized too big.

Peasant A blouse styled after European folkloric tops with long or three-quarter puffed sleeves and embroidered and ruffled trims.

Stock-tie Generally a plain blouse with an ascot or flip-tie neckline.

Tunic A blouse styled after the loose-fitting garments of ancient Rome and Greece. It may be front buttoning or pullover style and may or may not have a belt.

Tuxedo A woman's blouse imitating a man's formal dinner shirt with small pin tucks on the front.

Wrap A blouse that is generally cut on the bias, crosses over in the front or back, and ties at the waist. It may not have sleeves or they may be of varying lengths.

Boat neck (Bateau) A neckline slit over the shoulders in a boat shape that rests high on the front and back neck. A boat-neck top or dress would have this neck shape.

Bodice A close-fitting, upper-chest portion of a woman's dress or blouse.

Body dimension The actual measurement, the number in inches/centimeters, of a body at a body point of measurement.

Body form A dressmaking form made in the shape of a human body with legs on which a technical designer fits garments and a fashion designer or home sewer drapes fabric. These are also called dummy or model forms. Dress forms or dressmaker's dummies are generally body forms made without legs.

Body point of measure (body measurement) A measurement of a person's body at a specific point, e.g., the chest, waist, or hip.

Body prototype The model or body on which a dress form is patterned; a full-scale copy of a model's body.

Body shirt Refers to two different shirt styles: (1) a shirt that is fitted (also known as a fitted shirt) to conform to the body by slightly shaping the side seams or adding fitting darts/princess lines and (2) a blouse and leotard/bodysuit combination often seamed at or below the waist.

Body stocking A one-piece knitted garment with legs worn as an undergarment, sleep garment, or fashion garment. It may or may not have feet or sleeves and varying necklines.

Bodysuit A one-piece formfitting garment made without legs, often having a snap crotch opening.

Boy's wear Clothing designed to be worn by boys generally sold in sizes 4 to 7x and 8 to 20.

Bra top A dress or top where the bust portion has the appearance of a bra, but is meant as day/street wear.

Brand manager A person who is responsible for updating and maintaining the brand identity, including private label, of a line and is responsible for planning, sales, and marketing of the brand.

Brand/Branded merchandise A wholesale label or trade name used for distinguishing products to that of a particular company.

Bunny suit A one-piece garment often worn for sleeping or lounging, fashioned after the trademarked children's wear sleeper by Dr. Denton's.

Cardigan A slightly fitted hip-length jacket or sweater that buttons, sometimes having a small rolled collar. See *Classic cardigan.*

Center back (CB) The center of the garment, in back.

Center front (CF) The center of the garment, in front.

Children's wear Clothing for children, mainly used in a retail context.

Circular knit/knitting The construction of a knitted fabric or garment on a knitting machine in circular or tubular form.

Circular web A fabric knitted in a tubular form, then cut and sewn to construct a garment.

Circumference The perimeter of the garment, including the front and back measurements, in other words, the total measurement. [Note: To get the circumference measurement, the garment is measured once, across the front, then that number is doubled.]

Classic cardigan Named after the seventh Earl of Cardigan, this is a slightly fitted hip-length jacket or sweater generally made out of wool, buttons, and sometimes having a small rolled collar.

Close fitting A broad term used for a garment that fits very close or tight to the body, generally of fashion-forward design.

Coat An outerwear garment (with sleeves) designed to be worn over other clothing.

Balmacaan A loose-fitting coat with raglan sleeves and a turn-down collar, buttoning up to the neck. It may be made in wool or rain-resistant fabrics.

Cape A sleeveless outer garment that fits closely at the neck, with or without a collar, and hangs loosely over the shoulders.

Car A hip- to three-quarter-length coat styled for comfort while riding in a car.

Chesterfield A classic overcoat made of wool with a velvet collar; can be single or double breasted.

Classic A term that fits any basic coat style or a coat that has been in fashion for a long period of time.

Clutch A coat without front fasteners. It is generally held together by hand and may have a flared hemline.

Duster Generally water-repellent or raincoat made with a smock/flange on the back, raglan sleeves, shoulder epaulets, and a belt. Originally named for a vintage car coat to keep the dust off one's clothing.

Mackinaw A car-length coat or jacket made of thick, heavy plaid woollen cloth with a nap reminiscent of old Indian supply blankets.

Military Generally any coat that borrows details from coats worn by persons in the military, usually styles with gold buttons, epaulets, and a double-breasted front opening.

Parka A hip-length jacket or long coat with a hood often made of heavy wool or windproof or water-repellent material and lined and often trimmed with wool or fur; used in extremely cold temperatures.

Pea A short military-styled coat/jacket often of navy officer design.

Peasant A mid-length coat trimmed with real or fake fur and embroidered ribbon on the borders and cuffs.

Princess A long coat with princess seamed detail.

Raglan A coat with raglan-styled sleeves.

Stadium/Storm A coat often of quilted design made for warmth. It is often three-quarters in length and can have toggle front closures or a zip front.

Technical A coat or jacket that has been engineered with the latest waterproofing, moisture-wicking, breathability, stretch-ability fabrics, lightweight insulation, and more. Also know as a high-tech coat/jacket.

Tent A knee-length coat with a widely flared hem and raglan sleeves.

Toggle Any coat with toggle closures or a short car coat with toggle closures and a hood.

Wrap A coat of any length with a wrap closure and belt.

Codes The numbering (or lettering) system given to each of the measurement points.

Computer-aided design (CAD) Software that is used by designers, artists, and others to create precision drawings or technical illustrations; it can be used to create two-dimensional (2D) drawings or three-dimensional (3D) models.

Constructed (constructed garment) A term used for a garment that employs one or more of the following advanced sewing construction techniques: facings, linings, collars, sleeves, pockets, and waistbands.

Constructed waistband A waistband that is sewn with two or more parts.

Conversion A change in units or form.

Costing The process of achieving a total cost of goods by evaluating the materials, labor, shipping, and markup.

Cost sheet A name given to the page of calculations for the total cost of goods.

Cowl neck A draped neckline falling in soft folds and may be of a bias cut. A cowl-neck shirt or dress would have this neckline.

Crew neck A round neckline often finished with a self-bias or knit ribbing, originally derived from the neckline on crew racing shirts.

Cropped top A top with a shortened or cut off hemline, generally falling above the waistline.

Croquis A sketch of a subject (as used in this text, fashion figures).

Department merchandise manager (DMM) A person who manages a division or department of merchandise. This person manages several merchandisers and reports to a general merchandise manager.

Design ease Ease that is added to a garment for design or style, not fit.

Designer A person engaged in creating new and original clothing or accessories.

Design manager A person who sets the brand and/or private label fashion direction; manages all aspects of design and development; and has final approval of materials, colors, patterns, and silhouettes for the season.

Designer merchandise A term used for merchandise that is designed by a well-known or branded designer.

Dolman sleeve A sleeve that is fitted at the wrist and cut with a deep armhole, sometimes starting at the waist. The dolman sleeve is often cut as one piece with the bodice. A dolman-sleeve dress or blouse would have this sleeve.

Double-breasted blazer A slightly fitted blazer with a lapped-over front opening, fastened with two rows/sets of buttons.

Drafted/Drafting An industry term for the process of making a new pattern from a basic pattern or sloper.

Drape The hang or way a fabric falls when made into a garment; for example, chiffon has a delicate drape while horsehair canvas hangs stiffly.

Draping An industry term for the process of creating a garment by arranging and pinning fabric over a dress form to conform to the design of that garment. A garment made by this process is considered "draped."

Drawstring A closure for hems, necklines, waistlines, and cuffs made by inserting a cord or ribbon into a band of fabric, which is then pulled and tied. A drawstring skirt would have this closure on the waistband.

Dress Predominately a women's or children's item of clothing, made in one piece, or pieced at the waist, to resemble a top and a skirt.

Basic A-line (shift) A dress with a slightly flared skirt, having the illusion of the letter A in silhouette.

Caftan Traditionally a Moroccan-styled long and loose fitting dress with an embroidered, slit neckline.

Cardigan A dress that resembles the cardigan sweater in styling.

Coat A classic dress resembling a coat in styling. It may be single or double breasted and belted or unbelted.

Empire A dress having an empire or high waistline ending just under the bosom.

Granny An ankle-length dress often styled with a high collar, long sleeves, full skirt, and ruffled hem. It may have embroidered or ribbon trim.

One-shoulder A dress with an asymmetrical neckline, with one shoulder bare.

Polo shirt A dress that resembles a polo shirt in styling.

Poor-boy shift A dress resembling that of the early 1900s newsboy/poor-boy sweater.

Princess A dress styled with princess seams for shaping.

Safari Generally a tailored dress resembling a bush shirt or jacket, as worn on safari hunts.

Sheath A straight and narrow-fitting dress that is shaped to the body with vertical darts, princess seams, or a set-in waistline.

Shirt (shirtdress) A dress that resembles a blouse or man's shirt. It can be worn with or without a belt.

Slip A simple dress that is usually cut on the bias, fitted at the bust, is constructed with shoulder straps, and may resemble a slip or undergarment.

Sundress A dress in a strap, strapless, or halter style to be worn in warm weather.

Sweater A generic term for any knitted dress that resembles a sweater in styling.

T-shirt A dress that resembles a T-shirt in styling.

Tank A dress resembling a tank top in styling.

Torso/Dropped waist A loose-fitting dress that has an attached skirt below the waist.

Trumpet A slightly fitted dress with a flared flounce starting at the knees.

Waisted A generic term for any dress that has a constructed waistline.

Wedge A dress that is cut very full or wide at the shoulders, tapering down to a narrow or slim hemline, in a wedge/pie shape.

Wrap A generic term for any dress wrapping to either the front or the back, where an extension forms the closure.

Dress/body form A dressmaking form in the shape of a human body, used as a substitution for the body when draping or fitting clothing. It's also known as a dressmaker's dummy, dressmaker's form, dummy, or model form.

Ease The allowance added to patterns to accommodate for comfortable fit and ease of movement. See *Wearing ease.*

Elastic waist (elasticized waistband) A waistline/band used for pull-on garments, made by either inserting elastic into a casing, stitching elastic directly on to the fabric at the waistline, or shirring fabric to the elastic with two or more rows of stitching.

Exclusive Limiting a style, fabric, or name to a single company or group.

Extended measurement A measurement taken when the garment is stretched beyond the relaxed position, but not further than the natural extended position.

Factory Building or facilities for manufacturing.

Fashion director (coordinator) A person who works closely with the merchandisers, supplying important forecast information on color, trends, new fabrications, and market insights.

Fashion-forward A broad term for a garment (or person) that is more fashionable than most.

Fiberglass tape measure A narrow strip or tape (made more commonly of plastic than fiberglass) marked off in units of inches or centimeters for measuring.

Figure types Common combinations of typical body shapes or figure variations.

First patternmaker A person who works with the designer, or may be an assistant to the designer, who can construct actual pattern pieces for a new style by adjusting a sloper (basic pattern) for sample making.

Fit (n) The manner in which clothing is designed to look when worn; (v) adjust or adapt to an end design.

Fit Engineer A person whose sole responsibility is to conduct fit sessions, analyzing the garments and adjusting as needed.

Fitted A general term referring to a garment that fits closely to or hugs the body.

Fitted skirt A skirt that fits closely to or hugs the body. See *Body shirt.*

Flashdance Generally referring to the neckline of a top or dress popularized by the 1983 film *Flashdance.* These garments are often cut at the neck so that the garment falls off the shoulder on one side.

Flat knit The construction of a knitted fabric on a knitting machine in a flat form.

Fly away A garment inspired by the 1940s and 50s jackets of the same name that is full in either the front or back falling into soft pleats.

Fractional math Mathematical equations involving fractions.

Full fashioned A process of flat knitting in which fabric is shaped by adding or reducing stitches.

Fully graded specification A specification sheet listing the measurement points for pattern construction, including all applicable sizes.

Gathered skirt A skirt made from straight or full panels, shirred or gathered at the waist for shaping.

General merchandise manager A person who manages several divisions or departments of merchandise.

Gerber system A generic name used in the industry for all Gerber Technology, a division of Gerber Industry, hardware and software.

Grade rule A designated amount a pattern is made larger or smaller at a given point in order to make it fit a range of sizes.

Grading Increasing or decreasing pattern pieces and slope to achieve different sizes.

Girl's wear Clothing designed to be worn by girls generally sold in sizes 4 to 6x and 7 to 16.

Global sourcing Locating manufacturing facilities/factories to produce apparel merchandise worldwide.

Gross margin The retail industry's measure of profitability, using a percent of total sales (before expenses) as profit.

High point shoulder (HPS) The highest point on the shoulder seam slope, not including neck bindings or collars.

Hoodie A slang term used for a hooded sweatshirt, fleece, or knit jacket with or without a front opening.

Illustrator A person who illustrates for the designer, product development team, or technical team. Many illustrators work freelance. In the past, illustrators were known for creating illustrations for ads, catalogs, or presentations, while sketchers did sketches for design, product development, and technical teams. The terms *illustrator* and *sketcher* have sometimes blurred in their definition, as some illustrators sketch and some sketchers illustrate. See *Sketcher.*

Inert elastic Elastic in a relaxed position, before it has been stretched.

Jacket

Baseball A jacket resembling those worn by major league baseball players. It has a snap or zippered front opening, ribbed cuffs and waist, and often carries a team insignia.

Bike A traditionally styled jacket resembling those worn by a motorcyclist. It may be of leather or cloth and have shoulder epaulets, a buttoned sleeve cuff, and a ribbed waistband.

Bolero A waist- or rib-length jacket, collarless, with a rounded front and no fastenings, often embroidered around the edges to evoke a matador-like image.

Bomber Also called a flight jacket, it is sturdy, traditionally made of heavy leather, and having a fitted ribbed waistband, zippered front, and fleece or pile collar.

Chanel A cardigan-style jacket made of tweed without a collar and edged with boucle, braid, or chenille trim.

Denim Any western-style jacket or any jacket made out of denim.

Golf A jacket resembling those worn by golf players. It has a snap or zippered front opening and elastic cuffs and waist.

Karate A jacket originally styled like a short kimono worn for the sport of karate, also worn as a fashion styled jacket.

Safari A jacket styled after the bush jacket for safari hunts, introduced as a fashion item in the late 1960s.

Sweat (Sweat jacket) Similar to a sweatshirt in design, with a front opening and a hood.

Tyrolean An Austrian-inspired jacket made of fine wool with wide buttoning lapels, a Nehru collar, and wool binding on all the edges.

Jobber A manufacturer who generally does production work for several labels and customers. It may or may not own its own label.

Jumper A sleeveless dress meant to be worn over a blouse or sweater. It may or may not be belted.

Jumpsuit A one-piece garment that is a combination of a shirt and trouser, also known as a coverall.

Junior's A division of apparel aimed at female teenage customers who are too old for children's wear and too youthful for missy. Sizes generally range from 1 to 13.

Knit (n) A fabric that has been constructed by interlocking a series of loops (of one or more yarns); (v) to construct fabric by interlocking a series of loops (of one or more yarns).

Knitted course (also spelled coarse) A row of interlooping loops.

Knitting in the round A term for circular or tubular knitting.

Knockoff A copy of another's idea or design.

Large/Plus women's A size or segment of the industry for women with an ample girth or fit. Sizes generally range from 14W to 26W.

Line A designer's, manufacturer's, or retailer's collection of clothing offered for a specific season, linked by a common theme, such as color, fabric, or style. See *Product line.*

Loose fitting A general term referring to a garment that fits loosely on the body.

Manufacturer A company that produces clothing or clothing components, also called a contractor or jobber.

Manufacturing The process of making clothing or clothing components from raw materials, also a segment of the industry known for making clothing or clothing components from raw materials.

Manufacturing plant A place, factory, or workshop used for the manufacture of goods. See *Production plant.*

Marker A paper pattern, containing a fully graded size run, that provides the cutting lines for cutting stacked fabric in clothing production.

Marker yardage The amount of fabric needed to cut a fully graded size run.

Market (1) A segment of the fashion industry, (2) A place where buyers and sellers meet to potentially trade ownership of goods, (3) A demographic group of potential customers.

Measurement method The instructions or procedure for which a specific measurement is taken.

Measurement point A furnished point or position of which a measurement is taken. See *Point of measure.*

Measurer The title given to a person in the fashion industry whose sole responsibility is to measure garments and record those measurements on a spec sheet.

Menswear A size or segment of the fashion industry for men with an average size or girth or fit. Menswear is sized differently according to shirt, pant, suit, and sportswear.

Merchandise product director A person who provides leadership to the divisional managers by driving and managing the core vendor business to deliver sales and margin results.

Merchandiser A person who makes decisions concerning the direction of the company's line. The merchandiser will study market trends, conduct market research, work with the sales staff, and oversee product development. This person is responsible for merchandise numbers in terms of the product and the stockkeeping units (SKUs).

Middleman A dealer or an agent who intermediates between a producer of goods, a manufacturer, and a retailer or consumer.

Missy (misses) A size or segment of the fashion industry for women with an average girth or fit. Sizes generally range from 6 to 16.

Mock turtleneck A neckline/collar that stands on and fits close to the neck, but does not roll over like a turtleneck. A mock turtleneck sweater would have this neckline.

Natural relaxed position A garment set at ease or resting in a state that the inherent properties of the fabric or style allow.

Nehru A standing collar similar to the Chinese or mandarin but with rounded ends/edges in front; used mostly on blouses and jackets.

Newborn Clothing designed to be worn by young infants generally sold in sizes 0 to 3 months.

One-piece swimsuit (bathing suit) Any bathing/swim garment for women or children made in one piece. Classic one-piece suits include the tank and the maillot.

Outerwear Another name for a coat generally styled hip-length to full-length and designed to be worn over other clothing, also called an outercoat.

Outsourcing The concept of one business paying another company to provide services that the business might have otherwise employed its own staff to perform.

Overalls Pants with a bib top and shoulder straps, traditionally worn by farmers in blue denim or by painters (painter pants) in natural or white, and common styles in many fabrics for children.

Oversized A general term referring to a garment that fits very loosely on the body and may give the appearance of being sized too big.

Pants

Baggy (baggies) A pant that is cut full through the hips and tapers to a narrow opening at the ankle.

Bell-bottom (bell-bottoms) A pant that is cut with fullness at the hem on both the inner and outer seam, causing a perceived bell shape.

Blue jean/denim Pants originally styled for work, with top stitching, hip pockets, back pockets, a back yoke, and rivets; now refers to any pant made of denim.

Cargo Pants designed with several hip pockets and large below-thigh pockets, often banded at the bottom. Pant legs may or may not zip off into shorts.

Continental A pant with a man's trouser styling, fitted at the waistband without a belt. The pockets are often curved from the waist to the side seams.

Cropped A pant cut at a length ranging anywhere between the knee and the ankle.

Cuffed Generally refers to any classic pant with cuffs.

Harem/dhoti Bouffant-style pants gathered into bands at the ankles, often with a wide waistband and exaggeratedly long crotch.

Hip-hugger (low rise) A pant that sits at any point below the waistline, usually resting on the hip bones.

Jodhpur Riding pant that flairs at the side of the hips, are narrow through the calves and ankles, and have reinforced patches on the inseams at the knee.

Knickers A full pant of varying width fastened at the knee with a cuff.

Oxford A pant that follows a 1920s men's styling, with wide cuffed legs.

Palazzo A voluminous long wide-leg pant often worn for evening or loungewear.

Parachute/Zippered A pant made of parachute cloth, nylon, or "swishy" cloth, adorned with zippers and cuffs.

Sailor A pant styled after a navy sailor's pant, with flared/bell-bottom legs, a ten-button center front flap, and center back lacing.

Skinny A pant with a snug fit through the leg ending with a small leg opening, ranging from 9" to 20" depending on size. Also know as slim-fit pants.

Stirrup Pants generally made slim in design, with attached or detachable strap extensions under the instep, and made to be worn with boots.

Stovepipe A narrow-fitting pant with leg openings the same from the knee down.

Surfer/Bike Close-fitting pants extending to the knee, traditionally worn by surfers, bikers, and for exercise.

Western A slightly low-rising pant made traditionally of denim or gabardine, with topstitching accents and riveted detailing, named after the look of the pant worn by the Western United States cowboy.

Pattern A paper model designed and made into pieces to be used for making clothing.

Patternmaker A person who is in charge of making a sample pattern or final pattern for grading and production.

Peplum A short, flared ruffle or overskirt that is attached at the waistline of a blouse, dress, or jacket, often longer in the back than in the front.

Plain weave The construction of a woven fabric by passing filling yarns over and under warp yarns, one warp up and one warp down, in alternating rows.

Pleat Folds of fabric stitched into a garment.

Box Two pleats, one folded to the left, one folded to the right; the fabric in between forms the appearance of a box.

Envelope A large inverted pleat, often placed on the side of a garment, which generally reveals a pocket underneath.

Inverted Two pleats, one folded to the right and one folded to the left, that touch in the center.

Kick A flat pleat on the front or center back of a narrow skirt, which generally reveals a slit to make walking easier.

Kilt A series of flat pleats, covering one-half of the next pleat, all folded in the same direction.

Knife A series of pleats traditionally spaced one-half to one inch apart, all facing the same direction.

Plunging neckline A center front neckline with a low cut, often in a V shape that can extend to the waistline or below.

Point of measure A specific point or name of a point at which a garment is measured. See *Measurement point.*

Princess A style of women's clothing used in blouses, dresses, and coats characterized by the cut of vertical panels shaped to the body vertically through torso to hem without any horizontal seaming or darts.

Private label merchandise A category/line of merchandise that carries the name of or is owned exclusively by a retail store and meets its standards.

Product data management (PDM) The business function (usually within product lifecycle management) that is responsible for management and publication of product data.

Product developer A person who develops exclusive product lines, brands, or private label merchandise.

Product development The processes of developing a particular product line, brand, or private label merchandise.

Product development manager A person who oversees the development of an exclusive line and monitors its production to assure those garments meet the company's expectations.

Product lifecycle management (PLM) The processes of managing manufactured products from inception, through engineering, design and manufacture, to service and disposal.

Product lifecycle manager A person who manages the Product Lifecycle Management System, a computer system that tracks the product development process from the garment's conception through design, manufacture, service, and disposal.

Product line (collection) A designer's, manufacturer's, or retailer's collection of clothing offered for a specific season, linked by a common theme, such as color, fabric, or style. See *Line.*

Product manager An executive who heads the product development team and is responsible for helping to plan, develop, and oversee the consistency of a style message for an exclusive product, product line, brand, or private label.

Production plant A place, factory, or workshop used for the manufacture of goods. See *Manufacturing plant.*

Prototype An original model in which something is patterned or copied.

Pull-on (pullover, skirt/pant) A garment, without traditional openings and closures, that can be pulled on or pulled over a part of the body, e.g., a pull-on pant or pullover sweater.

Retail buying office (resident buying office) An association or group of retail stores working together under one organization for the purpose of sharing and providing services to member stores.

Retail standard Size and quality standards unique to a retailer's customer.

Rise The front and back seams on a pair of pants from the crotch to the waistband.

Romper A one-piece garment resembling a pajama-styled jumpsuit, with short legs or elastic-gathered leg openings.

Satin weave The construction of a woven fabric by passing filling yarns over and under warp yarns. This weave is generally constructed with five warps up and one warp down, repeating to create a smooth surface.

Season The apparel calendar for which a new line is presented, e.g., fall, winter, resort, holiday, spring, and summer.

Seat (1) The buttock portion of a pair of pants, (2) A hip measurement taken at a predetermined number of inches up from the crotch.

Selvage The finished edge on a cloth that prevents raveling or fraying.

Semifitted A general term referring to a garment that is somewhat fitted in style, yet hangs a little loose on the body.

Senior technical design manager A person who manages several technical design managers, makes executive department decisions, works with the divisional merchandise managers, and writes specification sheets as needed.

Shirring Multiple rows of gathering fabric.

Shrink A waist-length sweater or knit top, which may or may not have a ribbed hem and may or may not have sleeves, that looks as though it had been shrunk in the wash.

Side Seam Any garment seam running along the side of the body from under the arm to the ankle bone.

Silhouette The outline or contour of a figure or garment.

Size range The range of sizes to be cut within a size scale, e.g., small, medium, large.

Size scale The number of each size cut within a marker, e.g., three small, six medium, three large.

Size specification Accurate garment measurements.

Size specification analyst A person who analyzes garments, checking and adjusting fit as required and writing specification sheets. This person knows how to measure garments.

Size specification sheet A document listing the size standards, finished garment measurements, detailed technical diagrams, construction notes, and often fabric yields, material and trim details.

Sketch In fashion, a garment or silhouette drawing.

Sketcher A person who sketches for the designer, product development team, or technical team. Many sketchers work freelance. See *Illustrator.*

Skirt

A-line A slightly flared skirt having the illusion of the letter A in silhouette.

Asymmetric A skirt with a hemline that differs in length from the right to the left, often in a diagonal line. It may or may not have ruffles or flounces attached to the hemline.

Fitted (straight) A skirt that is close fitting, or is shaped to fit the body closely, any slim skirt.

Full circular skirt A skirt cut in a full circle or made with several widths of fabric, gores, or gathers to achieve the same circular effect.

Gored A skirt that is generally fitted through the waist, flaring out at the hem. It may be made by sewing together 4 to 24 gored skirt sections.

Granny A full-length gathered skirt, often styled with a ruffled hem.

Handkerchief A skirt with the hemline cut or sewn with gores to fall in points as if made of handkerchiefs.

Jean/Denim A skirt with blue jean styling or any skirt made of denim.

Kick pleated A skirt with a flat pleat on the front or center back of a narrow skirt, which generally reveals a slit to make walking easier.

Layered/Tiered A skirt with varying layers or tiers sewn together and placed on top of each other.

Pegged A skirt with a basic/classic fit at the waist and hips tapering inward to a very narrow hemline/sweep. It is usually constructed with knife pleats or a slit on the center back seam for movement.

Pleated A skirt with pleats. It may have box pleats, envelope pleats, inverted pleats, knife pleats, or kick pleats. See *Pleats*.

Sarong A wrapped skirt that ties at the waist often made of a bold cotton print, originally worn as a beach cover-up.

Slit A straight skirt made with a slash or slit for walking.

Straight (Fitted) A skirt that is close fitting, or is shaped to fit the body closely; any slim skirt. See *Fitted (straight)*.

Trumpet A straight-lined or gored skirt that flares out at the hem like an inverted trumpet.

Wrap A skirt that wraps around the body and fastens with buttons or ties. It is open from the waist to the hem and usually overlaps across the front or the back.

Yoke A skirt made with a yoke just under the waistband. The lower portion of the skirt is often gathered.

Skirt length The length of the skirt measured from under the waistband seam or stitching.

14" = Ultra-Mini

16" = Mini

18–20" = Short

22" = Knee length

26–28" = Midi/Traditional

36" = Maxi/Long

42" = Floor length

Slashed and spread A method of pattern alteration, cutting the pattern apart in the area that needs to be adjusted, spreading the pieces to obtain the desired results, then trueing the new line.

Sleeve cap (1) The extension of a shoulder seam into the sleeve, (2) The top curved portion of a sleeve pattern.

Sleeve cap slope The sleeve cap's degree of slant or curve.

Slide fastener (zipper) A fastener consisting of two rows of (metal or plastic) teeth or spirals, which draw closed or open by moving a sliding piece.

Slope The slant or incline of a garment or pattern.

Sloper A basic or foundation pattern created after standard body measurements have been designated. This pattern becomes the template for stylized patterns.

Softly tailored A term originally used for a garment of predominately curved lines and rounded shapes. It's now also used for a garment that possesses lightly tailored techniques, such as specialized cutting, fitting, sewing, and finishing. See *Tailored*.

Sourcing (1) Locating manufacturing facilities/factories to produce or assemble apparel merchandise, (2) Determining how and where merchandise or their components will be obtained.

Sourcing agent A person who locates manufacturing facilities/factories to produce or assemble apparel merchandise, or a person who determines how and where merchandise or their components will be obtained.

Specification (spec) sheet A standardized list of garment measurements. It consists of style information, technical renderings, points of measure, size ranges, and garment measurements.

Standard A measurement or value that is considered the usual or widely accepted kind, e.g., "standard width," "standard size," "standard grade."

Stockkeeping unit (SKU) Merchandise within a classification of merchandise to which an identifying number is assigned for the purpose of keeping sales and stock records.

Straight skirt Any slim, close-fitting, fitted, or semifitted skirt without fullness.

Style (n) The distinctive characteristics or appearance of a garment; (v) to give fashion features to a garment or line.

Style clerk A person working in a spec office that checks and records the style numbers of the garment for analysis.

Style name A name assigned to and used for identifying a particular style or garment.

Style number A number assigned to and used for identifying a particular style or garment.

Stylist A person who shops the market for style ideas that will fit the company's image, may translate those style ideas to fit the company's needs, giving direction to the design department or product development staff, and possesses a thorough knowledge of textiles and color.

Sweep The circumference of a hem, following the edge, straight or curved.

T-shirt (tee) A long- or short-sleeve knitted sport/casual shirt or dress with a ribbed, round, or V-neck neckline.

Tailored A term originally used for a garment of predominately straight lines and angled shapes and now also used for a garment that possesses tailoring techniques such as specialized cutting, fitting, sewing, and finishing. See *Softly tailored*.

Technical design The process of analyzing garments, checking and adjusting fit and writing specification sheets.

Technical designer A person who analyzes garments, checking and adjusting fit as required and writing specification sheets. This person also has a design background and can offer style changes as needed to solve production problems.

Technical design manager A person who manages several technical designers, makes final fit decisions, writes specification sheets, and evaluates potential production risks. This person works closely with the general merchandise manager, may offer style or design changes as needed for production, and sets the fit schedule.

Technical sketch A flat, proportioned drawing of a garment including all style details.

Teddy A relatively straight cut foundation garment combining the chemise with loose-fitting panties.

Template A pattern or guide that is used to draw or manufacture other objects with a similar shape.

Thread count (count of cloth) The number, or count, of warp and weft yarns per inch.

Toddler Clothing designed to be worn by small children generally sold in sizes 2T to 4T.

Tolerance The amount of acceptable measurement deviation, plus or minus, allowed during sewing.

Total measurement The perimeter of the garment, including the front and back measurements, in other words, the circumference. [Note: To get the total measurement, the garment is measured once, across the front, then that number is doubled.]

Trouser An item of clothing traditionally worn by men that covers the legs, with both an inner and outer seam.

Tube top A strapless top made of tight-fitting stretch or elastic-shirred fabric.

Turtleneck A neckline/collar that stands on and fits close to the neck and rolls over once or twice. A turtleneck sweater would have this neckline.

Twill weave The construction of a woven fabric by passing filling yarns over and under warp yarns, two warps up and one warp down, creating a diagonal effect.

Unconstructed jacket A jacket that is not constructed with advanced sewing techniques for facings, linings, collars, sleeves, and/or pockets.

Union suit A one-piece, front-buttoned, knitted garment of 1880s design worn for warmth. It may or may not have a drop seat.

V neck A neckline that is cut down in the front or back of a garment to a sharp point in the shape of a V. A V-neck T-shirt or dress would have this neckline.

V-neck cardigan A slightly fitted hip-length jacket or sweater that is cut down in the front to a point in the shape of a V. See *Cardigan*.

Vest A jacket- or sweater-style garment made without sleeves, meant to be worn over a blouse or knit top.

Wales The series of lengthwise loops or vertical stitches in knitted fabric.

Warm-up pant A casual pant generally made with a pull-on waist construction, often worn for exercise.

Warp knitting Knit produced with yarns running lengthwise, as warp-on beams are prepared with one or more yarns per needle.

Warp yarns (filling yarns) The set of yarns in a woven fabric that run from selvage edge to selvage edge.

Wearing ease The allowance added to patterns to accommodate for comfortable fit and ease of movement. See *Ease*.

Weft knitting Knitting produced on both flat and circular knitting machines using one continuous thread (yarn) making all of the loops in a course.

Weft yarns The set of yarns in a woven fabric that run lengthwise or parallel to the selvage.

Windbreaker A trademarked nylon jacket made for warmth and wind protection. It generally has a zip front opening, a hood, and a fitted waistband and cuffs. It has now become synonymous with any wind-protecting jacket.

Women's wear A size or segment of the industry for women with an ample girth or fit. Sizes generally range from 14W to 26W.

Work sketch or work photo A sketch or photo of a garment using the principles and elements of a style, without being a necessarily finalized design.

Yoke A separate seamed portion of the garment across the front and back shoulders.

Index

Across back, 28–29
blazers/unconstructed jackets, 199
fit in, 262
jumpsuits/one-piece garments, 115, 181
knit dresses, 100
knit tops, 69
outerwear/coats, 216
woven dresses, 166
woven tops, 142
Across back/center armhole, 28–29
blazers/unconstructed jackets, 199
jumpsuits/one-piece garments, 115, 181
knit dresses, 100
knit tops, 69
outerwear/coats, 216
woven dresses, 167
woven tops, 142
Across chest, 26–27
blazers/unconstructed jackets, 199
fit in, 262
jumpsuits/one-piece garments, 115, 181
knit dresses, 100
knit tops, 69
outerwear/coats, 215
woven dresses, 165
woven tops, 142
Across chest/center armhole, 28–29
blazers/unconstructed jackets, 199
dresses, 100
jumpsuits/one-piece garments, 115, 181
knit tops, 69
outerwear/coats, 216
woven dresses, 166
woven tops, 142
Across shoulder, 26–27
blazers/unconstructed jackets, 199
jumpsuits/one-piece garments, 115, 181
knit dresses, 100
knit tops, 69
outerwear/coats, 215
woven dresses, 165
woven tops, 142
See also Shoulder width
Applied pockets. *See* Pocket
Armhole, 33–35
blazers/unconstructed jackets, 200–01
fit of, 262–76
jumpsuits/one-piece garments, 116
knit dresses, 101
knit tops, 70–71
outerwear/coats, 217
woven dresses, 166–67
woven tops, 133
See also Across back/center armhole
Assistant designer, 7
defined, 371
Assistant merchandiser, 8
defined, 371
Assistant product developer/manager, 7
defined, 371
Assistant technical designer, 6
defined, 371
ASTM (American Society for Testing and Materials), 10, 12–13, 303

Back bodice length, 25–26
blazers/unconstructed jackets, 199
jumpsuits/one-piece garments, 114, 181
knit dresses, 100
knit tops, 69
outerwear/coats, 215
woven dresses, 165
woven top, 131
Back rise, 46–47
jumpsuits/one-piece garments, 119, 185
knit pants, 89
woven pants, 154
See also Rise
Back torso length, 60
jumpsuits/one-piece garments, 122, 188
Belt length/width, 52–53
blazers/unconstructed jackets, 203
jumpsuits/one-piece garments, 120, 186
knit dresses, 104
knit pants, 90
knit skirts, 83
knit tops, 73
outerwear/coats, 220
woven dresses, 170
woven pants, 155

woven skirts, 145
woven tops, 135
Belt loop length/width, 52–53
blazers/unconstructed jackets, 203
jumpsuits/one-piece garments, 120–86
knit dresses, 104
knit pants, 90
knit skirts, 83
knit tops, 73
outerwear/coats, 220
woven dresses, 170
woven skirts, 155
woven tops, 145
Belt loop placement, 57
Blazers and unconstructed jackets, 204–05
croquis for, 361–63
men's sportscoat, 253–54
types of, 371
Blouses, defined, 371–72
fit problems with, 266–75
See also Tops
Bodice, defined, 372
fit problems in, 274–75
See also Front bodice length; Side seam bodice length
Body dimensions, 10–14
Body form, 13–15
defined, 371
Bottom band circumference, 29
blazers/unconstructed jackets, 199–200
outerwear/coat, 216
woven tops, 132
Bottom band/ribbing height, 30–31
blazers/unconstructed jackets, 200
jumpsuits/one-piece garments, 119, 132
knit top, 70
outerwear/coats, 216
pants, 51
knit pants, 90
woven pants, 154
woven tops, 132
Bottom band width/circumference stretched, 30–31
blazers/unconstructed jackets, 200
outerwear/coats, 216
woven top, 132
Bottom opening/sweep, 30– 31, 42–44
blazers/unconstructed jackets, 200
fit problems with, 270–71
knit dresses, 103–04
knit skirts, 82
knit top, 70
outerwear/coats, 216
woven dresses, 169
woven skirts, 144
woven tops, 132
Brand manager, 7
defined, 372
Bust dart placement. *See* Dart placement
Button placement, 147
blazers/unconstructed jackets, 204
fit problems, 226
jumpsuits/one-piece garments, 121, 187
knit dresses, 106
knit tops, 74
outerwear/coats, 221
woven dresses, 171
woven tops, 136–37

Center back/front bodice length, 25
blazers/unconstructed jackets, 199
jumpsuits/one-piece garments, 114, 181
knit dresses, 100
knit tops, 69
outerwear/coats, 215
woven dresses, 165
woven tops, 131
Center back length, 25
blazers/unconstructed jackets, 198
knit dresses, 100
knit tops, 68
outerwear/coats, 215
woven dresses, 165
woven tops, 130
Center front/back skirt length, 44–45
knit dresses, 104
knit skirts, 82
outerwear/coats, 220
woven dresses, 169
woven skirts, 144
Center front length, 25
blazers/unconstructed jackets, 198
knit dresses, 99
knit tops, 68
outerwear/coats, 215
woven dresses, 165
woven tops, 130
Chest width, 26–27
blazers/unconstructed jackets, 199
circumference, 27
fit of, 266–267
jumpsuits/one-piece garments, 115, 181
knit dresses, 100
knit tops, 69
outerwear/coats, 215
woven dresses, 165
woven tops, 131
See also Across chest
Children's wear, 227, 229–41
body forms, 229–30
defined, 372
girls 4–6x, sundress, 235
girls 7–16, woven skirt, 237
grade charts, 303–12
juniors, knit dress, 240–41
newborn/infant, onesie, 231–32
spec sheets, 231–41
toddler, overall, 233–34
Circular bottom opening/sweep width, 30–31, 44–45
blazers/unconstructed jackets, 200
circumference, 31, 45
knit dresses, 103–04

knit skirts, 82
knit top, 70
outerwear/coats, 216
woven dresses, 169
woven skirts, 144
woven tops, 132
Coats. *See* Outerwear/coats
Codes, spec sheet, 15
defined, 373
Collar measurements, 38–39
blazers/unconstructed jackets, 202
jumpsuits/one-piece garments, 117, 183–84
knit dresses, 102–03
knit tops, 72
outerwear/coats, 219
woven dresses, 168
woven tops, 134–35
Computer Aided Design (CAD), 19
defined, 373
Costing, defined, 373
Croquis, 333–368
blazers/unconstructed jackets, 361–63
defined, 373
dresses, 351–57
jumpsuits/one-piece garments, 358–60
knit tops, 340–344
outerwear/coats, 364–68
pants, 347–51
skirts, 344–47
woven tops, 336–40
Crotch width, 60–61
jumpsuits/one-piece garments, 122, 188
Cuff height pants, 49–50
jumpsuits/one-piece garments, 119, 185
knit pants, 90
woven pants, 154
Cuff length sleeve, 36
blazers/unconstructed jackets, 201
jumpsuits/one-piece garments, 116, 183
knit dresses, 102
knit tops, 71
outerwear/coats, 217
woven dresses, 167
woven tops, 134
Cuff/ribbing height sleeve, 36
blazers/unconstructed jackets, 201
jumpsuits/one-piece garments, 117, 183
knit dresses, 102
knit tops, 71
outerwear/coats, 217
woven dresses, 167
woven tops, 134

Dart placement, 58–59
blazers/unconstructed jackets, 205
jumpsuits/one-piece garments, 121–122, 188
knit dresses, 106
knit pants, 91
knit skirts, 84
knit tops, 74–75
outerwear/coats, 222
woven dresses, 172
woven pants, 156
woven skirts, 146
woven tops, 137
See also Bust dart; Princess dart placement
Darts, fit of, 266–67
Department merchandise manager (DMM), 8
defined, 373
Distance between pleats, 50–51
blazers/unconstructed jackets, 203
jumpsuits/one-piece garments, 119–20, 186
knit dresses, 124
knit pants, 90
knit skirts, 83
knit tops, 72–73
outerwear/coats, 220
woven dresses, 170
woven pants, 154
woven skirts, 145
woven tops, 135
Dresses
croquis for, 351–54
knit, 96–106
spec sheets, 107–10, 173–76
types of defined, 373–74
woven, 161–72

Ease, missy allowance chart, 261
defined, 374
Elbow width, 34–35
blazers/unconstructed jackets, 201
circumference, 36
jumpsuits/one-piece garments, 116, 182–83
knit dresses, 101
knit tops, 71
outerwear/coats, 217
woven top, 133
woven dress, 167

Fashion director, 7
defined, 374
Final spec, 19
First patternmaker, 7
defined, 374
First sample, 19
Fit session worksheet, 17, 299
Fitting, 257, 259–98
common problems and solutions for, 266–97
conducting a fit session, 260, 298
fit defined, 374
fit evaluation sequencing, 259–60
generalized tips for, 264–65
pants, 282–97
rules for, 260–64
skirts, 276–82
tops and blouses, 266–76
Flange depth, 54–55
blazers/unconstructed jackets, 204
jumpsuits/one-piece garments, 140, 187

knit dresses, 105
knit tops, 73
outerwear/coats, 221
woven dresses, 171
woven tops, 136
Flounce/ruffle width, 52–53
jumpsuits/one-piece garments, 120, 186
knit dresses, 105
knit pants, 91
knit skirts, 83
knit tops, 73
woven dresses, 170
woven pants, 155
woven skirts, 146
woven tops, 136
Fly/zipper, 50–51
blazers/unconstructed jackets, 203
jumpsuits/one-piece garments, 119, 186
knit dresses, 104
knit pants, 90
knit skirts, 82
outerwear/coats, 220
woven dresses, 169
woven pant, 154
woven skirts, 145
Fractional math, 9
defined, 274
Front and center front bodice length, 25
blazers/unconstructed jackets, 198–99
jumpsuits/one-piece garments, 114, 181
knit dresses, 100
knit tops, 64–65
outerwear/coats, 215
woven dresses, 165
woven tops, 131
Front rise, 46–47
fit of, 290–91
jumpsuits/one-piece garments, 119, 185
knit pants, 89
woven pants, 153–54
Front torso length, 58–60
Jumpsuits/one-piece garments, 114, 122, 188

Gathers, fit of, 263
General merchandise manager (GMM), 8
defined, 374
Gerber, 19, 302
AccuScan, 300
system, defined, 374
Technologies, 21
Grading, 257, 300–31
Boys 8–20, 311–12
defined, 374
girls 4–6x and boys 4–7x, 306–08
girls 7–16, 309–11
juniors and missy/woman, 313–28
menswear, 329–31
newborns and infants, 303–04
toddlers, 305
Grain line, fit of, 263

Hemline, fit in, 276, 282
Hems, fit of, 263, 275
High point shoulder, bust dart. *See* Dart Placement
High point shoulder, hip width from, 41–43
circumference, 43
defined, 374
jumpsuits/one-piece garments, 184
outerwear/coats, 219
woven pants, 153
woven dresses, 164, 169
Hip measurements, menswear, 242
Hip seat width, 42–43
circumference, 43
jumpsuits/one-piece garments, 118, 184–85
knit pants, 89
woven pants, 153
Hip width, high/low, 40–41
circumference, 41
Jumpsuits/one-piece garments, 118, 184
knit dresses, 103
knit pants, 88–89
knit skirts, 82
outerwear/coats, 219
woven dresses, 168–69
woven pants, 153
woven skirts, 144
Hood measurements, 54–55
blazers/unconstructed jackets, 204
jumpsuits/one-piece garments, 120
knit dresses, 105
knit tops, 73
outerwear/coats, 221
woven dresses, 170–71
woven tops, 136

Illustrator/sketcher, 7
defined, 375
Inseam, 105
jumpsuits/one-piece garments, 118, 185
knit pants, 89
woven pants, 153

Jackets. *See* Blazers and unconstructed jackets
Juniors. *See also* Childrenswear
Spec sheet, 240
grading, 313–28
Jumpsuits/one-piece garments, 111–22, 177–88
croquis for, 358–60
spec sheets, 123–24, 189–94

Keyhole length, 39
jumpsuits/one-piece garments, 118, 184
knit dresses, 103
knit tops, 72
woven dresses, 168
woven tops, 135
Knee width, 47
circumference, 48–49
jumpsuits/one-piece garments, 119, 185
knit pants, 89

woven pants, 154
Knits, 63–64,
dresses, 96–106
jumpsuits/one-piece garments, 111–22
menswear, 244–48
pants, 87–91
skirts, 80–84
spec sheets, 76–79, 85–86, 92–95, 107–10, 123–24
tops, 65–75
Knitted courses, 64
fit of, 263

Lapels, fit of, 261
Lapel width, 29
blazers/unconstructed jackets, 202
jumpsuits/one-piece garments, 117, 184
knit dresses, 103
knit tops, 76
outerwear/coats, 219
woven dresses, 168
woven tops, 135
Leg opening width, 48–49
circumference, 48–49
jumpsuits/one-piece garments, 119, 185
knit pants, 88, 89–90
stretched and circumference, 48–49
vented and circumference, 48–49
woven pants, 154
Lectra, 19, 20
Lectra Modaris V7, 300
Linings, fit of, 264

Macy's, 4
Measurement,
basic points, 21–61
of model/body form, 13–15
preparation for, 22–24
Measurement method, 20
defined, 375
Measurer, 6
defined, 375
Menswear, 227, 242–256
defined, 375
grading, 302, 329–31
knit jog pant, 247–48
linen trouser, 251–52
mock-neck sweater, 245
short-sleeve linen shirt, 249–50
short-sleeve polo shirt, 246
size range conversion chart, 243
spec sheets, 244–56
T-shirt, 244
wool coat, 255–56
wool sportscoat, 253–54
Merchandise product director, 8
defined, 375
Merchandiser, 8
defined, 375
Metric to imperial conversion, 369–70
chart, 369–70
how to, 369
Misses figure type (sizes 2–20), 11–12
ease allowance chart, 261
grading, 313–328
Muscle width, 34–35
blazers/unconstructed jackets, 201
Circumference, 35
jumpsuits/one-piece garments, 116, 182
knit dresses, 101
knit tops, 71
outerwear/coats, 217
woven dresses, 167
woven tops, 133

Neckband fit, 261
Neckband length, 38
blazers/unconstructed jackets, 202
jumpsuits/one-piece garments, 117, 183
knit dresses, 102
knit tops, 72
outerwear/coats, 218
woven dresses, 168
woven tops, 131
Neckline, fit in, 261

OptiTex, 19, 21
Optitex PDS, 300
One-piece garments. *See* Jumpsuits/one-piece garments
Outerwear/coats, 210–22
croquis for, 364–68
fitting of, 265
defined, 372–73
mens, 255–56
spec sheets, 223–26
types of, 364
Out-of-tolerance column, 19
Outseam, 46–47
jumpsuits/one-piece garments, 118–19, 185
knit pants, 89
woven pants, 153

Pants
See Bottom band/ribbing height
croquis for, 347–51
See Cuff height
defined, 376
fit problems in, 282–97
knit, 87–91
menswear, 247–48, 252–52
spec sheets, 72–95, 157–60
types of, 347
woven, 151–56
Pant yoke depth. *See* Yoke depth
Patternmaker, 6
assistant and first, 7
defined, 376
Placket length/width, 39
blazers/unconstructed jackets, 203
jumpsuits/one-piece garments, 84, 118
knit dresses, 103

knit tops, 72
outerwear/coats, 219
woven dresses, 168
woven tops, 135
Pleat depth, 50–51
blazers/unconstructed jackets, 203
jumpsuits/one–piece garments, 119, 86
knit dresses, 104
knit pants, 90
knit skirts, 82–83
knit tops, 72
outerwear/coats, 220
woven dresses, 170
woven pants, 154
woven skirts, 145
woven tops, 135
See also Distance between pleats
Pleats placement, 55–57
blazers/unconstructed jackets, 204
jumpsuits/one-piece garments, 121, 87
knit dresses, 105–06
knit pants, 91
knit skirts, 83
outerwear/coats, 221
woven dresses, 171
woven pants, 155
woven skirts, 145–146
woven tops, 136
Pocket height/width, 50–51
blazers/unconstructed jackets, 204
jumpsuits/one-piece garments, 120, 187
knit dresses, 104
knit pants, 90
knit skirts, 83
knit tops, 73
outerwear/coats, 220
woven dresses, 170
woven pants, 155
woven skirts, 145
woven tops, 135
Pocket opening within seam, 50–51
blazers/unconstructed jackets, 203
jumpsuits/one-piece garments, 120, 186
knit dresses, 104
knit pants, 90
knit skirts, 83
knit tops, 73
outerwear/coats, 220
woven dresses, 170
woven pants, 155
woven skirts, 145
woven tops, 135
Pocket placement, 57
blazers/unconstructed jackets, 204
jumpsuits/one-piece garments, 121, 187
knit dresses, 106
knit pants, 91
knit skirts, 83
knit tops, 74
outerwear/coats, 221
woven dresses, 171
woven pants, 155
woven skirts, 146
woven tops, 137
Pockets, fit of, 263
Point of measure (POM), 15, 298
body point of measure, defined, 372
defined, 377
See Measurement point
Princess dart placement. *See* Dart Placement
Private label,
defined, 377
vs brands, 3–5
Product Data management, 19
defined, 377
Product development manager, 7
defined, 377
Product lifecycle management (PLM), 19
defined, 377
Product lifecycle manager, 7
defined, 377
Product manager, 7
defined, 377
Prototype garments, 5, 17
defined, 377
Pull-on styling, 94
defined, 377

Retailers, private label, 3–4
Retail standards, 4–5
Revised spec, 17–18
Rise. *See* Back rise; Front rise
Ruffles. *See* Flounce/ruffle width

Seams. *See* Inseam; Outseam; Side seam
Season, 15
defined, 377
Seat width. *See* Hip seat width
Senior technical design manager, 6
defined, 377
Shirts. *See* Blouses; Tops; Menswear
Shoulder pads, 54–55
blazers/unconstructed jackets, 204
fit of, 262
jumpsuits/one-piece garments, 120–21, 187
knit dresses, 105
knit tops, 74–75
outerwear/coats, 221
woven dresses, 171
woven tops, 136
Shoulder seams, fit of, 262, 268–69
Shoulder width, 26–27
blazers/unconstructed jackets, 199
jumpsuits/one-piece garments, 115, 181
knit dresses, 100
knit tops, 69
outerwear/coats, 215
woven dresses, 165,
woven tops, 132
See also Across shoulder; High point shoulder

Side length, 24
blazers/unconstructed jackets, 198
knit dresses, 100
knit tops, 68
outerwear/coats, 215
woven dresses, 165
woven tops, 130–131
Side seam bodice length, 26–27
blazers/unconstructed jackets, 199
jumpsuits/one-piece garments, 114–15, 181
knit dresses, 100
knit tops, 69
outerwear/coats, 215
woven dresses, 165
woven tops, 131
Side seam pockets. *See* Pocket opening within seam
Side seams, fit of, 263
Side skirt length, 44–45
knit dresses, 104
knit skirts, 82
outerwear/coats, 220
woven dresses, 169
woven skirts, 104
Size categories, 17
Size range, 17
defined, 399
men's conversion chart, 243
Size specification, 5–8
defined, 377
Size standards, 4
Sketch (work sketch), 17
See Croquis
Skirt lengths, defined, 378
See also Center front/back skirt length and Side skirt lengths
Skirts
croquis for, 384–46
defined, 377–78
fit of, 276–282
knit, 80–84
spec sheets, 85–86, 147–50
types of, 384
woven, 142–46
Skirt yoke depth. *See* Yoke depth
Sleeve lengths, 32–33
blazers/unconstructed jackets, 200
fit of, 262, 272
jumpsuits/one-piece garments, 182
knit dresses, 101
knit tops, 70
outerwear/coats, 217
woven dresses, 166
woven tops,
See also Muscle width
Sleeves, fit of, 262, 273
Slit. *See* Vent/slit
Sourcer/sourcing agent, 7
defined, 378
Specification (spec) sheet,
blazers/unconstructed jackets, 206–09
children's wear, 231–241
defined, 378
generic, 16, 18, 334–335
how to grade, 300–301
knit jumpsuits/one-piece garments, 123–24
knit dress, 107–10
knit pant, 92–95
knit skirts, 85–86
knit tops, 76–79
menswear, 244–256
outwear/coats, 223–226
using, 15–17
woven jumpsuits/one-piece garments, 189–94
woven dress, 173–76
woven pants, 157–60
woven skirts, 147–50
woven tops, 138–41
Specs. *See* size specifications
Standards, 4
ASTM body measurement table, 11–12
defined, 378
Store brands. *See* Private label
Straight armhole width, 33
blazers/unconstructed jackets, 200
circumference, 33
jumpsuits/one-piece garments, 116, 182
knit dresses, 101
knit tops, 70
outerwear/coats, 217
woven dresses, 166
woven tops, 133
Strap length/width, 52–53
jumpsuits/one-piece garments, 120, 186
knit dresses, 105
knit tops, 73
woven dresses, 170
woven tops, 136
Style, 15
defined, 378
Style clerk, 6
defined, 378
Stylist, 8
defined, 378
Sweep. *See* Bottom opening/sweep

Technical designer, 6
becoming, 8–9
defined, 378
Technical design manager, 6
defined, 379
Technical sketch, 17
defined, 378
Thigh width, 46–47
circumference, 46–47
jumpsuits/one-piece garments, 119, 185
knit pants, 89
woven pants, 154
Tie length/width, 52
blazers/unconstructed jackets, 203–04
jumpsuits/one-piece garments, 120, 186

knit dresses, 105
knit pants, 91
knit skirts, 83
knit tops, 73
outerwear/coats, 221
woven pants, 155
woven skirts, 145
woven tops, 136
Tolerance, 15
defined, 379
in grading, 302
"out-of", 19
Tops
children's wear, 236
croquis for, 336–44
fit problems with, 266–76
knit, 65–75
menswear, 244–46, 249–50
spec sheets, 76–79, 138–42
woven, 127–37
Torso length. *See* Back and Front torso lengths
Trousers. *See* Pants
Turtleneck, spec sheets for, 76–79
croquis, 343
dress, spec sheets for, 107–10
menswear, spec sheets for, 245

Vented bottom opening/sweep width. *See* Bottom opening/sweep
Vented leg opening width, 48–49
circumference, 48–49
jumpsuits/one-piece garments, 119, 185
knit pants, 89
woven pants, 154
Vent/slit, 50–51
blazers/unconstructed jackets, 203
jumpsuits/one-piece garments, 119, 186
knit dresses, 104
knit pants, 90
knit skirts, 82
knit tops, 72
outerwear/coats, 220
woven dresses, 169–70
woven pants, 154
woven skirts, 145
woven tops, 135

Waistband, fit of,
Waistband measurements, 39–41
circumference, 39–41
jumpsuits/one-piece garments, 118, 184
knit dresses, 103
knit pants, 88
knit skirts, 81
knit tops, 72
woven dresses, 168
woven pants, 153
woven skirts, 144
Waist width, 28–29
blazers/unconstructed jackets, 199
circumference, 28–29
jumpsuits/one-piece garments, 115, 181–82
knit dresses, 101
knit tops, 69
outerwear/coats, 216
woven dresses, 166
woven tops, 132
Women's wear, 17
defined, 379
See also Misses figure type
Wovens, 125–126
blazers/unconstructed jackets, 195–205
dresses, 161–172
jumpsuits/one-piece garments, 177–88
outerwear/coats, 210–22
pants, 152–156
spec sheets, 138–41, 147–50, 157–60, 173–76, 189–94, 205–09, 223–226
skirts, 142–146,
tops, 127–137

Yoke measurements, 30–31, 44–45
blazers/unconstructed jackets, 200
jumpsuits/one-piece garments, 115–16, 118, 182, 185
knit dresses, 101, 104
knit pants, 89
knit skirts, 82
knit tops, 70
outerwear/coats, 216
woven dresses, 166, 169
woven pants, 153
woven skirts, 144
woven tops, 132–33
Yoke, defined, 379

Zipper. *See* Fly/zipper